THE
SOCIAL DIMENSIONS
OF WORK

THE
SOCIAL DIMENSIONS
OF WORK

EDITED BY

Clifton D. Bryant

Western Kentucky University

P R E N T I C E - H A L L, I N C., Englewood Cliffs, New Jersey

Prentice-Hall Sociology Series
Neil J. Smelser, *Editor*

ISBN: 0-13-815605-0

Library of Congress Catalog Card Number: 74-163392

10 9 8 7 6 5 4 3 2 1

Printed in the United States of America

PRENTICE-HALL INTERNATIONAL, INC., LONDON
PRENTICE-HALL OF AUSTRALIA, PTY. LTD., SYDNEY
PRENTICE-HALL OF CANADA, LTD., TORONTO
PRENTICE-HALL OF INDIA PRIVATE LIMITED, NEW DELHI
PRENTICE-HALL OF JAPAN, INC., TOKYO

*This book is dedicated to
my daughters, Debbie and Diane,
with the hope that each will find
a life's work even partially as rewarding
as my life's work—
the sociological study of work.*

CONTENTS

The Sociology of Work

3

THE SOCIAL STRUCTURE OF WORK   121

Occupational Status and Role
A Longitudinal Perspective

Occupational Status and Role
A Comparative Perspective

Work Systems

xv

PREFACE

We never escape the shadow of work: it is one of our most pervasive and significant activities. Through work we derive sustenance and effect survival. As a collective enterprise, work has made possible our productive mastery of the elements and has afforded us a degree of control over our progress and destiny. The exercise of expertise in work provides intrinsic gratification as well as social recognition. One's standard of living, style of life, political ideology, basic value orientation, choice of friends and spouse, health, daily routine, mode of child rearing, and general satisfaction with life, to name only a few considerations, may well be the indirect, if not direct, results of one's work speciality. We are shaped, molded, regulated, even assimilated by our work. Work is our behavioral product, but so, too, are we and our lives in many ways the products of our work.

The recent broadening interest in the sociology of work has given rise to the publication of a number of excellent textual treatments of the topic. This anthology will supplement and complement both these recent volumes and the earlier, but still durable, texts on the subject. The extensive linking commentary in every section, and the book's overall organization should also make it well-suited for use as a course's principal text.

We have chosen to examine work more from the standpoint of structure and process than from a typological perspective. This text, therefore, begins with an examination of the social nature of work and then proceeds with a systematic exploration of work organization and process—and the inherent social relationships involved therein.

Although some of the articles included in this collection are well-known "classic" statements on various aspects of the sociology of occupations and professions, the majority are newer articles that either have not previously appeared in a collected anthology or are less well-known. A few of the selections are from relatively obscure sources such as foreign journals, and several selections were prepared especially for this volume.

All articles have been selected with an eye toward student interest, insightfulness, and readability. A wide range of different occupational specialties and work systems are represented and an attempt has been made to provide a balance between descriptive, and conceptual or theoretical, treatments of work. Thus the overall collection, hopefully, represents a fresh and stimulating set of illustrative materials that will simultaneously hold the student's attention and prove pedagogically useful.

I am particularly indebted to Alan Lesure for his interest in, and encouragement of, this volume and to Neil Smelser for his most helpful critical reviews. Special thanks are due my secretaries, Mrs. Katharine Van Eaton, Mrs. Elashia Jennings, and Mr. David Rowans for their labors on the clerical details of the book over the past two years.

C. B.

THE
SOCIAL DIMENSIONS
OF WORK

1

TOWARD A SOCIAL
INTERPRETATION
OF WORK

INTRODUCTION

Work may be viewed from many perspectives. It can be examined from
the standpoint of the physicist as force exerted and movement accomplished,
from the standpoint of the biologist as bio-physiological effort, from the
standpoint of the psychologist as task motivation and goal-oriented behavior, or from the newer and composite perspective of ergonomics as the
"physiological, psychological, anatomical and engineering features" of man
in his working environment.[1] Work can also be viewed in its social context,
as one is involved in it behaviorally with others. Inasmuch as work frequently occurs as group behavior—i.e., it is usually performed *by* some persons in connection or cooperation *with* other persons *for* the benefit of yet
still other persons, and often involves collective motivation, coordination,
and evaluation—it may be considered as a social activity. Work as social
activity is a pervasive phenomenon, and a significant portion of our life and
group existence is labeled as such. As O. G. Edholm has put it, "Work really
includes all, or nearly all, human activity. Birth, marriage, death mean work

1

for the midwife, priest and undertaker. One could even say that sex means work for the prostitute."[2] Work with its social implications has been responsible (directly or indirectly) for political movements, the promotion of wars, the growth of religious faiths, fluctuations in the content of art forms, and the existence of hierarchically ranked human populations.

On the personal level, work may engender great fame or fortune. Conversely, it may, by virtue of its limited rewards, bind one to a poverty level life style. It may dictate our daily routine, influence our choice of spouse and friends, shape our preference in leisure activities, and color our political and social views and behavior. For one individual, work may be sublimely satisfying, the chief activity in his existence; for another, the job may provide a singularly stultifying and frustrating experience in life. Work may even influence the likelihood and mode of our demise. Because it constitutes such a significant social factor in our lives, the field of work seems to be worthy of attention by the researcher or student of human social behavior.

Work is a basic human social process and is found in all societies, although the social concept of work does not necessarily exist in all of them. In some simple societies, for example, work may consist of mere specialization of function and be so completely integrated into the general fabric of social life that it is simply part of the experience of "total existence" and is not articulated as a separate and distinct category of social behavior. In such a society, where work is not compartmentalized as a particular variety of behavioral endeavor, values of good or bad, easy or difficult, honorific or menial cannot attach themselves to it; and it exists, as it were, as a value-free activity.

In the Western world, however, work historically has been associated with different value assessments; as brutalizing activity and painful drudgery by the Greeks; as religious calling and path to salvation by the early Protestants; as opportunity for creativity and self-realization by the Renaissance artisans.[3] In contemporary society, in contrast, work is conceptually defined as a sphere of social activity related to but separated from other modes of behavior, and as such is subject to a variety of meanings and assessments as part of the social definition. Not only has work tended to be compartmentalized as a special kind of human behavior and evaluated increasingly on the basis of its extrinsic characteristics, but the advances in machine technology, the mechanical-like nature of many job activities, and the vast bureaucratic structures in which much work occurs have all contributed to a loss of freedom and opportunity for creativity. Thus C. Wright Mills has spoken of the "big split" between work and play, and he and other observers have written of the profoundly unsatisfying nature of work today for many Americans. While work has become a negative cultural value for some, it nevertheless remains as a principal guiding force in our lives, and as an activity which frequently molds and affects our attitudes and perspectives, and patterns our social relationships with others. It is with this question of the social implication of work and the manner in which man is shaped by his particular variety of work that the readings included in this volume are concerned.

This chapter addresses itself to work and its social interpretation, beginning with the background of work. To be adequately understood, work must be viewed within the framework of the total culture. Raymond Firth's selection, "Anthropological Background to Work," seems a good starting point in this regard. Looking at the basic nature of work in both primitive and modern societies, Firth concludes that work involves a set of social relations as well as technological and economic relations.

In the next selection, Franz Baermann Steiner provides an intensive, and perhaps one of the more definitive, examination of the concept of labor (work) itself as well as of the division and organization of labor. Examining work both historically and anthropologically, he suggests that the major criteria for distinguishing work from other behavior is that it is a socially integrative activity associated with human subsistence, although the numerous occupations are only tangentially related to subsistence, and accordingly represent something of a problem in terms of classification. Viewed as an integrative activity, labor (work) "thus presupposes, creates, and recreates social relationships."

The next reading in this chapter, Walter S. Neff's "Work and Human History," provides a suitably expansive socio-historical overview of work and human technology. The general direction of the course of human development, the concomitant conceptions of work at different periods in history, and several theories of the social evolution of work are examined and discussed. What we would do well to keep in mind here is that the history of the world and of man may be usefully viewed as essentially a history of technology—a history, accordingly, of work. In the early stages of man's development, great advances were the direct result of the progress in technology and the resultant modification in man's work behavior. Man's ascent from the paleolithic hunting and food gathering stage to the neolithic agricultural stage was accompanied by formidable changes in the structure and quality of social life. Significant changes also took place simultaneously with the appearance of metal tools, the machine, atomic power, and, more recently, the computer. For better or worse, man's destiny is inextricably bound up with his technology and its influence on modes of work.

The next selection, "Work as a 'Central Life Interest' of Professionals," offers a comparative and more empirical treatment of the social interpretation of work. In this article, Louis H. Orzack takes up the question of the meaning and relevance of work to particular kinds of occupational categories, with special emphasis on the profession of registered nurses. This study was in large part a response to a previous research project by Robert

Dubin, who studied the meaning of work and the work place to industrial workers. Dubin had found that the majority of the industrial workers studied did not see their jobs as "important foci of concern." In contrast, for Orzack's professional nurses, the job and work place were central life interests; unlike the blue collar workers in Dubin's study, the nurses were more likely to "prefer work to non-work or community settings for their technological behavior and for their participation in formal organizations." One might conclude, therefore, at least insofar as we may compare the results in this study with those of the earlier Dubin research, that work takes on a somewhat different meaning for the professional than for the industrial worker; that while the professional lives to work, the industrial employee more likely works to live. (It should be noted, however, that not all would agree that nurses should be classified as professionals. In fact, considerable disagreement exists among sociologists as to which occupations may be appropriately classified as professions.)

If a man's work has a special set of meanings for him, so too does it have special meanings for other members of society who must necessarily and inevitably make observations and assessments concerning it. The members of society may react to a man's work in many ways; they may admire his work and honor him for it, or they may find it repulsive and avoid him because of it; they may attach great importance to it and reward him in a commensurate fashion, or they may view it as insignificant and consequently relegate him to an inferior social position. The general public may be fascinated and perhaps even thrilled by it to the extent that it becomes the preferred or ideal occupation, or they may perceive it as mundane and colorless, in effect an economic last resort. An occupational prestige system represents a consensual assessment of the different varieties of work extant in a given society. Evaluations change, however, and varieties of work and occupational specialties rise and fall in the public estimation; thus various workers from time to time may experience serious dislocations of privileges, deference, and rewards. Barbara G. Myerhoff and William R. Larson take up this development in the final reading of this chapter. In their treatment of the doctor and their evaluation of his occupational stereotype, they postulate two social models of the hero. One is the culture hero, who is a traditional composite of social virtues and approved characteristics and attributes; the other is the charismatic hero, who possesses extraordinary abilities and powers and whose authority rests on his "dedication to his mission of precipitating social progress and on the awesome, mysterious skills he brings to the task." The authors suggest that the doctor traditionally has been depicted in the mass media as a charismatic hero. The public's lack of sophistication concerning medical technology has permitted the doctor to appear almost magical and extraordinary in his ability to cure the sick. The recent television image of the doctor, however, has tended to emphasize his dependence on education and experience for his medical skills and competence. In effect, he has become more of a super technician than a super magician. This new image coupled with a more medically knowledgeable public (also the result of the mass media) has tended to routinize the doctor's charisma and to turn him more into a mundane culture hero. This shift in public evaluation, and the increased familiarity with the doctor and his virtues and vices, including his fallibility, are rightly the concern of sociologists of work, in that they will, for better or worse, have implications for the effectiveness of medical practice and the doctor-patient relationship.

Just as one man's work may be another man's drudgery, so too may one man's pride in pursuing a particular occupational specialty be matched by another's feeling only humiliation or embarrassment as a result of the low estimation or unfavorable stereotype which society holds of their common occupation. Some occupational pursuits carry with them a kind of social stain or stigma; still others may elicit undercurrents of social rejection and avoidance. A carnival executive of our acquaintance held an M.A. degree. He earned in excess of $60,000 annually and had supervisory responsibility over a massive corporate enterprise. Yet his own parents, he complained, had never told their friends and neighbors what he did for a living because they were ashamed of his occupation. Many rank-and-file "carnies" have experienced being classified as social freaks while visiting a community. Similarly, it may well be that young up-and-coming embalmers, despite the likelihood of their making a good living, are not always welcome as potential suiters by the middle-class parents of marital aged daughters. In the same vein, undertakers are among the few persons who are reluctant to visit their seriously ill friends in the hospital out of concern that their presence may be "unsettling" to their friends. I recall a chiropractor who changed his mind about purchasing a house in a particular neighborhood when he learned that his next door neighbor was a physician. It seems that he feared hostility and rejection on the part of the physician and his family and wished to spare his own family the indignities which he was certain were to come. Bartenders, prizefighters, tatoo artists, strippers, and faro dealers may all be in the unenviable position of being engaged in legal occupational pursuits which are socially marginal in terms of respect, acceptance, and emulation. Any discussion of the social assessment of work invariably leads to a consideration of the discomforts and dilemmas of work, and any examination of the nature of work must of necessity take up the question of the structure and internal processes of work. The work that a man does indeed weaves a sticky web of social influence that touches every aspect of his life and behavior. As Davidson and Anderson have put it:

A man's occupation exerts a most powerful influence in assigning [to] him and to his immediate family their place in society....

The work a man does to earn his livelihood stamps him with mental and physical traits characteristic of the form and level of his labor, defines his circle of friends and acquaintances, affects the use of his leisure, . . . limits his interest and attainment of his aspirations and tends to set the boundaries of his culture.[4]

The pervasiveness of work dictates that it must be examined in its entirety and as it relates to the larger patterns of the social enterprise if we are to acquire an adequate overview of its social import. It is hoped that the readings in this and subsequent chapters will provide such an overview.

Footnotes

[1] O. G. Edholm, *The Biology of Work* (New York: McGraw-Hill, 1967), p. 16.

[2] *Ibid.*, p. 7.

[3] See C. Wright Mills, *White Collar* (New York: Oxford University Press, 1951), esp. Chapter 10.

[4] Percy E. Davidson and H. Dewey Anderson, *Occupational Trends* (Stanford: Stanford University Press, 1940), p. 1.

The Background of Work

Anthropological Background to Work

RAYMOND FIRTH
London School of Economics
University of London

It is from societies simpler than our own that the anthropologist draws the bulk of his material. The significance of human activities can often be seen more clearly there than in all the complexities of an industrial society. My present intention is to consider, from the anthropologist's point of view, what we call "work." I shall deal with it as a social process—involving problems of incentive, organization and control—rather than as a technological or economic process.

What is "work"? We commonly use the term in two senses. The first and broader sense is that of purposive activity entailing the expenditure of energy at some sacrifice of pleasure. The second and narrower sense is that of income-producing activity. The latter is the more appropriate for our discussion. Any definition chosen must be arbitrary. It is, however, important to choose one which does not represent work simply as something people do not like doing.

We can start with the idea that any working group has certain elementary requirements. These include *incentives* to attract members to the work; an *organization* which will distribute tasks and arrange for their co-ordination; a *leadership* which will take the initiative; *controls* which will apply a spur if need be; and *technical standards* to which the work must conform. I hope to show that these requirements occur in the simplest as in the most complex types of working group.

First let us take a simple society where the use of money is unknown as a medium of exchange, and where to talk of the money incentive to work is meaningless. This is the situation in Tikopia, a remote island community

Reprinted from *Occupational Psychology*, Vol. 22 (1948), 94–102, by permission of the author and publisher.

on the fringe of the British Solomon Islands Protectorate. The people, some 1,300 tall, fair-skinned Polynesians, live on a diet of fish, fruit and vegetables. They wear a rough cloth made from the bark of the paper mulberry, and they use steel tools obtained from occasional exchange with the few European vessels that call. Of internal exchange of the ordinary kind there is very little; goods do change hands frequently, but nearly always by process of ceremonial gift and counter-gift. What are the essentials of the work situation in this community?

Theirs is no life of ease. They must often work hard and long to earn food for themselves. A variety of incentives actuates their labour. There is the immediate need for food and clothing. But it is difficult to separate this from other needs of a less personal but not less pressing kind. One of the characteristic features of this island culture is the elaborate set of ceremonies which mark such social events as marriages, funerals and the initiation of boys into young manhood. These ceremonies demand two things—feasting and the exchange of large quantities of bark-cloth and other property. For a funeral or a marriage, which take place equally suddenly and without warning in that community, practically all a household's stores of food and other goods are drained away. For an initiation ceremony, planned months in advance, extra gardens of vegetables are planted by the men and day after day the womenfolk prepare the masses of bark-cloth required. When the great occasion comes, bundles of all kinds are made up and borne off to the houses of the appropriate relatives—puddings and other cooked foods, sprouting coconuts, bark waist-cloths for men and bark shirts for women, and fine leaf mats. In return, wooden bowls, fish-hooks and fishing lines are handed over, on the spot or later on.

Work in food production thus gets in the end a material reward, though in an indirect way. And in the meantime the food serves to fulfil social obligations. It draws together and entertains large groups of people and so strengthens the social ties between them. Other factors come into the work, too. Even in such a simple economic system there is opportunity for superiority in hard work, in luck, or in skill to be shown up by results. And to some of these results tags of achievement are attached. When the flying fish season is on, a skilled crew can take a hundred fish in a night. When the fleet returns in the morning, their score, if it passes the hundred mark, is talked of all round the island—like that of a man who gets a century in a village cricket match. The bonito, a fast sporting fish, can be taken only with rod and line and by a very expert hand. When the day's fishing is over, any fisherman who has obtained a good catch—of ten fish or more—is entitled to stand his rod up in the stern of the canoe as he comes inshore. Such a man is known as "man of bonito"—a label with some prestige attached to it. Men who are noted fishermen can in this society even compose songs in their own honour and have them used as popular dance songs. A

certain amount of boasting is not merely allowed but is expected of someone who can deserve it. But if a man produced the song without the skill to
back it up he would be laughed to scorn over the whole island. Where
modesty and sensitiveness to criticism do come in is in the display of wealth.
What one is entitled to boast about here is not one's wealth but what one
does with it—feeding one's kinsfolk and strangers, for instance.

The simplicity of these symbols of achievement is interesting. The good
fisherman, the good gardener, gets no extra pay. One may wonder how the
simple act of sticking up one's fishing rod at the back of one's canoe should
be so highly prized, or the right to make a song about oneself. Yet it is precisely in these non-material ways that the human being in a society finds
some of his most cherished goals. And they are goals, of course, only because
he lives in a society. It is the opinion of his fellows that gives value to these
simple tokens. It is the rivalry of his fellows, expressed or not, which helps
to spur him on.

In a simple society of this kind the social controls of labour are often
directly evident. Labour is a scarce good in the economist's sense. One of
the ways by which it is secured is not to offer it any high material inducement, but to put it on a footing of social obligation. In particular, people
go and work for other people because they are relatives. Being relatives they
have a moral duty to help. For example, I have mentioned how important
is the preparation of food for the feasts which celebrate crucial social events.
For these feasts a great deal of work is involved in getting food ready for
the oven, cooking it, unwrapping and serving it. It is hot and often boring
work. But getting labour for it is simple. By convention, when a family holds
a feast the cooks are all the men who have married women of that family.
On the day appointed, each of these relatives in law goes along with his
bundle of firewood and his contribution of raw food to take part in the
work. The job is done under the direction of a chief cook who by custom is
the man married to the most important woman in the family. The bigger
the feast the more widely are the family connections traced out, so that even
the husbands of quite distant female cousins come into the scheme. They
have their reward. They get some food and a present in return. But what
really matters is the way in which from time to time their children are given
very substantial presents by their mother's family. This goes on through life
—at initiation, at marriage, or when a person is ill. So the labour of cooking
falls into place as just one item in a complex scheme of services and presentation which affects not only a man and his wife's kinsfolk, but also his
children.

In such societies work is not just an *economic* service, it is a *social* service. The pattern of employment is quite different from that which we know.
The basis of recruitment is not directly the offer of material reward, it is
the social relationship between the person who wants labour and the person

who has it to give. What makes the system work is that the relationship is reversible. He who employs one day may be a worker the next. The absence of a money reward means that output cannot be very carefully calculated in relation to costs. Moreover, to some extent it does away with the ability of the employer to dismiss marginal labour or reward it with less. On the other hand the system does mean that there is rarely a failure of labour, that not too great a strain is put on the physical and psychological capacity of the workers. It also means that relations between the workers and the person for whom the work is being done are good on the whole. The system is one of economic security. In the long run, one can really only withdraw from work by leaving the community. And so long as one stays in the community one is looked after, economically as well as socially. That, I think, is very important.

You may wonder that I have said nothing so far about superstition regulating work. In actual practice, religion and magic play a very great part in providing goals for work, and in giving people confidence. But on the whole they interfere very little with the actual processes of work, which are carried on in a way that we would describe as quite rational. There is one field, however, where religion does enter substantially—that is in setting aside certain days or periods as those on which no work should be done. And after all the derivation of our own word "holiday" is none other than "holy day," with a religious rule against work.

Let us now turn to consider the organization of work in a peasant society, such one meets among the Malays. This is intermediate between the very simple society just discussed and our own complex industrial society. A great deal is done in the way in which we are accustomed by giving a money reward. If a carpenter builds you a house, if you get a medicine man to cure your wife, you pay in money. As a rule some other inducement is offered as well—food, drink, or tobacco. But there are other features about work in such a society. There is little use of machinery, even of a simple kind. Perhaps even more important, there is little idea of the potentialties of machinery in aiding and lightening the work of the people themselves. At present machines are only on the fringe of the economy. Bicycles and buses are freely used, sometimes even bought. But there is hardly any conception of how tractors might be used for ploughing or oil engines for driving the fishing boats. In this sense many Malays are still in a pre-industrial economy. They have no idea of a constantly changing market for their capital, or of capital always looking for new avenues for investment. They do change their investments, but rarely in such a way as to cause any rapid fluctuations in employment of labour. Their capital goods are in fact controlled in ways different from ours. As they are Muslims by religious rule they cannot take interest in any obvious way, though they get the equivalent by roundabout means. The working unit is small and there is no clear-cut division into

manager, provider of capital, and manual worker. So, too, the divisions between profits, interest and wages coming out of the joint product are often
merged.

The society is still one where economic ties are largely personalized.
They do not rest on kinship to the extent found in the simpler Solomon
Islands community. But people usually work together for reasons other than
just money. They are terribly keen into the bargain, and they love haggling.
Yet they borrow from one another and lend to one another freely on the
most flimsy security—sometimes, apparently, no none at all. They attend
one another's feasts and contribute cheerfully to the cost, as a matter of
prestige or because of close relationship. On such ceremonial occasions they
give their labour, but they expect in due course to get a return in kind. In
other words, work and the use of wealth are to them governed by social,
community sanctions, and not by sheer economic individualism.

The difficulty comes when they try, as they are trying nowadays, to carry
on this system side by side with Western industrialism or to adapt their system to it. Throughout the Far East, as in Africa and elsewhere, we are faced
by the crisis of the peasantry. They have a low level of technology and a
comparatively low level of production. Yet their wants are continually expanding as they come more and more into contact with the West. Not only
do they want new kinds of food and clothes but they want modern transport,
cinemas, education, welfare services and a voice in government. To get these
things they must measure themselves against other producers in their own
country and outside. How to bring them up to modern production standards
is one of the real problems of the government concerned. It is the more
difficult, because in order to improve their level of work it looks as if it may
be necessary to break up their social system. Only by more individualistic
effort, it is argued, can a solution be found. Yet it seems very risky to apply
the individualistic idea to these peasant societies, just at the time when we
in Western Europe are feeling that individualism is not enough.

It should now be clear how the elementary labour situation works in
primitive societies. There is a variety of incentives, material and immaterial.
Organization, controls and leadership arise very largely from a close interlocking of social ties on a traditional basis, though there is room for personal
and individual enterprise. Technical standards are laid down primarily by
the needs dictated by community values, though here again individual skill
also comes in.

Now let us compare this with an industrial society. As one tours through
a modern factory, nothing seems to be more alien than the primitive or
peasant working community. Instead of that tightly knit group, bound together by a multitude of social ties, including often the ties of blood relationship and marriage, the factory is an even tighter aggregation of people but
with the primary tie between them only their joint contributions to a com-

mon product or set of products. Instead of a common background and
largely common aims the factory worker has a great diversity of individual
origins and interests; and instead of common knowledge of one another's
home life there is often the most profound ignorance. Membership of the
simple peasant type of group is ordinarily increased slowly by marriage and
by births, and diminished only by death; that of the industrial group may
be altered rapidly by "hiring and firing," or by the competing attractions of
other employments. I have shown that the economic functions of the simple
working group are often interchangeable, the worker of today being the
employer of tomorrow, and both labouring side by side on the job. The
factory has its hierarchy of clearly separable named functions, with often
a considerable gulf between them. While the simple working group relies
for the payment of its members on subtle interlocking services and mingles
the ideas of pay with those of giving presents, the factory has an elaborately
calculated system intended to relate reward as far as possible to the precise
amount of work done.

Yet despite these contrasts I think our analysis so far has some relevance
to modern industrial conditions. A factory is not simply a place where goods
are produced and wages are paid. It, too, is a little social world. Much as
they may rely on their families and on other associations outside for companionship, amusement and other human interests, the workers all depend
on the factory to some extent for some of these things. No one is insensible
to the opinions of his workmates, and one who tries to act as if he were is
apt to be a disturbing element. Those responsible for the organization of the
work tend to find that up to a point the attitudes among the workers resemble those in a family. Management tends to share in the workers' eyes
some of the attributes of the father, to be viewed on the one side with a
mixture of respect and resentment always accorded to authority, and on the
other to become a recipient of information or even confidences about some
of the personal problems of the workers. The larger the factory, the greater
the tendency to the de-personalization of relations. But the position is being
recognized nowadays more and more by the appointment of personnel managers or welfare officers, whose job includes some familiarization with the
character and situation of the individuals in the group.

But if we compare a factory with the simple working group we have
been discussing we see significant points of difference quite apart from size,
mechanization and division of labour. One lies in the difference between the
ability to evoke mechanical response as compared with ability to evoke
human response. It seems to me that the factory provides an opportunity for
knowledge and skill to show by calling out mechanical responses—by getting
the best out of the machines, as it were. But if the work is looked at in a
narrow way it may provide only a very poor chance for calling out human
responses. The corollary is that the worker often develops a proprietary,

quasi-social attitude to his machine. But most people like to be able to draw out their fellows, to exercise a power of attraction, of stimulus over them, to get their sympathy, even in the minute, trivial affairs of everyday life. It is presumably part of that general need for emotional response from other human beings which Linton has recently discussed as a basic psychic need. It also allows opportunity for exercise of leadership. The peasant system of work caters for this to a high degree; the traditional factory system hardly at all. Mechanical efficiency has to be the ultimate aim. It used to be generally thought that mechanical responses, of the machine to man, were the only test, the only significant element, in reaching that aim. Now we realize that human responses are a vital element, too. Rest pauses, factory sports teams, the wall newspaper, the dramatic society all give a chance for personal expression and responses.

To sum up: Work involves not only a set of technological and economic relations; it involves also a set of social relations. The character of these social relations, other things being equal, is a determinant of the employment into which the worker will enter and in which he will choose to remain. It also affects the quality of output. In one job I have seen a machine operator work with a girl who collects the product, which comes out in a steady stream. The feeling of partnership between them, I was told, is very important. Where the girl does not get on with the operator, all production falls off. Both become careless, they do not work together to correct faults, and so on. The feeling of loyalty, which depends on good social relations, may be important, too. There are jobs where slipshod work at one stage would ruin the next, and where part of the appeal to which the workers respond is not to let the other operators down.

Amenities of work, in the form of congenial physical surroundings—light and air; freedom from or minimization of dust and unpleasant noise; medical facilities—are very important. But whatever be the interest in them and appreciation of them when first introduced, they soon come to be taken for granted. When new to the worker, they are regarded as an asset; when he becomes accustomed to them they are regarded as a right. As the physical environment recedes into the background of interest the human environment comes more to the forefront.

Of what does this human environment consist? Workmates of course; and people directly or indirectly in control of the work—foremen, managers, directors. In one factory I visited I was told: "You really want to know everything about the background of this firm at the top to understand what is happening at the bottom." As part of the human environment of work there are also the conditions outside working hours. The home, clubs and other human contacts can directly affect the work situation. Behind this is what may be called the ideology of work—the attitudes towards work, resting on the social and political framework of ideas of the whole society.

In other words, in judging incentives to work it is not the factory situation only that matters; it is the total social situation. In this situation many of the possible incentives are group incentives. This can be seen if we review briefly some of the various types of incentive. First there is the material income. There is little doubt in my mind that this is the primary incentive in modern industry. If one asks workers why they choose a particular firm or a particular job, the answer commonly is in terms of the money. But another important incentive is security. In a way this is the material incentive in a kind of deferred form. People prefer a less well-paid job because they think that in the long run the total income to them will be greater. Other incentives of a personal kind include needs for physical and mental activity. How often has one not heard elderly people who could afford to retire say: "I must have something to do." Another personal factor is desire for variety of experience. This may range from the desire to have a completely new job to the wish for slight variation in the processes of work. This, of course, is associated with differences of temperament, and I have heard it suggested that women often deliberately prefer a task which has only the smallest variation in process. Aesthetic patterning of experience and activity would also appear to be a factor, though a subtle one. Associated with this may be the desire for an outlet for manual skill. One can imagine that a turner at a lathe finds attraction in the design of what he is doing as well as in the exercise of his fineness of judgment.

With some people, the opportunity to get some personal recognition and prestige for their work is undoubtedly attractive. Desire for companionship also may be important, as part of the more general need for emotional response which I mentioned earlier. Finally, the prospect of helping on some common aim, whether it be the war or the nation's recovery, may be for some individuals a powerful incentive.

It will be agreed that all the last set of factors mentioned are group incentives in that they depend basically upon a social background and are promoted by discussion among the workers themselves. Even the first, the material incentive, is not necessarily individualistic. Wife and family may be the real power behind the money drive. A works manager of long experience recently remarked: "The psychologists can say what they like, but after all money is the primary incentive." I would say that it is not money alone; it is money *plus* many of the other things mentioned. To use a very inexact analogy, the money element operates like a piston in a cylinder. It is the piston that rises and falls with a contraction and expansion of the working gases, and that seems to be responsible for the effect that gases are producing in driving the machine. Yet piston without cylinder is nothing; if the cylinder is cracked, the piston cannot work. So it is the social situation of values and relationships which surround the operation of the money element that gives the energy of the worker its significance.

Talk about incentives raises the question of leisure. There is an interesting difference here between the possible alternative uses of time in a peasant and an industrial society. Among most peasants, recreation is organized primarily in the intervals of their working time by those who have other jobs to do. When a Malay peasant has done his rice planting or his fishing for the day, he may bathe, change his clothes, take his drum and go off to take part in the orchestra of a shadow play. The shadow play artist himself may well be a fisherman; he almost certainly has some other occupation than that of purveying amusement. On holidays, laid down by religion as well as the need for rest, amusement comes largely in the same way. As in medieval Europe, when any amusement is provided by a body of people who make it their permanent job, they are normally travelling players.

In a modern industrial society leisure is coming to be regarded as a period to be filled by outside amusements. This is provided not by the workers but by others who specialize in amusement. They tend to be settled, because a large industrial society can give a fresh audience for every performance. And they are available when ordinary work is being carried on. So they provide competing attractions to that work. In the peasant society no individual can easily separate himself from the rest and go off to enjoy himself, because he relies on a team for his recreation. But in the industrial society with amusement as a full-time occupation, any individual can go off when he wants and find it ready made. This must affect his attitude to his work. The study of leisure is an important adjunct to the study of work.

Let me conclude with a general reflection which is not primarily anthropological. As I see it, there is no formula for the solution of the problem of industrial relations. Even the Soviet successes in industry would appear to be due not to their formula as such but to the realistic—some would say ruthless—way in which it has been put into effect. It may be, as is sometimes argued, that in modern industrial conditions improvement on any individual points will make no fundamental difference. Men may get on well with their workmates, they may feel part of a group, they may have diverse outlets for personal expression, leadership and the like. Their morale in a general sense may be very high. Yet they may go slow, or strike, precisely because they do feel themselves to be a group. Only in this case there may be a lack of intellectual and emotional association with management. And this may be very difficult to correct if every endeavour to bridge the gap is met with the view that there should be no party on the other side of the gap. It may be that it is the structure of society and not the structure of industry or the structure of incentives that is in need of overhaul.

The Nature of Work

Towards a Classification of Labour

FRANZ BAERMANN STEINER
Late of Oxford University

Labour, in the broadest sense possible, is associated with or conceived as a kind of subdivision of a still broader category concerning which the sociologist often exhibits signs of uneasiness, and towards which the social anthropologist has developed an attitude which resembles now a joking relationship, now pure avoidance. I am thinking of what is usually called "economics." The typical attitudes of anthropological uneasiness concerning economics can be summed up in two questions: (1) Can I give a true picture of a simple society when I leave out economics? (2) How far can I apply the economic concepts of contemporary industrial society to the life of a primitive group? The second was Malinowski's question. As to the first, since we know that we are not neglecting large bodies of field work data, what we are leaving out must be rather a systematic approach than the facts. In both questions, economics stands for an approach and a terminology, not for facts.

For the sociologist or anthropologist, there are no economic facts. We

Reprinted from *Sociologus*, Vol. 7, No. 2, (1957), 112–29, by permission of the publisher and Dr. H. G. Adler, Literary Executor of the Estate of Franz Baermann Steiner.

This paper is based on a series of eight lectures given by Dr. Steiner at the Institute of Social Anthropology, Oxford University, in 1952, a few months before his death. He considered them only a beginning of his comparative study of labour. In spite of the fact that I know he would consider this statement of his views inadequate, I have edited his lectures for publication. The main editing consisted in omitting detailed examples save for references; I have also omitted a few pages of the lectures which were in cryptic note form that could not be reconstructed without Dr. Steiner's own reanalysis. Thanks are due to Dr. H. G. Adler, Steiner's literary executor, for permission to publish this paper.—PAUL BOHANNAN, Princeton University.

can define economic relations as those relationships existing between human individuals and groups which can be best described in terms of values and non-human quantities. But these economic relationships are social ones. Both the values and quantities reflect cultural norms. From the sociologist's point of view, every economic statement is a shorthand account of human behaviour and relationships between individuals and groups. This statement applies to the law of supply and demand, to inflation, and to all the rest.

A whole complex of very complicated and misleading questions is simplified when we reduce it to one reasonable question: have those social relationships which we single out as economic relationships nothing more in common than the fact that they are amenable to description and treatment by one particular terminology? The position of the classical economist has been to answer in the affirmative and to seek the factual similarity in the supposed subsistence nexus of all economic "facts." My position is that when we deal with economic relationships we speak of social relationships which can be described in a certain way. The usefulness of a descriptive terminology varies with the society of discourse. After these terminological reminders, let us consider what is meant by labour.

Labour and Its Historical Meanings

The story of the definition of labour, particularly in the eighteenth and nineteenth centuries, is such a tangled and weary one, the thoughts put forward are so unattractive and contradictory, that to acquaint you with this part of the history of ideas would involve twenty times more space than we can spare and the building of a whole historical-critical apparatus which would be useful for no other purposes. Reading through that literature, one cannot suppress the suspicion that the people who tried to use the concept of labour were after several quite different things.

In the main, labour has been used in four different contexts. In each of these contexts, admirable use has been made of the word. But difficulties began when scholars tried to define labour in such a way as to account for more than one context—perhaps for three or even all four. I maintain that nothing connects the four contexts except the use of the same important and misleading word. As the resulting confusion has bedevilled anthropological discussion, I shall deal with the contexts briefly.

The first context (1) can be called that of the relation between occupational activities and status. In a society with a certain amount of social mobility and with a developing middle class (of course, the discussion in which all four contexts occur presupposes the existence of a middle class) there is bound to arise a situation in which the relative merits or demerits of occupations cannot be discussed in terms of an inherited status. Thus other terms must be sought. They comprise the supposed intrinsic qualities of those activities which constitute an occupation. In such a system of valued activities one might, as Cicero did, distinguish between the trading classes, by placing the great merchant above the retail trader, not because he is richer, not because he has inherited a higher status, but because, in the course of his activities, he is less likely to cheat than the retailer. Since his activities are more moral, they confer a greater dignity on the person. Cicero influenced Augustine; thence the idea served as a model throughout the Middle Ages, whenever the relative merits of professions were discussed. The last of the important books using such arguments is *The Perfect House-wife*, the work of the sixteenth century Spanish humanist, Fra L. de Leon. This book is, I believe, still given to girls in Latin America before they marry, as an introduction to their duties. We learn from it that the farmer is superior to the trader because in his toil he takes his gains from nature and not from man. Leon takes care to employ two sets of terms: one for the professions or occupations themselves, the other for the activities. Without this terminological separation the consistent value judgement would be impossible.

Quite a different context (2) is that of the so-called division of labour. This refers to the system of terms in which observations are made concerning social changes during which occupations and institutions become more specialized, tasks increasingly shared and subdivided. I will deal more fully with the concept later on; I pass it here, observing only that Aristotle has written very lucidly on the subject without finding it necessary to evolve a labour concept.

A third context (3) is that in which productive labour was distinguished from unproductive labour. Adam Smith is only partly responsible for this most enormous red herring of economics. It is the result of the discussion between the representatives of eighteenth century state capitalism and mercantilism on the one hand, and those of growing industrial capitalism on the other. For the former, productivity referred to the return in state revenue in an over-all estimate. Undertakings that did not fit into the scheme of wealth production were termed unproductive. Smith, however, applied this notion to the microcosm of economic activities rather than to taxation policy, thus creating a concept of an activity which can be either productive or unproductive. For an account of some of Smith's considerations, and at the same time for a muddled attempt to use this productivity notion in a modern context, I refer you to Marshall's well known text book.[1]

The fourth main context (4) is that in which we relate labour to nature on the one hand and to capital on the other. This is a use of the word which is quite necessarily (like the foregoing one) limited to societies of a certain type. There are innumerable occasions on which we make lists carefully under three separate headings: the resources which are given and can be used; the equipment, its values; and what has to be done. To define, revalue or reexamine an item means moving it from one to another of the three interdependent columns.

To sum up: we find labour used in theoretical contexts of four main kinds. In the first, labour relates to an activity, the moral perfection of which is supposed to indicate the status of the respective occupation or profession. In the second, a social process in the course of which human beings perform more and more specialized activities is discussed in terms of the division of something which, as a category, is called labour. In the third, economic processes are made relevant to political theory, and the smallest unit of such an economic process is called labour. In the fourth, attempts are made to analyze industrial production as economic processes (that is, transformation of one kind of value into another), and labour is called something of calculable value, which is distinguished from investment, commodities, profits, and from resources, but is related to them as something valuable.

There is no reason for being critical in the use of the word in any of the four contexts. Our criticism must begin, however, when definitions of labour are sought which intend doing justice to the use of the word in two, three, or all four of the contexts, especially when difficulties created by such a confusion begin to masquerade as genuine problems. There has been a tendency to fill the gaps between these contexts by noxious paddings and links, common sense reasoning of the worst kind, ideological fragments of secularized puritanism, psychological constructions such as the distinction between efforts concerning an aim in the future and others which are their own end (and therefore cannot be labour), or such as the theory of pain which is inflicted on every person who works, and which must be balanced somehow by the enjoyment occasioned by the fruits of this labour to make it—of all things—rational![2]

A Sociological Definition of Labour

Do we want to use the term "labour" as a sociological concept? If we do, we must not try to define several meanings of the word at the same time. Rather, we must relate—even contrast—the sociological meaning to others. With this idea in mind, we have a second list of contexts for the term "labour," which is of a different sort than the first list.

First, there is labour as an *ecological* concept: we may say that a colony of beavers does a measurable amount of labour or work, referring to the change of the environment of the colony's activities. Here the use of the word is legitimate because it is necessary. In the same ecological sense we talk about the labour of a human group.

Second, labour is also used in the *bio-physical*, or as some German schools had it, ergological sense, meaning a certain type of bodily function described in terms of that organism's nutrition and expenditure of energy.

Third, labour is used in *psychological* contexts where the use of the term presupposes knowledge of the drives of the respective individual, not mere surmise about conjectural "motives" behind a population's activities.

If we intend to use the term labour in a fourth sense, we must mean something not alluded to by the other meanings of the word. If that concept is to be a *sociological* one, we must mean something characteristic of social relationships and social groups. It is the purpose of the rest of this section and of the next to examine this context and to clarify this fourth sense of "labour."

There is no activity as such which could not be labour at one time and something quite different at another. We may make a distinction on the basis of the cash nexus and translate the latter into more economic terms. But even that does not cover such instances as the fishing and hunting performed as sport, the yield of which activities is nevertheless sold—a not uncommon occurrence. Or we may think of the often discussed distinction between the amateur and the professional sportsman, and go on distinguishing degrees of gainfulness among the so-called amateurs. Or we may think of the case of the priest celebrating a family ritual in his own house. The activities under varying circumstances of wet nurses and prostitutes could also be made the food for much profound thought. But not only is the cash nexus, where it occurs, insufficient for such distinctions—we have to deal with societies in which services are reciprocated and gifts exchanged, and where people are indemnified rather than remunerated. Moreover, the cases in which it is difficult to distinguish labour from sport and play are in those societies not, as they are in our own, restricted in the main to solitary activities. Quite the contrary. As one example for many, we can cite Firth's quotation from R. H. Matthews about a Maori fishing festival held in 1855.[3]

It seems to me to be impossible to distinguish, either with the help of Sombart's "objective" criteria, or with those of Firth, the labour element from the sport element in that instance. In general, I cannot see what purpose is served by classifying activities in terms of attitudes and supposed motives of the people who perform these activities. Looking beyond the social function and immediate social gratification seems particularly out of place in a primitive economy. In the long run, to distinguish labour from play and from sports is to be left with a riddle: how does labour, something so disagreeable, happen to be done at all? The historian of ideas recognizes the old argument: a natural existence of man without labour, hence labour as an unnatural element to be explained, an activity to which man must be forced if he is not to idle away his time in the most pleasant way he can think of. And perhaps the historian will agree with me in my preference for the original story of the Fall to this unpleasantly garbled secularization.

Labour as an Integrating Activity

When, in a sociological context, we say that an Eskimo watching an ice hole is performing labour, we do not mean that his motives for doing so are different from his motives in performing other activities, as this presupposes a choice having been made by the man, which is begging the question. Nor do we mean that in the tribe's language there is a formulated concept of *labour* which is used to differentiate that kind of activities from others. Nor do we allude to the fact that man needs food. When we single out this activity and call it labour, we mean that the Eskimo is doing something his household expects him to do; on his return home his wife will clean and unfreeze his gear and deal with the catch; the activities of the man and the woman are interdependent in a way which cannot be altered without affecting the social structure.

Thus, sociologically speaking, it is impossible to define labour and to discuss afterwards the way in which it is apportioned and divided. Contrarily, we have to describe labour as part of an activity which is divided and apportioned in a certain way. No psychological surmises can veil the tautology. Labour is an activity, interdependent with other activities of other people, which other activities in some cases belong to the same category as the first, in others they do not. The rules of apportionment of these activities are part of the given social system. Thus, when a man performs activities which are in accord with the laws of his society, and does so in order to gain his livelihood, we regard it as labour not merely because this is necessary to the man's physical survival, but because his society expects him to do something towards gaining his livelihood, and certain activities of others are performed under the condition that he behaves in the way described.

The difference between labour on the one hand and other activities on the other hand, including games or ritual activities of laymen, consists in the fact that the apportionment of the rôles and functions in the latter activities is regulated by other kinds of authorities or offices and connotes other sets of values. This is, as it were, the organizational aspect of labour.

Of labour itself, we can say—and this is the sum total of the preceding —that it is a socially integrative activity. It is a general feature of simpler society (and not only of the very simple ones) that we cannot discern inducements, incentives, motives, apart from the integrative function. The notion that, apart from the promise to make the labouring person a part of a whole to define his place among his fellows, society must hold out carrots or sticks in order to make its members work at all: this is a notion which, fortunately, makes sense only in a limited number of societies. Nor must we forget that, wherever European and other more complex societies have encountered primitive man, the carrot has been a bribe (and a pitiful indemnity) for those who must willingly neglect the performance of what are to them socially important functions so that they can perform during that time activities which are not integrative in their own society. To talk in terms of a more complex society: when a man makes a choice between a paid job and playing football (not as a professional) he is choosing between an activity which assures him of his rôle in his family group, among other things, and an activity which is irrelevant to this group, and his place in this group.

We have to assume that we can study, when dealing with an integrating activity, all its socially situational aspects, and can endeavour to relate them to some structural ramification. This, then, would be part of the sociology of labour in a narrower sense, and such a study could be distinguished from the economics of labour, again in a narrower sense. And this, finally, is my subject.

Division of Labour

The sociology of labour has been discussed in the past in terms of two concepts which sometimes accidentally, sometimes intentionally, are made to overlap: the division and organization of labour.

The idea of division of labour is familiar to most sociologists from the title of that misnomer, Durkheim's *Division du Travail Social*, a book which does not deal with labour at all. Durkheim, looking back on a long tradition of the use of this expression, hardly bothers to explain it. He speaks of the function of what he calls division of labour and, characteristically, thinks it necessary immediately to explain what he means by "function" but not what he means by "division of labour." From what he says later on, it becomes clear that by labour he means all social activities.

Durkheim himself cites Aristotle's Nichomachean Ethics (EN 1133a 16) to illustrate the antiquity of the idea, though he does not mention the relevant passages from the Politics. Moreover, he makes no reference to the long and learned discussion in Adam Ferguson's *Essay on the History of Civil Society*, where the phenomenon is called "separation of arts."

The two main influences on Durkheim and other nineteenth century writers on the subject were Comte and J. S. Mill, dissimilar as they were in many ways. Both these thinkers, because of their notions of progress and because of the function of economic speculation in these notions, derived not a small degree of precision from using economic processes with which they were familiar as prototypes of all social developments. (After all, nineteenth century economic determinism was only one of the ways, and perhaps the most reasonable one, of recognizing the prominence of some economic phenomena of the new industrial society.)

So, when the descendants of Mill and Comte talk about division of labour, a statement about industrial division of labour covers the division of all social activities, just as statement about the proportions of a skeleton applies to the proportions of the body inside which the skeleton is found.

Another feature of the division of labour problem is already obvious at the fountainhead: it is impossible to decide when these authors are thinking of principles of social organization and when of principles of social grouping. This confusion is more fully developed by Adam Smith himself: "The greatest improvements in the productive powers of labour, and the greater part of the skill, dexterity and judgment with which it is anywhere directed or applied, seem to have been the effects of the division of labour."[4]

Three factors were overlooked which refute this point of view. Firstly, the so-called sexual division of labour is a primary example of integrating activities. It conforms to the most general principle of complementary activities without ever giving rise to occupational specialization, either directly or indirectly.

Secondly, the value system of a people may lead to specializations which affect social organization, but be downright contrary to what the classicists meant by social growth. In a famous passage Adam Smith says that: "In a tribe of hunters and shepherds, a particular person makes bows and arrows, for example, with more readiness and dexterity than any other. He frequently exchanges them for cattle or for venison, with his companions; and he finds at last that he can, in this manner, get more cattle and venison than if he himself went to the field to catch them. From a regard of his own interest, therefore, the making of bows and arrows grows to be his chief business and he becomes a sort of armourer."[5]

Smith was wrong on this point. Obviously, the modern anthropologist cannot fathom a man dexterous in manufacturing bows giving up cattle in a cattle society, one where ritual values and status are connected with cattle, merely in order to make bows.

Finally, where primitive man invokes the help of his fellows he asks not for a complementary effort but rather for a quantity of energy which he cannot supply himself. The labour group of neighbours who work in unison, marked by the absence of dividing devices, is organizationally the most primitive form of labour, and the very negation of specialization. So the tendencies toward specialization and institutionalization do not coincide.

Smith's theory can be briefly summarized: man, not the "political man" of Aristotle, but the bartering animal, exchanges services; the unit of worthwhile exchange is also the basis of socially recognized occupational specialization. The basic assumption is that of the commodity character of services— it is this notion which creates the distinction between feudal and capitalistic concepts of labour. Smith projected this notion back into the childhood of man. Very ingeniously, his theory ties up with all major issues of eighteenth century trade-mindedness. But, of course, it does not fit primitive life as we know it.

The major critic of the classical theory was Karl Bücher. He pointed out in *Die Entstehung der Volkswirtschaft* (English translation, *Industrial Evolution*, pp. 284–86) that Adam Smith failed to distinguish between production which is separated into various departments in a single factory, and a tradelike situation in which a good undergoes one or several changes in proprietorship before it reaches the point at which it is ready to go to the consumer. Smith, in short, has two criteria: (1) a process of production and (2) ownership. Bücher separated them.

Bücher's idea is, today, as dated as Adam Smith's. When Bücher says "economic process" he invariably means "industrial processes." He thinks, not in terms of social relationships, but in terms of the actual changes taking place in the raw material, in the commodity, and in terms of disposition of working power. His analysis, which was at the time he did it enlightening and simplifying, now seems merely to get in our way. We are, however, permanently indebted to him for separation of "division of production" (*Produktionsteilung*) from "subdivision of labour" (*Arbeitszerlegung*). In an altogether different context and with a fully developed industrial society as his frame of reference, Max Weber has dealt with these points in the *Grundriss der Sozialökonomik*. As in all his general writtings on the sociology of labour, Weber bases his treatment on Bücher. I cannot, however, regard Weber's distinction between economic and technical division of labour as sound; this would give to his phrase (division of labour) too many functions.

Sexual Division of Labour

We are indebted to Bücher on another point: he was the first non-ethnographer to give attention to the sexual division of labour. However, since this phenomenon does not fit into what he described as division of labour—"increase of the number of labourers necessary for the accomplishment of a definite economic end, and at the same time . . . differentiation of work"—of course he cannot call it division of labour. And he does not. It is to him simply one of the phenomena of the sexual dichotomy. He relates it to other features of that dichotomy and regards it as something peculiarly primitive.[6]

This is a mistake we find in the whole earlier literature on the subject, and very understandable it is. The simpler a society is (that is, the fewer differentiating features there are), the more attention is given to the few.

Hence, in societies without professional grouping, without class or caste formation, without specialization of any kind, the allocation of different tasks to the different sexes seems a very prominent feature. And so it is. But the notion that the more primitive a society the more rigid its sexual division of labour does not follow from it.

The only English monograph on the subject is Dudley Buxton's *Primitive Labour*. He—like all who share his common sense approach—tries to establish classes of activities in terms of ends, finished products, categories of ecological entities or commodities, and then to centre each class of activities around one sex. He then tries to account for the exceptions in this classification by differences in the so-called cultural stages, which when examined closely turn out to be ecological types scarcely related to degrees of social or cultural complexity. With a few exceptions which we shall discuss later, no such permanent categories can be shown to exist. To cite one example for many: sexual division of labour in pastoral pursuits varies widely. It is possible to find, in Africa alone, (1) societies in which only men have to do with herds and women are excluded completely; (2) both sexes have duties with regard to cattle, but only men milk; (3) the same, but only women milk. These differences cannot be accounted for by any ecological theory or by any *one* principle.

If one reviews the relevant passages of a good many ethnographic monographs, one comes to the conclusion that there are several bases on which we might classify facts concerning the sexual division of labour. The first is what I have called integrative directives: what ideological factors lead to the integration? By and large, there are two: one is a space-sex reference, and the other is a tool-sex reference.

The space-sex directive is the more general. Perception of space is sharpened by associating some areas with one sex or the other. In the case of the Lele, reported by Mary Douglas, the spatial arrangement is into three spheres: village, scrub land and forest. Social space is made to coincide with the sexual spheres of activities (women work in the villages; men in the forest; both in the scrub). A similar element is apparent in Tepoztlan, described by Redfield: men's work is done in the field, and hence is subject to one rhythm; women's work, done in the house, is subject to a completely different rhythm.[7]

Second, we can classify by the organization of activities: whether the tasks of women and those of men are interlocking, parallel or separate. In the case of Eskimo division of labour, when the women unfreeze and repair the men's hunting gear on their return from the chase, the tasks are interlocking. Gutmann describes instances among the Chagga in which men and women do parallel work at the same time, but do not perform it together. And finally, one can find many examples of tasks which are performed solely by women, which do not interlock with those of men, and *vice versa*.

These two sets of criteria can be placed on a single chart for ease of characterization:

SEXUAL DIVISION OF LABOUR

	Activities		
	(1)	*(2)*	*(3)*
Intergrative Directives	*Interlocking*	*Parallel*	*Separate*
(a) Pragmatic (space-sex reference)	1 a	2 a	3 a
(b) Contextual (tool-sex reference)	1 b	2 b	3 b

[N.B.: 1 b and 3 a seem not to exist.]

It is useless to talk about the causes or origins of sexual division of labour. Although it is a complex matter, we can discern a few main principles which seem to rule it—but there may be more:

1. Biological. The female is excluded from a number of acts because of biological limits. This does not mean that women are "the weaker sex." This point has been greatly overemphasized: there is a difference between biological conditions and the rationalization of an existing mode of division. Professor Radcliffe-Brown was fond of pointing out that sexual division of labour related to the social personalities of men and women, and not to their bodily characteristics.

2. Psychological. There are groups of activities which are regarded as extensions of motherly functions, such as feeding the family. Therefore, they are woman's work in all societies. In all societies, women are excluded from killing (as labour) and activities derived from it.

3. In all societies there is a male sphere and a female sphere which are mutually exclusive, but not strictly so (though the concomitant ideology may claim that they are). There are rules for sharing the work, which tends to be stricter. Sexual division of labour connoted the two, supplied the terms in all societies for the two.

We have to assume that work cannot be done without minimum differentiation, and the sexual lines of cleavage make it possible for whole classes of activities to be added to those primarily identified with a sex. The result is a network of activities with polarity as organizing principle.

I have introduced into this discussion the concept of integrating directives: I noticed a pragmatic directive and a contextual one. The first referred to a linking of space and sex, the second of tools and sex. These integrating directives of the sexual division of labour relate to the social personalties of men and women of a society. I would be inclined to argue that we can, in regard to labour, discuss in terms of such directives, that is, the distribution of kinds of tasks within a group of human beings, division of labour in a narrow sense.

There is one last factor concerned in the sexual division of labour which must be mentioned here, although it will enter into the classification proposed in the next section: the prevailing division of labour does not apply to menial tasks or to persons in a servile status. An example from our own society will illustrate the point: however unwomanlike and "strenuous" a task which ought not to be performed by the housewife, it can be done by another female—the servant girl. A male servant finds it within his province to do some of the most extremely "womanish" work.

So far as the servant is concerned, the sexual division of labour of his master's group is a privilege from which he is excluded. This exclusion, making the servant into a sort of "sexless" person who ranks with the children, is a mark of servility easy to recognize.[8]

Organization of Labour

Only in the most primitive organizational types is it easy to distinguish division of labour from what is customarily called organization of labour. The difference is a conceptual one: organization of labour does not refer primarily to the apportionment of types of tasks to types of people, but to the way the allotted tasks are performed, either singly or in cooperation with other persons; the nature of the cooperation may lead to further qualifications. If we distinguish single work from group work, the first can be meaningfully subdivided in reference to control or supervision or their absence. The latter, group work, is more complex. Malinowski made a distinction between *communal* and *organized* labour, which led to valuable observations in his field work.

Organized labour, says Malinowski, "implies the cooperation of several socially and economically different elements." However, "when a number of people are engaged side by side, performing the same work, without technical division of labour, or social differentiation of functions,"[9] Malinowski terms it communal labour.

I find Malinkowski's terminology cumbersome and definitely misleading, for where a group of people engages in labour this performance can be called both organized and communal. I will use instead of Malinowski's communal, the word "uniform." Instead of organized, I will speak of "composite" labour. Both kinds are group labour. Group labour implies that the total of all the activities performed lies in one undivided social field of its own. This social field is conditioned by the other social fields in such a way that allotment of rôles and supervising activities which are part of the process do not exist independent of status relationships within the total structure. That is to say, we generally have to subdivide the forms of group labour first as to the uniformity or multiformity of the component individual tasks, and secondly as to the nature of control.

The distinction between series of interdependent tasks performed by several people, and the kind of labour which I have called composite, cannot be drawn by a hard and fast line. This is a case of gradual transition. It is these transitions which we are talking about when we discuss the technological developments of mankind, or the increasing "division of labour."

However, the difference between these two forms of labour on the one hand, and uniform labour on the other, seems so clear cut as to deserve theoretical comment. The main difference lies in the authority structures latent in the forms of group labour. In uniform labour processes, we commonly find a particularly loose and "unorganized" authority structure. The classic case is individuals performing together, for the sake of group stimulus, tasks which they may and do perform independently as well. To this class belong many female activities, particularly food-gathering, not ony in simpler societies but also, e.g., berry picking in country districts. The rota system of women spinning together was fairly widespread in Europe. Similar arrangements are resorted to in emergencies (mending or knitting in groups for soldiers). But even in the spinning meetings, at least in part of eighteenth century Germany, particularly in the Slav minority areas, a modification of the voluntary association is noticeable: it becomes the custom for the assembled girls to nominate one to be in charge of the procedure. This overseer had to warn slackers who were talking too much, and she had to use determination with male visitors who kept the girls from working properly.

On the whole, free working associations of this kind are appreciated for the semi-recreational character of the group activity (hop picking in England). Bücher was the first student to draw attention to the semi-recreational aspect of unison work. In his book, *Arbeit und Rhythmus*, he treated the whole range of phenomena from this point of view. He was the first to realize that uniform labour was a worldwide feature of human society, the more dominant the simpler the social organization of that society, and that all the world over this uniform work is very often unison work. He made the mistake of arguing that unison work of this type was the more primitive kind of work (which is wrong), that therefore it is the earliest kind of labour and represented the origin of labour (the more wrong), and that therefore labour can be proved to have originated in play.

This theory, the obvious errors of which must not blind us in our estimate of this pioneer work, of course angered the puritan sociologists who, for religious reasons they had long forgotten, preferred to see labour as a pain, the self-infliction of which had to be explained by hard necessity if not by the Fall. I would only point out what we all know: that Bücher's theory can be refuted out of hand by anthropological and ethnological evidence, especially from groups like the Pygmies and Bushmen.

The transition is gradual from this type to cases in which the labour group is performing work which, though consisting of many uniform individual tasks, could not be achieved by a single individual. The greater the discrepancy between the achievement which is within one individual's working capacity, and that of the group, the more permanent is the structure given to the work association.

In a later essay, Bücher made a further discovery, of what he called *Bittarbeit*, a term which Firth translates as "invitation labour". The invitation technique, the combination of labour with a feast, in which the man who needs the work done turns into a host, are archaic features found all the world over. They do not always disappear when a new evaluation of labour is introduced. Majumdar tells us that the Ho, a Munda tribe, having been throughly assimilated to wage labour, still practice agricultural assistance for which they insist on being "paid" with a goat, even though it is of much less value than they could receive for the same work at prevailing wage rates.[10] The preference for the goat payment seems absurd on economic grounds alone. We must realize that the goat is offered on the basis of reciprocal obligation, a sphere into which wage payment has not intruded.

"Invitation labour" must also be seen from the standpoint of the authority structures of the labouring group. Basically there are two major contexts for this sort of work: (1) reciprocal obligations (neighbours; kinsmen; age-sets and other associations may always act as uniform labour teams). (2) Chiefship. Malinowski, like Bücher before him, has stressed the great similarity between invitation labour (for in-laws) and tribute labour (for a chief). The difference between the two is that tribute labour is not on a basis of reciprocity, but the feast character of invitation labour is preserved in tribute labour. The chief may act as overseer or appoint one to act on his behalf or officially acknowledge foremen elected by the teams. This makes some difference in the authority structure of the teams, but does not constitute a different type of labour. Firth and Malinowski have confused the organizational (managerial) element contained in such supervision with the terminologically unsatisfactory distinction between communal and organized. This is the only difficult part in the functionalist theory—a difficulty, I maintain, which is merely verbal.

Firth gives an instance which illustrates very well how the chief, apart from being the recipient of tribute labour, may also be the work leader in other tasks, simply because of the association of political leadership with grouping, connected with uniform activities: every unison group is a potential army.[11] We may find this mode of work generally associated with the bidding of the chief or the claim of kinsmen or neighbours, performed by a corporate group with exclusively ritual functions.[12] Of the limits of the use of invitation labour we became aware when examining a case of a society where almost anybody can get invitation labour teams, with hardly any trouble. This is the case with the Tarahumara Indians of Northern Mexico.[13]

Uniform teams are often combined, and in some parts of Africa are combined on the basis of sexual division. The case of the Chagga was mentioned above.

Let us now turn to servile labour, and define it by our organizational approach. Here the difference between single uncontrolled work and single work which is controlled or supervised in various manners is of little importance. However, a further subdivision of the latter (controlled) form matters greatly: this is the kind of labour which is usually called *menial*. The word is used chiefly in reference to work done in the household, implying despicable work or drudgery. But the same work when done by the housewife according to the prevailing division of labour, is not regarded as menial. To understand the degradation, we must realize the servile implications of the absence of sexual division of labour.

Finally, there is the type of labour organization which we called composite labour. Examples are to be found when men combine to form a small boat's crew. They may divide carefully their functions in the fishing team, but they are held together by their organization only during a particular activity or a particular kind of activity. This does not mean that they are necessarily unrelated while not engaged in this activity—they may form a closed group or a kinship group, but the kinship unit is not identical with the fishing group. A very full description is given in Firth on making a canoe.[14]

Another example of composite labour is found in Japanese villages[15] in which a specialist carpenter is called in to oversee composite labour in house building.

The distinctions we have made are summarized in the following chart.[16]

CLASSIFICATION OF LABOUR TYPES

I.   Single individual task or group of tasks
    1.1   Independent of other tasks
        1.11   Uncontrolled
        1.12   Controlled
    1.2   Interdependent with other tasks
        1.21   Uncontrolled

Thus, to sum up, and giving the only possible sociological definition of labour, we may say: labour is any socially integrating activity which is connected with human subsistence. By "integrating activity" is meant a sanctioned activity which thus presupposes, creates and recreates social relationships. Only thus have we isolated a group of social phenomena which it is reasonable to treat separately. And if the nineteenth century economist and would-be philosopher, or his off-spring, were to approach us with some of their profounder questions such as "What about Robinson Crusoe, is he not working in his solitude? Is it not labour? What distinguishes this from the isolated farmer?" etc., etc.,—we can afford not to be amused, and to say that we are interested only in social phenomena.

Footnotes

[1] Alfred Marshall, *Principles of Economics*. Eighth Edition, 1949, pp. 54–56.

[2] Dr. Steiner here cited examples from W. Sombart, *Der moderne Kapitalismus*, 2nd edition, 1920, p. 72; Bronislaw Malinowski, an article in *Nature*, Vol. 25, 927; and Raymond Firth, *Primitive Economics of the New Zealand Maori*, 1929, p. 128.

[3] Raymond Firth, *op. cit.*, pp. 216–18.

[4] Adam Smith, *Wealth of Nations*. London: Henry Frowde, World's Classics Edition, 1904.

[5] *Ibid.*, p. 19.

[6] Karl Bücher, *Die Entstehung der Volkswirtschaft*, I, 30–31.

[7] Robert Redfield, *Tepoztlan*. University of Chicago Press, 1930, p. 84.

[8] For a further discussion of this point see Franz Baermann Steiner, *Prolegomena to a Comparative Study of Slavery*, forthcoming from the Clarendon Press.

[9] B. Malinowski, *Argonauts of the Western Pacific*, p. 159.

[10] D. N. Majumdar, *A Tribe in Transition*, London, 1937, p. 44.

[11] Raymond Firth, *Primitive Polynesian Economy*, pp. 223–24.

[12] E. H. Spicer, *Pascua*, pp. 52–5 ff.

[13] Bennett & Zingg.

[14] *Primitive Polynesian Economy*, pp. 118 ff.

[15] John Embree, *Suye Mura*, pp. 125–26.

[16] Like most of Dr. Steiner's manuscripts, this one becomes more cryptic as one approaches the end. Composite labour was dealt with only very superficially and needs a more thorough analysis, as Dr. Steiner would have been the first to insist.— P.B.

The Meaning and Motivation of Work

of Work

A Socio-Historical View

Work and Human History

WALTER S. NEFF
New York University

We know very little about the beginnings of work. The historians of the ancient world give us little information about how people worked or what they thought about the work they did. Similarly, the other great fields of knowledge which provide us with both direct and analogical information about man's past—archeology and anthropology—have largely concerned themselves with other things. Yet, even the meager and fragmentary evidence available leads to the inference that work has been construed in different ways at different times and in different types of societies.

A historical study of the meaning of work is not merely of abstract interest, because individuals in modern society attach quite different meanings to work in general and to different kinds of work in particular. Are these meanings intrinsic to the work-process itself, or have they merely become associated with work? Like all other aspects of human activity, work behavior is in part a function of the work-process itself and in part a function of how people regard the process. We are all, to some degree at least, creatures of our past. Human thoughts and feelings are not wholly determined by contemporary conditions. The ideas which surround human work are, in part, archaic survivals of periods of human history when very different conditions of work prevailed. . . .

Condensed and adapted from Walter S. Neff, *Work and Human Behavior* (New York: Atherton Press, 1968), copyright © 1968 by Atherton Press; Chapter 3, "Work and Human History: I," and Chapter 4, "Work and Human History: II," pp. 43–68. Reprinted with permission of the publisher.

Work and Social Organization

Whether we accept a developmental paradigm of human history, of the type suggested by V. Gordon Childe[1] or if we merely look at human societies cross-sectionally at the same point in time, it is evident that men have entered into an immense variety of forms of social organization. At the same time, it is also evident that human societies differ greatly in their internal complexity. At least one of the aspects may be observed in the means by which its members predominantly make their living. If we attempt to order societies in terms of levels or degrees of complexity (whether or not we can find a historical order in these levels), we can find at one extreme the relatively small tribal band which gains its subsistence by hunting and by the gathering of natural food products. At the other extreme, we can place the very large, heavily urbanized and industrialized societies of present-day Europe and North America. It is evident that the hunting and gathering forms of social organization are very ancient. They apparently prevailed during most of the half-million or so years that constitute the geological lifetime of the various hominid species and of the 50 to 100 millennia that make up the span of homo sapiens. At the other historical extreme, the industrialized society is very recent, having been in existence in its developed form hardly more than one or two centuries. Between these extremes, and starting with what Childe calls the Neolithic Revolution (circa 6,000 to 8,000 B.C. in Southwest Asia),[2] there have existed a wide variety of forms of social organization based on agriculture and the domestication of food-producing animals as the primary means of life. These latter societies vary enormously in development and complexity of structure, but the basic labor force in each is the agricultural and/or pastoral producer.

In the sections to follow, we shall attempt to characterize the kinds of work performed in various societies, with the objective of indicating the manner in which the meanings attached to work are, in a certain measure, reflections of culture. We may then begin to have some glimmerings of the reasons why human work, as we currently regard it, seems to have many meanings and implications, some of them contradictory, which contribute to many individuals' ambivalent and conflicting attitudes toward it.

Hunting and Gathering Societies

It is, of course, impossible to know anything of the attitudes toward work of our Paleolithic forbears. They left nothing behind them except the stones they worked, occasional skeletons, heaps of refuse, and a few draw-

ings and primitive inscriptions. The very little we know is a tribute to the
patience and in genuity of two or three generations of paleoarcheologists.
We know something of the tools and weapons they fashioned and of their
use of fire.[3] We can infer that they lived in very small bands and in a continuously migratory form of existence, following the wild game and bound
to the seasonal distribution of wild vegetables, cereals, fruits, and berries.
We can even guess something about the early development of religious and
spiritual beliefs, from the examination of burials. But everything else is lost.

In order to learn something of the nature of work behavior in human
groupings which are limited to hunting and gathering, we are forced to
turn to what can be learned from the small remnants of hunting and gathering folk which still exist in certain out-of-the-way corners of the earth. Of
course, there is a danger in this expedient, as anthropologists have frequently
warned. We cannot tell if a contemporary hunting and gathering people
constitutes a deteriorated and degraded remnant of what was once a more
developed and complex culture, or if they are, in reality, Stone Age survivals.
Typically, they continue to exist only because they occupy the most intractable and undesired habitats, where more developed subsistence technologies
are not easily applicable—the frozen tundras of the Arctic Circle, the almost
totally barren deserts of Southwest Africa and Central Australia, the dense
and virtually impenetrable rain forests of South America, Africa, and trop-
ical Asia. Whether they have been forced into these intractable areas or
simply could not escape from them is impossible to determine.

Contemporary examples of the hunting and gathering society are afforded by the more unacculturated aboriginal peoples of Central Australia,
by the surviving Bushmen of the Kalahari Desert in Southwest Africa, and
by the forest Pigmies of Central Africa. Illustrations of hunting and gathering peoples who are undergoing rapid acculturation or are already virtually
culturally extinct are the Eskimo of the Far North, certain Amerindian tribes
of the high, western plateaus adjacent to the Rockies (e.g., the Paiutes of
the Great Basin), and certain tribal groupings in the high rain forests of the
Malayan Peninsula.[4] What appears to be common to these people is that the
exigencies of securing the means of existence are so pressing and the resources available so limited that everyone in the tribal grouping is expected
to "work," even comparatively small children. These peoples live an extremely marginal existence, in highly inimical and impoverished environments. That they manage to exist at all in such hostile surroundings is a
tribute to human ingenuity. Within the limits of Stone Age technology and
with no motive power available other than human muscle, most of these
isolated groupings have manager to develop techniques of living which are
remarkably adaptive to their environments.[5] Nevertheless, these environments are so terribly inadequate that the maintenance of life is extremely
precarious. Compared to the physical size of the habitat, populations re-

main very small. Deaths from starvation and thirst are almost commonplace.

Under these conditions, it seems highly unlikely that the concept of work as a distinctive sphere of behavior was able to acquire any separate meaning at all. Where the labors of procuring the means of existence are so all-pervasive that everyone must participate and where need is so pressing that such labors may be virtually continuous, they may not be perceived as separate activities at all. Typically, the hunting and gathering tribe displays almost nothing resembling a division of labor, except between men and women.[6] Males are more heavily engaged in activities related to hunting and fishing and are, of course, the sole developers of the arts of warfare. Women are primarily engaged in the gathering of natural products, the fabrication of clothing and "household" implements, and the processing of foods for consumption. On the other hand, the manufacture of tools, weapons, and equipment is not otherwise a specialized function. Hunters make their own weapons and snares; women, their own implements. No one is exempt from some kind of labor, except very young children. There are no men who are specialized solely as weapons-makers or canoe-builders; everyone is a "jack-of-all-trades."[7] Similarly, to the degree that there are priests, chieftains, or other forms of political or social leaders, the activities attendant on these offices are carried out extra-curricularly, so to speak. Like their fellow tribesmen, even the shamans and war-leaders are *primarily* hunters or food-gatherers.

Language provides an indirect but impressive bit of evidence of the diffuseness of work in these societies. Their spoken languages do not have a distinctive term for "work," although there are usually extremely elaborate vocabularies for the various kinds of activities and objects involved in hunting, gathering, and the fabrication of implements. Boas has pointed out that the Eskimo have over a score of distinctively different words for "snow."[8] Correspondingly, there are many different words for the same animal, depending on its usefulness, potential for danger, sleeping or waking state, etc. Many preliterate tongues are extraordinarily rich in words to convey detailed information, and equally rich in terms implying social, spiritual, and religious abstractions.[9] However, work appears to be such a natural activity, akin to breathing or existing, that it does not require a distinctive term to describe it.

If contemporary hunting and gathering societies provide any clue to man's distant past, it is that the earliest meaning attached to work is hardly a distinctive meaning at all. It also seems likely that no distinction existed between work and nonwork, between labor and leisure. Herskovits carefully points out that the labors of primitive man are very arduous and virtually continuous.[10] Even when the hunt has been successful and the men are presumably merely "sitting about the campfire," they are usually occupied with something—making an arrow, chipping an arrow-head, shaping a scraper, etc. The women are continually busy. In one form or another, this implicit meaning of work—that work is a "natural" activity—persists to the present day. As we shall see, what was once conceived of as something that all men do became in time something that is only "natural" for certain men.

Work in Early Agricultural and Pastoral Societies

A more elaborate division of labor cannot appear until the techniques of food production become sufficiently advanced so that they are capable of producing a considerable surplus over the immediate needs of the primary producer. This advance in technique occurred at different times in different parts of the world and has not yet appeared in some places. However, it has been associated with a certain stage of development of the arts of agriculture and the taming of animals for food and labor. The earliest complex social organizations first appeared, naturally enough, within the fertile valleys of the great rivers of the Near East, China, India, and North Africa. These areas were marked by specially fortunate combinations of favorable climate, as well as the regular fertilization of soils through annual flooding, which made it possible for comparatively dense agricultural populations to develop. Similarly, the steppe and savannah areas of Central Asia and Africa proved to be ideal conditions for the development of powerful cultures based on pastoralism, once men learned to tame and breed animals for food and transport. Whether the particular form of society that gradually arose was predominantly based on cultivation, was primarily pastoral, or was mixed in type, what was clearly common to all of them was the provision of a relatively stable and ample supply of food and raw materials, a condition that is virtually unknown to the hunting and gathering society.

Under the conditions of an ample and stable supply of food, it was possible for men to be free from the necessity of full-time—or even part-time—production of the necessities of life. The society becomes productive enough not only to supply the needs of the primary producer and his immediate blood family or kinship group, but also to supply the needs of men who become entirely specialized for other occupations—craftsman, priest, political leader. Only at this point does work begin to acquire all sorts of distinctions and qualifications, as well as an increasingly complicated infrastructure of evaluative meanings. The hunting and gathering society is perfectly capable of distinguishing between men's and women's work. In fact, men of the hunting and gathering society will endure the most extreme privations rather than perform the kind of labor that is traditionally associated with the work of women; similarly, women never hunt (the male *berdache*, in Plains Indian societies, performed women's work and was often homosexual and transvestite as well). With the development of herding and agriculture, however, we not only find different kinds of work (with different evaluative meanings attached to each), but also distinctions between workers and non-workers, again with different evaluations related to a developing power structure.

According to Linton, the beginnings of systematic cultivation of cereals (barley, wheat, rice, etc.) and the domestication of food-producing and laboring animals (the cow, sheep, the goat, the water-buffalo, etc.) probably took place as more or less associated activities in the same areas of the world.[11] It appears likely that the first form of transition from the hunting and gathering society was the so-called Neolithic village, the earliest known signs of which date back some 8,000 to 10,000 years in the general region of Southwestern Asia.[12] This is the region roughly bounded by the Mediterranean on the west, the high central Asian mountains on the east, the Black and Caspian Seas on the north, and the belt of deserts ranging from Sinai to India on the south. In this area of a more or less uniform continental climate (hot summers and cold winters), the principal wild grasses which came under cultivation were barley and wheat, while the principal animals available for domestication were sheep, goats, cattle, and (for transport) the ass and the donkey. The early village economy was apparently a mixed economy, with the clear demarcation of agricultural and pastoral peoples being a later development.[13] Whatever the actual course of development, which undoubtedly depended on variations in climate and habitat, the relatively sparse groups of hunters and collectors gradually were replaced by numerically much more populous aggregates of village farmers. It is not even certain that the earliest cultivators were initially sedentary, although settled habitation was one of the ultimate consequences of cultivation. The final establishment of settled habitation was the precondition for everything else that followed: increasing density of population, a rapid development of technology, the consequent appearance of a division of labor, the rise of the early urban civilizations. As Neolithic farming spread into areas not quite suitable for it, adaptations and alterations took place. One of the most important of these differentiations was into cultures that were predominantly based on agriculture and those based on pastoralism. The semiarid steppe and savannah areas of Asia and Africa were poorly adapted for primitive cultivation but were immensely suitable for large-scale pastoral economies. Pastoral societies developed in just such areas in the late Neolithic, but their dependence upon a grazing animal made such new groupings quite the opposite of sedentary. Thus, the Neolithic Revolution gradually produced two quite different groupings of "farmers": the sedentary villager and the migratory pastoralist.

The consequences of the emergence of Neolithic farming were profound, although our brief sketch can hardly do justice to the complexities of the process. For our purposes we are interested not merely in the fact that improved food production permitted relatively enormous population increases, but that it created new kinds of men: not only people who specialized in quite different kinds of labor but also people who became specialized not to work at all, at least in the sense of physical work.

Undoubtedly, populations had to grow considerably and villages had to join together in more or less stable confederations before the need for such men became obvious. But, sooner or later, they appeared. It seems reasonable to suppose that one of the new divisions of labor that eventually arose, in addition to the ancient division between the sexes, was a division between the laborer and nonlaborer. Along with the gradual development of the material technology of food procurement, there must also have been a gradual development of knowledge. The ancient farmer not only had to know where to plant his seeds, he also had to know *when* to plant them. Apparently, the earliest efforts to acquire and maintain systematic knowledge of nature had to do with the succession of seasons—when major annual changes in temperature take place, when increases and decreases in rainfall are to be expected, when the flooding of rivers will occur. It is no accident that astronomy is the oldest of the exact sciences, since the apparent movements of the visible stars and planets are the most stable clues to the succession of the seasons. Men who became unusually expert in this kind of knowledge must early have been thought to possess the most magical of powers, since the entire welfare of the cultivating community depended on their decisions.

Since the borders between magic and knowledge were hardly distinguishable, it seems logical that the possessors and developers of early astronomical observation and calculation would be priests. Thus the shaman or medicine man—who is only a part-time diviner and controller of nature in the hunting and collecting society—eventually becomes a full-time priestly intellectual, as the agricultural economies develop. The earliest religions of which we have any record appear to be heavily tied to astronomical observation and the control of cultivation: the earliest evidence of centralized government appears to point to essentially theocratic forms of organization and control.[14]

The second kind of nonworker who gradually evolved from the mass of agricultural producers may have been the war-chief, who gradually moved into full-time political leadership as the regulation and control of society became more complex. As we have seen, such functions were part-time and temporary in the hunting and gathering societies. Among the predatory tribes of the American Plains, the war-chief was simply a more able and experienced warrior, who was temporarily appointed as a leader for particular raids or actions.[15] When conflict was not the order of the day, he was a hunter and food-collector like his fellows. However, as the Neolithic village grew in productive skills and population, and as villages began to band together for defense or conquest, the need for continuous military leadership must have gradually become a necessity. What probably began as a system of gifts and the lion's share of the loot must eventually have evolved into more or less formal systems of taxation: a fixed share of the social surplus is systematically drained off to maintain the growing institutions of priestly and military leadership which a denser and more productive population both produces and requires. Around these two functions, also, there arises an increasing network of attendant technicians: scribes, surveyors, clerks, weapon-makers, builders of public buildings and fortifications, tax-collectors, police and household-warriors, etc. The advantages of being freed from the exigencies of agricultural labor must soon have become intertwined with issues of social power and an early differentiation begins to take place between the noble—whose sole functions are the arts of government and war—and the commoner who functions as the primary producer of goods and services.

So far we have been discussing consequences which have the character of a developing distinction between mental and manual labor, although we should emphasize that the former was not considered work at all until comparatively modern times. However, within the sphere of work itself, other differentiations were taking place—the full-time craftsman, the full-time trader, the peasant, and the herdsman. Whereas the Paleolithic hunter and the early Neolithic villager was a jack-of-all-trades, the gradual development of population and technology made it possible for people to become specialists. It is probable that the early development of work specialization was on a tribal or village basis, with entire tribes or villages becoming specialists in certain occupations. In Bedouin Arabia and many parts of Africa today, special tribes, whose sole occupation is fabrication of weapons and implements, wander among the sedentary villagers and migratory herdsmen as the tinkers and metal-workers of the area.[16] Similarly, strategically situated villagers may have become specialized as merchants and seamen, giving up virtually all concern with food production to make their living by trade. As villages grew into towns and larger and more stable markets were provided, the migratory craftsmen and traders began to settle in the towns. The craftsmen and merchants who lived in the early urban centers of Asia Minor were most often depicted as outlanders—foreigners—who were not citizens of the community and were subjected to special taxes and exemptions. As time went on, however, the craftsman and the merchant eventually become indistinguishable parts of the general community, but are recognizable as distinct occupations.

We have briefly outlined the development of a division of labor because it bears upon the many meanings which have become associated with work. One of these meanings, which apparently made its appearance very early, distinguishes between occupations that are ignoble and degrading and those that are acceptable or even noble. Not always connected with the heaviness or monotony involved, the meaning has very particularized cultural origins. For example, the contemporary nomadic Bedouin in Central Arabia and North Africa are willing to labor very arduously in breeding and training the camels which are their primary sources of wealth and power, but they will not soil their hands with agriculture or the fabrication of weapons and equipment. To procure these necessities, they use slaves or serfs, secure the needed products by raids on sedentary villagers, or engage in trade.

This particular pattern of culturally derived attitudes toward different kinds of work is found—and appears to have existed for thousands of years —among many human groupings who have specialized in the domestication of food-producing or transport animals.[17] Contemporary accounts of the Masai and Watutsi of Central East Africa[18] or the Fulana of the Western Sudan[19] make one imagine that the same general pattern must have prevailed among such ancient peoples as the Aryan invaders of the Indian subcontinent, or the pre-Classical Greeks who came down with their herds of cattle on the Aegean.

Among many pastoral peoples, the successfully domesticated animal becomes not only the chief basis of wealth and power but a religious and cultural symbol as well—so much so that the breeding and care of the animal becomes the only acceptable occupation for the adult male. Where such pastoral people have conquered or subjugated more sedentary, agricultural peoples, they have either exterminated the latter or transformed them into servile food-producers. Witness the recent bloody struggles between the cattle-breeding Watutsi and the agricultural Bahutu of Central Africa. Apparently, following upon their conquest of the cultivating Bahutu a few centuries ago, the pastoral Watutsi were able to impose a feudal regime in which, as the master-tribe, they could spend all their time on the arts of war and government while remaining passionately devoted to their cattle; the semiservile Bahutu supplied everything else. We can speculate that the same sort of events may have taken place on an immense scale when the cattle-breeding Aryans subjugated the apparently agricultural Dravidian-speakers of ancient India.

However, many societies have existed—and still exist—where the land-holding tiller of the soil is the primary "citizen" of the society. Recall the Greek city-states of the early period, in which the landholding farmer was the only free citizen of the tribes and where other occupations—those of the craftsman, merchant, or even teacher—were relegated to the slave or outlander. But one of the early consequences of the massive division of labor into cultivating and pastoral peoples was a great initial advantage to the latter in the arts of war. Buxton points out that among early pastoral peoples the relatively great increases in population due to a guaranteed food supply, the comparative lightness of the work involved, the continuous need to defend the herds against animal and human enemies, their great mobility compared to the sedentary cultivator, and the continuous pressure to find more fertile grazing lands, have combined to make some pastoral nomads the most warlike peoples in history.[20] Many times in Africa, during comparatively modern times, the cattle nomad has conquered sedentary cultivators.

Of course, the classical example of the power of horse nomadism (a later development than domestication of the cow) is afforded by the Mongol conquests of all of Asia and parts of Europe just a few centuries ago. Whereas the hunting and gathering society simply exterminated its human enemies or used their bodies for food, when cultivation and pastoralism became successful ways of life, the military societies of the ancient world fairly quickly must have discovered new uses for subjugated peoples. While the original objective of the military raid may simply have been loot, it eventually became evident that the conquered sedentary cultivator can be disciplined or compelled to be a continuous source of food and labor. Thus, the institutions of slavery or other forms of forced labor became one of the early consequences of the large-scale development of agriculture, especially where successful cultivation of the soil or domestication of animals led to great spurts in population and consequent military power. Since the peasant farmer was the chief labor force of the ancient world, and since the pastoral conquerer did not regard the care of animals as work but rather as the noble occupation of the free warrior, it is easy to see how work began to take on a generally serville or degraded meaning, wherever the pastoral nomad managed to subjugate the sedentary cultivator.

The Grecian Example

The Proto-Grecian peoples who invaded the Aegean Peninsula in a series of waves during the third and second millennia, B.C., were apparently largely pastoral peoples, like the Aryan invaders of India. They may have developed a considerable culture in the steppe areas of Hither Asia and Eastern Europe, but it was a culture based largely on domestication of animals rather than than settled agriculture. Like many other pastoral and seminomadic peoples, the early Greek invaders must have had a developed and relatively efficient military organization, since we have seen that reliance on large-scale domestication appears generally congenial to the development of warriors.

Whatever the case, once the early Greek invaders reduced the indigenous population and divided the land and power among themselves, a new division of labor began to make its appearance. Even in the Homeric legends, it is perfectly appropriate for the Greek hero to care directly for his cattle and for his wife to perform certain household duties (the weaving of cloth, for example). All heavy agricultural pursuits were relegated to helots or slaves, who were often the conquered native peoples, sedentary cultivators of the soil. By the time the Greek city-states were fuly established, the free Greek citizen had managed to divest himself of all need to labor. This trend reached its apogee among the Spartans, but the Athenian did not lag far behind. The Classical Greek writings make it clear that all useful work in the Greek city-states—even the occupations related to trade and education— was performed by slaves, serfs, or outlander noncitizens. Under these circumstances, it is easy to see how Greek thought developed the conception that work is inherently servile and degrading. . . .

. . . It appears . . . that labor begins to taken on a servile cast in history only when one group of people manages to subjugate another and forces them to labor. Under these conditions, if one is a member of the dominant group, it may indeed be degrading to perform certain kinds of work, since to do so is to be akin to a slave or an alien.

Until a division of labor occurs between workers and nonworkers, with the former condition being associated with some kind of subjugation or dependent state, labor itself cannot be a "bad" thing. Once large-scale slavery or forced labor make their appearance, then the work that conquered or dependent peoples are forced to perform takes on a servile cast. Correspondingly, it then becomes noble to be freed from the necessity to labor. Gradually, new equations begin to arise (labor is equal to servility, freedom from labor equals nobility). Gradually, also, all sorts of institutions and cultural norms arise to support these equations. Thus, in modern times, the slaveowner of the pre-Civil War American South justified the "peculiar institution" by the fact that it freed the slaveowner from the necessity to labor, so that he could pursue knowledge, culture, and the full development of democratic institutions. Similarly, under quite different historical conditions, the Chinese mandarin grew his fingernails very long and bound the feet of his women, in order to prove to the world that he and his did not have to labor. We can find the same origins in the contempt held for any kind of work by the feudal aristocrat of medieval Europe, who felt degraded by any kind of work, even the labors of management and trade. It is interesting that quite similar attitudes still prevail among many cattle-breeding tribes of Africa, who have either been able to compel sedentary cultivators to perform labor for them or who relegate such tasks to their women.[21] Generally a militarily dominant people—who can force others to work for them—can develop the conviction that labor is servile.

The Grecian example provides us with the clearest case of the conditions under which work acquires totally negative meanings. We believe that it is not work itself which is degrading but the power relationships and social structures which surround it. Since the relationships of power and status differ greatly from society to society, we will expect the meanings ascribed to work also to differ.

The Rise of New Meanings

The meanings ascribed to work cannot be derived directly from the nature of the activity, but have many complex social and cultural determinants. Some further insight into these determinants can be gained by exploring how the meanings ascribed to work have changed since the Classical period of Greece and Rome.

If we restrict our study of work and human history to the European tradition, we find two apparently contradictory trends. On the one hand, the decline of cities after the fall of the Roman Empire, and the parallel consolidation of agrarian feudalism, greatly reinforced the conception of the landholding aristocracy that every kind of work was ignoble. On the other hand, new ideas about work began to appear in connection with the contemporary development of the great monastic brotherhoods, which gradually became great productive enterprises in their own right. In his rules for the behavior of monks, St. Benedict declared that both manual and intellectual labor was a religious duty. Rule XLVIII of the Benedictine Order reads as follows: "Idleness is the enemy of the soul and therefore, at fixed times, the brothers ought to be occupied in manual labor, and, again at fixed times, in sacred reading."[22] While the primary duties of the monk were directly religious, work was increasingly seen in the monastic orders as a way of serving the Lord. Idleness was condemned as opening the door to licentiousness. The function of work was not to secure material wealth, but to discipline the soul. Thus, work began to be conceived of as ennobling rather than degrading, as a way of serving God.

While it is customary to attribute these positive ideas about work to the rise of the Protestant Ethic, it is worth noting that they became current as early as the sixth century A.D. and can be considered an essential element in Roman Catholic doctrine. The difference is that initially these new ideas were confined to the members of the monastic brotherhoods and tended to lose their force as the monastic orders became rich and powerful. Luther declared that the monks had become idle and parasitic, living off the labor of the peasant just as the landlord did. By his time, however, the agrarian feudalism of the early Middle Ages had already undergone marked changes. Cities were in the process of re-establishing their sway over the countryside, as centers for trade and fabrication. While power and prestige were still largely in the hands of the landholding nobles and the high church dignitaries, the merchants and the master artisans were becoming increasingly wealthier and more numerous. The idea that work was ennobling began to pass from the monastic orders to these new men of the late Middle Ages— merchants, artisans, and traders—who wanted to find merit in their own pursuits. And, of course, the path to wealth and power for these new groupings in society was through work.

Although the Protestant Reformation did not itself invent the idea that work was ennobling, it was a very powerful force in spreading these new meanings of work. Historians of the rise of modern capitalism have offered different reasons for these changes. While Weber[23] finds the source of the new ideas about work in the religious controversy itself, Tawney[24] argues that the Protestant Reformation was an expression of the aspirations of the rising groups of merchants and craftsmen in the later period of medieval society. However, both of these historical interpretations tend to be one-sided. The idea that work was both ennobling and a path to salvation had its roots in the religious controversies but it also was congenial to the new citizens of the growing towns and cities. These were essentially landless people—many were runaway serfs and former feudal retainers—who could sustain themselves only through labor and had no reason to continue to consider it disgraceful. Compared to the hands of the landholding aristocrat, their hands were dirty, whether actually sullied through manual labor or metaphorically sullied through the mental operations of writing, reckoning, calculating, trading, or handling money.

What had formerly been largely a rule for monks, along with chastity and obedience, now began to acquire religious sanction as a way of life for the laity as well. The ideas of monastic Christianity, however, suffered something of a sea-change when they were taken over by their new advocates. The monks were ordered to work because Benedict believed that they could thereby better serve God. The merchants and artisans who became enthusiastic supporters of the Protestant reforms saw work as the path to *individual* salvation, both here on earth and in the after-life to come. These new attitudes to work and to life became most clear in the adherents of the sterner and more puritanical Protestant sects (e.g., Calvinism).

It is worth noting, however, that the religious content of the new ideas about work and their secular application were somewhat contradictory. Calvinist doctrine, for example, nowhere explicitly states that an industrious life is a prerequisite for salvation. In fact, the concepts of original sin and predestination imply that salvation is a matter of God's will and the elect are chosen in advance of their lives on earth. For the Protestant theologian, as well as his Catholic opponent, it was the after-life that counted. Devotion to God was still the only important aspect of man's life on earth. But what impressed the Protestant laity was the widespread belief that idleness was a path to damnation and work the path to salvation. In the Protestant countries, the moral ideal became that of the sober, prudent, and industrious Christian, who could pile up credit with the Lord by hard labor and "good works" in the world below.

Whether the sources of the Protestant Reformation were economic or ideological, or both, it seems clear that its outcome was the consolidation of new ideas about work. While labor was earlier considered simply as God's punishment for man's sins, or as a brutal necessity forced on the powerless by the powerful, it now acquired moral dignity in its own right. Thus, the countries in which the Protestant Reformation was most successful also became predominantly work-oriented societies, in which the general atmosphere was most conducive to the rapid breakup of agrarian feudalism and the most thoroughgoing industrial progress.

No sooner had the work concept acquired this "good" meaning than the rapidly developing division of labor in a manufacturing society began to invent additional subtleties of meaning. Distinctions began to arise between "mental" and "manual" labor, between skilled and unskilled work, between the labor of the manager of an enterprise and the labor of "hands" or "operatives." While all labor was now seen as "good," there were degrees of goodness. Mental work was better than manual work; skilled work better than unskilled work. Thus, within the framework of the new "positive" meaning of work, a hierarchy of evaluations of work reflected a status hierarchy in society. The outcome of the process is that today we assign social values to people not so much in terms of their religious beliefs, or their genealogical descent (these factors still have force, but not exclusively so) but in terms of what kind of work they perform. Whatever the meanings assigned to positions in this evaluative hierarchy, common to all its levels is the assumption that work is a necessary, even a desirable, aspect of the human condition. However, this concept is essentially modern and would have been wholly alien to the citizen of Classical Athens or the feudal noble of Medieval Europe.

Work in The United States

The conceptions of work which have so strongly influenced the history of the United States are, perhaps, the classical example of the change in its meaning. From the beginnings of colonial America, work has been persistently glorified as something intrinsically good in itself. The reasons appear fairly obvious in the special history of the settlement of North America. In the first place, the bulk of the original white settlers of North America were already convinced advocates of the Protestant Ethic. In the second place, the conditions they encountered were highly uncongenial to the establishment of any kind of agrarian feudalism, except under the special circumstances of black slavery in the South. Unlike the situation in parts of Central and South America, there were no dense populations of agricultural Indians who could be relatively easily enslaved or enserfed. The aboriginals of Northern and Eastern North America were relatively small in numbers and still largely at the hunting and gathering level of technical development. It was far easier to exterminate them or to drive them away than to transform them into servile laborers. Although attempts were made to introduce the manorial system, based on white indentured labor, they could not succeed. The abundance of open land, the extreme scarcity of labor, the early preoccupation with manufacturing and trade, combined with the general anti-aristocratic opinion which many settlers brought with them—all these factors very early established North America as the land where the path to success and security was through hard work.

Except for the slave-owning areas of the American South, no country has been as work-oriented as the United States. Although the idea that work is a virtue was brought to the New World from Europe, the special conditions of life in the United States greatly accentuated it and gave it a special quality. Even in the industrialized countries of Europe, there remained strong aristocratic traditions which maintained a very sharp distinction between intellectual and manual work. The professional or manager never worked with his hands and the manual worker was never expected to use his head. In America, however, this strong distinction between mental and manual work was never as sharp, in part because of the frontier tradition and in part because mechanical invention and tinkering with machinery were early seen both as a path to individual success and a contribution to the common good. The "rags to riches" success story became a great American theme and has been much more than merely a legend. The American of all classes was expected to be "good with his hands," even though manual work was understood to be just a side-line and a hobby for the educated elite. In no country has the inventive mechanic and the practical engineer reached as high status as in the United States and, in instances, as much monetary reward. In no country also has there been as much deliberate glorification of the "school of hard knocks" as compared to the university education. The other side of the coin, of course, was a tendency until comparatively recently to depreciate theoretical education as compared to practical experience on the job. In contrast to Europe, there was nothing at all invidious for an American to start out life as a laborer, although there was certainly no advantage in remaining one.

Although these traditions have somewhat weakened in present-day America and changed their internal character, they are still very strong. The idler tends to be derogated as a drone or parasite. If he is very poor, he is regarded with contempt as someone who doesn't *want* to work; if he is very rich, he is, at best, merely tolerated, but not really respected. Even the multimillionaire is expected to perform some kind of work, although it is no longer anticipated that he will work with his hands. The enormous pace of industrialization in the United States, however, has brought about something of a major shift in the evaluation placed on different *kinds* of work. While it is still more virtuous to work than to be idle, people are now evaluated in accordance with a very elaborate occupational hierarchy. Work is "good" but certain kinds of work are "better" than others. White-collar work is valued more than blue-collar work, and the executive has higher status than the subordinate. However, even the most exalted occupations in the United States are still looked upon as *work* and it is even believed that the top leaders of industry, government and science work harder than anyone else. Heavy manual labor has been stripped of whatever value it once may have had by the great advances in technology, but a man who puts in many hours at his desk or in his office is respected. The meaning of work in the contemporary United States is, therefore, in the sharpest possible contrast to its negative evaluation in Classical Greece and Rome....

Footnotes

[1] V. Gordon Childe. *Man Makes Himself.* London: Watts & Co., 1936; and *What Happened in History.* New York: Penguin Books, 1946.

[2] Cited in E. Anderson. *Plants, Men, and Life.* Boston: Little, Brown, 1952.

[3] W. Watson. *Flint Implements: An Account of Stone Age Techniques and Cultures.* London: British Museum, 1950.

[4] Cf. C. D. Forde. *Habitat, Economy and Society.* London: Methuen & Co., Ltd., 1934.

[5] Many writers have commented on the highly appropriate kinds of clothing, shelter, and weapons developed by the Eskimo tribes of the Far North; others have observed the intricate techniques for finding and storing water which the Bushmen have developed in the Kalahari Desert. These techniques are so impressive that many of them have been at once adopted by Europeans who have penetrated these areas in modern times. See for example: Forde, *op. cit.*; and M. J. Herskovitz. *Economic Anthropology.* New York: Knopf, 1952.

[6] See for example: Forde, *op. cit.*, and L. H. D. Buxton. *Primitive Labour.* London: Methuen & Co., Ltd., 1924.

[7] Herskovitz, *op. cit.*

[8] F. Boas. *The Mind of Primitive Man.* New York: Macmillan, 1911.

[9] A. P. Elkin. *The Australian Aborigines.* Sidney: Angus & Robertson, 1938.

[10] Herskovitz, *op. cit.*

[11] R. Linton. *The Tree of Culture.* New York: Knopf, 1955.

[12] Childe, *op. cit.*

[13] G. Clark. *From Savagery to Civilization*. London: Cobbett Press, 1946; and E. C. Curwen and G. Hatt. *Plough and Pasture: The Early History of Farming*. New York: Schuman, 1953.

[14] C. L. Wooley. *The Sumarians*. Oxford: Claredon Press, 1928; and H. Frankfort. *The Birth of Civilization in the Near East*. London: Williams and Norgate, 1951.

[15] J. R. Swanton. *The Indian Tribes of North America*. Washington. D.C.: The Smithsonian Institution, 1952; and M. E. Opler. *An Apache Life-way*. Chicago: University of Chicago Press, 1941.

[16] N. Glueck. *The Other Side of the Jordan*. New Haven: American School of Oriental Research, 1940.

[17] A. Musil. *The Manners and Customs of the Rawala Bedouin*. New York: Czech Academy of Sciences and Arts, 1928.

[18] Forde, *op. cit.*

[19] D. J. Stenning. *Savannah Nomads*. London: Oxford University Press, 1959.

[20] Buxton, *op. cit.*

[21] Elizabeth Marshall. *Warrier Herdsman*. New York: Knopf, 1965.

[22] H. S. Bettenson, ed. *Documents of the Christian Church*. New York: Oxford University Press, 1947.

[23] M. Weber. *The Protestant Ethic and the Spirit of Capitalism*. London: Allen and Unwin, 1930.

[24] R. H. Tawney. *Religion and the Rise of Capitalism*. New York: Harcourt Brace, 1926.

The Meaning and Motivation of Work

of Work

A Comparative View

Work as a "Central Life Interest" of Professionals

Louis H. Orzack
Rutgers—The State University
New Jersey

Robert Dubin's study of the "central life interests" of industrial workers concluded that work and the workplace do not generally constitute important foci of concern for this group.[1] As Dubin suggests, his study calls for replication with equivalent groups. It would seem desirable in addition to replicate with other components of the labor force. Our knowledge of the professions and of the pattern of commitment by professionals to work-centered goals is extensive.[2] This knowledge leads to the prediction that professionals would stress work and workplace as preferred locations for a variety of activities. Hence, work is more likely to be a "central life interest" for professionals than it is for industrial workers. This paper reports the results of an attempt to verify this prediction.

Categories of Work and Non-Work Experiences

Dubin reports four sub-patterns within the general finding. He classified experiences into the following categories: informal group participation; general activities which furnish personal satisfactions; involvement in formal organizations; and technological behavior.

Concerning informal social relations, Dubin found that a small minority of his subjects preferred to have their informal group life and social participation centered on the job. A parallel finding applied to personal satisfactions: industrial workers derive these from non-work connected experiences and relationships rather than from situations involving their work

Reprinted from *Social Problems*, Vol. 7, No. 2 (Fall 1959), 125–32, by permission of the author and the Society for the Study of Social Problems.

roles. Dubin contends, on the basis of these findings, that work is necessary for industrial workers but is "not valued" by them.

A related assertion is that individuals' attachments to nonvalued but mandatory situations, such as work, will be "... to the most physically and directly obvious characteristics of that situation." He then predicted that "... a significant proportion of industrial workers will score job-oriented for their [formal] organizational experiences" and for their experiences with technological aspects of their environment. His data generally bear out these predictions.

Professionals' Patterns

It can hardly be assumed that professionals do not value their work. They may in fact consider it an end-in-itself. For the professional, work is a focal center of self-identification and is both important and valued. Thus, we predict that professionals will be much more favorably oriented to work as a "central life interest" than are industrial workers.

Training as a professional may stress technological details as well as the learning of behaviors appropriate to future roles in work settings. Such training also encourages aspirants to professional status to prefer a work setting to other settings for the location of informal social relationships and as sources of personal satisfactions; these, however, are not as readily codified for transmission during training as are technology and prescriptions involving organization roles. At most, preferences for work rather than non-work settings as the environment for informal social relationships and for general personal satisfactions may be considered to be probable, if unintended, consequences of necessary segregation during training. Preferences of this sort are not the planned outcome of specific curricular features.

From these considerations, we expect the pattern among the four components of experiences which Dubin reported for industrial workers to be duplicated with professionals. Professionals will be quite likely to prefer the environment of the workplace as the setting for technological and organizational experiences. They will to a lesser degree locate informal social relationships and general personal satisfactions within the arena of work. In all four sectors, however, professionals should weight work settings more heavily than they weight non-work settings.

Sources and Methods

Questionnaires which contained Dubin's "central life interest" items were administered to registered professional nurses employed in public and private general hospitals and a state mental hospital in a midwestern city.[3] The cooperation of these institutions and of the registry organization of nurses employed on private duty in them was obtained. In all, 150 professional nurses completed questionnaires.

Scoring procedures were identical with those reported by Dubin, both for the calculation of the total pattern and for the sub-patterns. Results deriving from professional nurses, as well as those from Dubin's sample of industrial workers, are presented in Table 1.

Results

The most provocative finding concerns the total pattern. Dubin reported that "... for almost three out of every four industrial workers studied, work and the workplace *are not* central life interests." In contrast, for four of every five nurses studied, work and the workplace *are* central life interests.

TABLE 1

Total "Central Life Interests" and Subordinate Experience
Patterns, for Professional Nurses (Orzack) and Industrial
Workers (Dubin)

Pattern	Professional Nurses (Orzack) Percent	Industrial Workers (Dubin) Percent
Total "Central Life Interest"		
Work	79	24
Non-work	21	76
Informal Relations		
Work	45	9
Non-work	55	91
General Relations (Personal Satisfactions)		
Work	67	15
Non-work	33	85
Formal Organization Relations		
Work	91	61
Non-work	9	39
Technological Relations		
Work	87	63
Non-work	13	37
N	150	491

We may infer that these professional nurses are much more interested in their work than Dubin's factory workers were in theirs.

The responses for the four subcategories of experiences support in the main the relevant hypotheses. Informal social relations as well as general sources of personal satisfactions are less likely to be work or job-centered than are experiences involving participation in formal organization and technological behaviors. Professional nurses weight work settings more heavily than they weight non-work settings, with one exception: informal relations are somewhat more closely linked with non-work and community locations than is the case for general personal satisfactions. Nurses are overwhelmingly likely to prefer work to non-work or community settings for their technological behavior and for their participation in formal organizations.

The responses of these professional nurses regarding the preferred centers of informal social relations and the preferred sources of personal satisfactions are interesting. Some 45 percent of the respondents express a preference for work as the environment for informal social relations, with the remainder choosing non-work. About two thirds select work as the preferred source of personal satisfactions, with one third reporting that non-work sources are preferred for these satisfactions.

The relations between these are complicated and deserve further scrutiny. It might be expected that informal social relationships, probably primary group memberships, would furnish the individual with lasting personal satisfactions. However, many of these respondents locate their sources of personal satisfactions in environments other than those which they prefer for informal social relationships. In Table 2, the respondents' choices of work and non-work locations for the two items under consideration are cross-tabulated. Almost 60 percent select the same locations for both; of this group, virtually two fifths indicate that their greatest personal satisfactions

TABLE 2

Work and Non-Work Choices for Informal Group
Experiences and General Sources of Personal
Satisfactions, By Professional Nurses

Informal Group	*Sources of Personal Satisfactions*		
Experiences	Work	Non-work	N
Work	53	14	67
	(35%)	(9%)	
Non-work	48	35	83
	(32%)	(23%)	
N	101	49	150
			(100%)

and most preferred informal group experiences come to them outside the environment of work. Clearly, these are professionals whose outlook on their work can be expected to be somewhat distinctive. This outlook might stress what Habenstein and Christ have called the "utilizer" orientation toward a professional role.[4] Neither the pro-science and technique-committed "professionalizer" nor the warm-hearted "traditionalizer" could readily be expected to have such a perspective. These responses might be typical of professionals who are not engrossed in the area of work in any fundamental sense.

Somewhat similar problems arise in connection with the two other groups of nurses. One third of all nurse respondents indicate they prefer work as the setting from which they derive personal satisfactions, while preferring non-work locations for their informal group participation. Nine percent of the nurses make the opposite choices: they prefer work for informal group experiences, and non-work for their personal satisfactions. Thus, among these nurses with "deviant" orientations, the number who prefer work-centered personal satisfactions but non-work centered informal group experiences is roughly three and one half times as great as those who prefer the alternate locations for their satisfactions and group experiences.

Training as a professional may be expected to instill rather deeply-felt motivations toward personal satisfactions in work activities. However, the sense of colleagueship might not be as fully developed or intensified in nursing as in other professions. For many, nursing is simply back-stop protection against the hazards of widowhood, aging or spinsterhood. These professionals might be expected to have extensive memberships in what they would define as non-work groups, including their families and neighborhood associations. For many with tenuous commitments to nursing, the appeal of those memberships could far out-weigh the significance of colleagues.

These non-professional memberships may levy diffuse demands upon the individuals involved; the appropriate role behavior for them is learned gradually and usually unwittingly. In contrast, colleague groups demand patterned and specified behaviors; the associated roles are achieved through specialized instruction during a limited time span. The kinds of overlapping commitments to non-work groups and to colleague groups for this profession, at least, can be clarified by the results given above. Specialized training produces an individual with particular technological skills who has been taught to find the work rewarding and satisfying. At the same time, the profession does not have appeals sufficient to outweigh role obligations required by non-professional groups in which its members participate.

Such a pattern may be especially characteristic of professions with many females. The critical feature is the transiency of the professionals and the limited commitment that ties the person with the specialty. Or, the pattern might be characteristic of work specialities which have not achieved full status as professions. This implies that the ability of an aspirant profession to dominate the behavior of its members is not firmly established.

Low turnover, and the regular and persistent pursuit of occupationally-specified careers, are among the conditions that must exist for thriving loyalties to specialized occupations and professions. Without question, these are less characteristic of nursing than of most professions, or, indeed, of many crafts. In common with many other fields of work, the demand for increased technological specialization in nursing may in fact alienate the professional and limit the scope of felt rewards to personal satisfactions from technical achievements.

Discussion

Dubin's major hypothesis was that work roles are assigned merely segmental importance in our society and that work is only one competing area of socially-patterned personal identifications. Hence, he concluded, work may be but little valued by labor-force participants. The results reported here suggest that his generalizations need amplification. At least in terms of the technique employed in this study, work appears to be a major, if not dominant, interest of the professional nurses who constituted our sample.

It remains to be seen whether other professionals, for example, in a field which is predominantly male, or in fields which typically involve independent practice, such as optometry[5] or dentistry, reveal different patterns of preference for work locations. Unlike nursing, a dominant feature of such fields is the separation of work from a large organizational setting. The professional may work regularly with others such as receptionists and aides, both of whom he considers to be sub-professional. These are co-workers but not colleagues. At the end of a fatiguing work day, the professional optometrist or dentist may well prefer to relax with other people who are neither his non-professional work associates nor his professional peers. Responses to the "central life interest" inventory by these independent professionals might, as a consequence, show much less orientation to work than was evidenced by nurses.

Study of persons affiliated with other professions whose traditions do not stress independence from large organizations would provide an additional check on the results. Accountancy, where the major options appear to be employment in a department of a large corporation or affiliation with an accounting firm, or teaching, would be good examples of professions whose work occurs in organizational settings. In accounting, however, an historic ideal of independence has been taken over from the traditional ideology of small business ownership. Clinical psychology and social work are illustrative of the aspirant professions that have been tied in with organizational settings and have flourished and expanded in recent years as a direct result. A third interesting possibility is medicine, where hospitals provide large-scale settings for work. At the same time, that profession self-consciously asserts the independence of its members through the maintenance of separate offices, the vesting, in the hands of the medical societies, of critical power over hospitals, and the continuation of separate billing for professional services within hospitals.

Each of these several professions would be expected to have a somewhat different pattern. Medicine and accountancy have in common some tradition of independence in work. Accountancy appears to be less tenacious than medicine in using that tradition as the basis for the image of itself which it projects to the public. However, specialists in both fields usually perform their work in large and complicated organizational environments. It is probable that the unusual status concerns of physicians, coupled with their prestige and income, would result in a greater acceptance of work as a "central life interest" by them than by accountants.

In contrast, clinical psychology and social work have flourished within the context of large organizational settings and without the tradition of independence. Because of their fields' recent and very rapid growth, practitioners riding upon the success of these specialties might be expected to have intensive commitments to work and to their profession. Psychologists and social workers might be expected to show a greater concern for work than specialists in fields that have been stable for a longer period of time.

It may be appropriate to agree with Dubin's speculations that "the sense of attachment" to social organizations is a very important key to the understanding of contemporary industrial relations. For industrial workers, pride in work and in occupation may be less the center of personal identification than is pride in the organizations within the community to which they belong. In contrast to industrial workers, professionals still consider work and workplace as important and valued centers of their activity. Social relations within work settings are salient for professionals. Their specialized and prolonged training encourages the development of a commitment to work and to their professional community.

For industrial workers, mobility within the plant may mean a change from one level or type of job responsibility to another. Status within the factory implies interchangeability. Individuals cannot move easily from one profession to another, and advancements in ranks as a professional generally involve merely a higher degree of responsibility in the same area of work. Within health institutions, however, the emerging emphasis on the "health team" may ultimately lead to the blurring of the separate identities of the participants from several related professions. The long-run consequence may be the loss by the individual professions of what Everett Hughes calls their licence and mandate.[6] If that occurs, one outcome may be the reduction in the professional's attachment to his profession and the rise in his attachment to the organization which furnishes employment as well as to groups outside the field of work. The pattern reported here may then be replaced, in part at least, by that reported by Dubin.

It is not surprising to find that many professionals prefer to derive their personal satisfactions from work and workplace. This is a component of the emerging self-concept encouraged during training, if not specifically dictated by it. Nor is it surprising to find that a greater proportion of professionals than of industrial workers prefer work as locus for informal social relations. Results for the items on technological behavior and participation in formal organizations are also in accord with the hypotheses. Organizations are critical features of the work lives of many professionals. These professional nurses structure formal organizational activity in terms of their work behaviors. Knowledge of the range of controls which constrain these nurses makes this result expected. Further, the emphasis during training and post-training stresses the learning and repetition of certain behaviors and activities considered to be at the core of the profession itself. Technological behaviors such as are covered in the questionnaire are not excluded in socialization for non-work roles but are obviously not important as a component of them.

In the final analysis, the "central life interest" inventory is a measure of values. When it is used to compare professionals and industrial workers, we learn something about the values of these groups. The professional nurses studied here, in contrast to Dubin's industrial workers, do have an overriding preference for work. However, it is not merely technology and competence in dealing with the technological components of the field that binds the professional to his work. The total value commitment by professionals is shown in the greater tendency for professionals than for industrial workers to situate informal group experiences, personal satisfactions and formal organization attachments within the work environment.

As the movement of specialties toward professionalization continues, and as more technical specialties make claims as professions, we might suppose that work will have greater implications for the performance of non-work roles. It might be argued that the more highly organized and professionalized such fields become, the more frequent will be the tendency for work roles to create demands that affect the patterning of non-work activities. Such demands may, however, slacken off as the specialty nears the professional model, and as the professionals can afford, in consequence, to relax.

Perhaps this can be the explanation for the 21 percent of the nurses who did not portray work as a central life interest. These are the individuals who are unlikely to be dedicated professionals. This could be because of marital responsibilities, or beliefs that they will not remain within the field.

However, the deviants may reflect upon a characteristic of the professional community in another sense. As mentioned above, professional fields may well vary in their capacity to have non-work roles of their specialists influenced by work requirements and professional obligations. The ability of these fields to constrain the behaviors of their participants may vary. Nursing as a field is apparently moving toward increased professionalization. The result may be increased constraint upon those who remain in the field, and as a consequent reduction in the amount of deviancy tolerated.

The differences between Dubin's findings for industrial workers and the current findings for professional nurses imply a greater commitment to work by these and perhaps other professionals. Many facets of the professionals' lives are affected by the nature of their work and the extent of their commitment to it and to their places of work. Work is obviously a highly-valued, demanding and important feature of the many roles played in our society by professionals.

The professionals for whom work is a central life interest (not including lawyers) may consider participation in voluntary associations to be incompatible with their work obligations and an active involvement in community decision-making as an inappropriate and unnecessary use of time. Thus, they may withdraw or remain neutral on political issues. Such a disengagement can affect the level of public morality, as social power goes by default to others. In turn, sectors of the public may distrust the detached professionals and acutely resent even a rare venture into civic affairs. This view of professionals accompanies the belief that they ought to persist "until the work is done"; they *should* work more and harder than others; their satisfactions are not supposed to be primarily monetary. The underpayment of professionals, especially in fields where their associations do not significantly affect career entry or influence conditions of work, is a logical outcome.

Two circumstances suggest counter-balancing trends. One is the levelling effect on work roles of ubiquitous large-scale formal organizations. The contemporary professional is increasingly an "organization man," subject to job standardization procedures, personnel policies, and other structural coercions. His degree of participation in public matters may be much like that of other types of "organization man"; he may be resented as a member of the larger category of white collar workers, technicians and specialists. Second, professionals with deviant orientations to work may most readily come to the public's attention. The public may generalize to all professionals and believe them to be not very different from other categories of workers.

The outcomes of this study demonstrate the fruitfulness of re-casting generalizations derived from the study of particular groups as hypotheses for further research under changed conditions. One prospective possibility is to duplicate the technique used in this and in Dubin's study with other work groups, thereby broadening our knowledge of the several ways in which participation in and commitments to work and work activity may affect the other role behaviors of occupational and professional specialists.

Footnotes

This is part of a larger program of current research which analyzes and compares the role orientations of members of different professions. It is carried on with the support of the University of Wisconsin Graduate Research Committee and with a grant from the Wisconsin Department of Nurses.

[1] Robert Dubin, "Industrial Workers' Worlds: A Study of the 'Central Life Interests' of Industrial Workers," *Social Problems*, 3 (January, 1956), 131–142.

[2] See, for example, A. M. Carr-Saunders and P. A. Wilson, *The Professions* (Oxford: Clarendon Press, 1933).

[3] Some minor changes in wording were necessary. Industrial terms, such as "the plant," were replaced by terms appropriate to the organizations where these nurses are employed. Otherwise, the instrument was the same as that used by Dubin.

[4] Robert W. Habenstein and Edwin A. Christ, *Professionalizer, Traditionalizer, and Utilizer* (Columbia, Missouri: Institute for Research in the Social Sciences, University of Missouri, 1955).

[5] Louis H. Orzack and John R. Uglum, "Sociological Perspectives of the Profession of Optometry," *Reprint Series of the Industrial Relations Research Center, University of Wisconsin*, No. 58/1, 1958.

[6] Everett C. Hughes, "Licence and Mandate," in *Men and Their Work* (Glencoe: Free Press, 1958), pp. 78–87.

The Social Assessment
of Work

The Doctor as Culture Hero

The Routinization of Charisma

Barbara G. Myerhoff
University of Southern California
William R. Larson
California Polytechnic College
Pomona

The Culture Hero

Culture heroes have arisen in many areas and have been made known in many ways. At present, one of the most important sources of creating and perpetuating culture heroes is that of mass media, and of these, television in its scope and influence eclipses all others. Of the assorted social types presented as dramatic heroes on television programs, one has recently gained more and more attention—the doctor. From his previous status as an old standby, the doctor has become in the past few years a figure vying in popularity with the ubiquitous cowboy. At present in the United States there are seven regularly scheduled television dramas devoted to the exploits of the doctor. It is the purpose of this paper to examine the nature and function of two kinds of popular heroes, cultural and charismatic, and then to suggest that while the physician as currently depicted in mass media has attributes of both, he appears to be losing his charisma and becoming a culture hero. Finally, some implications of these changes for the practice of modern medicine will be explored.

Culture heroes typically function to promote social consensus, particularly in our society, in the form of mass idols presented by mass media which, as Duncan[1] points out:

> are of primary and crucial importance for the integration of diverse, secular worlds of modern man into cohesion and unity.

Reprinted from *Human Organization*, Vol. 24, No. 3 (Fall 1965), 188–91, by permission of the authors and the Society for Applied Anthropology.

The culture hero is a socializing agent who serves as a model, exemplifying how people should behave in recurring life crises—birth, love, death, illness. To paraphrase Burke[2] on great art, such heroes provide

> ...strategies for selecting enemies and allies, for socializing losses, for warding off evil eye, for purification, propitiation and desanctification, consolation and vengeance, admonition and exhortation, implicit commands or instructions of one sort or another.

The culture hero structures and defines the ingredients of typical situations, depicting appropriate behaviors and accompanying motivations and interpretations. People sharing the attitudes of loyalty, veneration, faith, and possessiveness toward culture heroes in general, and mass idols in particular, experience a sense of common identity and pride, as well as a shared perspective which makes collective action possible. Such a hero enables his public to bridge private experiences, and by participating in his life, to overcome the barriers of discrepant viewpoints. He prepares people to meet life crises which they may encounter, by rehearsing them in desirable responses. A manifest function of the culture hero for the individual is rhetorical—he provides a persuasive statement, a set of instructions, a role definition. A latent function of the culture hero for the society is that of fostering social integration by providing a basis of consensus within groups.

While the culture hero serves as a source of social control in most societies, there are certain features of our society which enhance his importance. First, so much of the culture of an urban, industrialized society is experienced differentially, that multiple rather than shared perspectives prevail, and social barriers abound. Second, the combination of social mobility and a rapid rate of change means that in the course of a single lifetime, an individual must often take many varying, even contradictory roles; he must acquire and discard numerous viewpoints, self-definitions and social values —a situation at best taxing, and at worst profoundly psychologically disruptive. Third, the society is essentially secular, in that no universally shared body of religious beliefs provides a set of ultimate values to serve as a guide in assimilating continual change. Finally, a democratic form of social organization means that, except in cases of illegal behavior, no coercive sanctions are applied to enforce social consensus. These conditions emphasize the importance of informal social controls, making it essential that there be agreement on a set of common definitions, which guide behavior and are authoritative because people voluntarily agree on their correctness. As Klapp[3] has pointed out, in a society as complex, heterogeneous, and unstable as ours, the burden carried by the popular hero as an agent of social integration is enormous.

The Charismatic Hero

In contrast to the culture hero, who is an embodiment of tradition, the charismatic hero is a force of social change. Weber's[4] classical definition of charisma is that it is the gift of grace, vouchsafed by God to an extraordinary individual. The charismatic hero, possessing superhuman and spiritual powers, arises during social crises when consensus has broken down and dissent prevails to the extent that radical changes are indicated. Charisma, in Weber's formulation, is not acquired through learning or training, but is awakened or endowed. The authority of the charismatic hero rests on his dedication to his mission of precipitating social progress and on the awesome, mysterious skills he brings to the task. His followers obey him with passionate devotion because of their belief in his unique, personal powers.

The vaunted status of the charismatic hero is short-lived, however, for

pure charisma exists only in the process of originating.

As the social crisis which gave rise to him subsides, he is beset with the necessity of consolidating the changes he has wrought and stabilizing the new social order. In coping with practical problems of administration, his charisma becomes routinized—transferred from his person to his position. When charisma becomes a transferable, objective entity which accrues to a position rather than an individual, Weber designates it as the charisma of office. The incumbent of a charismatic office is not responding to a divine call; he is rationally selected, trained to discharge mundane duties, and materially rewarded for his efforts. His followers continue to obey, but in a circumscribed, perfunctory manner. Their ardor is dissipated as their hero becomes more recognizably human, more nearly like themselves. This diminution of social distance is synonymous with the loss of charisma. If the formerly charismatic hero does not fade out of the public view entirely, he may in time become a traditional hero, an enduring representative of the stability of the new social order—in short, he may complete the cycle by becoming a culture hero.

The Television Doctor as a Hero

Where does the doctor, as a hero of mass media, fit into this frame of reference? Is he regarded as a saviour, following a call and endowed with unique and superhuman powers—or is he but an ordinary mortal, highly trained in a complex technology? Is his authority based on his personal charisma or on his incumbency of a charismatic position? The physician, it is suggested, has been traditionally depicted as a charismatic hero, a harbinger of progress, and a self-sacrificing, uniquely gifted semi-divine figure. This is true of shamans, medicine men, and witch doctors in many primitive societies, and until recent years was true of the physicians portrayed in mass media in our own society. Presently, this portrayal appears to be changing and the doctor can be seen to be losing his charisma and taking on more of the attributes of a culture hero. This is illustrated by the contrasts between Dr. Christian and Dr. Casey, between the original Dr. Kildare and his presentday counterpart. The earlier versions dramatized and emphasized the unlearned personal attributes of the doctor—his innate wisdom, his intuitive powers, his profound understanding of human nature. The present versions dwell at length on the doctor's acquired, technological skills. Operations, drugs, and machines are currently given so much time and attention on television programs that *they* emerge as the virtual heroes of modern medicine.

Of what, if any, importance is this change? Is there some reason why the doctor need be regarded as charismatic? Parsons[5] identifies certain requirements of the patient-doctor relationship which are seen as necessary for successful treatment of the patient. One of the most essential ingredients of this relationship is that of social distance between practitioner and client, a necessity stressed by social scientists and doctors alike, and recognized explicitly in nearly all societies. Drs. Burling, Lentz and Wilson[6] have remarked:

> ...we are coming to understand that faith in the doctor is a necessary element in cure, that he will not be able to exercize therapeutic leverage if we, as patients, regard him in too prosaic a light.

The medical practitioner is rarely a prosaic figure in any society. Doctors in primitive societies, as well as modern, occupy lofty positions and are set apart from common folk by prestige and appropriate material rewards. Numerous devices are used to emphasize this distinction. The Northwest Indians remove the future medicine man from his surroundings at birth and rear him away from his future patients to a avoid the familiarity which would undermine his authority. The wearing of masks, use of emblems, perfumes, and private languages are employed by contemporary doctors as well as by those in primitive societies. These techniques function to separate the familiar, fallible human elements from the venerated, powerful, and superhuman. The close alliance between religion and medicine in many cultures underlines the necessity for removing the curing role from the realm of the secular to the sacred.

Magic and Faith in Curing

In view of the importance of the doctor's function, it is not surprising that this should be so. He is the guardian of public and private well-being. The individual's health is in his hands, and insofar as sickness is a threat to the continuity of the social order, the physician is a protector of stability. His activities involve highly charged emotions, along with an uncertainty of outcome, since recovery can never be guaranteed. It is precisely this combination of strong emotion and unpredictability that is favorable to the development of magic, as Malinowski[7] has suggested. The doctor has always employed magic as well as science, for in curing technical competence and magic operate simultaneously and in a complementary manner. The gaps in the body of rational, tested techniques are filled in by magic, which is the expression of hope and desire. In the face of uncertainty, magic enables man to proceed with confidence—to overcome anxiety and despair. By ritualizing man's optimism and enhancing his faith, magic enables him to believe in the desired outcome, and so continue his life with equanimity and a sense of potency.

Without such an attitude of hope and belief on the part of the patient, his chances for recovery are greatly reduced. In most societies, it is felt necessary that he have faith in his doctor and believe in the certain success of the treatment. In our society, for example, it is not unusual for a doctor to refuse to continue to treat a patient who expresses doubt in his powers or who evidences a lapse of faith, by "shopping around" or calling in another doctor without his knowledge. The physician helps foster and enhance the patient's faith by surrounding himself with a body of rich magical symbolism that supports his authority. He maximizes his distance from the patient by enveloping himself in mysteries a layman cannot penetrate. Because the patient is inclined toward distrust and suspicion due to his technical incompetence, helplessness, and emotional involvement, it is essential that the doctor assist him in maintaining that attitude which will make it possible for him to respond to treatment. Since the scientific tradition defines reason and emotion as inimical, the continuity between magic and technical competence and the use of magic by the modern physician are explicitly ignored in our society.

Yet tacit recognition of the importance of magic is made by the doctor's insistence on the necessity for hope, faith, and belief on the part of his patient. Indeed, the doctor self-consciously uses the patient's faith in him as a positive technique in his repertoire. That the doctor feels his effectiveness is jeopardized without the social distance necessary to maintaining the patient's faith, is indicated by the current practice of referring intimates—friends and relatives—to other practitioners.

The Curer's Charisma

To indicate that a physician cannot be regarded in too prosaic a light is to suggest that he must be regarded as possessing considerable charisma. Presently, in our culture, a curious transformation is taking place. The doctor appears to be losing his charisma, which is passing into the "office" he occupies. We have, in our times, witnessed the transfiguration of the environment by applied science, which promises unlimited possibilities of nearly magical proportions. Increasingly, the glory of the doctor as a person fades, while his scientific practices glow with promise. Far from being seen as completely unique individuals, doctors are coming to be regarded as interchangeable because they all have approximately the same training—a belief, incidentally, which is self-consciously fostered by medical groups and institutions that socialize the practice of medicine. This is precisely what Weber called the routinization of charisma, the gift of grace being transferred from the man to his position. The doctor is not accorded unquestionable authority, rather it is the science that he applies which is the final authority. As medicine comes to be regarded as more science than art, it follows that doctors are felt to be made rather than born.

The tendency in mass media to emphasize the doctor's scientific skills at the cost of his personal powers is indicative of his passage from the status of a charismatic hero to a culture hero. The doctor is, by now, a very familiar social type, rather predictable, destinctly and recognizably human. So familiar is he that in dramatizations, his traits and responses may be merely adumbrated; the public can readily fill in the details. As he becomes a mundane and routine figure, his public's adulation fades, for it appears to be the case that he is no more semi-divine and extraordinary than any other applied scientist.

In his analysis of biographies in popular magazines, Lowenthal[8] finds parallel changes in heroes depicted before and after 1940. The heroes he examined evidenced the same loss of charisma, the same dwindling of extraordinary and awesome powers. Social distance between reader and hero has been reduced by what he calls the "especially for you" theme. The reader is introduced into the intimate and trivial details of the hero's habits of eating, dressing, and spending.

> There is nothing of the measured distance and veneration that a reader in the classics of biography had to observe before the statesman of the past, or the poet or the scientist. The aristocracy of a gallery of isolated bearers of unusual achievements seems to be replaced by a democratic meeting which requires no special honors or genuflections before the great.

Other writers have designated this extreme manifestation of democratization as "the cult of the common man."

The reduction of the hero's unusual gifts to vapid and common traits has the most profound implications for modern medical practice. There is every reason to think that as the doctor's popularity as a culture hero waxes, his charisma wanes. Further, as science takes on the charisma the doctor has lost, the use of magic to foster hope and courage and to maximize social distance between doctor and patient decreases. Indeed, as the public by means of mass media becomes increasing medically sophisticated and begins to penetrate the mysteries surrounding treatment, the belief in the charisma and authority of science may also fade, leaving the patient no basis for faith and hope whatsoever.

The process whereby a charismatic hero is transmogrified into a culture hero is significant practically as well as theoretically. It seems quite possible, even likely, that as the doctor appears in an increasingly prosaic light, he will lose his power to claim the patient's absolute confidence and in so doing will lose an essential ingredient of his success. Further, there has been a recent increase in the types and numbers of professionals depicted in heroic roles on television programs. Many of these, including psychotherapists, social workers, teachers, and lawyers, require a measure of charismatic authority and social distance in the course of their work. That which we have said about the implications of routinization for the doctor may be applicable to those professions as well.

So long as culture heroes were drawn primarily from historical situations —the cowboy and frontiersman, for example—or were mythical in origin— men and monsters from outer space, among others—public familiarity could not jeopardize occupational effectiveness. But when culture heroes are drawn from the contemporary scene and are depicted as dispensing essential social services, then we do well to inquire into the social price of their heroic status. We suspect that their occupational effectiveness will be impaired by their rapidly growing familiarity.

Footnotes

[1] Hugh Dalziel Duncan, *Language and Literature in Society*, University of Chicago Press: Chicago, 1953, p. 212.

[2] Kenneth Burke, *Philosophy of Literary Form: Studies in Symbolic Action.* Louisiana State University, Baton Rouge, 1941, p. 85.

[3] Orrin Klapp, "Creation of Popular Heroes," *The American Journal of Sociology*, LIV (September, 1948), 135–41.

[4] Max Weber, *The Theory of Social and Economic Organization*, Henderson and Parsons (trans.), Free Press, Glencoe, 1947.

5 Talcott Parsons, "Social Structure and Dynamic Process: The Case of Modern Medical Practice," *The Social System*, Free Press, Glencoe, 1951, pp. 428–79.

6 Temple Burling, Edith M. Lentz, and Robert N. Wilson, *Give and Take in Hospitals: A Study of Human Organization*, G. P. Putnam's Sons, New York, 1956, p. 71.

7 Bronislaw Malinowski, *Magic, Science and Religion*, Doubleday, Anchor, New York, 1948.

8 Leo Lowenthal, "Biographies in Popular Magazines," *American Social Patterns*, William Peterson (ed.), Doubleday, Anchor, New York, 1956, p. 106.

2

THE STUDY OF WORK

INTRODUCTION

As students of human social behavior, sociologists have long recognized the activity of work as a significant and pivotal force in the life and ethos of a society. Social philosophers and others who have addressed themselves to the behavior of man in his social milieu have long been cognizant of the vast social implications of the characteristic pattern of work for a given society. Even if we exclude the early Greek philosophers, we find that as early as the thirteenth century, Ibn Khaldun, the Arab social historian, had recognized the influence of an individual's livelihood on his character, noting that: "The difference between different peoples arises out of the differences in their occupations."[1]

In the centuries that followed, many of the early pioneer economists, sociologists, and even literary writers continued to perceive the social importance of work. For example, late in the eighteenth century, Adam Smith, the Scottish economist, suggested that: "... the very different genius which appears to distinguish men of different professions, when grown up to maturity, is not upon many occasions so much the cause as the effect of the division of labour."[2] During the next century, the industrial revolution and its social impact were to provide the impetus for many important works, both philosophical and literary, focusing on work and its effect on social life. *Das Kapital* resulted from Marx's reactions to the unhappy social conditions, which he saw as concomitant to the technological displacement characteristic of the industrial revolution. Charles Dickens, the English novelist, became a social critic through his novels; in *Oliver Twist, Hard Times,* and other of his writings he reacted to many of the same social conditions that followed the industrial revolution. In a similar vein, Émile Zola, the French novelist, and Samuel Butler and then D. H. Lawrence in England all had as a recurring theme in their writings the social dysfunctions of industrial life.

It is therefore surprising that modern sociologists were so late in conducting systematic studies on various aspects of the phenomena of work, as they had done with other areas of behavior. During the late years of the nineteenth century and the early decades of the twentieth, when the burgeoning field of sociology indicated a curious disinterest in work as a social phenomenon, American and European novelists, short story writers, and poets were developing keen insights into the social and socializing nature of work and building their creations around these insights. From Herman Melville to John Steinbeck and William Faulkner, we have an American literary tradition of using work and the social conditions surrounding work, as well as the impact of these conditions on the individual, as a backdrop if not a central theme of the novel. By including the waging of war as a variety of work, the list of recognized novels having work as one of the central themes is even further expanded. As a result, for those years prior to the modern era of sociological interest in work, the fictional literature of the period stands as an important source of information and insight concerning man and his work.

A few years prior to the turn of the century, the young French sociologist Émile Durkheim was to choose as a topic for his doctoral dissertation the division of labor in society, an undertaking in which he examined the relationship of social solidarity to the complexity of the division of labor in a society. Quite early in the twentieth century, the German sociologist Max Weber published his monumental *The Protestant Ethic and the Spirit of Capitalism.* His remarkable analysis of the interrelationship between Calvinism as a religious movement and capitalism as an industrial and economic development served to provide new understandings of the nature of work motivation and ideology in Western societies. Other significant contributions to the understanding of work include the writings of Thorstein Veblen, who examined the technological evolution of society and the "instinct of workmanship" which he saw as being present at certain levels of technological development. The pioneering scientific management studies of Frederick W. Taylor and the early time and motion studies of F. B. Gilbreth, his student, must also be included. The modern sociological study of work, however, had its genesis in two distinctive early research developments, the industrial productivity studies of Elton Mayo and the research thrust of the "Chicago School."

The so-called Mayo Studies were a series of industrial research projects conducted during the late 1920s and early 1930s by the Department of Industrial Research of the Harvard Graduate School of Business Administration, then directed by Elton Mayo, an Australian industrial psychologist. The studies, carried out at the Hawthorne Works of the Western Electric Company in Chicago, had been initiated as attempts to study the effects of differential environmental conditions and physical arrangements on worker efficiency and productivity. The first experiment of this series was designed specifically to examine the relationship of illumination to work output. Two rooms were used; one served as a control room where the level of illumination remained constant; the other was the experimental room where the lighting could be varied. It was hypothesized that as the lighting provided in the experimental room was increased, work output would likewise increase. Two sets of employees were selected for the two rooms and the experiment began. As anticipated, work output in the experimental room increased; but, to the surprise of the researchers, the output of the control room work group also went up. The level of lighting in the experimental room was alternately increased beyond and lowered below that of the control room. In both instances, the output of both work groups continued to rise. While the answer to this enigma was not immediately apparent to the researchers, the subsequent additional experimental projects were to yield a totally new perspective on work motivation. What was happening, evidently, was that the workers brought into the experiment as strangers were developing a familiarity with each other as the project developed, and consequently were also developing group structure and solidarity. By the same token, it has been argued that the workers' awareness of and sensitivity to their participation in the experiment (the so-called "Hawthorne Effect") was a significant factor in their increased productivity.[3] The group was, in effect, establishing work norms and enforcing them with various kinds of informal sanctions. The previously overlooked factor in work motivation and output was the social dimension. The early Hawthorne research was to provide the foundation for a whole new subdiscipline of sociology, that of industrial sociology. In the decades that have followed a voluminous literature dealing with industrial man and his work has accumulated.

Another significant development in the sociological study of work had begun to emerge in the United States when Robert Ezra Park gave up journalism and joined the relatively new Department of Sociology at the

University of Chicago, shortly before World War I. Vitally interested in people and their day-to-day behavior, Park was a vigorous advocate of field work and personal observation as an appropriate means of sociological research. His contagious enthusiasm for field research was a significant factor in the Chicago sociology department's becoming a center for the study of the city and the social behavior of its inhabitants. Although much of the early research focused on deviant behavior and examined gangs, hobos, and jack-rollers, among other subjects, some of these studies were at the same time studies of work or occupational specialties, even if deviant specialties. In any event, the end result of the research emphasis and approach at Chicago was to have a significant influence throughout the profession on the direction of subsequent research on the social aspects of work and occupational specialty. A literature on specific occupations, with the data primarily obtained from personal observation and contact, began to develop and continues its growth today. Prominent among sociologists interested in the study of work was Everett C. Hughes, whose students examined numerous occupations, ranging from janitors to physicians, and from jazz musicians to prostitutes. Perhaps more than any other single person, Hughes was responsible for the development of occupational sociology. With the increasing conceptual and methodological sophistication of sociological investigation of recent years, a variety of other social dimensions of work have been examined, including occupational structure and processes, occupational role integration in work systems, and the social relationships and interaction attendant to work.

Contemporary sociologists typically attach considerable significance to the study of work. Robert Dubin, for example, states: "We can tell a great deal about the life history of an individual if we know something about his occupational career."[4] In a similar vein, Everett C. Hughes comments that: ". . . a man's work is one of the more important parts of his social identity, of his self, indeed, or his fate, in the one life he has to lead, for there is something almost as irrevocable about choice of occupation as there is about choice of mate."[5] When one considers the prominent place of work in our daily lives as well as our preoccupation with its social implications, the sociological study of work appears patently relevant in our modern industrial and bureaucratic society.

The readings in this chapter address themselves directly to the study of work and provide examples of behavioral science approaches. The first selection, Elias H. Porter's engaging parable of "The System Thinkers," provides an interesting interdisciplinary perspective on the study of work and human relations problems in a restaurant chain. The president of a restaurant chain complains of strains in employee interrelationships, especially during the rush hours, and seeks the consultive aid of a sociologist, a psychologist, and an anthropologist. As a pedagogical device, Porter has us follow the analytical probings of these three types of social scientists into the problem. Although all three conceptualize the problem in terms appropriate to their discipline, together they arrive at a convergent and satisfactory solution on the basis of their analyses. After critiquing their analyses, Porter examines a fourth conceptual approach to the study of work, that of systems analysis, or the study of "the division of work between men and machines and how they are related one to the other." Systems analysis represents a synthesis of social science knowledge blended with engineering and natural science insights. The application of this frame of reference to the problems of work organizations takes the form of human engineering. For Porter the restaurant, like other work enterprises, represents a man-machine system and must be viewed in terms of the symbiotic relationships of its parts to each other and to the internal operations of the system as a whole.

The next reading, "Occupational Sociology: A Reexamination," by Erwin O. Smigel, Joseph Monane, Robert B. Wood, and Barbara Randall Nye, is a survey of the literature of the subdiscipline of occupational sociology during the middle and late 1950s. Previously, in the period from 1946 to 1952, the field had been studied in terms of the articles on occupational sociology published in several major American journals of sociology. During this period there was evidence of increasing research on occupations, particularly on status, mobility, careers, work forces, and professions. In much of the research, however, occupations were not the central concern, but were only a secondary focus. The article reprinted here surveys the literature on occupational sociology since 1953 and concludes that research interest in the field continued to grow; there was continued interest in professional and high status occupations; occupational research became more theoretically systematic and quantitative and occupations were studied more frequently in terms of their interrelationships with other aspects of culture.

In the final selection of this chapter, "The Study of Occupations," Everett Cherrington Hughes provides an overview of the sociological perspective on the social dimensions of work. He reviews some of the classical as well as some of the modern sociological concerns with work and examines some of the seminal concepts associated with work. In his discussion Hughes addresses himself to the division of labor and occupational specialization, the allocation of work rights and responsibility, and the work career, among other topics. He concludes that ". . . the study of careers, and of other facets of occupations and work, [is given] a certain timeliness and excitement that adds to their basic relevance for study of social and social-psychological processes."

Although relatively late in getting under way, the sociological study of work, and especially of occupations per se, has gained considerable momentum in recent years. Some evidence of the quantitative output in this research area can be noted by examining a government bibliography entitled

Sociological Studies of Occupations: A Bibliography, issued in 1965.[6] This bibliography runs to 87 pages and lists almost 1,000 references to occupational sociology studies which have appeared as journal articles, monographs, and theses. An indication of the relative sophistication as well as the degree of comprehensiveness of some of the studies is available in a volume of abstracts prepared on selected references from this bibliography.[7] The bibliography and the volume of abstracts represent only a selected portion of the literature, however, and concentrate primarily on sociological studies of occupation as opposed to the larger topic of the sociology of work. Since their publication, an impressive amount of new material has been published. In all likelihood this trend will continue, and, if anything, promises to significantly accelerate in the future as social scientists increasingly come to appreciate the social import of work. As Everett Hughes has put it:

> In our particular society, work organization looms so large as a separate and specialized system of things, and work experience is so fateful a part of every man's life, that we cannot make much headway as students of society and of social psychology without using work as one of our main laboratories.[8]

Footnotes

[1] Cited in Rollin Chambliss, *Social Thought: From Hammurabi to Comte* (New York: The Dryden Press, 1954), p. 305.

[2] Cited in Theodore Caplow, *The Sociology of Work* (Minneapolis: University of Minnesota Press, 1954), p. 124.

[3] For a detailed critique of these industrial experiments see Alex Carey, "The Hawthorne Studies: A Radical Criticism," *American Sociological Review,* XXXII, No. 3 (June 1967), 403–16.

[4] Robert Dubin, *The World of Work* (Englewood Cliffs, N.J.: Prentice-Hall, Inc., 1958), p. 150.

[5] Everett C. Hughes, "Work and the Self," in J. H. Rohrer and M. Sherif, eds., *Social Psychology at the Crossroads* (New York: Harper & Row, 1951), p. 314.

[6] Office of Manpower, Automation and Training (compiled by Robert P. Overs and Elizabeth C. Deutsch), *Sociological Studies of Occupations: A Bibliography* (Washington, D.C.: U.S. Government Printing Office, 1965).

[7] Robert P. Overs and Elizabeth C. Deutsch, *Abstracts of Sociological Studies of Occupations,* 2nd ed. (Milwaukee, Wisconsin: Curative Workshop of Milwaukee, 1968).

[8] Everett C. Hughes, "The Sociological Study of Work: An Editorial Forward," *The American Journal of Sociology,* LVII, No. 5 (March 1962), 426.

Approaches to the Study of Work

The Parable of the Spindle

ELIAS H. PORTER
Pacific Palisades
California

More and more we hear the word "systems" used in discussions of business problems. Research people are studying systems, experts are looking at organizations as systems, and a growing number of departments and companies have the word "systems" in their names.

Just what *is* a system in the business sense? What does it do? What good is it to management? To answer these questions I shall first use a parable from the restaurant industry. What, you may ask, can executives in manufacturing, retailing, or service systems learn from restaurant systems? I readily admit that if you envisage only menus, customers, waitresses, and cooks in a restaurant, you will find no transferable knowledge. But if you see (as I hope you will) inputs, rate variations, displays, feedback loops, memory devices, queuing, omissions, errors, chunking, approximating, channeling, and filtering in a restaurant system—then you should indeed find some practical value in my parable.

The implications of the parable will be discussed specifically in the second part of the article, after we have reduced it to a paradigm.

The Parable

Once upon a time the president of a large chain of short-order restaurants attended a lecture on "Human Relations in Business and Industry."

From Elias H. Porter, "The Parable of the Spindle," *Harvard Business Review*, XL, No. 3 (May-June 1962), 58–66. Copyright © 1962 by the President and Fellows of Harvard College; all rights reserved. Reprinted with permission of the author and the publisher.

He attended the lecture in the hope he would learn something useful. His years of experience had led him to believe that if human relations problems ever plagued any business, then they certainly plagued the restaurant business.

The speaker discussed the many pressures which create human relations problems. He spoke of psychological pressures, sociological pressures, conflicts in values, conflicts in power structure, and so on. The president did not understand all that was said, but he did go home with one idea. If there were so many different sources of pressure, maybe it was expecting too much of his managers to think they would see them all, let alone cope with them all. The thought occurred to him that maybe he should bring in a team of consultants from several different academic disciplines and have each contribute his part to the solution of the human relations problems.

And so it came to pass that the president of the restaurant chain and

his top-management staff met one morning with a sociologist, a psychologist, and an anthropologist. The president outlined the problem to the men of science and spoke of his hope that they might come up with an interdisciplinary answer to the human relations problems. The personnel manager presented exit-interview findings which he interpreted as indicating that most people quit their restaurant jobs because of too much sense of pressure caused by the inefficiencies and ill tempers of co-workers.

This was the mission which the scientists were assigned: find out why the waitresses break down in tears; find out why the cooks walk off the job; find out why the managers get so upset that they summarily fire employees on the spot. Find out the cause of the problems, and find out what to do about them.

Later, in one of the plush conference rooms, the scientists sat down to plan their attack. It soon became clear that they might just as well be three blind men, and the problem might just as well be the proverbial elephant. Their training and experience had taught them to look at events in different ways. And so they decided that inasmuch as they couldn't speak each others' languages, they might as well pursue their tasks separately. Each went to a different city and began his observations in his own way.

THE SOCIOLOGIST

First to return was the sociologist. In his report to top management he said:

> "I think I have discovered something that is pretty fundamental. In one sense it is so obvious that it has probably been completely overlooked before. It is during the *rush hours* that your human relations problems arise. That is when the waitresses break out in tears. That is when the cooks grow temperamental and walk off the job. That is when your managers lose their tempers and dismiss employees summarily."

After elaborating on this theme and showing several charts with sloping lines and bar graphs to back up his assertions, he came to his diagnosis of the situation. "In brief, gentlemen," he stated, "you have a sociological problem on your hands." He walked to the blackboard and began to write. As he wrote, he spoke:

> "You have a stress pattern during the rush hours. There is stress between the customer and the waitress. . . .
> "There is stress between the waitress and the cook. . . .
> "And up here is the manager. There is stress between the waitress and the manager. . . .

"And between the manager and the cook. . . .

"And the manager is buffeted by complaints from the customer.

"We can see one thing which, sociologically speaking, doesn't seem right. The manager has the highest status in the restaurant. The cook has the next highest status. The waitresses, however, are always 'local hire' and have the lowest status. Of course, they have higher status than bus boys and dish washers but certainly lower status than the cook, and yet they give orders to the cook.

"It doesn't seem right for a lower status person to give orders to a higher status person. We've got to find a way to break up the face-to-face relationship between the waitresses and the cook. We've got to fix it so that they don't have to talk with one another. Now my idea is to put a 'spindle' on the order counter. The 'spindle,' as I choose to call it, is a wheel on a shaft. The wheel has clips on it so the girls can simply put their orders on the wheel rather than calling out orders to the cook."

When the sociologist left the meeting, the president and his staff talked of what had been said. It made some sense. However, they decided to wait to hear from the other scientists before taking any action.

THE PSYCHOLOGIST

Next to return from his studies was the psychologist. He reported to top management:

"I think I have discovered something that is pretty fundamental. In one sense it is so obvious that it has probably been completely overlooked before. It is during the *rush hours* that your human relations problems arise. That is when the waitresses break out in tears. That is when the cooks grow temperamental and walk off the job. That is when your managers lose their tempers and dismiss employees summarily."

Then the psychologist sketched on the blackboard the identical pattern

of stress between customer, waitress, cook, and management. But his interpretation was somewhat different:

> "Psychologically speaking," he said, "we can see that the manager is the father figure, the cook is the son, and the waitress is the daughter. Now we know that in our culture you can't have daughters giving orders to the sons. It louses up their ego structure.
>
> "What we've got to do is to find a way to break up the face-to-face relationship between them. Now one idea I've thought up is to put what I call a 'spindle' on the order counter. It's kind of a wheel on a shaft with little clips on it so that the waitresses can put their orders on it rather than calling out orders to the cook."

What the psychologist said made sense, too, in a way. Some of the staff favored the status-conflict interpretation while others thought the sex-conflict interpretation to be the right one; the president kept his own counsel.

THE ANTHROPOLOGIST

The next scientist to report was the anthropologist. He reported to top management:

> "I think I have discovered something that is pretty fundamental. In one sense it is so obvious that it has probably been completely overlooked before. It is during the *rush hours* that your human relations problems arise. That is when the waitresses break out in tears. That is when the cooks grow temperamental and walk off the job. That is when your managers lose their tempers and dismiss employees summarily."

After elaborating for a few moments he came to his diagnosis of the situation. "In brief, gentlemen," he stated, "you have an anthropological problem on your hands." He walked to the blackboard and began to sketch. Once again there appeared the stress pattern between customer, waitress, cook, and management:

"We anthropologists know that man behaves according to his value systems. Now, the manager holds as a central value the continued growth and development of the restaurant organization. The cooks tend to share this central value system, for as the organization prospers, so do they. But the waitresses are a different story. The only reason most of them are working is to help supplement the family income. They couldn't care less whether the organization thrives or not as long as it's a decent place to work. Now, you can't have a non-central value system giving orders to a central value system.

"What we've got to do is to find some way of breaking up the face-to-face contact between the waitresses and the cook. One way that has occurred to me is to place on the order counter an adaptation of the old-fashioned spindle. By having a wheel at the top of the shaft and putting clips every few inches apart, the waitresses can put their orders on the wheel and not have to call out orders to the cook. Here is a model of what I mean."

TRIUMPH OF THE SPINDLE

When the anthropologist had left, there was much discussion of which scientist was right. The president finally spoke. "Gentlemen, it's clear that these men don't agree on the reason for conflict, but all have come up with the same basic idea about the spindle. Let's take a chance and try it out."

And it came to pass that the spindle was introduced throughout the chain of restaurants. It did more to reduce the human relations problems in the restaurant industry than any other innovation of which the restaurant people knew. Soon it was copied. Like wild fire the spindle spread from coast to coast and from border to border.

So much for the parable. Let us now proceed to the paradigm.

The Paradigm

Each of the three scientists had seen a different problem: status conflict, sex rivalry, and value conflict. Maybe it was none of these but simply a problem in the division of work between men and machines and how they are related one to the other: a problem of system design. Let us explore this possibility by observing the functions which the spindle fulfills.

FUNCTIONS SERVED

First of all, the spindle acts as a memory device for the cook. He no longer needs to remember all the orders given him by the waitresses. This makes his job easier and less "stressful"—especially during the rush hours.

Secondly, the spindle acts as a buffering device. It buffers the cook against a sudden, overwhelming load of orders. Ten waitresses can place their orders on the spindle almost simultaneously. The cook takes them off the spindle according to his work rate—not the input rate. This makes his job easier, more within reach of human capacity—especially during the rush hours.

Thirdly, the spindle acts as a queuing device—in two ways. It holds

the orders in a proper waiting line until the cook can get to them. When dependent on his memory only, the cook can get orders mixed up. It also does all the "standing in line" for the waitresses. They need never again stand in line to pass an order to the cook. This makes their jobs easier—especially during the rush hours.

Fourthly, the spindle permits a visual display of all the orders waiting to be filled. The cook can often see that several of the orders call for the same item. He can prepare four hamburgers in about the same time as he can prepare one. By reason of having "random access" to all the orders in the system at that point he is able to organize his work around several orders simultaneously with greater efficiency. This makes his job easier—especially during the rush hours.

To appreciate the fifth function which the spindle serves, we must go back to the procedures used before the advent of the spindle. In looking at these procedures we are going to examine them in "general system behavior theory" terms:

On the menu certain "information" exists in the physical form of printed words. The customer "transforms" this information into the physical form of spoken words. The information is once again transformed by the waitress. Now it exists in the physical form of written notes made by the waitress. Once again the information is transformed as the waitress converts her notes into spoken words directed to the cook. The cook transforms the information from the physical form of spoken words to the physical form of prepared food. We have an "information flow" which looks like this:

$$\text{Menu} \xrightarrow[\text{Words}]{\text{Printed}} \text{Customer} \xrightarrow[\text{Words}]{\text{Spoken}} \text{Waitress} \xrightarrow[\text{Notes}]{\text{Written}} \xrightarrow[\text{Words}]{\text{Spoken}} \text{Cook} \xrightarrow[\text{Food}]{\text{Prepared}}$$

Now every so often it happened that an error was made, and the customer didn't get what he ordered. Of course you and I would have been the first to admit that we had made an error, but not all cooks and waitresses have this admirable character trait. This is rather understandable since the waitress was trying to do things correctly and rapidly (she wanted all the tips she could get!), and when she was suddenly confronted with the fact that an error had been made, her first reaction was that the cook had goofed. The cook, on the other hand, was trying to do his best. He knew in his own heart that he had prepared just what she had told him to prepare. "It's the waitress' fault," was his thought.

So what did the cook and waitress learn? Did they learn to prevent a recurrence of the error? Indeed not! The waitress learned that the cook was a stupid so-and-so, and the cook learned that the waitress was a scatter-brained so-and-so. This kind of emotionalized learning situation and strainer-

of-interpersonal-relations any organization can do without—especially during the rush hours.

CHANGES EFFECTED

Consider now how the spindle changes all this. The waitress prepares the order slip and the cook works directly from it. If the waitress records the order incorrectly, it is obvious to her upon examining the order slip. Similarly, if the cook misreads the slip, an examination of the order slip makes it obvious to him. The fifth function of the spindle, then, is to provide "feedback" to both waitress and cook regarding errors. The spindle markedly alters the emotional relationship and redirects the learning process.

As errors are examined under conditions of feedback, new responses are engendered. The cook and waitress may find the present order slip to be hard to read, and they may request the manager to try out a different style

of order slip. Now they are working together to solve the system's problems rather than working against each other and disregarding the system's problems. Maybe they find that abbreviations cause some random errors. For example, it might be that HB (Hamburger) and BB (Beefburger) get mixed up just a little too often, so the cook and waitress get together with the manager and change the name of Beefburger to Caravan Special on the menu because the new symbol (CS) will transmit itself through the system with much less ambiguity—especially during the rush hours.

Handling Overload

Had I been asked a few years ago to advise on human relations problems in the restaurant industry as a professional psychologist, my approach would have been limited to what I now call a "component" approach. My thinking would have been directed at the components in the system—in this case, the people involved. I would have explored such answers as incentive schemes, human relations training, selection procedures, and possibly some time-and-motion studies. My efforts would have been limited to attempts to *change the components to fit in with the system as designed no matter how poor the design might be.*

But now I would first concern myself with the "information" which must be "processed" by the system. My concern would be centered on the functions which would have to be performed by the system and how they might best be performed. I would concern myself especially with how the system is designed to handle conditions of information overload.

It is significant that in our parable the three scientists each discovered that the human relations problems arose mostly during the rush hours, in the period of "information overload." How a system responds to conditions of overload depends on how the system is designed. Let us look at how various design features permit the handling of conditions of overload in a number of different kinds of systems.

INCREASE IN CHANNELS

One of the most common adjustments that a system makes to an excess input load is to increase the number of "channels" for handling the information. Restaurants put more waitresses and cooks on the job to handle rush-hour loads. The Post Office hires extra help before Christmas. The telephone system has recently introduced automatic-switching equipment to handle heavy communication loads; when the load gets to a certain point, additional lines are automatically "cut in" to handle the additional calls. Even our fire departments increase "channels." If there is not enough equipment at the scene, more is called in. Department stores put on additional clerks to handle holiday crowds. Military commanders augment crews in anticipation of overload conditions. Extra communication lines may be called up. More troops are deployed.

Almost everywhere we look we see that systems are very commonly designed to increase or decrease the number of channels according to the load.

WAITING LINES

But there comes a time when just increasing the number of channels is not enough. Then we see another common adjustment process, that of "queuing" or forming a waiting line. There are few readers who have not had the experience of waiting in a restaurant to be seated. Other examples are common. Raw materials are stored awaiting production processes. Orders wait in queue until filled. Manufactured goods are stored on docks awaiting shipment. The stock market ticker tape falls behind.

We have already seen how the spindle makes it unnecessary for the waitresses to queue to give orders. And we are all familiar with the modern cus-

tom in most restaurants of having a hostess take our names and the size of our party. What happens when the hostess takes our names down on paper? For one, we do not have to go through the exasperating business of jostling to hold our position in line. Also, the "holding of proper position" is done by machine; that is, it is done by the list rather than by our elbows.

USE OF FILTERING

The hostess' list also illustrates the way in which a system can make still a third type of adjustment, that of "filtering." Because she jots down the size of the group, she can now selectively pull groups out of the queue according to the size of the table last vacated. Some readers will recall that many restaurants used to have all tables or booths of the same size and that everyone was seated in turn according to how long he had waited. It used to be infuriating for a party of four to see a single person being seated at a table for four while they continued to wait. The modern notion of accommodations of varying sizes, combined with the means for filtering, makes the use of floor space much more efficient and the waiting less lengthy. We can see filtering in other systems as well:

- The Post Office handles registered mail before it handles other mail, delivers special delivery letters before other letters.

- In the case of our other most important communication system, the telephone system, there is no way for dial equipment to recognize an important call from an unimportant call: it cannot tell whether a doctor is dialing or the baby is playing. However, where long-distance calls must go through operators, there is a chance for filtering. For instance, in trying to place a call to a disaster area the operator may accept only those calls which are of an emergency nature.

- Military systems assign priorities to messages so as to assure differential handling.

- Orders may be sent to production facilities in bunches that make up a full workday rather than in a first-in-first-out pattern. Special orders may be marked for priority attention.

VARIATIONS OF OMISSION

A system can be so designed as to permit "omissions," a simple rejection or nonacceptance of an input. The long-distance operator may refuse to accept a call as a means of preventing the lines from becoming overloaded. The dial system gives a busy signal and rejects the call. A manufacturing organization may reject an order it cannot fill within a certain time. A company may discontinue manufacture of one line temporarily in order to catch up on a more profitable line that is back-ordered.

As another example of how the design determines what adjustments the system can make, consider the way the short-order restaurant system design utilizes the omission process:

> If waiting lines get too long, customers will turn away. That is not good for business, so restaurants often practice another kind of omission. On the menu you may find the words, "No substitutions." Instead of rejecting customers, the restaurants restrict the range of inputs they will accept in the way of orders. Thus time is saved in preparing the food, which in turn cuts down the waiting time in the queue.

The goal of most restaurants is to process as many customers per unit time as is possible. With a fixed profit margin per meal served, the more meals served, the more profit. But when people are in the queue, they are not spending money. One solution to this is the installation of a bar. This permits the customers to spend while waiting. It is a solution enjoyed by many customers as well as by management.

Chunking and Approximating

Another big timesaver in the restaurant system is the use of a fifth adjustment process, that of "chunking." Big chunks of information can be passed by predetermined arrangements. You may find a menu so printed that it asks you to order by number. The order may be presented to the cook as "4D" (No. 4 Dinner), for example. The cook already knows what makes up the dinner and does not need to be told each item with each order. Preplanning permits chunking, and chunking frees communication channels.

Somewhat akin to the chunking process is a sixth adjustment process, "approximating." To illustrate:

- A business forecaster may not be able to make an exact count of future sales, but he may predict confidently that the sales will be small, moderate, or large.

- An overburdened Post Office crew may do an initial sorting of mail as "local" or "out of town."

- An airborne radar crew may report a "large formation" headed toward the coast.

- An intelligence agency may get a report of "heightened" air activity in a given area.

- An investment house may predict "increased" activity in a certain line of stocks.

- Stock market reports state that industrials are "up" and utilities are "down."

Approximating thus means making a gross discrimination of the input rather than making a fine discrimination.

TRADING ERRORS

A rather unusual adjustment process that a system can adopt to cope with overload is to accept an increase in the number of errors made. It is almost as if systems said to themselves. "It's better to make mistakes than not to deal with the input." For example, the sorting of mail is not checked during rush periods. Mail which is missent must be returned, but in a rush that risk is worth the cost; more mail gets sent where it is supposed to go even though there are more errors. Thus, quality control is given up for the sake of speed. On the other hand, some systems are so designed as to be insensitive to errors. The telephone system will permit you to dial as many wrong numbers as you are capable of dialing.

It is interesting to see in the restaurant system design a deliberate making of errors of one sort in order to prevent the making of errors of another sort during rush hours:

> Picture yourself and a couple of friends dropping into a restaurant during the middle of an afternoon. You are the only customers there. The waitress takes your order. You ask for a hamburger with "everything on it." The next person asks for a hamburger but wants only lettuce and a slice of tomato on it. The third person asks for a hamburger but specifies relish and mayonnaise. The work load is low. There is time to individualize orders.
>
> But during rush hours it would be too easy to make errors. Then the cook prepares only the meat and bun. The waitress goes to a table where there are bowls with lettuce leaves and tomato slices and little paper cups of relish and mayonnaise. On each plate she places a lettuce leaf, a tomato slice, a cup of relish, and a cup of mayonnaise. In most instances she will have brought something that the customer did not order, and in this sense she would have made an "error"; but she would have avoided the error of not bringing the customer something he *did* want.

Other examples of the same type are common. For instance, a sales department sends out brochures to everyone who inquires about a product so as not to miss someone who is really interested. Again, the Strategic Air Command, as a central policy, uses this deliberate making of one type of "error" to avoid a possible error of more severe consequences. The commander may order the force launched under "positive control." It is better to have launched in error than to be caught on the ground and destroyed.

Conclusion

And so we see that there is a new frame of reference, a new point of view coming into use in approaching the problems of organizations. This new frame of reference looks at organizations as systems which (1) process information, transforming the information from one form into another, and (2) are or are not designed to cope with the conditions of overload that may be imposed on them. This new frame of reference is expressed as an interest in how the structure or design of an organization dynamically influences the operating characteristics and the capacities of the system to handle various conditions of information overload.

At the University of Michigan there are some 50 scientists whose primary interests lie in looking for similarities and differences in system behavior at all levels. They examine single cells, whole organs, individuals, groups, and societies for the manners in which these systems cope with their environments in common and in unique ways. They search the work of other scientists for clues to system behavior at one level that is followed at higher or lower orders of organization. As for the application of this "system frame of reference," one finds such organizations as System Development Corporation, the RAND Corporation, and the MITRE Corporation using it in approaching the complex problems of advanced military systems. Here is just a sampling of specific development that bear close watching:

- Because it is possible to view organizations as systems which process data in a continuous sequence of "information transformations" and which may make numerous types of adjustments at the points of transformation, a wholly new concept of training has arisen. In the past, training in business and industry as well as in the military was largely limited to training a man or men to do a given task in a certain way. Now training can be provided that teaches a man or men to adopt adjustment processes suited to the design of the system and the condition of overload. In other words, training for flexibility rather than rigidity is now possible. It should not be long before internal competition is replaced by internal cooperation as the main means of enhancing production.

- Because it is possible to view a business or industry as an information processing system, it is possible to simulate the information flow on digital computers and, by controlling the adjustment processes at each point where the data are transformed, to learn what

effects and costs would be involved in change. The manager will then be able to test his policies realistically on the computer before committing himself in action. A computer program called SIMPAC (Simulation Package) has already been developed at System Development Corporation for this purpose.

• A digital computer program capable of "learning" has been developed. By analyzing how data can be sensed, compared with other data, and stored in the computer's "memory," scientists have been able to "teach" a prototype computer program to recognize letters of the alphabet, cartoon characters, and spoken words. One can look forward to the day when, opening a bank account, he will be asked to sign his name in a variety of situations—e.g., standing, sitting, bending over, and maybe even after a couple of martinis. The computer will learn to recognize his signature from these samples, and at the clearinghouse, after that, his account will be automatically debited and the payee's account automatically credited.

Ludwig von Bertalanffy, the father of general system theory, predicted that general system theory would unify the sciences, thus making it possible for a scientist trained in one area to talk in common terms with another scientist trained in another area.[1] It also seems certain that business and industry will soon profit from the application of the theory of how systems behave.

Footnotes

I am indebted to Robert Mitchell for the sketches which enliven this article and to William Foote Whyte of Cornell University for having developed the spindle in real life.—ELIAS H. PORTER

[1] "General System Theory," *General Systems*, Volume I (Ann Arbor: Society for General Systems Research, 1956), 1–10.

The Sociology of Work

Occupational Sociology

A Reexamination

Erwin O. Smigel
New York University
Joseph Monane
Boston State College
Robert B. Wood
Rochester, New York
Barbara Randall Nye
La Mesa, California

It is important that a discipline take stock of itself from time to time, noting where it has been and where it is going. This task of inventory was undertaken for the years 1946–1952 by one of the authors.[1] The chief sources of data used were articles on occupational sociology (for the seven year period, 1946–1952) published in four major journals of American sociology: the *American Sociological Review*, the *American Journal of Sociology, Social Forces*, and *Sociology and Social Research*, and M.A. and Ph.D. dissertation titles for the years 1946–1952, as listed in the *American Journal of Sociology*.

For purposes of comparison, the 1946–1952 period was divided into two sub-periods: 1946–1949, and 1949–1952. It was found that investigations in occupational sociology were becoming "methodologically more rigorous and theoretically more sophisticated . . . [with] an increased use of sampling procedure, primary sources of data, statistical analysis, frames of reference, and an increased emphasis on the theoretical aspects of occupational sociology."

Evidence of increasing research in "occupational status and mobility, some growth in the investigation of careers, and continuing concern with both working force studies and professions," was also indicated. High status occupations were studied most often. It was revealed, too, that in many of the articles examined, occupations were a secondary rather than a primary focus: race, family, and industrial sociology appeared frequently as central considerations. Little research was discovered on such areas as "the relationship of the client to the occupation, occupation and crime, inter-occupational relations, occupational associations, professionalization, images

Reprinted from *Sociology and Social Research*, Vol. 47, No. 4 (July 1963), 472–77, by permission of authors and publisher.

of occupations, social distance between occupations, the military as an occupation, occupational ethics, and historical and cross-cultural comparisons."

What has happened since 1953? In what directions has occupational sociology moved? Have the earlier trends continued? What new elements have entered the milieu? These are the questions which concern us here. Critical evaluations of the various works in occupational sociology lies outside the scope of the present investigation.

To answer the questions raised above, we have returned to the original sources of data: these titles and articles in the same four major journals previously studied, but now for the seven year period, 1953 through 1959. As in the earlier investigation, the following course description was used as a guide in determining whether articles properly belonged within the realm of occupational sociology:

> Occupational Sociology: An analysis of the professions and occupations; the study of the range, history, social origins and typical career patterns of selected occupations; the influence of factors such as sex, education and minority group membership upon a profession or occupation and on its selection; and the effect of professions and other occupations upon social structure.

I. Extent of Research

Research interest continues in the field of occupational sociology. There has been an increase of 10 percent in the number of articles published in this area between 1953–1959 (195) over the period 1946–1952 (177).

This increase, however, is roughly in line with the growth in the total number of articles in all fields published in the four journals (1510 during 1946–1952, 1650 during 1953–1959). It is in graduate theses that the most conspicuous and meaningful growth of interest in occupational sociology is found—a rise of 44 percent (from 198 in 1946–1952 to 286 in 1953–1959) as against 28 percent for theses in all fields (from 2261 in 1946–1952 to 2893 in 1953–1959). Since theses are a prime source of future articles, we should expect the representation of occupational sociology in the professional journals to proceed with heightened impetus.

A trend also of interest is the spread of graduate research in occupational sociology throughout the American academic world. In the 1946–1952 survey, half of the graduate theses in this field came from five universities: Chicago, New York, Columbia, Wisconsin, and Illinois. Chicago led the field with a fourth of them. By 1953–1959, a far broader academic representation appears. Less than a third of the theses are produced at the five universities mentioned. And Chicago's dominance dwindles to 15 percent of the total.

II. Occupations Studies

Interest during the 1953–1959 period, though less than during the earlier period, continues to center in the high socioeconomic level represented by the professions, and this holds for both articles and theses (Table 1). A partial explanation for continued interest in high-status occupations may be that the glamour and prestige surrounding many professions and professionals in American society influence the researcher and his choice of subject matter. It is possible, too, that professionals are relatively convenient to reach, receptive, of comparable socioeconomic background to the researcher and empathetic to his research goals.

We may note (Table 1) a growth in the proportion of articles and theses devoted to unskilled workers as well as in the proportion of theses concentrating upon clerks and kindred workers: research interest in skilled

TABLE 1

ARTICLES AND THESES DEALING WITH SPECIFIC OCCUPATIONS
CLASSIFIED BY THE EDWARDS' SOCIOECONOMIC SCALE

	Articles		Theses	
	1946– 1952	1953 - 1959	1946– 1952	1953– 1959
Edwards' Socioeconomic Scale	Percent	Percent	Percent	Percent
Professional persons	58.0	47.5	58.6	56.1
Proprietors, managers, and officials	18.0	22.2	13.5	13.8
Clerks and kindred workers	3.0	2.0	2.2	8.7
Skilled workers and foremen	3.0	2.0	11.3	6.6
Semi-skilled workers	8.0	7.1	5.3	6.6
Unskilled workers	1.0	10.1	3.8	6.1
Military*	9.0	9.1	5.3	2.1
Total percent	100.0	100.0	100.0	100.0
Total number of research items concerning specific occupations	(100)	(99)	(133)	(194)

*Military as an occupation was added to the list but not scaled.

workers and foremen appears to be waning. A similar slackening of research interest in the military, measured by theses though not by articles, is also found. Thus articles on the military—insofar as they may originate as theses, and unless sponsored by the military or related agencies—may conceivably decline. This is of interest in view of the increased social significance of the military in America and the world.

III. Major Areas of Subject Matter

Our data show (Table 2) the research interest in working force, occupational images, occupational comparisons, and client-professional relations to remain about the same from 1946–1952 to 1953–1959. A significant drop-off (from 23 percent in 1946–1952 to 13 percent in 1953–1959), however, occurs in the proportion of articles devoted to careers, and to ethnic groups and occupations (from 14 to 8 percent). A rather distinct rise, as indicated in Table 2, conversely, appears in the attention given to the areas of occu-

TABLE 2

Major Areas of Subject Matter in Occupational
Sociology Articles, 1946–1952 and 1953–1959

Area Studied	1946–1952 Percent	1953–1959 Percent
Career	23.2	12.9
Occupational status and mobility	14.1	21.0
Ethnic group and occupations	13.6	8.2
Working force	10.7	8.2
Occupational role and personality	8.5	16.4
Occupational images	6.8	5.1
Occupational comparisons	3.9	5.1
Methodology	3.9	7.7
Client-professional relations	2.8	1.0
Occupational culture and ethics	2.3	9.8
Miscellaneous	10.2	4.6
Total percent	100.0	100.0
Total number of articles	(177)	(195)

pational status and mobility, occupational role and personality, occupational culture and ethics, and methodology. It may be that the subjects of status, role, mobility, personality, and methodology are in themselves gaining in research interest. Their occupational components may thus have become part of this interest-growth pattern.

IV. Theoretical Frames of Reference

Our data indicate that occupational sociology is growing in scientific maturity insofar as the latter is reflected in the use of theoretical frames of reference. In the period 1946–1952 it was found that a fourth of the articles in the field lacked a theoretical frame of reference; in the period 1953–1959, less than a twentieth of the articles lacked such a conceptual framework.[2] It is noteworthy that this movement towards scientific systematization represents a continuation of a trend observed in the earlier study for the 1946–1952 period. It is likely, too, that it reflects a growing orientation towards theory in sociological research as a whole.

Especially apparent in our data is an increased use of the social structural frame of reference—from 13 percent in 1946–1952 to 31 percent in 1953–1959. Role theory has shown a comparable growth (from 7 percent to 21 percent), while the historical approach finds itself in diminishing favor (10 percent to 4 percent). All three of these trends appeared also in the earlier study for the period 1946–1952. Their continuation here may throw some light on the possible future course of occupational sociology. A tentative hypothesis in this regard is that theoretical frames of reference are subject to the forces of fashion. Those applied to a segment of a discipline (in this case occupational sociology as a segment of general sociology) may tend roughly to follow those in vogue for the discipline as a whole.

V. Collection and Analysis of Data

Our evidence reveals a continued emphasis on the use of primary sources of data (interview, observation, etc.) for the years 1953–1959. As in the earlier period, two-thirds of all studies make use of primary materials.

A finding of special significance is the great increase in the proportion of reports utilizing some form of statistical approach to the data. Less than a third of the published papers in 1953–1959 make no use of statistics. In 1946–1949, however, over half were non-statistical, and in 1949–1952 37 percent. This important trend towards heightened quantification in occupational sociology may parallel a similar trend and in sociology as a whole.

Summary and Conclusions

Noteworthy among the findings of the present reexamination are:

1. Research interest in the field of occupational sociology continues to grow.

2. Though less than formerly, research emphasis continues to center upon the professions.

3. Occupations are being increasingly studied in their interrelationships with other aspects of culture.

4. Occupational sociology grows more systematic with heightened use of theoretical frames of reference.

5. Occupational sociology grows more quantitative. Some use of statistical data appears increasingly.

Although changes occurred, many of the trends noted in the earlier study are corroborated by the present reexamination. Our prediction is that several of the noted trends will continue. It is likely, for example, that occupations will be increasingly studied in their interactive milieu and that more and more research in the field will be solidly grounded in some theoretical frame of reference. And it is likely also that the growing quantification in social science generally will be reflected in occupational research. With the growth of interest in such fields as medical sociology, educational sociology, and the sociology of law, moreover, we may look forward to an increased research attention to the occupational components of these areas.

Footnotes

[1] Erwin O. Smigel, "Trends in Occupational Sociology in the United States: A Survey of Postwar Research," *American Sociological Review*, 19 (August, 1954), 398–404. All quotations, unless otherwise noted, come from this article.

[2] It should be noted in this connection that different personnel worked on the 1946–1952 and 1953–1959 studies. This may serve to explain some of the variation observed in the extent of theoretical orientation. The overall direction of movement, however, we believe to be clear-cut; it is the extent of this direction which conceivably reflects evaluative differences among judges.

The Study of Occupations

EVERETT CHERRINGTON HUGHES
Boston College

Any occupation in which people make a living may be studied sociologically. Many have been so studied in recent years, especially those which are undergoing changes in techniques and social organization and in their social and economic standing. Sometimes the study is instigated by those in the occupation; sometimes by people not in it but affected by it. The motive may be immediate practical advantage; it may be greater understanding and general social advantage. Sociology has much to gain from such studies, provided that those who undertake them make and keep a sociological bargain with those who support them and those who allow themselves to be studied. The maximal gain can be reached, however, only when the sociologist keeps clearly in mind his ulterior goal of learning more about social processes in general.

In the following pages, we are frankly preoccupied with this ulterior goal of learning about the nature of society itself from the study of occupations.

The Labor Force

Modern industrial and urban societies and economies, no matter what the political systems under which they operate, are characterized by a wholesale mobilization of people away from traditional and familial activities into more formally organized work activities. These activities are named and

Reprinted from *Sociology Today*, Chapter 20, edited by Robert K. Merton, Leonard Broom, and Leonard S. Cottrell, Jr., © 1959 by Basic Books, Inc., Publishers, New York.

categorized in payrolls, organization charts, and union-management contracts, and in income-tax, licensing, and social-security legislation.

In the sense that they work at some times in their lives in this system
of things, more people are engaged in occupations than in other kinds of
societies and at a greater variety of occupations. In industrial countries, the
census more and more serves the end of informing government and business
about the actual and potential labor force and about the actuarial problems
of providing for people who are not at work, whether because of age, physical condition, lack of the skills needed in a changing technology or simply
because they live in the wrong place. Race, sex, marital status, and other
characteristics formerly determined civil estate quite directly; now it is work
that counts (although it has always been a great determiner of status), and
the other characteristics take their importance by virtue of their influence
on one's place in the labor force.[1]

It also seems that everyone who is not too young, too old, too sick, or
too burdened with household duties is rather expected to have an occupation in the sense indicated. In Soviet Russia, this expectation has become
compulsion; a man may not stay away from his work without a doctor's
certificate, and the physician who gives such certificates too freely is called
on the carpet.[2] In this country, those who look to our national resources
have lately added womanpower to the list, not because women did not work
in the past and are now expected to do so, but because they have become
mobilized away from the household and into the labor force in greater proportion and for longer periods of their lives than previously.[3]

I leave to others the task of counting the occupations in industrial economies and the changing numbers of people engaged in each of them, and
the tiresome business of fitting the many occupations into a small enough
number of categories to permit crowding them into tables. I can think of
no set of categories that has been given such heavy sociological work to do,
both theoretical and practical, as those of occupations in census tables.
Measures of social stratification and of mobility, both territorial and social,
are based upon them, as are international comparisons. They are used as
independent variables against which to weigh differences of political opinion,
taste, religion, and many other things. One is tempted to ask whether they
are equal to the burden; it is a question on which many people are very
competently breaking their heads.

Work and Leisure

Oddly enough, at a time when nearly everyone is being drawn into the
labor force, the proportion of a man's daily, weekly, annual, and life time
that he is expected to devote to work is falling so drastically that the days of

leisure in each seven may become nearly equal to the days of work. Already the waking hours spent away from work are, for many people, more than those spent at work, even on working days. At the same time, a new concept has been introduced, that of underemployment. It refers not to hours, weeks, and months of idleness so much as to the supposed underuse of human effort; the standard of efficient use applied is that of an economy which, like ours, provides great amounts of capital per worker and thus allows great per-man-hour production. The underemployed man may put forth great effort, but his product is small. It is as if the famed Protestant ethic had been transferred from the individual to the system; it is the machinery which is supposed to put in seven days a week and almost, if not quite, 52 weeks a year. The machine-tenders can take it easier at work, although they are expected to keep their eyes and ears piously glued to the "media" so that they may keep their consumption up to expectation. For, as G. Tarde said in his *Psychologie économique*,[4] a return to the early evangel, with its belief in the vanity of human desires, would be the death of modern industry.

Although the great masses of people who are occupied are taking it easier, a minority appears to be bound to the tireless wheels of the machines. Those who manage the machines and the organization required to keep them and their products moving appear to require an extra dose of a certain brand of the Protestant ethic, a brand which does not leave time for prayer or other solitary and idiosyncratic activities. The new distribution of work and leisure in the life of the individual, and as between people in various positions in our society and economy; the new concepts, values, and expectations with respect to them, and to the levels and kinds of effort expected or required of people in the various positions; these are fundamental problems of society and of occupations. The change of balance between work and leisure has given new emphasis and a new turn to studies of leisure. The demand for men of unlimited ambition and drive to fill certain of the positions in our economy of abundance has, in its turn, given a new impulse to studies of social mobility into the higher ranks of management.

The Division of Labor

Division of labor, one of the most fundamental of all social processes, finds one of its most explicit expressions in occupations. The phrase, however, is but a poor term for differentiation of function in a social whole. It is poor because it emphasizes the divison and neglects the integration, the relations among the functions so divided or differentiated. All organization of behavior consists of differentiation of function. Economic division of labor is but a special case, or a special aspect of it.

An occupation, in essence, is not some particular set of activities; it is the part of an individual in any ongoing system of activities. The system may be large or small, simple or complex. The ties between the persons in different positions may be close or so distant as not to be social; they may be formal or informal, frequent or rare. The essential is that the occupation is the place ordinarily filled by one person in an organization or complex of efforts and activities. Sociologically speaking, the division of labor is only incidentally technical. It consists, not of ultimate components of skill or of mechanical or mental operations, but of the actual allocation of functions to persons. Individual components of motion or action are combined in ways that sometimes appear fearful and wonderful to a mechanically oriented or rational and detached mind. The logic of the division and combination of activities and functions into occupations and of their allocation to various kinds of people in any system is not to be assumed as given, but is in any case something to be discovered. Likewise, the outward limits of a system of division of labor are not to be assumed but are to be sought out. Analysis of systems whose limits have not been determined can be very deceiving.

Homans[5] has recently emphasized exchange as a basic social process the analysis of which might bring us closer to a sound general theory of social behavior. Although this is not an entirely novel idea, it is an important one and especially pertinent to the analysis of division of labor. Where there is differentiation of function, there is exchange—and exchange not merely of money, goods, or tangible and easily described services. Durkheim's book, let us remember, is entitled *De la division du travail social*—on the division of social labor. And although it may be true that more and more kinds of exchange tend to have an expression in money, it is also true that it is very difficult to keep money exchanges free of other kinds.

One of the problems of the purest markets is to limit exchanges to the purely economic. Glick has recently found this to be so in the market in egg futures.[6] The rules and signals for buying and selling are made explicit so that the dealers will not be able to give private information or to exchange favors on the floor. I mention this case only to emphasize that the division of labor involves many kinds of exchange, many of them not at all apparent, and that several kinds may go on at once. This is true of occupations as well as of those differentiations of functions found in families and other systems of relationship. In many occupations, the exchanges occur on at least two levels. There is exchange between a person and the various others with whom he interacts in his occupational role. It is of this exchange that Henderson wrote in "Physician and Patient as a Social System."[7] It is also described in studies of industrial relations, and especially of the informal relations among people in the same work situation. One must remember, however, that much interaction occurs in formally defined relationships and that much involves persons not in personal contact with one another. The other level is that of exchanges between the occupation and the society in which it occurs; they underlie those characteristic features of certain occupations, license and mandate.

License and Mandate

An occupation consists in part in the implied or explicit *license* that some people claim and are given to carry out certain activities rather different from those of other people and to do so in exchange for money, goods, or services. Generally, if the people in the occupation have any sense of identity and solidarity, they will also claim a *mandate* to define—not merely for themselves, but for others as well—proper conduct with respect to the matters concerned in their work. They also will seek to define and possibly succeed in defining, not merely proper conduct but even modes of thinking and belief for everyone individually and for the body social and politic with respect to some broad area of life which they believe to be in their occupational domain. The license may be merely technical; it may, however, extend to broad areas of behavior and thought. It may include a whole style of life, or it may be confined to carrying out certain technical activities which others may not carry out—at least not officially or for a reward. The mandate may be small and narrow, or the contrary.

License, as an attribute of an occupation, is usually thought of as specific legal permission to pursue the occupation. I am thinking of something broader. Society, by its nature, consists in part of both allowing and expecting some people to do things which other people are not allowed or expected to do. Most occupations—especially those considered professions and those of the underworld—include as a part of their being a license to deviate in some measure from some common modes of behavior. Professions, perhaps more than other kinds of occupation, also claim a broad legal, moral, and intellectual mandate. Not only do the practitioners, by virtue of gaining admission to the charmed circle of the profession, individually exercise a license to do things others do not do, but collectively they presume to tell society what is good and right for it in a broad and crucial aspect of life. Indeed, they set the very terms of thinking about it. When such a presumption is granted as legitimate, a profession in the full sense has come into being. The nature and extent of both license and mandate, their relations to each other, and the circumstances and conflicts in which they expand or contract are crucial areas of study, not merely for occupations, but for society itself. Such licenses and mandates are the prime manifestation of the *moral division of labor*—that is, of the processes by which differing moral functions are distributed among the members of society, as individuals and as categories of individuals. These moral functions differ from one another in both kind and measure. Some people seek and get special responsibility for defining values and for establishing and enforcing sanctions over a certain aspect of life; the differentiation of moral and social functions involves both the area of social behavior in question and the degree of responsibility and power.

Since this is the aspect of occupations to which I give most emphasis in this paper, I will illustrate it in a manner which I hope will stimulate discussion and research.

Many occupations cannot be carried out without guilty knowledge. The priest cannot mete out penance without becoming an expert in sin; else how may he know the mortal from the venial? To carry out his mandate to tell people what books they may or may not read and what thoughts and beliefs they must espouse or avoid, he must become a connoisseur of the forbidden. Only a master theologian can think up really subtle heresies; hence Satan is of necessity a fallen angel. A layman would be but an amateur with a blunderbuss where a sharpshooter is wanted. The poor priest, as part of the exchange involved in his license to hear confessions and to absolve and his mandate to tell us what's what, has to convince the lay world that he does not yield to the temptations of his privileged position; he puts on a uniform and lives a celibate existence. These are compensating or counter-deviations from the common way of dressing and living; they would not be admired, or perhaps even tolerated, in people who have no special function to justify them. The priest, in short, has both intellectual and moral leeway, and perhaps must have them if he is to carry out the rest of his license. He carries a burden of guilty knowledge.

The lawyer, the policeman, the physician, the reporter, the scientist, the scholar, the diplomat, the private secretary, all of them must have license to get—and, in some degree, to keep secret—some order of guilty knowledge. It may be guilty in that it is knowledge that a layman would be obliged to reveal, or in that the withholding of it from the public or from authorities compromises the integrity of the man who so withholds it, as in the case of the policeman who keeps connections with the underworld or the diplomat who has useful friends abroad. Most occupations rest upon some bargain about receiving, guarding, and giving out communications. The license to keep this bargain is of the essence of many occupations.

The prototype of all guilty knowledge is, however, a different, potentially shocking, way of looking at things. Every occupation must look relatively at some order of events, objects, or ideas. These things must be classified, seen in comparative light; their behavior must be analyzed and, if possible, predicted. A suitable technical language must be developed in which one may talk to his colleagues about them. This technical, therefore relative, attitude must be adopted toward the very people whom one serves; no profession can operate without license to talk in shocking terms behind the backs of its clients. Sometimes an occupation must adopt this objective, comparative attitude toward things which are very dear to other people or which are the object of absolutely held values and sentiments. I suppose that this ultimate license is the greatest when the people who exercise it, being guardians of precious things, are in a position to do great damage. (No one is in so good a position to steal as the banker.)

Related to the license to think relatively about dear things and absolute values is the license to do dangerous things. I refer not to the danger run by the steeplejack and the men who navigate submarines, for that is danger to themselves. (Even so, there is a certain disposition to pay them off with a license to run slightly amok when the one comes down and the other up to solid ground.) I speak, rather, of the license of the doctor to cut and dose, of the priest to play with men's salvation, of the scientist to split atoms; or simply of the danger that advice given a person may be wrong, or that work done may be unsuccessful or cause damage.

License of all these kinds may lie at the root of that modicum of aggressive suspicion which most laymen feel toward professionals, and of that raging and fanatical anger which burns chronically in some people and which at times becomes popular reaction. Many antivivisectionists, according to Hughes,[8] do not love beasts more but love doctors less, suspecting them of loving some parts of their work too much. It is a chronic protest. Of course there are people who believe that they have suffered injury from incompetent or careless work or that they have been exploited by being acted upon more for the professional's increase of knowledge or income than for their own well-being.

Herein lies the whole question of what the bargain is between those who receive a service and those who give it, and of the circumstances in which it is protested by either party. Of equal or greater sociological significance is the problem of a general questioning of license or mandate. Social unrest often shows itself precisely in such questioning of the prerogatives of the leading professions. In time of crisis, there may arise a general demand for more conformity to lay modes of thought and discourse.

One of the major professional deviations of mind, a form of guilty knowledge, is the objective and relative attitude mentioned above. One order of relativity has to do with time; the professional may see the present in longer perspective. The present may be, for him, more crucial in that it is seen as a link in a causative chain of events; the consequences of present action may be seen as more inevitable, rippling down through time. The emergency, in this sense, may appear greater to the professional than to the layman. In another sense, it appears less crucial, since the professional sees the present situation in comparison with others; it is not unique, and hence the emergency is not so great as laymen see it.

Something like this seems to lie in the attack upon the Supreme Court following its decisions on civil rights and upon professors who insist on freedom to discuss all things in this time of Cold War. They are thought to be playing legal and academic tunes while the Communists plaster us with firebombs. In time of crisis, detachment appears the most perilous deviation of all, hence the one least to be tolerated. Their deviation, in these cases, consists in a drastic reversal of what many laymen consider the urgent as against the less urgent aspects of our situation. And it arises from their license to think in different terms.

Militant religious sects give us an instructive illustration. They ordinarily, in Christianity at least, consist of people convinced that they are all in imminent danger of damnation. So long as they remain militant sects, they are in chronic crisis. It is perhaps not without sociological significance that they do not tolerate a clergy, or much differentiation of function at all. It is as if they sense that professionalizing inevitably brings some detachment, some relative and comparative attitude. In a large society the clergy are generally more ardent than the laity; a sect might almost be defined as a religious group in which the opposite is true. Inquisitions to the contrary, it is probable that the professional clergy tend to be more tolerant than ardent laymen. Although it may seem paradoxical to suggest it, one may seriously ask under what circumstances religious people tolerate a professional clergy.

The typical reform movement is an attempt of laymen to redefine values and to change action about some matter over which some occupation (or group of occupations or faction within an occupation) holds a mandate. The movement may simply push for faster or more drastic action where the profession moves slowly or not at all; it may be a direct attack upon the dominant philosophy of the profession, as in attempts to change the manner of distributing medical care. The power of an occupation to protect its license and to maintain its mandate and the circumstances in which licenses and mandates are attacked, lost, or changed are matters for investigation. (And one must not overlook movements within a profession.) Such work is study of politics in the fundamental sense—that is, in the sense of studying constitutions. For constitutions are the relations between the effective estates which *constitute* the body politic. In our society, some occupations are among the groups which most closely resemble what were once known as estates. While there has been a good deal of study of the political activities of occupational groups, the subject has been somewhat misunderstood as a result of the strong fiction of political neutrality of professions in our society. Of course, a certain license to be politically neutral has been allowed some occupations, but the circumstances and limits of such neutrality are again a matter for study. Special attention should be given to the exchanges implied and to the circumstances, some of which we have mentioned, in which the license is denied, and the ways in which it is violated and subverted, from within or without.

One can think of many variations of license and mandate, and of the relations between them. School teachers in our society have little license to think thoughts that others do not think; they are not even allowed to think the nastier thoughts that others *do* think. Their mandate seems limited to minor matters of pedagogy; it does not include definition of the fundamental issues of what children shall be taught. Educational policy is given into their hands very grudgingly, although they have a good deal of power by default. Mandate by default is itself a matter for study. The underworld, to take another example, has a considerable license to deviate; in fact, members get paid to help respectable people escape the norms of everyday life. But the license is not openly admitted. The manner in which the people of the underworld find spokesmen and the nature of the exchanges involved have often been discussed as a pathology of politics. The full circle of exchanges is seldom analyzed with an eye to learning something significant about the very nature of social exchanges. Study of the license of artists and entertainers could also yield much knowledge concerning the degrees of conformity possible in a society and the consequences of trying to reduce deviation to something like zero. For these occupations seem to require, if they are to produce the very things for which society will give them a living of sorts (or, in some cases, unheard-of opulence), at least some people who deviate widely from the norms more or less adhered to and firmly espoused by other people. Their license is, however, periodically in a parlous state, and there seems no guarantee that it will not, at any moment, be attacked. There has recently been a case which turns upon whether poetic license includes speaking for an enemy country in time of war.

Occupations and Social Matrices

If an occupation is a more-or-less standardized one-man's part in some operating system, it follows that it cannot be described apart from the whole. A study of occupations, then, becomes in part a study of the allocation of functions and the consequent composition of any given occupation.[9]

Although an occupation may conceivably consist of but one activity in a narrow and mechanical sense, it takes an extremely rationalized organization to keep it so. Most occupations consist of a number, a bundle, of activities. Some may be bundled together because they require similar skills; others, simply because they can conveniently be done at one place, or because taken alone they do not occupy a man's full time; still others, because they are, or seem to be, natural parts of a certain role, office, or function. The physician's repertoire, for example, includes technically unrelated activities, bound together by the demands of his basic function. Only in those specialties which can be practiced without personal contact with patients can physicians group their activities on strictly technical lines. One might, indeed, try to scale occupations according to the dominance of technical as against role factors in determining combinations of activities.

The extreme of technically rational division and grouping of activities, under conditions of constant and aggressive invention of new machines and forms of organization, would lead to continual destruction and reforming of occupations.[10] The problems of adjusting self-conceptions and social roles in such a case have been much studied lately. The opposite of this would be a system of strongly traditional and entrenched occupations whose activities, whether bound together by technical considerations or not, are considered to belong rightfully and naturally together.

This leads us to the distinction between historic and less historic occupations. An historic occupation is historic, not because its chief activity is an old one but because it has long had a name, a license, and a mandate, a recognized place in the scheme of things. In the extreme case, an historic occupation has a strong sense of identity and continuity; a galaxy of historic founders, innovators, and other heroes, the saints or gods of the trade; and a wealth of remembered historic or legendary events, which justify its present claims. The aspirant to such a trade is expected to acquire a strong sense of belonging to an historic estate, somewhat set off from other men. New occupations, like new families, seek an heroic genealogy to strengthen their claims to license and mandate. Occupations vary greatly in the degree to which they become the master determinants of the social identity, self-conception, and social status of the people in them.

In an occupation which is strongly historic, one would expect the combination of activities also to have a certain historic quality, reinforced by a traditional logic. Historic or not, occupations vary greatly in their autonomy in determining what activities are their duty and prerogatives. One would, however, expect occupations of long standing to resist attempts, especially of outsiders, to determine the content of their work or the rules governing it.

The various activities which make up an occupation are, of course, given varying values both by the people inside and by others. Sometimes the name of the occupation expresses an emphasis upon one rather than other activities; note the use of "preacher," "priest," and "pastor" in referring to clergy of various denominations, and the insistence of some gynecologists upon being called gynecological surgeons. Some one activity may be symbolically valued beyond its importance in the present complex of activities. Changes in technology, economics, and organization may change the balance between the named symbolic activity and others; in extreme cases, the symbolic activity may be lost or dropped from the repetory of the occupation while the name persists.

Nursing is a striking example of such a series of shifts. The word has a certain connotation in the lay mind; it refers to a role and an attitude, but also to certain comforting activities considered consonant with the role. The elaboration of the organization of hospitals, clinics, and public-health agencies, combined with great technological change in medicine and an immense increase in the demand for medical services, has led to a great reshuffling of functions in the whole medical system. Doctors need much more technical help than before; the system also requires much more administrative activity. A host of new occupations has arisen. The physician has passed along many activities to the nurse; the nurse has in turn passed along many of hers to other occupations. The result has been upward mobility of the nurse, since a good number of the new occupations stand below her in the hierarchy and since there are some posts of high prestige, income, and authority to which nurses alone may aspire. But there has been a certain dissociation of the occupation called nursing from the activities traditionally associated with it in the lay mind. The case is not peculiar, but it is so clear cut as to allow sensitive observation.

Every occupation has some history which may in part be described in terms of changes in the bundle of activities, in the values given them, and in the total system of which the occupation is a part. Changes may occur in ownership and control over access to appropriate tools (pulpits, operating rooms, law libraries, stages and properties, Univacs and laboratories), methods of payment and exchange, the formal authority and status systems in which work is done, the terms of entry to the occupation, and competition among individuals, occupations, and whole complexes of goods and services for the patronage of consumers. Of course, these same matters are crucial to study of an occupation at present; but sociologists have to be reminded of the pertinence of history rather more than of present doings.

I hope I have not put so many things into the last few paragraphs that the main points will be overlooked: namely, that the items of activity and social function which make up any occupation are historical products. The composition of an occupation can be understood only in the frame of the pertinent social and institutional complex (which must in turn be discovered, not merely assumed). The allocating and grouping of activities is itself a fundamental social process.

The Work Situation

I should at this point mention work situations as systems of interaction, as the setting of the role-drama of work, in which people of various occupational and lay capacities, involved in differing complexes of *Lebenschancen*, interact in sets of relationships that are social as well as technical. Some of the best work in contemporary sociology[11] is being done in such settings and is giving us new knowledge of reciprocal expectation of role performance, definition of roles, group solidarity, and development and definition of reference groups. We are by this time alerted to the value of work situations as posts for observing the formation of groups and the generation of social rules and sanctions. I am not sure that we are using the findings of such observation vigorously enough in building our theories of social control and of the larger legal and political processes.

A Man and His Work

Let me conclude with some remarks on the individual and his occupation and his career. Career, in the most generic sense, refers to the fate of a man running his life-cycle in a particular society at a particular time. The limitations put upon his choice of occupation by his own peculiarities (sex, race, abilities, class, wealth, access to and motivation for education, and access to knowledge of the system itself) in interaction with the "times" have been the object of many studies. Not all the problems of logic and method involved in such studies have been adequately attacked or solved.

Occupations vary in their strength as named reference-groups, as the basis for full and lasting self-identification and firm status. They vary also in their demand for full and lasting commitment and in the age and life-phase at which one must decide to enter training for them. Some occupations are more visible to young people than are others, and effective visibility varies also by class and other social circumstances. The inner working of the best known cannot be seen by outsiders. Add to this the fact of changes in even the most historic occupations, and it is evident that young people must choose their occupations, as they do their wives, largely on faith (if, indeed, they choose at all). The career includes not only the processes and sequences of learning the techniques of the occupation but also the progressive perception of the whole system and of possible places in it and the accompanying changes in conceptions of the work and of one's self in relation to it. A good deal of work is being done on these matters; the phrase *adult socialization* is being applied to some of the processes involved.[12]

The processes are complicated by the fact that some occupations, strong as their symbols of common identity (their license and mandate) may be, are inwardly very heterogeneous. Within medicine, there is wide choice of specialties; each of them is not merely a unit of technical work but a position in the huge and complex system of health institutions. They offer alternative career lines, some of them mutually exclusive from an early stage. These career lines are variously ranked within the profession itself as well as outside; the people in each of them have their own ethos and sometimes their own variant system of relative values concerning many things in medicine. They differ, for example, in their notions of what knowledge and skills should be taught in medical schools. How these factors act upon and are reacted to by students who are in the process of choosing their specialties is discussed in a current paper.[13] A part of the individual's career may be the making of the finer decisions concerning his hoped-for place within an occupational system, the projecting of his self-image in the direction of one rather than others of the available models of mature members of his occupation.

Career involves, at each stage, choices of some rather than other activities in one's economy of effort. A career consists, in one sense, of moving —in time and hence with age—within the institutional system in which the occupation exists. Ordinarily, career is interpreted as progress upward in the system, but a man can make progress in a number of ways. He may become more skillful at the basic activities of the occupation; the increase of skill may be rewarded by increase of income, security, and prestige among his fellows. If his occupation is practiced directly with customers or clients, he may get more of them and better ones. However, progress and advancement also consist in part of change in the proportions of time and effort devoted to various activities, and even in rather complete change of organizational function or role.

Sometimes the greater success is paid for by a complete abandonment of the activities symbolically most closely associated with the occupation, a consequent loss of skill in those activities, and passage from identification with the basic colleagueship to some other. This is a career contingency of much importance to the individual's self-conception. It often creates severe guilt. We might expect the severity of such crises to vary with the sense of commitment and the strength of the colleague-group as a significant other for its members. Some occupations appear intense, others weak and indifferent, in commitment. In some there is a casual attitude toward particular activities and perhaps a full acceptance of the right of employers to determine just what work one shall do. In others, there is a rich culture and a strong sense among the members of being different from other people. There are songs and lore about logging, railroading, and going to sea. In these occupations there are strong feelings about who really shares in the dangers and fate of the group, and who consequently has a right to the name. Jazz musicians, who live life wrong-end-to—for their night is day, and other people's pleasure is their work—have a similarly strong sense of who is and who is not one of them. Some of the professions also have a sense of identity and a tendency to be self-conscious about who is a true member of the group.

Today, there are great numbers of people in occupations which are, in fact, products of modern industrial and business technology and organization and in which there appears to be little sense of belonging to a closed circle of people with a peculiar fate. The sense of identification of such people with their work, or with classes and categories of people at work, is a matter for study. Many of them are said to be alienated both from their work fellows and from society. Not the least problem of such people is the balance between work and leisure—not merely as proportions of their lifetimes, years, weeks, and days, but in terms of their importance and meaning. This is also, in the broad sense, a problem of career, of a man and his work seen in the perspective of his ongoing life and life chances. We may then think of man and his work, of careers, as an immense area of problems, embracing a great many of the problems of formation of social personality and of adjustment of individuals to their social surroundings. Careers in various occupations are patterned in varying degree. In the narrowest sense, career—as Mannheim wrote—is a predictable course through a bureaucracy.[14] But the patterns, the possible positions and sequences in work systems, themselves change. And each human career is worked out in some particular historical phase. Ours is a rapidly changing phase, which means that careers and career contingencies are changing, too. This gives the study of careers, and of other facets of occupations and work, a certain timeliness and excitement that adds to their basic relevance for study of social and social-psychological processes.

Footnotes

[1] See Evelyn M. Kitagawa, *The Family as a Unit in the Work Force: A Review of the Literature*, Population Research and Training Center, University of Chicago, 1956.

[2] Mark G. Field, "Structured Strain in the Role of the Soviet Physician," *Amer. J. Sociol., 53:5* (1953), 493–502.

[3] National Manpower Council, *Womanpower*, Columbia University Press, 1957.

[4] Paris, 1902, Vol. 1, p. 186. Tarde's chapters on the economic role of desires and beliefs are good reading for those who are working on a theory of consumption and leisure.

[5] George C. Homans, "Social Behavior as Exchange," *Amer. J. Sociol., 53* (1958), 597–606.

[6] Ira O. Glick, "Futures Trading: A Sociological Analysis," unpublished Ph.D. dissertation, University of Chicago, 1957. See also Max Weber, "Die Boerse" (1894),

in *Gesammelte Aufsaetze zur Soziologie und Sozialpolitik*, Tuebingen, 1924, pp. 256–322.

[7] L. J. Henderson, "Physician and Patient as a Social System," *N. E. J. Med., 212* (1935), 819–23.

[8] Helen Hughes, "The Compleat Anti-vivisectionist," *Sci. Mon.*, N.Y., *65:6* (1947), 503–7.

[9] Throughout this paper, but especially in what follows, it would be hard for me to distinguish what is, at least in some small sense, my own combining of ideas and what I owe to my colleagues in recent studies, Howard S. Becker, Blanche Geer, and Anselm Strauss. I am sure that many of my former students and other colleagues will have reason to think that I am borrowing liberally from their work.

[10] Georges Friedmann has been the leading student of this problem. See his *Où Va le Travail Humain?*, Paris, 1950; *Problèmes Humains du Machinism Industriel*, Paris, 1946; and *Travail en Miettes*, Paris, 1956. He has also written a fundamental criticism called "La thèse de Durkheim et les formes contemporaines de la division du travail," *Cahiers Internationaux de Sociologie, 19* (1955), 45–58.

[11] See Erving Goffman, *Presentation of Self in Society*, University of Chicago Press, 1956.

[12]Howard S. Becker and Anselm Strauss, "Careers, Personality, and Adult Socialization," *Amer. J. Sociol., 72* (1956), 253–63. See also Robert K. Merton, George Reader, and Patricia Kendall (eds.), *The Student Physician: Introductory Studies in the Sociology of Medical Education*, Harvard University Press, 1957.

[13] Kurt W. Back and Bernard S. Philips, "Public Health as a Career of Medicine: Specialization within a Profession," paper read at the annual meetings of the American Sociological Society, 1957.

[14] Karl Mannheim, "Über das Wesen und die Bedeutung des wirtschaftlichen Erfolgsstrebens," *Archiv für Sozialwissenschaft und Sozialpolitik, 63:3* (1930), 449–512.

3

THE SOCIAL
STRUCTURE OF WORK

INTRODUCTION

Work, like other social behavior, is structured. That is to say, it is performed according to certain social rules, by specially designated persons who usually possess appropriate skills and expertise and who relate to other workers as well as to their clientele in a hierarchically prescribed fashion involving constrained cooperation. Work takes place within socially approved contexts, is often integrated with other activities labeled as work, and is subject to monitoring and control during and after its occurrence. The needs of society are many and complex, ranging from the need to obtain subsistence and make it available to the population, to the requirement of appropriately disposing of the dead. The population on various occasions must be entertained, protected, cured, fed, buried, or incarcerated. To accomplish such tasks requires a complex division of labor and an elaborate social structuring of work. Purposefully structured as opposed to randomly organized work activity is quite essential if the socially required tasks are to be performed by qualified persons in the appropriate times and under the right circumstances, and, most important, in the desirable quantities, sequences, and proportions.

As structured behavior, work is usually compartmentalized in a fashion that permits ease of learning as well as of performance. Toward this end work is compartmentalized into specific social roles that facilitate the socialization of its skills and norms by the persons who will practice it. This compartmentalization into social roles plays a part both in the performance of work and in the process by which work can be monitored and evaluated in terms of prestige by members of the larger community.

This chapter takes up the question of the social structuring of work and looks at a variety of structural forms, beginning with work statuses and roles. It then moves on to examine other more elaborate configurations of work organization and other dimensions of work structure. The first two articles examine the status and roles of three female occupational specialties and serve as specific illustrations of the structure and dynamics of work role behavior. They also provide a contrast in perspective in that one views occupational status and role longitudinally and the other takes a comparative approach to status and the resulting work role. The first of these two articles, Helena Znaniecki Lopata's "The Life Cycle of the Social Role of Housewife," looks at that role in terms of the various stages or plateaus of patterning and development of role behavior required of the housewife at various times in her life cycle. The work role is thus viewed as changing during the lifetime of the housewife, involving "shifts in the components of [her] role clusters" from time to time that require her to learn the new role demands and to make the necessary adjustment to the role changes.

The subsequent selection, "The Call Girl and the Dance Teacher: A Comparative Analysis," examines occupational status and role by comparing and contrasting the work roles of two other female occupations. In this article, Mary Gray Riege focuses on certain basic similarities and differences between the two occupations in terms of services rendered, earnings and expenses, social class origins, recruitment and training, social mobility, and occupational ideology. Although there is implicit sexuality involved in ballroom dancing, the dance teacher does not provide actual sexual service to her students. The call girl, on the other hand, offers physical sex to her clientele, but has to simulate the sexuality. The occupational role structures of the two specialties function in such a manner as to bifurcate sex and sexuality effectively, emphasizing one and preventing the other. Both the call girl and the professional dance teacher, however, Riege concludes, respond to "the need for friendship formation in the large city." Persons working in the city may find their friendship formation limited to a restricted choice by their work role.

Although work may occur as an individual status and task assignment, it often takes place within the context of larger social configurations. Frequently a number of individuals occupying various work statuses that are linked together in a symbiotic fashion will perform their specialized roles as part of a team effort to accomplish some overall set of work tasks. Such sets of linked work statuses can be called work systems. Work systems may be relatively small, involving only a few persons, as in the small "six stooler" short order restaurant with a four-man work force including the busboy-dishwasher, the cook, the waitress-cashier, and the owner-manager. Some work systems, on the other hand, may have extremely large work forces, such as a factory with several thousand employees. Jerome J. Salomone's article "The Funeral Home as a Work System: A Sociological Analysis," considers yet another kind of work system—that of the funeral home, which has as its principal work tasks the processing of the dead and assisting in the management of the grief of the bereaved. This selection examines the various occupational specialities that work within the setting of the funeral home and the symbiotic relationship that exists among these individuals as members of a work team. Most of the occupational specialties concerned with the processing of the dead are internal to the funeral home; however, there are several specialties that are external, but are temporarily integrated into the work system for the purpose of assisting in the necessary activities and ceremonies attendant to death and bereavement. The funeral home, with its occupational staff and ancillary outside specialties, usually functions smoothly and efficiently as an integrated work system to accomplish the many and varied tasks attendant to processing the dead.

As we saw in the selection about the restaurant in Chapter 2, many work systems are, in effect, man-machine systems that rely not only on their human components but also on a variety of mechanical devices to facilitate, pattern, or accomplish work. On occasion employers or the owners of business establishments may pattern work in order to effect some desired work routine or work tempo as a means of making the work system more efficient. This may be done in a variety of ways, including the adjustment of office or plant layout, the implementation of certain procedures, or the use of different kinds of apparatus. For example, industrial plants may attempt to regulate the speed of their workers by regulating the speed of the assembly lines. A typical pattern might be to begin the day with a moderately slow assembly line rate, speed it up as the day goes on, slow it down just before and after lunch, speed it back up in the afternoon, and slow it down again just before quitting time. In this way the employees are barely aware that they are being manipulated by the speed of the machines.

Such techniques of industrial engineering have as their goal increased work efficiency through improved procedures and layout. Many of the same techniques can also be applied to a business's clientele, in which case they are perhaps more appropriately termed stimulus structuring or situation manipulation. For example, some chain cafeteria sandwich shops use the device of a recorded message, which plays over and over in the background, urging the patrons to hurry through the line and to make their selections quickly. The customers usually respond to urgent directions and "process" through the shop as rapidly as possible. Another unusual device for a contrived patterning of work is recorded background music, which has been used quite successfully for controlling the work tempo and mood of office workers as well as factory workers. By playing music with a fast tempo in restaurants it is possible to induce the customer to eat faster and leave sooner, for the customer tends to chew in tempo with the music. This is desirable at the lunch meal, which is often a standardized "plate lunch" at which customer volume is important. At evening time, in contrast, the customer eats to relaxing music such as waltzes, lingers over his meal, and is more likely to spend on a la carte dishes. Background music service is used by a variety of businesses. Curiously enough, it was reported a while back that a brothel in Stutgarde, Germany, rented background music service and requested a "light industrial" music program. As will be seen in the next reading, Clifton D. Bryant's "Sawdust in Their Shoes: The Carnival as a Neglected Complex Organization and Work Culture," a work situation can be so patterned as to make the product seem extremely attractive to the clientele to the point where they will partake of the product in a highly predictable fashion even though they may later come to regret their expenditure.

Work organizations, like other social structures, often have elaborate cultural components. An exemplary case in point is that of the carnival. The fourth reading addresses itself to a descriptive analysis of the carnival as a work system, subculture, and complex organization. The carnival, contrary to popular belief, is not a single economic entity owned by one individual or corporation. Rather, it is an assemblage of many diverse but related economic activities owned for the most part by individual, independent entrepreneurs. The transient nature of carnival life and the latent exploitive orientation of the carnival enterprises make for discernible social distance between carnival workers and patrons, but in compensation foster a strong in-group solidarity and a sense of occupational community. In addition to a colorful material culture, the carnival population has also, in response, developed an extensive nonmaterial culture, including a rich technical argot and detailed value and norm systems. The patrons are likely to view aspects of only the material culture—the sights, sounds, tastes, and smells so distinctive and characteristic of the midway—whereas the social scientist's interests lie more with the nature of the social structure of the carnival.

Work traditionally has been a significant factor in social differentiation and thus a major criterion for one's placement in the stratification structure. Societal or community estimates of the desirability or undesirability of a particular kind of work, the economic rewards, or the honor and deference that accrue to the work all figure in the status ranking of an individual who practices that particular kind of work. Just as community or societal stratification produces a hierarchical ranking of various occupations, so too there is prestige differentiation *within* occupations. One aspect of work culture is the informal ranking system or structure that develops within the occupational organization of certain kinds of work. Robert A. Stebbins takes up this topic in his "Class, Status, and Power Among Jazz and Commercial Musicians." In this selection he examines jazz musicians as an occupational group and "status community," comparing and contrasting them with commercial musicians in terms of general community class standing, various socio-economic dimensions, and a variety of attitudinal orientations. Jazz musicians, he finds, tend to form into specialized status communities. Although they were ranked higher than commercial musicians in terms of class, status, and power in the jazz community, they tended to rank lower in the broader community.

Much work in today's society occurs within the framework of formal bureaucracy, and for many people even life outside of work is lived in large measure within a bureaucratic milieu. Religion, politics, education, and leisure all occur under a bureaucratic umbrella. The next reading, Alan Harrington's "Life in the Crystal Palace," provides some of the flavor of work life in a bureaucracy. In this instance, the bureaucracy is a corporation with a new and modern suburban home office, a "crystal palace," as it were. While some writers, notably William H. Whyte in his *Organization Man*, have painted a picture of bureaucratic life involving overtly enforced regimentation, conformity, intense pressure, and a fast pace of work routines, Harrington, on the other hand, gives us a glimpse of an entirely different kind of bureaucratic existence. There is conformity in the crystal palace, but it is a voluntary variety, not so much enforced as produced by a subtle kind of indoctrination and socialization that resembles "brainwashing." There is no apparent pressure in this company, only a kind of lethargic, insulated, almost pathological security. Dwellers in the crystal palace experience a degree of remoteness from life, are surrounded by an office subculture that emphasizes politeness and cooperation (although this atmosphere is largely contrived by the firm), and live out their days in a sort of corporate limbo. Life in the crystal palace denies the employees their individuality and the opportunity to realize their creative potentiality. This bureaucratic existence erodes the self, drains the employees of their vital elan, and robs them of a "fullness" in life which they might possibly otherwise experience.

The final selection in this chapter, "Professionalism and Occupational Associations" by George Strauss, is concerned with the growth of professionalism and the development and functions of white-collar occupational associations. The author first examines three relatively "pure" occupational categories in the corporate setting in terms of their orientation and their occupational associations: the assembly-line worker, the executive or line manager, and the research scientist. He then takes up the case of several "in between" occupations, such as clerical workers and foremen ("who are neither fully employees nor fully managers"), functional staff men ("who are in managerial positions yet aspire to professional status"), and craftsmen ("who are primarily workers, yet to some extent accept professional values"). Like executives, workers in these "in between" occupations aspire to professionalism, and their occupational associations tend to promote this aspiration. Strauss suggests that employee professionalization will necessitate increasing diversity in company policy because jurisdictional disputes, questions of departmental autonomy, and complications in developing corporate teamwork will arise with the growth of this "professional pluralism."

Not only is work structured and patterned by means of occupational statuses and roles, work systems, and such formal organizational rules as one finds in bureaucracies, it is also informally patterned by workers themselves, who affect informal structure in their work activities as a means of bypassing burdensome formal procedures and channels as a device for alleviating monotony and a way of asserting some control on their part over the work situation. This topic will be taken up in depth in the next chapter.

Occupational Status and Role

and Role

A Longitudinal Perspective

The Life Cycle of the Social Role of Housewife

HELENA ZNANIECKI LOPATA
Loyola University
Chicago

This article[1] is devoted to the analysis of the life cycle of the social role of housewife, and of its placement in the role cluster of performers at different stages in their life cycles.[2] It thus combines the concepts of social role and role cluster with three sets of life cycles: that of the role, that of the social person bearing the title of the role, and that of the participants in the social circle. The analysis is based upon the Znaniecki definition of social role as a set of patterned relations between a social person and participants of the social circle, involving sets of duties which are the functions of the role, and the sets of rights which enable their performances.[3] In all but new roles, a social role in entered into when more than one "other" (or Parson's alter") accepts a person into culturally defined relations after tests have indicated that he is fit to carry out the duties and to receive the rights. The title of the role is assigned to this person who is the center of the relations, toward whom rights are directed and from whom duties are expected. The role is based upon cultural expectations, but it is the actual set of relations. Members of the society and sociologists select only certain generalized and patterned actions in describing a role and in indicating it by the use of the title.

Although the title of a social role is assigned to the one person who is the center of the relations, the role does not exist if only that person carries out a system of actions.[4] It requires at least two more persons who interact within him because of the role. Thus roles require relational duties and, usually, task duties, but never the latter alone. The rights include the per-

Reprinted from *Sociology and Social Research*, Vol. 51, No. 1 (October 1966), 5–22, by permission of the author and publisher.

mission to carry out the duties, certain actions by circle members, and the facilities they provide in order to enable the functioning of the role.

Social roles can be located in a variety of systems. They are always assigned positions in status or prestige systems and, in the case of associational groups, in organizational charts.[5] They can also be seen as having location in clusters of all the social roles carried out by their participants. Each human being performs, usually, if not always, several social roles at any stage of his life, each role within a different social circle, but often among the same aggregates of human beings. The role clusters tend to be focused by the individual around a central role, with relative degrees of importance assigned by him to other roles which are placed in different locations from this center. Each role, of course, can take the center stage briefly every time attention is focused on it. However, it is the thesis of this paper that the individual tends to focus on one or at the most two, roles in any cluster he maintains. The life cycle of a human being can be seen as involving shifts in the components of his role cluster new roles are added and old ones dropped, and shifts in the location of each role in the cluster. Modifications in the characteristics of each role occur as the individual enters different stages of its life cycle or changes his definition of the role, or as a consequence of shifts in the cluster. Changes in the role definition can, of course, be brought about by events external to the person, such as modifications in the components or characteristics of the social circle or in their definitions of the role or of their part in it.

The title "housewife" is assigned, in Western European and American societies, to women who are, or have been, married and who "run" their own households, clearly differentiating between them and daughters who care for the homes of their fathers, "housemothers" in sororities, or "housekeepers" running the households of their employers.[6] The matter of proprietal rights over the household is an issue in our society, as evidenced by the aged mother who feels that she has lost some vital rights as a housewife when she moves into the household of her daughter. A person may be designated as a housewife even when she no longer performs the role of wife, although it is assumed that only women who have been married are rightful holders of the title.

The social role of housewife is an indeterminate one, to use Mack's classification of occupations, binding together a variety of "others" through diversified sets of relations.[7] The role cannot be performed by a woman herself, although she may carry out many of the actions through which the maintenance of the home is accomplished without the immediate presence of others. It requires that several persons relate to the title holder through the duties and the rights. The housewife in modern American society maintains her home for and/or with the cooperation of: members of her family of procreation and other residents; guests, such as kin, neighbors, friends,

husband's work associates, persons involved in the lives of offsprings, mem
bers of voluntary associations, etc.; persons or groups who enter the hom
to provide services, such as servants, repair experts, or delivery men; an
persons or groups whose services or goods she seeks outside of the home i
order to maintain it.

The social role of housewife has an interesting cycle compared to othe
roles, involving relatively little anticipatory socialization, very brief tim
devoted to the "becoming" stage and a rather compressed and early pea
It can be performed during the major part of the life cycle of a wome»
yet its entrance, modifications, and cessation are usually not a consequenc
of its own characteristics or rhythm but of those of other roles.

"Becoming a Housewife"[8]

The first stage of any role which is to become important for the perso
is really composed of two phases, frequently lumped together under th
term "novice." It involves not only the process of learning to perform th
duties and to receive the rights in a satisfactory and unselfconscious c
sophisticated manner, but also the process of gradual placement of the se'
within the role. The latter phase requires the ability to see the self as
"natural" center of a role circle and the role as a part of one's own ro
cluster.

The dual aspect of the first stage are in great evidence in the socia
role of the housewife. In modern American society a young woman typicall
enters the role upon marriage, due to the neo-local residence of each famil
of procreation. The housewife is not "adequately" trained for the role ac
cording to Chicago urban and suburban women whose depth interview:
collected over the past few years form the base of this paper,[9] and to nume»
ous other commentators.[10] Although each young girl usually lives in a hom
run by her mother up till the time of marriage, the American system c
education and occupation removes her from its walls for most of her con
scious hours starting at the age of five, and even impinges upon her tim
within it. Training in "home economics" and the voluntary learning c
homemaking skills are not highly evaluated by the society and especially b
teen-aged school-work-boy-leisure oriented girls. Attention tends to be di
rected "outside" of the home, and the focal point of interest in the rol
cluster of each teen-ager tends to be not a role, but the individual.

The process of becoming a housewife includes the phase of the learnin
the various skills used in maintaining the home and relating to those wh
are involved in its maintenance. The process of shifting identifications an
space placements is also important to the young woman. The stress upo»

the location of the self "inside" the home as opposed to "outside" life roles, or persons, so important to housewives in the next stage of the cycle, begins with a gradual shift of the image of the self from a rather functionally diffused "outside" existence to a role-focused and geographically placed identity within a home.

The newly married bride, still engaged in occupational or school roles typical of the American pattern, sees herself as located outside of the home. Living in her own place is important, but it is seen mostly as part of being a wife, and then in terms of primary relations with the husband, rather than as a potential center of multiple relations. She talks of her life in terms of personality changes and feelings to a degree not used again till very old age.

The role of housewife begins to enter her life pattern with a grow-awareness of the complexity of duties involved in the role of wife, duties beyond those of primary attitudes, and, with shifting significance, the role of customer. The meaning of money does change, reflecting and perhaps even leading the changes in the role cluster. The role of worker becomes used more instrumentally than before, as a source of obtaining means for housekeeping activities. The role of consumer begins to involve purchasing for a unit, budgeting, and accounting to the self for expenditures. The role of customer no longer serves only the ends of personal pleasure and adornment. Although "fixing up the apartment" is accomplished with external eyes, the process of bringing the self and purchases "inside" the house begins to acquire a symbolic tone.

The shifting of roles into new clusters often results in the placement of the role of wife in the center, and in the pushing of the roles of daughter, worker, and colleague into the background. The role of housewife or "homemaker" and of consumer are gradually pulled into the foreground.

The Expanding Circle

The increase of importance assigned to the role of housewife in the role cluster comes with pregnancy. Outside employment "fades out" as an important role for most women, and the role of mother antecedes actual birth. The length of time involved in pregnancy performs the important function of "anticipatory socialization."

As LeMasters points out, and interviewees emphatically echo, the birth of the first child is a dramatic event, changing the whole life pattern of the woman.[11] One of the consequences is the shift of focus in the cluster of roles as new ones are added and old ones are dropped. Because of the utter dependence of newborn infants upon practically 24 hour care by an adult, the number of activities such care necessitates, and the society's preference for its being undertaken by the biological mother, the young housewife suddenly finds herself confined to her house, carrying on a variety of housekeeping tasks; often inexpertly and alone.

Not only does the infant require many housewifely actions, and its birth expand the social circle to include new people, but new sets of duties arise in new role relations with people already present in other circles. The husband now becomes also the father of the child and must relate to the mother on that level. The shift of attention often pushes the role of wife to the background, temporarily if not permanently.[12] One of the characteristics of the role of housewife is the fact that competence acquired in the previous stage of the role may not actually help the new mother. A housekeeping schedule, for example, may be dysfunctional to, or made ineffective by, the demands of a newborn baby in a society which stresses its needs above those of adults.

The Peak Stage

The stage of the role of housewife in which the woman has several small children, that is, the peak stage, varies considerably in actual practice, depending on a combination of the following factors:

1. The number and ages of the children.

2. Their special needs.

3. The kinds of duties undertaken by the housewife in relation to these children, because of societal, circle, or self-imposed demands.

4. The kinds of duties undertaken by the housewife in relation to other members of the household.

5. The size of the home which must be maintained.

6. The number of items which must be maintained and the activities required to keep them in a desired condition.

7. The number of persons helping in the performance of the duties and the type of assistance each provides. Such assisting circle segments may include employees, relatives, friends and neighbors, and members of the household involved in a regular or emergency division of labor.

8. The number and variety of "labor-saving" devices or "conveniences" designed to decrease the effort or the time required to perform any of the tasks.

9. The location of the household and of each task in relation to the assisting segment of the circle and to the useful objects, plus the versatility of these services as a source of shifting duties and activities.

The role of housewife, being an indeterminate one, can be performed in a variety of styles, with great complexity or with simplified standards of care of the house and persons within it.

The "Full House" Plateau

The next major stage in the role of housewife starts, according to interviewers, when the youngest child enters school and ends when the children start leaving home to live somewhere else. The women with small, preschool children had anticipated this stage with hopes for "relaxation" and "time for myself." Their statements reflected their reaction to the stage in which they were engaged, one of shift from "outside" to "inside," accompanied by the addition of new roles and hectic hours.

The stage when there are no babies in the home is not reached for most women as soon as the Glick tables of average life cycles led us to expect.[13] At least, the range of time between the birth of the first child and the year when the youngest child starts school, for the 1,000 Chicago interviewees, indicates wide variations in the ages of women when this stage occurs.

Furthermore the "full house" stage does not turn out to be as restful as the mothers of pre-schoolers had anticipated. It seems to be true that, as children grow older, the housewife tends to be relieved of certain household activities. A child's gradual increase in self-control, and in the ability to care for himself and his belongings, plus the decrease in the amount of time he actually spends in the home, may decrease the number or complexity of actions performed by the adult in the house. However, the presence of school-aged children often results in the expansion of the housewife's circle with additions of duties toward each member. Playmates, teachers, tutors, or organization leaders may ask for special attention or impose special demands upon the child, requiring more work of its mother. Other roles may impinge on the time she has to devote to housekeeping tasks. For example, many of the interviewed mothers stated that the supervision of their teen-aged daughters, who are entering a new stage of life, took more time than the supervision of small children. Allowing for the warping of memory and for the probability that these women are not really talking of the amount of time involved in direct supervision but of the amount of worry and conflict, we still must caution ourselves from accepting an over-simplified image of the "full-house" stage of the role of housewife —one of decreased activity and increased leisure.

The housewife's activities in this stage, when new members are not likely to be added to the household through birth, and when residing members are all still there and functioning in a relatively self-sufficient manner, are highly dependent on the size of the social circle, the cultural and personal demands as to what she must do for each person, the kind and amount of assistance provided her, and the time other roles leave her for this function.

For example, the career cycle of the husband is likely to have resulted in a consistent improvement of the family's economic position, due to increased expertness in occupational role performance or upward mobility in role sequences. Such affluence was frequently mentioned by interviewees, but its consequences upon the role of housewife varied; it became a source of more work, if more objects were added for the sake of beauty, comfort, or class status; or a source of less work if the money was converted into services or work simplifying objects.

Standard variations in the role of housewife in the "full-house" stage depend also on solutions to a "inside-outside" continuum of role clusters. The fact that the husband and the children are now all "outside" of the home a great deal of time, and have many outside identifications and orientations may leave the housewife as the only person with a basically "inside" location. She can continue focusing on any of the three roles of wife, mother, or housewife. An interesting focus is developed by women who generalize their relations with the husband and with each child into "family" relations, involving mostly the performance of duties for it. Such women tend to separate themselves, as performers of certain home maintaining-actions, from those who are the recipients, defining all as "the family" and seldom during the interview, if ever, isolating individual relations. Such women speak of "cooking for the family," "sewing for the family," or "waiting for the family to come home."

Other women with growing children place themselves on the "outside" of the home for the majority of the day, taking full-time employment or devoting themselves with complete dedication to volunteer work. As a number of sociologists have pointed out, especially in the analysis of The Working Mother,[14] the kinds of outside roles undertaken, and the ways in which these are clustered depend on several factors. We can analyze the influence of these by seeing how they contribute to the balance between the pull of the activities and gains from each direction. Some women never become "inside-located," so that the return to work or other community life after the birth of children is rapid and complete. Women who have placed themselves in the home and for whom the housewife role became important may be attracted to the outside or forced out of the inside by a feeling of obligation to help in the financial support of the family, or through crises such as widowhood. This study of housewives suggests that the factor of personal influence is very important in furnishing a bridge and an impetus for the breaking down of psychological barriers between the home and the rest of the world. The example and urging of friends and relatives who return to work help offset inertia of a woman who fears that she could no longer function in the occupational work. As in other instances of personal influence, decisions to undertake new roles requiring new skills and behavioral traits tend to take the form of fashion.[15]

Those who do not go out completely, but do so part-time include women who have never cut off ties with the outside, or who develop new lines of connection. They most frequently combine both orientations through the addition of some outside roles, such as that of PTA member, or part-time worker, without letting such identifications grow into total commitments. They continue their focality of a home based role, such as a wife, mother, housewife, or "carer" of the family. The women utilizing the last two categories of role foci tend, however, to least often combine inside with outside orientations, and they continue being home oriented.

One of the factors which must be considered in the analysis of role clustering on the part of women who no longer have small, dependent children and who have a choice in activities they may undertake is the low, if not negative, evaluation of the role of housewife in American society. Such an evaluation has been built up into whole systems of ideology by such writers as Betty Friedan.[16] The role tends to be seen as an instrumental, or servile one, whose function is to help other people perform more vital and interesting roles—away from the home.

Some prestige can come to a housewife if she runs the home of persons judged important by the society. The increase in the number of persons benefiting from the activities of a housewife is also a source of prestige, as it is assumed to increase the significance of what she does. So are, to some extent, the degree of dependency of these people, and the excellence of performance of the role.

All of these bases for prestige in the role of housewife make difficult the next stage for women who have invested their lives in that role, as many have, and who do not have alternative sources for the focusing of identity. The number of alternatives, however, decreases with increased separation from the "outside." The role of mother cannot become a satisfactory focus at this stage of the child's life, because, in American society especially, one of its basic functions to decrease its own importance.

The Shrinking Circle

The next stage in the social role of housewife starts when the first child is married or when he has left home. The previous years actually prepared the way for this stage, since modern American children tend to spend less and less time in the home as they progress through their teens. This stage can last for many years; and it often contains a pause after the last child has left and before the death of the husband.

The shrinking of the circle seriously affects the role. It removes many of the sources of prestige without any choice or control on the part of the woman whose identity is bound with it. No matter how well she performs it, how many and how important are the persons for whom it is performed, or how significant is the role in the lives of recipients, modern society automatically decreases the ability of the role of housewife to serve as a center of relations. The housewife ceases to perform the role at a peak, and even at a high plateau level, long before capacity to carry out its duties decreases, providing a reason or excuse for its cessation. Changes in the role come basically and primarily from changes in characteristics of the circle prior to any changes in her which could provide justification for decreasing functionality.[17]

The shrinking of the role importance of housewife and mother cannot always lead to a shift of self and of role-focus to a concentration on the role of wife, if such an emphasis was absent, since the husband tends still to be highly involved in his role of worker. Thus a gap develops between importance assigned to the husband's functions and those of his wife. She now has the time she desired before, but not necessarily the means of converting it into meaningful roles. An increase in self-directed or in house-directed activities is not a source of roles unless it is accomplished by entrance into new circles. In the case in which the woman does not have satisfactory role substitutions, or in which she does not have an acceptable reason for not being the center of several circles, the life cycle of the role and of the person are not synchronized. This withering of roles and circles leaves her feeling useless and functionless. It is within this stage of the role's cycle that a sharp difference in expressed life satisfactions occurs among different women because of availability of alternative activities and of expectations. Barring ill health, the women who can be located in the higher socioeconomic strata express greater enjoyment of their lives than their less well-positioned counterparts. They make frequent references to the tasks of entertaining and visiting, and to community activities. They look forward to their husbands' vacations and future retirement. As one interviewee explained: "I have the ability, both physical and financial, to do and go pretty much as I please." On the other hand, women of the lower socioeconomic strata tend to list more dissatisfaction with life, and to either see the future in negative hues, or to refuse to predict changes in it.[18]

A source of satisfaction for some women whose circles inside the home had shrunk was that of grandmother. The interview did not specifically refer to this role, so we cannot know why so few women who had children 25 years of age or over, and who can be presumed to be grandmothers, actually spoke of the role. Older women tended to make more references to it, regardless of the age or number of children. Future studies will attempt to learn more of the significance of this role. An interesting hypothesis is that younger women do not identify with the role of grandmother, either because of its aging stereotype, or because they are so busy with other roles as not to assign much significance to it. The distance between the family units is, of course, one factor. It is possible that the present trends in marriage and child bearing are producing grandmothers who are too young to take up the role voluntarily until the grandchildren are too old to need them.

The role of worker does not draw positive comments from women in this stage of life, except on the part of the few who identify with their occupation, all of whom are in professional roles. Most women see their jobs as a source of money and personal contact, but, as they get older, they refer to the role more frequently as something they can leave, or from which they may retire. The comments bear some analysis, since they are very different from the desires of younger women with small children, who see happiness in future roles away from home; and since they indicate a probable source of difference in attitudes of men and women facing retirement.

Women with shrinking housewife roles who are working outside the home, frequently explain that they want to "return home" where they "belong," and where they "always wanted to be." They feel that they have been deprived of a certain set of rights because they "had to go to work." Previous complaints about home restrictions (if actually made by the same woman) are forgotten, and working away from home is seen as an imposition, not a choice. It is quite possible that the man, lacking this feeling of rightfully belonging in the home, has a much more difficult time adjusting to the substitution of this location of the "self" for one in the "world of work." Retirement automatically tends to place the focus of life inside the home. The woman who has always had the role of housewife, with its location "inside," as one of the roles in her cluster and sometimes as the focal role, finds herself inside the home more comfortably than the man for whom this focus is foreign.

The first phase of the "shrinking circle" stage in the social role of housewife ends with her adjustment to the absence of the last child to leave home. During the pause preceding the next stage when she is left alone in the home, before aging becomes a real problem, and if she is not bothered by special difficulties as ill health, the housewife tends to experience gradual changes due to the process of growing older. The factors bringing about these changes and the manner in which aging is evaluated by those who experience it, is of particular interest to modern society because of the increasing percentages of populations who do, or will, face the variety of problems connected with it. Sociological literature dealing with the process is recent, but expanding.[19] This study of the life cycle of the role of housewife indicates that there are several phenomena connected with not only the process but also with the societal and self definitions of its characteristics, stages, and consequences. Such definitions influence social roles in several different ways.

The roles a person performs are affected, of course, by physiological processes experienced in aging, since certain duties are no longer possible or have become modified. The interviewees who were in their latter 60's for example, frequently commented on the fact that they were getting "slower" or that it was taking them longer to do the things they had to do, although the evaluation of this fact ranged from negative, through neutral to even positive.

The societal definition of "symptoms" of aging and classification of a person who has reached a certain chronological age as "old" may have any of the additional consequences upon social roles:

One, it may result in modifications in permitted duties or in rights offered within roles which the person is already performing. Fewer demands for help or for entertaining may be made on the part of offsprings of a housewife. She may even be forbidden to perform certain actions. Women mentioned that they now were "eating out" a lot, or that husbands wouldn't let them shop alone.

Two, the person may be removed from certain social roles because of the assumption on the part of others, or of the self, that qualifications necessary for satisfactory behavior in those roles are lost. The interviewees frequently referred to retirement, or withdrawal, from active participation in voluntary association and "community life," due to aging.

Three, the person may be assigned special social roles due to the societal assumption that the process of aging automatically develops qualities judged necessary for the roles. As many observers have pointed out, the American society has no social role for the aged person, not even a *status role*.[20] It does not have a function to be performed by an aged person. It does not even have a noun which could be the title of such a role, toward which preparatory stages would train the candidate.

Finally, it may make necessary a shift in the concentrations or clusters of social roles, with or without serious modifications of their components.

The aging housewife experiences all forms of changes but the process is gradual and the phenomena connected with it so complex that, until the final stages, its relation to the life cycle is not automatic and the manner in which it affects a particular woman depends upon many factors. A surprising finding was the level of satisfaction expressed by many women in their 50's and 60's who have remained healthy, have husbands still living and no serious problems. Aging frequently provides a rational and virtuous excuse for not expanding roles. Statements by women in this phase of the stage often lack the implication of emptiness and on nonfunctionality of statements made by women in the early phase of circle decrease. Fewer decision-making problems, a lack of pressure from demanding and often conflicting roles, satisfaction with past performance of the role of housewife and with the products of the role of mother, and prior adjustment to the lack of centrality in the lives of children, have all contributed to a relatively high degree of satisfaction contained in the interviews with women in this segment of the cycle. For those who are not widows, the focality of the role of wife is increased with the retirement, or "fade-out" from occupational roles on the part of the spouse. The roles of grandmother and of association member continue to provide sources of satisfaction but demand decreasing contribution. Actions are slowed down gradually so that regular self and house maintenance activities take more time and attention, and are less frequently seen as things which must be finished in order to clear the ground for something "important."

Widowhood causes a major transformation in the social role of housewife, especially if it occurs after everyone else but the couple have left the household. Being a widow with small children is very different from becoming one in later life, when the removal of the role of wife is likely to be permanent and when it adds to the effects of the prior withering of the social circle of housewife.

The Minimal Plateau

The final stage in the role of housewife can be delineated as one in which she is the only person for whom the house is regularly maintained, though others still contribute to the performance of the role and enter it as guests or in order to provide services. It lasts until the death of the housewife, or until the time she breaks up *her* household and moves into a residence being "run" by someone else, be it an offspring or a paid administrator. For its duration the woman tends to devote decreasing energies to external affairs and she tends to see and relate to a decreasing number of persons, depending upon size and closeness (both social and geographic) of kin and friends.[21] The society expects of her lessening contributions while it increases her rights. No one seriously expects the "old widow" or "old woman" to be giving a role outside of her home the focal place in her cluster. The process involves some "disengagement" from organized "outside activities" but it basically changes role clusters.[22] The society, and, reflectively, she herself, justifies her existence in terms of itself, and her functionality in terms of self maintenance. The older she gets, the more pride she can gain from such tasks, and from continued contacts with others. Strain occurs if her expectation of what roles she should perform or what level of performance can be expected of her, does not match that of her social circle which either "restricts" her, or does not grant her "sufficient consideration" rights. The society has not, as the students of aging have pointed out, developed a satisfactory set of sub-roles or standardized variations of regular roles for its older persons. The lack of *status roles* or of other functional assignments for the aging may thus be only part of the problem facing the society and the person. It is possible that more attention ought to be paid by problem solvers to the development of, and training into, satisfactory modifications of on-going in addition to the creation of new roles for our aged population.

One of the basic problems leading to difficulties in role assignment or modifications is the fact that this stage of life is surrounded, as Goffman has pointed out, by "stigma" of such proportions that younger circle members are often incapable of understanding the needs of a mother, hostess, customer, etc., who obviously looks old.[23] The emphasis upon idiosyncratic characteristics of appearance and the suspicion of on-coming senility interfere with role relations.

The end result of this process of adjustment of performance is that no social role is expected to form the focus of the role cluster of the very aged. The person is considered as not "having to" or not "needing to" be vitally concerned with any role. The role of wife and mother have already been left behind entirely or significantly. The role of worker and association member are no longer a source of action or identity. The role of daughter as well as many others are impossible to maintain. Because of concern with the self, because of the slowness with which tasks are performed, and because of the relative isolation of an old woman from the flow of active adult life, she is often described in terms quite similar to those assigned to teenage girls.[24] The content and the location of the roles each undertakes in her cluster are almost exclusively different. Both women, however, are expected to be concerned mostly with themselves and society assigns neither a focal role nor a focal place in its scheme. The society excuses each if she neglects some aspects of a role and even expects negligence—if such behavior provides the active, often harried adult with a motivation to "keep his shoulder to the wheel." Role-oriented, wheel pushing activity belongs to those who prove virtue by non-negligence and who judge themselves as well as being judged by others on the basis of their performance within specific social roles, of the unique roles they select, or of the unique clusters they make of them.

A right which is often taken away from the aging housewife is that of running her own home or of deciding the duties she should undertake to run it. When this happens she loses one of the important rights by which housewives contrast this role to that of working outside, the right to "be my own boss," to "plan my own work."

Summary

The social role of housewife is, in summary, peaked early in the life cycle of a woman, preceding sufficient anticipatory socialization, training, and identification. She must "be" a housewife before she has shifted her role clusters and herself inside the home through a process of "becoming." Placement of the self in the home as the center of its relations, because of house maintenance functions, is frequently a slow and painful process for the young American woman. Her successful adjustment to such placement may not, however, draw societal approval after the period of time judged normal, especially if it involves additions of "extra children." Some women never move inside. They do not build role clusters around the role of house-wife or even assign it an important location. A number of women combine "inside" and "outside," especially after the peak stage, due usually to the influence of friends, neighbors, or relatives, and to the outside location of husband and children. Most of the Chicago interviewees, even those who had full-time employment outside of the home, expressed an "inside" identity. Such a placement did not necessarily solve all strains as it involves several roles and is often combined with some external activities. Thus, in all but the last two stages the housewives felt rushed and busy, expecting the next stage to give them "time for themselves." Many expressed the desire to "go out," especially during the peak period, but not in terms of a complete shift in the role cluster.

Footnotes

Appreciation is expressed to Erving Goffman and Joseph Gusfield for their advice concerning the role monograph which was the foundation of this and of other role papers.

[1] Revised version of paper read in the Sociology of Aging session of the Midwest Sociological Society meetings in April, 1965, in Minneapolis, Minnesota.

[2] The major contributor to the concept of life cycle of the family is Paul Glick, both in his *American Families* (New York: John Wiley and Sons, 1957) and in articles, including: "The Family," *American Sociological Review*, XII (April, 1947), 164–74, and "The Life Cycle of the Family," *Marriage and Family Living*, XVII (February, 1955), 3–9. Most of the textbooks on the family rely on this concept. This is a major focus of Evelyn Duvall's *Family Development* (New York: J. B. Lippincott, 2nd edition, 1962); and Robert Winch uses it throughout his *The Modern Family* (New York: Holt, Rinehart and Winston, Inc., 1963). See also J. S. Slotkin's "Life Course in Middle Age," *Social Forces*, XXXIII (December, 1954), 171–76, for reference to the concept of "life course" developed in Germany by Charlote Bühler.

[3] The definition and the theoretical framework for the concept of social role are contained in the work of Florian Znaniecki. They first appeared in English in *The Method of Sociology* (New York: Farrar & Rinehart, 1934) and were developed fully in his posthumous *Social Relations and Social Roles: An Unfinished Systematic Sociology* (San Francisco: The Chandler Publishing Company, 1965). The last prior published reference to it is contained in "Basic Problems of Contemporary Sociology," *American Sociological Review*, XIX, No. 5 (October, 1954), 519–42.

[4] The assumptions that a role can be limited to expectations of actions, or to the behavior of one person, or to the consequences of status placement is an important factor in the inability of sociologists to utilize it meaningfully in their analyses of social interaction. This defiiciency results in an uneven and restricted use of a concept which could be vital to the field and renders comparisons of roles impossible or at best limited.

[5] See Helena Znaniecki Lopata, "A Restatement of the Relation Between Role and Status," *Sociology and Social Research*, XLIX (October, 1964), 58–68, for the theoretical foundation and definition of *status role*.

[6] American women often react negatively to the term "housewife." Women's magazines have used the word "homemaker" to accentuate creativity and action, but pilot interviews indicated that the women themselves find the term artificial and seldom use it to define their role. The objection to the term "housewife" is not due to the presence of a more satisfactory title, one suspects, but to the low level of prestige assigned to the role.

[7] Raymond W. Mack, "Occupational Determinateness: A Problem and Hypotheses in Role Theory," *Social Forces*, XXXV (October, 1956), 20–24.

[8] The term "becoming" is not meant to indicate a teleological reaching for completed bloom of being, the closed frame of existentialistic writers. Howard Becker's "Becoming a Marihuana User," *American Journal of Sociology*, LIX (November, 1953), 235–42, expresses more of the intended stress upon a process involving self-indication and placement.

[9] The study involves 1,000 interviews with Chicago area housewives. The first 300 were obtained with the help of funds from the *Chicago Tribune* and formed an area probability sample drawn from newly developed sections of 12 socioeconomically divergent suburbs. It included only full time housewives who owned their homes and hard pre-high-school children. The additional 700 interviews came from as broad a range of racial, ethnic, socioeconomic, residential and role focusing women as available in the Chicago area and to Roosevelt University students.

[10] The most famous proponent of "home economics" training for women was Lynn White, Jr. His *Educating Our Daughters* (New York: Harper and Brothers, 1950) created a storm of controversy over the relative value of different systems of education for future homemakers. Practically every study of role expectations and preparation on the part of American girls concludes that training in housekeeping knowledge and skills is not a present focus of choice or even interest, although the

popularity of "adult education" courses in related fields indicates increasing interest in later years.

[11] E. E. LeMasters, "Parenthood as Crisis," *Marriage and Family Living*, XIX (November, 1957), 352–55.

[12] Two-thirds of the Chicago area women interviewed in this study, as reported in Helena Znaniecki Lopata, "Secondary Features of a Primary Relation," *Human Organization* (Summer, 1965), pp. 116–23, did not assign the role of wife first place when asked to list the roles of women in order of importance.

[13] Paul Glick, "The Life Cycle of the Family," (*op. cit.*), 4.

[14] The lack of importance given to their occupational roles, and especially to the task components of such roles, on the part of American women is a conclusion researched by many sociologists, as reported in F. Ivan Nye and Lois W. Hoffman, eds., *The Employed Mother in America* (Chicago: Rand McNally and Company, 1963). The same point is made by Cumming and Henry, especially in their chapter on "Retirement and Widowhood." Elaine Cumming and William E. Henry, *Growing Old* (New York: Basic Books, Inc., 1961).

[15] The Elihu Katz and Paul E. Lazarsfeld statement of the significance of informal communication appeared in *Personal Influence* (New York: The Free Press, A Division of the Macmillan Co., 1955), and it has been the foundation of a great deal of research, especially in consumer behavior. I had the pleasure of participating in a search for an effective technique for getting to the content of "the recommendation process" through interviews, under the direction of Nelson Foote of General Electric in the summer of 1955. This experience, combined with the study of Polish-American associations, "The Function of Voluntary Associations in an Ethnic Community: Polonia" in Ernest Burgess and Donald Bogue, *Contributions to Urban Sociology* (Chicago: University of Chicago Press, 1964) and the study of housewives have convinced me of the importance of friends and other personal links between the woman and any form of "outside" activity.

[16] Betty Friedan, *The Feminine Mystique* (New York: W.W. Norton and Company, Inc., 1963). See also Simone de Beauvoir, *The Second Sex* (New York: Alfred Knopf, 1953).

[17] One must bear in mind that the fact the circle shrinks through a decrease in the number of persons within it may not automatically decrease the signifiance of the role to the person, even when the society evaluates roles by using the numbers game.

[18] The importance of a feeling of competence in life satisfaction has been of interest to several University of Chicago social scientists, including Nelson Foote, Robert Havighurst, and Bernice Neugarten. Lee Rainwater, Richard Coleman, and Gerald Handel contrast *The Workingman's Wife* (New York: Oceana Publications, 1959) whom they find filled with feelings of inadequacy, powerlessness, and incompetence with the middle-class woman who expects to be able to deal with the world and to solve problems.

[19] The aging literature which is most pertinent to this study includes: James Birren, ed., *Handbook of Aging and the Individual* (Chicago: University of Chicago Press, 1959); Clark Tibbits, ed., *Handbook of Social Gerontology* (Chicago: University of Chicago Press, 1960), especially Ch. 9 by Richard Williams; Clark Tibbits, Wilma Donahue, eds., *Process of Aging*, Vol. I (New York: Atherton Press, 1963); E. W. Burgess, ed., *Aging in Western Society* (Chicago: University of Chicago Press, 1962); Peter Townsend, *The Family Life of Old People* (London: Routledge and Kegan Paul, 1957); Elaine Cumming and William E. Henry, *op. cit.*; and Arnold Rose in Arnold and Warren Peterson, *Old People and their Social World* (Philadelphia: F.A. Davis Co., 1965).

[20] Helena Znaniecki Lopata, "A Restatement of the Relation between Role and Status." *op. cit.*

²¹ The importance of kin for the older person is indicated in the national and cross-cultural research of Ethel Shanas, in the Cumming and Henry and in the Townsend studies. Marvin Sussman and Eugene Litwak have also contributed to our understanding of the interaction with, and assistance dependencies of, members of a kin.

²² The theory of disengagement, as developed by the several authors of *Growing Old*, suffers from a confused use of the concept of social role. Based on the ideal-typical Parsonian separation of roles on the basis of a single dimension, for example, "instrumental-emotional"—a separation that speaks only of the manner of behavior or attitude forming part of the duties or means—they neglect to distinguish between several forms of role-related phenomena. They thus speak of disengagement as involving the following processes as if they were all the same: a decrease in the number of duties which are performed, a change in the manner in which all duties are performed, a change in the manner in which rights are granted and received, shifts in the relation between one role and another performed simultaneously or in sequence by one person, the shifting focus of life from one role to another, the dropping of roles entirely, and the removal of persons with whom the individual is involved in a multiplicity of roles as if his absence eliminated only one role.

²³ Erving Goffman, *Stigma* (Englewood Cliffs, New Jersey: Prentice-Hall, Inc., 1963).

²⁴ Although Cumming and Henry draw a comparison between the old person and the child, my interviewees lead me to the comparison of the old woman to the teen-age girl because my population contained only housewives. Those women who were judged able to perform this role, to run a home, at least in a minimally effective manner, by those who would have had the right to remove them from the role, or to encourage or permit them to remove themselves had not disintegrated in their abilities sufficiently to warrant analogies of child-like behavior or attitudes.

Occupational Status and Role

A Comparative Perspective

The Call Girl And The Dance Teacher

A Comparative Analysis

MARY GRAY RIEGE

Northern Arizona University

Introduction

In his introduction to The Taxi Dance Hall, Burgess (1932) states:

> The taxi dance hall is an example of the failure of the tradi-
> tional devices of social control to function in a culturally hetero-
> geneous and anonymous society. Conventional avenues for forming
> friendship are deficient in the city, and taxi dance halls, lonesome
> clubs, and matrimonial advertising bureaus appear.

Burgess might have included the branch studios of national dancing school
chains and professional prostitution in his list of examples, since these are
also phenomena of large cities and are also a-conventional responses to the
felt need for friendship formation.

In this context, this paper is a comparative analysis of the occupational
roles of the call girl and the female ballroom dance teacher employed by a
national dance school chain. Both professions fall under the broad heading
of service occupations, defined by Becker (1966) as:

> in general, distinguished by the fact that the worker in them
> comes into more or less direct and personal contact with the ulti-
> mate consumer of the product of his work, the client for whom he
> performs the service.

Both professions may be considered the upper echelon of their occupational sphere. One typology of prostitution (Minnis, 1963) divides this

Reprinted from *Cornell Journal of Social Relations*, Vol. 4, No. 1 (Spring 1969),
58–71, by permission of the author and publisher.

occupation into seven subgroups of which the pony girl and the call girl are the elites.[1] Although there is no comparable study in the sociological literature describing strata among ballroom dance teachers, it is generally accepted that there is a sharp division between those girls who are employed by national chains of ballroom dance schools, such as Arthur Murray or Fred Astaire, and those who work for independent schools. The Murray or Astaire teacher receives extensive professional training in dancing, teaching, salesmanship, grooming, etc. Her dance training is standardized according to a "dance manual" issued to each branch studio of the national chain, and is extensive in that she is able to dance and to teach a wide range of dances at a standard of excellence ranked by professional judges. She earns an average-to-good salary based on an hourly wage as well as commissions for selling additional lessons to the students assigned to her.

At a lower level are those girls employed by independent dance studios. These are of two types—those that attempt to establish themselves in competition with Murray or Astaire schools (and frequently fail), and the resort-type school, usually in business only for "the season." The primary reasons for distinguishing between teachers in national and independent schools are (1) independent schools generally have a short life, while national chains have been in operation for several decades; (2) the training program for teachers in independent schools is generally catch-as-catch-can, not extensive, and usually confined to teaching "what the student wants" rather than a broad academic-type general knowledge of ballroom dances; and (3) the female teachers are sometimes ex-employees of national chains who have been fired for one or another reason, or, sometimes, near-prostitutes—that is, girls who use the contacts they make at the school for personal profit.

Having identified the subgroups among prostitutes and dance teachers whose roles will be compared in this paper, we now turn to a discussion of the foci within which these occupations are to be examined. As stated earlier, both the dance teacher and the call girl are reflections of occupations which have grown up within large cities as a spurious response to the need for friendship formation "in a culturally heterogeneous and anonymous society." In this paper, particular interest is focused on the ideology of both occupations and on how that ideology is manifested in the occupational roles of call girls and dance teachers. Neither of these occupations provide genuine friendship—but both sell, along with their manifest service, a simulated friendship. Further, in both cases there is a sexual component which differentiates these services from non-sexually or a-sexually oriented service occupations.[2] While the sexual component of the call girl's role is obvious, it may not be so apparent in the role of the dance teacher. However as Lopata and Noel (1967) state:

> In our society, one of the forms of interaction in primary relations with members of the opposite sex . . . is ballroom dancing. An

important factor distinguishing this form of interaction from others
... is the fact that it involves physical contact on the part of a
man and a woman who are supposedly attractive to each other.
... Its sexual connotations are implicit in the attitude of members
of the society toward two women who dance together and in the
refusal of men to dance with each other.

Cottle (1966) also notes that:

> The inherent intimacy ... makes dancing uniquely different
> from most other observable social interaction.

How does—or indeed, how can—a professional ideology support the
sale of simulated friendship in a sexually oriented occupation? (At first
thought, this would seem to be a case of fraud at worst, or hypocrisy at
best.) This matter is of special interest since sexual behavior is one common
aspect of primary relationships and, as such, is incompatible with the notion
of simulated friendship. Lopata and Noel (1967) discuss this situation:

> "Primary relations" ... are viewed as involving affection, per-
> sonality-directed goals, pleasure in the relationship itself, and trust
> in its symmetry or reciprocity. Partners in a primary relationship are
> expected to commit themselves to equal involvement and to be con-
> cerned over each other's feelings. *The presence* of commercial lonely
> hearts clubs and *ballroom dance studios violates this distinction*
> [between primary and secondary relationships] since they supposedly
> attract defenseless people who want primary relations so badly that
> they are willing to use secondarily designed organizations to buy
> them. (Emphasis added.)

According to Becker and Geer (1966):

> It makes some difference in a man's performance of his work
> whether he believes wholeheartedly in what he is doing or feels that
> in important respects it is a fraud.

While we can readily agree that the sale of simulated friendship is fraudulent, we may wonder what differences there might be in the occupational
behavior of (1) the call girl, around whom there is only minimal organizational framework for support, and whose ideology directly acknowledges the
fraud involved in her work, and (2) the dance teacher, surrounded by a
complicated organizational framework so structured as to keep her from
awareness of the fraud involved in her work. Other similarities and differences, regardless of "official" ideologies found in these two occupations,
will also be explored below.

Two Cultural Factors

1. SEX AND SEXUALITY

While there are many superficial similarities between the roles of dance teacher and call girl (to be illustrated below), there is an essential difference in the area of what Masters and Johnson (1966) have called the disparity in our culture between sex and sexuality. These authors demonstrate that sexuality and sex are not synonymous but that they do lie on a continuum— a fact not recognized in our society. They contend that while we educate our children about sex (largely in the form of "reproduction education") we fail to educate them about sexuality. As a result, they state, we fail to produce mature adults, capable of forming adequate interpersonal relationships including tenderness, intimacy, warmth, or responsible and intelligently managed sex behavior. Using Masters and Johnson's framework, the property space below illustrates how sex and sexuality are differentially bifurcated in the occupations of the call girl and the dance teacher.

	Call Girl	Dance Teacher
Sex	Provided	Not Provided
Sexuality	Simulated	Genuine

Interestingly, since it is implicit in Masters and Johnson's argument that sex without sexuality is a fraud, as is sexuality without sex, the call girl's culturally disapproved occupation actually comes closer to the desired state of affairs than does the dance teacher's culturally approved occupation. Although simulated sexuality may be a fraud-within-a-fraud, at least it is coupled, however spuriously, with sex itself. This is not the case for the dance teacher, in whose occupation sex and sexuality are totally dichotomized.

2. WORK AND FUN

Both the call girl and the dance teacher view their occupational specialties as providing "fun" for the client. The call girl is consistent in her behavioral implementation of this idea. That is, "success" is not expected or demanded from the client; he does not work, nor is he expected to, to obtain fun. Conversely, she provides the work and he has the fun. The dance teacher, on the other hand, is inconsistent in her behavioral implementation of this idea. Learning to dance is seen by her as hard work, something eminently worth doing well, and something which takes a long time in order to be "successful." (The call girl does not teach her client, except perhaps incidentally, and the provision of fun is immediate.)

The paradoxical attitude of the dance teacher and the consistent attitude of the call girl may be seen as differential reflections of lower-class vs. middle- and upper-class values in our culture. In the latter classes, there is a general trend (if not a manifest predilection) toward making work of everything which would customarily be considered play or fun. In the middle and upper classes, play (including dancing) is not spontaneous. In the lower class, however, there is a countervailing attitude which holds that fun is, by definition, spontaneous. Interestingly, comparisons of dancing styles among lower-class Negroes and middle- and upper-class whites reveal that it is only in the lower-class Negro's style that there is a large element of spontaneity. Cottle (1966) finds that:

> Pure innovation occurs primarily in the lower class, where innovators transmit interpretive findings and readings to their groups, but social norms control this activity as well. A great male dancer, for example, is heralded in lower classes, held suspect in middle classes, and is nonexistent among elites.

It is not surprising, therefore, that it is from the lower-class groups that innovations in dancing steps and styles most frequently arise—which are then "learned" and "perfected" by middle- and upper-class dancers.

These notions lead to the conclusion that the call girl's occupational behavior reflects a consistency of attitude similar to that of the lower-class Negro, i.e., that fun is a spontaneous happening. The dance teacher's occupational behavior reflects, on the other hand, an incongruous attitude similar to the middle- and upper-class feeling that having fun is something to be worked at—i.e., non-spontaneous. This paradox may reflect an overgeneralization of the Protestant Ethic in our culture, where success is an important element of all behavior, where work is highly valued for its own sake, and where the impetus to successful work becomes extended to the point that one is expected to be "good at" having fun!

Other Similarities and Differences

1. SOCIAL CLASS ORIGINS

In view of the discussion above, it is curious that in one extensive study of call girls (Greenwald, 1958), 85 percent were found to have middle- or upper-class backgrounds—quite the converse of what might have been expected. While no data are available on the social class background of dance teachers, it is the impression of the present writer that most dance teachers come from middle-class families.[3] There is a relationship between the clientele served and the class origin of the teacher. Clients who can afford lessons at an Astaire or Murray studio are generally middle- or upper-class themselves.[4] Greenwald (1958) points out the relationship between class origins of call girls and their clientele. He states:

> Girls from [middle and upper] classes are usually more willing than others to provide the variety of sexual activities frequently required by middle- and upper-class males.

2. Recruitment, Training, and Role Sets

Dance teachers are usually recruited through newspaper want-ads. Careful screening eliminates the physically unattractive, unpoised, or in any way undesirable applicants. Those who are considered suitable for training are then given an extensive course of instruction in teaching ballroom dancing as well as in other skills (see above, page 147). When the trainee is considered ready to teach, she is officially hired. However, training continues after hiring, taking up a large part of the time the teacher spends in the school.

The new teacher is inculcated with upper-class attitudes toward her students and toward her own role. The professional stance, as Lopata and Noel (1967) point out, includes:

> ... no derogatory or degrading remarks about the activity of ballroom dance teaching ... the regular or "long course" student who dances well as a source of pride.... The highly professional studio ... the rules forbidding outside, non-studio sponsored contact, demands non-sexual connotations in the student-teacher relations, and has a non-cynical attitude toward dancing and toward the student. It tends to [have] a high morale and strong skill orientation on the part of teachers....

During the training period, the novice-teacher becomes acquainted with members of the studio staff who form her elaborate role set. These are:

> 1. The studio receptionist, who will book appointments and on whom she is dependent not only for this function but also for "keeping the student happy" while he waits for his lesson in the reception room of the studio;

2. The studio manager, who is her direct employer, and who will provide sales training and orient her to the value system of the studio;

3. The dance director from whom she receives her ongoing training in both dancing and teaching;

4. The senior interviewer(s) who is the first salesperson the incoming student encounters in the studio, and on whom the new teacher is thus dependent for her clientele;

5. The junior interviewer(s) who teaches the first several lessons of a new student's course, and who is a secondline salesperson, "extending" the course of lessons originally purchased into a longer, tailormade program, before the student is assigned a regular teacher;

6. The supervisor whose function is to help the teacher obtain "renewals"—i.e., to sell additional courses of lessons;

7. The guest director, who encourages students, teachers, and trainees to bring guests to the studio in order to provide opportunities to enroll them for courses;

8. Other trainees and regular teachers with whom she will be working, once hired, and finally;

9. Students assigned to her, and other teachers' students.

Call girls are usually recruited into the profession by other call girls or by men connected with call girl circles. Bryan (1965) describes the standard structure of the apprenticeship period as follows:

> The novice receives her training either from a pimp or from another more experienced call girl, more often the latter. She serves her initial two to eight months of work under the trainer's supervision and often . . . in the trainer's apartment. The trainer assumes responsibility for arranging contacts and negotiating the type and place of the sexual encounter. . . . The content of the training pertains both to a general philosophical stance and to some specifics (usually not sexual) of interpersonal behavior with customers and colleagues.

Bryan describes the interpersonal techniques as consisting primarily of "pitches," telephone conversations, personal and sometimes sexual hygiene, rules against alcohol or drugs while with clients, how and when to obtain fees, and specifics concerning sexual habits of particular customers, although specific sexual techniques are very rarely taught. He states further:

> It appears that the primary function of the apprenticeship, at least for the trainee, is building a clientele. . . . The novice call girl

is acclimated to her new job primarily by being thoroughly immersed in the call girl subculture, where she learns the trade through imitation as much as through explicit tutoring.

During her apprenticeship, the call girl becomes acquainted with other members of her rather small role set.[5] This consists largely of clients and other call girls. An attorney may be a member of the role set, although his services are infrequently used. In some cases there may also be a pimp, though he generally functions as a paid lover rather than as a procurer at this level of prostitution (see Greenwald, 1958).

3. Mobility

Upward mobility is quite limited for both the dance teacher and the call girl, but downward mobility is commonplace in both occupations.

Among dance teachers, for instance, former employees of other schools are seldom hired by national chains which prefer to train their teachers themselves. Even between the two major studios (Murray and Astaire) very little cross-hiring is done.

Regarding the call girl, Greenwald (1958) states:

It should be noted that one does not become a call girl by working one's way up the economic ladder of prostitution. Call girls usually start at that level.

As noted above, in both occupations downward mobility is fairly common among those who do not leave their work for marriage or some entirely different occupation. One factor here would seem to be length of time involved. Both dance teachers and call girls need to be fairly young and at least moderately attractive in order to meet the expectations of their respective publics. If a call girl stays "in the life" too long, she may find her clientele diminishing to the point where she "automatically" moves down the ladder—i.e., becomes a B-girl or, should she lose her attractiveness through excessive drinking, drug use, etc., she may be eventually reduced to the status of a streetwalker. The dance teacher is usually not "in the business" for many years. Most leave the profession to take other kinds of jobs or to marry. However, those who are fired from a national chain and who wish to stay in the business—or those who are interested in a less stable job that may offer more short-range financial reward—may move down the occupational ladder to another type of dance studio.

Within the dance studio, however, upward mobility is possible. That is, the teacher may become a salaried supervisor, interviewer, studio manager, or may purchase a franchise from the national chain (though this is rare for women). Since the role set within the dance studio is a large one, there are many possible within-situs moves. No comparable situation exists for the call girl, since her role set is extremely small, and she is not equipped to occupy any of the other roles within her occupational situs (e.g., pimp, attorney, etc.) although a small percentage may become "madams" when age or unattractiveness limit her earning capacity.

4. COMPARISON OF EARNINGS AND SPECIAL EXPENSES

While the call girl earns a great deal more than does the average dance teacher,[6] her expenses are also much higher though the earnings of both are spent for similar occupational necessities. Both the call girl and the dance teacher must maintain extensive and glamorous or semi-glamorous wardrobes. Laundry and cleaning bills, cosmetics, perfumes and beauty shop expenditures account for a much higher percentage of both the call girl's and the dance teacher's earnings than, for example, the average office secretary would spend. As may well be imagined, the dance teacher's expenses for shoes alone is considerably higher than average. In addition to the foregoing, the call girl's expenses include large bills for telephone service, often including an answering service; for maintenance of an attractively furnished apartment in an appropriate location; for medical expenses including not only frequent "regular" checkups but sometimes for abortions and sometimes special treatment for venereal disease. The call girl also pays protection or bribe money to the local police, and has large expenses in the form of tips to elevator men, doormen, etc.

5. ASSOCIATIONS

Dance teachers' contacts with "respectable society" are limited. This is largely a function of the unusual working hours they keep. Customarily, a teacher begins work at one o'clock in the afternoon and leaves the studio after ten o'clock at night. Since this schedule is out of pace with a normal nine-to-five working day, contacts with those working regular hours are restricted. Thus, they necessarily associate with others who have late schedules—i.e., musicians, bartenders, etc. Not infrequently, dance teachers use open-all-night beauty shops and, since these are also often used by prostitutes, the two professions come into contact, however fortuitously. Goffman (1963), commenting on the management of spoiled identity, notes that:

> the prostitute, particularly the call girl, is supersensitive in polite society, taking refuge in her off hours with . . . artists, writers, actors [etc.]. There she may be accepted as an off-beat personality, without being a curiosity.

Because of the above-mentioned unusual working hours of the dance teacher, she frequently spends her leisure time in places where prostitutes and other "off-beat personalities" gather, and because of the inability of the public to differentiate visually between the call girl and the dance teacher, the latter may be seen as a marginal case of spoiled identity, in Goffman's terms. In the eyes of the layman, she is as off-beat as her associates and thus is stigmatized.

6. Occupational Attitudes Toward the Motives of the Public

Caplow states (1954) :

> It is by consensus and by the sharing of attitudes that occupational groups ... become sociologically meaningful. ... Even the most loosely organized occupational group will share certain attitudes toward ... the motives of the public.

Intra- and inter-occupationally, call girls and dance teachers share the view that their clients feel the need for friendship along with the manifest occupational service. The need for a listening ear, for appreciation, for "romance," for feeling wanted, are frequently attributed to their clients by call girls (McManus, 1960; Greenwald, 1958; Stearn, 1956). Bryan (1966) reports that when his sample of call girls was asked to give what they thought were justifying reasons for the existence of prostitution, one of several stereotypic answers given was that men don't just frequent call girls for sex, but also for companionship. Thus, they feel that they are functioning as "someone to talk over problems with." The dance studio's attitude toward students' needs is summarized by Lopata and Noel (1967) :

> The studio sees the student as a lonely person who needs the interaction provided by its activities. ... The assumption is that the student is in the studio because of his inability to relate to people in a satisfactory manner ... [and] that the student deeply needs primary relations.

Ideology and Its Implementation through the Role Set

When Bryan (1966) asked his sample of 52 call girls about their attitudes toward their profession, he found certain responses to be stereotypically frequent. His subjects stated that:

1. Prostitution serves important social functions because of man's varied and extensive sexual needs, protecting individuals and social institutions from destructive ruptures;

2. Prostitution takes care of the socially stigmatized (freaks, isolates, etc.), and prevents rapes, murders, perversions, etc.;

3. Because of prostitution, marriage is made more enduring (the prostitute sees herself as more effective in saving marriages than a marriage counselor) and;

4. Prostitutes serve as important psychotherapeutic agents, giving comfort, insight, and satisfaction to those men too lonely, embarrassed, or isolated to obtain interpersonal gratification in other ways.

Compare the foregoing ideological stance with the following brief description of the ideology of the dance studio, taken from Lopata and Noel (1967):

> The studio sees itself as providing important services, increasing the person's self-confidence and poise, and teaching him or her to relate others in new ways in addition to providing fun for persons who do not have much of it in their lives. The ideology of the studio thus stresses multi-level help to students who are [seen as] unhappy without it.

While the parallels in these occupational ideologies are striking, Bryan (1966) finds that call girls do not internalize their professional perspective. He states that once entrance into prostitution has been accomplished, there are many reasons for rejection of such beliefs which, for instance, attempt to justify exploitation of customers on the ground that the role of the prostitute is no more immoral than the role of the "square" and that colleagues are more honest than women outside the profession. Prostitutes, feeling that they perform a necessary, even therapeutic service, state that they should not be stigmatized. However, since prostitution at the call girl level is loosely organized and cooperative interaction with colleagues is required only for short periods of time and usually within restricted circumstances, no critical dependence upon particular individuals is developed. Thus, in spite of ideology, the everyday life of the call girl is to a great extent designed to avoid public revelation and is generally successful in this effort. Moreover, much of the interaction of client and prostitute is specifically oriented toward the reduction of the stigma attached to both roles, according to Bryan (1966), each pretending that the other is fulfilling a role more obscure than that which is apparent. "The call girl rarely experiences moral condemnation through interpersonal relations, thus reducing the need for justification. This may further lessen the impact of attempts at occupational socialization." Bryan finds that the group as a whole fails to identify with colleagues.

Conversely, the elaborate role set and intricate system of interdependency within the dance studio contributes toward an ongoing reinforcement of the ideology of the professional dance studio in the attitude of its teachers.

The role sets of call girl and dance teacher are presented diagrammatically below:

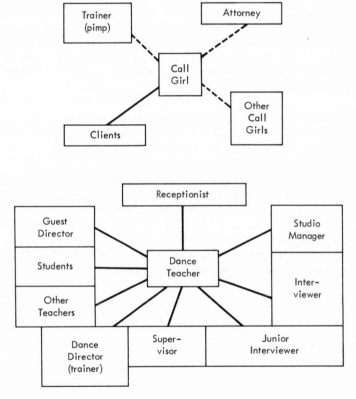

Dotted lines indicate members of the role set who are infrequently and sometimes never encountered. Since, in the dance studio, all role set members interact frequently with all other members, solid lines could be drawn showing all interconnections.

Earlier we noted the *implicit* sexuality involved in ballroom dancing and questioned how the ideology of a profession could support and sustain a condition of "unawareness" of this sexuality. The answer lies in the elaborate system of controls imposed on studio personnel, and in the reinforcing nature of the large role set with its high interaction frequency. The studio controls do not deny the sexual component of the occupation; rather, they impose strong negative sanctions against any *explicit* evidence of it in the behavior of their teachers, either within or outside of the school. Teachers are trained to discourage sexual advances in extremely tactful ways, and to keep the student's attention centered on dancing. Studios forbid teachers to date students, or even to be escorted to or from studio functions by students. For failure to comply, the teacher will be fired. Lopata and Noel (1967) state:

> The constant training of teachers stresses that they must look and act as "gentlemen and ladies." The total atmosphere attempts to be controlled and dignified without involving sexual or deeply personal feelings.

Interdependence on other staff members is deliberately fostered by the studio, and this acts as another form of control. Lopata and Noel (1967) explain:

> Each teacher is encouraged to build up the image of other members of the studio in the eyes of the student. . . . Thus, although the students tend to be relation-oriented at the beginning, increasing participation leads them to become competitively skill-oriented. The studio management is aware of this fact and is probably . . . right in stating that the long-term courses are most likely to produce the best students—not only in terms of money, but in justifying the studio, and maintaining the rationale.

Summary and Conclusions

Although there is a large body of sociological literature about the prostitute, including historical background, cross-cultural comparisons, etc., there is little or no comparable data about dance teachers. Therefore, several dimensions of possible comparison or contrast between the professional prostitute and the professional dance teacher have been neglected in this paper. We have not inquired directly into codes of ethics, or possible psychological reasons for recruitment; neither has the aspect of deviance in the roles of either dance teacher or call girl been fully explored; nor has the importance of female attractiveness, so strongly emphasized in our culture, been investigated as it relates to either of the professions of interest here.

We have, however, presented a discussion of:

1. how both the professional prostitute and the professional dance teacher function in their occupational roles as a-conventional responses to the need for friendship formation in the large city—in particular, how both roles are examples of pseudo-primary relationships within secondary relationship systems;

2. how both occupations differentially reflect the bifurcation of sex and sexuality in American culture; and

3. how both occupations differentially reflect class differences in adherence to the Protestant Ethic and its extensions in American culture.

Additionally, we have examined similarities and differences between call girls and dance teachers along the dimensions of social class origins, recruitment, training, role sets, occupational mobility, associations, occupational attitudes toward motives of the public, stigmatization and its management, and finally, professional ideology.

We have indicated that the professional ideology of call girls, while known to them, does not play a large part in their lives, and that the reason may lie in the very loose organization of the profession, combined with the fairly close internal consistency of the role behavior with certain cultural values. On the other hand, the professional ideology of the dance teacher, in the structural/functional sense, indicates a "need" for an elaborate role set and for a strong system of controls to support it, since it reflects some rather basic inconsistencies. We are not suggesting a causal relationship between relative size of role sets and professional ideologies in any direction, or with any particular level of fraud or hypocrisy involved. However, there does appear to be a revealed correlation in this area, within the two occupations of interest in this paper.

While Becker (1966) was referring to the specific case of the jazz musician in the following quotation, it would seem to have particular relevance to the subject matter of concern here:

> It may be suggested that similar conflicts are to be found in other service occupations and that research in such areas could profitably focus on such matters as the professional's conception of his client, the manner in which the client impinges on (or, from the professional's point of view, interferes with) his work, the effects of such conflicts on professional organization, with particular reference to the defensive tactics employed by the profession, and the relation of such dilemmas to the individual's participation in the life of the larger society.

Selected References

BECKER, HOWARD S. 1966. "Performing Arts—Music," in *Professionalization*, Howard M. Vollmer and Donald L. Mills, Eds., Englewood Cliffs, N.J., Prentice-Hall, Inc.

BECKER, HOWARD S. and BLANCHE GEER, 1966. "Medicine," in *Professionalization*, Howard M. Vollmer and Donald L. Mills, Eds., Englewood Cliffs, N.J., Prentice-Hall, Inc.

BRYAN, JAMES H. 1965. "Apprenticeships in Prostitution," *Soc. Probl.*, 12, 3, Winter, 287–297.

BRYAN, JAMES H. 1966. "Occupational Ideologies and Individual Attitudes of Call Girls," *Soc. Probl.*, 13, 4, Spring, 441–450.

BURGESS, ERNEST W. 1932. Quoted in *Sociology*, Leonard Broom and Philip Selznik, New York, Harper and Row, 3rd Ed., p. 611 (Cressey, Paul G., *The Taxi Dance Hall*, Chicago, University of Chicago Press.)

CAPLOW, THEODORE 1954. *The Sociology of Work*, McGraw-Hill Book Co., University of Minnesota Press.

COTTLE, THOMAS J. 1966. "Social Class and Social Dancing," *Sociol. Quart.*, Spring, 179–196.

GOFFMAN, ERVING S. 1963. *Stigma: Notes on the Management of Spoiled Identity*, Englewood Cliffs, N.J., Prentice-Hall, Inc.

GREENWALD, HAROLD 1958. *The Call Girl: A Social and Psychoanalytic Study*, New York, Ballantine Books.

LOPATA, HELENA ZNANIECKI and JOSEPH R. NOEL 1967. "The Dance Studio—Style Without Sex," *Trans-Action*, Jan.-Feb., 10–17.

MASTERS, W. H., and VIRGINIA E. JOHNSON 1966. "Sex and Sexuality—the Crucial Difference," *McCalls*, Nov.

McMANUS, VIRGINIA 1960. *Not For Love*, New York, Dell Publishing Co.

MINNIS, MHYRA S. 1963. "Prostitution and Social Class," *Proc. S.W. Sociol. Assoc.* 13, 1–6.

STEARN, JESS 1956. *Sisters of the Night*, New York, Gramercy Publishing Co.

Footnotes

[1] A brief description of the roles of the pony girl and the call girl will indicate why the focus in this paper is on the call girl rather than the pony girl:

> The prostitute who considers herself above the ordinary prostitute is the call girl. In some cases, this aristocrat of prostitution considers herself not a prostitute at all. She restricts herself to a limited number of contacts with patrons whom she may know over long periods and who pay a high fee. Second to the pony girl, this class is the elite of the prostitution world. (Minnis, 1963)

The pony girl actually has two occupations—she is either model-and-prostitute or entertainer-and-prostitute. The prostitution in which she engages is sporadic and not her sole or primary source of income. Thus, she falls into a category which is less comparable to that of the female dance teacher than the call girl who, like the dance teacher, usually has only one occupation from which she derives her entire income.

[2] Non-sexual or a-sexual service occupations are too numerous to mention. Other

sexually oriented service occupations are few. The Playboy Bunny type of cocktail waitress is one example.

[3] This impression was gained over a 15-year employment span with the Fred Astaire Dance Studios.

[4] Lessons range in price from $10 to $18 per hour with the mean considerably closer to the upper end of this range. Comparatively, the call girl's average fee for services is not lower than $20.

[5] Curiously, while the organization is rather loosely structured around the call girl and rather tightly structured around the dance teacher, Caplow's comment (1954) below would seem to apply more to the call girl than to the dance teacher! He states:

> The specifications for the control of behavior in a well organized occupation are exceedingly numerous. Indeed training for such an occupation . . . consists primarily in learning the rules governing the exercise of a function rather than in rehearsing the function itself.

[6] Greenwald (1958) estimates the average call girl's income at $20,000 per year.

Work Systems

The Funeral Home as a Work System

A Sociological Analysis

JEROME J. SALOMONE

Louisiana State University in New Orleans

Introduction

This essay is about death, which ranks in importance with birth as one of the two greatest and most significant facts of all existence. These enormously important existential conditions have given rise, according to Herbert Spencer, to pervasive and timeless fears—the fear of living which becomes the basis of political institutions, and the fear of death which becomes the basis of religious institutions.[1] Indeed, birth and death are thought to be so critical throughout the world that everywhere religious belief systems support the notion that these events are in fact sacred phenomena.[2]

Turning exclusively to death, the subject of this paper, we find that contemporary beliefs and rites vary widely in the manner in which the dead are treated. Moreover, these beliefs and rites are subject to slow, unplanned, and usually unconscious change, both cross-culturally and, from time to time, even within the same society.

In general, it can be observed that the less advanced technologically the society, the more consonant the beliefs and rites regarding death within the society. This means, for example, that in agricultural societies both the beliefs and rites related to death and the disposition of the dead tend to be predominantly, if not exclusively, sacred or religious in nature, with the shaman or priest clearly in unchallenged control over the funeralization process. By contrast, in more technologically advanced, industrial societies the beliefs tend to remain sacred while the rites assume a more secular or materialistic aura, with the funeral director substituting for the clergyman in managing the funeral ceremonies. In fact, the funeralization process in

An original article prepared especially for this volume.

contemporary America has come under heavy criticism recently because of the alleged commercialization and materialization of what historically has been, and should remain, according to the argument, an entirely religious process.[3]

The elaboration of the procedures and rituals associated with the disposition of the dead has reached the point where it requires, for its efficient performance, a coterie of occupational specialists who operate as a coordinated team and whose overall goal is to process the corpse from death to the grave.

STATEMENT OF PURPOSE

This essay undertakes, first of all, to describe the various work statuses and roles of the different major occupational specialties within the funeral home setting. The funeral home is described and analyzed as a work system composed of various occupational specialties which are integrated and coordinated in such a manner that the task of processing the dead is accomplished in a team fashion. A second objective is to delineate and specify those occupational specialties that are internal to the funeral industry—like funeral director, embalmer, hearse driver, and receptionist—from those that are externally related to it—for example, florist, cemeterian, clergyman and insurance salesman.

My intention in this descriptive essay is to be suggestive rather than definitive. The article, therefore, is perhaps as noteworthy for what it excludes as for what it treats. A selected bibliography is included for the interested reader who would like to follow up leads suggested here.

Types of Funeral Homes

Robert Habenstein has called attention to two ideal types of funeral establishments, which can be labeled mass mortuaries and local mortuaries.[4] They are distinguishable from one another on the basis of five criteria: (1) In mass mortuaries first contact with the bereaved family is made by a staff of salaried specialists; in local mortuaries contact is first made by the owner-operator of the establishment. (2) Mass mortuaries do not reflect community values; locals do. (3) Mass mortuaries treat each case "in the spirit of formalistic impersonality"; local mortuaries "have an obligation to the family." (4) The goal of mass mortuaries is "a business unlimited" ethic; whereas that of the locals is not. (5) Mass mortuaries are organized bureaucratically; locals are organized traditionally.

The trend within the industry is away from local and toward mass mortuaries. However, local mortuaries overwhelmingly outnumber mass mortuaries at this time, as the preponderance of funeral homes is still small, family-owned and -operated establishments located in small towns across the length and breadth of this country.

There are pronounced operating differences between local and mass establishments. Locals usually operate an ambulance service as an expensive, and usually unprofitable, adjunct to the funeral home, whereas in the metropolis, where mass mortuaries are found, this service is usually provided by hospitals. Locals are single units, while mass mortuaries spawn branch units in various sections of the city and region. While both local and mass mortuaries frequently operate an insurance department in conjunction with the funeral business, mass mortuaries are more likely to do so than local establishments. Locals own their own rolling stock (hearse and limousines), whereas mass mortuaries are more likely to rent theirs from a separate corporation which provides such equipment. The division of labor is less precise and more flexible in locals than in mass mortuaries. For example, in locals the embalmer may also double as gardener, ambulance driver, and general handyman around the funeral home, while his counterpart in the large city probably embalms exclusively. Many local establishments do not have resident embalmers. They hire them on a piece-rate basis when needed. Mass mortuaries, on the other hand, always employ resident embalmers.

The Internal System

FUNERAL DIRECTOR

Just as the handling of illness is rapidly becoming an institutional matter, with the hospital rather than the family caring for the sick, so also is the funeral home replacing the family as the agent in handling the dead. This transformation is virtually complete in large urban centers where overwhelmingly the home has given way to the funeral home as the environmental setting for the ceremonies accompanying the disposition of the dead.

As a consequence, the funeral home has become a rather elaborate work system with its own peculiar occupational subculture. At the heart of this activity is the modern American funeral director, who is in overall operational charge of the activities associated with processing the dead. As such, he is a central figure in a fascinating, if not unique, work culture.

The funeral director is the organizational representative who is the gobetween linking the funeral home with the family of the dead person. As the person in managerial control of the ceremonies, he plays a public relations role in the funeralization process.[5] Future funerals are sold on the basis of how past and current funerals are conducted. One of the main means of advertising in the industry is the production of the funeral itself. Adverse criticism, therefore, must be kept to a minimum, as its deleterious affects would be difficult to overcome. Indeed, price advertising is altogether prohibited by an industry-wide code of ethics, and advertising in general is allowed for informational purposes only. Competitive advertising is disallowed through the application of strong internal negative sanctions. Violation of these expectations or norms constitutes grounds for the possible dismissal of a funeral director from the several professional associations in the industry.

The funeral director receives the call from the bereaved family announcing the death. Subsequently it is he who interviews the survivors charged by the family with making the arrangements for the funeral. The funeral director's supervisory role includes managerial responsibility over the following lengthy list of disparate activities:

Attend to the immediate needs of the bereaved.

Notify the family's clergyman.

Call the coroner if this is deemed necessary.

Notify the relatives and friends of the deceased. Send necessary wires.

Secure death certificates, burial permit, and release.

Remove remains from home, hospital, or depot.

Bathe, shampoo, shave, and manicure the body.

Perform necessary dermasurgery.

Prepare, restore, and preserve the body.

Consult with the family for vital information and details.

Notify local and distant newspapers for printing of obituary and funeral notices.

Contact cemetery for grave opening—arrange for use of cemetery equipment.

Meet trains and airplanes bringing out-of-town relatives and friends. Arrange for family's flowers.

Contact pallbearers and vocalist.

Contact military and fraternal organizations.

Receive, arrange, and remove flowers; retain flower cards.

Provide acknowledgment, mass cards, memorial folders, and similar items.

Provide visitor's registration book.

Provide equipment for various religious and lodge services.

Provide seating, special lighting, and casket carriage.

Make shipping and other arrangements if the deceased is to be interred at a distant point.

Arrange for transportation for the family, if needed.

Arrange appropriate music for service.

Advance the honorarium for the clergy, soloist, cemetery, florist, transportation, and other cash items ... as an added convenience for the family.

Provide casket coach, sedan passenger car, transportation for the clergy and the floral tributes.

Provide parking space and personnel.

Direct and supervise funeral service according to particular religious, national, and local customs.

Arrange for church or home service.

Arrange auto cortege.

Notify family attorney, bank, and insurance agent.

Assist in securing Social Security and Veterans' Benefits as well as insurance claims.

Provide Notary Public service.

Advise as to any other benefits which will be due to the family.

Assist with any personal problems that fall within his province.[6]

Funeral directors must be licensed according to state law. In general, they must be high school graduates, or, increasingly, college graduates with one or two years' experience as an apprentice director. Licensed embalmers are also eligible to become funeral directors. Historically, the practice was that embalmers and funeral directors were one-in-the-same person. In time, the jobs split. When that first happened, the usual career line followed by practitioners in the industry was from embalmer to funeral director. But current practice is different, as will be explained in a later section.

The Embalmer

There are state licensing requirements[7] for embalmers which include graduation from an accredited college of embalming. Additionally, every state has established certain minimum academic educational prerequisites which must be met before matriculating in an embalming college. Since these academic standards are set on the state level, as might be anticipated, they vary considerably from one state to another. Prospective student embalmers are required to complete high school or its approved equivalent (for example, the high school equivalent examination given in the Armed Forces), or to complete one or two years of academic college before admittance to an embalming college.

Approximately one-third of the states now require two years of college prior to admittance to a college of mortuary science and the trend is in the direction of more and more emphasis on academic educational prerequisites.

There is also a period of apprenticeship during which the embalming student receives on-the-job training under the tutelage of a licensed embalmer. The length of the apprentice or interne training program varies from twelve to thirty-six months. The various states are about equally divided between twelve and twenty-four months' apprenticeship requirements, with only two states having a thirty-six months' practicum. The internship is variously administered across the country. Some require its completion before enrollment in embalming college; some after graduation; and some split the internship, requiring that it be completed partly before and partly after completion of the embalming curriculum.

The embalmer is caught in the middle insofar as his career aspirations are concerned. The funeral industry is moving from a small family owned and operated business to a large corporate enterprise. In the process, managerial entrepreneurs are emerging within its bureaucratic framework. These funeral management specialists are recruited from college campuses more and more, in contradistinction to what was found historically, where one moved up from an embalmer in the preparation room (embalming room) to a funeral director in charge of directing the drama that is the modern funeral service.

> The emergence of new types of funeral management executives has had the effect of reducing the status of the embalmer to that of "technician." The result of this has been to curtail the supply of qualified embalmers. Schools of mortuary science have been reporting shortages in applicants, and several schools have closed. The future of the embalmer seems dim. Capital outlay for the business is large and the corporate structure is more and more in evidence in funeral service. This means that only a limited number of em-

balmers and funeral directors can be expected to be in positions of ownership; the embalmer appears to be more and more relegated to the role of hard working, poorly paid employee. The advent of unionization in some of the larger cities reflects this trend.[8]

The trend toward more stringent educational prerequisites prior to matriculating is accompanied by increased educational demands on the student when he enters embalming college. Once there, his curriculum includes study in the basic sciences of anatomy, physiology, and chemistry; in the public health sciences of microbiology, hygiene, and pathology; in the mortuary arts and sciences, including the elementary and advanced principles of embalming, and the application of embalming principles in the restorative arts (i.e., modeling) ; in funeral management, such as business and mortuary law, accounting, psychology, and the principles of funeral directing and management.[9]

There is no mystery as to why educational requirements are becoming more demanding. Funeral educators are, like everyone else, intent on professionalizing the industry. Their conviction that this should be done precisely at a time when opportunities for upward mobility for embalmers are diminishing introduces into the industry an occupational incongruity of the greatest magnitude.

The embalmer's training is intended to prepare him eventually for a managerial position in the funeral industry, though the future holds dim prospects that he will ever get out of the embalming room. As this realization becomes more widespread, embalmers come to view themselves as "locked into" their jobs. As of this writing, funeral educational curricula have not adjusted to this industry-wide trend. They still require training in areas outside the purely technical skills required for preparing the dead for viewing.

Two types of skills are central to the embalmer: dermasurgical skills and cosmetological skills. Dermasurgery refers to skills required to restore, through surgery, any deformities or abnormalities associated with a corpse. Especially important are certain parts of the anatomy, like the face and hands, which are exposed during viewing. Sometimes great skill and artistry are required to remake a face deformed in an accident or to rebuild a countenance emaciated through some prolonged terminal illness.

Cosmetology refers to the application of cosmetics in preparing the body for viewing. For example, where beauticians are not subcontracted, embalmers do the actual facial make-up, using rouge, lipstick, etc., in the preparation of the body.

Dermasurgery and cosmetology are collectively considered the skills that comprise, what is called in the industry, the *restorative arts*. The restoration of the body to a lifelike resemblance of the dead person is considered of the utmost importance since, according to the funeral industry, it is in this way the family experiences the benefits of *grief therapy*.

THE SOCIAL PSYCHOLOGY OF DEATH

Proper grief therapy, it is believed, is obtained through the restorative arts by returning the dead person to a natural and lifelike resemblance of his former self. Through proper restoration of the corpse the bereaved survivors experience an indelible "memory picture" of the dead person which is said to have positive psychological consequences.

This entire philosophy of viewing is heavily dependent on embalming skills, and as such as determined by the level of sophistication of the technological tools available in the industry and known to the embalmer. Since the embalmer is the *technical expert* responsible for preparation of the corpse, it is quite logical that his occupational skills are crucially important in the over-all funeralization process.

But grief therapy is not entirely dependent on the memory picture and the preparation of the dead person. The funeral director must also be expert in *social relational skills*. The proper application by him of psychological and sociological principles in handling the funeral ceremonies contributes to a gestaltist perception on the part of the bereaved that the funeralization process is a worthwhile and valuable experience. It should be clear, then, that the funeral director takes over or enters where the embalmer leaves off or exits. The two occupational encumbents, together, constitute a team—with the embalmer and his technical expertise behind the scenes and the funeral director and his expertise in social relationships on the scene in the drama of the funeral.

Although the other employees who assist in funeralizing the dead are not the central figures in these activities, they nevertheless make a major contribution toward achieving the overall desired effect of leaving all the participants—bereaved and sympathizers—with a wholesome image of the ceremonies. They accomplish this goal primarily in *the manner in which certain services are provided.*

The receptionist at the funeral home, the driver of the hearse and limousines, and the funeral director's assistants are expected to perform their assigned tasks with a solemnity, courtesy, kindness, promptitude, and conviction characteristic of people who sincerely want to please those they serve. This occupational attitude on the part of the entire funeral home staff contributes to the memory picture and feeling the participants have toward the mortuary establishment itself. Their roles, therefore, complement those of the embalmer and funeral director, in guiding the bereaved, through grief therapy, toward a satisfactory post-funeral psychological adjustment.

Funeralizing the dead, it is believed, satisfies certain needs of the bereaved; it is therefore considered a necessary process that provides a friendly environment within which the grief-stricken can work through their feelings of loss, emptiness, or void occasioned by death. As such, funerals are thought to be therapeutic in eight ways.

The bereaved experiences an emotional catharsis through the *therapy of direct expression.*

When the grief-stricken "talks to himself" or communicates with others he benefits from the *therapy of language.*

Emotional, physical, and financial support received by the next of kin constitutes the *therapy of sharing.*

Survivors are "forced" out of their immobility and are required by custom to participate in the funeral rituals; this is considered the *therapy of activity.*

The memory picture of a lifelike, but sleeping corpse together with the comfort, quiet, and beauty of the funeral home (in America) constitutes the *therapy of aesthetics.*

Seeing the "remains" itself makes up the *therapy of viewing.*

The *therapy of ceremony* is an ennobling and glorifying experience from which the grievers benefit.

Guilt feelings and our reactions to them during funeralization constitute the *therapy of self-denial and suffering.*[10]

The External System

CLERGYMEN

The funeral director's responsibilities involve him in a network of institutional relationships with representatives of other community organizations and agencies. Foremost among these external contacts is the funeral director's association with clergymen.

Fulton reported that "criticism of the funeral director and of funeral practices by the clergy is both intensive and extensive in America." The principle complaints of American ministers, he found, revolve around three themes. First, the clergy object to what they consider an overemphasis on the body with the subsequent diminution of attention to the spiritual meaning of the funeral. Second, clergymen throughout the nation have negative attitudes toward the funeral director because the funeral director is involved in the dual role of businessman and professional man. As a businessman he is involved in the commercial end of the funeral; as a professional man he is seen by the clergy as identifying with the sacred aspects of the funeral. Thus, the ambivalence of the funeral director's professional role gives rise to an attitudinal ambivalence on the part of the clergy toward the funeral director. Third, Fulton says:

> For the individual clergyman, the funeral is one of the most significant ceremonies in his church. Moreover, by the very nature of faith he believes that his church's particular rites, ceremonies and beliefs command what has been called a "priority of sanctity" over all other churches. There is as a consequence, a fear of taint that is evidenced sometimes when a clergyman or relative requests or insists that the funeral director be of the same faith as the deceased. It seems that when the funeral director makes his services available to people of different faiths, or relates all funerals past and present in an apparent effort to establish the claim of equal sanctity for all of them, he leaves himself open to the charge of paganism from clergymen of different persuasions.[11]

Another point at which funeral directors and clergymen are apt to differ relates to the preparation of the body. Clergymen feel that the purpose of preparation of the body is to improve appearance, while the funeral director favors preparation designed to create the illusion of life.[12]

Still another source of difficulty between these two occupational practitioners has to do with relative emphases between the wake and the funeral service. The wake is primarily a secular ceremony over which the funeral director has complete charge. It is customarily scheduled in the evening hours when it is more convenient for accommodating sympathizers. The funeral service, on the other hand, is by tradition a sacred rite, conducted by a clergyman and is held prior to interment, the morning after the wake, when people are working and are consequently less likely to be able to attend. The greater attendance at the wake over the funeral service results in a shift in the emphasis of the supervisory roles of the funeral director and the clergyman, with the funeral director emerging in the ascendant position.

Finally, the modern funeral director, guided by contemporary social science, is expected to supervise the funeral ceremonies in such a manner that they do not play harshly on the emotions. He rejects the previous crude emphasis on sorrow, guilt, and fear encouraged by some clergymen of a previous era. Clergymen agree with funeral directors in that they believe the entire funeralization process contributes to the amelioration of grief among the survivors. But, clergymen feel, of the three elements comprising the funeral ceremonies (the wake, the funeral service, and the interment service), the wake plays a relatively insignificant role in the social-psychological adjustments of the bereaved to a world devoid of a recently lost love object. The funeral director, by contrast, emphasizes the therapeutic role of the wake in aiding the bereaved survivors.

But the controversial relationship between clergymen and funeral directors is more latent than manifest, more private than public, and more institutional than personal. From all outward signs they work harmoniously and cooperatively together, as the clergyman offers prayers and comfort to the survivors at the wake, and as he conducts his religious ceremonies during the funeral and interment service—all the while, of course, with the funeral director inconspicuously standing by orchestrating the whole process.

GOVERNMENT PERSONNEL

Besides the clergyman, the funeral director is continuously in close liaison with cemeterians and governmental officials. His relationship with both classes of worker is purely administrative. The cemeterian must work with the funeral director to insure that the cemetery is prepared to receive the encasketed remains upon the arrival of the funeral cortege. In this regard timing is of the utmost importance. Any disjunction between the plans of the funeral director and those of the cemeterian would result in confusion and delay at a time when emotions are running high. Teamwork and coordination between the two are therefore held as inviolate virtues to be compromised under no circumstances.

The connections between funeral directors and governmental officials have been summarized by Bowman, who observes:

> Advice is given to clients in the matter of benefits and proceedings of which they may not have been aware. These include old age insurance for surviving spouses and children under eighteen years of age, old age assistance, veterans' rights, and local welfare benefits. Advice is given also on matters in which government agencies may be involved, such as procedures in respect to wills, laws of inheritance, and settling estates. The advice that is given involves only a limited knowledge of social security, welfare, and law; but, coming at the time it does, it is important.[13]

Summary

This descriptive essay highlighted selected characteristics of the funeral home as an environmental setting within which is located a special occupational subculture. Of particular concern were the internal and external dimensions of the funeral home as a work system. The funeral director and the embalmer were considered the central occupational characters involved as a team in processing the dead. The funeral director was defined as the social relations expert who, in addition to this role, also was in overall supervisory charge of the funeralization process. In carrying out these responsibilities, the funeral director is, in fact, also serving in a public relations capacity for his firm and the entire industry.

The technical expert charged with preparing the dead person for viewing is the embalmer, who, together with the funeral director, is responsible for cultivating among the bereaved survivors a wholesome image of the dead person known as a memory picture, which presumably will aid the bereaved in working through their grief.

The funeral director is the link between the funeral home and persons and/or institutions connected with, but external to, the funeral industry. In this regard, the funeral director is in close outward cooperative contact with the clergyman, who nevertheless harbors certain latent critical reservations concerning the funeral director. Whatever differences exist between them are the result of two considerations: (1) the gradual usurpation by the funeral director of the supervisory functions of the funeral, which were formerly monopolized by the clergy, and (2) relative secular orientation of the funeral director as opposed to the sacred orientation of the clergyman. Finally, an administrative connection between the funeral director and the cemeterian and representatives of government was mentioned, with special emphasis on the critical importance of timing in coordinating the activities of everyone concerned, so as to minimize the probability of disruption and confusion that would disturb the bereaved and distort their memory picture.

Footnotes

[1] Herbert Spencer, *The Principles of Sociology*, Vol. 1, reprinted in Robert Bierstedt (ed.), *The Making of Society* (New York: Random House, 1959), 255.

[2] See Émile Durkheim, *The Elementary Forms of the Religious Life*, especially the Introduction and Book I, entitled "Preliminary Questions on the Connection Among Values, Belief, and Religion" (London: George Allen and Unwin, Ltd., 1915), pp. 1–64.

[3] The most vocal and perhaps antagonistic contemporary critic is Jessica Mitford, *The American Way of Death* (Greenwich: Fawcett Publications, Inc., 1964).

[4] Robert W. Habenstein, "The American Funeral Director: A Study in the Sociology of Work" (unpublished Doctor's dissertation, University of Chicago, 1955).

[5] The entire funeralization process is understood to include the wake, the funeral service, and the interment service.

The term "wake" is an Anglo-Saxon word which literally means "to watch a corpse." It is a custom of unknown origin and antiquity, although waking the dead almost certainly was invented before the advent of civilization and is found all over the world. It used to be an uninterrupted vigil of relatives and friends over the human remains from death until committal of the body: this custom, relatively unmodified by time, still exists in many societies around the world as well as among many Americans, especially among those of African, Irish, and Italian descent. See William S. Walsh, *Curiosities of Popular Customs* (Philadelphia: J.B. Lippincott Company, 1925), pp. 790–92. By wake we understand that period when the dead person is exposed for public viewing sometime between death and disposition. It might be an all night affair, determined by the family of the dead person and/or the funeral director handling the funeral.

By the funeral service is meant a ceremony, usually religious, held in a church or, increasingly, in a special room in the funeral home called a funeral chapel, and which ordinarily is held immediately before the interment service.

The interment service refers to the final ceremony of the dead at which time the body is committed to the ground.

[6] John T. Arends, "The Great Controversy Relating to Funerals" (printed brochure, Decatur, Illinois, n.d.), pp. 17–19. This brochure is part of the funeral industry's public relations program of public education. Its contents, therefore, must be evaluated in that light.

[7] Information in the following three paragraphs is synthesized from *Design for Learning*, College Catalogue of the Cincinnati College of Embalming, School of Art and Science (n.d.).

[8] This quotation taken from William H. Porter, "Some Sociological Notes on a Century of Change in the Funeral Business," unpublished paper presented at the Meetings of the Southern Sociological Society, March-April, 1967, Atlanta, Georgia. A revised version of this paper has subsequently been presented in *Sociological Symposium*, No. 1 (Fall 1968), 36–46.

[9] *Design for Learning, op. cit.*, pp. 29–39.

[10] Robert W. Habenstein and W. M. Lamers, *Funeral Customs the World Over* (Milwaukee: Bulfin Printers, Inc., 1960), pp. 763–70.

[11] Robert L. Fulton, "The Clergyman and the Funeral Director: A Study in Role Conflict," *Social Forces*, XXXIX (May 1961), 317–23.

[12] Paul E. Irion, *The Funeral: Vestige or Value?* (Nashville, Tennessee: Abingdon Press, 1966), pp. 47–51.

[13] Leroy Bowman, *The American Funeral* (New York: Public Affairs Press, 1964), pp. 62–63.

Selected References

ARROYO, EDDIE, AARON BROUSSARD, LINDA CRAIG, *et al.* "A Sociological Study of the Funeral Industry." n.p., 1969 (Mimeographed).

BOWMAN, LEROY. *The American Funeral, A Way of Death.* New York: Paperback Library, Inc., 1964.

Design for Learning. College Catalogue of the Cincinnati College of Embalming, School of Art and Science (n.d.).

DURKHEIM, ÉMILE. *The Elementary Forms of the Religious Life.* London: George Allen and Unwin, Ltd., 1915.

ELIOT, THOMAS D. "Bereavement: Inevitable but not Insurmountable," in *Family Marriage and Parenthood*, ed. Howard Becker and Reuben Hill. Boston: D.C. Heath and Company, 1948, pp. 641–69.

FAUNCE, WILLIAM A., and ROBERT L. FULTON. "The Sociology of Death: A Neglected Area of Research," *Social Forces*, XXXVI (March 1958), 205–9.
FULTON, ROBERT L. "The Clergyman and the Funeral Director: A Study in Role Conflict," *Social Forces*, XXXIX (May 1961), 317–23.
————. *The Sacred and the Secular: Attitudes of the American Public Toward Death*. Milwaukee: Bulfin Printers, Inc., 1963.
————, ed. *Death and Identity*. New York: John Wiley & Sons, Inc., 1965.
HABENSTEIN, ROBERT W., and WILLIAM M. LAMERS. *The History of American Funeral Directing*. Milwaukee: Bulfin Printers, Inc., 1955.
————. *Funeral Customs the World Over*. Milwaukee: Bulfin Printers, Inc., 1960.
IRION, PAUL E. *The Funeral and the Mourners, Pastoral Care of the Bereaved*. Nashville, Tennessee: Abingdon Press, 1954.
————. *The Funeral, Vestige or Value?* Nashville, Tennessee: Abingdon Press, 1966.
JACKSON, EDGAR N. *For the Living*. Des Moines, Iowa: The Meredith Press, 1963.
KEPHART, W. M. "Status After Death," *American Sociological Review*, XV (October 1950).
KRIEGER, W. M. *Successful Funeral Management*. Englewood Cliffs, N.J.: Prentice-Hall, Inc., 1951.
LINDEMANN, ERICH. "Symptomatology and Management of Acute Grief," *American Journal of Psychiatry*, CI (1944), 141–48.
MITFORD, JESSICA. *The American Way of Death*. Greenwich: Fawcett Publications, Inc., 1964.
PORTER, WILLIAM H., JR. "Middleville Morticians: Some Social Implications of Change in the Funeral Business in a Southern City." Unpublished Doctoral Dissertation, Louisiana State University, Baton Rouge, 1958.
————. "Toward a Theory of Possession Control." n.p., 1966 (Mimeographed).
————. "Some Sociological Notes on a Century of Change in the Funeral Business." *Sociological Symposium*, I (Fall 1968), 36–46.
SALOMONE, JEROME J. "An Attitudinal Study of Funeral Customs in Calcasieu Parish, Louisiana: A Sociological Analysis." Unpublished Doctoral Dissertation, Louisiana State University, Baton Rouge, 1966.
————. "The Status of Funerals and Funeral Directors," *The American Funeral Director* (October 1967), pp. 69–74.
————. "An Empirical Report on Some Controversial American Funeral Practices," *Sociological Symposium*, I (Fall 1968), 47–56.
SPENCER, HERBERT. *The Principles of Sociology*, Vol. I, reprinted in Robert Bierstedt, ed., *The Making of Society*. New York: Random House, 1959, pp. 255–73.
VOLKART, EDMUND H., and STANLEY T. MICHAEL. "Bereavement and Mental Health," in *Explorations in Social Psychology*, ed. A. H. Leighton, J. A. Clausen, and R. N. Wilson. New York: Basic Books, Inc., 1957, pp. 281–307.
WALSH, WILLIAM S. *Curiosities of Popular Customs*. Philadelphia: J. B. Lippincott Company, 1925.

The Culture of Work

Sawdust in Their Shoes

The Carnival as a Neglected
Complex Organization and Work Culture

CLIFTON D. BRYANT
Western Kentucky University

The Carnival as Industry

The carnival is a neglected major American industry.[1] Each year it assembles a labor force numbering in the hundreds of thousands, sells its goods and services to millions of people for about six months (except for Florida fairs, which provide an opportunity for some carnivals to operate year round), grosses hundreds of millions of dollars profit, and then ceases operation until the next year.[2] The carnival is a part of a large industrial complex known as the outdoor amusement industry, increasingly known in recent years as the "fun industry," which includes circuses, amusement parks, racing, air expositions, etc., but it differs from these others in a number of unique ways.

The carnival is a mobile work system and this mobility contributes in a significant way to its distinctive work culture and the strong sense of occupational community and "in-group" identity that is characteristic of its work force. As a mobile work system it becomes, in effect, a kind of "community-like" social entity, with a variety of collective needs that must be met through social entity, with a variety of collective needs that must be met through the development of particular institutionalized devices. Although the organizational make-up of the carnival is relatively unbureaucratized in comparison to many other large contemporary work systems, its structure would seem to be sufficiently elaborate to qualify it as a complex organization.

In view of its size, economic importance, prominence on the American leisure scene, and unique work organization and culture, it is surprising that it has been almost totally neglected as an object of study by sociologists.[3]

The descriptive observations and impressions of this work organization in this paper are offered in the hope that they might stimulate some interest in the carnival as a research setting.

The Socio-Historical Background of the Carnival

The history of the carnival stretches far back into antiquity.[4] In ancient times in the Middle East, jugglers and acrobats might perform for a few coins in the marketplaces of the towns. By the medieval period and even earlier, bands of strolling players, musicians, and performers would provide amusement for the population in attendance at market times and on the occasions of festivals.

In Europe, fixed places of amusement grew up near the cities and provided recreation for the urban dwellers. These early day amusement parks were known as "pleasure gardens" and offered games, displays, exhibitions of wild animals, acrobatic and high wire acts, and by the late 1700s were also the scene of free balloon ascensions and parachute jumps. Even to this day most European cities boast at least one large amusement park.

According to Mangels, however, the European pleasure gardens were not so much the forerunner of the American amusement parks as were the early picnic groves where social societies and fraternal organizations held their annual outings.[5] On these festive occasions, beer and other refreshments were available. Various kinds of competitive activities took place, such as bowling, athletic games, and shooting matches, and primitive amusement and pleasure devices such as simple swings and crude merry-go-rounds provided fun for the young and young in heart. As time passed these picnic groves took on a more permanent nature; more elaborate recreational facilities were constructed, new attractions and amusements appeared, and they developed ultimately into the amusement parks of modern times.

In lieu of the fixed amusement parks near the large cities, the smaller communities in the rural areas were served by traveling theatrical groups, "medicine shows," gypsy bands, and groups of performers who went from town to town, staging their shows under local auspices. These groups of performers devised more elaborate acts, acquired various fun devices and games of chance and skill, and by the end of the nineteenth century had developed into "carnival companies"; the first such company was organized in 1894. Frequently following a circuit of street fairs and agricultural expositions, the carnival companies grew in size and number and became major purveyors of fun and recreation to rural America. Some evidence of the carnival's impact on the American recreational scene is the fact that in many states the occasion of a state or county fair often is declared a local holiday in order that the population, and especially school children, may take in the carnival. Chartered school buses may bring children from more than a hundred miles away. The county or state fair is often one of the more significant events in the annual calendar, and families in some regions save their money for some weeks prior to the fair in order to be able to have ample funds to expend while in attendance. The carnival stands as a signal recreational and festive event for a significant proportion of American society.

Work Organization of the Carnival

Contrary to popular belief, the carnival is not a single economic entity under unified ownership. Rather, it is an assemblage of many independent economic enterprises operating in a coordinated fashion under a centralized administration.

Usually the "owner" of a carnival will own the majority of the rides, some or most of the shows, all of the logistical equipment such as lighting, generators, etc., and such transportation equipment as is necessary to move his own rides and shows.[6] The carnival "owner" also owns the name or marque of the show, and in this connection many carnivals have been in the same family for generations. The remainder of the carnival is owned by a number of private entrepreneurs known as "concessionaires."

Carnivals can be divided into two basic categories depending on their principal mode of transportation. Some of the larger carnivals rely almost exclusively on rail transportation and usually own their own rolling stock. Other shows rely on tractor-trailer trucks. Rail transportation is the traditional mode of transportation and railroad carnivals, which are frequently the larger shows, are considered to be more prestigious than truck shows. Railroad show employees contemptuously refer to truck-transported carnivals as "bicycle" or "gilly" shows.[7]

The carnival owner contracts to lease the fairgrounds or carnival site from a state, municipality, or private owner. He then, in turn, leases space within the site to private concessionaires and to persons who have rides, shows, or other attractions necessary to make the over-all carnival complete. Space may be leased on a front-foot basis, as in the instance of concessionaires, or it may be leased for consideration of a percentage of the proceeds, as in the case of rides and shows. (Carnies refer to the commission fee as the "nut."[8]) To insure receiving an honest and accurate percentage of the proceeds, the carnival management will issue rolls of official tickets to be sold to the operators of the rides and shows. These tickets are sold to the public, and taken up at the tent door or upon entering the ride, and the stubs are dropped into boxes, locked by the carnival management. Each day the carnival management and ride or show operators will jointly count the stubs, and the percentage owed is based on the stub count. A ride or show operator who attempts to retain the tickets rather than dropping them in the locked box, and then subsequently resells them, is said to be "rehashing" tickets and is guilty of violating one of the occupational mores of the carnival.

Carnival enterprises are erected in an elongated semi-circular shaped arrangement around an open area known as a "midway." Various other establishments are located in the center of the midway so that the remaining open space is a horseshoe shaped passage. "Midways" are designed to be either "left-handed" or "right-handed" depending on how the patrons are to be funneled along through the carnival attractions. The classical midway arrangement is to have fair or agricultural exhibits in the front of the lot with food and souvenir concessions at the beginning of the midway, followed by game concessions. Directly following the game concessions are the low rides and some of the smaller shows. Next are the large shows, and to the extreme rear of the midway are the tall rides, like the ferris wheels. The tall rides are purposely placed so as to serve as a beacon and "draw" the crowds down through the midway all the way to its rear.

A particular blend and balance of rides, shows, and concessions for each show date is considered essential for a successful carnival. The carnival owner books a series of "fair dates" and "still dates" (carnival dates that do not involve fairs or expositions; they are less profitable than "fair dates"), and he will then advertise his route and date schedule in the industry trade publication, *Amusement Business* (known formerly for many years as *Billboard*), indicating which kinds of independently owned rides, shows, and concessions he will need for particular fair dates to insure a complete show. A typical ad might indicate that the carnival needs particular rides such as a Scrabler, a Paratrooper, or a Round-Up, as well as specific kinds of shows such as a Monkey show or a Grind show. Such ads also frequently ask by name for specific individuals to return and associate themselves with the show as concessionaires or to be reemployed.[9] In theory a carnival is made up of a slightly different mix of rides, shows, and concessions for every show date, as well as a different set of independent concessionaires and ride and side show owners. In actuality, however, many such persons stay with the same carnival for whole seasons, year after year. This appears to be especially true with the larger railroad shows.[10]

The backbone of the carnival is the rides. The greatest attraction of the carnival, as well as the largest source of income is the rides. All else is secondary and supportive. Rides include the classical variety such as the vener-

Source: Amusement Business, May 20, 1967, p. 37, Reprinted by permission of Mr. Irwin Kirby, Editor.

able merry-go-round and the ferris wheel, the small size "kiddy rides," and the newer, more elaborate rides such as the roll-o-plane, caterpillar, and roller coaster.

The side shows constitute a second major type of carnival attraction. Various categories of "backend" shows are the "ten in one" or freak shows[11] (including fat and midget), the "girlie" or musical review shows, the animal (including monkey and snake) shows, the thrill shows, such as the motor-drome or midget car racing show, and the educational or historical display show. Usually all the various shows will attempt to attract customers by providing a sample or skit of the regular performance outside on the "Bally-Platform." This preview performance or free show is known as the "Bally." Some of the side show also will offer a special performance at the end of the regular performance, for which additional admission charge will be made, and in which the customers are led to believe that they will see something of an extraordinary or "forbidden" nature. This frequently occurs with the "girlie shows" and the extra performance is purported to be one where the girls will completely strip or perform in an obscene manner. (Such additional shows are known as a "blow-off.")

The remaining attractions on the carnival midway consist of the various concessions which feature different kinds of competitive games of chance and skill, as well as the food and souvenir concessions. These ancillary concessions, along with the rides and shows, and supported by the logistical activities, make up the carnival.

Occupational Argot

Carnival people, like persons in other occupations, have developed a rich and colorful argot which serves both as technical language for those in the business, and to differentiate between the outsider and those "with it."[12] In describing the various enterprises on the midway, they speak of the "pig iron" (rides) or more specifically a "chump heister" (ferris wheel), or "simp twister" or "jenny" (merry-go-round), the "ding" shows (exhibit-type shows that appear to be free upon entrance, but actually require a "donation" upon leaving), the "jig" shows (Negro musical reviews), the various "hanky panks" (concessions featuring inexpensive games of skill) where a winning customer is rewarded with "slum" (cheap prizes such as whistles or chalk animals), the "corn game" (bingo establishment), or "flat" and "alibi joints" (concessions that involve deception or dishonest games of skill or chance). Food concessions include "grab joints" (centrally located snack stands) which sell "pale meat" sandwiches (anemic hamburgers), "flukem" (fruit flavored soft drinks), or, for those desiring something more substantial, a "royal gorge" (a full meal). Also in the refreshment line, carnies speak of "pudding wagons" (frozen custard trucks), "dentist friends" (candy apples), and "sweetened air" (cotton candy).

An equally colorful vocabulary is applied to the various kinds of carnival employees and concessionaires. A "catrack queen" refers to the female agent on a ball-throwing concession. The "patch" or "fixer" is the carnival's legal counsel. The big boss is the "gaffer," "geeks" are performers who eat live chickens or other animals, and "laundry queens" are the girl show dancers. A "mule skinner" is a tractor driver and the "midway snitch" is the carnival press agent who reports the news. The announcer on the stage in front of the shows who presides over the outside "free show," which is designed to arouse interest in the inside show, is not called a barker (this term refers to a circus announcer), but rather a "talker," and his verbal endeavors to attract and interest patrons are called "building a tip."

Formal Authority Structure

The carnival owner or manager represents the apex of authority and control in the work structure. Directly under him in the line organization is the lot boss who is the general superintendent of the entire midway enterprize. Large carnivals may also have an officer or administrative supervisor who is directly under the owner or general manager. At the next lower level of supervision are the various ride foremen and show managers. These individuals in turn supervise the ride-boys and laborers or "gazoonies" in the instance of rides, and the performers, operators, and entertainers in the case of the shows. By way of staff organization the owner or manager usually has several individuals assisting him, including persons in charge of transportation, routing, ticket sales, bookkeeping, public relations, and perhaps an advance man. The lot boss has as his assistants various technicians and logistical personnel such as electricians, mechanics, neon lighting specialists, plumbers, and sign painters. Show managers may in some instances have a small staff including animal trainers, show directors, or a musical conductor. The concessions, while administratively autonomous and independent, are actually operationally under the supervision of the lot boss and, as such, make up a third functional division along with the rides and shows. The concession owners and managers may, in turn, have their own employees.

The carnival as a work structure generates and sells a highly perishable and intangible product called "fun." To accomplish this, it relies on a highly routinized but largely unformalized set of work procedures. Carnies, as a general rule, from lot boss to "gazoonie," work with a minimum of direction and supervision. They man a mobile work system on a seasonal schedule in an outdoor setting, all of which can be highly demanding both in a physical as well as a mental sense. In the tradition of "showmanship" with which they tend to identify, they feel an obligation to their craft and take considerable pride in their work at all levels.

The Function and Appeal of the Carnival

The "fun" carnivals produce is made up of excitement, thrills, suspense, erotic stimulation, competition, symbolic achievement, as well as visual, audio, and olfactory stimulation. When asked what was the appeal of the carnival to people, one carny replied:

> I would think the lights, the color, and the music; the element of chance—people thinking they are going to come out and get something for nothing from the various games. They don't really think they are going to get something for nothing, they just hope they will.

The carnival, with its cacophony of stimuli, a total sensory and emotional experience, provides a "trip," if you will, and permits a release or respite from the drabness and monotony of the daily routine of many people.[13] In keeping with the universal concept of carnival, *the* carnival affords reveling, festivity, merrymaking, and has traditionally given temporary release from the stern dictates of the protestant ethic. In addition to its major manifest function of recreation, the carnival fulfills a number of secondary functions such as affording an opportunity for courtship interaction for the young, providing some educational benefits in the form of exhibits and even sideshows, and promoting an increase in business in the local community. Basically, however, the latent function of the carnival lies in its ability to provide emotional catharsis in the form of a temporary escape from the harshness of everyday reality, and in this sense the carnival has more of a therapeutic rather than a recreational function.

The Carnival Clientele

Carnival workers and their patrons share a degree of mutual hostility. Much of this can be traced to an early history of mutual exploitation and both retain a degree of residual cynicism about the other. This is demonstrated by the comments of a carnival informant who stated that:

The public will take advantage of you, is what I'm trying to say! Not all of them [however]. Then—I assume—in the early years of our business we took advantage of the public too. We don't deny that. When I say we—I have to say we—because I was part of the business; but that's very rare anymore. Most shows are legitimately operated.[14]

At one time relations between carnies and the citizens of the towns they visited were so strained that local newspapers would not even accept ads for the carnivals that told of their coming. Also many of the local merchants felt that a carnival in town tended to divert money from the local economy and thus viewed the carnies as direct and even unfair competitors. The attitudes of the locals toward the carnies then were often unfavorable. In addition, the carny realized that the patron often viewed him as a kind of undesirable cultural freak. On the other hand, the low esteem in which a carny holds the patrons is demonstrated by his jargon terms for patrons or towners: "apes," "squares," or "suckers." Carnival people consider themselves to be highly independent and they hold members of conventional occupations in contempt because they believe such persons are "suckers" to tolerate the work routine and other demands that their occupations place on them.[15] The carny knows also that his customer is likely to be suspicious of him and often resentful after he has spent his money at the show or concession, feeling that "it was a gyp." Carnival people take exception to suggestion of their shows and concessions being "gyps." As they view the situation the patron who feels this way is simply being unreasonable and unrealistic. One informant addressed himself to this question and explained that:

In the latter years, there was no concessions that I know of that were gyps. They [the public] have to realize that the man running those concessions is buying the prizes; he's making a living off of them: he's got someone else that's making a living off them, and there's several people that are making a living off that one concession. So the man comes up to spend fifty cents to win a teddy bear —he cannot expect to win one every time . . . and we find that the public, as an over-all . . . does not expect to. Most of them come to the carnival or the county fair with the thought of spending so much money. If they win, that's good; if they don't, they don't think nothing about it. We want 'em to win, I mean that . . . if people don't win in a stand we don't . . . people don't play the stand. As far as being a gyp, everything is mathematically regulated—I mean the odds are naturally in favor of the operator. He has to make a living off that stand. The teddy bears, they don't get them for fifty cents or a dollar as some of the public thinks. They become quite expensive; they come anywhere from five, six, eight, ten, twelve dollars apiece, depending on the size of them. So everyone does not win one; they can't win one.[16]

While carnies do not usually feel that a customer gets his money's worth in prizes, they do feel that the customer gets his money's worth in prizes *and entertainment*.

Carnival people are most emphatic about the fact that carnivals today, in contrast to former times, are operated in a legitimate fashion. As one carny put it:

> As I keep saying, it is a good business. It has become what we call a legitimate business since the war. Prior to that the carnival business was a rough business—I mean it was a—We take pride in saying that we have cleaned it up and made it respectable. There are still some unscrupulous operators and—but the majority of them are doing the best they can. Sometimes the public won't let you be as honorable as you want to be—In most cases you can be.

Most of the patently exploitative practices of the early carnivals have since been discarded and many carnivals today pride themselves on being "Sunday-School Shows" (a Sunday School show is one where "the games are not rigged and the girls don't take everything off"). In this regard also, many carnivals today, when advertising for concessions, specifically indicate "no flats and alibis [rigged concessions] wanted!"

The awareness of potential or real hostility and suspicion toward them on the part of their patrons, coupled with their own contemptuous assessment of the "sucker's" way of life, tends to promote a strong in-group identity and sense of occupational community. The following poetic lines provide some suggestion of the awareness of occupational solidarity:

> They'll run you out of this here town,
> They'll tear your goldarn midway down,
> So spake a man with a hoary head,
> But the showman merely winked and said,
> "Hey Rube."[17]

In spite of the potential or real hostility, the carny depends on his patrons for his living and he must avoid offending the customer. Instead he must be able to manipulate the customer in such a way that the customer will spend his money freely and leave satisfied. The carny sees himself in "show business." He is creating an illusion for his clientele. In this regard the carny features himself as something of a craftsman who, as previously mentioned, is selling an intangible product in the form of "fun." The carny prides himself on his ability to help create the illusion of "fun" for the customer. Since his product is extremely perishable and the customers in some instances regret their extravagance after their money is gone, the carnival worker is faced with the dilemma of attempting to maintain his craftsmanship in the face of a potentially unappreciative clientele. This he accomplishes through the use of several well institutionalized devices of "cooling the mark out,"[18] such as "awarding" some cheap prize for "winning" at the concession booth.[19] Furthermore, as the carny has a work image of himself as being shrewder than his clientele, he can rationalize that his customer is, in fact, getting his money's worth, because he, as a "showman," is providing a product, thrills and fun, whether the patron knows it or not.

Although there is a real or potential strain in the role relationship between carny and patron, this strain does not necessarily extend to the carny's relationship with outsiders when they are not *patrons*. Many carnival people, especially those who follow a similar route each year, tend to meet and develop friendly relationships with persons in the different communities they visit. In such instances their contact is usually not in the formal context of carny-patron, but rather in the informal context of resident and casual acquaintance who returns for a brief visit year after year. In describing these local acquaintances one carny said:

> But the people were quite interesting, I mean, and it was something to go in a town and you would be there a week and you'd meet people and you would be surprised how you would look forward to going back and seeing that same group of people in another year. Even though your acquaintance with them would be quite casual—but you'd look forward to 'em. It would be kinda like going home in the fall: you're ready to go home but after a couple of weeks, that was long enough to be there, because after all you traveled all your life, but then that was the same way about going on the route. You'd be looking forward to seeing the people and they would be glad to see you. It was kind of a different friendship than you would have at home, but it was still a close and good friendship.[20]

Some managerial level carnival people felt that relatively few persons, and then only persons connected with the management of a carnival, would have the opportunity of meeting townspeople on an intimate basis. In this vein one observed:

> I would say there is practically no fraternizing out on the road other than with the management level. Naturally being in the ownership as I was and all, well I would fraternize with the local officials, the people that you would meet by going to town so much and they would have you out to supper—to their homes and you would enjoy it—but what keeps that to a minimum, you don't have

time—you're just—in a country fair you go work at 9 or 10 o'clock in the morning and work to 12 or 1 at night. After the customers go home, you still have work to do. You don't have too much time when you're on the road.[21]

Such an observation was by no means widespread, however. Practically every carny that I spoke with told of having non-carny acquaintances and friends scattered throughout the country whom they had met while "on the road." In the final analysis it would seem that carnival people, when not playing the carny role, tend to relate to outsiders in a conventional manner.

Informal Social Structure

The carnival labor force constitutes a kind of over-all occupational "community," but for carnival people the individual carnival is like a mobile small town—their occupational "home town," so to speak. This occupational home town, like any other small community, operates on a *gemeinschaft* model and the presence of primary group controls operates to provide social identity and internal cohesion. As Krassowski describes:

> To a carny, a carnival is a tight little community, in which he lives, earns his living, and has friends, and in which he may find his future wife and make a home and bring up children. A large number of carnivals have a larger population than numerous towns and villages. Carnies are attached to their communities. They are proud of belonging to them and enthusiastic when they develop and occupy a leading position among other units operating in the same or neighboring territory. They have pride, problems and attachments similar to those exhibited by the inhabitants of small towns and communities.[22]

While entrance into the occupation is relatively easy and entails little more than "coming on the road," membership in the larger occupational group and particularly in the smaller carnival "communities" carries with it certain obligations and role demands. To be accepted into the "community" the individual is expected to comply with the occupational norms and to display a "professional" (i.e., real show business) orientation toward his work. Failure to do so may result in non-acceptance into the group, the application of informal sanctions, or expulsion from the "community." As one informant put it:

> I had 150 employees; well, that was just like a little town of 150 people. We had some good people, we had some excellent peo-

ple, we had some people who were just average, then we had some
that we were not too proud of. Those that we were not too proud
of, we would try and get rid of.[23]

A carny is also expected to reject the way of life of the ordinary people
in the outside world. As one carny put it, "Any person who isn't shifting,
drifting, and lifting for a living [is a sucker]."[24] Although the application of
informal group sanctions are usually sufficient to effect and maintain social
control in the carnival communities, formalized mechanisms are used occasionally. In "Big Show," for example, the carnies staged their own show,
after closing on Saturday nights, both for recreation and as a means of
raising money for various carnival charity and relief causes. These after
hours performances also served as social control devices. Persons who had
committed mild violations of the norms were ridiculed and made sport of
in stage skits and jokes. In some instances, a humorous "kangaroo court"
was staged and errant carnies were "fined" (either cash or a contribution
of liquor to be auctioned off for the charity) for their offenses.

There is a certain element of latent feudalism in some of the small
"communities." In some instances carnivals have been owned by members
of the same family for several generations. In such cases the owner and particularly the owner of one of the large carnivals may demand and receive
a kind of manorial deference from his employees as the "big boss," but with
a relatively short line organization he may have to supervise many of the
ongoing activities in a rather direct fashion, including the planning and
coordination of the over-all season's operation. A carnival owner-operator
bears some resemblance to a Chinese war lord, a panzer general, or a feudal
nobleman overseeing his fief in performing his work role; but even though
he can act in a highly autocratic fashion, he usually elects not to. In most
instances the owner relates to his employees and other carnival personnel in
a rather informal and democratic fashion, often allowing them considerable
autonomy in carrying out his directives. Krassowski, for example, quotes a
carnival ride boy in commenting on his relationship with the "boss." The
ride boy observed that:

> He owns this outfit and in carnival things, he is the boss. I have
> to mind what he says and do it. But how I do it, that's none of his
> business.... If he keeps his nose too high all the guys would leave
> and he will be stuck with his _____ wheels. We are a tight bunch
> you see, and he has to be one of us if he wants the work done.[25]

The carnival population is a highly heterogeneous group of individuals.
Persons of all educational levels, with diverse geographical origins and a
wide variety of occupational backgrounds, are encountered.[26] Also found
occasionally are individuals who have experienced scandal, had brushes with

the law, or been failures in some other occupational endeavor.[27] Employment (or joining in the case of concessionaires) with a carnival frequently involves a minimum of formalities and usually no investigation of the applicant's past. Once hired, an individual is assured of anonymity if desired and knows that no one will pry into his past history or personal business. In a sense, the carnival is a kind of occupational "foreign legion." Perhaps the strongest norms to be found in carnival culture are the prohibition against the invasion of another individual's privacy and anonymity, intolerance toward another carny, the imposition of one's own views or orientation on others, and the absolute requirement to render help and assistance to fellow carnies. The privacy and anonymity of other carnies is always respected, and a person must be judged on his attitude and behavior toward other carnies rather than on the basis of his past. His personal affairs both past and present are his own business and no one else's. Toleration toward other carnival people includes toleration toward their physical abnormalities (in the case of the freaks), their race, and their religion.[28] One of Krassowski's interviewees, in speaking of religious toleration, summed it up by saying:

> See, kid, we don't care if you believe in God or you don't. We don't care either how you believe and if you go to church or not. ... That's your own business. Everyone of us has the right to do, to think, and to believe the way he _____ please. Ain't gonna try to convert you and you better don't try to pull me over to your side. "People" outside the midway are too _____ busy worrying about other people's religion. I would tell them to keep away.[29]

As Krassowski puts it, "Carnies do not wish to be forced to live in terms of social conventions, and they do not attempt to force these conventions on others."[30] The values of carnival culture, which dictate a respect for the privacy and integrity of other members, are simply an extension of this basic conviction. In short, as Krassowski sums it up:

> One should be completely free to do things the way he wants to do them, providing that they do not produce any harmful effects on other members of the carnival community. The freedom of action of any individual carny with the stated limitation is considered the basis on which the whole occupation is built.[31]

Finally and perhaps most important of all, the carny must never forget that he is tied to other members of the "carnival community" by bonds of mutual obligation and expectations. He must stand ready at all times to render assistance or help, either financial, physical, or psychological. Like pioneer families, carnival families and individuals will readily lend a hand to repair a booth after a storm, give relief at a stand, or provide a financial "lift" (it is not called a loan) to another carny family which has some financial problem. Infact, carnies never worry about being broke inasmuch as they can count on financial assistance from their colleagues and co-workers. If necessary, carnies are also obligated to go to the physical assistance of other carnival members if danger threatens.[32]

As a small community, the carnival provides opportunities for young people to meet, engage in courtship, marry and raise families, and as in any small community, there are norms governing appropriate courtship behavior. The carnival community, recognizing the vulnerability of the single girls on the midway, assumes an especially protective posture toward them.

The carnival community collectively chaperones the single girls in the work groups. If the girl were annoyed by a male customer, someone would quickly intervene and, if necessary, eject the offensive individual. By way of protection from the exploitative single male carny, the informal norm dictates that if a single carny girl and a single carny boy wish to date, they must "go steady" for the duration of the time they are on the road for one season.[33] This rule deters fickleness on the part of both young people and prevents friction and fights among the boys for the favors of the girls. The requirement for season-long relationships tends to stabilize courtships and calls for serious reflection on the part of the young people. Such season-long courtships often lead to marriage and, in some cases, the carnival owner may give the bride away in the absence of her parents. On the occasion of an engagement, the carnival community helps equip the young couple with elaborate household gifts.

Carnival marriages appear to be stable, more equalitarian than most marriages, and usually constitute a working partnership. The wives frequently work in the show or concession, or perhaps sell tickets at some other ride Babies are often born on the road and the mother's and baby's return to the carnival is usually the occasion of an elaborate baby shower, with everyone again being expected to participate. Children are raised "on the lot" and as infants may be kept in the concession booth or sideshow where the working parents can watch them. As the children grow older they have the run of the midway, and are watched and cared for by the other members of the carnival community. In this sense the carnival work group resembles an extended kin group all of whom serve as surrogate parents in the temporary absence of the real parents. In years past, carnival children traveled with the parents throughout the entire season. This necessitated their going to different local schools every week, a patently unsatisfactory arrangement. Today, however, most carnival children travel with the show only during the summer months and in the fall return to their permanent winter home and attend school there on an annual basis. While in the past it was traditional for carnival children to follow in the footsteps of their parents and pursue the carnival life, there is more of a tendency today for parents to send their children to college and prepare them for other kinds of careers.

Since the carnival season lasts only part of the year, the carnies repair at the end of the season to their "winter quarters" where they live during the winter months. Florida is the principal "winter quarter" state, with Miami, Tampa, and Gipsontown being particularly popular cities for carnival people. Some individuals have second businesses such as growing citrus fruits, while others simply vacation during the off season. Almost all of the carnies with whom I spoke told of their attempts to integrate themselves into the community life of their winter quarter towns. They are apparently active in community affairs such as volunteer fire departments, local politics, and charitable cases.[34]

The Carnival as Refuge for the Handicapped, Haven for the Deviant, and Therapeutic Milieu

Perhaps the most sociologically interesting and significant characteristics of the carnival as a work system and subculture are its ability to absorb and utilize the physically and mentally handicapped, to tolerate certain patterns of deviancy, and the degree to which it serves as a therapeutic milieu.

The carnival has traditionally employed and continues to employ freaks or persons who have some extraordinary physical abnormality. These abnormalities may range from grotesque dermatological conditions (a so-called "alligator boy") to that of a person with a partial second body growing out of his trunk. The most classical type of freak, however, is the midget, although the "fat lady" might constitute a close second. Such persons are hired to exhibit themselves or perform "ten in one" freak side shows or in shows that feature midgets or obese persons exclusively. Thus the carnival becomes a significant employer of the handicapped. Krassowski speaks of this in his thesis and states:

> In connection with the freaks (in the physical sense), a seldom recognized circumstance is the fact that carnivals throughout America are hiring thousands of handicapped persons who would find it difficult to earn a living on the outside. Here they make fifty to a hundred dollars a week and do not have to accept charity. Within the carnival society a freak is treated as a completely "normal person," who earns a living, by all carnies who belong to the same carnival unit.[35]

All freaks are not born, however; some persons turn themselves into freaks voluntarily (these are called "gaffs" in carnival jargon). An example here is the person who has himself tatooed from head to toe and displays himself in the freak show. The so-called wild boy and jungle girl are other examples of individuals who in their behavior become a kind of freak. Perhaps the most bizarre of all "gaffs" is the "geek," or person who bites the heads off live chickens or snakes as part of his act. Such an act often attracts a large crowd of morbidly curious patrons who are usually horrified by the genuine performance.[36]

In addition to employing the physically handicapped, carnivals, with their need for relatively unskilled labor to use as "ride boys" and general handymen, frequently employ persons who may be mentally retarded or mentally handicapped to some degree. Often a "gazoonie" of substandard mentality may be a midway "character," but as long as he performs his duties satisfactorily he is tolerated, accepted, and given support if necessary. Every carnival has its share of mental defectives who may not be capable of handling the responsibility of a regular job, but who instead exist by doing odd jobs for the other carnies for small tips, and by "mooching" meals and small amounts of money. In this sense the carnival becomes a kind of "sheltered workshop" of significant size and proportion among industrial and business work systems.

It has been said that carnival people have "soft hearts" and are "soft touches." If they are particularly tolerant of others and especially of handicapped persons, it may well be because of having played the role of "oddities" themselves. One informant suggested that in the earlier years people in the carnival business experienced non-acceptance. Townspeople would stare at them, shun them socially, and say insulting things to them and about them. Having experience as "cultural freaks," they may be better able to empathize with those persons who are actually mentally or physically afflicted.

If the carnival can absorb the physically and mentally handicapped, so too does it attract and absorb various kinds of deviants who find that they can operate satisfactorily without their deviant behavior serving as a handicap. A case in point is the alcoholic. Whereas few work systems could and would tolerate the chronic alcoholic because of his lowered standards of efficiency and his undependability, the carnival often accomplishes this rather handily. Although most carnival owners and managers try to avoid hiring alcoholics, many do slip in and find that their drinking will be tolerated as long as they can maintain even a minimum standard of efficiency or dependability. Should they stay on a lengthy drunk and be fired, there are always some other shows that will hire them with few questions asked. The two principal criteria for being tolerated are that the individual try to do his job even at a minimum level of efficiency and, most important, that he do nothing to harm or bother other carnies or betray their trust.[37]

As has been previously suggested, the carnival worker demonstrates considerable tolerance. He refrains from intervening in the business of his co-workers and colleagues, is especially protective of those who are helpless or inept, and stands ready at any time to help and assist the others in the carnival community. As a member of a mobile work system constantly facing the rigors of the elements and a potentially hostile clientele, he sustains himself with the knowledge that the other members of the group stand behind him, and he is secure in the fact of the social solidarity of the work group.

Aware that a low level of efficiency will draw little criticism and that almost complete irresponsibility in all matters other than his relationships with other carnies will be ignored, the habituated or deviant individual in the carnival community would seem to be in the midst of a therapeutic milieu, at least to the extent that he is "carried," tolerated, and supported by his fellow carnies. The carnival work culture, like many other work cultures, may very well provide a setting in which many individuals can operate in a day to day fashion who might not be able to do so in other circumstances. In a setting where one's personal idiosyncracies, abnormalities, and aberrations are discounted or overlooked, the individual surely enjoys a "therapeutic milieu."

Summary

The carnival, as a major American industry, a complex work organization, a historically significant American leisure institution, whose product is illusionary, perishable, and transitory, a work structure which attracts and maintains a wide variety of physically, mentally, and socially handicapped persons, a mobile "near-community," a social group with intense solidarity, and a highly distinctive subculture, veritably invites the sociological researcher to "get sawdust in his shoes."

In view of the many sociologically relavant dimensions of this work system, and the strong probability of applicability of research findings on the carnival to other areas of social behavior, additional research of an intensive nature would seem to be indicated and could well prove profitable.

Selected Readings

Books

BOLES, DON. *The Midway Showman.* Atlanta: Pinchpenny Press, 1967.
BRAITHWAITE, DAVID. *Fairground Architecture: The World of Amusement Parks, Carnivals and Fairs.* New York: Frederick A. Praeger, 1968.

CARRINGTON, HEREWARD. *Sideshow and Animal Tricks*. Kansas City: A. M. Wilson, 1913.

CLAUSEN, CONNIE. *I Love You Honey, But the Season's Over*. New York: Holt, Rinehart, & Winston, 1961.

DADSWELL, JACK. *Hey There Sucker*. New York: Bruce Humphries, 1946.

DE BELLE, STARR. *Dictionary of Midway Slang: Webster Was a Sucker*. Cincinnati: Billboard Publications, 1946.

DOC AND THE PROFESSOR. *Hurry, Hurry, Hurry: A Handbook of the Modern Carnival Midway*. Providence: Pyramid Publishers, 1939.

FROST, THOMAS. *The Old Showmen and the Old London Fairs*. London: Chatto and Windus, 1881.

GRESHAM, WILLIAM LINDSAY. *Monster Midway*. New York: Rinehart & Company, Inc., 1953.

HOLTZMAN, JERRY, and HARRY LEWISTON. *Freak Show Man*. Los Angeles: Holloway House Publishing Co., 1968.

LEWIS, ARTHUR H. *Carnival*. New York: Trident Press, 1970.

MANGELS, WILLIAM F. *The Outdoor Amusement Industry*. New York: Vantage Press, Inc., 1952.

MANNIX, DAN. *Step Right Up*. New York: Harper & Brothers, 1951.

Articles and Chapters in Books

ANONYMOUS. "I'll Gyp You Every Time," *The Saturday Evening Post*, September 17, 1949.

BILLITER, BILL. "Business With Pleasure: The Fair as a Money Mover," *The Courier-Journal & Times Magazine*, August 20, 1967.

CUBER, JOHN F. "Patrons of Amusement Parks," *Sociology and Social Research*, XXIV (1939), 63–68.

EASTO, PATRICK C., and MARCELLO TRUZZI. "Towards an Ethnography of the Carnival Social System," in *Anthropology On American Social Life*. Englewood Cliffs, N.J.: Prentice-Hall, Inc., 1971.

GRESHAM, WILLIAM LINDSAY. "Its Magic is the Magic of Life," *New York Times Book Review*, March 13, 1960, pp. 34–35.

———. "The World of Mirth," *Life*, September 13, 1948.

HARPER, (MR.). "After Hours," *Harper's Magazine*, October 1948.

JONES, J. P. "Carnival Comes on Cat Feet," *Christian Science Monitor*, July 26, 1947.

KLEIN, FREDERICK C. "Step Right Up: How 'Heels' Shapiro Makes a Tidy Living Off a Carnival Game," *Wall Street Journal*, September 30, 1969, pp. 1, 16.

KOBLER, J. "World's Biggest Show: Royal American Shows," *Cosmopolitan*, November 1953, pp. 78–83.

Life. "Great American Midway," December 22, 1958, pp. 8–23.

———. "Structure of Entertainment," December 22, 1958, p. 52.

MANNIX, DANIEL P. "The Games People Can't Win." *True*, May 1969, pp. 64–67, 87, 90.

———. "A Rare Look at Rare People," *True*, January 1964, pp. 60–61, 92–96.

———. "Two-Legged Fox of the Midway," *True*, July 1961, pp. 46–48, 92–97.

———. "Sex on Sawdust," *Playboy*, June 1958, pp. 17–18, 28, 64–65.

———. "Strange People," *True*, September 1948, pp. 34–35, 63–68.

MILLSTEIN, GILBERT. "Carnie Biz—Bigger Than Ever," *New York Times Magazine*, May 18, 1952.

Maurer, David W. "Carnival Cant: A Glossary of Circus and Carnival Slang," *American Speech*, VI (1931), 327–37.

Mockridge, Norton. "Carnival," *The American Way* (published by American Airlines), May 1970, pp. 18–21.

New York Times Magazine. "Circus in Close-Up" February 25, 1962, p. 6.

Oliver, Raymond. "More Carny Talk from the West Coast," *American Speech*. XLI (1966), 278–83.

Poling, James. "Sawdust in Their Shoes," *The Saturday Evening Post*, April 11, 1953.

Scarne, John. "Carnival, Fair, Bazaar, Arcade and Amusement Park Games," in his *Scarne's Complete Guide to Gambling*. New York: Simon & Schuster, 1961, pp. 456–523.

Skardon, J. A. "Carney Kids," *Coronet*, December 1957, p. 57.

Taylor, R. L. "Profiles: N. Eagle, Last of The Great Carnival Talkers," *New Yorker*, April 19, 1958, pp. 47–84.

Time. "The Last Individualists," August 30, 1956, pp. 38–39.

———. "No More Rubes," September 29, 1958, pp. 41–42.

Truzzi, Marcello. "The American Circus as a Source of Folklore: An Introduction," *Southern Folklore Quarterly*, XXX (1966), 289–300.

Ward, Donald J. "The Carny in the Winter," *Western Folklore*, 21 (1962), 190–92.

Wisehart, M. K. "Behind the Midway," *Pathfinder*, June 1, 1949.

Zinzer, William K. "A Lot of Quarters," *Look*, September 5, 1967, p. 18.

Papers

Bryant, Clifton D. "Sawdust in Their Shoes: The Carnival as a Neglected Complex Organization and Work Culture." Paper presented at the Southern Sociological Society meetings, Atlanta, Georgia, April 1970.

Easto, Patrick C. "The Carnival Subculture: A Neglected Area of Study." Paper presented at the Ohio Valley Sociological Meetings, Akron, Ohio, April 1970.

Krassowski, Witold. "Social Structure and Professionalization in the Occupation of the Carnival Worker." Unpublished Master's Thesis, Purdue University, 1954.

Footnotes

Portions of this article were read as a paper at the thirty-third annual meeting of the Southern Sociological Society, Atlanta, Georgia, April 11, 1970. The information and impressions for these observations on the carnival derive from several sources. Mr. E. E. Farrell of Jackson, Mississippi, a retired carnival owner, graciously consented to a lengthy interview conducted by my student assistant, Mr. Tom Matthews. Another ex-carny, Mr. Gordon Adams, of Pelehatchie, Mississippi, a retired concessionaire, also acted as an informant and shared many reminiscences of his carnival days with the author. Mr. Hal Eifort, General Manager of the Gooding Amusement Company, owners of several carnivals, took time from a busy executive schedule to grant a lengthy and insightful interview. However, many of the observations in this paper are the result of several days of informal interviewing and participation in some "back lot" activities on the midway of one of the large railroad shows several years ago. For purposes of anonymity, I will simply identify the carnival as "Big Show." These informative experiences were shared with Robert G. Brown, now Chairman of the Department of Sociology at George Washington University. Dr. Brown and myself were fortunate to make the acquaintance of many "show people" that week, and our conversations with lot bosses, menagerie keepers, strippers, talkers, and many other persons on the midway proved to be most enlightening. Apparently the only sociological study of the carnival was a Master's thesis done some years ago (see Witold Krassowski, "Social Structure and Professionalization in the Occupation of the Carnival Worker," Master's Thesis, Purdue University, May, 1954), and I have drawn heavily upon Professor Krassowski's findings and comments in shaping my remarks in this paper. (After this paper was read, another paper on the carnival was given. See Patrick C. Easto, "The Carnival Subculture. A Neglected Area of Study," paper presented before the Ohio Valley Sociological Meetings, Akron, Ohio, April 1970.) Several nonscholarly but informative books about carnivals exist and provide some interesting insights about carnival structure and culture; see, for example: William Lindsay Gresham, *Monster Midway* (New York: Rinehart & Company, Inc., 1948); also Dan Mannix, *Step Right Up!* (New York: Harper & Brothers, 1950); and Jack Dadswell, *Hey There Sucker* (Boston: Bruce Humphries, 1946). A recent and highly relevant trade book on carnival life is Arthur H. Lewis' *Carnival* (New York: The Trident Press, 1970). A bibliography of carnival articles from popular periodicals and trade books is found at the end of this paper.

[1] There are presently more than 400 carnivals operating in the United States. (Easto suggests that there are eight hundred to a thousand carnivals in the United States; see Easto, *op. cit.*).

[2] A large state fair such as the Kentucky State Fair may have a week's attendance in excess of 500,000 persons. It has been estimated that upwards of 85,000,000 people attend carnivals each year.

[3] With the exception of the previously mentioned Master's Thesis (Krassowski, *op. cit.*) and the more recent Easto paper (Easto, *op. cit.*).

[4] A definitive history of the carnival is found in William F. Mangels, *The Outdoor Amusement Industry* (New York: Vantage Press, Inc., 1952). See also Patricia Nothe, "Carnivals, also Fairs, Circuses, and Amusement Parks: A Historical Perspective," Master's Thesis, University of California, Berkeley, 1969.

[5] Mangels, *The Outdoor Amusement Industry*, p. 17.

[6] The logistical support necessary to operate the average carnival is staggering. The elaborate lighting and electrically motorized equipment requires an electrical generating capacity sufficient to supply power needs of a town of perhaps several thousand. If water is not available, a carnival may have to drill its own well. The complex electrical and mechanical equipment requires the maintenance services of a whole range of technicians, including neon lighting specialists, diesel motor mechanics, tent repairmen, sign painters, welders, tire repairmen, and even wild animal keepers if a menagerie show is included. The food, health, sleeping, and sanitation needs of upwards of 2 thousand persons in some instances (and occasionally an elephant herd) must be accommodated. The transportation problem alone necessitates whole fleets of tractor trailer trucks, and in the case of the big rail shows, the carnival may own and maintain its own train.

[7] According to Easto, these are also called "Rag-Bags" or "Forty-Milers." He comments that "Larger truck shows call smaller outfits gillies, rag-bags, or forty-milers. On most of these forty-milers or rag-bags there are fewer license plates and chauffeur's licenses than there are tractor-trailers. The result is that there is a lot of 'doubling back' to pick up the rest of the show. The doubling-back operates to limit the size of the move or 'jump'! Therefore the name 'forty-miler.' " (From personal communication to author.)

8 Easto takes issue with this and contends that "I have always heard 'nut' used to refer only to the privilege [paying by the foot or another flat rate type privilege]. The P.C. [percentage] cannot 'be made' in the sense in which Nut is used." (From personal communication to the author.)

9 A typical page of such ads is reproduced on page 184.

10 Larger truck-moved shows also are quite stable in terms of the same population during season, or from season to season for that matter.

11 According to Marcello Truzzi, in circuses the ten in one is called a side show because such shows were always located along the side of the entrance to the Big Top. (From personal communication from Patrick C. Easto to author.)

12 For an amusing glossary of carnival argot, see Starr DeBelle, *Webster Was a Sucker: Dictionary of Midway Slang* (privately printed by the author and not dated). A somewhat dated but more definitive treatment of this topic is David W. Maurer, "Carnival Cant: A Glossary of Circus and Carnival Slang," *American Speech*, VI (June 1931), 327–37. A particularly interesting aspect of carnival language is a form known as Z-Latin, which has some similarity to Pig Latin. Z-Latin is known as "carny" and has a set of rules governing its use. For details see Easto, *op. cit.*, especially pp. 10–13. Also consult Raymond Oliver, "More Carny Talk from the West Coast," *American Speech*, XLI (1966), 278–83.

13 Curiously enough, the lights, color, and music of the carnival seem to provide a "trip" for the carnies as well as for the patrons. During the day when there are no lights, color, and music, the carnies themselves seem depressed, loggy, and frustrated. It is at night when the lights and music come on that they seem to "come alive." Several of my informants admitted this. One said that it was the color and the sounds of the caliope that kept him with the carnival. In a more cynical vein Gresham comments that, "Carnivals exist by giving the public what it wants, in the teeth of professional moralists. The sober fact of that matter is that in this great democracy of ours, the majority of young men like to gamble and like to look at girls taking their clothes off. A serious discussion of the ethics of carnival games brings us into deep waters: theories of government, ethics and sociology. None of these speculations troubles the carnies." Gresham, *op. cit.*, p. 262.

14 This informant illustrated his views by referring to the youngster who comes to the carnival with a ten dollar bill. His parents had told him to spend several dollars and bring the change home. The youngster spends all of the money, returns home, and reports that he had been "short-changed," thus transferring the guilt. Almost all of the carnies I spoke with told of instances where patrons had purposely extorted money from ticket sellers by claiming they had given a larger bill than was actually the case, and then threatening to call a law enforcement officer if the ticket seller did not pay them the "change." Since the law enforcement officers would usually side with the patron, the ticket seller would have no other recourse but to let himself be victimized. (Another informer, however, doubts this anecdote. As he put it, "I'm suspicious about your respondent. My first job on the carny was a ticket seller. At age 12 I exemplified the old carnie adage: 'A carnie kid can make change for a buck before he can write his name.' One of the first things I learned was how to short-change the marks. The youngster's remark is more probably TRUE.")

15 Gresham comments on this independence and says: ". . . the carny is one of the last stands of rugged individualism." He also points out that persons become carnies in order ". . . to get away from the deadly routine of a farm or factory and their binding restrictions and to remove themselves from their quiet desperation of everyday boredom." Gresham, *op. cit.*, pp. 17 and 18.

16 Much of the strain between carny concessionaire and patron revolves around the different conceptions held by each of what and how often an individual should win at some game. (Another carny informant felt that the individual quoted here

was purposely overestimating the cost of plush bears for my benefit. In the opinion of this second carny plush bears are not quite as costly as this man told me.)

17 DeBelle, *op. cit.*, p. 1 ("Hey Rube!" is the traditional carnival call for help which must be answered by any who hear it.)

18 A full discussion of this concept can be found in E. Goffman, "On Cooling the Mark Out," *Psychiatry*, XV (1952), 451–63.

19 The gaily painted chalk animal or doll "won" at the carnival remains as a principal *objet d'art* and symbol of competitive achievement in many American homes today.

20 Excerpt from interview with Mr. Farrell.

21 *Ibid.*

22 Krassowski, *op. cit.*, p. 69.

23 Excerpt from interview with Mr. Farrell.

24 DeBelle, *op. cit.*, p. 5.

25 Quoted in Krassowski, *op. cit.*, p. 51. In "Big Show" the owner was a young man whose father had founded the carnival and made it into one of the largest in the country. Many of the employees had been with the show for many years before the elder man had died. They had known the son since he was a baby and had helped raise him in a sense. As the big boss he demanded and received the appropriate deference, but many of the older employees still called him by his childhood name and chide him about his behavior if necessary. It was a curious mixture of feudal deference and paternalistic benevolence, reminiscent of the relationship between Scarlet O'Hara and her "mammy" in *Gone With the Wind*.

26 Some of the carnival owners that I talked with or heard about had multiple college degrees, and several of my informants made reference to having known persons in the carnival world who had been ministers, lawyers, and even college professors. Krassowski mentions numerous such examples. See *op. cit.*, p. 90.

27 In "Big Show" several of the carnies made reference to their transportation manager and alluded to the fact that he had, at one time, been a physician. Although everyone was very vague about the details, the implication was that this individual had been involved in a scandal involving professional medical ethics and had been forced to leave the profession. In good carnival tradition, however, no one ever inquired about the details.

28 Although practically every informant I spoke with vehemently insisted that carnival people did not discriminate and that they were completely tolerant of race, the fact remains that Negroes are definitely in the minority as carnival employees. If they are employed, it is usually in some menial position or as a performer in a "jig show." In one carnival I visited I observed that the entertainers in the Negro musical review show had their own cook tent and ate their meals apart from the white employees. The carnival lot boss assured me that this segregation was voluntary and that " 'the colored' prefer to eat by themselves where they can cook the special foods that they like." I do admit, however, that I saw no evidence of the white employees attempting to enforce segregation and Negro carnies would eat and congregate with whites in a casual manner in the midway "grab joint."

29 Quoted in Krassowski, *op. cit.*, p. 87.

30 *Ibid.*, p. 85.

31 *Ibid.*, p. 93.

32 One of my informants told me that in pre-World War II days, carnival people were so used to giving and receiving financial assistance that in bad times he and many of his friends would take turns working and being broke, living as it were in a kind of communal financial fashion. In regard to physical assistance, the informant's wife who was listening to the interview interjected that one of the main

reasons that her husband had stayed with carnival life was that he had liked to fight so well. There were apparently many occasions to go to the help of a fellow carny or protect a show girl from the improper advances of a patron. From his descriptions of some of the altercations he experienced, they sounded like the barroom free-for-alls in a John Wayne movie.

³³ This quaint custom was no doubt the inspiration for the title of a book about life in the outdoor entertainment industry. See Connie Clausen, *I Love You Honey, But the Season's Over* (New York: Holt, Rinehart & Winston, 1961).

³⁴ A particularly engaging account of a carnival couple (in this instance two freaks: a giant man and his wife whose body ends at the hips) who live conventional lives and engage in community activities is found in Gresham, *op. cit.*, pp. 108–12. One informant recalled that when he was a younster, his mother belonged to P.T.A. at his public school during the winter season and even filled an officership of some kind. During the carnival season, however, she was one of the featured "ecdysiasts" in the girlie show.

³⁵ Krassowski, *op. cit.*, p. 60.

³⁶ "Geeks" are often addicts or alcoholics who cannot find or keep regular employment and who require a regular supply of whiskey or drugs. Such persons will resort even to the repulsive act of eating live animals if this is their only means of supplying their alcohol or drug needs. Mentally retarded persons are also easily recruited as "geeks." Some "geeks" have been attempted special spectacular acts such as eating a whole live chicken, feathers and all, but the act to end all "geek" acts was one reported in the *Atlanta Journal and Constitution* in September 1960. The newspaper article told of a "geek" act where the grand finale was the eating of a live pig. An interesting poetical view of the "geek's" dilemma is given in David Rowans' poem, "The Weeping Greek,"

> The geek sat alone in his tent after each performance
> Digging at the shrunken limbs for a vein to be pumped with horse.
> Mounting the stallion, he rode on calliope chords
> The length of the midway stealing cotton candy
> Until it was time for the suckers to stare at the gaffs.
> He sank to his knees in the sawdust and wept.
> The gazoonies passed him by—laughing.

Maurer provides some historical background on the geek and relates that "the word is reputed to have originated with a man named Wagner of Charleston, West Virginia, whose hideous snake eating act made him famous. Old Timers still remember his ballyhoo, part of which ran:

> Come and see Essau
> Sittin on a see-saw
> Eatin' 'em raw"

Maurer, *op. cit.*, p. 331.

³⁷ One informant told of an incident where an individual who was an alcoholic and apparently mentally disturbed, had been hired as a workman; everyone knew of his problems and tolerated and accepted him, and there possible tried to help and support him. Unfortunately, he lured the young son of another carny into the portable men's rest room on the midway, sexually assaulted him, and then strangled him. He was quickly arrested by the authorities, who were barely able to get him off the lot because of the crowd of carnival people who wanted to kill him. The informant said that he and several would gladly have killed the individual earlier had they known that he might have done what he did.

Occupational Stratification

Class, Status, and Power
Among Jazz and Commercial Musicians

ROBERT A. STEBBINS
Memorial University of Newfoundland

To most people, sociologists and laymen alike, the world of the jazz musician has seemed a mysterious place with a number of clandestine overtones. Jazz has been accepted in America, as well as elsewhere, as a true art form, but its physical surroundings have remained in doubt. Too often jazz musicians have been associated with narcotics, murky slum-area bars, prostitutes, the criminal element, loose morals, and the renegades of society. They play a music originated and supported by Negroes. Jazz musicians are often young, single, and footloose. Like homosexuals, criminals, nudists, political radicals, and the mentally ill, jazz musicians are often regarded as one of society's deviant groups and part of its social problems.

And, yet, there are indications, amid the occasional arrests for the use of marijuana, that there is a very definite trend toward respectability among the inhabiltants of the jazz world. Jazz musicians are graduates from the highly respected Julliard School of Music these days; many of them are highly trained. Even at the local level of jazz life, these professional musicians are found giving performances in the established concert halls of the community. There is evidence among them of a great deal of family life and an interest in middle-class values. More and more of those who play jazz also teach music, and, where their training is sufficient, they do so in the public schools.

It seems, then, that a reappraisal of the jazz musician is in order. Have there been changes in his economic life, in his attitudes toward society, in his relationships with the conventional world? Are we correct in labeling him as a deviant? An attempt will be made in this study to answer these

Reprinted from *The Sociological Quarterly*, Vol. 9, No. 3 (Summer 1968), 318–31, by permission of the author and the publisher.

questions with respect to one group of jazzmen, those who currently play jazz in the historically active jazz center of Minneapolis.

Theoretical Background

To its practitioners, jazz tends to be an all-absorbing set of interests. Like any participants in some form of play or art, a large number of the producers and consumers of jazz are concerned with it for its own sake and not for some exterior reason. To the extent that this true, the line between work (which is concerned with instrumental values) and leisure (which is concerned with intrinsic values) tends to be blotted out, and making a living becomes possible while doing what one enjoys.

This ideal, however, is not always realized, and musicians are often forced to play commercial music because a satisfactory livelihood cannot be obtained from jazz. In this case, the sphere of the instrumental values expands at the expense of the intrinsic values of jazz. It is the fundamental thesis of this study that their concern with making a living dissociates some musicians from the jazz community; commercial musicians are or become different from jazz musicians.

These ideas are not new in the sociology of jazz. Cameron has employed the term "controlled schizophrenia" to describe the dualistic life of jazz artists who alternate between commercial and jazz music.[1] The inability to care when playing jazz and not to care when working a commercial job may lead to serious disorganiation and adjustment problems. Howard Becker suggested two modes of thought which are prevalent in this situation: the desire to be creative and to become an artistic success, and the awareness of the many forces which affect commercial playing and which result in a loss of creativity to a greater or lesser extent.[2] Both jazz and commercial musicians recognize and feel these themes or pressures in their work, but the former emphasize the creative principle, and the latter choose to bow to the demands of the audience and the night club owners. Stebbins found that the intrinsic values of jazz were carried over into the jazz musician's leisure time in the form of musically related activities when compared with the leisure time of commercial musicians.[3] The opposition of jazz and commercial values may even be extended to the sphere of family life.[4]

The intrinsic values of jazz form the core around which the jazz community develops. A number of authors have observed this tendency toward community formation. They emphasize the social segregation of the jazz musician as a result of his deviant behavior,[5] greater social freedom,[6] and the threat of jazz to white culture.[7] Others have concentrated on various internal aspects which lead jazz musicians to isolate themselves, such as lack of formal education,[8] jazz as a form of revolt and protest against society,[9] and the individual possession of a specialized talent.[10]

However, communities in general are more than a simple collection of values and attitudes. While values and attitudes are a vital part of the culture of a community, it also has a structure of statuses and roles which, when linked with their corresponding norms, take on institutional form. All genuine communities have institutionalized behavior in three critical areas of life: education of newcomers in the appropriate values, attitudes, and behavior; provision of food and shelter; decision-making and decision-enforcement. These three areas of life are referred to respectively as the institutions of socialization, mastery of nature, and social control.[11] In the jazz community, they take the following form:

1. Institutions of socialization—cliques

2. Institutions of the mastery of nature—jazz jobs

3. Institutions of social control—cliques, jazz, jobs, jam sessions, after-hours social life, and the musician's union

These are the core institutions of the jazz community because they are most basic to the life of the jazz musician. Certain peripheral institutions also exist in the form of the jazz musician's family and commercial music jobs.

Of course, certain principles of community formation must be in operation before a true community can take shape. Habits must be stabilized. Institutions may be defined as standardized solutions to the problems of collective life; these solutions often become embedded in the habits of the individual and the customs of the group. Furthermore, because the stabilization processes in one area of life eventually intersect with those of other institutional areas, there must be interinstitutional consistency. Finally, the core institutions of a community, as solutions to the collective problems of life, must be complete beyond a certain degree. The modification of the institutions of socialization, mastery of nature, and social control has a lower limit of efficiency below which the community as a complete way of life cannot survive.

The jazz community is most accurately depicted as a specialized status community. In the words of Max Weber,

> *Status groups* are normally communities. They are, however, often of an amorphous kind. In contrast to the purely economically determined "class situation," we wish to designate as "status situation" every typical component of the life fate of men that is determined by a specific, positive or negative, social estimation of honor.[12]

In the development of a status community two secondary principles of community formation are involved—social differentiation and closure. All communities have systems of stratification based on the differential access to wealth, esteem, and power. Differentiation occurs in stratification competition. Once status groups form, further social differentiation continues to take place within them: there is differentiation both within the larger community and within the status group. In this study, both levels were investigated.

From whatever point it begins, fusion on all three dimensions can occur, thereby closing the circle. We are speaking here of "closure" or the simultaneous operation of the principles of institutional stability and interinstitutional consistency which insures against disintegration from within and disruption from without.[13]

The jazz community does not completely fulfill these requirements. Yet it is not a mere institution, for it consists of a series of related structure such as bands, cliques, jam sessions, and so forth, and it has its order of merit. The persons and activities involved in jazz occupy some kind of intermediate situation between a congeries of institutions and a full-fledged community. It is perhaps best described as a semi-community—a tendency toward community formation which, because of the conditions of its origin and development, cannot become total. Many of the institutions necessary to any complete community, such as a fully developed economy and politics, are present only in rudimentary form. The fact that the jazz musician must occasionally turn to commercial music indicates that the chief institution of the mastery of nature, the jazz job, is incomplete.

The Hypotheses and the Design

The preceding discussion has concerned itself with the theory of the jazz community and then only in an abbreviated way.[14] This brings us to a statement of our research intentions: (1) to determine the position of the jazz musician in the larger society; and (2) to determine the extent of community formation among jazz musicians. Several propositions have been selected for investigation, with those falling under category I being related to number 1, above, and those falling under category II being related to number 2.

I. Jazz musicians as an occupational group hold a lower rank on the basic dimensions of general community stratification than commercial musicians.

A. Jazz musicians hold a lower status rank in the general community than do commercial musicians.

    B. Jazz musicians hold a lower class rank in the general community than do commercial musicians.

    C. Jazz musicians have less power in the general community than do commercial musicians.[15]

II. Jazz musicians are more than an occupational group; they are members of an organized subcultural or status community.

    A. The jazz community has a specialized class, status, and power system.

    B. Jazz musicians occupy higher rank in the strata of their subcommunity than outsiders.

        1. Jazz musicians occupy a higher class position in their status community than do commercial musicians.

        2. Jazz musicians occupy a higher status position in their community than do commercial musicians.

        3. Jazz musicians occupy a higher power position in their status community than do commercial musicians.[16]

These hypotheses, if confirmed, would provide additional evidence for the notion that a jazz community exists in Minneapolis. This evidence would be provided by establishing the relationship between jazz musicians (core members of the jazz community) and commercial musicians (marginal members).[17] If jazz musicians are different from commercial musicians, that is, if they form into status groups while commercial musicians do not, then we could expect them to hold different positions on the wider community dimensions of class, status, and power. It has been predicted here that they will be lower on these variables than their commercial colleagues. On the other hand, since it has been theorized that jazz musicians form themselves into communities and that all communities exhibit some sort of internal differentiation, then one could expect that jazz musicians would hold a higher position on the class, status, and power dimensions within their group than marginal members such as commercial musicians. It was predicted that jazz musicians would be higher on these internal community variables.

In this fashion, this study was constructed to assess, from two different perspectives, the general proposition that jazz musicians form into specialized status communities as well as more clearly defining the inner structure of these communities. The principle of status community formation, social differentiation, operates among jazz musicians in such a way as to set them off from the wider community and from other night club musicians.

Two groups of musicians, one jazz and one commercial, were isolated for study under field conditions. To this end, what Chapin called an *ex-post-*

facto experimental design was used.[18] The commercial musicians were assumed to live "off" of music while the jazz musicians lived "for" music. The former became the control group and the latter the experimental group. The independent variable was the decision whether or not to devote one's life to the pursuit of the intrinsic values of jazz.[19] The dependent variable is a whole host of effects centering around core or peripheral membership in the jazz community, including differential position on the dimensions of class, status, and power.

The two sample groups were randomly selected from among the jazz and commercial musicians in Minneapolis during April, 1964. For the purpose of the selection of jazz musicians, a special study was conducted to determine the number and identity of active jazz musicians in the city. The jazz musicians of the community were identified by a special panel of recognized jazz musicians. The panel was instructed to designate as a "jazz musician" all those who were known to play some form of modern jazz and were "active," that is, they were seen regularly on steady jazz jobs of one or more nights per week, or they were known to go to jam sessions frequently. A similar list of commercial musicians was prepared from the local union bulletin. Every commercial musician was playing steady and a large majority were musically employed on a full time basis. In this manner, a sampling universe for jazz and commercial musicians was developed.

A total of seventy respondents were interviewed for some phase of the study, twenty-five jazz musicians and twenty-five commercial musicians participating in the questionnaire survey. There were ten jazz and commercial musicians who participated in the pretest and the validation of scales. The remaining ten persons were used in the special survey done to establish the number of jazz musicians in Minneapolis.[20]

The questionnaire, used to gather data for our hypotheses, was made up of a series of ordinal or summated scales. Each hypothesis was operationalized in terms of a number of scales which were expected to differentiate jazz and commercial musicians along the dimensions of class, status, and power in the wider community and within the jazz community. Each item was assigned a set of weights ranging from 1 to 5; theory and practical knowledge dictated how the weighting was to be assigned. An item assigned a weight of 1 represented the ideal anticipated response for a commercial musician, while a response to an item which had a weight of 5 was the ideal anticipated response for a jazz musician. When each item or scale was answered, it was expected that the jazz musicians would have a significantly higher total item score than the commercial musicians. These scales were validated in the pretest of the questionnaire.

A chi-square analysis was undertaken to establish if statistically significant differences existed between the two sample groups with respect to the various scales. For this purpose the scales were broken down into two-by-two contingency tables on the basis of the distribution of the respondents around the scale mean. The null hypothesis was rejected at the .05 level of significance.

Findings

A series of scales was constructed to measure the general community class standing of jazz and commercial musicians in terms of housing characteristics, employment and income, characteristics of automobile ownership, and other material possessions: ownership of television sets and boats.

There were a number of these which were statistically significant. Jazz and commercial musicians in Minneapolis have a different class standing in the general community with respect to type of dwelling lived in (apartment, fourplex, duplex, rented, or owned house), number of automobiles owned, cost of newest automobile, and number of television sets owned. Jazz musicians ranked lower on these items than did commercial musicians (Table 1). Thus, 8 out of 25, or 32 percent, of the jazz musicians owned their own homes while 21 out of 25, or 84 percent, of the commercial musicians were home owners. Out of the two sample groups, 12 percent of the jazz musicians owned two or more automobiles as compared with 48 percent of the commercial musicians. There were 9 out of 25 jazz musicians who had paid $2,000 or more for their newest automobiles. Twice as many commercial musicians, 18 out of 25, paid over $2,000. Sixteen percent of the jazz musicians owned two or more television sets to 44 percent of the commercial musicians in that category.

Although some of these items did not turn out to be significantly differ-

TABLE 1

SUMMARY OF THE CHI-SQUARES AMD LEVELS OF SIGNIFICANCE
FOR THE ITEMS PERTAINING TO GENERAL COMMUNITY
CLASS STANDING

Items	X^2*	Level of Significance
Type of dwelling	9.88	$.005 > p. > .001$
Number of automobiles owned	6.10	$.01 > p. > .005$
Cost of newest automobile	6.60	$.01 > p. > .005$
Number of television sets owned	3.43	$.05 > p. > .025$

*For chi-square, the Yates correction for small frequencies was used. Each test was one-tailed and had one degree of freedom.

ent, none of them varied in the opposite direction of the predictions. Two items, weekly family income and estimated home and property value, showed chi-square differences significant at 10 percent and 15 percent levels, respectively.

Six scales were used to measure the status of the two sample groups in the wider community: attitudes and behavior toward marriage, attitudes toward the two moral issues of free love and use of drugs, and religious behavior. Both items in the scale of moral issues were significant at well below the .05 level. These were two of the strongest findings of the study. Each respondent was asked to answer the following two questions on moral issues in terms of a five point scale ranging from "strongly agree" to "strongly disagree":

1. Free love is a good thing, and should be established in America.

2. It is immoral to use drugs such as heroin or marijuana.

The results are presented in Tables 2 and 3.

While neither of the scales concerning religious behavior was significant, the item pertaining to church attendance varied in the predicted direction: jazz musicians attended church less often than commercial musicians. However, 68 percent of both groups were members of a church. It had been hypothesized that jazz musicians would belong to a church less often than commercial musicians.

Marriage may be thought of as a status criteria; being married is of higher status than bachelorhood. It was predicted that jazz musicians would have negative attitudes toward marriage and, consequently, they would be

TABLE 2

JAZZ AND COMMERCIAL MUSICIANS' RESPONSES TO
QUESTION ON FREE LOVE

Responses		Jazz Musicians	Commercial Musicians	Total
Strongly Agree	(5)	2	0	2
Agree	(4)	7	2	9
Uncertain	(3)	7	0	7
Disagree	(2)	5	10	15
Strongly Disagree	(1)	4	13	17
Totals		25	25	50
Scale mean = 2.3			$X^2 = 14.67 ;^*$ p. $< .001$	

*For chi-square, the Yates correction for small frequencies was used. Each test was one-tailed and had one degree of freedom.

TABLE 3

JAZZ AND COMMERCIAL MUSICIANS' RESPONSES TO
QUESTION ON DRUG USE

Responses		Jazz Musicians	Commercial Musicians	Total
Strongly Agree	(1)	8	11	19
Agree	(2)	5	9	14
Uncertain	(3)	0	0	0
Disagree	(4)	7	4	11
Strongly Disagree	(5)	5	1	6
Totals		25	25	50
Scale mean = 2.4		$X^2 = 4.37$;* $.025 > p. > .01$		

*For chi-square, the Yates correction for small frequencies was used. Each test was one-tailed and had one degree of freedom.

more apt to be single. However, only six jazz musicians were unmarried compared with 4 commercial musicians. The item measuring attitude toward marriage was not significant, but there were indications that it was too general to produce accurate responses.

There were ten scales measuring the power of the sample groups in the wider community:

1. Number of organizations of which one is a member

2. Number of offices held in organizations

3. Frequency of meetings attended in organizations

4. Political activity other than voting

5. Political activity of wife other than voting

6. Number of close friends active in politics

7. Friends who are elected officials in government

8. Close friends who hold office in an organization

9. Possession of own lawyer

10. Close friend who is a lawyer

The results from these scales were ambiguous, and for this reason no conclusions could be drawn about the differences in power between the two groups. There were no statistically significant differences either in the direction of prediction or in the opposite direction.

TABLE 4

Types of Records Purchased by Jazz and
Commercial Musicians

Types of Records		Jazz Musicians	Commercial Musicians	Total
Modern jazz	(5)	22	3	25
Swing or dixieland jazz	(3)	0	2	2
Other ; seldom or never				
buy records	(1)	3	20	23
Totals		25	25	50
Scale mean = 3.1			$X^2 = 25.92$;* p. < .001	

*For chi-square, the Yates correction for small frequencies was used. Each test was one-tailed and had one degree of freedom.

TABLE 5

Duration of Employment of Jazz And
Commercial Musicians

Length of Job		Jazz Musicians	Commercial Musicians	Total
Under 3 months	(5)	10	3	13
3 to 6 months	(4)	3	2	5
7 mos. to 1 year	(3)	3	0	3
13 mos. to 2 years	(2)	4	9	13
25 months or more	(1)	4	11	15
Totals		24	25	49
Scale mean = 2.8			$X^2 = 9.07$;* p. < .005	

*For chi-square, the Yates correction for small frequencies was used. Each test was one-tailed and had one degree of freedom.

At this point the analysis shifted to the internal structure of the jazz community. Two class scales were constructed to measure the predicted differences between jazz and commercial musicians within the Minneapolis community. Two items in the questionnaire gathered data for these scales: types of recorded music purchased and duration of musical employment. Both items showed a statistically significant difference between the two sample groups in the direction predicted (Tables 4 and 5).

Jazz community power, which is almost entirely noncoercive, was measured in two ways: demonstration of the existence of a hierarchy of cliques and demonstration of the existence of a small group of influential musicians established by consensus of the sample groups as to who was a good musician (either jazz or commercial) in Minneapolis. The attempt at determining whether a hierarchy of cliques was present among the jazz musicians was not successful. A sociometric device was employed here, but only on the sample groups. Each respondent was asked to name those musicians whom he associated with most frequently after hours or during the day.[21] It has since been determined that a much larger proportion of the universe of jazz musicians is needed before any conclusive evidence can be gained. However, the author's observations support the predictions that cliques do exist in Minneapolis.

However, a small group of influential jazz musicians was found. No such phenomenon was discovered among the commercial musicians sample. Each respondent was asked the following question: In your opinion, who are three good musicians who play either jazz or commercial music in Minneapolis on the following six instruments (piano, tenor sax, trumpet, drums, bass, and trombone)? Twelve jazz musicians were selected by ten or more other jazz musicians for their music ability. One individual was mentioned 21 times out of a possible 25. In contrast, the commercial musicians had only one such person; he was selected ten times. Only ten commercial musicians were considered good by jazz musicians. On the other hand, a large number of jazz musicians were chosen for their musical ability by commercial musicians. Even the commercial musicians of Minneapolis recognized the superior musical qualities of certain jazz musicians.[22]

A specialized status system was found in the Minneapolis jazz community. Four types of scales were developed to measure this aspect of the jazz life: the importance of creativity for the respondent's music (jazz or commercial), playing jazz for its own sake and not for some instrumental reason, the amount of practicing done, and the dislike for audience requests.

TABLE 6

JAZZ AND COMMERCIAL MUSICIANS' RESPONSES TO QUESTION ON
PLAYING JAZZ FOR ITS OWN SAKE

Responses		Jazz Musicians	Commercial Musicians	Total
Strongly Agree	(5)	14	2	16
Agree	(4)	7	6	13
Uncertain	(3)	2	0	2
Disagree	(2)	1	14	15
Strongly Disagree	(1)	1	3	4
Totals		25	25	50
Scale mean = 3.4			$X^2 = 11.82$;* p. $< .001$	

*For chi-square, the Yates correction for small frequencies was used. Each test was one-tailed and had one degree of freedom.

The responses to two items relating to creativity and playing jazz for its own sake were found to be significant. The items, answered in terms of the "strongly agree—strongly disagree," scheme are as follows:

3. In (commercial music, jazz) creativity is important.

4. (Commercial music, jazz) is so exciting to you that you would like to play it as a leisure time activity.

The results from item (4) are presented in Table 6. The status scale of the amount of practicing done varied in the expected direction, but was not significant. The status scale of dislike for audience requests showed only slight power to discriminate between the two sample groups.

Summary and Conclusions

This study centered around the following two research interests: (1) What is the position of the jazz musician in the larger society? (2) To what extent do jazz musicians tend to form into communities of their own? After having developed a theory of the jazz community, six hypotheses were derived and tested by means of an *ex-post-facto* study design. It was predicted that jazz musicians would rank lower than commercial musicians on the major social dimensions of class, status, and power in the wider community and higher than commercial musicians on these same dimensions within the jazz community. In general, this study confirmed these hypotheses on a single population of jazz and commercial musicians.

Additional evidence has been provided for the general proposition that jazz musicians form into specialized status communities. Also, we have more clearly defined the inner structure of these communities. Previous authors have observed that jazz musicians differ from other musicians in their values and attitudes and from the general population, that is, they have viewed the world of jazz as a subculture. However, an assemblage of unique values and attitudes is not a community in-and-of-itself but only an important part of it. In this paper, we have added another critical element to the idea of the jazz community by confirming the existence of a community structure.

While there is sufficient evidence to support the proposition that Minneapolis jazz musicians form into status communities while commercial musicians from the same city do not, the standing of the former in terms of wider community standards is more in doubt. The following points lend support to the *ad hoc* hypothesis that there is a trend toward respectability among the practitioners of jazz in Minneapolis. (1) None of the general power scales were statistically significant although six out of ten varied to a certain degree in the predicted direction. However, two of the remaining four were almost significant in the direction opposite of the hypothesis, and the other two had virtually the same distribution. (2) While the majority of the general status scales were either significant or close to it, the remaining two scales—church membership and marital status—showed an even distribution. (3) A special analysis revealed no differences between Negroes and whites on the variables studied, a situation which, if it had turned out differently, could be used to explain the findings on status location which indicate a lower-class existence. (4) Some of the differences found in the general class scales may also be explainable in terms of the age difference between the two sample groups. (5) Jazz in Minneapolis is no longer strictly associated with lower-class surroundings, but has been making its way into some of the nicer night clubs and the concert halls.[23]

These points plus some current observations on the jazz scene[24] lead one to the conclusion that if there is not a trend there is at least a shift toward respectability and a middle-class existence. What effect this may have on the community characteristics of jazz musicians remains to be seen. This situation harmonizes with Stone and Form's ideas on the social location of the various status groups in American society, among which they include jazz musicians. These collectivities are usually found outside of the main status hierarchy of the community, and they are composed of members from many different walks of life.[25] The core of such groups of jazz musicians is likely to be made up of those musicians working on the creative fringes of jazz, whose compositions and playing are too radical to be acceptable to the general public and who are, consequently, not likely to make much money.[26] It seems possible that the jazz community might survive even under middle-class conditions.

Several precautions must be heeded in connection with this research. First of all, it should be mentioned that the questionnaire items which gathered the data to be used in the scales were not selected in the usual manner. While these items were validated by appropriate methods, they were not chosen from a large pool of items as having the greatest power to discriminate. Instead, the items used in the questionnaire were seen as likely to discriminate between the two groups on the basis of the theory of the jazz community. Perhaps if the conventional procedure of an item pool had been used, a greater proportion of the scales would have turned out to be significant.

Another limitation was the lack of complete success in enumerating the active jazz musicians in Minneapolis. This was caused, in part, by too small a panel of judges and too high a cut-off point. During the course of the study the investigator became aware of a number of new and young jazz musicians who were not listed by the judges or listed only a few times so as to be below the cut-off point. This means that not everyone in the universe of active jazz musicians had an equal chance of selection in the random sampling process. A similar criticism can be made of the sampling procedure for commercial musicians, since the union bulletin list of musicians currently employed is usually inaccurate to some extent. These lists, however, were the best available at the time.

There is always the possibility of a third limitation because of some peculiar characteristic of Minneapolis. For example, it has a comparatively small Negro population, which partially eliminates one of the chief factors in the past in jazz community life. Yet, cities the size of Minneapolis are numerically more prevalent in the United States than the cities the size of the jazz giants, New York, Los Angeles, and Chicago. It is not inconceivable that Minneapolis is more typical or jazz life across the nation than these "meccas" are.

It is obvious that this study requires replicative research in other jazz communities to determine the strength of our theory. Most useful to the sociology of jazz will be those studies which concentrate on cities like Minneapolis which are numerically most prevalent. Unfortunately, these communities have been studied the least.

The internal structure of jazz community life has barely been touched in this study. A rich array of investigations awaits centering on the structure of cliques, norms, values, and institutions. A social psychological approach to the sociology of the jazz musician could also be fruitfully undertaken. In this area there are possibilities for studying cliques as reference groups, as miniature social systems, as units of socialization and social control. There remain opportunities for studying the self conception of the jazz musician, as well as his role-playing and role-taking abilities both within and outside of the jazz community.

There is a paucity of demographic data about jazz musicians. There is a need for a representative investigation of levels of education and intelligence. More accurate data is needed on age and marital status as well as racial composition and size of professional group. An interesting research question arises from the conflict between the intrinsic and the instrumental values of jazz and commercial music, and the personality changes, if any, brought about by this situation.

Footnotes

The author wishes to thank Don Martindale for his stimulating criticisms and encouragement in the course of this research.

1 William Bruce Cameron, "Sociological Notes on the Jam Session," *Social Forces*, 33:182 (1954).

[2] Howard Becker, "The Professional Dance Musician and His Audience," *American Journal of Sociology*, 72:140 (1951).

[3] Robert A. Stebbins, "The Conflict Between Musical and Commercial Values in the Minneapolis Jazz Community," *Proceedings of the Minnesota Academy of Science*, 30:76 (1962).

[4] Howard Becker, *Outsiders* (New York: The Free Press of Glencoe, 1963), pp. 114–19.

[5] Aaron M. Esman, "Jazz: A Study in Cultural Conflict," *American Imago*, 8:221 (1951).

[6] Cameron, *op. cit.*, p. 181.

[7] Sidney Finklestein, *Jazz: A People's Music* (New York: Citadel, 1948), pp. 28f.

[8] Esman, *op. cit.*, p. 222.

[9] A. P. Merriam and R. W. Mack, "Jazz Community," *Social Forces*, 38:218 (1960).

[10] Becker, in *American Journal of Sociology*, 72:139.

[11] Don Martindale, *American Society* (Princeton, N.J.: Van Nostrand, 1960), pp. 256–65.

[12] Max Weber, *From Max Weber*, trans. by Hans Gerth and C. Wright Mills (New York: Oxford Univ. Press, 1958), pp. 186–87.

[13] Don Martindale, *American Social Structure* (New York: Appleton-Century-Crofts, 1960), pp. 454–55.

[14] For a more complete discussion of the theory of the jazz community see Robert A. Stebbins, "The Jazz Community: The Sociology of a Musical Sub-Culture," unpublished Ph.D. dissertation, University of Minnesota, 1964, chap. 2.

[15] The definitions of the concepts of class, status, and power in this study follow those of Max Weber. A class situation is the typical chance for a supply of goods, external living conditions, and personal life experience as determined by the market place. Status is viewed as a common component in the life of a group of men seen in terms of a positive or negative social estimation of honor. By power is meant "the chance of a man or number of men to realize their own will in communal action even against the resistance of others who are participating in the action." Weber, *op. cit.*, pp. 180–87.

[16] It will become apparent to the reader as he studies the operationalization of these concepts that there are actually several kinds of power under consideration. Goldhamer and Shils, whose general definition of power is much the same as Weber's, distinguish three major forms of power: "force" or the influencing of behavior by the physical manipulation of the subordinated individual; "domination" or the influencing of behavior by making explicit what the power-holder wants done (command, request, etc.); "manipulation" or the influencing of behavior without making explicit what the power-holder wants done. To the extent that there is power among jazz and commercial musicians in the wider community, it will predominately take the form of force and to a lesser extent domination. Within a jazz community, however, power is usually exhibited in the form of manipulation, with some domination being manifested as well. See Herbert Goldhamer and Edward A. Shils, "Types of Power," *American Journal of Sociology*, 45:171–72 (1939).

[17] Commercial music is popular music designed for a sale to the mass public. In this study, it specifically refers to a form of music played predominately in the finer night clubs to older patrons. In general, it is two-beat instead of four, sometimes improvised, seldom very fast or slow, and made up of tunes familiar to the listeners' younger days and of the less raucous popular songs of the day. A commercial musician is often an erstwhile jazz musician who has relied on commercial

music so long that he has lost contact with the jazz community. These commercial musicians are either in transit or have already made the transition from the jazz community to the wider community: they are essentially middle-class. Also included here are those commercial musicians who never have been members of the jazz community but have always played this form and other forms of music.

[18] F. Stuart Chapin, *Experimental Designs in Sociological Research*, rev. ed. (New York: Harper & Bros., 1955), chaps. 5 and 10. A thorough discussion of the research design and techniques is available in Robert A. Stebbins, "A Historical and Experimental Design for the Study of a Jazz Community," *Indian Sociological Bulletin*, 2:228–42 (1965).

[19] One of the limitations of the present study is its cross-sectional characteristics: the consideration of the state of jazz and commercial musicians at one particular time only. For the purposes of the research problem, this is quite adequate, but such a design omits certain processual features of jazz life such as Becker's notion of careers. It has been stated here that the individual respondents made a choice between jazz and commercial music. One should not overlook the fact that the same jazz musicians of today may be some of tomorrow's commercial musicians.

[20] An additional seven informants were interviewed for the purposes of developing a local history of jazz. Stebbins, "The Jazz Community: The Sociology of a Musical Sub-Culture," chap. 4.

[21] This is the only meaningful way to establish the existence of cliques in a small jazz community. It is true that in larger communities the cliques function as informal employment agencies and reference centers, and usually a jazz musician works jazz jobs with members of his own clique. But, in smaller jazz communities, musicians take the best men available regardless of their clique identification. There are simply not that many good performers to choose from.

[22] The question arises as to just how jazz musicians are influential. Since the top figures in a jazz community embody most perfectly the major values of this subculture (ability to play jazz and resistance to the call of commercialism), they become the ultimate judges of the other jazzmen in town. Recognition from leading members of the jazz community can do more to raise a man's status within the hierarchy than can anyone from a lower level.

[23] Stebbins, "The Jazz Community," pp. 130–37.

[24] For an account of an organized attempt to revive jazz in Harlem under the Harlem Youth Act see Nat Hentoff, "Harlem Sounds," *The Reporter*, vol. 42 (Dec. 3, 1964); or that of a lunch-hour bandstand in New York see the *Christian Science Monitor*, for Tuesday, Oct. 12, 1965, p. 12, sec. B.

[25] Gregory P. Stone and William H. Form, "Instabilities in Status," *American Sociological Review*, 18:160 (Apr., 1953).

[26] Andre Hodeir, *Toward Jazz* (New York: The Grove Press, 1962), p. 200. Jazz musicians like Cecil Taylor, Thelonius Monk, and Ornette Coleman fall into this category.

Bureaucracy

Life in the Crystal Palace

ALAN HARRINGTON

The Crystal Palace is one of America's great corporations. We who earn a living in such companies have been characterized variously as corporation men, organization men and women, and (inaccurately) as wearers of charcoal-gray suits. For some years now we have been living under glass. Through our transparent walls observers have been peering, as they would into an ant palace, to discover what in the world animates this strange new being, the corporation person.

I don't blame them for studying us. From the outside looking in we must appear to be a rather peculiar bunch of people. Is it true that we are collectively different from our fellow countrymen? Are we in our corporate glass houses separated from the life going on outside our walls? Not being a sociologist, I can't say with authority whether corporation life has produced a new species of American. But from my own experience at our company I feel that it has.

I think that our new species may be distinguished from other American working people at least in one way, by an absence of nervousness. We are not worried about our jobs, about the future, about . . . much of anything. This is a curious sensation, not to have any real worries. Try to imagine it. How are you going to get ahead? The company will decide. *Quo vadis?* The company will take care of that too. Furthermore your affairs will be ordered fairly and squarely with maximum sympathy for your well-being.

This sort of good-fortune cannot help but separate our species from others who are not so lucky. We are like a man in an electrically-cooled suit,

Adapted and reprinted from *Life in the Crystal Palace*, by Alan Harrington, pp. 3–5 and 7–21. Copyright © 1958, 1959 by Alan Harrington. Reprinted by permission of Alfred A. Knopf, Inc.

or in winter an electrically-heated suit, wondering why others are perspiring and shivering and why they are running about and jostling each other in animated dispute.

Our protected man is a good person. He faces the world with all-purpose amiability. Assail his position and he will readily agree that you have a point. Swing your fists at the company itself and the answer to your primitive behavior will come in the form of courteous public relations. But how unreasonable to attack him! He is polite, decent and cooperative, and eager to be a good citizen. Besides, your assault will be unfair. *He* is not responsible for the policies that govern his life. No one is. These policies have been formed over the years by ten thousand committees. Like this nice man or not, with each passing year you see more of him. Ask, if you will, whether our founding fathers would draw back in dismay or whether they would be pleased to have the future of the United States entrusted to his care.

As the great companies and their subsidiaries have extended their operations across the country and overseas, hundreds of private enclaves have come into being. (Indeed in some instances they resemble private company-states, insofar as employees hardly exist outside of them.) Mark these enclaves as small circles on the map and you will see the number of circles from Maine to California increasing every year. I am reporting from one such enclave, not as an expert but as an insider looking out. The writer is knocking on the picture window trying to get attention. He is saying: "Here, look. This is the way we live and how we feel about it."

"Happy families are all alike," said Tolstoy. Whether this is true of great corporations I don't know, because I have belonged to only one. The company I have been with for more than three years is one of the world's largest, having some thirty-four thousand employees in the United States and overseas. There are more than five hundred of us here at headquarters —and we are a happy family. I say this without irony, not for the reason that I am in the public-relations department, but because it is the truth. We give every appearance of happiness. We are also in many respects pretty much alike, at least on the surface.

It is not that our company makes us behave in a certain way. That kind of thing is out of date. Most of our people tend to live and talk alike, and think along the same general lines, for the simple reason that the company treats us so well. Life is good, life is gentle. Barring a deep depression or war, we need never worry about money again. We will never have to go job-hunting again. We may get ahead at different speeds, and some will climb a bit higher than others, but whatever happens the future is as secure as it can be. And the test is not arduous. Unless for some obscure reason we choose to escape back into your anxious world (where the competition is so hard and pitiless and your ego is constantly under attack) we will each enjoy a comfortable journey to what our house organ calls "green pastures," which is, of course, retirement.

"Is this sort of existence worth living?" you ask. I think that depends on who you are and also on the person you could become. There are two ways of looking at it: (1) If you are not going to set the world on fire anyway, it is better to spend your life in nice surroundings; (2) looking back, you *might* have had a more adventuresome time and struggled harder to make your mark in the world if the big company hadn't made things soft for you.

But it is all too easy to be glib in disapproving of the kindly corporation. We are then in the position of scorning the earthly paradise, and that cannot be done lightly. To be honest, we should put aside the convenient clichés—that big business firms, for example, are by their very nature heartless, exploitative, enforcers of conformity, etc. It is commonly assumed that a big, apparently impersonal authority is made up of bad fellows. How much more bewildering and exasperating to discover that they are good fellows!

I went into my job at the corporation with a poor spirit. I was suspicious of large companies, and swore that nobody was going to turn me into a robot. My situation was untenable anyway. I had just sold my first novel, a satire about a man who, under the pressure of business, had turned himself into a Nothing. In a year the grenade would go off, and of course the writer would be fired.

Particularly disconcerting in the early days was the gentleness of my new associates. Most public-relations offices are filled with edgy, hustling people. Here there was such courtesy and regard for your comfort . . . it was unfair. When I arrived, everyone turned and smiled, and they all came over to say how glad they were than I was with them. The boss took my arm and had me in for a long talk. "We want you to be happy here," he said earnestly. "Is there anything we can do? Please let us know." When you discover that the members of the company team really care about you it is a shock to the nervous system. The skeptical newcomer stands there, shifting his feet, not knowing what to do with his preconceived resentment.

I went through the orientation course, and completed all the forms and saw that I was protected against everything. I had a momentary fearful sensation of being enfolded in the wings of the corporation and borne aloft. "How's everything going?" inquired one of the orientation men, and I grunted at his civil question.

Now I was one of the group, hunched gloomily over a typewriter amid smiling faces. With the exception of the department head and assistant manager, our public-relations staff worked in one large room. We did our jobs in leisurely fashion with a carpet of non-glare fluorescent lighting above and a thick wall-to-wall carpet below. The usual office noises were hushed. Typewriters made a faint clack. Our mild jokes were lost in the air. It seemed to me a strange pressure chamber in which there was no pressure. This was a temporary arrangement. Next year the company was moving to a new office building in the suburbs, and it would be a fabulous place—a great office-palace on a hilltop surrounded by fields and woodlands. Everybody talked about the palace and what a marvelous headquarters it would be. The enthusiasm bored me, and I thought: "Well, I'll never see it."

That was a long time ago. Today I continue to live in the city but commute in reverse to the suburbs, and every weekday I sit down to work in the country palace. Here, after three years, are some general impressions of our corporate life:

The Corporation Is Decent. Most of our men have deep, comfortable voices. You have stood beside them in slow elevators, and heard these vibrant tones of people whose throats are utterly relaxed. And why shouldn't they be relaxed? Once you join our company, so far as the job is concerned, you will have to create your own anxieties. The company won't provide any for you.

There is no getting around it—our working conditions are sensational. The lower and middle echelons arrive at nine and, except in very rare instances, go home at quarter-to-five. Many of the higher executives work longer and harder, according to their inclinations, but seldom in response to an emergency. Rather it is a pleasure for them.

This is a company whose products move easily in great packages across the continent. Demand is constant and growing, since our products are good for people and contribute to the nation's health and well-being. The supply is adjusted from time to time in order to keep prices at a reasonable level. There is no reason for anyone to kill himself through overwork.

The savage, messianic executive of the type described in Rod Serling's *Patterns* would find himself out of place here. In fact, he would be embarrassing. In the unlikely event of his coming with us, the moment he started shouting at anybody he would be taken aside and admonished in a nice way. (We do have one high-ranking officer a bit like that, but he is old and close to retirement. He is very much the exception.)

A full recital of our employee benefits would—and does, in the indoctrination period—take all day, but here are just a few of them. We have a fine pension fund, a fantastically inexpensive medical program for you and your family, and a low-premium life-insurance policy for double your salary. The company will invest five percent of your pay in blue-chip stocks and contribute on your behalf another three percent. The company picks up half of your luncheon check. When we moved to the suburbs, the company paid its employees' moving expenses and helped them settle in their new homes. For those who didn't wish to move . . . a bus waits at the railroad station for commuters from the city and drives them to the hilltop office building.

The only unsatisfactory working condition, I think, is that you must be content with a two-week vacation until you have been with the company for ten years. In other words, the experience you may have gained elsewhere, precisely the experience the company has *bought*, counts for nothing in terms of vacation time. But this policy is fairly standard practice. It certainly inhibits a man's desire (say, after nine years) to change companies for a better job. Thus, it is at least a minor pressure against free-spirited enterprise. All the benefits exert pressure, too. There is nothing sinister about them, since admittedly they are for your own material comfort—and isn't that supposed to be one of the goals of mankind? What happens is that, as the years go by, the temptation to strike out on your own or take another job becomes less and less. Gradually you become accustomed to the Utopian drift. Soon another inhibition may make you even more amenable. If you have been in easy circumstances for a number of years, you feel that you are out of shape. Even in younger men the hard muscle of ambition tends to go slack, and you hesitate to take a chance in the jungle again.

On top of all this, it is practically impossible to be fired. Unless you drink to alcoholism or someone finds your hand in the cash box, the company can afford to keep you around indefinitely. Occasionally under great provocation—such as a scandal that reaches the tabloids—there may be a transfer. Once in a while a prematurely crusty old-timer is retired. Otherwise the ax will not fall.

Every so often I hear my seniors at the corporation inveigh against socialism, and it seems strange. I think that our company resembles nothing so much as a private socialist system. We are taken care of from our children's cradles to our own graves. We move with carefully graduated rank, station, and salary through the decades. By what marvelous process of self-deception do we consider our individual enterprise to be private? The truth is that we work communally. In our daily work most of us have not made an important decision in years, except in consultation with others.

Good People Work Here. Since joining the company I have not heard one person raise his voice to another in anger, and rarely even in irritation. Apparently when you remove fear from a man's life you also remove his stinger. Since there is no severe competition within our shop, we are serene. We do compete mildly perhaps, by trying to achieve good marks in the hope that our department head will recommend a promotion or an increase to the Salary Committee. Cutting out the other fellow and using tricks to make him look bad is hardly ever done. At higher levels, now and then, executive empires will bump into each other and there will be skirmishes along the border. But these are for the most part carried on without bullying and table-pounding, and the worst that can happen to the loser is that he will be moved sideways into a smaller empire.

It would be wrong to say that our employees are not lively. They smoke and drink and love, and go on camping trips, go skiing, and operate power boats, and read things and go to the movies, and ride motorcycles like anybody else. In the office they know what to do (usually after consultation) in almost any circumstance. What a great many of them have lost, it seems to me, is temperament, in the sense of mettle. We speak of a mettlesome horse. Well, these are not mettlesome people. They lack, perhaps, the capacity to be mean and ornery when the ego is threatened—because at our company we do not threaten people's egos. Rather the ego tends to atrophy through disuse.

Another curious thing is our talent for being extremely friendly without saying anything to each other. I remember a conversation that went something like this:

"Jim! Where did you come from? I haven't seen you in—I guess it's been about a year and a half."

"Just about that, Bill. A year and a half at least."

"What are you up to, for goodness' sake?"

"I've been in Washington, and now I'm going back overseas."

"Always on the move!"

"Well, I guess I am. I just thought I'd come down and have a chat with you before leaving."

"It's great that you did. How's your family?"

"Fine, Bill, how is yours?"

"They're fine, too."

"The years go by, don't they?"

"They sure do."

"Well. . . ."

"Well. . . ."

"Well, I guess I'd better be moving along."

"It's been wonderful talking to you, Jim. Look, before you get on the plane, why don't you come down for another talk?"

"I will, boy. You can count on it."

Also common among our employees is a genuine and lively interest in the careers of upper-level executives whom they may never have laid eyes on. As the gentlemen move from one station to another, their progress is followed with exclamations and inside comments. "Hmm, Jackson has moved to Purchasing! I thought so." "Look at Welsh—he's taken over the top spot in Patagonia. Anybody can tell that they're setting him up for a vice-presidency." Who *cared* about Jackson and Welsh? At one point, I did.

I had to prepare a press release about them, and update—add two more lines to—their official biographies.

The role of the corporation's top directors in our cosmos is an interesting one. In our company, members of the board are not remote figures from outside who drop in to attend meetings now and then. They are on the job every day. They recognize us, nod, and often say hello. I have found these august gentlemen to be amiable and even shy in the presence of their inferiors, but their appearance on the scene is the occasion of total respect, body and soul, such as I have never witnessed outside the army. They are not feared either. They conduct themselves in a friendly, most democratic manner. It is not awe they inspire but, so far as I can see, pure admiration. I was once talking to a young man in the employee-relations department when his eyes, gazing over my shoulder, suddenly lit up with joy. I turned, expecting to see our pretty receptionist, but it was a director passing by and giving us a wave of his hand.

Team Play Is the Thing.   Team play means that you alone can't get too far out ahead of the troops. You can't, because in our company it is necessary to consult and check over everything. Someone will ask whether this doesn't lead to a certain amount of mediocrity. It does. We have a substantial number of mediocre people in the company—that is, men and women of ordinary ability who would probably never originate anything under any circumstances.

But where organizing an effort is concerned it is sometimes better to have mediocre talent than a bunch of creative individuals who disturb the situation by questioning everything. In terms of performance, if you have a slow but sure operation, mediocre personnel, including your nephews, can carry it out beautifully. In *planning*, mediocrity has and still does hurt the company.

Our method is to get together and talk it out, each one of us contributing his mite. Why have one man make a decision when thirty-three can do it better? The consequence of this policy is that our executives commit few errors—although sometimes they arrive at the right decision three years too late. But the sure markets for the company's products bring in so much money that the mistake is buried under mountains of dollar bills. Our interminable round of conferences may also be counted on to produce by default serious errors of omission. These don't hurt noticeably either, for the reason cited above.

I got over my impatience at the slow pace of things, but I felt it once at a lecture given to senior and junior executives on the new central filing system that would go into effect when we reached the palace. A fierce little girl, a vestal of the files, told us how it was going to be. We sat, without anyone suggesting it, according to rank, and I could work out the possible course of my company career, if I stayed with it, just by looking at the assemblage of heads in front of me—bald and white in the front rows, then pepper-and-salt, and gradually back where I was, the black, brown, and blond heads of hair. I thought of my own head, slowly changing through the years as I moved up a row or two, with never a chance by a brilliant coup of jumping while still brown-headed—or even pepper-and-salt—over several rows and landing among the white thatches. How could I make such a leap when anything I accomplish I do as a member of a group?

A Little More Tension Would Be Welcome.   This may be based on fragmentary evidence, but I suspect that when people are not placed under at least a minimum of tension they seek it out in their dreams. One day I overheard our press-relations man conferring with our public-relations manager, Mac Tyler, who said: "Maybe next time, Walt, you had better try it the other way." The press man came out of the office and saw me. "Boy!" he said, "I sure got a bawling out on that!"

Another man of some rank joined his local Democratic Party, and worked hard at it during the presidential campaign. But he felt guilty about what he had done. Finally he rushed upstairs and confessed to the president of the corporation. "Gosh," he told me afterward in a disappointed tone, "he didn't mind at all. He just put his hand on my shoulder and said: 'Don't worry, Fred, I'm a Jeffersonian Republican myself!' "

We Conform by Choice.   Critics of big business are constantly on the watch for the kind of over-cooperation that a company explicitly demands of its members. Our company doesn't demand anything. Oh, there is tactful pressure on us to join the annuity and insurance program, and a rather strong insistence on Red Cross and Community Chest contributions, but nothing serious.

What you have to watch out for is the amount of compliance you fall into by yourself, without realizing it. Something like this almost happened to me when my book was published. Far from resenting the satire, most of our employees who read it enjoyed the book. I was asked to autograph dozens of copies, and several were bought and prominently displayed in the company lending library. I had thought of myself as a writer in temporary captivity. Now that was no longer possible. A captive of what? Good Will?

I began to feel what I now recognize was a gradually deepening contentment. If you are on the watch for the symptoms, here are a few: (1) You find that you are planning your life defensively, in terms of savings plans and pensions, rather than thinking speculatively of moving up fast—faster than the others. (2) You become much less impatient over inefficiency, shrug your shoulders and accept it as the way things are. (3) Your critical faculties become dull; you accept second-best; it seems unsporting to complain. (4) Nothing makes you nervous. (5) You find that you are content to talk to people without saying anything. (6) You mention something like (improvising now) "our Human Development Department" to outsiders and learn with surprise that they think you have made a joke.

During this period of contentment, which lasted quite a few months, I did not concern myself with anything beyond the requirements of my job. I became easy-going and promiscuously nice, and had a harmless word for everybody. Finally, I was reminded that this sort of thing was the mark of a fat soul. A succession of incidents helped indicate what was wrong.

We Are Remote from the Lives of Others. Shortly before we moved to the country the press-relations man and I were looking out of our eleventh-floor window in the direction of the waterfront. We saw a half-circle of men gathered on a far-off pier. "Isn't that what they call a shape-up?" he asked with faint curiosity. It was easy to tell that he barely imagined that these men existed and that their quaint customs were real.

Some weeks before, I had looked down on a gentleman in a homburg and cutaway, running among the crowds in the financial district. He carried a bouquet of red roses wrapped in green paper. You don't associate this street with flowers, and it was exciting to see him running, holding his green wrapping like a torch of something beautiful in this place. And then he died on his feet, twisting over and slumping to the pavement. His head rested against the wall of a building. He rested with the flowers flung across his knees and his fine hat askew, and the absurd and living gallantry that produced this death *could* only be nothing to us or to anyone in the crowds that simply swerved around him and kept going, because of the way we are concentrated and oriented away from things like that.

How remote we were too from the crazy musicians who arrived on a blustery fall day with the idea that, since this was a financial center, there would be a rain of coins from the tall buildings in response to their trumpet, guitar, and bass fiddle. The wind swirled jazz among the canyons. I saw that no one was paying them the slightest attention. Feeling guilty, I threw them a quarter, but they didn't see it. They danced and made jazz in the cold, while upstairs we went on with our work, and they didn't exist, and it was nobody's fault.

It isn't that we should have been expected to know about longshoremen, or care particularly about the man in the homburg, or throw coins to the brave musicians, but we have simply, systematically, avoided letting these aspects of life into our field of vision. We came in from the suburbs and plundered the city, and left each night without having the least idea of what was going on there. Even our daily experience in the rapid transit was spent behind a newspaper; taxis shielded us from the bad sections of town. We never heard guitars strumming on the dirty doorsteps, nor comprehended the possible excitement of disorderly feelings that make other people so much more alive than we are.

And when the corporation moved to the country our isolation from all that became completely splendid. Now most of us could anticipate fifteen- and thirty-minute rides in car pools from our suburban homes to a suburban office. You could almost hear an official sigh of contentment on the day that we moved.

This Way to the Palace. Point your car along a winding drive-way up the green hillside shaded with great elm trees. Enter the wide and friendly doorway and look at the murals in our lobby. They will tell you the story of our industry. As you go through the offices, you will probably marvel as we did at all the comforts and services we have. Imagine a sea of blond desks with tan chairs, outdoor lighting pouring in everywhere, roomy offices with individually-controlled air-conditioning and area-controlled Music by Muzak coming out of the walls. We need few private secretaries. All we have to do is pick up a phoning device and dictate our message to a disc that whirls in a sunny room in another part of the building. Here a pool of stenographers type all day long with buttons in their ears. We don't see them and they don't see us, but they know our voices.

A high-speed pneumatic tube system winds through the entire building. We send material from one office to another not by messenger but by torpedo containers traveling twenty-five feet a second. Simply have the attendant put your paper, magazine, or memo in the plastic carrier. He inserts the container in the tube, dials the appropriate number, and, whoosh, it is shot across the building. There is a complete sound system throughout headquarters. If, for example, a bad storm is forecast, there will be an "Attention Please," and you may go home early. At noon, enjoy movies in an auditorium the size of a small theater, visit the library, watch the World Series on color TV, or play darts and table tennis in the game room. The finest catering service and a staff of friendly waitresses bring you luncheon. Then go to the company store, pitch horseshoes, or take a brief stroll under the elms.

What happens to an office force when it is offered facilities like these? At first there were a few small complaints. The main difficulty is that we find it all but impossible to get off the campus. You can speed several miles to town for a quick lunch. Otherwise you stay on the grounds until closing. City employees everywhere have the chance to renew, at least slightly, their connection with the world during lunch hour. When we first came many of us rambled in the woods and picked flowers, but we seldom do that anymore.

As for our work-efficiency, I think it has diminished a bit as a result of what one of my friends calls "our incestuous situation." When you are isolated in the country it is not easy to feel that sense of urgency that distinguishes most businessmen.

I sometimes have a feeling of being in limbo. More than ever one feels

—ungratefully—over-protected. While on the job, I actually can't feel hot or cold. I can't even get sick. This will sound ridiculous, but when the company obtained a supply of influenza shots, I found myself in the absurd position of refusing one. For some reason I wanted a chance to resist the flu in my own way.

What is the moral of all this? I am not quite sure, but some time ago Dostoevsky put it in *Notes from Underground:*

> Does not man, perhaps, love something besides well-being? Perhaps he is just as fond of suffering? Perhaps suffering is just as great a benefit to him as well-being? . . .

> . . . In the "Crystal Palace" [suffering] is unthinkable. . . . You believe, do you not, in a crystal palace which shall be forever unbreakable—in an edifice, that is to say, at which no one shall be able to put out his tongue, or in any other way to mock? Now, for the very reason that it must be made of crystal, and forever unbreakable, and one whereat no one shall put out his tongue, I should fight shy of such a building.

Work Associations

Professionalism and Occupational Associations

GEORGE STRAUSS
University of California
Berkeley

Once it was possible to think of just two main occupational groups in business, the managers, who gave the orders, and the workers, who took the orders (and belonged to unions).[1] The growing proportion of salaried white-collar workers has made this division an oversimplification. In recent years, a good many students of collective bargaining have turned their attention to white-collar and engineering unions, while personnel men have switched their emphasis from the selection and training of hourly paid employees to management selection and development. The management of professional engineers has become a field in itself, with a considerable literature.

Nevertheless, the typical personnel or industrial relations text still devotes the bulk of its attention to blue-collar workers; white-collar problems are relegated to the category of "special cases," to which the traditional blue-collar analysis can be applied with appropriate modifications. The time is now ripe for industrial relations students to fashion new frameworks which will deal with all categories of employees, not just with blue-collar employees, but with the whole range of salaried employees, from office clerks through commission salesmen, engineers, staff men, lower- and middle-level executives to top management itself.

The analysis which follows makes no pretense of providing a complete framework. But as a step in this direction I shall consider three developments which such a framework should eventually take into account: (1) the growth of professionalism, (2) the development of occupational associations, which are, in a sense, a partial substitute for unions in white-collar

Abridged and reprinted from *Industrial Relations*, Vol. 2, No. 2 (May 1963), 7–31, by permission of the author and publisher.

fields, and (3) the growing ambivalence among "in-between" occupational groups which are not entirely management, worker, or professional.

This paper . . . considers the variety of occupational groups existing in industry today, and in each case analyzes the extent of professionalization and the role of occupational associations. . . .

The discussion which follows should not be considered a scholarly report on research findings. I intend to paint with a broad brush and call attention to what appear to be emerging trends and patterns of change—patterns from which there are many deviations.

Professionalism

The rapid growth of professional influences in business has been one of the most striking developments of recent years. The forecast of an English author thirty years ago seems to be coming true: "Under a system of large-scale commercial and industrial organization, all those who occupy important positions will gradually come within professional associations—or at least under professional influence."[2] Today almost every occupation— from rodent killer on up—calls itself a profession. But the weight of academic thought regards true professionalism as involving at least four values, derived in part from the self-employed professional and the university.[3]

> 1. The professional claims that his occupation requires *expertise*, that is, specialized knowledge and skills which can be obtained only through training (usually academic).[4] As a consequence, he seeks to restrict entry into his profession to those who can demonstrate their proficiency. (In many cases, too, he seeks to control the training process as well.)

> 2. The professional claims *autonomy*, the right to decide how his function is to be performed and to be free from lay restrictions.

> 3. The professional feels a *commitment* to his calling. In Merton's terms he is likely to be a "cosmopolitan" rather than a "local," that is, he is more likely to identify with members of his profession in other organizations than with his own organization.[5] "Getting ahead" to him may mean winning esteem in the eyes of his fellow professionals as much or more than advancement in his own company.

> 4. Finally, he feels a *responsibility* to society for the maintenance of professional standards of work. Thus he supports professional self-discipline and codes of ethics.

Each of these values conflicts with a traditional bureaucratic value. Most managers feel that (1) management alone should decide who is competent for a job, (2) and how it will be done, and that (3) an individual's loyalty should be to his own company, and (4) management alone should be responsible for discipline. Many of the most difficult problems in managing salaried employees arise from this conflict of values.

Actually two processes seem to be at work: the bureaucratization of the professionals and the professionalization of the bureaucrats. On one hand, the growing importance of research and technical processes has brought a tremendously greater number of engineers and scientists into business. But the professional traditions these men bring with them from the self-employed professions and from the university clash with the bureaucratic traditions of management. Considering the nature of the work which professionals do in industry, neither professional nor bureaucratic approaches to administration are fully appropriate. As a consequence, both parties make a not-fully-satisfactory compromise.

On the other hand, as we shall discuss below, those who engage in traditional bureaucratic, functional staff jobs, such as purchasing and personnel administration, are beginning to aspire to professional status.

Occupational Associations

Emphasis on unions, because they are the common form of employee representation, has tended to obscure the wide variety of other occupational associations which, in one way or another, represent the interests of their members. To take an extreme example, in the hospital we see a vast proliferation of professional and semiprofessional associations covering almost every occupation from physician and hospital administrator down through housekeeper, medical records librarian, and laboratory technician. Each association fights for the economic and social welfare of its members, and many seek the full accounterments of professionalism, such as certification, professional training, a code of ethics, and the right to exclude nonprofessionals from their special work. Unskilled workers comprise about the only hospital group which is not widely organized.[6] Professional and quasiprofessional organizations of all kinds abound in industry, and even occupational groups, such as foremen (whose professional interests are fairly minimal), are represented by associations.

Occupational associations form a continuum, from the learned society (which exists only to advance knowledge) at one extreme, to the economically oriented union at the other. Among other things, they may function to provide a means for: (1) social fraternization, (2) occupational identification, (3) raising the occupation's status in the organization and in the community, (4) furthering professional objectives by self-regulation and restriction of entry, or (5) advancing the economic interests of members, e.g., through gaining salary increases, processing grievances, and so forth. Such associations are sometimes halfway houses on the road toward unionism. As such they may either block or facilitate the development of more traditional unions.[7]

Just as individual employees are in a sense "split personalities," torn among professional, managerial, and employee values, so occupational associations are also divided as to values. These conflicts appear perhaps most dramatically in the professional unions, as we shall see.

Various Occupational Groups

In the pages which follow we shall first look briefly at three relatively "pure" occupations, those of (1) the assembly-line worker, who represents the employee orientation, (2) the executive or line manager, who represents the managerial orientation (but there is evidence that management itself is becoming professional), and (3) the research scientist who represents the professional orientation (though some insist that the term "professional" be reserved for those who *apply* knowledge). Then we shall consider some

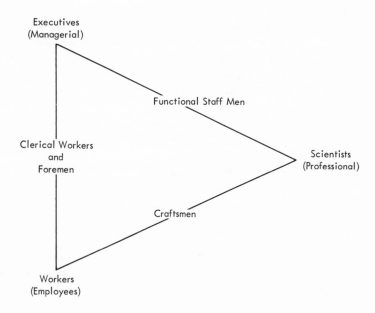

in-between occupations, which, in effect, suffer "split personalities" and are torn between several values: (4) clerical workers and foremen, who are neither fully employees nor fully managers, (5) craftsmen, who are primarily workers, yet to some extent accept professional values, [and] (6) functional staff men who are in managerial positions, yet aspire to professional status. . . .

The diagram [above] is based on the assumption that one can conceive of three continua, one being employee-professional, another employee-managerial, and the third managerial-professional. This presents a vastly oversimplified picture of the relationships involved. In reality individuals are scattered over the three sides of the triangle and at many points within it. Furthermore, there are many dimensions not represented. (For example, industrial relations students have made almost no studies of the motivation and behavior of salesmen, though salesmen may constitute a category very different from any of those discussed below.)

Relatively Pure Cases

PRODUCTION WORKERS

For the purposes of this paper it is enough to use the production worker as a base and to point out what he is not. The worker on the assembly line is often considered to be the archetype of the production worker and his job has been intensively studied.[8] The research suggests that he has little feeling of being an expert, of commitment to calling, of autonomy on the job, or of obligation to turn out high quality work. In other words, he has little sense of being a professional. In addition, he has little or no sense of identification with the company for which he works, nor does he feel that he is part of management.

His occupational association is, of course, his union. The union is concerned with economic questions and with protection of its members against management; it shows little interest in enhancing the position of assembling as a line of work or in making what I shall later call "professional demands."

EXECUTIVES

The contrast between the production worker and the executive is very sharp.[9] The executive's job permits substantial discretion. He is restlessly ambitious and expects to get ahead on his own. For him success is measured by salary and position within the company. He is strongly job and company oriented. The relatively low evaluation he gives to family and community ties is shown by his willingness to transfer from community to community on short notice.

There is increasing talk in some circles of creating a management profession. "The burgeoning body of literature on the professionalization of management expresses the view that administratives as well as staff positions are governed to an increasing extent by professional standards. The school of business seeks to make administration an exact science."[10]

Since to some, management professionalism may seem almost a contradiction of terms, it might be useful to inquire how such a movement could develop. Top managements of many corporations today are self-perpetuating groups which own relatively few shares of stock in the corporations they control. Since the source of their power is not clearly legitimatized, many managers feel it necessary to justify their social role. At least for publication, they seem to worry increasingly about their social obligations. In addition, corporate objectives are less clear than they once were. Growth, share of the market, company (and managerial) prestige are partially supplanting the goal of maximizing profits, and some managers claim that their function is to act as trustees for a number of interests (some of which admittedly conflict).

Furthermore, as the number of managers increases, and as the problems which they face become more technical, the feeling rises that management calls for special skills, formal training, and apprenticeship. As one manager commented, "Perhaps the most provocative—and important—idea on which we are proceeding is that managing should be regarded as a distinct type of work, with its own disciplines, its own criteria for achievement; something which is both learnable and teachable."[11]

Managerial conferences, such as those sponsored by the American Management Association, help managers develop a sense of occupational identity. In this sense, at least, the AMA is an occupational association. (If one can make a distinction—and I think one can—the National Association of Manufacturers is not an occupational association, since it represents company interests, not those of managers as managers.)

SCIENTISTS

Relatively few "pure" scientists work in industry. Yet the "pure" scientist (more likely to be found in a university) provides a model for many with professional backgrounds or aspirations, especially engineers and scientists employed in industry.[12] The scientist is as dedicated to his job as the executive, but success to him means advancing knowledge and winning respect from his professional colleagues.[13] While he does not disdain making more money, a higher salary in itself is not nearly as important a criterion for success as it is for the executive. He wants to win the respect of his scientific colleagues more than he wishes to advance in the corporate hierarchy; he feels loyalty to his science, not to his firm.

Understandably there are numerous areas of friction between the scientist and the manager. The scientist seeks to advance and disseminate knowledge for its own sake; the manager seeks to direct the scientist to areas which will be most profitable for the company. The scientist seeks to publish; the manager wants to protect trade secrets. In management, successful accomplishment is rewarded by promotion; but to promote a scientist may mean that the organization loses a good scientist and gains a poor administrator. The scientist expects his boss to be a senior colleague, not an overseer. Juniors feel free to criticize their seniors. "Authority does not rest in socially powerful individuals, but in observed fact. . . . Any decisions affecting all scientists are the consequences of the 'weight of scientific opinion' rather than of individual authority. . . . The concept of 'management' or 'supervision' is absent from and alien to the organizational traditions of science."[14] Naturally all this conflicts with the hierarchical boss-subordinate relationships upon which organizations are traditionally built.

The learned societies are the scientists' occupational associations. These provide a sense of identity as well as a forum in which work may be disseminated and appraised.

In-Between Cases

CLERICAL EMPLOYEES

Clerical employees are the first example of an in-between group, in this case part management, part employee.[15] At one time white-collar work was highly desirable. Being an office worker meant that one avoided the long hours, hard work, unpleasant working conditions, and general stigma attached to working in a factory. White-collar workers associated with management, made minor decisions, and many times had a chance to move into management—or at least dreamed of doing so. Consequently they identified with management.

Events in recent years have done much to shake this close identification and to reduce the relative attractiveness of white-collar work. In the first place, factory work is less undesirable than it used to be: factory wages and fringe benefits are much improved, supervision is substantially more humane, and factories are becoming increasingly safe and pleasant places in which to work. Meanwhile, office automation has reduced employee discretion in many white-collar jobs to the point where there is little difference between the white-collar employee on a computer and the blue-collar worker on an automated production line. And as the numbers of white-collar workers rise year by year, being a white-collar worker has provided a much less secure claim to social prestige, while the opportunity for close social contact with the boss has declined. Also, for those without a college education, the opportunities to move into management are growing smaller.

As yet there is little evidence that clerical employees have come to look upon themselves as workers. Quite the contrary. Clerical employees cling adamantly to middle-class values even when their aspirations for moving into management become unrealistic.

In spite of recent gains by white-collar unions (particularly among governmental employees), the degree of office unionization is much less than it is in the factory.[16] The explanations for this are well-known: the white-collar identification with management, the higher percentage of females among office workers, and the recent unfavorable social climate for unions. Still another factor must be considered: some union organizers adopt the same techniques with white-collar workers that they would use in the factory. They seek to build up hostility to the boss. They point to the large gains won by industrial workers and urge white-collar workers to jump on the bandwagon ("You can get it, too" is a recurring theme in organizing pamphlets). They utilize large meetings and blustery speeches. Such approaches are not notably successful.

Other organizers try to give the union a middle-class appeal. This is not always as difficult as it sounds—the middle class is a "joining" class. For the working white-collar girl, the union can conceivably be the equivalent of the afternoon bridge club; for the white-collar male, it can be his Rotary Club or professional association. Respectability can be enhanced merely by a change of name or terminology. There is the Newspaper Guild and the Office Employees International Union; among organized insurance agents, the grievance committee is called the "office relations committee," and the international bargaining committee is the "presidents' committee."

Organizers who follow the middle-class approach mention economic themes, but they speak of protection rather than of fighting the boss. They point out how a union can provide security and eliminate favoritism, how it will bring wages up to a "decent" or "professional" level. At times they even brag about the number of their members who move into management. They de-emphasize the class struggle and even imply that top management is really in favor of the union.

Not even this sort of approach is particularly successful at the moment, but there is every reason to believe that if white-collar workers are ever organized it will be by unions which take a distinctively white-collar approach—perhaps organizations which shun the word "union" and are not affiliated with the main body of organized labor. Just as the old craft unions were unable to organize the mass-production workers during the twenties, and new forms of unionism had to be developed, so it seems likely that completely new techniques and organizational structures will be required before white-collar workers will become active in occupational associations.[17]

Once organized, white-collar unions often behave quite differently from blue-collar unions. In general their approach is more conservative. Demands for seniority, for example, are less insistent. But, since the problems of white-collar unions are in many ways similar to those of professional unions, there is little point in discussing the matter at length here.[18]

Does union membership mean that white-collar workers forego a sense of identification with management? Limited research suggests that it does not. "We still think ourselves part of management," a time-study man who served as union vice-president commented (and his comments seem typical). "Many times we have to make decisions against production people, and this is what we are going to continue to do."

FOREMEN

Foremen present another in-between case not too different from that of clerical workers.[19] A half-century ago the foreman's status was not in doubt. To the men on the factory floor he exemplified management: in many companies he had the right to hire, fire, and set production standards; singlehandedly, he took care of all the activities which are now called scheduling methods, safety, wage administration, and quality control.

But over the years, staff departments have taken over many of these functions. Hiring and discipline—once the foreman's main sources of prestige and authority—today are often handled by the personnel department. The advent of the union has further lowered the foreman's status; no longer are his orders obeyed unquestioningly, and the contract restricts his freedom on all sides. Further it has become increasingly clear that in many companies higher level jobs are reserved for college graduates; the foreman now has a dead-end job.

During World War II all these frustrations, plus the frantic pressures of war production, plus the fact that wage controls at times held foremen's wages below those of some of the men they supervised, led many foremen to join a newly organized union, the Foreman's Association of America.[20] This development, coming less than ten years after the success of the CIO, was a shock to management. Its reaction was to take advantage of the newly passed Taft-Hartley Act and defeat the Association.[21]

But many companies also resolved to take constructive measures to increase the foreman's status and authority, or at least to make him *feel* that these had been increased. Management newsletters, clubs, conferences, and training programs began to mushroom, designed in part to include the foreman in the management group. Efforts have been made, with various degrees of sincerity and success, to improve communications upwards and downwards. In some cases policies of decentralization have led staff departments to transfer decision-making powers back to foremen. In short, most progressive companies have tried to do something about the foreman problem.

These measures have had varying degrees of success, but the foreman in a unionized plant is still in a uniquely frustrating position. He alone, among all levels of management, must deal with subordinates who are protected by a union contract and who show relatively little interest in pleasing their boss to win a promotion. The foreman is often subject to pressures from above which he is in no position to pass on down. Being at the end of the communications channel, he often feels left out. The non-college foreman also finds that his chances for promotion are growing ever slimmer. In addition, as old-timers in higher management retire, he finds himself surrounded by college men who have different interests and, in effect, speak a different language from his.[22]

Many companies have set up foremen's clubs or encouraged their foremen and other lower levels of management to join a YMCA-sponsored Industrial Management Club or the independent National Management Association (formerly the National Foreman's Association). Some foremen attend meetings of these "occupational organizations" because of management pressure, but I am convinced (on the basis of having taught courses of various lengths for eleven different such organizations) that there are other reasons for the enthusiastic participation which sometimes occurs. These clubs provide fellowship and identification for non-college men (college graduates are rarely active). Classes and speakers are looked upon as means of improving managerial skills.

But foremen's associations may also function as a sounding board for frustrations. In one case I observed, a so-called "management night," to which the plant manager had been invited, "degenerated" into what, in other contexts, would have been called collective bargaining for an across-the-board salary increase. I know of two personnel directors who refused to sponsor foremen's associations in their companies on the grounds that these might develop into unions.

Informal conversation at foremen's meetings often turns to the question, "How can we get management to appreciate our problems?" In formal classroom discussion of collective bargaining, considerable ambivalence is shown: when the discussion concerns discipline, in general foremen identify with management; but when it concerns wage increases, then sympathies seem to lie with labor. To be sure, the union is the enemy, yet the foremen often feel socially closer to the union's leaders than they do to higher management.

Looked at from one point of view, foremen's associations are quasi-unions (though very weak ones); from another point of view they are quasi-professional associations (particularly since they sponsor classes and discuss technical problems). Both management and foremen look upon such organizations primarily as a means of developing closer ties with management.[23]

CRAFT WORKERS

Few observers consider craftsmen to be professionals. And yet if we take the building tradesman as the classic example of the craftsman, we find that he behaves in many ways like a professional. For this reason we can think of him as occupying a position on the continuum between the production worker and the pure professional.[24]

> 1. Certainly he feels his job requires specialized knowledge and skill which can be obtained only through training (though he receives his training through apprenticeship, not at a university). The closed shop (particularly when it is combined with an examination for admission into the union) permits entry to be restricted to those who can demonstrate proficiency at the trade (sometimes, of course, there is favoritism).

> 2. Craftsmen like to decide how they will do their work. Normally building tradesmen (and also skilled maintenance men in industrial plants) receive much looser supervision than do mass-production workers.[25] Building tradesmen normally take orders only from foremen of their own craft.

> 3. The building tradesman strongly identifies with his craft. In frequent cases his family has followed the craft for generations. The casual nature of his employment makes him feel closer to his fellow craftsmen than to any firm. Pride in craft is also shown in the attention many tradesmen give to training apprentices.

> 4. The true craftsman feels a sense of responsibility for turning out a high-quality product. It is hard to induce him to work faster and turn out a sloppy product. And in some cases the union penalizes incompetent craftsmen or encourages foremen to do so.

It is true that much of this "professional" behavior is motivated by economic self-interest. Even so, it is clear that building tradesmen feel strong pride and identification with their work.

There is no need to point out that the craft union is the building tradesmen's occupational association. But it should be noted that craft unions perform certain quasi-professional functions: they promote and enforce standards of training; they seek to advance the status of the craft in the community; they protect the autonomy of their members; they prevent "non-professionals" from doing "professional" work; at times, they serve as a forum in which technical (in addition to economic) occupational problems can be discussed; and, on occasion, they enforce "professional" standards of workmanship.

Following roughly the above analysis, several observers have suggested that professionalism is spreading to other blue-collar activities which require a high degree of training and involve considerable responsibility.[26] Recent years have seen the establishment of special skilled trades units within the United Automobile Workers and the spread of the principles of exclusive craft jurisdiction among skilled trades groups in manufacturing generally.[27] Although these developments have been largely motivated by economic considerations, they are not inconsistent with an emerging sense of professionalism.

FUNCTIONAL STAFF MEN

Just as craft workers represent a point on the continuum between production workers and true professionals, so members of functional staff groups (particularly those with management responsibilities) fit on another continuum, this time between pure management and pure professionals.

Not long ago the vast majority of employees in most companies belonged to the line, i.e., were engaged in the firm's primary function—production in a factory, sales in a store, etc. But the picture is changing fairly rapidly in many organizations today. Staff or functional groups—concerned with accounting, personnel, quality control, research, development, and the like— are growing in size and status; at times staff seems to be the tail which wags the dog. And, as we shall see, many of these functional groups aspire to professional autonomy.[28]

In large departments today, staff tends to deal not with line, but with other staff departments. Take a routine activity: sales lands a big order; sales liaison passes it on to production scheduling, which in turn asks engineering for blueprints and specifications; engineering writes specifications, on the basis of which production scheduling writes requisitions; with these requisitions in hand, purchasing places an order for components. Thus up to a dozen functional departments may be involved in the work flow.

Normally, interdepartmental work-flow relations are smooth, but even in the best-run organizations there is considerable pulling and hauling between departments. Naturally each functional group seeks to protect its own autonomy and advance its own point of view. Design engineering, for example, looks for technical perfection, industrial engineering for manufacturing ease, and marketing for sales appeal. In addition to differences in point of view, there are status conflicts: each functional group feels that its importance is not fully recognized by other functional groups and by top management. Departmental loyalties flourish at the cost of an identification with the organization as a whole. Departmental loyalties are further facilitated by the fact that heads of functional departments often have dead-end jobs.

There is reason to believe that many functional groups look on professionalization as a means of bolstering self-esteem, raising status, strengthening a position as against other departments, and, at times, protecting autonomy from top management interference. Professionalization may be one of the "dramaturgical techniques and ideological arguments [which functional groups use] to support their claims for increased jurisdiction."[29] Engineering and accounting have already achieved professional status; purchasing and to a lesser extent, personnel, among others, are striving in that direction.

Each occupation hopes that once it is accepted as a profession, other departments will be less likely to dispute its professional judgment. Furthermore, as a profession it will be able to keep nonprofessionals from poaching on its preserves and will be able to disregard orders from higher management which would require it to engage in unprofessional acts. "Management at Chrysler was able to tell purchasing from whom to buy," a purchasing agent commented, "and look at the scandal. I bet they couldn't get away with telling a professional accountant to falsify the books—or if he did he would go to jail. With professional standards we could eliminate unprofessional practices."

Occupational associations exist for many functional activities. They promote professional identity and solidarity and help staff men to become "cosmopolitans" rather than "locals." Informal conversation at association meetings gives members a chance to exchange woes in brotherhood with those who have similar problems, i.e., to let off steam in a safe environment.

Associations often meet real educational needs. Formal programs provide training for younger members. Officers and members learn about human relations, public speaking, and organizational skills. And many members exchange information and tricks of the trade in informal conversation around the bar before and after meetings. Since individuals in functional departments often have dead-end jobs, being elected to association office may provide the means for "getting ahead" which is absent within the company. Furthermore, association membership provides the contact which may ease the way to finding a new job.

Such organizations often make active efforts to enhance the profession's status in the eyes of others. Through its Professional Development Committee, for example, the National Association of Purchasing Agents seeks to persuade educational institutions to establish courses in "purchasing science."

"As purchasing goes in our colleges and universities," one publication put it, "so will it go in the business world of tomorrow."[30]

Finally, professional associations sometimes seek to control entry into the profession. The National Association of Purchasing Agents has given considerable thought to setting up a series of examinations leading to a certificate in purchasing, and an experimental program has been started in the field of governmental purchasing. Some members talk of starting education campaigns to induce employers not to hire uncertified purchasing agents. If doctors, lawyers, engineers, and accountants all have licensing or certificate requirements, it is argued, why should not purchasing agents, as professionals, have the same thing?

Not all purchasing agents agree with this program, it should be emphasized. Purchasing agents, and presumably all staff men, have conflicting self-images. Many argue that their primary loyalty should be to management, not to a profession. They would like to get ahead within higher management, but are trapped in dead-end jobs. They recognize that it may take years before they receive the same kind of respect as do the traditional professions. ("After all," commented a frustrated purchasing agent, "the man in the street thinks any housewife can do purchasing, and it will take a long time to change people's opinions.") Yet professionalism beckons as a means of raising status and winning autonomy—if the occupation can get away with it.

Thus top members of functional groups, individuals who clearly have management status, are pulled between professional and managerial objectives. Subordinates in these departments at times feel that they are only employees. . . .

Conclusion

Increasingly it is more realistic to think of the corporation not as a unified organization of individuals with a common loyalty, but as an amalgamation of partially self-governing power groups—many claiming to be professional—which compete for status and authority. Just as we have become accustomed to thinking of pluralism in our larger society, so should we think of it within the organization.

There are a number of factors which explain the growth of professional pluralism. The very size and complexity of large corporations make it easier to develop loyalty to sub-units than to the whole. The human relations movement fosters a permissive atmosphere in which various occupational groups state their claims. More people are going to college and taking courses which lead to their thinking of themselves as professionals: once in industry they expect to be treated as such (in particular, to be granted a high order of autonomy). Finally, the technical nature of modern industry encourages specialization, and specialists often find that it is easier to get ahead by finding a job with another company than by winning promotion to a somewhat different job in their own company; to the extent that such an expectation prevails, it leads to professional rather than organizational identification. In any case, we see a wide variety of groups claiming to be professions (or at least to be crafts). These claims: (1) help win autonomy for the group, (2) tend to raise the group's status in the eyes of management, other occupational groups, and the general public, and (3) enhance the meaning individuals give to their work.

Occupational associations promote professionalism: they help protect the occupation's autonomy and raise its status. These professional objectives are often more objectionable to management than are purely economic demands. Thus a company representative spoke of how his engineering union "threatens teamwork with accounting, operating personnel, and other management people. . . ."[31]

Whether occupational associations become increasingly powerful would seem to depend on several factors. Foremen's clubs, professional associations, and some engineering unions would find it hard to exist without management's tolerance and support. Generally, management is pleased when employees take part in such extracurricular activities and feels that such organizations are desirable from a morale standpoint. Perhaps were managements more aware of the long-run implications of professionalism they might withdraw support. But as the factors making for professionalism become increasingly prevalent, employees may come to think of the opportunity to take part in occupational associations (even on company time) as a fringe benefit or even as a vested right.

The immediate future of white-collar and professional unions is hard to forecast. It depends, in part, on the general public attitude toward unions, economic conditions, and the level of government space and defense expenditures. Certainly most managements are aware of the possibility of being unionized and, in general, are making considerably more effort than in the past to improve morale (although layoffs due to computerization are a complicating factor). Furthermore, many managements are prepared to battle strenuously against any union which tries to enter their organization.

History suggests that eventually white-collar workers will be organized, but I have a hunch that, for the most part, the associations they join will not be affiliated with blue-collar unions or even call themselves unions. Yet, as white-collar workers get to be more like blue-collar workers, white-collar associations (regardless of their name) may behave more like blue-collar unions. Possibly research and development engineers may come to view "sounding boards" as an acceptable way to compromises between their professional and employee interests. . . .

Professionalism—with or without associations—will make management's job harder. In the first place, it introduces a note of collegial self-government *within* each occupation and practically forces supervisors to use participative rather than authoritarian forms of leadership. Secondly, it complicates the task of developing teamwork *between* occupations.[32] Each profession tends to develop a parochial, specialized point of view. As a result jurisdictional disputes become more common, and the over-all organization starts to break down into a number of semiautonomous departments (which keep each other in line through a series of checks and balances).

The principles of departmental self-government and autonomy are well established in universities, and to a lesser extent in hospitals. These two institutions may well provide models for companies to follow in administering highly professional departments. Just as substantially different policies are applied to managerial and hourly-paid employees, so a third, very different set of policies should be developed for professional groups. But, in addition to this, if my thesis is correct, we shall see a growing number of "in-between" groups; for these, "in-between" policies must be worked out. One thing seems sure: diversity rather than uniformity will become increasingly common in company policies in the future.

Footnotes

[1] The author is indebted for helpful suggestions on the preparation of this paper to Professors Vaughn Blankenship and F. T. Malm and to Mr. Arnold Nemore, all of the University of California, Berkeley.

[2] A. M. Carr Saunders and P. A. Wilson, *The Professions* (Oxford: Clarendon Press, 1933), p. 493.

[3] William Kornhauser, *Scientists in Industry* (Berkeley: University of California Press, 1962), and Everett C. Hughes, *Men and Their Work* (Glencoe, Ill.: Free Press, 1958).

[4] Some authorities suggest that a profession must rest on a body of rational theory. But such a narrow definition would exclude all creative and performing artists, as well as perhaps clergymen.

[5] Robert Merton, "Patterns of Influence: A Study of Interpersonal Influence of Communications Patterns in a Local Community," in Paul F. Lazersfeld and Frank Stanton, editors, *Communications Research, 1948–49* (New York: Harpers, 1949).

[6] For a discussion of hospital occupational associations, see David Kochery and George Strauss, "Non-Profit Hospitals and the Union," *Buffalo Law Review*, VII (Winter, 1960), 255–282.

[7] For the view that "white-collar unionism may develop through professional organizations unaffiliated with national labor federations," see Daniel H. Kruger, "Bargaining and the Nursing Profession," *Monthly Labor Review*, LXXXIV (July, 1961), 699–705.

[8] For careful studies of assembly-line workers, see Charles R. Walker and Robert Guest, *The Man on the Assembly Line* (Cambridge, Mass.: Harvard University Press, 1952), and Ely Chinoy, *The Automobile Worker and the American Dream* (New

York: Doubleday, 1955). Robert Blauner suggests that the assembly line represents an extreme rather than a typical example of production work. See his "Work Satsifaction and Industrial Trends in Modern Society," in Walter Galenson and S. M. Lipset, editors, *Labor and Trade Unionism* (New York: Wiley, 1960).

9 To the extent that the executive is subject to professional influences he is not a pure case and cannot be considered as occupying one of the three points on the employee-manager-professional triangle. Perhaps the proprietor or the Schumpeterian entrepreneur represents a purer case. Nevertheless, in spite of the executive's recent professional tendencies, it may be convenient to think of him as being relatively unprofessional.

10 Kornhauser, *op. cit.*, p. 6.

11 Harold F. Smiddy, Vice President of General Electric, quoted in Herbert Harris, "How Managers Are Made," *Nation's Business* (March, 1956), p. 91.

12 Some observers contrast the professional with the pure scientist. The professional, they say, is concerned with the *application* of knowledge, and professional problems are largely those of client-professional relationships. The pure scientist is interested in science for its own sake and therefore has patrons, perhaps, but not clients. See William M. Evan, "Role Strain and the Norm of Reciprocity," *American Journal of Sociology*, XLVIII (November, 1962), 346–354. Nevertheless, the pure scientist provides a role model which professionals seek to follow.

13 Among the most interesting work in this field is that of Herbert Shepard. See his, "Basic Research and Social System of Pure Science," *Philosophy of Science*, XXIII (November, 1956), 48–57; "Nine Dilemmas in Industrial Research," *Administrative Science Quarterly*, I (December, 1956), 295–309; and "Superiors and Subordinates in Research," *Journal of Business*, XXIX (October, 1956), 261–267.

14 Shepard, "Superiors and Subordinates . . . ," pp. 262–263.

15 This section is based in part on George Strauss, "White Collar Unions Are Different!" *Harvard Business Review*, XXXII (September, 1954), 73–82. The growth of secretaries' associations, some of which offer courses and grant certificates of proficiency, suggests that professionalism is entering this area too.

16 White-collar workers are fairly well organized in many parts of Europe, and some of their unions are militant.

17 There is reason to believe that a substantial proportion of white-collar organization today is via the back door; that is, production unions place direct pressure on employers rather than trying to induce white-collar workers to join unions voluntarily.

18 See Strauss, *op. cit.*, pp. 78–79.

19 See Burleigh Gardner and William F. Whyte, "The Man in the Middle: Position and Problems of the Foreman," *Applied Anthropology*, IV (Summer, 1945), 1–8; Fritz J. Roethlisberger, "The Foreman: Master and Victim of Double Talk," *Harvard Business Review*, XXIII (May, 1945), 283–298; Floyd G. Mann and James K. Dent, "The Supervisor: Member of Two Organizational Families," *Harvard Business Review*, XXXII (November-December, 1954), 103–112; and Amatai Etzioni, "Human Relations and the Foreman," *Sociological Review*, I (Spring, 1958), 33–38.

20 Charles P. Larrowe, "A Meteor on the Industrial Relations Horizon: The Foreman's Association of America," *Labor History*, II (Fall, 1961), 259–294.

21 First-level supervisors in construction, the printing trades, the railroads, the maritime industry, and the post office all commonly belong to unions today.

22 See George Strauss, "The Changing Role of the Working Supervisor," *Journal of Business*, XXX (July, 1957), 202–211.

23 Strange as it may seem, a union may exist for the purpose of winning management status for its members. One of the primary objectives of the American Radio Association-CIO was to win for its members the status of ship's officers. Jane

Cassels Record, "The Marine Radioman's Struggle for Status," *American Journal of Sociology*, LXII (January, 1957), 353–359.

[24] This section is based on George Strauss, *Unions in the Building Trades* (Buffalo, N.Y.: University of Buffalo Studies, 1958); Joel Seidman, Jack London, Bernard Karsh, and Daisey Tagliacozzo, *The Worker Views His Union* (Chicago: University of Chicago Press, 1958), Chap. 3. These characteristics are most noticeable in sections of the building industry where high skills are required; they would probably be less evident in mass-production house building, for example. Railroad men seem to share many professional characteristics with building tradesmen. See William F. Cottrell, *The Railroader* (Stanford: Stanford University Press, 1940).

[25] "Decisions, which in mass production were outside the work milieu and communicated bureaucratically, in construction work were actually part of the craftsmen's culture and socialization, and were made at the level of the work crew." Arthur L. Stinchcombe, "Bureaucratic and Craft Administration of Production: A Comparative Study," *Administrative Science Quarterly*, IV (September, 1959), 180.

[26] Nelson Foote, "The Professionalization of Labor in Detroit," *American Journal of Sociology*, LVIII (January, 1953), 371–380; Howard M. Vollmer and Donald L. Mills, "Nuclear Technology and the Professionalization of Labor," *American Journal of Sociology*, LXVIII (May, 1962), 690–696. On the other hand, the introduction of mass-production techniques into home building may have reduced the sense of craft identification and professionalism among building tradesmen working in these areas.

[27] The claim by groups, such as screw-machine operators, for craft status, is somewhat analogous to claims by groups such as purchasing agents for professional status.

[28] This section is based largely on the author's research on purchasing agents. See George Strauss, "Work-Flow Frictions, Interfunctional Rivalry, and Professionalism," *Human Organization*, 23 (Summer, 1964), 137–49. Further study is needed of the attitudes towards professionalism of other functional groups. There is considerable interest in professionalism among technical journals, but those who write in these journals hardly represent a cross-section of any occupation.

[29] W. Richard Scott, in reviewing Victor Thompson: *Modern Organizational Theory*, in *American Journal of Sociology*, LXVII (May, 1962), 713.

[30] *Purchasing News* (July 27, 1959), p. 28.

[31] T. E. Shea, "The Implications of Unionism: Western Electric Experience," *Research Management*, II (Autumn, 1959), 155.

[32] In addition, as the supervisory role becomes less important as a source of status, one may expect that occupational status may become relatively more important, and so status rivalries between occupational groups may become more intense.

4

THE SOCIAL PROCESSES
OF WORK

INTRODUCTION

Occupational structures, like any social system, articulate several of their internal components at one time. That is to say, it is through their interdependent processes that the various components of the system are linked so as to accomplish certain system maintenance functions. The occupational structure must have an ongoing supply of new members, and it must also train and otherwise socialize the new members into the occupational culture, to the point that they will reflect the appropriate ideology and attitudes necessary for satisfactory role performance. The occupational structure also must establish the necessary control mechanisms to insure conformity to the norms, thereby insuring collective attainment of work goals as well as protecting the occupation both from internal disruption through excessive competition and from external attack from other occupations or sources. A division of labor within the occupation, along with a system of differential rewards and opportunities for social mobility, result in differential career patterns, while the competition of one occupation with other occupations for deference and technical competency results in the trend toward professionalization. In this connection, the present chapter will examine the processes of: selection, socialization, the internalization of occupational perspective, control, careers, and professionalization.

In a society as large as ours, with its labor force of many millions and more than twenty-five thousand different occupational specialties, the matching of man to job is obviously a complex process. Although many persons speak of "choosing a job," this is perhaps not a totally appropriate label for job-seeking activities, inasmuch as it implies that individuals are completely free to search and select, "cafeteria-fashion," from a total array of occupational opportunities. Most persons, however, are quite limited in terms of the actual vocational opportunities existing for them. A number of factors may operate to prevent a person's entrance into a particular line of work, including sex, age, race, physical condition (and appearance), intelligence, education, temperament, and manual dexterity. For example, federal nondiscriminatory hiring practices notwithstanding, some jobs are simply not going to be open to an "inappropriate" sex. A restaurant is hardly likely to consider hiring a male for a topless waitress position or a female as attendant in the men's rest room. More seriously, there is a tendency to think in terms of certain occupational specialties as calling for members of one sex only, either because of physical or temperament requirements. Nursing, for example, has traditionally required a "woman's touch," as does the job of airline stewardess, office secretary, or interior decorator. Cabdriving, police work, traveling saleswork, and being an airline pilot, on the other hand, called for male practitioners. While we have seen numerous exceptions to these generalizations in recent years, the fact remains that sexual stereotyping of occupations continues to operate as a factor in restricting the entrance to an occupation by a person of the "wrong" sex.

Many occupations may be open only to persons of certain physical size, shape, weight, and appearance, and thus closed to persons who do not measure up or down to the appropriate physical criteria. Chorus girls usually must be tall and "leggy," jockeys must be short and light, some police and military positions call for specific minimum heights and weights, just as airline stewardess jobs specify both maximum and minimum heights. Other jobs may require particular weights, bodily proportions, or certain standards of physical attractiveness. Some persons may, however, be able to overcome these obstacles by altering themselves physically, by gaining or losing weight, firming up flabby muscles, having their teeth capped and their hair styled, or in the case of the underendowed would-be "topless" go-go girls, by having silicone injections to increase breast measurements. But these cases are the exception rather than the rule.

Many occupations are strictly age graded in terms of minimum or maximum age requirements. Most elected governmental positions, such as representative, senator, and president, have minimum age requirements, just as other jobs have strictly enforced maximum age levels, such as airline pilot and military officer. (Most ranks have "over-age in-grade" provisions for mandatory retirement or release from active service.) Age grading may also exist at an informal level with entrance to a given occupation barred to those deemed to be "too young" or "too old."

The complexity and intricacy of many occupational tasks may preclude persons who lack the necessary mechanical aptitude, manual dexterity, and native intelligence. On the other hand, the technical, verbal, and social requirements of other occupations may limit the entrants to only those who possess the necessary knowledge, sensitivity, and skills that college education may provide.

In addition to all these external factors operating to prevent the entry of an individual into an occupation, there are also factors internal to the individual that may color his perception of available opportunities. Because of ethnic or regional bias, social class perspective, individual temperament and experiences, cultural provincialism, or educational outlook, the individual simply may fail to perceive the existence of certain occupational opportunities, find them idiosyncratically objectionable or unacceptable, or consider them too unattainable or requiring too great an expenditure of time and effort. Thus again, using the cafeteria analogy, the individual is not totally free to select and choose, but can be instead likened to an individual who, through selective inattention, ignorance of the foods, or unknowledgeable objections, considers only a small portion of the total fare in front of him. He will find that his choices are restricted, and what is more, his resources may permit only a limited selection from those left.

In the first article in this chapter, "Occupational Choice: A Conceptual Framework," Peter M. Blau and his colleagues address themselves to an analytical and conceptual overview of the varied factors which influence an individual's selection of an occupation. Using an interdisciplinary approach and examining both individual factors of choice and selection as well as historical, economic, and social determinants, the authors conclude that "occupational choice is a developmental process that extends over many years." Lack of knowledge about existing opportunities tends to restrict occupational choice, which, as a result, "does not necessarily involve conscious deliberations and weighing of alternatives." Occupational choice is apparently affected by "the matrix of social experiences" channeling "the personality development of potential workers," and by "conditions of occupational opportunity" limiting "the realization of their choices."

To function effectively in an occupational status, an individual must acquire the necessary skills and learn to perform the occupational tasks in a satisfactory manner; in effect, he must be socialized into the occupational culture. Edward Gross has suggested that the necessary skills may be divided into three categories: regular technical skills, tricks of the trade, and social skills.[1] The acquisition of these skills can be accomplished as part of either a formal or an informal socialization process. In the instance of some occupational specialties, the requisite skills may be well defined and the means by which these skills (at least the technical ones) are to be acquired may be quite specific and highly institutionalized. A case in point is the lengthy and specific professional socialization of the physician involving exposure to an elaborate academic curriculum in college and medical school, followed by an intensive and rigorous apprenticeship experience in acquiring the actual technical and social skills while interning and serving a residency. In other occupations there may be no provision for occupational socialization other than "on-the-job training" after entrance to the occupation. An illustration of such an occupation is that of the pawnbroker. There is no formalized training mechanism to learn the necessary skills. A recent Associated Press article described this problem as related by a veteran pawnbroker, who said:

> Pawnshop operators simply aren't available anymore. . . . You just can't find them. . . . Nobody's going into the business. To be a pawnbroker you have to be able to evaluate instantly a diamond or a hi-fi or a mink stole.
> You have to be an amateur detective and a psychoanalyst. Everybody has a story. There isn't anything I haven't heard. . . . [The] Job is [an] art.[2]

In the absence of formal socialization mechanisms, many occupational specialties must rely on informal (but usually equally effective) procedures. Such an occupation is that of the prostitute. There are no technical schools for prostitutes as there are for physicians, attorneys, or even barbers. Yet they must learn their trade if they are to survive and succeed in the occupation. Accordingly an informal apprenticeship system has developed within the occupation.[3] The apprenticeship experience provides training in good grooming and personal hygiene, exotic sexual practices, the appropriate "professional" attitudes toward clientele, and methods of handling the economic relationship with their clientele. Prostitution seems to be "technically a low level skill" and the informal apprenticeship arrangements appear adequate to the task of equipping the individual for pursuing this occupational endeavor.

In the second selection in this chapter, " 'Breaking Out': An Apprenticeship System Among Pipeline Construction Workers," Bennie Graves describes another occupational setting where the socialization process is effected at an informal level. Although it is possible to acquire appropriate welding skills in trade schools, individuals are able to accomplish this informally by "breaking out on the line." The pipeline work culture looks with disfavor on trade school welders; accordingly, "breaking out" is seen as a preferred way of acquiring correct welding skills and attitudes. The neophyte must establish a "training-strategic" friendship (i.e., an intimate relationship which facilitates opportunity for learning pipelining skills) with an experienced pipeliner who will impart the necessary knowledge and skills to him over a period of time, mostly during breaks and slack periods. The neophyte or "bronc," as he is known, must acquire suitable attitudes and relate to his trainer in a deferential fashion. Ultimately the "bronc" develops the necessary competence to be able to work as a skilled worker at least part of the time and to be recognized as such. Unfortunately, this final period of apprenticeship sometimes produces friction between the "bronc" and his trainer for the apprentice may now be placed in a competitive situation with his former trainer.

In "The Naval Recruit Training Center: A Study of Role Assimilation in a Total Institution," Louis A. Zurcher, Jr., provides an account of a different type of occupational socialization—in this case, the highly formalized and institutionalized training situation of naval boot camp. The boot camp undertakes as its first task to "de-civilianize" or role-dispossess the entering individual. The goal here is to wipe away the old civilian identity in preparation for providing a new naval identity. Boot camp as a "total institution"[4] provides a highly routinized and standardized set of daily activities in a socially isolated setting. After entering boot camp, the new recruit begins an intensive phase of his training known as Receiving and Outfitting, in which he experiences not only a loss of civilian identity but also a sharp break with his former life and past experiences. After Receiving and Outfitting, the boot camp defines new roles, attempts to create new group loyalties, new expectations, and a new identity for the recruit as he gradually becomes indoctrinated in the new naval culture and is given an opportunity to rationalize his new role enactment. The recruit emerges from the total socializing experience of boot camp as a true "seaman."

In boot camp, as in other total institutions, socialization is effected with a zeal seldom found outside of such settings. One researcher, however, has reported that in sales organizations that rely on home-parties to display their line, an attempt is made to indoctrinate the sales personnel with company ideology through a socialization process that relies on religious revival techniques and evangelical zeal.[5] In the case reported—that of a manufacturer of plastic bowls—the company held sales meetings and promotion rallies which they termed "jubilees" and "pilgrimages," at which they urged their saleswomen "demonstrators" to "believe in" the product and to "believe in what it can do for you." The bowl manufacturer stressed the esthetic beauty and "sacredness" of their products and attempted to transmit a feeling of "reverence" and "awe" about the bowls to their consumers as well as to their salespersons. It appears that the company was quite effective in using religious revival techniques to implant desired company ideology in the saleswomen in question.

This case is significant because successful socialization into an occupational culture and subsequent acceptance of the neophyte by the members often calls for an appropriate ceremonial event or "rite of passage," as it is termed by anthropologists. In boot camp, when the individual "died" as a civilian and was "reborn" as a seaman, the final formal parade review was the ceremonial rite of passage. Weiss has reported on similar symbolic occupational deaths and rebirths in an army airborne unit. Airborne training culminates in a formal review ceremony where the men receive their "wings" insignia and an informal "prop blast" where the new paratroopers engage in drinking, singing, and frivolity with their former instructors.[6]

Whether the socialization is informal or formal, low-key or religious revival in tone, whether it occurs over a long period of time or quickly within a total institution, the ultimate goal is to transmit the necessary knowledge and techniques and to help the person develop an appropriate self-image, occupational rationalization, and ideology. Norman R. Jackson, Richard O'Toole, and Gilbert Geis address themselves to the question of occupational ideology in "The Self-Image of the Prostitute." Using interview data from fifteen prostitutes, the authors advance three propositions concerning the self-image and ideology of the prostitute: (1) the prostitute as an isolated individual is more likely than a less isolated person to engage in condemned behavior; (2) even the isolated prostitute experiences the impact of the general social values and must thus rationalize her occupational behavior; and (3) in rationalizing their violation of social taboos, prostitutes tend to emphasize other values, such as financial success and the financial burden of supporting others. The authors also identify two principal types of reference group orientation, which they label the *criminal world contra-culture*, in which the prostitutes tend to associate and identify with "those on the edge of the criminal world"; and the *dual worlds* in which the prostitutes display middle-class values and have a strong identification with their families. Thus the prostitutes apparently had dichotomized their existence and played two roles, a depersonalized prostitute role with which they tended to disassociate, and a family role with which they could more comfortably identify. A third type of reference group orientation, that of *alienation*, was also discerned. This is found in the prostitute who, because of her violation of laws and sexual norms, is able to maintain a satisfactory self-image by internalizing an appropriate occupational ideology which permits her to rationalize and justify her activities.

Members of all work organizations find themselves subject to a variety of social control processes. Control mechanisms are employed as a means of coordinating the collective efforts of the individual members in order to insure conformity to the norms of the work organization and to assist in the securing of its work goal. Edward Gross has dichotomized occupational controls into two varieties—controls from within the occupation, and controls that emanate from outside the occupation.[7] Examples of the first general variety might include the formal rules of the work organization such as military regulations or official "company policy," as well as the informal work norms that employees often develop among themselves and enforce as a means of regulating their work output. The second variety of controls can be illustrated by governmental regulation of certain occupational enterprises, including licensing, price controls, building codes, and minimum standards of sanitation and health (e.g., health cards for restaurant employees). Other controls from outside might include control by clients, pressure from other occupations or organizations and from the public, and controls applied by unions and other occupational associations. Professional controls such as codes of ethics are, in one sense, controls internal to the occupation, but in another sense they may represent controls that are external to the work organization in which the professional operates.

The next selection, Warren Breed's "Social Control in the Newsroom: A Functional Analysis," takes up the question of how internal controls are enforced in the face of possible conflict with outside controls. Breed points out that a newspaper publisher as owner of the enterprise has the right to set publishing or editorial policy as well as to see that his policy is enforced. Other control systems may operate to prevent conformity to publishing policy, however. These might include ethical journalistic norms, attitudes of reporters and other subordinates more liberal than those of the publisher, and thus a reliance on ethical norms to justify anti-policy writing, as well as ethical norms on the part of the publisher which would prevent his directly ordering subordinates to conform to his policy. Rather than being directly told of paper policy, the neophyte "staffer" has to acquire knowledge of it indirectly as part of his *occupational socialization*. As he learns policy, he also internalizes it and learns how he is expected to perform if he is to win rewards and avoid punishments. Through exposure to newspaper policy via conferences with executives, house organs, general reading, the paper itself, and executives' expressions of editorial position, the neophyte learns policy. A number of factors are present that facilitate conformity to policy, including feelings of obligation and esteem for superiors, desire for mobility, and institutional authority and sanctions, among others. To be sure, there are certain situations where the staffer may be able to deviate from editorial policy without penalty. Among the possibilities here are the situations where the norms of policy are not always clear, where executives may be ignorant of particular facts, or where the staffer has "star" status and is more privileged and immune to sanctions than a cub reporter. Breed concludes that "the newsman's source of rewards is located not among the readers, who are manifestly his clients, but among his colleagues and superiors," and accordingly "the publisher's policy . . . is usually followed."

After "selecting" an occupation, an individual will enter its ranks, acquire the necessary skills, attitudes, and perspectives through socialization, and will come to internalize these attitudes and perspectives and to manifest them as an occupational ideology, with a resultant occupational image of self. As part of the socialization process, the individual will also come to perceive and understand the occupational control systems operant on him and either will learn to conform to them or will learn ways in which they may be circumvented without sanction. The individual will move through the early learning phases of his occupational experience and in many instances, ideally, will take on successive job statuses with increasing responsibility, authority, and rewards. Ultimately, the individual will vacate his last occupational status because of failing health, or age, and will terminate his work experience with retirement. The process of selecting a work specialty, being socialized into its culture, and passing through a series of successively more prestigeful statuses within an occupation (or moving through a series of different occupational statuses,[8] or for that matter pursuing one's life work always in one particular occupational status) is termed an individual's *career*. The concept of career often carries the connotation of successful upward mobility, which may in fact be the case, although some persons in their careers experience unfavorable, disruptive, or disastrous career contingencies, with the result that their career pattern may encompass downward mobility at some point.

Such an instance is examined in the selection by Douglas M. More. In "Demotion," More addresses himself to downward career mobility and develops a conceptual scheme to classify the forms of demotion. He also considers the question of what conditions tend to increase the likelihood of demotion. Demotion, according to More, "must be seen only as a special instance of downward social and occupational mobility." Finally he discusses the consequences of demotion for both the individual affected and his employing firm.

The final selection in this chapter is M. Lee Taylor and Roland J. Pellegrin's, "Professionalization: Its Functions and Dysfunctions for the Life Insurance Occupation." No discussion of work processes is complete without making mention of professionalization, or the attempt on the part of many occupational groups to increase the specialized knowledge and services of their vocation as well as to elevate its prestige and respect to a level commensurate with that accorded to the traditional professions like law and medicine. As occupations make significant progress in terms of requiring advanced education, training, and technical skills of their members, they tend to seek professional status including "legal certification and its accompanying monopolistic advantages." The process of professionalization is often difficult, and Taylor and Pellegrin examine some of the difficulties encountered by insurance men in the professionalization process. As the authors point out, the life insurance occupation has two major goals—first, to "extend life insurance protection to all socio-economic groups in the population," and second, "to promote professionalization." In some ways, efforts to achieve the second goal may be dysfunctional in terms of achieving the first goal. For some years, life insurance salesmen have been able to avail themselves of a comprehensive study program which leads, when successfully completed, to the designation C.L.U. (Chartered Life Underwriter). The C.L.U. program, while a legitimate and significant step toward professional status, unfortunately orients many of its recipients to want to serve only a professional or business level clientele. Yet the great future market for life insurance is with the middle- to low-income segment of the population, and thus this is also where the most lucrative occupational prospects lie. Many insurance men do not aspire to selling insurance on the debit to these classes, indicating instead a desire to be an *estate consultant*. With this kind of orientation on the part of its agents, the life insurance industry will not be able to extend insurance coverage service to more and more people, especially in the low and middle income levels. Taylor and Pellegrin also suggest that another dysfunctional aspect of professionalization for the occupation involves the self-image that the life insurance man has of himself as a professional. Many newcomers to the industry apparently have a *career-professional* image of themselves and are more concerned with security and fringe benefits than with sales. The older image of the life insurance salesman was that of *rugged individualist* who desired "freedom of opportunity to make his own fortune," rather than "a guaranteed average salary." Accordingly, some members of the industry have concerns about the new image affecting the vitality of the occupation. The authors conclude that "the dynamics of professionalization involve more than agreement on a certain number of 'steps' through which an occupation must develop or which it must fulfill and then, as a matter of course, proclaim its new elevated status." In the instance of life insurance men, "the disproportionate promotion of one goal, professionalization, has precipitated a growth of dysfunctions for other occupational goals." As will be observed in subsequent chapters, the processes of work structurally relate the individual to a variety of other persons and flavor the nature of this relationship. The processes of work are in some instances dysfunctional to both the individual and the occupational system, as will also be seen.

Footnotes

[1] Edward Gross, *Work and Society* (New York: The Thomas Y. Crowell Company, 1958), pp. 130–33.

[2] Ted Simmons, "Pawnbroker Says Job Is Art (AP)," *Bowling Green* (Ky.) *Daily News*, March 26, 1970, p. 10.

[3] James H. Bryan, "Apprenticeships in Prostitution," *Social Problems*, XII, No. 3 (Winter 1965), 287–97.

⁴ The concept of "total institution" was popularized by Goffman. See especially Erving Goffman, "On the Characteristics of Total Institutions," *Asylums: Essays on the Social Situation of Mental Patients and Other Inmates* (Garden City, N.Y.: Doubleday and Company, Inc., 1961), pp. 1–124.

⁵ Dorothy E. Peven, "The Use of Religious Revival Techniques to Indoctrinate Personnel: The Home-Party Sales Organization," *The Sociological Quarterly*, IX, No. 1 (Winter 1968), 97–106.

⁶ Melford S. Weiss, "Rebirth in the Airborne," *Trans-action*, IV, No. 6 (May 1967), 23–26.

⁷ Gross, *op. cit.*, pp. 134–39.

⁸ The concept of "career" is subject to various interpretations by different writers. Some especially take exception to the suggestion that a series of different occupational statuses occupied by an individual may constitute a "career." They would perhaps choose to label such phenomena as simply "work." Many of our society's political leaders, however, can show a work history which may include many different occupational statuses, such as educator, attorney, elected official, and so forth. It would seem inappropriate to call such a succession of statuses simply "work," and from our viewpoint such a work history would just as surely constitute a "career" as that of the individual who remained and progressed in one firm, agency, or occupational specialty.

Occupational Selection and Recruitment

Occupational Choice

A Conceptual Framework

PETER M. BLAU
Columbia University
JOHN W. GUSTAD
Kansas State College at Fort Hays
RICHARD JESSOR
University of Colorado
HERBERT S. PARNES
RICHARD C. WILCOCK

Why do people enter different occupations? The problem of explaining this can be approached from various perspectives. One may investigate, for example, the psychological characteristics of individuals and the processes of motivation that govern their vocational choices and, for this purpose, consider the social and economic structure as given conditions which merely impose limits within which these psychological processes operate. It is also possible to examine the ways in which changes in the wage structure and other economic factors channel the flow of the labor force into different occupations, in which case the psychological motives through which these socioeconomic forces become effective are usually treated as given. Still another approach would focus upon the stratified social structure, rather than upon either the psychological makeup of individuals or the organization of the economy, and would analyze the effects of parental social status upon the occupational opportunities of children. Each of these perspectives, by the very nature of the discipline from which it derives, excludes from consideration some important variables which may affect occupational choice and selection. For this reason, representatives from the three disciplines—psychology, economics, and sociology—have collaborated in the development of a more inclusive conceptual framework, which is presented in this paper.[1]

Reprinted by permission of the authors and publisher from the *Industrial and Labor Relations Review*, Vol. 9, No. 4 (July 1956). Copyright © 1956 by Cornell University. All rights reserved.

Conceptual Scheme

It should be stressed that we are proposing a conceptual framework, not a theory of occupational choice and selection. A scientific theory must, in our opinion, be derived from systematic empirical research. To be sure, many empirical studies have been carried out in this area, and a variety of antecedents have been found to be associated with occupational position, such as intelligence,[2] interests,[3] and job-market conditions,[4] to name but a few. The identification of isolated determinants, however, cannot explain occupational choice; indeed, it may be highly misleading. While it is true that Negroes are less likely to become surgeons than whites, this finding does not mean what it seems to imply (namely, that race determines the capacity to develop surgical skills). To understand this correlation, it is necessary to examine the intervening processes through which skin color affects occupational position, notably the patterns of discrimination in our society and their implications for personality development. In general, theory is concerned with the order among various determinants, that is, the interconnections between direct and more remote ones. The function of a conceptual scheme of occupational choice and selection is to call attention to different kinds of antecedent factors, the exact relationships between which have to be determined by empirical research before a systematic theory can be developed.[5]

Occupational choice is a developmental process that extends over many years, as several students of the subject have pointed out.[6] There is no single time at which young people decide upon one out of all possible careers, but there are many crossroads at which their lives take decisive turns which narrow the range of future alternatives and thus influence the ultimate choice of an occupation. Throughout, social experiences—interactions with other people—are an essential part of the individual's development. The occupational preferences that finally crystallize do not, however, directly determine occupational entry.[7] Whether they can be realized, or must be modified or even set aside, depends on the decisions of the selectors, that is, all persons whose actions affect the candidate's chances of obtaining a position at any stage of the selection process (which includes, for instance, acceptance in a teachers college as well as employment as a teacher). Of course, the candidate's qualifications and other characteristics influence the decisions of selectors, but so do other factors which are beyond his control and which may even be unknown to him, such as economic conditions and employment policies. Hence, the process of selection, as well as the process of choice, must be taken into account in order to explain why people end up in different occupations. Moreover, clarification of the selection process requires analysis of historical changes in the social and economic conditions of selection, just as study of the choice process involves analysis of personality developments.

The social structure—the more or less institutionalized patterns of activities, interactions, and ideas among various groups—has a dual significance for occupational choice. On the one hand, it influences the personality development of the choosers; on the other, it defines the socioeconomic conditions in which selection takes place. These two effects, however, do not occur simultaneously. At any choice point in their careers, the interests and skills in terms of which individuals make their decisions have been affected by the past social structure, whereas occupational opportunities and requirements for entry are determined by the present structure. The values that orient a person's efforts and aspirations may have developed in a period of prosperity, but he has to find a way to make a living in a depression.

This twofold effect of the social structure is schematically presented in Figure 1. The left side suggests that the molding of biological potentialities by the differentiated social structure (Box 3) results in diverse characteristics of individuals (Box 2), some of which directly determine occupational choice (Box 1). At the same time, as indicated on the right side, the social structure changes (Box III), resulting in a socioeconomic organization at any point in time (Box II), some aspects of which directly determine occupational selection (Box I).[8] These two developments, separated only for analytical purposes, must be joined to explain entry into occupations. The explication of the schema may well start with the process of entry, presented at the top of the chart.[9]

Processes of Choice and Selection

A choice between various possible courses of action can be conceptualized as motivated by two interrelated sets of factors: the individual's valuation of the rewards offered by different alternatives and his appraisal of his chances of being able to realize each of the alternatives.[10]

These valuations and appraisals of chances are acquired through and modified by social experience, and both are conceived to be roughly ordered in hierarchical fashion for each person—a hierarchy of preferences (valuations) and a hierarchy of expectancies (appraisals). The course of action upon which an individual decides will reflect a compromise between his preferences and his expectations (an attempt to maximize expected value). Thus, his actual choice will probably not be identical with his first preference if his expectation of reaching the preferred goal is very low.

Before applying this formulation to the study of occupational choice, some possible objections must be met. Katona's distinction between habitual

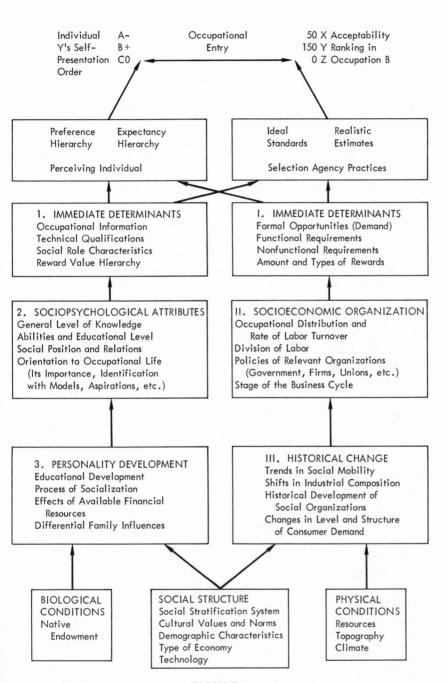

FIGURE 1

Schema of the Process of Occupational Choice and Selection

action, which is not preceded by *deliberate* decisions, and problem-solving behavior, which is governed by explicit choices,[11] raises the question whether some people do not simply drift into jobs without ever having made explicit choices between alternative occupations. Indeed, Reynolds' findings suggest that this is the case for many workers, since they do not have sufficient information about the range of alternative opportunities to make deliberate rational choices in their careers.[12] This calls attention to the importance of taking labor market information into account in the study of occupational choice, because a person can obviously choose only among the alternatives known to him. Within the limits of their information, however, potential workers do take action by seeking jobs in one occupation rather than another, and prior to any action, as Parsons and Shils have noted, "a decision must always be made (explicitly or implicitly, consciously or unconsciously)."[13]

Even if an individual has not made a deliberate occupational choice and is not aware of the factors that induced him to look for one kind of job instead of others, these factors are subject to scientific inquiry, and the conception of a compromise between values and expectations suggests one method by which such inquiry can proceed. (The utility of this conception depends on the possibility of actually obtaining empirical data on the compromise process, a research problem which is discussed below.) To be sure, if it is a matter of *complete* indifference to a worker which of several occupations he enters, we cannot analyze the choice he made between them, but neither could he possibly have made such a choice. To the extent to which complete indifference prevails, it can only be the selection process (or fortuitous circumstances) which accounts for workers being in one occupation rather than another.

In sum, occupational choice is restricted by lack of knowledge about existing opportunities; it does not necessarily involve conscious deliberation and weighing of alternatives; and in the polar case of complete indifference, no choice between occupations does in fact take place. Variations in knowledge, in rationality, and in discrimination between alternatives constitute, therefore, the limiting conditions within which individuals choose occupations by arriving at a compromise between their preferences and expectancies. This compromise is continually modified up to the time of actual entry, since each experience in the labor market affects the individual's expectations, and recurrent experiences may also affect his preferences.

Let us examine, as a simplified illustration of this compromise process, a graduate of the Fashion Institute whose training as a designer included learning the various skills needed for making dresses. His first preference would be to become a fashion designer, but his expectation of getting a job in this most desirable occupation in the garment industry is so low that he does not even apply for one. The first occupational position for which he presents himself as a candidate is that of sample maker, which ranks lower on his preference hierarchy but where his expectation of success is somewhat greater. Unable to get such a position (A on top of the chart), he tries to find work as a finisher, another skilled trade that may lead to a career as a designer. Since he obtains employment as a finisher (B), what position he would have looked for next (C) is irrelevant; indeed, this third alternative may not have crystallized in his own mind.

This account of why an individual chooses a given occupation must be supplemented by an explanation of why he is selected for it. Let us assume that the employment practices in the industry have the result, whether achieved by deliberate effort or inadvertently, that persons with certain characteristics, including considerable practical experience, have the greatest chance of being hired as finishers. Since only fifty candidates of this type present themselves for two hundred openings (X), employers also accept 150 applicants whom they consider not quite as suitable for the job, such as individuals with more than adequate training but without experience (Y). Having found a sufficient number of workers, employers are not forced to lower their requirements further and hire persons who are not properly trained (Z). There is probably a floor below which employers would not be willing to drop their requirements. The closer the qualifications of applicants approach this floor, the greater is the likelihood that employers will redefine the entry situation by increasing rewards in order to attract better qualified workers.

Occupational choice, then, can be conceptualized as a process involving a series of decisions to present oneself to employers or other selectors as a candidate for a number of more or less related occupations. Each decision is governed by the way in which the individual compromises his ideal preference and his actual expectations of being able to enter a given occupation, the latter being conditioned by previous rejections and other experiences. Occupational selection, on the other hand, consists of successive decisions of employers (or other selectors) about applicants for jobs. The decision concerning each candidate is guided by the employer's ideal standards and by his estimate of the chances that a better qualified candidate than the one under consideration will present himself in the near future. The process of occupational selection involves a regression from ideal standards (or an increase of rewards), the limits of which are defined by the occupational choices of potential workers. Correspondingly, the process of occupational choice involves a descent in a hierarchy of preferences (or the acquisition of new qualifications), which comes to an end, at least temporarily, by being selected for an occupation.

Determinants of Occupational Entry

Eight factors, four pertaining to occupations (Box I) and four characterizing individuals (Box 1), determine occupational entry. First, the demand for new members in an occupation is indicated by the number of vacancies that exist at any one time, which can be more easily ascertained, of course, for the employed than for the self-employed. The size of the occupational group, its tendency to expand, and its turnover rate will influence the demand for new members. The second factor, functional requirements, refers to the technical qualifications needed for optimum performance of occupational tasks. The third one, nonfunctional requirements, refers to those criteria affecting selection that are not relevant to actual performance, such as veteran status, good looks, or the "proper" religion. Fourth, rewards include not only income, prestige, and power, but also opportunities for advancement, congenial fellow workers, emotional gratifications, and indeed, all employment conditions that are defined as desirable.

Turning now from the attributes of occupations to those of potential workers, a fifth factor that influences occupational entry is the information people have about an occupation—their knowledge about the requirements for entry, the rewards offered, and the opportunities for employment and advancement. Two characteristics of individuals are complementary to the two types of occupational requirements, namely, their technical skills to perform various occupational duties and their other social characteristics that influence hiring decisions, such as a Harvard accent or skin color.[14] Finally, people's value orientations determine the relative significance of different kinds of rewards and thus the attractive force exerted by them.[15]

To be sure, many other characteristics of individuals influence their careers—their level of knowledge, ability, and education, their social position and relationships, and their orientation toward occupational life, to cite only the most general ones (Box 2). It may be hypothesized, however, that the effects of all other factors can be traced through the immediate determinants of occupational entry. In other words, unless a social experience or attribute affects the information individuals have about occupations, their technical or social qualifications for entry, or their evaluation of occupations, it is not expected to influence their careers. Similarly, whereas many aspects of the socioeconomic organization (exemplified in Box II) must be examined to explain the four characteristics of occupations outlined in Box I, it is these four (plus the four directly relevant characteristics of individuals) that directly account for occupational entry, according to the hypothesis advanced here.

Problems for Research

It is evident that the significance of such a conceptual scheme depends entirely on whether the empty categories it supplies can be "filled" through empirical research and, if so, whether theoretical propositions that explain occupational choice and selection can be derived from the data. The conceptual framework merely suggests the variables to be taken into account, but the crucial theoretical question concerning the relative influence of these various determinants of occupational entry cannot be answered by conceptual analysis but only on the basis of empirical research. The type of research needed for this purpose may be briefly illustrated.

As a starting point, one could select a town in which most of the labor force is employed by a few large companies. Interviews with a sample of high-school students would be designed to determine the four factors in Box 1; that is, the information they have about working conditions and opportunities in different occupations, their occupational skills and qualifications, their other social characteristics that may influence employment chances, and the value they place upon different kinds of rewards. Since reward is defined as an employment condition that contributes to satisfaction, an important function of the interview would be to identify the various conditions that constitute rewards for different individuals. Three of the four items called for in Box I could be obtained from personnel officers in the various companies: the number and types of vacancies to be filled, the qualifications required to fill each type, and the rewards offered by each position (including under rewards again all working conditions that may contribute to satisfaction). The remaining factor, nonfunctional requirements, would be determined in a follow-up interview with the student respondents after they entered the labor market. By comparing applicants who were rejected with those who were accepted for a given position, it would be possible to discern the social characteristics that do, in fact, govern hiring practices, whether the selectors are aware of it or not. The occupational positions of the respondents, also ascertained in the follow-up survey, would constitute the criterion for constructing a theoretical model that makes it possible to predict occupational entry on the basis of a knowledge of the eight determinants. To validate this model, the predictions made with it in *other* studies *prior* to obtaining data on occupational entry would have to be confirmed by these data.[16]

The research outlined does not take into account the social and psychological processes through which the determinants affect occupational entry. An empirical investigation of the process of choice as here conceptualized would have to inquire, first, whether individuals actually rank occupations in a hierarchy of preferences and a hierarchy of expectancies, and, second, what the nature of these hierarchies is. One method for doing this is to administer questionnaires employing paired comparisons of occupations to young people prior to entry into the labor market. The instructions, which would be designed to control one of the two variables while measuring the other, might read, respectively: "If you had an opportunity to get either of these two kinds of jobs, which one would you prefer?" and "Without considering which job you like better, which one of these two would you have the best chance of getting?" Respondents would be permitted to state that they are indifferent to the two alternatives.

Answers to such questions raise problems of validity as well as reliability. Repeating the same procedure after a month or so could furnish a check on its reliability, that is, on whether the answers are meaningful or sheer guesswork. Validation would consist of determining whether the data on preference and expectancies, properly weighted, make it possible to predict the occupational positions for which respondents later actually present themselves as candidates. If this is not possible, improved instruments for measuring preferences and expectancies might be devised. For example, short descriptions of different kinds of work could be substituted for occupational labels, which often have little meaning, particularly for less educated respondents. As a matter of fact, a comparative analysis of the rankings obtained by using occupational labels and different descriptive statements would itself help to clarify the character of preferences and expectancies.

Of course, not all people end up in the first occupation for which they present themselves. Many are not accepted; others quit or are fired after a brief trial period.[17] The individual's second choice, however, is not likely to be governed by the same preferences and expectancies as his first one, since his experiences in the labor market, and possibly elsewhere, have probably given rise to changes in his expectations and even his preferences.

These socially induced changes in the two hierarchies constitute the core of the compromise process.[18] To study this process, repeated intensive interviews with entrants into the labor market would have to discern how modifications in occupational expectations and values are produced by various social experiences, such as inability to get a job, expulsion from professional or vocational school, being repelled by unanticipated aspects of the work, and many others. Also of interest would be an analysis of the contingency factors that influence the compromise process. For instance, what is the significance of differences in the tenacity with which an individual adheres to his first choice despite continuing inability to realize it? What difference does it make whether initial expectations are more or less realistic, as indicated by a comparison between an individual's expectations and the actual occupational chances of persons with his qualifications and social characteristics?

Inasmuch as the compromise process is conceived as an intervening variable between various determinants and occupational entry, its relationships to these antecedents raise a host of additional problems for research. What are, for example, the effects of differences in knowledge of employment and working conditions on preferences and expectancies? How does the importance his career assumes in the thinking of an individual influence the compromise process? What differences are there between socioeconomic classes with respect to evaluation of various rewards, preferential ranking of occupations, and discrimination made in these rankings? Do members of the working class generally discriminate less in their occupational preferences, or do they make finer discriminations than middle-class people between different working-class occupations? What is the relative significance of income and education in producing these differences between socioeconomic classes? How is the process of occupational choice affected by other social characteristics, such as ethnic background, rural-urban residence, religious affiliation, and frequency of church attendance?

Empirical investigation of the processes of occupational selection is, perhaps, even more complicated than that of choice processes. At this point, a few illustrations to indicate the range of research problems in this area must suffice. How are selection practices changed in response to a shortage of skilled workers? Specifically, under what conditions does such a shortage result not in increased rewards, but in a reorganization of the production process that makes it possible to employ workers with lesser qualifications? (The answer to this question has far-reaching implications for economic theory as well as for social welfare.) If nonfunctional barriers to occupational entry (such as sex, age, or skin color) are withdrawn during a temporary labor shortage, what determines whether these nonfunctional requirements are reintroduced once the labor shortage subsides? Are the differences in nonfunctional requirements between occupations greater than those between employers within each occupation? (Only if analysis of variance gives an affirmative answer to this question is it permissible to speak of differences in nonfunctional requirements between occupations.)

Research might also test the hypothesis that the greater the rewards offered by an occupation, the more pronounced are the barriers to entry that are unrelated to technical qualifications. Cases of persisting shortages in essential occupations, such as nursing and teaching, could be investigated to determine the political and social factors that prevent the so-called law of supply and demand from increasing rewards sufficiently to overcome the shortages. The impact of bureaucratization on the selection process might be studied by comparing hiring procedures, say, for typists in the federal government, in a large private concern, and in a sample of small firms. Corresponding comparisons could be made to examine the influence of labor unions on occupational selection.

The Historical Dimension

We must now turn our attention to the developments that precede the period of occupational entry, to which only occasional references have been made so far. On the chart, the time dimension is presented as cut between the second and third boxes. The upper part indicates the social and psychological conditions of choice and selection; the lower part, the developments that produce these conditions. Thus, the family's position in the stratified social structure determines the financial resources available for preparing children for their careers. It is also reflected in the parents' value orientations, their child-rearing practices, the number of children, and the likelihood that the family is organized along authoritarian rather than egalitarian lines. These elements of family structure affect the process of socialization, in which biological potentialities are transformed into personality traits. Of course, the process of socialization is not confined to the home; associations with peers and teachers constitute other important socializing experiences for an individual, but these are not independent of the neighborhood in which his family lives, the attitudes toward people it has instilled in him, and the behavior patterns that it has cultivated and which encourage one kind of person instead of another to befriend him. With advancing specialization, the individual's educational development in school assumes increasing significance as a ladder for occupational mobility or as a barrier against it.[19] The internal conditions that govern occupational entry are the result of these different processes of personality development (Box 3), and the external conditions that govern entry have their roots in historical changes in the social structure (Box III).[20]

It is an oversimplification, however, to conceive of occupational choice and selection as occurring at one point in time, even if this is defined as a limited time interval rather than an instant, and even if the effects of earlier developments are taken into consideration. To think of the transition from graduation from medical school to the establishment of a medical practice as the time of occupational choice, and of entry into medical school as merely one of the factors that influenced it, is hardly realistic; but to treat entry into medical school as the point of choice is not a satisfactory procedure either, since not all students become physicians. A series of successive choice periods must be systematically analyzed to show how earlier decisions limit or extend the range of future choices.

This requires the repeated application of the conceptual scheme at crucial stages in the individual's development. Thus, choice of high-school curriculum could be investigated (see Box I) by examining the information pupils have about each curriculum and its vocational significance, their grades, their role characteristics and relationships with other pupils and teachers in different programs, their value orientation toward education and occupational life, and the social experiences that gave rise to these characteristics, as well as the direct influence parents exerted on choice of curriculum. Of equal relevance would be (see Box I) an analysis of the existing opportunities for entering various high-school programs, the grades needed for acceptance, the other criteria that govern selection, the rewards offered by different programs (including parental resources or scholarships that permit a pupil to anticipate going to college), and the historical trends that produced these conditions in the educational system.[21] Once the curriculum has been decided upon, the consequent diverse experiences at high school become part of the developments of individuals that affect the immediate determinants of subsequent choices.

The study of the process of occupational entry itself often involves more than one application of the schema. An individual who is not accepted in the first occupation for which he presents himself may have to retrace his steps before he can choose another, by reorienting his thinking or acquiring new skills. Hence, a new choice situation, influenced by the earlier rejection and the actions it stimulated, must be investigated the next time he presents himself as a candidate for an occupation. Indeed, there is no reason to discontinue the analysis with the first full-time job. The schema can be applied again to explain how shifts to new occupations result from the modifications of immediate determinants produced by the experiences during previous employment and the contemporaneous changes in social conditions.[22] The comparison of choice patterns at successive stages in the life history of individuals will indicate the way in which the relative significance of each determinant changes, and the contrast of patterns under varying socioeconomic conditions will suggest how such conditions affect the relative significance of the determinants. Technical qualifications, for example, may be of decisive importance at one stage or under certain conditions, but relatively unimportant at another stage or under different conditions.[23]

The study of historical trends in occupational selection also involves analysis of the processes through which the patterns of selection at an earlier period influence those at a later one. For example, interviews with high-school teachers and students could be designed to determine how differences in personality and conduct between natural science and social science instructors—differences which are expressions of earlier selection processes—affect occupational selection in the next generation by attracting different types of youngsters to work in the two fields. Another project might be concerned with the effects that the contrasting social characteristics of the members of various occupations have upon the public image of these occupations and with the implications of differences in public image for occupational entry. A related question is that of the significance of upward mobility into an occupation for subsequent selection. If two professions are compared, one with many members who originated in lower socioeconomic strata and one with only few such members, is there any distinction between the criteria that govern the selection of future colleagues in the two groups? (A parallel problem is posed by the impact of upward mobility on occupational *choice*, which could be examined by contrasting the occupational choices of children whose fathers, although holding similar occupational positions now, had different socioeconomic origins.) As a final illustration of research in this area, a hypothesis may be suggested for investigation: the influence of parental social class on occupational selection is partly due to the fact that the common interests of individuals reared in the same social class affect their chances of being accepted in an occupational group.[24] Interviews with students in professional schools, repeated at successive stages in their training, could furnish data to test this hypothesis. Confirming evidence would consist of finding that there is a relationship between parental social class and failure to complete professional training, but that this relationship disappears if either degree of acceptance by fellow students or extent of common interests with them is controlled.

Summary and Conclusion

The main points of this paper can be briefly outlined:

1. The conceptual scheme presented is not a substitute for a theory of occupational choice and selection, but merely a framework for systematic research which, in due course, will provide the material needed for constructing such a theory.

2. The social structure affects occupational choice in two analytically distinct respects: as the matrix of social experiences which channel the personality development of potential workers, and as the conditions of occupational opportunity which limit the realization of their choices.

3. Although four characteristics of individuals and four of occupations have been specified as determinants of occupational entry, the two crucial questions are: what developments in the lives of potential workers and in the history of the socioeconomic organiza-

tion determine these characteristics, and what are the processes of choice and selection through which they affect occupational entry?

4. Occupational choice is conceived as a process of compromise between preferences for and expectations of being able to get into various occupations. This compromise is continually modified, since the experiences of individuals in the course of searching for suitable careers affect their expectations and often also their preferences.

5. Lest the complicated and extended developmental process that culminates in occupational choice be oversimplified, it is necessary to consider it as a series of interrelated decisions rather than as a single choice. The repeated application of the suggested framework for analysis at crucial turning points in the lives of individuals makes it possible to trace this development and to show how earlier decisions, by narrowing the range of future possibilities, influence the final choices of occupations.

6. The analysis of the processes by which individuals choose one occupation in preference to others must be complemented by an analysis of the processes by which some individuals, and not others, are selected for a certain occupation. To be sure, it is legitimate scientific procedure to treat the actions of selectors as given conditions in the investigation of occupational choice, and it is equally legitimate to treat the actions of choosers as given conditions in the investigation of occupational selection, but only the combination of both procedures makes it possible to explain why people end up in different occupations.

Although this article is concerned with the determinants of occupational entry, not its consequences, the distinction between the latter and the former breaks down once historical developments are taken into account, since the consequences of earlier occupational choices and selections become determinants of later ones. A labor shortage may result in changes in the wage structure or in technological reorganizations that permit the employment of less skilled workers—new conditions which help determine future occupational entry. When it becomes generally known that dissatisfaction with their career is less prevalent among the members of one occupation than of another, these psychological consequences of occupational entry become one of the rewards the anticipation of which influences the occupational choices of the next generation. Whether a person experiences upward mobility or finds his aspirations frustrated in his career will also find expression in the orientation toward occupational life that he transmits to his children and thus in their occupational choices. At these points where consequences turn into determinants, the study of occupational choice and selection merges into the economic study of labor markets, the psychological study of personality adjustment, and the sociological study of social mobility.

Footnotes

1 We gratefully acknowledge the assistance of the Social Science Research Council, which sponsored the interuniversity summer research seminar (1954) that provided the opportunity for our collaboration. Although one member of this seminar, Leonard Reissman, has not joined the rest of us in the authorship of this article, we are indebted to him for his help in formulating many of the ideas in it.

2 Naomi Stewart, "A.G.C.T. Scores of Army Personnel Grouped by Occupation," *Occupations*, Vol. 26, 1947, pp. 5–41; Carroll D. Clark and Noel P. Gist, "Intelligence as a Factor in Occupational Choice," *American Sociological Review*, Vol. 3, 1938, pp. 683–694.

3 Edward K. Strong, "Predictive Value of the Vocational Interest Test," *Journal of Educational Psychology*, Vol. 26, 1935, pp. 331–349.

4 Donald E. Super and R. Wright, "From School of Work in the Depression Years," *School Review*, Vol. 49, 1940, pp. 123–130.

5 For a discussion of the distinction between conceptual scheme and systematic theory, see Robert K. Merton, *Social Theory and Social Structure* (Glencoe: Free Press, 1949), pp. 83–96.

6 See especially Eli Ginzberg, *et al.*, *Occupational Choice* (New York: Columbia University Press, 1951); and Donald E. Super, "A Theory of Vocational Development," *American Psychologist*, Vol. 8, 1953, pp. 185–190.

7 Several studies have shown that occupational preferences are "unrealistic," that is, fewer students become professionals than had aspired to do so; for instance, Earl D. Sisson, "Vocational Choices of College Students," *School and Society*, Vol. 46, 1937, pp. 763–768. This disproportionate attractiveness of some occupations is, of course, the expected result of the fact that they offer much higher rewards than others. Occupational expectations, on the other hand, are much more realistic than aspirations; see, for example, E. S. Jones, "Relation of Ability to Preferred and Probable Occupation," *Educational Administration and Supervision*, Vol. 26, 1940, pp. 220–226.

8 The lists of factors in the second and third boxes are illustrative rather than exhaustive.

9 The oversimplification involved in treating occupational entry as occurring at a single point in time will be dealt with presently.

10 This conceptualization constitutes a point of convergence between recent economic and psychological formulations concerning the conduct of individuals in choice situations that involve some risk. See Samuel P. Hayes, "Some Psychological Problems of Economics," *Psychological Bulletin*, Vol. 47, 1950, pp. 289–330; John von Neumann and Oskar Morgenstern, *Theory of Games and Economic Behavior* (Princeton: Princeton University Press, 1944); Kurt Lewin, *et al.*, "Level of Aspiration," in J. McV. Hunt, *Personality and the Behavior Disorders* (New York: Ronald Press, 1944); Julian B. Rotter, *Social Learning and Clinical Psychology* (Englewood Cliffs, N.J.: Prentice Hall, 1954); and Egon Brunswik, *The Conceptual Framework of Psychology* (Chicago: University of Chicago Press, 1952).

11 George Katona, "Rational Behavior and Economic Behavior," *Psychological Review*, Vol. 60, 1953, pp. 307–318.

12 Lloyd G. Reynolds, *The Structure of Labor Markets* (New York: Harper & Brothers, 1951).

13 Talcott Parsons and Edward A. Shils, eds., *Toward a General Theory of Action* (Cambridge: Harvard University Press, 1951), p. 89.

14 Discrimination and nepotism illustrate how the relationship between nonfunctional requirements and role characteristics—being a Jew or a nephew, respectively—influences chances of entry.

[15] Indeed, these values determine which employment conditions constitute rewards; for instance, whether working in a group is more rewarding than working alone.

[16] To demonstrate that the model contains all immediate determinants of occupational entry, it would be necessary to show that the correlation between occupational position and any other antecedent factor (not included in the model) disappears if the variables included in the model are controlled.

[17] In any research on occupational choice, it has to be decided how long an individual must have remained in an occupation before he is considered to have entered it rather than merely to have tried it out or to have been tried out for it in the process of choice and selection. Various studies have shown that first jobs are not indicative of future careers. See, for example, Reynolds, op. cit., pp. 113–114, 127–133; and Gladys L. Palmer, *Labor Mobility in Six Cities* (New York: Social Science Research Council, 1954), pp. 135–136.

[18] Super, loc. cit., p. 187, emphasizes the importance of investigating the compromise process and criticizes Ginzberg, et al., op. cit., for failing to do so. We are here suggesting some conceptual tools with which the empirical investigation of the compromise process could be carried out.

[19] The growing significance of specialized formal education first reduces the family's influence on careers but later enhances it again. At an early stage, it means that the school has become the substitute for parents as the provider of vocational skills. Once this is an accomplished fact, further specialization in the educational system has the consequence that educational decisions made before the child can act independently have crucial implications for his subsequent occupational life.

[20] Changes in the social structure also affect the course of personality development, as previously mentioned, and basic historical change, in turn, may well be contingent on the emergence of new personality patterns. See on this point Erich Fromm, *Escape from Freedom* (New York: Farrar and Rinehart, 1941).

[21] For two studies of the significance of social class for the selection process in high school, see A. B. Hollingshead, *Elmtown's Youth* (New York: Wiley, 1949), and W. Lloyd Warner, et al., *Who Shall Be Educated?* (New York: Harper & Brothers, 1944).

[22] The experience can be "negative," such as the absence of expected promotions.

[23] In addition, variations in the relative significance of determinants exist among occupational groups. Thus, technical qualifications are not equally important for entry into all occupations, and discrimination against ethnic minorities is more prevalent in some than in others.

[24] On the relationship between occupational entry and having interests in common with the successful members of an occupation, see Edward K. Strong, *Vocational Interests of Men and Women* (Stanford: Stanford University Press, 1943).

Occupational Socialization
Informal

"Breaking Out"

An Apprenticeship System Among Pipeline Construction Workers

BENNIE GRAVES
Central Michigan University

This paper undertakes a description of the social relationships involved in becoming a skilled pipeline construction worker. The industry offers a convenient opportunity to study the informal and direct recruiting of workers.[1] Construction companies do not sponsor formal training programs, yet most of the skilled workers in pipelining probably were trained on the job while working as laborers. Moreover, the skills are fairly complex and in order to learn one of them, the learner must have instruction and he must have access to the equipment and materials with which to practice. The process of skill-learning, then, has been examined in terms of the trainee's status relationships to: (1) previously trained workers who can give or withhold instruction, (2) supervisors who control access to the materials and equipment for practice, and (3) inspectors who control work quality.

The Setting "Pipelining"

Most pipeline construction work is done by construction companies which are owned and operated independently of pipeline transmission companies. The transmission companies usually award contracts to the lowest bidding construction companies.

The "spread," which consists of an organization of enough men and equipment to build a single pipeline, is the pipeline work plant. It is divided into eight or ten gangs, organized around general tasks in construction.

Reprinted from *Human Organization*, Vol. 17, No. 3 (Fall 1958), 9–13, by permission of the author and the Society for Applied Anthropology.

Each gang, directed by a foreman, usually contains a combination of unskilled, semi-skilled, and skilled workers. A "spread man" coordinates and directs the work of all the gangs.[2]

Transmission company inspectors enforce their companies' policies and work quality requirements on the operating spread. In order to do this, they may require that certain technical procedures be followed and that some tasks be recompleted. They sometimes direct work in much the same way as do contracting company foremen. Most important for this discussion, however, they often pass on the hiring of workers, and they have the power to fire any worker whom they believe to be doing faulty work.

Only about one-half of the workers on any job are in-group "pipeliners." The remaining workers are "common hands" who are recruited from towns near a particular job. A few common hands remain in the occupation and eventually become "professional pipeliners," but most of them simply ricochet off the line. In-group workers are recruited for each new job by way of an informal grapevine which extends at least throughout the Southwest. Workers may be hired through phone calls or letters between themselves and friends or relatives at the job location or through direct phone calls to contractors, spreadmen, or foremen. *The Pipeliner*, a trade magazine, publishes information on jobs in progress and on proposed jobs. Included are the names of spreadmen and foremen. Most of the named supervisors are fairly well known in the industry and have different reputations. "*Who* has the dope?" (who is the dope foreman) or "*who* has the pipe?" (pipe gang foreman) etc., and "*who* all are going up there?" are important questions for in-group pipeliners when they seek jobs.

Cliques of families and individuals often travel together from job to job. In this way, the groups remain fairly cohesive in spite of the frequent moves which must be made. This is fortunate for the pipeline apprentice because he is very dependent upon such primary groups throughout most of his training. The group usually contains his main instructor and it keeps him informed about new jobs and jobs in which he may practice his goal skill. In addition, friendship-kinship group members often supplement his salary by furnishing him with food, lodging, and money for other expenses. Even with his advantages, the trainee, like other workers, often is unemployed. Consequently his laborers' salary alone is not always enough to meet his expenses.

The pipeline skill aspirant may learn a trade in one of four generally recognized skill categories. These are, in the descending order of their relative status among the workers: welder, heavy equipment operator, pipe processing machine operator, and truck driver. He may acquire the necessary training in trade schools (welders only), in other industries, or by "breaking out on the line" while working as a laborer.

Most skilled workers probably are trained on the line while working as laborers. Trade school welders are not favored and, in spite of the fact that most of the pipeline skills are found extensively in other industries, entry of outside trained workers is restricted by pipeliners' unfavorable attitudes toward them, attitudes which probably are reinforced by outside trained workers' initial ignorance of pipeline routines. Outsiders are seen as inferior in skill and as workers who will not live up to their obligations to contractors and the transmission companies. "Not only is their work bad, but they don't give a damn."[3] An observer can hear a number of statements such as "I never saw a trade school (or shop) welder who was worth a damn." "The only time I've ever worked a trade school welder was when I was in union territory." "They know everything, you can't tell them nothing; send them to the dope gang to weld a piece of equipment, they can't find it; you got to show them. They don't know a dope pot from a granny rag.[4] And besides it's not just knowing how to weld, you got to know the pipeline."

An incident which occurred between two unemployed tractor operators demonstrates some of the attitudes held by in-group pipeliners which help to restrict jobs to those workers trained on the line. The two workers were sitting around talking and drinking whiskey in an apartment house living room. Although getting off the subject occasionally, the conversation remained generally on pipelines and pipeliners. One of the men, becoming expansive, stood up and said in a loud voice, "If I don't get a job pretty soon, I ain't gonna' remember how to pull them levers (steering devices on a tractor)—better get a little practice." He then got two chairs, set them side by side in front of another chair, sat in the third chair, and began to operate the imaginary tractor. He furnished sound effects and mock exertions. In a little while, another unemployed worker, affecting what was taken for the walk and speech of a farmer, walked up to the "tractor operator" and asked: "You reckon a feller could get a job on this here pipeline?"

"Had any experience?" asked the operator.

"Shore have," answered the farmer. "I reckon I've drove them Farmalls a thousand miles."

"How many levers them Farmalls got?" asked the operator.

"Bout as many as this here Caterpillar," replied the farmer.

"Well," said the operator, "you can go to work but you'll have to get used to these levers; the first one will be a 'idiot stick' (long-handled spade) and then sort of work up to these here on a tractor."

Breaking Out

Upon first examination, pipeline skill-learning appears to be loose and unorganized because unskilled workers seem to pick up skill techniques just here and there. Pipeliners themselves tend to see the acquisition of skill as a cumulative experience on the pipeline plus the help of skilled workers. This seems essentially to be true but getting a trade is selective rather than random, and it is made to conform to workers' beliefs about what it takes to be a pipeline welder or an operator.

The social relationships involved in pipeline skill-learning may be described as a series of changing status-role relationships between the trainee and the people who help him to break out: skilled workers, supervisors, and inspectors. The process seems to consist of at least three distinct stages. First, and with few exceptions, the trainee must be a kinsman or a friend of some pipeliner who can either train him or of someone who can arrange to have him trained. Next, he goes through a period of training and practice in which he is a laborer officially, but in which he has special privileges and duties other laborers do not have. During this time, he is recognized as a "bronc breaking out"[5] and other workers are obligated to help him whenever they can. He is among the last of the laborers to be laid off during the progress of the job, and he is hired over other laborers on new jobs. The third, and most critical, stage is that in which he must make a transition from dependency to competitive relationships with bosses and other workers.

The First Stage

There is little need to distinguish a first stage if the trainee is kin to the person who helps him most. If, however, he is not kin to someone who can help him, he must establish a training-strategic friendship with some pipeliner or become a member in a pipeliner clique. Of course, all such friendships are not made by skill aspirants; nevertheless, it is acceptable on the pipeline to "get next to somebody who can break you out." Because some unskilled workers seem deliberately to establish friendships in order to break out, this may be considered as a first stage in some workers' training.

If the way in which a skill aspirant goes about getting next to someone is conspicuous, he may be seen in one of two ways by in-group workers. He may "grape up" to a skilled worker. This is conspicuous, but not censured. He may "suck up" to a boss, in which case he is a "brown nose." This is censured and the subject is exposed to frequent and colorful innuendoes concerning his relationship to his benefactor. He is able to learn a skill but his progress depends largely upon a single in-group pipeliner.

The opportunities for establishing training-strategic friendships may be found both during and after the work day. Recreation places and restaurants are convenient locations for friendships to be established. Local hands often help the unmarried pipeliners to find dates in towns near the job. A local hand's instrumental value as a go-between may turn into a friendship which may later permit him to learn a skill.

⁻ The work day affords opportunities to establish friendships through "horseplay." A worker may get himself typed as a "smart aleck" or a "pretty good old boy" depending upon the way he enters into horseplay. Horseplay on the line consists of hitting, wrestling, clod throwing, name calling, tightening vises with long "cheater pipes," and urinating on welding rods (dried urea is invisible on the rods and it produces a strong and startling odor when the welder fires up). Horseplay is permitted on the line if it does not interfere with work. Consequently, much of it is not formally controlled, but the informal control of horseplay approximates something like the "pecking order" found among chickens.[6] It is often carried on between status unequals, but the low status person does not initiate it. There are long-standing friendly feuds among workers but the time and place for acting these out are chosen by the upper status workers when status discrepancies are broad, as in a feud between a laborer and an operator.

The time and place control of non-technical behavior by upper status workers sometimes extends to conventionalized greetings as in the following example: During a lull in the work, a fairly new laborer walked up to a truck in which a welder and the observer were sitting. He asked the welder: "Who is the bird with you, is he worth a damn for anything?" (A common innocuous remark on the line.) The welder neither answered nor looked at the worker! The worker stood with his foot on the truck's running board for a few minutes and then walked away. During the next few days that he worked on the spread, the laborer made several other attempts to enter into the horseplay and banter of the in-group workers. It is doubtful whether he was rebuffed so completely as he was by the welder, but within a few days he "drug up (quit) for no reason and borrowed money to get home on."

A foreman, commenting on the worker, said: "I've seen that kind before; they get out on the line and want to fool around. Who the hell does he think he is?" The fooling around that the worker tried to do was apparently no more than the horseplay that in-group workers carry on, but he was labeled an "overbearing smart aleck" because "common hands don't act like they owned the pipeline." Out-group workers are pulled in; they don't push in.

The extent and manner in which an unskilled worker enters into horseplay is perhaps more of an index to his standing than it is a means to achieve status, but decorous participation may enhance his chances of getting next to a strategic person. For the most part, this means that he must wait for time and place cues, and be a cheerful target for practical jokes.

There are at least two other types of work situations in which an unskilled worker may become a friend of some pipeliner who can help him break out. Probably the most common is that in which a skilled worker trains his helper. This seems especially to be true of welders. Physical stress situations, such as river crossings, also give some outsiders an opportunity to become in-group pipeliners. Once started, many crossings must be completed before the workers quit work for the day. Consequently, they often spend many continuous hours on a crossing with only the sleep afforded by thirty or forty minute naps taken in pickup trucks, on tractor and dope pot tracks, and on the damp river sand. There is an apt saying among pipeliners that a river crossing "separates the men from the boys." Many unskilled workers are free to "go to the house" (quit for the day) during a crossing and those who remain on the job for continuous periods of up to 80 hours gain some prestige. At least their names become known to other pipeliners. Workers may even be recognized as in-group pipeliners because "only a 'pipeliner' is that crazy about overtime."

In addition to proving their physical prowess and becoming known by being seen continuously, laborers who work on river and difficult road crossings have the advantage of a less rigid informal status system. Although formal work roles are maintained, normal work routines are changed. Social distance between bosses and workers, and between high and low status workers, is lessened perceptibly. In-group-out-group distinctions seem to disappear altogether. Workers become more and more compatible with one another as their fatigue increases. Any joke, no matter how old and often heard, produces laughter. Workers become tolerant of each others' mistakes and clumsiness. The laborer who was unable to enter into the horseplay during a regular work day probably could have done so easily during a river crossing. Group morale seems to be higher on crossings than it is in other work situations. This high spirit and cordiality may be caused in part by the overtime pay that workers get on crossings. Or it may be a reaction to the danger of "getting on each other's nerves." In either case, it seems that such physical stress situations offer important opportunities for the induction of out-group workers.

The Second Stage

Once the trainee becomes recognized as a man breaking out (the second stage) he learns by instruction and practice of the skill. If he is learning to weld, he can observe the techniques employed in that skill daily. At slack moments in the day's work, he can weld on scrap pipe and perfect his own technique. If he is learning to operate a side boom or dozer, the practice consists of operating the machine where expert work is not too important. During this stage, the trainee may receive instruction and supervised practice from several skilled workers in a single day. Indeed, under certain conditions, any skilled worker is obligated to help the trainee. For example, if an operator has a task to do in which the work need not be expert and there is a trainee present who needs the practice, the skilled operator is more or less obligated to let him do the work. In many cases, it might seem that being thus "spelled" (relieved) by a trainee gives the skilled operator an opportunity to rest, but often it is an added responsibility: ". . . it is easier to do the work yourself than to worry around with some bronc."

This seems true for all trainees except those learning to weld. Welder trainees, although they may not be trained by the kinsman or friend who helped them to get in, tend to get their training from a single welder. Whereas operator trainees enjoy fairly free access to equipment, welder trainees are more restricted as to the equipment they may use and the conditions under which they may use it. This, perhaps, is due to the fact that most pipeline welders own their own rigs whereas the tools used by other skilled workers are owned usually by the contracting company.

Occasionally, trainees are restricted to bits of technical information, doled out piecemeal. One welder sent his helper-trainee back to the welding truck several times to get a single piece of equipment. A part of the running conversation between welder and trainee during the incident was approximately as follows:

Welder: "Get me a 'round about.' "
Trainee: "What's a round about?"
Welder: "It's in the truck, get me a round about."
Welder: After trainee returns with the wrong tool. "That ain't no round about."
Trainee: "Well, I don't know what a round about is."
Welder: Walking to the truck to get the tool (a device used to mark pipe for cutting). "Boy, if you gonna' weld on the pipeline, you gonna' hafta learn what a round about is."

Perhaps such instruction helps to account for the fact that it often takes up to four years to master pipeline welding. The foregoing example is not, however, simply the result of pure malice on the part of the welder. Many such deliberate blocks to skill-learning seem to be based upon the assumption that "you oughtn't to have to show a bronc everything."

Throughout the second stage of training, the trainee's status is recognized by management largely through supervisors' implicit permission to use time, expendable materials, and equipment in practicing. It is recognized by owning company inspectors through their tolerance of substandard work.

Often the supervisors participate more actively in the bronc's training. For example, if an assignment does not interfere with other work, a skilled worker will sometimes be assigned to a special task admittedly because he is breaking out a bronc. Road crossings furnish an especially convenient setting for welder trainees. Very often a welder on a crossing will be waiting more than working, thus giving his bronc a chance to practice on scrap pipe. In addition to time, the pipe is placed inside of a protective casing which is made and fitted to the particular road. Since its main function is to keep dirt from scraping the dope from the pipe, the welding does not have to be expert, and the trainee can do much of the actual work.

Management's support is not entirely due to direct kinship or friendship ties. Most managers have attained their own position through one, or a series, of on-the-job apprenticeships. Consequently, the trainee has the advantage of the belief that such training is the only way to become adequately skilled. In addition, after the trainee has worked as a laborer for several weeks, he usually has acquired some knowledge of the routines of pipelining. As a result, he is sometimes assigned to straw boss groups of laborers on special jobs which are not handled directly by any of the standard gangs.

The inspector's interest in the bronc's achievement usually is more remote than is that of the contracting company boss. Inspectors tend to remain in one area. Consequently, they are much less likely to be kind to the trainee than are bosses. Occasionally, an inspector will arrange to have one of his kinsmen trained by a pipeline skilled worker, but the key to the inspector's participation in the apprenticeship system seems not to be in any extra job relationship between him and the trainee; rather, it comes about as a result of his necessary cooperation with contracting company managers. Superficially the interests of managers and inspectors are antagonistic. Managers want to make a profit as quickly as possible, whereas inspectors want enough time spent to maintain their companies' standards. But, in order to get the work done, the two groups of workers cooperate in many ways. For example, they must deal often with recalcitrant private property owners and public officials. Much of this cooperation is necessarily covert and informal because some of the negotiations are against transmission company policies, or they are illegal (e.g. frequent bribery). It seems that the inspectors' support of the bronc is an extension of this cooperative tendency. That is, it seems to be a situation in which the inspectors reason: "You help me out, and I'll help take care of your boy."

The Third Stage

The third stage of the trainee's progress seems to be the most critical. He works as a skilled worker whenever he can, but often he must work as a laborer. He may go from company to company trying to find skilled jobs in which more expert workers are unavailable. The trainee and the people who have helped him sometimes judge his competence differently and there is more interpersonal conflict in this stage than in the other two. This is illustrated in the following lament by a foreman who helped the subject of his comments.

> I broke that bastard out on a dozer: know what he done? Tried to get me to put him on a dozer on that B_____ job. You know yourself it takes a "operator" for a job like that. He couldn't understand that. Hell no, he's going to take a dozer and go out and conquer the world. Hasn't spoke to me since; to hell with him!

In addition to differing judgments of competence, the trainee may not understand adequately the changed role expectations which apply to him and to people who have helped him. At this stage, he is thrown into the competitive labor pool without the necessary competence and with his source of help cut off by prohibitions with respect to the "brother-in-law" hiring of skilled workers.

When nepotism extends into a skilled position, as in the following incident, there may be a lack of consensus among workers. The contractor wanted to finish a job before the end of the day. This, and an agreement with the inspectors, caused the spreadman to hire a trainee as a fully-paid welder for the part day. The inspectors agreed on condition that the bronc "set up on two." The other welders were "setting up on three." That meant that the bronc would make only two-thirds as many welds as the other welders. The inspectors' reasoning was: "If he sets up on two he may be able to do good work; just make sure you plug up his holes; you pay the salaries."

The welder with whom the observer was working at the time was unhappy at the arrangement, and the fact that he had to reweld some of the trainee's welds during the day caused him to be more dissatisfied. He admittedly tried to have the trainee fired. He criticized him at every opportunity. Each time inspectors came by the welder made statements such as: "Boy, this is the first time I ever saw a welder get by with pure murder; welding over his puddles is like trying to weld up a screen door." Each time the spreadman came by he said something like: "Boy, it must be nice, knocking down a welder's salary without doing anything."

The disgruntled welder's complaints were not entirely personal. Bosses do "get talked about" and occasionally reprimanded by superiors for hiring "phoney hands." The welder called repeatedly upon standards of competence which would have applied under slightly different circumstances. After the work day he tried to solicit support for his criticisms. The other welders agreed with him outwardly but one of them told the observer later that he couldn't see anything wrong with the bronc's working and that the critical welder "just hates to see anybody get something he don't get."

The friction which often marks the third stage of training seems due to the uncertainty arising from two sets of hiring standards in pipelining: that of trainees in terms of relationship criteria, and that of other workers in terms of production criteria. The two sets of standards are fairly well segregated throughout the first and second stages, but their distinction tends to become obscured among both workers and managers during the third. This is due perhaps to the lack of any "graduation" ritual or other very clear symbolism which might mark a transition from bronc to full skill status.

Broncs who can do skilled work, "but not too good," are sometimes advised to go to other companies and not to work for the one in which they broke out until they "get pretty good." The assumption among workers is that "you learn faster when you get out on your own." Aside from its effect upon learning-speed, leaving the primary group probably serves the important function of taking the newly trained worker out of uncertain relationships wherein "old buddies all of a sudden start throwing their weight around." Moreover, it probably relieves some supervisors of the uncertainty of their roles with respect to trainees. As long as the trainee is clearly recognized as a man-breaking-out, the supervisor can treat him in terms of *who* he is or *whose boy* (protégé) he is. But, when the trainee begins to compete with skilled workers, supervisors are expected to view him in terms of production criteria. In addition, the supervisor's confusion often is compounded by his own kinship to the trainee during the third stage of training.

Most pipeline workers probably are hired without regard to their extra-job relationships to bosses and other workers. Such hiring ranges all the way from a foreman's offhand judgment of a worker's strength to the impersonal verdict of an x-ray machine.[7] In spite of this dominant mode of hiring, however, the apprenticeship system remains nepotistic. Common-sense observation has produced the statement that "it's not *what* you know, but *who* you know"[8] that often accounts for your getting ahead; but both workers and managers recognize the threat of wholesale nepotism to contracting companies. The belief in this threat may be seen in comments about unsuccessful contractors. For example, "the woods are full of contractors who went broke because of too many phoney personnel," or too many "brothers-in-law." A spreadman told the observer how he "learned his lesson." "I run a old boy off once just so Old B_____ could have the job, I don't know why I did it; to this day, I can't look that man in the face. A boss who'll do that's got no business pushing men."

Conclusion

Rather than being as disruptive as it might seem, the apprenticeship system seems to circumvent a great deal of conflict which might otherwise result from large kinship groups working in a highly competitive industry. By absorbing much of the kinship-friendship hiring, it probably keeps incompetent workers from doing much inadequate or damaging work and it keeps them from competing "unfairly" with skilled workers. Moreover, the trainee trains when there is "not much else to do and it won't hurt." His training can be set aside at any time for "more serious business." His special privileges are given to him at such a low level that the efficiency of the spread probably is not diminished.

The apprenticeship system frees bosses from having to decide whether or not to hire workers on a kinship-friendship basis or to hire more skilled workers. In many cases, bosses may hire workers on the basis of both sets of hiring standards if kinsmen or friends can be placed in skill-learning situations. The boss is expected only "to use his head." This means that he must be able to distinguish those situations in which trainees may be dealt with in terms of relationship criteria and those in which they must be dealt with in terms of production criteria.

Footnotes

This paper is based upon the writer's experience of eleven months as a pipeline worker in two Southwestern contracting companies, and upon his contacts with pipeliners over the past seven years.

The writer is very grateful to three people for their encouragement and assistance in the project. Professor Walter Firey of the Department of Sociology, University of Texas, Professor John Walter of the Department of English, University of Texas, and Mr. Robert Pace of the Anthropology Department of the Veterans Administration Hospital, Downey, Illinois.

The writer selected the data and made the conclusions. He is solely responsible for defects in both.

1 This conception of recruiting is taken largely from Theodore Caplow, *The Sociology of Work*, The University of Minnesota Press, Minneapolis, 1954, pp. 102–106.

2 *A Primer of Pipeline Construction*, issued by the Petroleum Extension Service, The University of Texas, Austin, The Pipeline Contractors Association, Dallas, and the Texas Education Agency, Trade and Industrial Service, Austin, 1952, p. 12. This pamphlet contains a list of the work gangs and a description of their activities.

3 Datum statements quoted in the paper were recorded as accurately as memory over several hours permitted. The paper probably contains inaccuracies in wording, but working with subjects over a long period of time furnished repeated opportunities to check recorded statements. Some of the statements used are composites of more extended conversations with workers.

4 *Primer, op. cit.* This pamphlet contains a partial glossary of pipeline argot.

5 The trainee is called a bronc, a name he shares with all workers who are "green" and with the infant children of pipeliners.

6 C. Murchison, "The Experimental Measurement of a Social Hierarchy in Gallus Domesticus," *Journal of General Psychology*, XII (1935), 3–39; *Journal of*

Social Psychology, VI (1935), 3–30; *Journal of Genetic Psychology*, LVI (1935), 76–102.

[7] Transmission companies often require that welders have their specimen welds examined by x-ray and other equally searching techniques as a condition for employment.

[8] This "social logic," with only slight grammatical differences, is discussed with respect to social mobility in W. Lloyd Warner, *Democracy in Jonesville: A Study of Quality and Inequality*, Harper & Bros., New York, 1949, p. 296.

Occupational Socialization

Formal

The Naval Recruit Training Center

A Study of Role Assimilation in a
Total Institution

Louis A. Zurcher, Jr.
University of Texas

No "landlubber" civilian can go from the recruiting office directly to duty as an enlisted man aboard a vessel or installation of the United States Navy. He must first spend nine weeks, sometimes less in time of war, at a naval recruit training center. There he will undergo the now traditional "Boot" indoctrination process that will, upon his successful completion, qualify him for a place in the fleet. ("Boot" is an argot name for recruit. The term originates from the leggings, resembling boots, worn by recruits as part of their uniform. Naval recruit training centers are, therefore, called "Boot Camps.")

Every man who joins the Navy comes to it with a "presenting culture," an elaborate set of values, beliefs, roles, norms, and expectations which lead him to behave in certain ways with regard to certain perceived social stimuli. Always in peacetime, and largely in wartime, the Navy consists of volunteers. Thus, it might be expected that the individual who enlists for a tour of active duty (four years) has already begun the process toward enactment of the role of sailor. In the main, however, because he really doesn't know the expectations of the Navy, the volunteer is a civilian person, sees himself as such, and plays his roles in life accordingly.

The day-to-day conduct of a civilian, guided as it is by relative freedom of decision, cannot be tolerated in a total institution if it is to remain total. Therefore, the first and major task of the training center, or boot camp, is to "decivilianize," to role-dispossess, the entering individual.

The enlistee, while he is going through the paper-processing stage of joining the Navy, will probably not notice any radical changes from his

Originally published in *Sociological Inquiry*, Vol. 37, No. 1 (Winter 1967), 85–98. Reprinted by permission of the author and publisher.

usual civilian interpersonal and intraorganizational experiences. He will have several forms to fill out, some examinations to take, physical and mental, but the officials still call him *Mr.* Jones, and he may still decide, for example, the time and day he wishes to report for other parts of the enlistment process, and when he wishes to go on active duty.

After all the paper work has been finished, and the scheduled day for formal enlistment arrives, the individual is shown, together with several other enlistees, into a room, on one of the walls of which is a large American flag and a copy of the oath of service.

> "Before I administer the oath service to you, gentlemen, are there any of you who wish to reconsider? If so, please feel free to speak up. No? Very well, gentlemen, I will give you the oath. Raise your right hands, please, and repeat after me:
>
> "I, (name), do solemnly swear that I will bear true faith and allegiance to the United States of America, and that I will serve them faithfully and honestly against all their enemies whatsoever, and I will obey the orders of the officers appointed over me according to the rules and articles for the governing of the Navy.
>
> "Now, Boots, you belong to the Navy! Knock off the chatter and get your scrawny tails into that bus!" (Field notes)

Depersonalization has begun. The "boot," now in the charge of the physically largest member of the enlistee group, who has been given the position of leader, boards transportation which will take him to the naval recruit training center—the "Boot Camp."

Goffman has defined a total institution as a place "of residence and work where a large number of like-situated individuals, cut off from the wider society for an appreciable period of time, together lead an enclosed, formally administered round of life."[1] He describes some general characteristics of the total institution as follows:

1. All aspects of life are conducted in the same place and under the same single authority.

2. Each phase of the member's daily activity is carried on in the immediate company of a large batch of others, all of whom are treated alike and required to do the same thing together.

3. All phases of the day's activities are tightly scheduled, with one activity leading at a prearranged time into the next, the whole sequence of activities being imposed from above by a system of explicit formal rulings and a body of officials.

4. The various enforced activities are brought together into a single

rational plan purportedly designed to fulfill the official aim of the institution.

5. There is a sharp split between the supervisors and the members, with social mobility between the two groups being highly restricted.

6. Information concerning the fate of the member is often withheld from him.

7. The work structure in the total institution, geared as it is to a twenty-four hour day, demands different motives for work than exist in the society at large.

8. There are usually real or symbolic barriers indicating a break with the society "out there."[2]

In the light of these criteria, the naval recruit training center can be seen to be a total institution. All aspects of the boot's life are conducted in the same place (the center) and under a single central authority (the center commander, or, more broadly, the U.S. Navy). The recruit does *everything* in the company of others, and the expectations for his particular recruit behavior are the same for all his fellow recruits. The day's activities tick off "by the numbers," everything done at the proper time in the proper place, according to an elaborate "plan of the day," published daily and posted by order of the commanding officer. There is a single rational plan (to create sailors out of civilians) purportedly designed to fulfill the official and instrumental function of the center (to supply the fleet with manpower). The supervisors have their own quarters, mess, and recreational facilities, are allowed to leave the training center, and cannot be approached by the recruit without strict adherence to the "chain of command" and to "military courtesy." A supervisor is *anyone* who is not a recruit. The boot seldom can be certain what is in store for him from one moment to the next. He is told to fall in, to march, and finds out his destination when he gets there. The work structure is based on a twenty-four hour day of classes, drill, physical training, and watches; and the recruit reminded that he "belongs to the Navy even when sacked out."[3] Barriers separating the training center and the recruit from society at large are tangible in the form of barbed wire and armed Marine guards.

At the beginning of his first week in boot camp, the recruit is assigned to "R and O" (Receiving and Outfitting).[4] In "R and O" the boot lives, along with approximately sixty other members of his recruit company, in a section of the training center which is literally isolated from the remainder of the center. The "R and O's" (as they are called by the staff and by the more advanced boots) have their own mess hall, their own medical facility, their own "grinders" (marching fields), and are not allowed access to the center-at-large. The ostensible purpose of this isolation is to prevent the spread of any contagious diseases the new men might be carrying, while at the same time issuing these men their clothing, giving them an extensive physical examination, administering General Classification Test Batteries, giving them haircuts and shots, and getting them acquainted with the general rules, schedules, and with marching as a group. But something more is happening than these obvious elements of organizational design. It is during this "R and O" phase that the challenge to the civilian self begins in earnest.

From the point of view of the training center, the boot has come through the gates with a well-developed personality, a civilian frame of reference, and a set of cultural values and expectancies that are not compatible with the center's objective and organization. The adjustment problem for the recruit consists in reorienting his behavior from a civilian frame of reference to the military standard. Such an adjustment is no easy task, considering the demands of the training process.

Some behavioral scientists have observed the threat to self which is posed by the military training center, and although the following reports are not based upon Navy personnel, they are both appurtenant and revealing: The new recruit is a "lone individual, hopelessly insecure in bewildering newness and complexity of environment . . . powerless . . . subjected to 'shock treatment'."[5] He is taken "away from civilian life contacts and abruptly placed into a new routine, without customary individualistic responsibilities and dependent upon superiors for orders. . . . The recruit becomes depressed and disorganized."[6] The process of recruit training is "analogous to major crises in childhood, puberty, and adolescence. . . . [It is] a strict discipline plus the end of opportunities for self-expression and impulse gratification. . . . [It engenders] mass frustration."[7] The method of indoctrination in such centers is one of "rigid discipline . . . [and] is feudalistic."[8] The fact that the institution is "governing the life of the individual when he is not on actual work duty . . . [is a sharp] contrast to normal civilian social controls. . . . Aspects of daily life considered by civilians to be solely within the realm of private discretion are regarded as fit subjects for regulation. . . ."[9] The training center not only requires of its recruits a "lapse of civilian occupations and avocations, but also involves the increasing decline of the social controls of the family and the neighborhood. . . . There is a knifing off of past experiences . . . nothing in one's past seems relevant. . . . [The recruit is] thrust into a completely alien role . . . he experiences feelings of isolation . . . impersonality . . . atomizing . . . personal degradation."[10] During the first part of recruit training "so much happens to the person in such a short time that his reactions tend to be confused. . . . The perfectly trained member of the military organization is one who has had his civilian initiative reduced to zero."[11]

Dornbusch, in a paper on the assimilation of the new cadet into the Coast Guard Academy, reports that the "swab" (the Academy's equivalent of "boot") is, for the first two months after his arrival, not allowed to leave base or to engage in social intercourse with non-cadets. This process purports to provide, within a short period of time, a "clean break with the past" and a "loss of identity in terms of preexisting statuses."[12] Thus, the individual is "softened up" and made receptive to the role expectations of the organization of which he is a recruit.

In general, the pressures of the recruit training center, especially the "R and O" phase, *challenge*, after Goffman, four areas in the boot's life that have much influenced his understanding and acceptance of himself as a "civilian," and which have provided a foundation for and a reinforcement of his concept of self: (1) autonomy of action (self-determination, responsibility for own behavior, feeling relatively free to express himself and to make choices, feeling personal integrity); (2) personal economy of motion (feeling free to move spontaneously toward, away from, or against a given experience according to his preference, able to set own activity pace, to control and vary own rate of locomotion); (3) privacy (having opportunity for physical and mental privacy, having places where he can be alone and "get away from it all"); (4) individual's picture of himself as a physical person (seeing himself in his usual choice of clothing, degree of neatness, tonsorial demeanor).[13] The following are some examples, taken from the writer's field notes, of challenges to these self-sustaining areas which are encountered by the "R and O":

Challenge to Autonomy of Action

1. The "R and O" finds that he cannot choose the people with whom he will experience everyday life. He must be a "shipmate" to anyone assigned to his recruit company.

2. Hours for sleeping, hours for eating, hours for the use of the "head" (toilet facilities), frequency of shaves, smoking, and other similarly previously autonomous actions are now rigidly scheduled.

3. The recruit is told that he *will* write a letter home each week; thus a measure of control is established over his interaction with the original primary group.

4. All clothing, all bedding, and all personal gear must be stored in exactly the prescribed manner. Any individual deviations result in punishment for the entire company of recruits. In controlling the condition and position of the boot's personal effects, authority strengthens its control over the condition and position of the boot, who has invested some element of himself in his belongings.

5. "You have been issued five pairs of shorts. Put one pair on each shoulder, one pair in your teeth, and hold one pair in each hand. Now, do you have a pair of shorts on each shoulder, in your teeth,

and in each hand? Good! Put them in the sea bag. Next, you have been issued six pairs of stockings. . . ."

6. Every morning, all the "R and O's" must stand inspection for uniforms, shaves, shoes, etc. One of the positions assumed during the inspection procedure is a rigid stance at attention, the left hand holding the white hat bottom side up at elbow's length, the thumb of the right hand hooked underneath the collar of the "skivvy shirt" (undershirt), turning the material outward, so that the inspector can check both hat and shirt in one quick glance. Thus, the recruit's responsibility for personal cleanliness is challenged.

7. "Forget your name! All you have to remember is the number of the square on which you are now standing. I'm going to let you fall out, then have you fall back in. Return to the same numbered square. Understand? Ready? Fall out!"

Challenge to Personal Economy of Motion

1. "When I give the command 'Attention!' you will bring your heels together sharply, toes at a 45 degree angle. Your hands will be by your sides, in a natural position, with your thumbs lined up with the seams in your trousers. You will pull your stomach in, push your chest out, keep your shoulders back and your body straight. I don't want to see any daylight between your knees. Keep your head and eyes forward at all times. And keep your mouths closed. If I haul out of here for a week-end liberty while you're at attention, you had better be in that same position when I get back!"

2. "When the Captain comes by your position for inspection, don't blink and don't breathe! Make that uniform look good!"

3. Everywhere the boot goes, he must march in formation. If for some administrative reason he must go somewhere alone, he will be given a "walking chit" (permit), stating his point of origin, his destination, a time limit, and who has given him permission to walk independently.

4. The boot is constantly kept active and moving. The pace never seems to slacken. "You're not standing around on corners now!" He does not pause for rest unless the company is ordered to fall out or stand-at-ease.

5. "When they walk, when they sit, sailors are tall!"

Challenge to Privacy

1. "There's a folder up in the administration office. We know more about you than you do!"

2. "Remove all of your clothes, sit over there on that bench, and wait until you are told to line up facing the doctor."

3. "Get a load of the perfume on this one, guys! It's from his girl!"

4. "You with the dreamy look in your eyes! What are you thinking about!"

5. "Hey, mate, throw me your soap, will you?"

Challenge to the Individual's Picture of Himself as a Physical Person

1. Within a matter of hours after arrival at boot camp, the new recruit is told to remove all of his civilian clothes, his jewelry, religious medals, etc. and place them, along with wallet, comb, key ring, and the like into the shipping box that has been given to him. He stands there nude and wraps and addresses the box containing the accouterments of his civilianity. When finished he proceeds through a line in which he is issued his naval attire.

2. There is nothing at all distinctive about the clothes he now puts on. The blue dungarees and blue chambray shirt (R and O's are not allowed to wear the Navy blues or whites they have been issued), the identical underwear, the white hat, the black socks and shoes, look exactly like everyone else's. The clothing is untailored, and will remain so for about two weeks. "It's not that the clothes don't fit you, boot. You don't fit the clothes! We'll shape you up!"

3. The haircut takes about thirty seconds. Full length mirrors are conveniently placed around the barber shop. The reflection of the shorn head, the baggy clothes, the drawn features, makes its point; you *are* a boot!

4. "You boots with the lard tails will knock off at least twenty pounds, and you beanpoles will gain at least twenty, before you get off these grinders!"

5. "You're going to discover muscles you never knew you had before!"

Assault after assault is made on the new recruit's "presenting culture" self. It seems that many of his responses to situations which had served him well in civilian life are now inappropriate or ineffective. He seems to be unable to do anything right. Everywhere he goes, everyone he must deal with, reminds him that he is not an individual but an "R and O" boot, the lowest of the low. Even other recruits, those who are on the other side of the isolation fence, shout derisions at his clumsiness, his appearance, his confusion. The new recruit's company is marched over to the end of the isolation area facing the main drill field. There he and his company mates stand in their ill-fitting, stiff dungarees, arms still burning from shots, heads cold and itching from the haircut, tired, lonely, and lost. On the main drill field, company after company of sharp-stepping, cadence-singing seventh and eighth-week recruits parade smartly by to the thundering drum of the center band. The company commander (himself an enlisted man) points to the experienced recruit companies and expresses doubt that his charges, those miserable "R and O's," will ever look *that* good. The role is being defined. The expectations are becoming clearer. The recruit thinks to himself, as he watches through the fence, "Someday, maybe. . . ."

In the society at large the civilian compartmentalizes his roles. He can be student, son, sweetheart, part-time grocery-clerk; and he understands a set of reciprocal expectations for each of these roles. Similarly, he comes to expect compartmentalized authority over him. The professor may be able to set down limits for his classroom performance, but the professor cannot tell him what, where, and when, for example, to eat.

In the naval training center, the boot has a single role (the expectations of which are painfully vague at first), and the authority over him is not compartmentalized. Any member of the staff can correct him for any offense at any time.

"During the "R and O" phase of recruit training, the boot has been pushed, pulled, and badgered from five in the morning until ten at night (and is awakened from sleep to stand watches). He has been challenged in his previous expectations of autonomy of action, personal economy of motion, privacy, and his picture of himself as a physical person. He has found that the confidence he had in himself as a civilian is no longer supportive, that in the training center environment his previous pattern of behavior leaves him powerless, isolated, in conflict with the sanctioned norms, and makes most of the center's day-to-day events appear meaningless. In short, if the purposes of the center have been realized, the recruit's phenomenal experience of identity has been muddled, the comfortable feeling of knowledge of himself has been taken away, and he begins to reject his earlier conception of self and civilian expectations as being ineffective. If the "R and O" process is fruitful, the boot should be somewhat of a depersonalized and role-dispossessed shell, searching hungrily for the security and certainty of a sanctioned role which he can enact.

During the "R and O" phase, the role of sailor has been constantly presented—in the physical environment, in the example of the company commander, in the glimpses the "R and O" gets of advanced recruits. But the emphasis (not necessarily to be construed as intentional or by design) was on role-dispossession; and the major result, from the point of view of the recruit, is confusion rather than enactment of the sailor role. Hollingshead points out that in the training center, though the opportunity to attain military status is present, the meaning of military status does not grow clear for some time. When the recruit realizes that he is in a military situation and that his old civilian life is behind him, that he is "in the Navy now," the "self will begin to appraise itself in relation to the new situation, and to adjust, or to figure out ways to evade the situation."[14]

It would not be correct to say that for *every* boot the "R and O" phase represents depersonalization and role-dispossession, and the advanced recruit stage (last six weeks) represents a clearer presentation of the center's role expectations meant to fill the gap. Rather, role dispossession and role enactment exist on a continuum, varying in time and degree for each recruit. However, examination of the structure and scheduling of the two phases of recruit training reveals the "R and O" period of the process as functional largely in decivilianizing the recruit, while the advanced period is functional largely in defining the expectations of the sailor role.

Upon the completion of "R and O," the recruits move to new quarters in the main area of the training center, shed their dungarees for blue or white uniforms (depending upon the time of year), and are issued a colorful company flag. Their company is now in official competition with the advanced recruit companies for the weekly honors awarded with great ceremony at the Saturday brigade review. The boot begins to see· himself and his mates in a different light. Where before there was confusion, clumsiness, individual isolation, and general uncertainty, now there are the "men of Company 123." The company becomes the center of orientation. Hollingshead posits that there is a group substitute for the shattered civilian self.[15] Brotz and Wilson observed that "the complete severance of accustomed social relations finds compensation in part in the acquiring of 'buddies.' "[16] To the recruit, the term" buddy" applies to every man in the company. The hours of drilling and exercising together, the constant exhortations to "move as one man," work as a unifying discipline. Marching may be joked about, points out Warren, but let another man get out of step as the company passes in review and the in-step recruit "curses under his breath."[17]

The low status held by the recruit in "R and O" makes the new uniforms, the company flag, the new quarters in the main part of the training center, and a place among the advanced recruits seem like a giant step upward. Dornbusch observed a similar phenomenon in the Coast Guard Academy where the assignment of low status to the "swab" was "useful in producing a correspondingly high evaluation of successfully completing the steps in an Academy career."[18]

The recruit finds himself united with his mates in Company 123 to "bilge the other companies" for the weekly honor prize (which is symbolized by a streamer or star affixed to the company flag; the flag is carried by the guideon bearer, who marches at the head of the company). One observer describes this "we feeling" in infantry training:

> By sharing experiences, they have a feeling of closeness and begin to feel that they form a select group. This *esprit de corps* rein-

forces their new conceptions of themselves because the rifleman gets collective support from the sense of belonging with others.[19]

Air Force men are "sloppy," "airdales," "flyboys." Marines are "jar-heads," "jungle-bunnies," "sea-going bell hops," "gung-ho." Coast Guardsmen are "fresh water sailors," "lighthouse keepers." Soldiers are "dogfaces," "female marines."[20] But *we* are *sailors*, the men of Company 123. Heels pounding in cadence unison, company flag snapping in the breeze, Company 123 now takes its turn marching fiercely past the "R and O" company standing in ragged lines on the other side of the chicken-wire fence.

Got no women, got no dough,
But at least we're not in R and O
Sound off! Sound off!
Cadence count![21]

Goffman states that the member of the total institution regains stability of self as he learns the institutional privilege system.[22] This system is presented by formal training (classroom and field) and informal instruction (examples set by staff and more advanced recruits or "bull" sessions) and makes possible a clearer understanding of the role expectations involved in the role of sailor, thus providing a framework for personal organization.

The boot now attends daily classes in naval tradition and customs, in gunnery, first aid, seamanship, naval history, military conduct, shipboard organization, etc. He finds himself proud of his knowledge and likes to demonstrate his prowess in sailor skills, such as knot tying, flag signaling, and so on. Warren reported this kind of behavior when he observed trainees in naval candidate schools "competing with each other on shipboard knowledge during their off-duty hours."[23] The boot is a member of a boat crew, a fire-fighting team, a rifle squad, and a watch section, in each of which he clearly knows what is expected of him and what he can expect of his teammates. He learns naval argot and finds that he can communicate with the "real sailors" who are his instructors. Automatically now the floor is a "deck," the ceiling is "overhead," the flight of stairs a "ladder." It is not "right and left" but "starboard and port," not "front and back," but "fore and aft." He comes to be familiar with argot terms for many of the physical objects around him which previously had civilian names. Various events and sequences of behavior unique to the military are now understood by the recruit in single terms such as "taps," "AWOL," "liberty," "square away," "field day," etc. Frederick Elkin has demonstrated that the recruit's acceptance of military language patterns reflects an image of solidarity and an admission of a break with civilian society.

The use of so-called "taboo" language is significant of a freedom from certain restraints of the civilian culture. "The most significant feature of such expressions is that . . . they give . . . a unique universe of discourse which helps distinguish him (the member of the military), and thus they become a binding-in-group force."[24] Some authors vividly describe the obscenity of the language of the military man, and explain it in terms of expression of aggression, traumatic regression to an earlier level of impulse gratification, negativism, need to express virility in the threat of a purely masculine society, etc.[25] These certainly may be factors in the frequent use of tabooed language by the member of the military, but the importance of role expectations must not be overlooked. Elkin also points out that the obscene terms come into universal and relatively indiscriminate usage and thus lose their original sexual significance. The words merely become the language of a social group.[26] There seems to be no one emotion expressed by a given obscene term. One given word can be used positively, negatively, or as a neutral expression. Sometimes the obscenity will be an adjective, sometimes a noun, sometimes a verb, and sometimes an expletive. Such terms may come at the beginning of sentences, at the end of sentences, between words, or even between the syllables of words. Such lability of use indicates a probable social variable as well as any psychodynamic variable which may engender the use of such language. The sailor is expected to swear. The boot, then, observing the language habits of "real sailors," and having a need to communicate with them, picks up the use of obscenities along with such terms as "bulkhead" for wall and "scuttlebutt" for drinking fountain or rumors.

Ceremonies and rituals become less strange and more a part of every-day life. The Company Commander seems less "different" and less fear-some now, and "sea stories" about his prowess have become a central topic for bull sessions. Isolation among the members of the company diminishes and is replaced by fraternization, as the company develops acceptable counter mores and finds new others with whom they can contrast them-selves. All these occurrences present the boot with a clearer definition of the role he is expected to enact in the training center and the role the training center will play for him. "You boots keep it up," the Company Com-mander comments, "and you just might turn out to be sailors!"

Each of the boots comes to the recruit training center with a relatively unique self-concept, based upon an individual organization of his past ex-periences. He has some needs that differ from those of his peers and some that are similar to theirs, but all his needs express themselves through his uniqueness. Each recruit has a different facility for enacting roles, a different degree of toleration for threats to and demands for change of his self-con-cept. When the "R and O" phase of boot camp calls for dispossession of the civilian role, each recruit, in accordance with his perception of the role expectations and possible role and role-self conflicts, and with his level of flexibility for role enactment, will work out a solution for adjustment. This adjustment might occur in the "R and O" phase, during the advanced phase, or not at all.

According to Sarbin, there is a continuum of role behavior, ranging from a differentiation of role and self (minimal involvement, few organic systems aroused, little effort engendered; e.g., role of customer in a super-market) to a state where role and self are undifferentiated (maximal involvement, entire organic system involved, much effort engendered; e.g., role of accursed in Voodoo death).[27] Goffman has described four points on such a continuum, ways in which an individual who is undergoing role dis-possession-repossession within a total institution might react: (1) situational withdrawal; (2) intransigent role; (3) colonization; and (4) conversion.[28] These four categories of behavior can be observed in the total institutional setting of the naval recruit training center.

In the first type of reaction, situational withdrawal, the training center's challenge to the comfortable civilian self of the recruit encourages him to retreat within the walls of his civilianity—to shut himself off from the threat of depersonalization. Such an individual may be administratively discharged from the Navy during the "R and O" phase. If not, he suffers internal torment for the first three weeks of boot camp, and then, as the rest of the company members enact their new roles in the second phase, he suffers additional torment as an ostracized "other."

The intransigent recruit vociferously verbalizes his gross discontent with the Navy and its ways; but he becomes, in fact, deeply involved in the total institution. His careful study of institutional expectations in order to protest them serves to contribute to his enactment of the very expectations he is admonishing.

The colonized recruit "finds a home in the Navy." His previous experience with civilian society has been one marked by relative deprivation, and Navy life provides him with the first real security he has ever known. As one chief petty officer put it:

> I left the cotton fields and joined this man's Navy. They gave
> me a place to sleep, good clothes, and all I could eat. Then, one day,
> they paid me, and I thought they were crazy![29]

In conversion as a method of adjustment, the recruit becomes "gung ho," a "red hot." He completely accepts and performs the role in accordance with the expectations of the training center. He wears his hat at the same angle as the Company Commander, emulates his jargon, gestures, and perhaps even his seamanlike gait. The convert is often rewarded with minor positions of authority within the recruit company.

These four reactions can be seen to fit a continuum of role-self interaction. There is, however, the problem of knowing just how much the sailor role, or any role, has been internalized—has become part of the individual's concept of self. It is quite possible, for example, that the individual could overtly be a convert and covertly be laughing at the whole recruit process. If then he is "playing at" the role of sailor, he must provide himself with some reason for his doing so—some rationalization. The following are examples of rationalization observed in the recruit training center:

1. Well, you see, there was this girl . . .

2. I'll be darned if I was going to let the Army draft me!

3. Me? I want to see the world.

4. I didn't join the Navy, I bought the G.I. Bill!

5. I figure I had to do it sooner or later. I'm just putting in my time.

The training center staff is not concerned about the individual's motivation or rationalization for performing the sailor role—just as long as their expectations for that role are met. As Janowitz observes, when a general gives an order specifying advance or attack, he doesn't care *why* the individual soldier fights, just so he *does* fight![30]

In summary, then, the naval recruit training center, operating as a total institution, rigidly controls the environment of the recruit. During a nine-week period, the function of the center can be viewed as challenging the boot's initial civilian self-concept, attempting to depersonalize and role-dispossess him, offering the sanctioned role of sailor to him for enactment, and giving him the opportunity, if necessary, to rationalize this role enactment.

After completion of the ninth week in the center, the recruit graduates. The commencement ceremony is dramatized by drums, flashing swords, banners, "Anchors Aweigh," speeches of the "now you are a man" type, and is culminated with the recruit's stripping off his boots and hurling them into the air.

At last, splendid in his pressed dress blue uniform, arm heavy with the two shiny white stripes seaman apprentice, and seabag on his shoulder, he is ready to go "down to the sea in ships."

Footnotes

This paper is based on the writer's unpublished master's thesis titled "The Sailor Aboard Ship: A Study of Role Behavior in A Total Institution," University of Arizona, 1963. Data for the thesis were drawn from interviews, relevant documents and publications, and from field notes collected by the writer during four years of active duty as an enlisted man in the United States Navy. Appreciation is expressed to Drs. Robert Blauner, Raymond Bowers, Richard Coan, Lewis Hertz, and Stuart Queen, who critically reviewed the thesis, and to Dr. Salvatore Zagona, who directed it. This paper was written while the author was on the faculty of The University of Arizona.

[1] Erving Goffman, *Asylums*, New York: Doubleday, 1961, p. xiii.

[2] *Ibid.*, p. 5.

[3] Field Notes.

[4] During the second and third week of training, the boots are relatively less isolated, but are still referred to as "R and O's" by the "advanced" recruits (fourth through ninth week) and by the staff. Therefore, in this paper the "R and O" phase will be taken to include training weeks one through three.

[5] Samuel Stouffer, *et al.*, *The American Soldier*, Volume 1, Princeton: Princeton University Press, 1949, pp. 411–412.

[6] S. Kirson Weinberg "Problems of Adjustment in an Army Unit," *American Journal of Sociology*, 50 (January, 1945), p. 272.

[7] Irving L. Janis, "Psychodynamics of Adjustment to Army Life," *Psychiatry*, 8 (May, 1945), p. 159.

[8] Arnold Rose, "The Social Structure of the Army," *American Journal of Sociology*, 51 (March, 1946), pp. 363–364.

[9] Anonymous, "Informal Social Organization in the Army," *American Journal of Sociology*, 51 (March, 1946), p. 366.

[10] H. Brotz and E. Wilson, "Characteristics of Military Society," *American Journal of Sociology*, 51 (March, 1946), pp. 372–374.

[11] August Hollingshead, "Adjustment to Military Life," *American Journal of Sociology*, 51 (March, 1946), p. 440.

[12] Sanford Dornbusch, "The Military Academy as an Assimilating Institution," *Social Forces*, 33 (May, 1955), p. 317.

[13] Goffman, *op. cit.*, pp. 237–238.

[14] Hollingshead, *op. cit.*, p. 442.

[15] *Ibid.*, p. 447.

[16] Brotz and Wilson, *op. cit.*, p. 374.

[17] Roland R. Warren, "The Naval Reserve Officer: A Study in Assimilation," *American Sociological Review*, 11 (April, 1946), p. 205.

[18] Dornbusch, *op. cit.*, p. 317.

[19] Anonymous, "The Making of an Infantryman," *American Journal of Sociology*, 51 (March, 1946), p. 378.

[20] Field Notes.

[21] *Ibid.*

[22] Goffman, *op. cit.*, p. 51.

[23] Warren, *op. cit.*, p. 205.

[24] Frederick Elkin, "The Soldier's Language," *American Journal of Sociology*, 51 (March, 1946), p. 414.

[25] See Janis, *op. cit.*, pp. 172–174, and H. Elkin, "Aggressive and Erotic Tendencies in Army Life," *American Journal of Sociology*, 51 (March, 1946), pp. 408–413.

[26] Frederick Elkin, *op. cit.*, p. 419.

[27] Theodore Sarbin, "Role Theory," in Gardner Lindzey, editor, *Handbook of Social Psychology*. Cambridge, Massachusetts: Addison-Wesley, 1954, pp. 233–234.

[28] Goffman, *op. cit.*, pp. 61–63.

[29] Field Notes.

[30] Morris Janowitz, *The Professional Soldier*, Glencoe: The Free Press, 1960, p. 174.

Occupational Ideology and Identity

The Self-Image of the Prostitute

Norman R. Jackman
California State College at Hayward
Richard O'Toole
Case Western Reserve University
Gilbert Geis
California State College at Los Angeles

Sexual behavior represents one of the most sensitive areas in American life. Within this sphere, professional promiscuity on the part of females stands as a striking deviation from what a large segment of the society declares to be acceptable sexual performance. Prostitutes are undoubtedly well aware of the prevailing social attitudes toward their behavior. It would seem, therefore, that these women develop a set of beliefs which counteract the social anathema attached to their way of life. This set of beliefs allows them to continue their behavior and to face and retaliate against persons who share the dominant and negative social values toward them.

Analyses of prostitution have generally employed a socioeconomic or a psychological frame of reference. The socioeconomic approach has ranged from Marxist[1] through ecological[2] to sophisticated structural-functional interpretations.[3] Other attempts at causal explanations have stressed mobility[4] and have concentrated on detailed life histories.[5] In addition, there is a wide range of psychoanalytical approaches, including those on frigidity,[6] Oedipal fixation,[7] maternal rejection,[8] homosexuality,[9] "social-existential" castration,[10] and restrictive ego-ideals combined with revenge motives.[11] Nowhere in the literature is there more than a hint of the manner in which the prostitute forms and supports her self-image.[12]

Two questions appear to be central to the problem of the prostitute's self-identity. First, since most Americans scorn prostitutes and these dominant social values travel throughout the society, how are women recruited to prostitution? Second, since a high degree of conformity to the dominant, middle-class American society is considered necessary for the maintenance

Reprinted from *The Sociological Quarterly*, Vol. 4, No. 2 (Spring 1963), 150–61, by permission of the authors and publisher.

of self-esteem, how do prostitutes rationalize their violation of a dominant social norm?

Interview Phase

Fifteen prostitutes were interviewed for periods averaging two hours each. Thirteen interviews were obtained while these women were held in the city jail awaiting the results of clinical tests. Two other women were interviewed in night clubs.[13]

Open-ended questions were employed for interviewing. The questions were used only to get the respondents to talk: everything they said was recorded and subsequently coded. Standard profile questions were asked (name, age, education, marital status, number, sex, and age of children, religion, etc.) followed by a series of questions organized around certain principal topics. These were (*a*) account of career, (*b*) self-conception, (*c*) group identifications, and (*d*) role expectations. Specific but unformalized questions were asked in each of these major areas, such as childhood experiences, recruitment to prostitution, attitudes toward clients, police, neighbors, etc., relationships with parents, husbands, children, relatives, other prostitutes, etc., attitudes toward work, future hopes, fears and plans, moods, fantasies, daydreams, and recreation.[14]

Analysis of the Data

The three following propositions concerning the formation and the structure of the self-image of the prostitute emerged from the data.

1. *The more isolated girl in urban society comes to define as acceptable patterns of behavior condemned by general social values more readily than does the less isolated individual.* Evidence indicated that the respondents were alienated from their parents following a break with the father toward whom they all expressed extreme hostility. After their introduction to prostitution, many of them became reconciled with their mothers, though they all maintained that they had kept knowledge of their activities from the mother:

> I would go through hell for my mother, but my father is a bastard. Every time my mother got pregnant [respondent has five siblings] my father went out with other women.
> My parents were divorced when I was eight. I lived with relatives and in an orphan home until I was thirteen and then I went

to live with my mother. . . . My father was cruel to me. . . . I hated my father and stepfather. . . . I was glad when my father died. . . .

My father was a carpenter and a gambler. . . . He always treated me like I was strictly from age two. But I got along good with my mother.

Alienation during the period of entrance into prostitution was indicated by the respondents' statements that they associated with people who meant little to them, or that they had no friends at all. In every case they felt that they stood alone against a hostile or indifferent world, though some of them were introduced to semi-criminal groups with which in time they came to identify themselves.

I ran around with a girl who started and so I started, too. She had a lot of friends. . . . I got to know a lot of people in the hustling racket.

I just been runnin' around with rum-dums all my life, I guess. . . . There was a fellow once in San Antone—I came in off a box car, believe it or not, and I met him in honky-tonk.

I was hanging 'round bars in Tulsa just looking for kicks. I had no place to go, like. It was strictly from hunger, man.

I figgered it was easy money—prostitution. . . . Nobody cared what I did anyway, and I knew a fellow who would set it up for me.

2. *The general social values, nevertheless, have some impact on the isolated individual. Therefore, the violation of these values must be rationalized by the individual.* The violation of sexual values is justified in two ways: (*a*) Everyone is rotten. Hence, prostitutes are no worse than other people, and they are less hypocritical. (*b*) Society doesn't really scorn prostitutes. Every prostitute interviewed expressed some degree of guilt feeling about her activity. This attitude ranged from mild expressions of guilt to statements like the following.

I will rot in hell for what I am doing. If you don't know what you are doing is sinful, then it is not so bad. But it is an unpardonable sin if you know what you are doing is sinful and keep on sinning.

My father told me two things: "Don't ever become a prostitute and don't marry a nigger."

Several respondents reflected in their defensive attitudes their imputation of middle-class disapproval on the part of the interviewers. These responses took the form of an attack on men or women, the world in general, or they reflected the attitude that prostitution did not mean a person was bad.

Men are . . . shrimps. Show me the man that's worth killing and I'll do the job.

Little chippies in bars give it away for a couple of beers.

This business doesn't keep you from having good children. Religion is right. It's a good thing. What we do doesn't affect religious feelings—being a wife, mother, housewife.

Other people look down on you. Deep down inside it hurts, but you ignore it . . . biggest majority are nice people. Several of the vice squad men hold the squad car door open for me [when they arrest her].

3. *The rationalization by prostitutes violating social taboos against commercial sex behavior takes the form of exaggerating other values,*[15] *particularly those of financial success, and for some the unselfish assumption of the financial burden of people dependent upon them.* Support for these justifications is found through reference groups, real or fictional, whose values the prostitute internalizes and thus is able to act in a consistent and "normal" manner. The behavior of prostitutes is not abnormal given the norms of those groups with which they identify themselves.

We identified two principal types of reference group orientations: one we labeled the *criminal world contraculture* and the other *dual worlds,* the world of prostitution and the middle-class world of American society.

THE CRIMINAL WORLD CONTRACULTURE

The principal characteristic of this type of prostitute is a strong identification with criminals and with those on the edge of the criminal world—Hobohemians. Yinger argues for the use of the concept *contraculture* for this type of group identification:

> . . . I suggest the use of the term contraculture wherever the normative system of a group contains, as a primary element, a theme of conflict with the values of the total society where personality variables are directly involved in the development and maintenance of the group's values, and wherever its norms can be understood only by reference to the relationships of the group to a surrounding dominant culture.[16]

This group had the greatest contempt for middle-class, "proper" people, whom they felt to be dull, frightened, and hypocritical. On the other hand, they made some attempt to justify their behavior by appealing to such dominant social values as financial success, their ability to move in "big business" circles, and being good mothers.

One respondent in this group said that prostitution was a means to secure money for her husband and herself so that they could lead an exciting life. Her husband is her procurer, and the group with which they associate is composed of people connected with prostitution. They are heavy drinkers, and many of them are addicts. They appear to be carefree and irresponsible, deciding at a moment's notice to go off on trips together. A vice squad officer related an incident wherein this group decided to dig a swimming pool in a back yard. They dug intermittently for several weeks, but finally gave up the project and left on a trip.

Another respondent stated that she liked the easy money. She had gotten tired of working twelve to fourteen hours a day as a waitress.

Another respondent displayed a great deal of satisfaction from claiming to be a big spender, wearing good clothes, and going to expensive restaurants and night clubs. She also associated with a semi-criminal group. She bragged about X,

> . . . a very wealthy businessman who pays me twenty-five to thirty dollars an evening just for my company. He takes me to the best places in town for dinner and dancing, and buys me expensive gifts. And I've never been in bed with the man! He told me that I mingled well with the finest people. He said once, "You act like a lady."

She also mentioned a boy friend who was in trouble with the Kansas City police.

This respondent, the only one in the criminal subculture who had children, stated that she was "a good mother" who visited her children regularly. However, her account of the break-up of her first marriage indicated that this self-evaluation, as well as the characterization that she acted like a lady, might be questioned.

> My husband started running around. I wanted to make him leave so I could keep the children. I cut him off, cursed him, and cut him with a knife, but I couldn't make him go.

Her children lived with her first husband and his second wife. When she visited her children once, she told her ex-husband that his present wife, "had better be good to my kids or I'll stomp her in a mudhole."

The final respondent in this group also stressed the luxurious life she leads as a prostitute and aligned herself with a criminal group. Like the second respondent she stressed her claim to association with the "best" people in the city and her attendance at social functions where such people gather. A vice squad officer said that she had been arrested while they were investigating a tip that she was harboring a criminal who was a known drug peddler.

These four respondents were generally friendly in their feelings toward their clients and middle-class society in general. As indicated above, they maintained with considerable pride that they associated with the best people. Toward their clients they expressed some ambivalence:

> Most of my clients are nice guys. . . . Most of them are married. . . . I like older men because younger men look down on you.
> Some men take it out on you because they feel guilty about cheating on their wives. . . . I don't hold it against married men for going to prostitutes. Actually, it teaches them the values of affection because prostitutes are so cold. . . . All in all they are pretty nice.

DUAL WORLDS

The five cases which fell into this category were characterized by a strong identification with their families and a rejection of the world of prostitutes which they were in, but not of. Two of the respondents claimed to be supporting their husbands and children, while the other two lived alone and claimed to be supporting children in other states whom they visited occasionally. The two married prostitutes said that their husbands acted as procurers for them, but for no other women. This group strongly and consistently expressed middle-class values. Unlike those in the criminal subculture, they never swore or used obscene words. They sought constantly to assure the interviewers that they were excellent mothers who made great sacrifices for their husbands, children, and relatives. They professed religious beliefs, and the two married respondents claimed that their associates (with the exception of their husbands) were not prostitutes or criminals. The two single prostitutes said that they associated with no one except their families whom they visited occasionally in another town. They resisted questions about their clients and other aspects of the business of prostitution. In short, they have seemingly dichotomized their world successfully by depersonalizing their prostitute roles and living almost entirely in the dominant world of American middle-class values.

Sherif and Cantril have noted that the ego can be dissociated from the self under certain extreme situations, and they illustrated this concept with a reference to the autobiography of a London prostitute who wrote, "I have moments when I realize that I am a person to no one. . . . The act of sex I could go through because *I hardly seemed to be taking part in it. . . . Indeed, it was scarcely happening even to me: It was happening to something lying on a bed that had a vague connection with me. . . .*"[17]

All of the respondents reported a certain amount of dissociation in their initial commercial experience. What would seem to distinguish the *dual worlds* groups from other groups was that this initial dissociation was continued and strengthened. The other two groups reported varying degrees of dissociation or none at all, some respondents claiming that they occasionally participated emotionally in the sex act and enjoyed it. Because of their middle-class moral values most of the *dual worlds* group avoided the topic of sex completely. The members of this group had successfully repressed their prostitute role and justified it as a self-sacrificing necessity to support those who were helpless and dependent upon them.

One of the married prostitutes in this group said that when she became pregnant her husband left her. She became a prostitute to support herself and her child. Her present husband is an unemployed tile-setter. She apologized for her husband by saying that there isn't too much demand for tile-setters. She claimed that she was supporting six persons and herself.

> They don't know what I do for a living, except my husband. I see my little girl often. About once a week. I don't work weekends so I can go see her.
> ... My sister just got a job, but she's not on her feet yet. She has a tiny baby. Her husband is in the penitentiary. [Embarrassed laugh.]

The other married prostitute also claimed to be supporting an unemployed husband, two children, and her mother. Her mother takes care of her children and none of them knows that she is a prostitute:

> I think that I am a good mother who takes care of her children. I love my family very much. I have a normal family life other than being a prostitute. I hope that my husband can find a job and gets to working steadily against so I can be an ordinary housewife.

Of the single prostitutes in this group, one had five children by a previous marriage and the other had never been married. The first strongly identified herself with her children, while the second strongly identified herself with her parents. Neither of them associated intimately with other people. Both claimed they had become prostitutes in order to care for their children or their parents.

> I am very proud of my family. Even though the mother is a prostitute it doesn't reflect on her family—this business doesn't keep you from having good children. I keep my children in the best private schools and colleges in Texas. One of them married very well. They don't know what I do.

The respondent who identified herself with her parents maintained that her father had given her the best of everything as a child, but she had failed to live up to his expectations because she was too much like him. Nevertheless, she helped both parents financially:

My parents are the most wonderful people alive. I like 'em both but my mother is easier to get along with. Dad and I fight like cats and dogs. Both alike. He thinks I'm two years old. He said, "I knew the day you was born you'd be just like me." He's got suspicious of my work, but not my mother. She had an operation—cancer of the brain. I gave him [father] four hundred dollars and three hundred more after I came back from Chicago. He said, "Myra, I know what you're doing, but for God's sake don't let your mother know."

All four respondents in the *dual worlds* category expressed middle-class values:

I have some friends, some are married women, and some work.

My husband and I run around with other couples where the wife isn't a prostitute.

I got lots of friends not even connected with hustling. Went with a Kansas City dick for a long time.

I don't associate with hustling people. Half their husbands are in McAlester [state penitentiary] or the county jail.

ALIENATION

The six respondents who fell into this group were characterized by feelings of normlessness, apathy, lack of direction or future goal orientation. They identified themselves with no one and felt their lives to be empty and meaningless. Two of them were young: one an eighteen-year-old who was new to the profession, and the other a nineteen-year-old who had been a prostitute for one year. It is possible that the newest recruit's sense of alienation will become modified as she becomes less a stranger to her environment. The third respondent had been a prostitute for ten years. The length of time in prostitution is evidently not a factor in alienation, however, since the second youngest respondent in this group had been a prostitute for one year, and the prostitute with the longest record (eleven years) seemed to be well integrated in a criminal subculture. As noted above, all of this group dissociated themselves from the sex act.

Their conditions of alienation may be summarized by the following selected quotations:

I been in this racket ten years, I guess it's too late to get out. . . . I got no future; I been married four times and that's enough. . . . I don't care. I spent a hundred and fifty dollars over the weekend on drinking and gambling. I can't save. But I kicked the habit cold turkey. [Another respondent in the *dual worlds* category, who knew this prostitute, said: "Hustling's got the best of Jerry. She's drunk all the time. Girls like that are weak. They got no will power."] I got no friends; everybody's rotten, anymore. Women are as bad as men. Women ain't worth a damn. I'm usually too drunk to know what's going on [sex act].

I live by myself and have no friends. I just sleep and hustle at the night club. No, TV shows and books just bore me. Daydreams? Why daydream when you can't be out doing the things you day-dream about? ... Just before you came in, I was out standing in the rain watching the world cry because it's been so screwed up by all the bastards in it. [This respondent was interviewed in a night club.]

I was drunk when I was arrested—had been drinking for several days. I was too drunk to care. I don't live with anybody. I don't know anyone in this town, except the porter [procurer]. My parents don't care about me, they put me in an Indian boarding school and I ran away from it. Drinking is very bad. I've been so bad I decided I might as well go all the way. I used to walk around town late at night and once a porter from one of the hotels stopped me and tried to get me to start working. He asked me twice. I felt it didn't matter. I was sober when I started, but I had to get drunk to finish it.

Summary and Conclusions

The present study is mainly heuristic. We have been concerned with the problem of self-respect. Assuming that commercialized sexual activity is condemned by general social norms in the United States, how do prostitutes maintain a consistent self-image?

The interviews with fifteen prostitutes provided us with data which we feel are related to these questions. The interviews provided support for the following propositions:

1. The more isolated individual in the urban society comes to define as acceptable patterns of behavior condemned by general social values more readily than does the less isolated individual.

2. The general social values have some impact on the isolated individual. Therefore, the violation of these values must be rationalized by the individual.

3. The rationalizations by prostitutes violating sexual taboos against commercial sex behavior take the form of exaggerating other values, particularly those of financial success, and for some the unselfish assumption of the financial burden of people dependent upon them.

Two types of reference group orientation important for self-justification were identified: the *criminal world* and the *dual worlds* categories. A third category of alienated individuals was discerned.

We have drawn other tentative conclusions regarding various hypotheses culled from the literature of prostitution. The following hypotheses await further investigations:

1. Prostitution is not a function of ecological factors. Evidence indicates that there exists at the present time a kind of "white collar" prostitution. These are secretaries, stenographers, and file clerks in large corporations who work as call girls in their off-hours in first-class metropolitan hotels.

2. Not all prostitutes are recruited from the economically deprived. The rationalization for prostitution may occur at all occupational and income levels because of urban anonymity and the weakening of traditional religious and moral values.

3. Most prostitutes have normal intelligence and average educational backgrounds.

4. Personality factors, early socialization, childhood sexual experiences, and adult marital relations are insufficient explanations of recruitment to prostitution. The selection of prostitution as an occupation from available alternatives must be sought in the individual prostitute's interaction with others over a considerable time span.

5. Self-denigration is only one of several alternatives available to the prostitute who is "hooked." Her prostitute's role may be sustained through interaction with others who are important to her, or a fantasy world may sustain a satisfactory self-image.

Further research is planned on a larger scale in view of the results reported in this preliminary study. It is believed that the frame of reference employed here can be useful in a synthesis of existing empirical insights concerning behavior in this area.

Footnotes

The authors are indebted to the Oklahoma City and the Norman Police Departments for their co-operation. Police Inspector E. B. Giddens, Oklahoma City, was extremely helpful in arranging interviews with prostitutes held on vagrancy and disorderly conduct charges. Inspector Giddens clearly expressed to the investigators and the respondents the right of any prisoner to refuse to be interviewed. Our thanks are also extended to the personnel of the vice squad and the matrons of the Oklahoma City jail. Officer Terry Sharp, Norman Police Department, and Robert Bristow contributed as graduate students to this research. Acknowledgment is also due the Faculty Research Fund of the University of Oklahoma for partial financial aid.

1 W. A. Bonger, *Criminality and Economic Conditions* (Boston: Little, Brown, 1916), pp. 321–56.

2 Robert E. Park and Ernest W. Burgess, *Introduction to the Science of Sociology* (Chicago: Univ. of Chicago Press, 1921); Park, Burgess, and Roderick D. McKenzie, *The City* (Chicago: Univ. of Chicago Press, 1925); Nels Anderson, *The Hobo: The Sociology of the Homeless Man* (Chicago: Univ. of Chicago Press, 1923); Walter C. Reckless, *Vice in Chicago* (Chicago: Univ. of Chicago Press, 1933).

3 Kingsley Davis, "The Sociology of Prostitution," *American Sociological Review*, 2:744–55 (Oct., 1937).

4 Edwin H. Lemert, *Social Pathology* (New York: McGraw-Hill, 1951), p. 233.

5 W. I. Thomas, *The Unadjusted Girl* (Boston: Little, Brown, 1924).

6 Karl Abraham, *Selected Papers on Psycho-Analysis* (London: Hogarth Press, 1927), p. 361.

7 Edward Glover, "The Abnormality of Prostitution," in A. M. Krich, ed., *Women* (New York: Dell, 1953), pp. 247–73; and Glover, *The Psychopathology of Prostitution* (London: Institute for the Study and Treatment of Delinquency, 1957).

8 Harold Greenwald, *The Call Girl* (New York: Ballantine Books, 1958), p. 94.

9 Frank S. Caprio, *Female Homosexuality* (New York: Citadel, 1954).

10 T. Agoston, "Some Psychological Aspects of Prostitution; The Pseudo-Personality," *International Journal of Psycho-Analysis*, 26:62–67 (1945).

11 Helen Deutsch, *The Psychology of Women* (New York: Grune and Stratton, 1944), vol. 1.

12 Cf. David W. Maurer, "Prostitutes and Criminal Argots," *American Journal of Sociology*, 44:546–50 (Jan., 1939). On rationalization by juvenile delinquents, see Gresham M. Sykes and David Matza, "Techniques of Neutralization: A Theory of Delinquency," *American Sociological Review*, 22:664–70 (Dec., 1957).

13 During the jail interviews only the investigating team was present. In two night club interviews patrol car officers were also present but not in a position to hear the conversation.

14 We were not concerned with the literal "truth" of respondents' statements. We accepted the statements at their face value since we were concerned with the prostitutes' self-image, however fantastic. Where pertinent, however, we have employed police records for validation or further information.

15 Gresham M. Sykes and David Matza, *loc. cit.*

16 J. Walton Yinger, "Contraculture and Subculture," *American Sociological Review*, 25:625–35 (Oct., 1960).

17 Muzafer Sherif and Hadley Cantril, *The Psychology of Ego-Involvements* (New York: Wiley, 1947), p. 387.

Work and Social Control

Social Control in the Newsroom

A Functional Analysis

WARREN BREED

Scientific Analysis Corporation
San Francisco, California

Top leaders in formal organizations are makers of policy, but they must also secure and maintain conformity to that policy at lower levels. The situation of the newspaper publisher is a case in point. As owner or representative of ownership, he has the nominal right to set the paper's policy and see that staff activities are coordinated so that the policy is enforced. In actuality the problem of control is less simple, as the literature of "human relations" and informal group studies and of the professions[1] suggests.

Ideally, there would be no problem of either "control" or "policy" on the newspaper in a full democracy. The only controls would be the nature of the event and the reporter's effective ability to describe it. In practice, we find the publisher does set news policy, and this policy is usually followed by members of his staff. Conformity is *not* automatic, however, for three reasons: (1) the existence of ethical journalistic norms; (2) the fact that staff subordinates (reporters, etc.) tend to have more "liberal" attitudes (and therefore perceptions) than the publisher and could invoke the norms to justify anti-policy writing; and (3) the ethical taboo preventing the publisher from commanding subordinates to follow policy. How policy comes to be maintained, and where it is bypassed, is the subject of this paper.

Several definitions are required at this point. As to personnel, "newsmen" can be divided into two main categories. "Executives" include the publisher and his editors. "Staffers" are reporters, rewrite men, copy readers, etc. In between there may be occasional city editors or wire editors who occupy an interstitial status. "Policy" may be defined as the more or less

Reprinted from *Social Forces*, Vol. 33, No. 4 (May 1955), 326–35, by permission of the author and publisher. Copyright © 1955 by the University of North Carolina Press.

consistent orientation shown by a paper, not only in its editorial but in its news columns and headlines as well, concerning selected issues and events. "Slanting" almost never means prevarication. Rather, it involves omission, differential selection and preferential placement, such as "featuring" a pro-policy item, "burying" an anti-policy story in an inside page, etc. "Professional norms" are of two types: technical norms deal with the operations of efficient news gathering, writing, and editing; ethical norms embrace the newsman's obligation to his readers and to his craft and include such ideals as responsibility, impartiality, accuracy, fair play, and objectivity.[2]

Every newspaper has a policy, admitted or not.[3] One paper's policy may be pro-Republican, cool to labor, antagonistic to the school board, etc. The principal areas of policy are politics, business, and labor; much of it stems from considerations of class. Policy is manifested in "slanting." Just what determines any publisher's policy is a large question and will not be discussed here. Certainly, however, the publisher has much say (often in veto form) in both long-term and immediate policy decisions (which party to support, whether to feature or bury a story of imminent labor trouble, how much free space to give "news" of advertisers' doings, etc.). Finally, policy is covert, due to the existence of ethical norms of journalism; policy often contravenes these norms. No executive is willing to risk embarrassment by being accused of open commands to slant a news story.

While policy is set by the executives, it is clear that they cannot personally gather and write the news by themselves. They must delegate these tasks to staffers, and at this point the attitudes or interests of staffers may—and often do—conflict with those of the executives.[4] Of 72 staffers interviewed, 42 showed that they held more liberal views than those contained in their publisher's policy; 27 held similar views, and only 3 were more conservative. Similarly, only 17 of 61 staffers said they were Republicans.[5] The discrepancy is more acute when age (and therefore years of newspaper experience) is held constant. Of the 46 staffers under 35 years of age, 34 showed more liberal orientations; older men had apparently "mellowed." It should be noted that data as to intensity of attitudes are lacking. Some staffers may disagree with policy so mildly that they conform and feel no strain. The present essay is pertinent only insofar as dissident newsmen are forced to make decisions from time to time about their relationship to policy.[6]

We will now examine more closely the workings of the newspaper staff. The central question will be: How is policy maintained, despite the fact that it often contravenes journalistic norms, that staffers often personally disagree with it, and that executives cannot legitimately command that it be followed? The frame of reference will be that of functional analysis, as embodied in Merton's paradigm.[7]

The present data come from the writer's newspaper experience and from intensive interviews with some 120 newsmen, mostly in the northeastern quarter of the country. The sample was not random and no claim is made for representativeness, but on the other hand no paper was selected or omitted purposely and in no case did a newsman refuse the request that he be interviewed. The newspapers were chosen to fit a "middle-sized" group, defined as those with 10,000 to 100,000 daily circulation. Interviews averaged well over an hour in duration.[8]

There is an "action" element inherent in the present subject—the practical democratic need for "a free and responsible press" to inform citizens about current issues. Much of the criticism of the press stems from the slanting induced by the bias of the publisher's policy.[9] This criticism is often directed at flagrant cases such as the Hearst press, the *Chicago Tribune* and New York tabloids, but also applies, in lesser degree, to the more conventional press. The description of mechanisms of policy maintenance may suggest why this criticism is often fruitless, at least in the short-run sense.

How the Staffer Learns Policy

The first mechanism promoting conformity is the "socialization" of the staffer with regard to the norms of his job. When the new reporter starts work he is not told what policy is. Nor is he ever told. This may appear strange, but interview after interview confirmed the condition. The standard remark was "Never, in my——years on this paper, have I ever been told how to slant a story." No paper in the survey had a "training" program for its new men; some issue a "style" book, but this deals with literary style, not policy. Further, newsmen are busy and have little time for recruit training. Yet all but the newest staffers know what policy is.[10] On being asked, they say they learn it "by osmosis." Sociologically, this means they become socialized and "learn the ropes" like a neophyte in any subculture. Basically, the learning of policy is a process by which the recruit discovers and internalizes the rights and obligations of his status and its norms and values. He learns to anticipate what is expected of him so as to win rewards and avoid punishments. Policy is an important element of the newsroom norms, and he learns it in much the following way.

The staffer reads his own paper every day; some papers *require* this. It is simple to diagnose the paper's characteristics. Unless the staffer is naive or unusually independent, he tends to fashion his own stories after others he sees in the paper. This is particularly true of the newcomer. The news columns and editorials are a guide to the local norms. Thus a southern reporter notes that Republicans are treated in a "different" way in his paper's news columns than Democrats. The news about whites and Negroes is also of a distinct sort. Should he then write about one of these groups, his story will tend to reflect what he has come to define as standard procedure.

Certain editorial actions taken by editors and older staffers also serve as controlling guides. "If things are blue-pencilled consistently," one reporter said, "you learn he [the editor] has a prejudice in that regard."[11] Similarly an executive may occasionally reprimand a staffer for policy violation. From our evidence, the reprimand is frequently oblique, due to the covert nature of policy, but learning occurs nevertheless. One staffer learned much through a series of incidents:

> I heard [a union] was going out an strike, so I kept on it; then the boss said something about it, and well—I took the hint and we had less coverage of the strike forming. It was easier that way. We lost the story, but what can you do?
> We used a yarn on a firm that was coming to town, and I got dragged out of bed for that. The boss is interested in this industrial stuff—we have to clear it all through him. He's an official in the Chamber. So . . . after a few times, it's irritating, so I get fed up. I try to figure out what will work best. I learn to try and guess what the boss will want.

In fairness it should be noted that this particular publisher was one of the most dictatorial encountered in the study. The pattern of control through reprimand, however, was found consistently. Another staffer wrote, on his own initiative, a series about discrimination against Jews at hotel resorts.

> It was the old "Gentlemen's Agreement" stuff, documented locally. The boss called me in . . . didn't like the stuff . . . the series never appeared. You start to get the idea. . . .

Note that the boss does not "command"; the direction is more subtle. Also, it seems that most policy indications from executives are negative. They veto by a nod of the head, as if to say, "Please don't rock the boat." Exceptions occur in the "campaign" story, which will be discussed later. It is also to be noted that punishment is implied if policy is not followed.

Staffers also obtain guidance from their knowledge of the characteristics, interests, and affiliations of their executives. This knowledge can be gained in several ways. One is gossip. A reporter said:

> Do we gossip about the editors? Several of us used to meet— somewhere off the beaten path—over a beer—and talk for an hour. We'd rake 'em over the coals.

Another point of contact with executives is the news conference (which on middle-sized papers is seldom *called* a news conference), wherein the staffer outlines his findings and executives discuss how to shape the story. The typical conference consists of two persons, the reporter and the city editor, and can amount to no more than a few words. (Reporter: "One hurt in auto accident uptown." City editor: "Okay, keep it short.") If policy is at stake, the conference may involve several executives and require hours of consideration. From such meetings, the staffer can gain insight through what is said and what is not said by executives. It is important to say here that policy is not stated explicitly in the news conference nor elsewhere, with few exceptions. The news conference actually deals mostly with journalistic matters, such as reliability of information, newsworthiness, possible "angles," and other news tactics.

Three other channels for learning about executives are house organs (printed for the staff by syndicates and larger papers), observing the executive as he meets various leaders and hearing him voice an opinion. One staffer could not help but gain an enduring impression of his publisher's attitudes in this incident:

> I can remember [him] saying on election night [1948], when it looked like we had a Democratic majority in both houses, "My God, this means we'll have a labor government." (Q: How did he say it?) He had a real note of alarm in his voice; you couldn't miss the point that he'd prefer the Republicans.

It will be noted that in speaking of "how" the staffer learns policy, there are indications also as to "why" he follows it.

Reasons for Conforming to Policy

There is no one factor which creates conformity-mindedness, unless we resort to a summary term such as "institutionalized statuses" or "structural roles." Particular factors must be sought in particular cases. The staffer must be seen in terms of his status and aspirations, the structure of the newsroom organization and of the larger society. He also must be viewed with reference to the operations he performs through his workday, and their consequences for him. The following six reasons appear to stay the potentially intransigent staffer from acts of deviance—often, if not always.[12]

1. INSTITUTIONAL AUTHORITY AND SANCTIONS

The publisher ordinarily owns the paper and from a purely business standpoint has the right to expect obedience of his employees. He has the power to fire or demote for transgressions. This power, however, is diminished markedly in actuality by three facts. First, the newspaper is not conceived as a purely business enterprise, due to the protection of the First Amendment and a tradition of professional public service. Secondly, firing is a rare phenomenon on newspapers. For example, one editor said he had fired two men in 12 years; another could recall four firings in his 15 years on that paper. Thirdly, there are severance pay clauses in contracts with the American Newspaper Guild (CIO). The only effective causes for firing are excessive drunkenness, sexual dalliance, etc. Most newspaper unemployment apparently comes from occasional economy drives on large papers and from total suspensions of publication. Likewise, only one case of demotion was found in the survey. It is true, however, that staffers still fear punishment; the myth has the errant star reporter taken off murders and put on obituaries—"the Chinese torture chamber" of the newsroom. Fear of sanctions, rather than their invocation, is a reason for conformity, but not as potent a one as would seem at first glance.

Editors, for their part, can simply ignore stories which might create deviant actions, and when this is impossible, can assign the story to a "safe" staffer. In the infrequent case that an anti-policy story reaches the city desk, the story is changed; extraneous reasons, such as the pressure of time and space, are given for the change.[13] Finally, the editor may contribute to the durability of policy by insulating the publisher from policy discussions. He may reason that the publisher would be embarrassed to hear of conflict over policy and the resulting bias, and spare him the resulting uneasiness; thus the policy remains not only covert but undiscussed and therefore unchanged.[14]

2. Feelings of Obligation and Esteem for Superiors

The staffer may feel obliged to the paper for having hired him. Respect, admiration, and gratitude may be felt for certain editors who have perhaps schooled him, "stood up for him," or supplied favors of a more paternalistic sort. Older staffers who have served as models for newcomers or who have otherwise given aid and comfort are due return courtesies. Such obligations and warm personal sentiments toward superiors play a strategic role in the pull to conformity.

3. Mobility Aspirations

In response to a question about ambition, all the younger staffers showed wishes for status achievement. There was agreement that bucking policy constituted a serious bar to this goal. In practice, several respondents noted that a good tactic toward advancement was to get "big" stories on Page One; this automatically means no tampering with policy. Further, some staffers see newspapering as a "stepping stone" job to more lucrative work: public relations, advertising, free-lancing, etc. The reputation for trouble-making would inhibit such climbing.

A word is in order here about chances for upward mobility. Of 51 newsmen aged 35 or more, 32 were executives. Of 50 younger men, 6 had reached executive posts and others were on their way up with such jobs as wire editors, political reporters, etc. All but five of these young men were college graduates, as against just half of their elders. Thus there is no evidence of a "break in the skill hierarchy" among newsmen.

4. ABSENCE OF CONFLICTING GROUP ALLEGIANCE

The largest formal organization of staffers is the American Newspaper Guild. The Guild, much as it might wish to, has not interfered with internal matters such as policy. It has stressed business unionism and political interests external to the newsroom. As for informal groups, there is no evidence available that a group of staffers has ever "ganged up" on policy.

5. THE PLEASANT NATURE OF THE ACTIVITY

a. *In-Groupness in the Newsroom.* The staffer has a low formal status vis-a-vis executives, but he is not treated as a "worker." Rather, he is a co-worker with executives; the entire staff cooperates congenially on a job they all like and respect: getting the news. The newsroom is a friendly, first-namish place. Staffers discuss stories with editors on a give-and-take basis. Top executives with their own offices sometimes come out and sit in on newsroom discussions.[15]

b. *Required Operations Are Interesting.* Newsmen like their work. Few voiced complaints when given the opportunity to gripe during interviews. The operations required—witnessing, interviewing, briefly mulling the meanings of events, checking facts, writing—are not onerous.

c. *Non-Financial Perquisites.* These are numerous: the variety of experience, eye-witnessing significant and interesting events, being the first to know, getting "the inside dope" denied laymen, meeting and sometimes befriending notables and celebrities (who are well-advised to treat newsmen with deference). Newsmen are close to big decisions without having to make them; they touch power without being responsible for its use. From talking with newsmen and reading their books, one gets the impression that they are proud of being newsmen.[16] There are tendencies to exclusiveness within news ranks, and intimations that such near out-groups as radio newsmen are entertainers, not real newsmen. Finally, there is the satisfaction of being a member of a live-wire organization dealing with important matters. The newspaper is an "institution" in the community. People talk about it and quote it; its big trucks whiz through town; its columns carry the tidings from big and faraway places, with pictures.

Thus, despite his relatively low pay, the staffer feels, for all these reasons, an integral part of a going concern. His job morale is high. Many newsmen could qualify for jobs paying more money in advertising and public relations, but they remain with the newspaper.

6. NEWS BECOMES A VALUE

Newsmen define their job as producing a certain quantity of what is called "news" every 24 hours. This is to be produced *even though nothing much has happened*. News is a continuous challenge, and meeting this challenge is the newsman's job. He is rewarded for fulfilling this, his manifest function. A consequence of this focus on news as a central value is the shelving of a strong interest in objectivity at the point of policy conflict. Instead of mobilizing their efforts to establish objectivity over policy as the criterion for performance, their energies are channeled into getting more news. The demands of competition (in cities where there are two or more papers) and speed enhance this focus. Newsmen do talk about ethics, objectivity, and the relative worth of various papers, but not when there is news to get. News comes first, and there is always news to get.[17] They are not rewarded for analyzing the social structure, but for getting news. It would seem that this instrumental orientation diminishes their moral potential. A further consequence of this pattern is that the harmony between staffers and executives is cemented by their common interest in news. Any potential conflict between the two groups, such as slowdowns occurring among informal work groups in industry, would be dissipated to the extent that news is a positive value. The newsroom solidarity is thus reinforced.

The six factors promote policy conformity. To state more exactly how policy is maintained would be difficult in view of the many variables contained in the system. The process may be somewhat better understood, however, with the introduction of one further concept—the reference group.[18] The staffer, especially the new staffer, identifies himself through the existence of these six factors with the executives and veteran staffers. Although not yet one of them, he shares their norms, and thus his performance comes to resemble theirs. He conforms to the norms of policy rather than to whatever personal beliefs he brought to the job, or to ethical ideals. All six of these factors function to encourage reference group formation. Where the allegiance is directed toward legitimate authority, that authority has only to maintain the equilibrium within limits by the prudent distribution of rewards and punishments. The reference group itself, which has as its "magnet" element the elite of executives and old staffers, is unable to change policy to a marked degree because first, it is the group charged with carrying out policy, and second, because the policy maker, the publisher, is often insulated on the delicate issue of policy.

In its own way, each of the six factors contributes to the formation of reference group behavior. There is almost no firing, hence a steady expectation of continued employment. Subordinates tend to esteem their bosses, so a convenient model group is present. Mobility aspirations (when held within limits) are an obvious promoter of inter-status bonds as is the absence of conflicting group loyalties with their potential harvest of cross pressures. The newsroom atmosphere is charged with the related factors of in-groupness and pleasing nature of the work. Finally, the agreement among newsmen that their job is to fasten upon the news, seeing it as a value in itself, forges a bond across status lines.

As to the six factors, five appear to be relatively constant, occurring on all papers studied. The varying factor is the second: obligation and esteem held by staffers for executive and older staffers. On some papers, this obligation-esteem entity was found to be larger than on others. Where it was large, the paper appeared to have two characteristics pertinent to this discussion. First, it did a good conventional job of news-getting and news-publishing, and second, it had little difficulty over policy. With staffers drawn toward both the membership and the reference groups, organization was efficient. Most papers are like this. On the few smaller papers where executives and older staffers are not respected, morale is spotty; staffers withhold enthusiasm from their stories, they cover their beats perfunctorily, they wish for a job on a better paper, and they are apathetic and sometimes hostile to policy. Thus the obligation-esteem factor seems to be the active variable in determining not only policy conformity, but morale and good news performance as well.

Situations Permitting Deviation

Thus far it would seem that the staffer enjoys little "freedom of the press." To show that this is an oversimplification, and more important, to suggest a kind of test for our hypothesis about the strength of policy, let us ask: "What happens when a staffer *does* submit an anti-policy story?" We know that this happens infrequently, but what follows in these cases?

The process of learning policy crystallizes into a process of social control, in which deviations are punished (usually gently) by reprimand, cutting one's story, the withholding of friendly comment by an executive, etc. For example, it is punishment for a staffer when the city editor waves a piece of his copy at him and says, "Joe, don't *do* that when you're writing about the mayor." In an actual case, a staffer acting as wire editor was demoted when he neglected to feature a story about a "sacred cow" politician on his paper. What can be concluded is that when an executive sees a clear anti-policy item, he blue-pencils it, and this constitutes a lesson for the staffer. Rarely does the staffer persist in violating policy; no such case appeared in all the interviews. Indeed, the best-known cases of firing for policy reasons—Ted O. Thackrey and Leo Huberman—occurred on liberal New York City dailies, and Thackrey was an editor, not a staffer.

Now and then cases arise in which a staffer finds his anti-policy stories printed. There seems to be no consistent explanation for this, except to introduce two more specific subjects dealing first, with the staffer's career line, and second, with particular empirical conditions associated with the career line. We can distinguish three stages through which the staffer progresses. First, there is the cub stage, the first few months or years in which the new man learns techniques and policy. He writes short, non-policy stories, such as minor accidents, meeting activity, the weather, etc. The second, or "wiring-in" stage, sees the staffer continuing to assimilate the newsroom values and to cement informal relationships. Finally there is the "star" or "veteran" stage, in which the staffer typically defines himself as a full, responsible member of the group, sees its goals as his, and can be counted on to handle policy sympathetically.[19]

To further specify the conformity-deviation problem, it must be understood that newspapering is a relatively complex activity. The newsman is responsible for a range of skills and judgments which are matched only in the professional and entrepreneurial fields. Oversimplifications about policy rigidity can be avoided if we ask, "*Under what conditions* can the staffer defy or by-pass policy?" We have already seen that staffers are free to argue news decisions with executives in brief "news conferences," but the arguments generally revolve around points of "newsiness," rather than policy as such.[20] Five factors appear significant in the area of the reporter's power to by-pass policy.

1. The norms of policy are not always entirely clear, just as many norms are vague and unstructured. Policy is covert by nature and has large scope. The paper may be Republican, but standing only lukewarm for

Republican Candidate A who may be too "liberal" or no friend of the publisher. Policy, if worked out explicitly, would have to include motivations, reasons, alternatives, historical developments, and other complicating material. Thus a twilight zone permitting a range of deviation appears.[21]

2. Executives may be ignorant of particular facts, and staffers who do the leg (and telephone) work to gather news can use their superior knowledge to subvert policy. On grounds of both personal belief and professional codes, the staffer has the option of selection at many points. He can decide whom to interview and whom to ignore, what questions to ask, which quotations to note, and on writing the story which items to feature (with an eye toward the headline), which to bury, and in general what tone to give the several possible elements of the story.

3. In addition to the "squeeze" tactic exploiting executives' ignorance of minute facts, the "plant" may be employed. Although a paper's policy may proscribe a certain issue from becoming featured, a staffer, on getting a good story about that issue, may "plant" it in another paper or wire service through a friendly staffer and submit it to his own editor, pleading the story is now too big to ignore.

4. It is possible to classify news into four types on the basis of source of origination. These are: the policy or campaign story, the assigned story, the beat story, and the story initiated by the staffer. The staffer's autonomy is larger with the latter than the former types. With the campaign story (build new hospital, throw rascals out, etc.), the staffer is working directly under executives and has little leeway. An assigned story is handed out by the city editor and thus will rarely hit policy head on, although the staffer has some leverage of selection. When we come to the beat story, however, it is clear that the function of the reporter changes. No editor comes between him and his beat (police department, city hall, etc.), thus the reporter gains the "editor" function. It is he who, to a marked degree, can select which stories to pursue, which to ignore. Several cases developed in interviews of beat men who smothered stories they knew would provide fuel for policy—policy they personally disliked or thought injurious to the professional code. The cooperation of would-be competing reporters is essential, of course. The fourth type of story is simply one which the staffer originates, independent of assignment or beat. All respondents, executives and staffers, averred that any employee was free to initiate stories. But equally regularly, they acknowledged that the opportunity was not often assumed. Staffers were already overloaded with beats, assignments, and routine coverage, and besides, rewards for initiated stories were meager or non-existent unless the initiated story confirmed policy. Yet this area promises much, should staffers pursue their advantage. The outstanding case in the present study concerned a well-educated, enthusiastic reporter on a

conventional daily just north of the Mason-Dixon line. Entirely on his own, he consistently initiated stories about Negroes and Negro-white relations, "making" policy where only void had existed. He worked overtime to document and polish the stories; his boss said he didn't agree with the idea but insisted on the reporter's right to publish them.

5. Staffers with "star" status can transgress policy more easily than cubs. This differential privilege of status was encountered on several papers. An example would be Walter Winchell during the Roosevelt administration, who regularly praised the president while the policy of his boss, Mr. Hearst, was strongly critical of the regime. A *New York Times* staffer said he doubted that any copy reader on the paper would dare change a word of the copy of Meyer Berger, the star feature writer.

These five factors indicate that given certain conditions, the controls making for policy conformity can be by-passed. These conditions exist not only within the newsroom and the news situation but within the staffer as well; they will be exploited only if the staffer's attitudes permit. There are some limitations, then, on the strength of the publisher's policy.

Before summarizing, three additional requirements of Merton's functional paradigm must be met. These are statements of the consequences of the pattern, of available alternative modes of behavior, and a validation of the analysis.

Consequences of the Pattern

To the extent that policy is maintained, the paper keeps publishing smoothly as seen both from the newsroom and from the outside, which is no mean feat if we visualize the country with no press at all. This is the most general consequence. There are several special consequences. For the society as a whole, the existing system of power relationships is maintained. Policy usually protects property and class interests, and thus the strata and groups holding these interests are better able to retain them. For the larger community, much news is printed objectively, allowing for opinions to form openly, but policy news may be slanted or buried so that some important information is denied the citizenry. (This is the dysfunction widely scored by critics.) For the individual readers, the same is true. For the executives, their favorable statuses are maintained, with perhaps occasional touches of guilt over policy. For newsmen, the consequences are the same as for executives. For more independent, critical staffers, there can be several modes of adaptation. At the extremes, the pure conformist can deny the conflict, the confirmed deviate can quit the newspaper business. Otherwise, the adaptations seem to run in this way: (1) Keep on the job but blunt the sharp corners of policy where possible ("If I wasn't here the next guy would let *all* that crap go through . . .") ; (2) Attempt to repress the conflict amorally and anti-intellectually ("What the hell, it's only a job; take your pay and forget it . . .") ; (3) Attempt to compensate, by "taking it out" in other contexts: drinking, writing "the truth" for liberal publications, working with action programs, the Guild and otherwise. All of these adjustments were found in the study. As has been suggested, one of the main compensations for all staffers is simply to find justification in adhering to "good news practice."

Possible Alternatives and Change

A functional analysis, designed to locate sources of persistence of a pattern, can also indicate points of strain at which a structural change may occur. For example, the popular recipe for eliminating bias at one time was to diminish advertisers' power over the news. This theory having proved unfruitful, critics more recently have fastened upon the publisher as the point at which change must be initiated. Our analysis suggests that this is a valid approach, but one requiring that leverage in turn be applied on the publisher from various sources. Perhaps the most significant of these are professional codes. Yet we have seen the weakness of these codes when policy decisions are made. Further leverage is contained in such sources as the professional direction being taken by some journalism schools, in the Guild, and in sincere criticism.

Finally, newspaper readers possess potential power over press performance. Seen as a client of the press, the reader should be entitled to not only an interesting newspaper, but one which furnishes significant news objectively presented. This is the basic problem of democracy: to what extent should the individual be treated as a member of a mass, and to what extent fashioned (through educative measures) as an active participant in public decisions? Readership studies show that readers prefer "interesting" news and "features" over penetrating analyses. It can be concluded that the citizen has not been sufficiently motivated by society (and its press) to demand and apply the information he needs, and to discriminate between worthwhile and spurious information, for the fulfillment of the citizen's role. These other forces—professional codes, journalism schools, the Guild, critics and readers—could result in changing newspaper performance. It still remains, however, for the publisher to be changed first. He can be located at the apex of a T, the crucial point of decision making. Newsroom and professional forces form the base of the T, outside forces from community and society are the arms. It is for the publisher to decide which forces to propitiate.

Suggestions for Validation

The Merton paradigm requires a statement concerning validation of the analysis. Checks could be forthcoming both from social science researchers and from newsmen. If the latter, the newsman should explicitly state the basis for his discussion, especially as regards the types of papers, executives, and staffers he knows. A crucial case for detailed description would be the situation in which staffers actively defied authority on policy matters. Another important test would be a comparative description of two papers contrasted by their situation as regards the six factors promoting conformity, with particular reference to the variable of obligation and esteem held toward superiors, and the factors permitting deviation. In any event, the present exploratory study may serve as a point of departure.

A second type of validation may be suggested. This would focus on the utility of the paradigm itself. Previous studies have been based on functional theory but before the development of the paradigm.[22] Studies of diverse social systems also lend themselves to functional analysis, and such comparative research could function not only to build systematic theory but to test and suggest modifications of the paradigm. Situations characterized by conflict and competition for scarce goals seem particularly well suited to functional analysis. Several points made in the present essay might have been overlooked without the paradigm.[23]

Summary

The problem, which was suggested by the age-old charges of bias against the press, focussed around the manner in which the publisher's policy came to be followed, despite three empirical conditions: (1) policy sometimes contravenes journalistic norms; (2) staffers often personally disagree with it; and (3) executives cannot legitimately command that policy be followed. Interview and other data were used to explain policy maintenance. It is important to recall that the discussion is based primarily on study of papers of "middle" circulation range, and does not consider either non-policy stories or the original policy decision made by the publishers.

The mechanisms for learning policy on the part of the new staffer were given, together with suggestions as to the nature of social controls. Six factors, apparently the major variables producing policy maintenance, were described. The most significant of these variables, obligation and esteem for superiors, was deemed not only the most important, but the most fluctuating variable from paper to paper. Its existence and its importance for conformity led to the sub-hypothesis that reference group behavior was playing a part in the pattern. To show, however, that policy is not iron-clad, five conditions were suggested in which staffers may by-pass policy.

Thus we conclude that the publisher's policy, when established in a given subject area, is usually followed, and that a description of the dynamic socio-cultural situation of the newsroom will suggest explanations for this conformity. The newsman's source of rewards is located not among the readers, who are manifestly his clients, but among his colleagues and superiors. Instead of adhering to societal and professional ideals, he re-defines his values to the more pragmatic level of the newsroom group. He thereby gains not only status rewards, but also acceptance in a solidary group engaged in interesting, varied, and sometimes important work. Thus the cultural patterns of the newsroom produce results insufficient for wider democratic needs. Any important change toward a more "free and responsible press" must stem from various possible pressures on the publisher, who epitomizes the policy making and coordinating role.

Footnotes

[1] See, for instance, F. J. Roethlisberger and William J. Dickson, *Management and the Worker* (Cambridge: Harvard University Press, 1947); and Logan Wilson, *The Academic Man* (New York: Oxford University Press, 1942).

[2] The best-known formal code is The Canons of Journalism, of the American Society of Newspaper Editors. See Wilbur Schramm (ed.), *Mass Communications* (Urbana: University of Illinois Press, 1949), pp. 236–38.

[3] It is extremely difficult to measure the extent of objectivity or bias. One recent attempt is reported in Nathan B. Blumberg, *One-Party Press?* (Lincoln: University of Nebraska Press, 1954), which gives a news count for 35 papers' performance in the 1952 election campaign. He concluded that 18 of the papers showed "no evidence of partiality," 11 showed "no conclusive evidence of partiality," and 6 showed partiality. His interpretations, however, are open to argument. A different interpretation could conclude that while about 16 showed little or no partiality, the rest did. It should be noted, too, that there are different areas of policy depending on local conditions. The chief difference occurs in the deep South, where frequently there is no "Republican" problem and no "union" problem over which the staff can be divided. Color becomes the focus of policy.

[4] This condition, pointed out in a lecture by Paul F. Lazarsfeld, formed the starting point for the present study.

[5] Similar findings were made about Washington correspondents in Leo C.

Rosten, *The Washington Correspondents* (New York: Harcourt, Brace, 1937). Less ideological conflict was found in two other studies: Francis V. Prugger, "Social Composition and Training of the Milwaukee Journal News Staff," *Journalism Quarterly*, 18 (Sept. 1941), pp. 231–44, and Charles E. Swanson, "The Mid-City Daily" (Ph.D. dissertation, State University of Iowa, 1948). Possible reasons for the gap are that both papers studied were perhaps above average in objectivity; executives were included with staffers in computations; and some staffers were doubtless included who did not handle policy news.

⁶ It is not being argued that "liberalism" and objectivity are synonymous. A liberal paper (e.g., *PM*) can be biased too, but it is clear that few liberal papers exist among the many conservative ones. It should also be stressed that much news is not concerned with policy and is therefore probably unbiased.

⁷ Robert K. Merton, *Social Theory and Social Structure* (Glencoe: Free Press, 1949), esp. pp. 49–61. Merton's elements will not be explicitly referred to but his principal requirements are discussed at various points.

⁸ The data are taken from Warren Breed, "The Newspaperman, News and Society" (Ph.D. dissertation, Columbia University, 1952). Indebtedness is expressed to William L. Kolb and Robert C. Stone, who read the present manuscript and provided valuable criticisms and suggestions.

⁹ For a summary description of this criticism, see Commission on the Freedom of the Press, *A Free and Responsible Press* (Chicago: University of Chicago Press, 1947), chap. 4.

¹⁰ While the concept of policy is crucial to this analysis, it is not to be assumed that newsmen discuss it fully. Some do not even use the word in discussing how their paper is run. To this extent, policy is a latent phenomenon; either the staffer has no reason to contemplate policy or he chooses to avoid so doing. It may be that one strength of policy is that it has become no more manifest to the staffers who follow it.

¹¹ Note that such executives' actions as blue-pencilling play not only the manifest function of preparing the story for publication but also the latent one of steering the future action of the staffer.

¹² Two cautions are in order here. First, it will be recalled that we are discussing not all news, but only policy news. Secondly, we are discussing only staffers who are potential non-conformers. Some agree with policy; some have no views on policy matters; others do not write policy stories. Furthermore, there are strong forces in American society which cause many individuals to choose harmonious adjustment (conformity) in any situation, regardless of the imperatives. See Erich Fromm, *Escape From Freedom* (New York: Farrar and Rinehart, 1941), and David Riesman, *The Lonely Crowd* (New Haven: Yale University Press, 1950).

¹³ Excellent illustration of this tactic is given in the novel by an experienced newspaperwoman: Margaret Long, *Affair of the Heart* (New York: Random House, 1953), chap. 10. This chapter describes the framing of a Negro for murder in a middle-sized southern city, and the attempt of a reporter to tell the story objectively.

¹⁴ The insulation of one individual or group from another is a good example of social (as distinguished from psychological) mechanisms to reduce the likelihood of conflict. Most of the factors inducing conformity could likewise be viewed as social mechanisms. See Talcott Parsons and Edward A. Shils, "Values, Motives and Systems of Action," in Parsons and Shils (eds.), *Toward a General Theory of Action* (Cambridge: Harvard University Press, 1951), pp. 223–30.

¹⁵ Further indication that the staffer-executive relationship is harmonious came from answers to the question, "Why do you think newspapermen are thought to be cynical?" Staffers regularly said that newsmen are cynical because they get close enough to stark reality to see the ills of their society, and the imperfections of its

leaders and officials. Only two, of 40 staffers, took the occasion to criticize their executives and the enforcement of policy. This displacement, or lack of strong feelings against executives, can be interpreted to bolster the hypothesis of staff solidarity. (It further suggests that newsmen tend to analyze their society in terms of personalities, rather than institutions comprising a social and cultural system.)

16 There is a sizeable myth among newsmen about the attractiveness of their calling. For example, the story: "Girl: 'My, you newspapermen must have a fascinating life. You meet such interesting people.' Reporter: 'Yes, and most of them are newspapermen.'" For a further discussion, see Breed, *op. cit.*, chap. 17.

17 This is a variant of the process of "displacement of goals," newsmen turning to "getting news" rather than to seeking data which will enlighten and inform their readers. The dysfunction is implied in the nation's need not for more news but for better news—quality rather than quantity. See Merton, *op. cit.*, "Bureaucratic Structure and Personality," pp. 154–55.

18 Whether group members acknowledge it or not, "if a person's attitudes are influenced by a set of norms which he assumes that he shares with other individuals, those individuals constitute for him a reference group." Theodore M. Newcomb, *Social Psychology* (New York: Dryden, 1950), p. 225. Williams states that reference group formation may segment large organizations; in the present case, the reverse is true, the loyalty of subordinates going to their "friendly" superiors and to the discharge of technical norms such as getting news. See Robin M. Williams, *American Society* (New York: Knopf, 1951), p. 476.

19 Does the new staffer, fresh from the ideals of college, really "change his attitudes"? It would seem that attitudes about socio-economic affairs need not be fixed, but are capable of shifting with the situation. There are arguments for and against any opinion; in the atmosphere of the newsroom the arguments "for" policy decisions are made to sound adequate, especially as these are evoked by the significant others in the system.

20 The fullest treatment of editor-reporter conferences appears in Swanson, *op. cit.*

21 Related to the fact that policy is vague is the more general postulate that executives seek to avoid formal issues and the possibly damaging disputes arising therefrom. See Chester I. Barnard, *Functions of the Executive* (Cambridge: Harvard University Press, 1947).

22 References are cited in Merton, *Social Theory and Social Structure, op. cit.,* and also in the works of Talcott Parsons.

23 That the paradigm might serve best as a check-list or "insurance," or as a theoretical guide to fledgling scholars, is shown by the excellence of an article published before the paradigm—and quite similar to the present article in dealing with problems of policy maintenance in a formal organization: Edward A. Shils and Morris Janowitz, "Cohesion and Disintegration in the Wehrmacht in World War II," *Public Opinion Quarterly*, 12 (Summer 1948), pp. 280–315.

Work Careers

Demotion

Douglas M. More

Northern Illinois University

There are many studies in the fields of business and of industrial psychology that assess individual abilities related to requirements for promotion within the business hierarchy. While some conditions contributing to downward movement in the occupational system have been specified, rarely do we find mention of demotion as an instrument of industrial control, or even as a distinct phenomenon occurring within industry. Nowhere do we find specific attention given to the various forms of demotion that occur, or the conditions under which businesses may and do use demotion in handling the management group.[1] Some attention has been given to the psychological consequences of loss of occupational status. Even this is, in our opinion, quite incomplete, tending to emphasize the negative consequences of such loss, rather than giving systematic attention to any of its possible consequences. In one instance it has been pointed out that downwardly mobile people tend to have lower rates of mental disorder than those who are upwardly mobile.[2] Our purposes in this paper are: (1) to lay out a scheme of the forms of demotion that we have observed; (2) to indicate the conditions which increase the likelihood of demotion being used as a business process; and (3) to analyze the consequences of demotion on the individuals demoted and on the company organizations in which this takes place.

In the past several years we have had the opportunity to observe intimately, over sufficient periods of time, the processes of promotion and demotion in a wide range of businesses. These include many companies in the small class from $100,000 to $1,000,000 yearly sales volume, 9 in the class from $1,000,000 to $6,000,000, over a dozen companies in the range from $6,000,000 to $20,000,000, 13 in the range from $20,000,000 to $60,000,000,

Reprinted from *Social Problems*, Vol. 9, No. 3 (Winter 1962), 213–21, by permission of the author and the Society for the Study of Social Problems.

and 14 very large corporations, among the five hundred largest in the United States. In about half of these, covering this entire range, we did not observe dramatic forms of demotion. In the other half, one or more of the forms of demotion classified below occurred with sufficient frequency to constitute a company-wide phenomenon of note and importance. In the former group, the lack of demotion as a phenomenon can be attributed in most cases to consciously adopted policies of dismissing a man after he has been found wanting in a position, rather than demoting him to a lower level job. Such companies make this policy because they feel, and often state, that it is more detrimental to company morale to demote a person from a management position than it is to dismiss the individual involved and to seek a replacement for him.

In one organization we have recently studied, which lies in the yearly dollar volume group from $20 to $60 million, we learned that out of 70 individuals who had had more than five years of service in management positions, roughly one-third had experienced one or another obvious form of demotion in the course of their employment with the company. This is only one among many companies in which we observed demotion, and perhaps it is one in which this occurs strongly. Nonetheless, demotion appears as a sufficiently common business process to have deserved more intensive analysis than it has received. Perhaps we have avoided studying demotion, because it is one of those unpleasant topics, just as in psychology we can observe that there are far more studies of highly intelligent and gifted children than there are studies of feeble-minded and defective children.

Before proceeding to a consideration of the forms of demotion, it is necessary to define the term in a general sense. We consider it as a process in business and industry in which an individual is reduced to a lower grade or classification of function, or has his relative position in the hierarchy decreased as a result of surrounding forces. Both promotion and demotion are results of external forces, or authorities, acting on individuals. A man cannot be promoted to a higher position or demoted to a lower position by his efforts alone, but must be acted upon by some other person who has this authority. Demotion in this sense includes a wide range of changes of behavior or status within a company, all the way from those which imply minimal change up to, but not including, outright dismissal from the company.

The Forms of Demotion

The forms of demotion we have observed are:

1. *Lowered job status with continuation of the earlier compensation.*

This is the case when a man is demoted from a position of general foreman to line foreman in the department but, at the discretion of the president of the company, earns the same amount of money at the lowered status.

2. *Lowered status with decreased compensation.* This particular form of demotion seems to be the most characteristic one to define the term itself. We doubt, however, that it would be the commonest form, if it were possible to achieve an accurate count. As an example, we have noted the situation in which a general superintendent, paid at the rate of $13,500.00 per year was demoted to the status of a divisional superintendent with a cut in pay to $10,800.00 per year. As an interesting sidelight, it was found necessary to raise the salary of a parallel divisional superintendent from $9,600.00 per year to $10,800.00 per year when this move was made, in order that the two men should have the same compensation on the same level.

3. *Retained status with decreased compensation.* Strictly, perhaps this should not be considered a form of demotion because the individual involved retains the same level of prestige and functional authority that he previously had, but is merely being paid less to do the job. We include it here for completeness, but would not insist on maintaining this form in our over-all scheme. It is not common except with men of advanced years who are "semi-retired."

4. *Being "bypassed" in seniority for promotion.* Although in this kind of case there is no objective change in an individual's status, there is apparently a loss in a person's reputation and his strength to influence operations within a company. In a very obvious sense, to anyone who knows the situation this can be seen as a "slap in the face." Commonly we note that men in this category seem to give up hope for promotions in the age range from 50 to 55 years.

5. *Change of job to a less desirable function.* A particular instance we observed recently involved this form of demotion for a chief engineer in the company. Originally he was in charge of an engineering development group. When the project his group had been assigned bogged down and he seemed incapable of moving ahead with it, the project was reassigned to another engineering group. The engineer in question was removed from his position and, without change of level in formal company status or compensation, was moved to a position in charge of plant maintenance engineering, while one of his former subordinates was promoted to the position he had vacated.

6. *Maintained formal status with decreased span of control.* An example is of a single individual who had general charge of market research, marketing programs, advertising, and the sales force. In a subsequent period he retained line direction of the sales force, another individual, reporting to the President, was named Director of Marketing.

7. *Exclusion from a general salary raise.* In the past several years our expanding economy and increased inflationary pressures have produced

several rounds of salary raises in most large firms, especially for important executive positions. From time to time we have observed instances in which particular individuals have been excluded from a general salary raise often with a side comment running somewhat as follows, "Everybody is getting a raise this year end, but we just can't see giving Joe Smith a raise at this time. We currently are paying all we can for the job he is doing."

8. *Increased steps in the hierarchy above given position.* This phenomenon frequently occurs in small to medium sized companies that are expanding rapidly. As the complexity of the company's operations increases with increasing size, the necessity for greater diversification of management talents and specialization by departments increases. Technological advances have made impossible further honoring of the maxim to promote from within. Frequently, new positions are created in the managerial hierarchy, particularly at intermediate levels, so that such departmentalization can proceed smoothly. Everyone below the position created may be considered as having had a demotion, in the sense of being removed one further step from possibly moving to a very high position in the company. Such instances should be considered important demotion phenomena when it is apparent that a position has been created in the company hierarchy to prevent the advance of certain key people at lower levels.

9. *Movement from line to staff authority, but with the same compensation.* Generally such moves in a company are tantamount to demotions in the sense of removing the individual from the possibility of advancing in the power hierarchy of the company. In many modern organizations which are strongly research-oriented and research-directed, this may not be the case.

10. *Retention of the same job level, with same compensation, and carrying with it equal authority and responsibility, but transfer out of direct line of promotion.* This is distinguished from the preceding statement, because there is no implication that the person has changed his job function. We have in mind the case that we observed recently of an individual who was moved from being a general manager of a major metal fabricating plant in close connection with the main offices of the company to a position in charge of an even larger branch plant in a distant rural area. He was effectively severed from informal, social relationships with people in powerful positions in the home office, and consequently had his chance of advancement through such informal processes severely decreased.

11. *Position elimination and reassignment.* This kind of demotion occurs most commonly in major company reorganizations. These are frequently a consequence of management efficiency studies and the like. It is found that certain positions in the firm are totally unnecessary. Because the individual occupying such a position may have considerable tenure in the company, it frequently is deemed possible to reassign him to another job. The

course of reassignment in which this connotes demotion is such that the person is moved into a department with a loss of senior rank or a decreased level of function within the company power structure.

Conditions Increasing the Likelihood of Demotion

We have assembled in the following, those conditions we have found in a variety of businesses to be associated with demotion as it has been outlined above. Not all the conditions we list here may apply in any given case. It is our experience that some of them, either in combination or separately, occur in every instance in which demotion is a highly visible or reasonably recognizable feature. These points again are phrased in a descriptive way, rather than attempting at this early stage to create a logically parsimonious set of limiting conditions.

1. *Extreme paternalism as the company "climate."* This is a frequently observed feature of companies in which demotions are common. Paternalism is not simply an attitude of management; it also reflects acceptance on the part of lower levels of management and workers of a filial role toward the parental head of the company. It is precisely this emotional acceptance of the paternalistic image that permits the punitive practices of demotion to occur and to be accepted by the management and worker groups.

2. *Seductive benefit programs.* In many companies, although benefit programs seem to operate to the direct benefit of the employee, it is possible for an individual to accrue a considerable retirement benefit with a company after he has been with it a number of years. This tends to increase the likelihood that a person will accept a change of status downward in order to remain with the company to be able to participate to the full in his anticipated benefits. Especially is this true when he would receive only a percentage of final benefits were he to leave the company prior to full retirement age.

3. *Scarcity of positions outside the company to which men might move.* Demotion can occur in instances such as this when a company controls virtually all the jobs of importance in a given area. When this is the case, if a worker leaves a company, he is put to considerable hardship to move himself and his family some distance from his present location in order to find work concomitant with his level of training and ability. This increases the possibility that a company may be able to deal with its workers in an arbitrary way.

4. *High average age in supervisory personnel.* Above age fifty foremen, supervisors, and others in the company middle management levels find it

relatively difficult to move from a job in one company to a similar or better position in another company. Although a person may be well qualified for a job, companies, as much because of the folklore of employment practices as anything, exhibit reluctance to employ people over age forty. This is so severe a question that some states have legislated against employment discrimination toward a senior citizen. When high average age among supervisors occurs in a firm, it is possible for the company to demote individuals without them feeling that they have any chance of moving elsewhere. These men seem to feel that they have to take it as it is dished out to them.

5. *Sharply fluctuating work load.* This is a condition that tends to permit demotion, particularly in industries that are strongly influenced by seasonal changes, because of varying contractual loads as is the typical case of the job shop. A job shop is dependent on contracts from clients, and when it doesn't get them, it is forced to lay off workers and often to decrease the size of the supervisory staff. During such a layoff, persons at one of the higher supervisory levels may be stepped down to jobs at lower levels, at least temporarily. The way this process increases the likelihood of demotion is that certain individuals the company may have decided to cut back need not be promoted back to former levels of authority when there is the next major buildup in employment.

6. *A company condition of loss or non-profit.* This condition frequently necessitates a reduction in management overhead. As the phrase goes, men who have been "taking it easy behind the desk" may have to roll up their sleeves and get back to work.

7. *Mergers producing an over supply of managerial personnel to staff the available positions.* This often occurs in mergers of companies of approximately equal size in the medium to large ranges. In such conditions, unless there is a clearcut continuation of a division of products and services, the merged company does not need, for example, two vice-presidents in charge of sales. After mergers there is commonly a great deal of loss of morale in middle management ranks, as the two companies who have been merged begin to shake down. Everyone seems to be watching closely to see who it is that is going to move into a position or retain his former position, and which members of the two company managements are going to have to take a back seat.

8. *Belated recognition that certain men have been promoted beyond their capacities.* This often results in what business has come to phrase as "restructuring of job content," in which the expectations of the company toward the man in a position are realigned to be more realistically in accord with what the person can do. Whenever there is an intensification of specifications laying out the duties inherent in a position, this tends to remove authority and responsibility from the position itself. For a company to have to spell out a man's job for him in considerable detail, means that it has

removed from him the possibility of exercising independent judgment, initiative, or discretionary behavior.

9. *Broad company reorganizations of management structures and functions.* Demotions occur in these instances because company officials come to realize that management efficiency may have to be improved. Such management improvement programs often result in decreased need numerically for managers as such. When meaningful studies of efficiency are completed it is often found that there are individuals in the group who are in nonfunctional, or at least minimally effective, positions. Demotions and reassignments frequently follow.

10. *Position obsolescence.* This often occurs as a consequence of mechanization or automation. In these instances, companies—since warm-heartedness rather than cold-heartedness seems to be the current business philosophy —often tend to try to "make" positions in order to retain people on the staff, to avoid creating economic hardship among employees who have been with them some time. The fact is, however, that these men must be seen as demoted as regards their actual levels of functioning in the company.

11. *A contracting economy in the company's area of activity.* In a rapidly changing economy there are many entire industries that are decreasing while others increase. Frequently this happens as new inventions and new methods make possible the displacement of them in the market. For example, extruded and molded plastics are rapidly displacing many items that formerly were produced in the glass and metal industries. Those segments of the glass and metal industries, in proportion, exhibit a contracting number (or proportion) of management jobs available. The status of a contracting aspect of an industry complex tends to decrease vis-a-vis other parts of the same industry complex. As its status decreases, the amount that a company is willing to allocate to executive salaries in that area of its operation correspondingly is constricted. Railroading, and those companies supplying to the railroads, present this feature rather clearly at this time, and have over the past decade.

Consequences of Demotion

In this section we wish to take the third step in our analysis of demotion in two respects. First, we consider the way demotion affects the individual demoted, and then the effects of demotion on the company as a whole.

When a person is demoted, this generally is the result of a negative evaluation of him or his job by his superiors. Such an implicit or explicit negative evaluation tends to increase the individual's feelings of anxiety about his job, to lead him to question his own worthfulness. The person may show, as a consequence, increasing negativism, bitterness, resistance to direction within the firm, and may go so far as to express a defeatist attitude with respect to his total life goals. Frequently we have noted demotion to result in widespread lethargy in a person's behavior, almost amounting to an inability to function. Often, individuals who feel especially bitter toward their companies for having demoted them show tendencies toward sabotage, in an effort, in effect, to get even with the company for the hurt and damage it has done to them.

The above are rather blatant results. In our experience there is often a more subtle effect of affective withdrawal of the person from group contacts. While the person may continue to work, and work well, at his job, this withdrawal process results in a kind of non-communicative blandness in social contacts in the work situation. Psychologically speaking, this may result because the individual feels he must maintain self-esteem by withdrawing from any contact in which he might be subject to further negative interpersonal evaluations. It may also represent a retreat into a wishful fantasy life, a la Walter Mitty, rather than a concentration on the objective requirements of the work role.[3]

Although negative effects of demotion are probably more pronounced, in a significant minority of cases there are definite positive effects. The demotion can act as a spur to work hard to recapture former status, resulting in increased effort and output. The man may become more realistically self-critical and may drive himself toward more thoroughness and perfectionism. He may readjust his aspirations to more realistic levels, and, as a result, improve his functioning to the point that he can be promoted back to former status.

In a third group there appear to be feelings of contentment. This most often occurs to men who have been demoted from positions which were extremely burdensome to them, given their abilities and talents. The demotion represents to them a release from tension-producing burdens of authority and responsibility they were unable to handle. These men express a sense of comfort at being able to return to familiar, easier tasks. In retrospect we learn that these are the men who have expressed at the time of their promotions some resentments against the company and their superiors for having pushed them into positions they felt they were unprepared to handle.[4]

There are levels of negative and positive effects to be distinguished. Quite commonly we note an intensification of the "climate of authoritarian paternalism" and the implied consequences of such a system. With increased authoritarian paternalism we often find an increased cohesiveness in the worker groups at the bottom of the company, and consequent increased conflict between worker groups and management. Top management tends to lose bargaining power, in part because it loses the loyalty of middle management. Foremen may become unwilling to "administer" a labor contract. This trend also leads to placing greater burdens of decision making and communication on one or a very few people at the top of the firm. This can easily decrease the over-all efficiency of the company organization.

Another effect on a company as a result of established demotion practices is a loss of morale in all levels of management below the very top. Specific effects that we would lump under this general term are:

1. Decreased individual productivity.

2. Decreased creative efforts from men in positions that require creative work.

3. Loss of loyalty to the company, a feeling that the company no longer deserves the emotional attachment the person had given it earlier.

4. An increase in turnover in middle management and in supervisory positions.

5. Increased chronic illnesses and absenteeism, as a result of the unwillingness of people to come to work, because they feel that the work is not worthy. Interestingly this may be seen as actual chronic illness, or merely reported chronic illness.

6. Increase in abuse of privileges—tendency to stretch out the lunch hour, rest periods, and coffee breaks to unreasonable length; decreased attention to the work itself; increases in petty theft; use of the company's facilities for personal interests.

7. Moonlighting. In companies that have a history of demotion, and in which the process of demotion is well-established, it is our impression that, except in those companies that rigidly restrict the worker's right to work anywhere else, there is a high frequency of outside work and outside business interests. Men often will give more time or energy to such interests than they will give to their main jobs.

8. Formation of protective power cliques. The *informal* structures of supervision tend under demotion to become more and more rigid as sub-groups coalesce in an attempt to secure sufficient power for themselves to insure personal continuance as small, entrenched enclaves in the management hierarchy.

Some results of a system of demotion may be seen as positive. There may be a clear gain in morale, rather than a loss, when the persons demoted are individuals who are responsible for major problems in the company. If the manager demoted was one who was unable to make decisions, or to institute action, and his replacement can do so, there is a sharp increase in morale. This results in better definition of work roles, decrease of confusion resulting from ambiguity. Few things are more destructive of morale than a vague, diffuse, and ambivalent definition of the work situation. Corresponding to such gains in morale there may be gains in efficiency and productivity throughout the firm.

Another kind of gain that may occur under demotion depends on the prior establishment of a well-publicized promotion-demotion system. This permits moving men up to positions temporarily for training purposes, then demoting them to former jobs. This allows a company to develop a body of trained managers on which to draw for expansion or replacement when needed. For this to have positive effects, it must be recognized and accepted in middle management, and there must have been time for the men involved to see that the system does indeed operate to create opportunities within the company. To be realistic a company must make it clear that these are trial or training assignments, not final promotions. Demotion out of the position, then, is not seriously taken, and perhaps should not be seen as fitting into the broad picture of demotion as we have outlined it.

Summary

In the above we have attempted to lay out a descriptive scheme of the forms of demotion, as used in business and industries we have observed, and to specify the conditions, limits, and mechanisms that appear to be associated with demotion. Finally, we indicated the apparent consequences of demotion on individuals and companies. We can in no sense pretend that our scheme approaches a theoretical statement. It is a first level of inference from widely scattered and discontinuous observations. Any further development toward a theory applicable in this area will have to be integrated, in our opinion, with general theory of vertical movement. Demotion must seen only as a special instance of downward social and occupational mobility. The total theory will have to take into account the economics of the firm, the labor market, and other general changes in the occupational system. This we have hesitated to attempt at this early stage.

Footnotes

The writer is deeply indebted to Nathan Kohn, Jr., and Harry Morley for critical evaluation of an early draft of this paper in January, 1960. The present draft was presented at the meetings of the Midwest Sociological Society, Omaha, Nebraska, April, 1961.

[1] Strictly, demotion is a part of the general study of administrative succession.

Fundamental contributions to this area have been made by Alvin Gouldner, *Patterns of Industrial Bureaucracy*, Glencoe, Ill.: The Free Press, 1954; Norman Martin and Anselm Strauss, "Patterns of mobility within industrial organizations," in W. L. Warner and N. H. Martin (eds.), *Industrial Man*, New York: Harper and Brothers, 1959, pp. 96–100; and, Oscar Grusky, "Administrative succession in formal organizations," *Social Forces*, Vol. 39, No. 2, Dec. 1960, pp. 105–115.

[2] This conclusion can be made from the studies by Hollingshead and colleagues in their survey of class, mobility, and mental illness in New Haven. Cf. A. B. Hollingshead, R. Ellis, and E. Kirby, "Social mobility and mental illness," *American Sociological Review*, Vol. 19, No. 5, October 1954, pp. 577–584; A. B. Hollingshead and F. C. Redlich, *Social Class and Mental Illness*, New York: Wiley, 1958. Studies of social mobility and related phychosomatic illness also support such a conclusion. See especially Jurgen Reusch, *et al., Duodenal Ulcer*, Berkeley: Univ. of California Press, 1948, pp. 86–91, in which the rate of duodenal ulcer is reported to be less than one-third as great for "decliners" as it is for "climbers" and "static" persons. In an earlier study, Reusch, *et al.*, "Chronic disease and psychological invalidism," *Psychosomatic Medicine Monographs*, New York: American Society for Research in Psychosomatic Problems, 1946, pp. 103–124, ratings on mobility of cases of delayed recovery resulted in a distribution of 45 percent "static," 39 percent "climbers," 12 percent "decliners," and 4 percent "mixed." It is worth adding that the "decliners" have the worst prognosis for psychotherapy. S. Lipset, *Social Mobility in Industrial Society*, Berkeley: Univ. of California Press, 1959, pp. 251–252, concurs with the conclusion on this evidence; the writer feels the evidence weak, if not insufficient, at this date.

[3] Martin and Strauss (*op. cit.*) suggest that class background of the demotee strongly influences the type of negative reaction, lower class people more prone to act out and higher class men more apt to withdraw.

[4] The extent to which a sample of demotees contains a high percentage of these "contented" ones may be involved in the conclusion that downwardly mobile people exhibit low frequencies of mental disturbance (see note 2 above). Further studies of emotional adjustment as related to vertical mobility probably should attend to some classification, such as we suggest, into reaction types.

Professionalization

Professionalization

Its Functions and Dysfunctions for the
Life Insurance Occupation

M. LEE TAYLOR
Louisiana State University in New Orleans
ROLAND J. PELLEGRIN
University of Oregon

The rising tide of professionalization is one of the most striking characteristics of contemporary occupational organization.[1] Associated with it is increasingly specialized knowledge and service as well as elevated prestige for professionals and would-be professionals. The trend toward an ever expanding number of professions continues almost unabated as numerous occupational groupings among white collar workers and specialists seek professional status. Indeed, in modern society the traditional distinctions between professions and nonprofessions have become quite tenuous. There is a tendency for all occupations that require advanced education, training, or technical skill to put forth claims to professional status.[2] It has also become common practice to seek legal certification and its accompanying monopolistic advantages.[3] An evaluation of the situation leads one readily to the conclusion that, while professions are growing quantitatively, their qualitatively distinct characteristics have become diluted and their influence on occupational behavior precarious. It has in fact been asserted by one authority that the distinction between occupations and professions is invidious.[4]

Despite the impressive increase in the number of occupations that are called professions by their practitioners, there are numerous difficulties encountered by an occupation that seeks to achieve professional status and recognition. Professionalization can hardly be achieved through study of lists of characteristics of professions[5] and the development of a program which seeks to attain these characteristics as though they were "steps" in the achievement of professional status.

Reprinted from *Social Forces*, Vol. 38, No. 2 (December 1959), 110–14, by permission of the authors and publisher. Copyright © 1959 by the University of North Carolina Press.

It is the purpose of this paper to bring into view some of the dynamics of the difficult professionalization process as revealed by an investigation of life insurance men.[6] This study calls to attention the conflict of two major goals of the occupation: to promote professionalization, and to extend life insurance protection to all socio-economic groups in the population. For the occupation the trend toward professionalization is functional[7] in that it heightens occupational status; however, it is dysfunctional for both the occupation and society in that it is incompatible in certain respects with service to a greater number of people.

Data and Methodology

Data used in this study were obtained primarily from two sources. First, a selective survey was made of the wealth of literature concerning the life insurance industry in general. This literature consisted of historical, statistical, ideological, professional, propagandistic, and other materials; but none was primarily sociological.[8] A second source of data was confidential depth interviews with 64 life insurance men taken in the fall of 1957 in a prominent southern city. Respondents represented companies domiciled in all regions of the nation; companies founded prior to the mid-nineteenth century and those founded in the twentieth century; some of the largest and smallest companies; some of the most conservative and some of the most liberal companies; and ordinary, industrial, and combination companies. The interviewees represented the following categories of practitioners (inclusive of intermediate categories where they exist, e.g., men between the categories of old-timers and newcomers): (1) 20 administrators, or home, regional, or local office men, and 44 agents, or members of the agency or sales forces; (2) 50 (78 percent) old-timers, or men who had been in the occupation three years or longer, and 14 (22 percent) newcomers, or men who had been in the occupation less than three years; (3) 2 company presidents and 7 parttime agents; (4) 4 Chartered Life Underwriters and 28 men with no training; (5) 20 (31 percent) college graduates and 44 (69 percent) noncollege educated men; and (6) 39 (61 percent) members of professional associations and 25 (39 percent) nonprofessional association members. This study, then, is not limited either to field agents, to home office personnel, or to some other category of practitioners within the occupation.

The Life Insurance Situation

Life insurance as an *occupation*[9] is relatively new; it can be said to have emerged gradually in the nineteenth century. The original life insurance men were home office officials concerned with organizing a business. *Agency forces* were first employed in the 1840's; and after the turn of the century, soliciting agents gradually acquired a distinctive occupational identity. The prominence of agents in the life insurance industry has increased until today some investigators, perhaps in myopic judgement, consider them *the* real life insurance men. A more penetrating analysis of the occupation, however, shows that both agents and home office men collectively constitute the occupational practitioners.

As occupations mature out of their pre-history and develop a consciousness of their existence, there are some practitioners who come to see the occupation as a whole and for whom the occupation becomes virtually an end in itself. In the early days of this occupation some life insurance men began to view their occupation in the above manner. These perceptive individuals were innovators and leaders in the founding of trade organizations and, eventually, professional organizations. The overt aims of the trade and professional organizations were to improve the service of the life insurance men to their policyholders. However, motives were far from being completely altruistic, and there are some suggestions that even the earliest efforts at organization were intended to elevate the status of the occupation and expand the business.

In 1927 the American College of Life Underwriters was founded. It has since become one of the occupation's leading promoters of professionalism. The conviction motivating its founders was that the proper fitting of life insurance protection to individual and business needs should be elevated above the level of mere salesmanship. Moreover, it was thought that life insurance should be conceived of as a profession in which underwriters, expertly trained in financial and security matters and pledged to high ethical idealism, would counsel and guide their clients.[10]

These idealistic aims of the American College of Life Underwriters reveal no perceived conflict between the promotion of professionalization and the extension of sales and service to an ever greater mass of people. Far from suggesting any conflict, they suggest an ideological compatibility between these diverse goals. The sociological problem is one of ascertaining what differences, if any, exist between this statement of the *ideal* occupational structure and the *actual* occupational organization. The present investigation revealed considerable divergence between the ideal and actual patterns, manifested in the form of dysfunctions for the occupation.

There are multiple dimensions related to the process of professionalization, two of which are treated in the discussion which follows. The first dimension of professionalization of pertinence here concerns the increased training which is encouraged for life insurance men. The second involves the image the life insurance man has of himself as a professional.

Training vs. Service for All

Prominent in the thinking of certain life insurance men has been the idea that one of the most propitious ways to elevate their occupational status was to develop an extensive training program for all practitioners. Accordingly, in 1927 an idealistic and comprehensive study program was launched to provide a professional standard of education for life underwriters. This course of study, which leads to the C.L.U. (Chartered Life Underwriter) designation, is said to be equivalent to the C.P.A. (Certified Public Accountant) or even to the Master of Arts degree awarded by universities. The prestige of the C.L.U. may be exaggerated by such comparisons; but its attainment does require comprehensive knowledge, and it is the highest designation the occupation bestows on its practitioners. The course of study is quite comprehensive, ranging over topics which in some cases are but indirectly related to the technicalities of insurance and selling. Included are such subjects as business law, banking and corporation finance, social insurance, tax law, and investment policy, as well as others.

In actuality the C.L.U. training requirements are so comprehensive that there is much objection to them. The negative criticisms most frequently voiced by more than 40 percent of the interviewees in this study are that C.L.U. is "strictly an academic organization and has not done a thing for the policyholder," that the program is "exclusive and discriminatory," restricting membership to a certain few. The view was expressed that "only a certain few will ever be accepted, no matter how hard individuals study."

The empirical situation is this: As life insurance men become more career-professionally oriented, they tend to become selective in their service to clients. This is to say that they prefer to sell life insurance to a professional clientele—doctors, lawyers, or engineers—or to industrialists and other big executives. Typical comments of more than 37 percent of the professional men concerning their choices of clients were: "I prefer to serve the professional and business classes; most of my clients are physicians"; "Most of my clients are heavily propertied men"; "I serve the upper class"; "Business and professional men come to see me"; and "Most of my clients are middle-class professionals and businessmen." Several of the respondents who expressed these views are Chartered Life Underwriters; one was formerly a lawyer and another at one time an engineer. It is also to be noted that the highly educated men that the occupation attracts select clients from the higher socio-economic classes. Usually, the college graduate who goes into life insurance (and there are few of them, although the number is increasing) wants to become an *estate consultant* (75 percent of the respondents) rather than a debit man. It is, however, pointed out to life insurance men by fellow practitioners that over half of the families in the United States are in the middle to low income categories. This means the big potential market for life underwriters is among families with middle incomes or lower, while possibilities of making sales to industrialists and professionals are necessarily limited. The extent to which advanced professional training of life insurance men influences them to become *estate consultants* to the exclusion of soliciting most small policy business must be viewed as dysfunctional in terms of the avowed occupational goal of serving an ever greater number of people.

It is also recognized by some life insurance men that as the life insurance industry fails to provide adequate insurance coverage for middle and low income people, and as social insurance makes more such provisions, the private life insurance market is diminished. In other words, agents usually understand that the average family will invest only a certain relatively small proportion of its income in life insurance. Consequently, as social security benefits are increased to cover many lower income families, the probability of selling them additional private life insurance is lessened. Some life insurance men (22 percent of the interviewees) view this situation as a threat to the industry, and they actively encourage the extension of life insurance protection to more and more clients rather than to a select few who can afford large policies. The average agent, however, sees social security as an aid to his business and asserts that it has made people aware of the need for insurance. Despite this fact, it is worth noting that there is considerable opposition in the insurance industry to the extension of present social security benefits.[11]

Ultimately, objections to the relatively idealistic C.L.U. program became so ubiquitous throughout the occupation and the felt need for a more practical sales course so widespread, that in 1947 the L.U.T.C. (Life Underwriter Training Council) was established as an admittedly nonprofessional course. Its objective is to improve sales techniques. The advantages of L.U.T.C. are readily perceived by the life underwriter, and his willingness to take this study course is generally greater than his desire to take the C.L.U. program which is recommended by a more intangible value to its recipient.

In further contrast and opposition to the tendency to develop an "elite class" of life underwriters who are extensively trained and who limit their service to the few, there are practitioners who are proponents of what can be called the "humanitarian" approach to life insurance. This type of life insurance man often has a religious fervor for his occupation and feels *called* to render an invaluable service to all his fellow men, no matter what their socio-economic class or status. To this type of man, sophistication in training, programming, or estate counseling is far less important than the making of a sale—even the most simple "package deal"—which he believes to be a fundamental human service. Spokesmen for this humanitarian approach make their position clear. They believe that life insurance protection should be extended to more and more people; that emphasis should be on the number of policies sold and less on programming and estate counseling.[12] Life insurance men so oriented have recently taken steps to glorify the position of the *debit man*, who most frequently sells to low and middle income families, and who in the past has frequently been the man of lowest status in the occupation.

Study of the occupation shows, however, that while two goals—professionalization and service to a greater number of people—are both explicitly stated, and both to an extent achieved, the professionalization goal currently receives dominant emphasis.

The Professional Self-Image

The second dimension of professionalization which reveals dysfunctional aspects for the occupation is the image the life insurance man has of himself as a professional. For some time many life insurance men (22 percent of the respondents) who see their occupation in perspective have manifested considerable apprehension concerning the *career-professional* image and its impact on the vitality of the occupation. Not infrequently old-timers in the occupation remark that as neophytes are recruited they are carefully and highly trained—if not coddled—and as a result they become more interested in security and fringe benefits, as a part of their professional ideology, than in an opportunity to make sales. The new professional orientation is in contrast to the old image of the salesman as a *rugged individualist*, a man who did not want a guaranteed average salary, but, instead, freedom of opportunity to make his own fortune. The new professionally oriented life insurance man, often a C.L.U., is implicitly if not explicitly accused of wanting to emulate the executive, the desk man, the decision maker, rather than be an aggressive salesman. The accusation that the new career or security-professional approach offers the salesman little motivation is widely made in many sales occupations.[13]

The extent to which the observation that professionalization reduces sales vitality is correct is also the extent to which this dimension of the professionalization process is dysfunctional for the occupation. However, the evidence of asserting that "securityism" is in opposition to the making of a good, producing salesman is conjectural. Logically there is no reason to conclude that the man who is tense and insecure is more highly motivated to be a high production salesman than the man who enjoys a reasonable security in his occupation. The existing evidence lends caution to extreme assertions on this point.

Discussion

The analysis of the program for professionalization demonstrates that there is a reciprocal relation between the internal structure and the external functions of the occupation. Consequently, it is not practical for members of an occupation to decide that, for a variety of arbitrary reasons, they should develop a program of professionalization and *ipso facto* expect it to be successful. The success of planned changes for an occupational structure is necessarily limited and largely determined by the functions of the occupation for the greater society. Therefore, when certain professionally oriented life insurance men inaugurated the Chartered Life Underwriter training program and endeavored to promote it, there was soon to develop sharp opposition to the program. The opposition, an inevitable outgrowth from the occupational culture, was soundly based on the argument that most life insurance men could sell their product and service almost as well, and in some cases better, without having the advanced training. The objective fact is that in a sales occupation most practitioners have far greater need for new sales techniques than for training in business law, banking and corporation finance, and a number of other specialized areas of study that constitute the core of C.L.U. training.

The Chartered Life Underwriter designation actually serves more as a prestige factor or status identification within the occupation than as a method of increasing the service of the practitioner to the average policyholder. While professional prestige is a powerful driving force, the C.L.U. designation has often been viewed as a price too great to pay for prestige alone.

The evidence in the case of the life insurance occupation points clearly to the reciprocal relations between social structure and social function. The principle to be observed is that the degree of counteraction that an occupational goal (in this case professionalization) will evoke is related to its arbitrary support beyond its objective justifications. In the case of life insurance men the disproportionate promotion of one goal, professionalization, has precipitated a growth of dysfunctions for other occupational goals. Practitioners not only are bound by their occupational culture but must operate within the framework of the various institutions of their society. Only within this framework can practitioners plan and establish new occupational goals.

The dynamics of professionalization involve more than agreement on a certain number of "steps" through which an occupation must develop or which it must fulfill and then, as a matter of course, proclaim its new elevated status. Professionalization is far from being this arbitrary. Instead it is to be properly understood as a social product of the reciprocal interrelations between the occupational structure and social institutions.

Footnotes

Read before the twenty-second annual meeting of the Southern Sociological Society in Gatlinburg, Tennessee, April 18, 1959.

[1] For studies of the growth, development, and status of the professions, see A. M. Carr-Saunders and P. A. Wilson, *The Professions* (London: Oxford University Press, 1933); Roy Lewis and Angus Maude, *Professional People* (London: Phoenix House, Ltd., 1952); and Talcott Parsons, "The Professions and Social Structure," *Social Forces*, 17 (May 1939), pp. 457–467.

[2] A. M. Carr-Saunders, "Metropolitan Conditions and Traditional Professional Relationships," in Robert Moore Fisher (ed.), *The Metropolis in Modern Life* (New York: Doubleday and Company, 1955), pp. 280–281.

[3] An impressive and revealing discussion of occupational licensing and its consequences is found in Walter Gellhorn, *Individual Freedom and Governmental Restraints* (Baton Rouge: Louisiana State University Press, 1956), chap. 3.

[4] Donald Young, "Universities and Cooperation Among Metropolitan Professions," in Fisher, *op. cit.*, p. 290.

[5] Listings of the characteristics of the professions are found in Edward Gross, "Some Suggestions for the Legitimation of Industrial Studies in Sociology," *Social Forces*, 33 (March 1955), pp. 234–235; Myron Lieberman, *Education as a Profession* (Englewood Cliffs, N.J.: Prentice-Hall, Inc., 1956), pp. 2–6; and Lewis and Maude, *op. cit.*, pp. 55–56.

[6] See M. Lee Taylor, "The Life Insurance Man: A Sociological Analysis of the Occupation" (unpublished Doctor's dissertation, Louisiana State University, Baton Rouge, 1958).

[7] For a discussion of the concepts of functionalism, see Robert K. Merton, *Social Theory and Social Structure* (rev. and enl. ed.; Glencoe, Ill.: The Free Press, 1957), pp. 19–84.

[8] A book by Edward A. Wood, *The Sociology of Life Insurance* (New York: D. Appleton and Company, 1928), is not the exception to our statement that the title implies. This book is important, but it is not a treatment of the occupation; nor was that its purpose. Wood's study focuses primarily on the history of the industry and discussions of various types of life insurance. Also, a doctoral dissertation in progress by Robert Ketcham Bain, "The Process of Professionalization: Life Insurance Selling" (University of Chicago), gives insight into the professionalization of the occupation, but it is not the intent of the author to treat the occupation *per se.*

[9] In the sociology of occupations it is desirable to differentiate the business from the occupation as clearly as possible. In the case of life insurance the principles of the business were known and considerably systematized for some time prior to the growth of a body of practitioners who were conscious of their common existence, occupationally, as life insurance men. Here we are concerned with this latter development.

[10] For a discussion of the objectives of the American College of Life Underwriters, see *Working Together for Professional Growth* (Philadelphia: American Society of Chartered Life Underwriters, n.d.), p. 6.

[11] See R. E. Wood, "No Social Security Boost Needed," *Life Association News*, 53 (August 1958), p. 24, for a report of recent action by life insurance men to contain the Social Security threat to their occupation.

[12] Julius C. Greer, "Blue Print for Progress," *The Life Insurer* (March 1957).

[13] "Help Wanted: Sales," *Fortune*, 45 (May 1952), pp. 102 ff.

5

WORK AND SOCIAL
RELATIONSHIPS

INTRODUCTION

Work, like any social behavior, involves a person with others. Although at times individuals may work alone, frequently even in these instances they may perform their work as part of a larger group effort. Work involvement may take the form of a team effort to accomplish some unified goal, such as an industrial assembly line force, in which each member individually performs a minute, specialized task, while collectively the group accomplishes the construction of a complex product. In such a situation, work activities must necessarily be carried out in a closely coordinated fashion. On the other hand, work goals may be accomplished largely as the result of many individuals pursuing their specialties in a completely individual and largely unconnected fashion. An example here might be a number of general practitioners who treat their patients in an independent and individual manner. These independent physicians use medical techniques quite similar to those of other physicians, and thus, when one considers their common, shared skills, may be seen to be dealing with human illness in a collective fashion. Fellow workers who have different specialties are termed co-workers, but those who pursue similar occupational specialties are called colleagues.

One's co-workers and, to a lesser degree, one's colleagues usually are not selected by choice; rather, they are more likely to be selected by necessity as dictated by the needs of the work situation itself. Although an individual may take up work with his fellow workers as strangers, in time the close daily association of working with them may result in the development of a strong social bond. The shared stimulation or monotony of work frequently makes for a kind of "consciousness of kind" and generates an occupational group awareness on the part of those involved. For some, the lack of meaning in monotonous and unstimulating work may be offset only by the fact that interaction with other persons at the work place may be rewarding. Thus the frequent interaction with fellow workers often provides the foundation for the development of primary informal work groups within the larger formal structure. These informal work groups, like other primary groups, perform several functions, one of the more significant of which is to provide the individual with meaningful personal gratifications. The work group, then, may become, along with the family, one of the more significant social entities of which the individual is a member. This fact may explain the occasionally observed phenomenon of individuals in some work situations—warehouse crews, military personnel, to mention two—who, on their day off, return to the work place, watch their fellow employees work, interact with them, and not infrequently pitch in to help with the work.

These ties that bind fellow workers together may strengthen over time to the point where it becomes painful and even traumatic for the worker to sever them by leaving the work place. The relationships between co-workers may be so close that, in some extreme situations, an individual may make the supreme sacrifice of life in behalf of a fellow worker. There have, for example, been battle situations where a soldier may in an instant of decision throw himself on a hand grenade that has landed among a group of his "buddies," saving their lives at the cost of his own. There are numerous examples of military personnel who endanger themselves in other ways to bring back wounded friends to the safety of their own lines. An historical illustration involving the concern for the life or safety of a fellow worker is that of the famous railroad engineer, Casey Jones, who, when confronted with the prospect of having his train collide with another, elected to stay at the controls of the engine in a heroic last-minute effort to prevent the crash. One of his last acts was to order his Negro fireman, Sim, to jump just before the crash.

On the other hand, interaction with fellow workers may be exasperatingly routine in terms of the work itself, such as assembly line work, or in terms of verbal interaction in which the repertoire of jokes, humorous banter, and other informal interchange may be very limited.

The first selection in this chapter, Don Roy's "Banana Time" deals with a group of factory machine operatives and their informal interaction during a two-month observation period. These individuals were engaged in work of a simple and highly repetitive nature and they turned to informal group interaction for relief. They were able to alleviate the monotony of the work day and make their daily routine more stimulating by creating games out of their work and devising colorfully-named work breaks. They were thus able to "gentle the beast of boredom."

Colleagues, individuals who practice a similar occupational specialty but who may not necessarily work together in team fashion, also develop a strong identity with each other as well as with the occupation. As an occupational practitioner, an individual develops skills appropriate to his work and similar to that of his colleagues: he encounters a similar clientele, frequently works under similar circumstances, and faces similar difficulties and challenges. He receives similar status recognition, remuneration, and work satisfaction. It is perhaps not surprising, then, that a bond of occupational awareness and solidarity develops among colleagues. Becker, and others, have spoken of the sense of occupational community that develops among jazz musicians[1] to the extent that they even resent the intrusion of the clientele who, on the one hand, provide their income, but who, on the other hand, frequently want them to produce music that is distasteful to their own esthetic sensibility. Thus, occupational practitioners frequently think of themselves as members of a select fellowship or brotherhood of occupational specialists who, on one level, have a vested interest in protecting the name and fame of colleagues inasmuch as the individual well-being of the colleagues represents the collective good of the occupational group as a whole, and thus, ultimately, of themselves.

The second selection deals with some observations on a group of petroleum industry occupations which are the technical and professional level occupations that make up the so-called exploration branch of the petroleum industry. This group of occupations includes, among others, petroleum geologists, petroleum land scouts, petroleum engineers and geophysicists, and petroleum landmen, with whom this essay is especially concerned. Those individuals in the exploration branch of the oil industry are concerned solely with the finding and extraction of oil. The petroleum landmen with their colleagues and co-workers collectively are responsible for the location and development of oil fields that yield billions of dollars to their companies. This aspect of the petroleum industry has a colorful and exciting history, and both the historical residue and the close involvement with the actual drilling and discovery aspects of the industry combine to produce strong subcultural characteristics among individuals in the exploration branch of the industry. For a number of reasons explained in the article, oil people come to think of themselves as a special kind of occupational community and refer to themselves as "the oil fraternity."[2] As is also noted in the article, this clannishness and exclusiveness is functional to the petroleum occupations for several reasons, one of the chief reasons being a high rate of geographic mobility among oil people which tends to place them frequently in new and unfamiliar social surroundings as they relocate from community to community. Fortunately for them, the social devices developed by the "oil fraternity" help them overcome the problems of an alien social setting.

Just as work routinely involves one with his fellow workers, so too does it routinely involve the practitioner with his client, customer, or patron. For many occupational practitioners the relationship with clients may involve little more than the perfunctory processing of some item or the rendering of some modest service for them. The checkout clerk at a grocery counter does little more than ring up the amount of the sale and issue a mechanical greeting to the customer. In other instances, the practitioner may perform a variety of services or be confronted with the necessity of providing a particular item or goods to the customer in a variety of forms. The social relationship between practitioner and patron or customer is frequently routinized and structured, sometimes subject to manipulation by one or the other member of the dyad, and occasionally the object of strain or discomfort to one or both. Where the service rendered by the practitioner represents a highly specialized and not easily obtainable service—particularly where the service involves occupational "secrets" in the form of esoteric knowledge and techniques—the practitioner is well equipped to manipulate the customer relationship. As receiver of the physician's services, the patient is ill-equipped to diagnosis and treat his own ailment, and thus he must rely rather completely on the competence and advice of his physician; thus the patient must respond in a more or less subordinate fashion if he is to continue receiving the services and counsel of his physician. To trust one's physician is to place oneself completely in his hands and care. Of course, the patient does have some leverage in manipulating the relationship between himself and the physician. He can exert economic pressure by withdrawing from the relationship and seeking the service of some other physician who may be more sympathetic to his idiosyncratic complaints or his hypocondriasis. Thus to at least some degree the physician is under pressure to attempt to adapt his treatment to accommodate the fancy of the patient, lest he lose him to a competitor.

While the possession of secret knowledge or techniques provides the practitioner with an advantageous position in the bargaining situation, so too does actual possession of the object being serviced. As an example, consider the individual who drives his automobile to a garage for repair, lacking the knowledge and ability to repair the automobile himself. He must turn the automobile over to the mechanic, who must dismantle it to some degree in order to diagnose its problems. If, after hearing the diagnosis and estimate of repair cost, the customer is unhappy with the cost, he has little other recourse than to have the repair work done or to pay the cost of having his automobile reassembled, inasmuch as he can hardly carry his dismantled automobile home in a sack. By the same token, the funeral director or mortician has considerable control over the practitioner-client relationship once he has "body control." It is hardly practicable to have poor deceased Uncle John put back in one's station wagon in order that one may shop around for a better price on the funeral services. Furthermore, as Bowman points out, the funeral director deals with his clientele—that is, the family of the deceased—at a time when grief and bereavement render them ineffective in a bargaining situation.[3] Recognizing that at this time the family and kinsmen may be particularly vulnerable to feelings of guilt, it is possible for him to urge upon them a more extravagant service or more expensive casket than they might otherwise have chosen. Thus, just as the physician is able to use fear of illness, discomfort, and death as a means of manipulating the clientele, so too can the mortician utilize guilt as a means of manipulating the bargaining situation.

The relationship between practitioner and clientele, however, may not have any of the features of dependency we have just described. There are numerous other forms such relationships may take. Fred Davis, in his article about cabdrivers and their fares, tells of a practitioner-client relationship that is "random, fleeting, unrenewable, and largely devoid of socially integrative features" conducive to "constraints and controls between the parties to the transaction." The cabdriver has almost no control over the selection of clientele, and in large measure neither do the clientele have any control over the selection of a driver (other than to refuse to use the cab, which may be inconvenient). The cabdriver is subject occasionally to physical danger from his clientele, and may have to tolerate criticism or belligerency from them. Frequently the cabdriver may be treated simply as a "nonperson" who is merely an extension of the automobile. The nature of the practitioner-client relationship can be critical for the cabdriver, however, especially in terms of whether it is conducive to his getting a tip. To this end cabdrivers are able to classify riders in terms of the likelihood of their tipping and also have developed ways of manipulating the situation and the fare in such a fashion as to ensure a favorable tipping outcome. Thus the cabdriver by the use of a variety of interpersonal strategies is often able to cope with the regulative imbalance inherent in the relationship of practitioner and clientele.

The next reading, John P. Reed's "The Lawyer-Client: A Managed Relationship?", takes up the question of whether lawyers manage their clients. Based on data obtained from 125 civil lawyers, Reed concludes that the lawyer-client relationship is now, as historically it has been, among other things a business relationship. Professionalization among lawyers may have modified the lawyer-client relationship but it has not created a new relationship. Through a variety of screening and management techniques, the lawyers are apparently able to select a preferred clientele and effectively "engineer and control the lawyer-client relationship rather than leave its development and outcome to chance."

If an individual is affected by his work in terms of altered life chances, the special work routines or job conditions imposed, or the need to engage in role behavior appropriate to his occupation, then so too is his family. The family residually bears the same occupational label as the individual, shares indirectly if not directly any of the work benefits enjoyed by the breadwinner, and, if the job imposes any special requirements or conditions upon the worker, the family will have to adapt itself accordingly. The family of a college professor must get used to having him around all the time while the family of a sea captain or an over-the-road truck driver must get used to his prolonged absences. The traveling salesman must often be gone from Monday till Friday and the night shift worker goes to work when his family goes to bed and he sleeps while they are awake. They must, accordingly, learn to be quiet around the house during the day. Some persons run a business in their home; others have a home in their business and use the family members to help out. Other persons must move very frequently, thus uprooting their family often. The wife of today's large-scale organization middle management man may discover that she must play a corporate role as well as her husband in terms of having dinners and cocktail parties to entertain clients and customers. In his novel *The Jungle*, Upton Sinclair has one of his characters begin work in a fertilizer mill; when he went home after work, he smelled so bad that he affected the taste of the food at the table and made his family vomit.[4] Of course, this is an extreme case. Some amusing vignettes of the impact of a man's work on his family are contained in McDill McCown Gassman's biography of her father, a small town undertaker.[5] As she relates it: "There was always somebody dead at our house. There was eternally a body in the house—for Daddy was undertaker and we lived upstairs over the funeral parlor." This girl had a difficult time keeping boyfriends, since they had to call for her and perhaps wait for her in the "parlor" of the "establishment." They seemed to especially resent this if there happened to be a "client" lying in the parlor. Her friends did, however, like to come to her home on halloween, for it seemed the most appropriate place for a party. There were other compensations also for being the undertaker's daughter: her mother trimmed the caskets with cloth, and she got the leftover scraps of crepe cloth for making doll dresses.

The next selection is a biographical account of family life as influenced by the father's occupation. In this instance, Janet Kern, in her "A Doctor in the House," tells of the adjustments that she and her family had to make because of her physician father. Physicians' families have to learn never to stay on the telephone too long; there might be a patient trying to call. Physicians' families also, it seems, have to endure their own sicknesses as the father has "real" patients to tend. This physician's family complained that they were used as guinea pigs by the father, who tried out all new sample drugs on them. The physician's family must also accustom itself to the interuption of any family activity whenever the doctor is called out on a case. The life of a physician's daughter apparently can be as much of a trial as that of an undertaker's daughter, only in different ways, imposed by the nature of the respective father's work.

The final selection in this chapter, Arlie Hochschild's "The Role of the Ambassador's Wife: An Exploratory Study," focuses on the elaborate sociability role requirements of the wife of an ambassador. According to Hochschild, the ambassador's wife plays a significant part in the diplomatic process by informally and indirectly communicating political and social messages through the use of a "covert message system." Her role is challenging and requires expertise in recognizing and interpreting "the larger meanings of small signs." In the final analysis, this wife's role "simply accentuates the diplomacy of everyday life."

The performance of work behavior inevitably and inextricably relates us indirectly if not directly with numerous other persons; those who work with us including superiors, peers, and subordinates; those who follow a similar calling and who thus share a set of skills, a socialization experience, and a clientele; those who receive the products and services of our work, our patrons, customers, and clients; other occupational specialists whose work is integrated with our own in a symbiotic fashion, such as the druggist who compounds the specific medication prescribed by the physician; our spouses, offsprings, relatives, and even friends who often reflect the impact and influence of our work. Research on work and social relationships should prove to be a fertile source of insights into the social dimensions of work.

Footnotes

[1] Howard S. Becker, "The Professional Dance Musician and His Audience," *American Journal of Sociology*, LVII, No. 2 (September 1951), 136–44.

[2] Strictly speaking, the other oil occupations are co-workers rather than colleagues to the landmen; however, landmen as well as the other oil specialists are inclined to think of the different occupational specialties as merely different specialties of the "oil fraternity"; thus they tend to view these other occupational specialties as colleagues as much as co-workers.

[3] Leroy Bowman, "The Bargaining Situation: Family and Undertaker," *The*

American Funeral: A Way of Death (New York: Paperback Library, Inc., 1964), pp. 37–60.

⁴ Upton Sinclair, *The Jungle* (New York: The Viking Press, Inc., 1946), pp. 129–31.

⁵ McDill McCown Gassman, *Daddy Was an Undertaker* (New York: Vantage Press, Inc., 1952).

Colleagues and Co-Workers

"Banana Time"

Job Satisfaction and Informal Interaction

DONALD F. ROY
Duke University

This paper undertakes description and exploratory analysis of the social interaction which took place within a small work group of factory machine operatives during a two-month period of participant observation. The factual and ideational materials which it presents lie at an intersection of two lines of research interest and should, in their dual bearing, contribute to both. Since the operatives were engaged in work which involved the repetition of very simple operations over an extra-long workday, six days a week, they were faced with the problem of dealing with a formidable "beast of monotony." Revelation of how the group utilized its resources to combat that "beast" should merit the attention of those who are seeking solution to the practical problem of job satisfaction, or employee morale. It should also provide insights for those who are trying to penetrate the mysteries of the small group.

Convergence of these two lines of interest is, of course, no new thing. Among the host of writers and researchers who have suggested connections between "group" and "joy in work" are Walker and Guest, observers of social interaction on the automobile assembly line.[1] They quote assembly-line workers as saying, "We have a lot of fun and talk all the time,"[2] and, "If it weren't for the talking and fooling, you'd go nuts."[3]

My account of how one group of machine operators kept from "going nuts" in a situation of monotonous work activity attempts to lay bare the tissues of interaction which made up the content of their adjustment. The talking, fun, and fooling which provided solution to the elemental problem of "psychological survival" will be described according to their embodiment

Condensed from "Banana Time," *Human Organization*, Vol. 18, No. 4 (Winter 1959–60), 158–64, by permission of the author and the Society for Applied Anthropology.

in intra-group relations. In addition, an unusual opportunity for close observation of behavior involved in the maintenance of group equilibrium was afforded by the fortuitous introduction of a "natural experiment." My unwitting injection of explosive materials into the stream of interaction resulted in sudden, but temporary, loss of group interaction.

My fellow operatives and I spent our long days of simple, repetitive work in relative isolation from other employees of the factory. Our line of machines was sealed off from other work areas of the plant by the four walls of the clicking room. The one door of this room was usually closed. Even when it was kept open, during periods of hot weather, the consequences were not social; it opened on an uninhabited storage room of the shipping department. Not even the sounds of work activity going on elsewhere in the factory carried to this isolated work place. There were occasional contacts with "outside" employees, usually on matters connected with the work; but, with the exception of the daily calls of one fellow who came to pick up finished materials for the next step in processing, such visits were sporadic and infrequent.

Moreover, face-to-face contact with members of the managerial hierarchy were few and far between. No one bearing the title of foreman ever came around. The only company official who showed himself more than once during the two-month observation period was the plant superintendent. Evidently overloaded with supervisory duties and production problems which kept him busy elsewhere, he managed to pay his respects every week or two. His visits were in the nature of short, businesslike, but friendly exchanges. Otherwise he confined his observable communications with the group to occasional utilization of a public address system. During the two-month period, the company president and the chief chemist paid one friendly call apiece. One man, who may or may not have been of managerial status, was seen on various occasions lurking about in a manner which excited suspicion. Although no observable consequences accrued from the peculiar visitations of this silent fellow, it was assumed that he was some sort of efficiency expert, and he was referred to as "The Snooper."

As far as our work group was concerned, this was truly a situation of laissez-faire management. There was no interference from staff experts, no hounding by time-study engineers or personnel men hot on the scent of efficiency or good human relations. Nor were there any signs of industrial democracy in the form of safety, recreational, or production committees. There was an international union, and there was a highly publicized union-management cooperation program; but actual interactional processes of cooperation were carried on somewhere beyond my range of observation and without participation of members of my work group. Furthermore, these union-management get-togethers had no determinable connection with the problem of "toughing out" a twelve-hour day at monotonous work.

Our work group was thus not only abandoned to its own resources for creating job satisfaction, but left without that basic reservoir of ill-will toward management which can sometimes be counted on to stimulate the development of interesting activities to occupy hand and brain. Lacking was the challenge of intergroup conflict, that perennial source of creative experience to fill the otherwise empty hours of meaningless work routine.[4]

The clicking machines were housed in a room approximately thirty by twenty-four feet. They were four in number, set in a row, and so arranged along one wall that the busy operator could, merely by raising his head from his work, freshen his reveries with a glance through one of three large barred windows. To the rear of one of the end machines sat a long cutting table; here the operators cut up rolls of plastic materials into small sheets manageable for further processing at the clickers. Behind the machine at the opposite end of the line sat another table which was intermittently the work station of a female employee who performed sundry scissors operations of a more intricate nature on raincoat parts. Boxed in on all sides by shelves and stocks of materials, this latter locus of work appeared a cell within a cell.

The clickers were of the genus punching machines; of mechanical construction similar to that of the better-known punch presses, their leading features were hammer and block. The hammer, or punching head, was approximately eight inches by twelve inches at its flat striking surface. The descent upon the block was initially forced by the operator, who exerted pressure on a handle attached to the side of the hammer head. A few inches of travel downward established electrical connection for a sharp, power-driven blow. The hammer also traveled, by manual guidance, in a horizontal plane to and from, and in an arc around, the central column of the machine. Thus the operator, up to the point of establishing electrical connections for the sudden and irrevocable downward thrust, had flexibility in maneuvering his instrument over the larger surface of the block. The latter, approximately twenty-four inches wide, eighteen inches deep, and ten inches thick, was made, like a butcher's block, of inlaid hardwood; it was set in the machine at a convenient waist height. On it the operator placed his materials, one sheet at a time if leather, stacks of sheets if plastic, to be cut with steel dies of assorted sizes and shapes. The particular die in use would be moved, by hand, from spot to spot over the materials each time a cut was made; less frequently, materials would be shifted on the block as the operator saw need for such adjustment.

Introduction to the new job, with its relatively simple machine skills and work routines, was accomplished with what proved to be, in my experience, an all-time minimum of job training. The clicking machine assigned to me was situated at one end of the row. Here the superintendent and one of the operators gave a few brief demonstrations, accompanied by bits of advice which included a warning to keep hands clear of the descending hammer. After a short practice period, at the end of which the superintendent expressed satisfaction with progress and potentialities, I was left to develop my learning curve with no other supervision than that afforded by members of the work group. Further advice and assistance did come, from time to time, from my fellow operatives, sometimes upon request, sometimes unsolicited.

The Work Group

Absorbed at first in three related goals of improving my clicking skill, increasing my rate of output, and keeping my left hand unclicked, I paid little attention to my fellow operatives save to observe that they were friendly, middle-aged, foreign-born, full of advice, and very talkative. Their names, according to the way they addressed each other, were George, Ike, and Sammy.[5] George, a stocky fellow in his late fifties, operated the machine at the opposite end of the line; he, I later discovered, had emigrated in early youth from a country in Southeastern Europe. Ike, stationed at George's left, was tall, slender, in his early fifties, and Jewish; he had come from Eastern Europe in his youth. Sammy, number three man in the line, and my neighbor, was heavy set, in his late fifties, and Jewish; he had escaped from a country in Eastern Europe just before Hitler's legions had moved in. All three men had been downwardly mobile as to occupation in recent years. George and Sammy had been proprietors of small businesses; the former had been "wiped out" when his uninsured establishment burned down; the latter had been entrepreneuring on a small scale before he left all behind him to flee the Germans. According to his account, Ike had left a highly skilled trade which he had practiced for years in Chicago.

I discovered also that the clicker line represented a ranking system in descending order from George to myself. George not only had top seniority for the group, but functioned as a sort of leadman. His superior status was marked in the fact that he received five cents more per hour than the other clickermen, put in the longest workday, made daily contact, outside the workroom, with the superintendent on work matters which concerned the entire line, and communicated to the rest of us the directives which he received. The narrow margin of superordination was seen in the fact that directives were always relayed in the superintendent's name; they were on the order of, "You'd better let that go now, and get on the green. Joe says they're running low on the fifth floor," or, "Joe says he wants two boxes of the 3-die today." The narrow margin was also seen in the fact that the superintendent would communicate directly with his operatives over the public address system; and, on occasion, Ike or Sammy would leave the workroom to confer with him for decisions or advice in regard to work orders.

Ike was next to George in seniority, then Sammy. I was, of course, low man on the totem pole. Other indices to status differentiation lay in informal interaction, to be described later.

With one exception, job status tended to be matched by length of workday. George worked a thirteen-hour day, from 7 a.m. to 8:30 p.m. Ike worked eleven hours, from 7 a.m. to 6:30 p.m.; occasionally he worked until 7 or 7:30 for an eleven and a half- or a twelve-hour day. Sammy put in a nine-hour day, from 8 a.m. to 5:30 p.m. My twelve hours spanned from 8 a.m. to 8:30 p.m. We had a half hour for lunch, from 12 to 12:30.

The female who worked at the secluded table behind George's machine put in a regular plant-wide eight-hour shift from 8 to 4:30. Two women held this job during the period of my employment; Mable was succeeded by Baby. Both were Negroes, and in their late twenties.

A fifth clicker operator, an Arabian *emigré* called Boo, worked a night shift by himself. He usually arrived about 7 p.m. to take over Ike's machine.

The Work

It was evident to me, before my first workday drew to a weary close, that my clicking career was going to be a grim process of fighting the clock, the particular timepiece in this situation being an old-fashioned alarm clock which ticked away on a shelf near George's machine. I had struggled through many dreary rounds with the minutes and hours during the various phases of my industrial experience, but never had I been confronted with such a dismal combination of working conditions as the extra-long workday, the infinitesimal cerebral excitation, and the extreme limitation of physical movement. The contrast with a recent stint in the California oil fields was striking. This was no eight-hour day of racing hither and yon over desert and foothills with a rollicking crew of "roustabouts" on a variety of repair missions at oil wells, pipe lines, and storage tanks. Here there were no afternoon dallyings to search the sands for horned toads, tarantulas, and rattlesnakes, or to climb old wooden derricks for raven's nests, with an eye out, of course, for the telltale streak of dust in the distance which gave ample warning of the approach of the boss. This was standing all day in one spot beside three old codgers in a dingy room looking out through barred windows at the bare walls of a brick warehouse, leg movements largely restricted to the shifting of body weight from one foot to the other, hand and arm movements confined, for the most part, to a simple repetitive sequence of place the die, —————— punch the clicker, —————— place the die, —————— punch the clicker, and intellectual activity reduced to computing the hours to quitting time. It is true that from time to time a fresh stack of sheets would have to be substituted for the clicked-out old one; but the stack would have been prepared by someone else, and the exchange would be only a minute or two in the making. Now and then a box of finished work would have to be moved back out of the way, and an empty box brought up; but the moving back and the bringing up involved only a step or two. And there was the half hour for lunch, and occasional trips to the lavatory or the drinking fountain to break up the day into digestible parts. But after each momentary respite, hammer and die were moving again: click, —————— move die, —————— click, —————— move die.

Before the end of the first day, Monotony was joined by his twin brother, Fatigue. I got tired. My legs ached, and my feet hurt. Early in the afternoon I discovered a tall stool and moved it up to my machine to "take the load off my feet." But the superintendent dropped in to see how I was "doing" and promptly informed me that "we don't sit down on this job." My reverie toyed with the idea of quitting the job and looking for other work.

The next day was the same: the monotony of the work, the tired legs and sore feet and thoughts of quitting.

The Game of Work

In discussing the factory operative's struggle to "cling to the remnants of joy in work," Henri de Man makes the general observations that "it is psychologically impossible to deprive any kind of work of all its positive emotional elements," that the worker will find *some* meaning in any activity assigned to him, a "certain scope for initiative which can satisfy after a fashion the instinct for play and the creative impulse," that "even in the Taylor system there is found luxury of self-determination."[6] De Man cites the case of one worker who wrapped 13,000 incandescent bulbs a day; she found her outlet for creative impulse, her self-determination, her meaning in work by varying her wrapping movements a little from time to time.[7]

So did I search for *some* meaning in my continuous mincing of plastic sheets into small ovals, fingers, and trapezoids. The richness of possibility for creative expression previously discovered in my experience with the "Taylor system"[8] did not reveal itself here. There was no piecework, so no piecework game. There was no conflict with management, so no war game. But, like the light bulb wrapper, I did find a "certain scope for initiative," and out of this slight freedom to vary activity, I developed a game of work.

The game developed was quite simple, so elementary, in fact, that its playing was reminiscent of rainy-day preoccupations in childhood, when attention could be centered by the hour on colored bits of things of assorted sizes and shapes. But this adult activity was not mere pottering and piddling; what it lacked in the earlier imaginative content, it made up for in clean-cut structure. Fundamentally involved were: (a) variation in color of the materials cut, (b) variation in shapes of the dies used, and (c) a process called "scraping the block." The basic procedure which ordered the particular combination of components employed could be stated in the form: "As soon as I do so many of these, I'll get to do those." If, for example, production scheduled for the day featured small, rectangular strips in three colors, the game might go: "As soon as I finish a thousand of the green ones, I'll click some brown ones." And, with success in attaining the objective of working with brown materials, a new goal of "I'll get to do the white ones" might be set. Or the new goal might involve switching dies.

Scraping the block made the game more interesting by adding to the number of possible variations in its playing; and, what was perhaps more important, provided the only substantial reward, save for going to the lavatory or getting a drink of water, on days when work with one die and one color of material was scheduled. As a physical operation, scraping the block was fairly simple; it involved application of a coarse file to the upper surface of the block to remove roughness and unevenness resulting from the wear and tear of die penetration. But, as part of the intellectual and emotional content of the game of work, it could be in itself a source of variation in activity. The upper left-hand corner of the block could be chewed up in the clicking of 1,000 white trapezoid pieces, then scraped. Next, the upper right-hand corner, and so on until the entire block had been worked over. Then, on the next round of scraping by quadrants, there was the possibility of a change of color or die to green trapezoid or white oval pieces.

Thus the game of work might be described as a continuous sequence of short-range production goals with achievement rewards in the form of activity change. The superiority of this relatively complex and self-determined system over the technically simple and outside-controlled job satisfaction injections experienced by Milner at the beginner's table in a shop of the feather industry should be immediately apparent:

> Twice a day our work was completely changed to break the monotony. First Jennie would give us feathers of a brilliant green, then bright orange or a light blue or black. The "ohs" and "ahs" that came from the girls at each change was proof enough that this was an effective way of breaking the monotony of the tedious work.[9]

But a hasty conclusion that I was having lots of fun playing my clicking game should be avoided. These games were not as interesting in the experiencing as they might seem to be from the telling. Emotional tone of the activity was low, and intellectual currents weak. Such rewards as scraping the block or "getting to do the blue ones" were not very exciting, and the stretches of repetitive movement involved in achieving them were long enough to permit lapses into obsessive reverie. Henri de Man speaks of "clinging to the remnants of joy in work," and this situation represented just that. How tenacious the clinging was, how long I could have "stuck it out" with my remnants, was never determined. Before the first week was out this adjustment to the work situation was complicated by other developments. The game of work continued, but in a different context. Its influence became decidedly subordinated to, if not completely overshadowed by, another source of job satisfaction.

Informal Social Activity of the Work Group:
Times and Themes

The change came about when I began to take serious note of the social activity going on around me; my attentiveness to this activity came with growing involvement in it. What I heard at first, before I started to listen, was a stream of disconnected bits of communication which did not make much sense. Foreign accents were strong and referents were not joined to coherent contexts of meaning. It was just "jabbering." What I saw at first, before I began to observe, was occasional flurries of horseplay so simple and unvarying in pattern and so childish in quality that they made no strong bid for attention. For example, Ike would regularly switch off the power at Sammy's machine whenever Sammy made a trip to the lavatory or the drinking fountain. Correlatively, Sammy invariably fell victim to the plot by making an attempt to operate his clicking hammer after returning to the shop. And, as the simple pattern went, this blind stumbling into the trap was always followed by indignation and reproach from Sammy, smirking satisfaction from Ike, and mild paternal scolding from George. My interest in this procedure was at first confined to wondering when Ike would weary of his tedious joke or when Sammy would learn to check his power switch before trying the hammer.

But, as I began to pay closer attention, as I began to develop familiarity with the communication system, the disconnected became connected, the nonsense made sense, the obscure became clear, and the silly actually funny. And, as the content of the interaction took on more and more meaning, the interaction began to reveal structure. There were "times" and "themes," and roles to serve their enaction. The interaction had subtleties, and I began to savor and appreciate them. I started to record what hitherto had seemed unimportant.

TIMES

This emerging awareness of structure and meaning included recognition that the long day's grind was broken by interruptions of a kind other than the formally instituted or idiosyncratically developed disjunctions in work routine previously described. These additional interruptions appeared in daily repetition in an ordered series of informal interactions. They were, in part, but only in part and in very rough comparison, similar to those common fractures of the production process known as the coffee break, the coke break, and the cigarette break. Their distinction lay in frequency of occurrence and in brevity. As phases of the daily series, they occurred almost hourly, and so short were they in duration that they disrupted work activity only slightly. Their significance lay not so much in their function as rest pauses, although it cannot be denied that physical refreshment was involved. Nor did their chief importance lie in the accentuation of progress points in the passage of time, although they could perform that function far more strikingly than the hour hand on the dull face of George's alarm clock. If the daily series of interruptions be likened to a clock, then the comparison might best be made with a special kind of cuckoo clock, one with a cuckoo which can provide variation in its announcements and can create such an interest in them that the intervening minutes become filled with intellectual content. The major significance of the interactional interruptions lay in such carryover of interest. The physical interplay which momentarily halted work activity would initiate verbal exchanges and thought processes to occupy group members until the next interruption. The group interactions thus not only marked off the time; they gave it content and hurried it along.

Most of the breaks in the daily series were designated as "times" in the parlance of the clicker operators, and they featured the consumption of food or drink of one sort or another. There was coffee time, peach time, banana time, fish time, coke time, and, of course, lunch time. Other interruptions, which formed part of the series but were not verbally recognized as times, were window time, pickup time, and the staggered quitting times of Sammy and Ike. These latter unnamed times did not involve the partaking of refreshments.

My attention was first drawn to this times business during my first week of employment when I was encouraged to join in the sharing of two peaches. It was Sammy who provided the peaches; he drew them from his lunch box after making the announcement, "Peach time!" On this first occasion I refused the proffered fruit, but thereafter regularly consumed my half peach. Sammy continued to provide the peaches and to make the "Peach time!" announcement, although there were days when Ike would remind him that it was peach time, urging him to hurry up with the mid-morning snack. Ike invariably complained about the quality of the fruit, and his complaints fed the fires of continued banter between peach donor and critical recipient. I did find the fruit a bit on the scrubby side but felt, before I achieved insight into the function of peach time, that Ike was showing poor manners by looking a gift horse in the mouth. I wondered why Sammy continued to share his peaches with such an ingrate.

Banana time followed peach time by approximately an hour. Sammy again provided the refreshments, namely, one banana. There was, however, no four-way sharing of Sammy's banana. Ike would gulp it down by himself after surreptitiously extracting it from Sammy's lunch box, kept on a shelf behind Sammy's work station. Each morning, after making the snatch, Ike would call out, "Banana time!" and proceed to down his prize while Sammy made futile protests and denunciations. George would join in with mild remonstrances, sometimes scolding Sammy for making so much fuss. The banana was one which Sammy brought for his own consumption at lunch time; he never did get to eat his banana, but kept bringing one for his lunch. At first this daily theft startled and amazed me. Then I grew to look forward to the daily seizure and the verbal interaction which followed.

Window time came next. It followed banana time as a regular consequence of Ike's castigation by the indignant Sammy. After "taking" repeated references to himself as a person badly lacking in morality and character, Ike would "finally" retaliate by opening the window which faced Sammy's machine, to let the "cold air" blow in on Sammy. The slandering which would, in its echolalic repetition, wear down Ike's patience and forbearance usually took the form of the invidious comparison: "George is a good daddy! Ike is a bad man! A very bad man!" Opening the window would take a little time to accomplish and would involve a great deal of verbal interplay between Ike and Sammy, both before and after the event. Ike would threaten, make feints toward the window, then finally open it. Sammy would protest, argue, and make claims that the air blowing in on him would give him a cold; he would eventually have to leave his machine to close the window. Sometimes the weather was slightly chilly, and the draft from the window unpleasant; but cool or hot, windy or still, window time arrived each day. (I assume that it was originally a cold season development.) George's part in this interplay, in spite of the "good daddy" laudations, was to encourage Ike in his window work. He would stress the tonic values of fresh air and chide Sammy for his unappreciativeness.

Following window time came lunch time, a formally designated half-hour for the midday repast and rest break. At this time, informal interaction would feature exchanges between Ike and George. The former would start eating his lunch a few minutes before noon, and the latter, in his role as straw boss, would censure him for malobservance of the rules. Ike's off-beat luncheon usually involved a previous tampering with George's alarm clock. Ike would set the clock ahead a few minutes in order to maintain his eating schedule without detection, and George would discover these small daylight saving changes.

The first "time" interruption of the day I did not share. It occurred soon after I arrived on the job, at eight o'clock. George and Ike would share a small pot of coffee brewed on George's hot plate.

ᶠ Pickup time, fish time, and coke time came in the afternoon. I name it pickup time to represent the official visit of the man who made daily calls to cart away boxes of clicked materials. The arrival of the pickup man, a Negro, was always a noisy one, like the arrival of a daily passenger train in an isolated small town. Interaction attained a quick peak of intensity to crowd into a few minutes all communications, necessary and otherwise. Exchanges invariably included loud depreciations by the pickup man of the amount of work accomplished in the clicking department during the preceding twenty-four hours. Such scoffing would be on the order of "Is that all you've got done? What do you boys do all day?" These devaluations would be countered with allusions to the "soft job" enjoyed by the pickup man. During the course of the exchanges news items would be dropped, some of serious import, such as reports of accomplished or impending layoffs in the various plants of the company, or of gains or losses in orders for company products. Most of the news items, however, involved bits of information on plant employees told in a light vein. Information relayed by the clicker operators was usually told about each other, mainly in the form of summaries of the most recent kidding sequences. Some of this material was repetitive, carried over from day to day. Sammy would be the butt of most of this newscasting, although he would make occasional counter-reports on Ike and George. An invariable part of the interactional content of pickup time was Ike's introduction of the pickup man to George. "Meet Mr. Papeatis!" Ike would say in mock solemnity and dignity. Each day the pickup man "met" Mr. Papeatis, to the obvious irritation of the latter. Another pickup time invariably would bring Baby (or Mable) into the interaction. George would always issue the loud warning to the pickup man: "Now I want you to stay away from Baby! She's Henry's girl!" Henry was a burly Negro with a booming bass voice who made infrequent trips to the clicking room with lift-truck loads of materials. He was reputedly quite a ladies' man among the colored population of the factory. George's warning to "Stay away from Baby!" was issued to every Negro who entered the shop. Baby's only part in this was to laugh at the horseplay.

ᶠ About mid-afternoon came fish time. George and Ike would stop work for a few minutes to consume some sort of pickled fish which Ike provided. Neither Sammy nor I partook of this nourishment, nor were we invited. For this omission I was grateful; the fish, brought in a newspaper and with head and tail intact, produced a reverse effect on my appetite. George and Ike seemed to share a great liking for fish. Each Friday night, as a regular ritual, they would enjoy a fish dinner together at a nearby restaurant. On these nights Ike would work until 8:30 and leave the plant with George.

Coke time came late in the afternoon, and was an occasion for total participation. The four of us took turns in buying the drinks and in making the trip for them to a fourth floor vending machine. Through George's manipulation of the situation, it eventually became my daily chore to go after the cokes; the straw boss had noted that I made a much faster trip to the fourth floor and back than Sammy or Ike.

Sammy left the plant at 5:30, and Ike ordinarily retired from the scene an hour and a half later. These quitting times were not marked by any distinctive interaction save the one regular exchange between Sammy and George over the former's "early washup." Sammy's tendency was to crowd his washing up toward five o'clock, and it was George's concern to keep it from further creeping advance. After Ike's departure came Boo's arrival. Boo's was a striking personality productive of a change in topics of conversation to fill in the last hour of the long workday.

THEMES

To put flesh, so to speak, on this interactional frame of "times," my work group had developed various "themes" of verbal interplay which had become standardized in their repetition. These topics of conversation ranged in quality from an extreme of nonsensical chatter to another extreme of serious discourse. Unlike the times, these themes flowed one into the other in no particular sequence of predictability. Serious conversation could suddenly melt into horseplay, and vice versa. In the middle of a serious discussion on the high cost of living, Ike might drop a weight behind the easily startled Sammy, or hit him over the head with a dusty paper sack. Interaction would immediately drop to a low comedy exchange of slaps, threats, guffaws, and disapprobations which would invariably include a ten-minute echolalia of "Ike is a bad man, a very bad man! George is a good daddy, a very fine man!" Or, on the other hand, a stream of such invidious comparisons as followed a surreptitious switching-off of Sammy's machine by the playful Ike might merge suddenly into a discussion of the pros and cons of saving for one's funeral.

"Kidding themes" were usually started by George or Ike, and Sammy was usually the butt of the joke. Sometimes Ike would have to "take it," seldom George. One favorite kidding theme involved Sammy's alleged receipt of $100 a month from his son. The points stressed were that Sammy did not have to work long hours, or did not have to work at all, because he had a son to support him. George would always point out that he sent money to his daughter; she did not send money to him. Sammy received occasional calls from his wife, and his claim that these calls were requests to shop for groceries on the way home were greeted with feigned disbelief. Sammy was ribbed for being closely watched, bossed, and henpecked by his wife, and the expression "Are you man or mouse?" became an echolalic utterance, used both in and out of the original context.

Ike, who shared his machine and the work scheduled for it with Boo, the night operator, came in for constant invidious comparison on the subject of output. The socially isolated Boo, who chose work rather than sleep on his lonely night shift, kept up a high level of performance, and George never tired of pointing this out to Ike. It so happened that Boo, an Arabian Moslem from Palestine, had no use for Jews in general; and Ike, who was Jewish, had no use for Boo in particular. Whenever George would extol Boo's previous night's production, Ike would try to turn the conversation into a general discussion on the need for educating the Arabs. George, never permitting the development of serious discussion on this topic, would repeat a smirking warning, "You watch out for Boo! He's got a long knife!"

The "poom poom" theme was one that caused no sting. It would come up several times a day to be enjoyed as unbarbed fun by the three older clicker operators. Ike was usually the one to raise the question, "How many times you go poom poom last night?" The person questioned usually replied with claims of being "too old for poom poom." If this theme did develop a goat, it was I. When it was pointed out that I was a younger man, this provided further grist for the poom poom mill. I soon grew weary of this poom poom business, so dear to the hearts of the three old satyrs, and, knowing where the conversation would inevitably lead, winced whenever Ike brought up the subject.

I grew almost as sick of a kidding theme which developed from some personal information contributed during a serious conversation on property ownership and high taxes. I dropped a few remarks about two acres of land which I owned in one of the western states, and from then on I had to listen to questions, advice, and general nonsensical comment in regard to "Danelly's farm."[10] This "farm" soon became stocked with horses, cows, pigs, chickens, ducks, and the various and sundry domesticated beasts so tunefully listed in "Old McDonald Had a Farm." George was a persistent offender with this theme. Where the others seemed to be mainly interested in statistics on livestock, crops, etc., George's teasing centered on a generous offering to help with the household chores while I worked in the fields. He would drone on, *ad nauseam*, "when I come to visit you, you will never have to worry about the housework, Danelly. I'll stay around the house when you go out to dig the potatoes and milk the cows, I'll stay in and peel potatoes and help your wife do the dishes." Danelly always found it difficult to change the subject on George, once the latter started to bear down on the farm theme.

Another kidding theme which developed out of serious discussion could be labelled "helping Danelly find a cheaper apartment." It became known to the group that Danelly had a pending housing problem, that he would need new quarters for his family when the permanent resident of his temporary summer dwelling returned from a vacation. This information engendered at first a great deal of sympathetic concern and, of course, advice on apartment hunting. Development into a kidding theme was immediately related to previous exchanges between Ike and George on the quality of their respective dwelling areas. Ike lived in "Lawndale," and George dwelt in the "Woodlawn" area. The new pattern featured the reading aloud of bogus "apartment for rent" ads in newspapers which were brought into the shop. Studying his paper at lunchtime, George would call out, "Here's an apartment for you, Danelly! Five rooms, stove heat, $20 a month, Lawndale Avenue!" Later, Ike would read from his paper, "Here's one! Six rooms, stove heat, dirt floor. $18.50 a month! At 55th and Woodlawn." Bantering would then go on in regard to the quality of housing or population in the two areas. The search for an apartment for Danelly was not successful.

Serious themes included the relating of major misfortunes suffered in the past by group members. George referred again and again to the loss, by fire, of his business establishment. Ike's chief complaints centered around a chronically ill wife who had undergone various operations and periods of hospital care. Ike spoke with discouragement of the expenses attendant upon hiring a housekeeper for himself and his children; he referred with disappointment and disgust to a teen-age son, an inept lad who "couldn't even fix his own lunch. He couldn't even make himself a sandwich!" Sammy's reminiscences centered on the loss of a flourishing business when he had to flee Europe ahead of Nazi invasion.

But all serious topics were not tales of woe. One favorite serious theme which was optimistic in tone could be called either "Danelly's future" or "getting Danelly a better job." It was known that I had been attending "college," the magic door to opportunity, although my specific course of study remained somewhat obscure. Suggestions poured forth on good lines of work to get into, and these suggestions were backed with accounts of friends, and friends of friends, who had made good via the academic route. My answer to the expected question, "Why are you working here?" always stressed the "lots of overtime" feature, and this explanation seemed to suffice for short-range goals.

There was one theme of especially solemn import, the "professor theme." This theme might also be termed "George's daughter's marriage theme"; for the recent marriage of George's only child was inextricably bound up with George's connection with higher learning. The daughter had married the son of a professor who instructed in one of the local colleges. This professor theme was not in the strictest sense a conversation piece; when the subject came up, George did all the talking. The two Jewish operatives remained silent as they listened with deep respect, if not actual awe, to George's accounts of the Big Wedding which, including the wedding pictures, entailed an expense of $1,000. It was monologue, but there was listening, there was communication, the sacred communication of a temple, when George told of going for Sunday afternoon walks on the Midway with the professor, or of joining the professor for a Sunday dinner. Whenever he spoke of the professor, his daughter, the wedding, or even of the new son-in-law, who remained for the most part in the background, a sort of incidental like the wedding cake, George was complete master of the interaction. His manner, in speaking to the rank-and-file of clicker operators, was indeed that of master deigning to notice his underlings. I came to the conclusion that it was the professor connection, not the strawboss-ship or the extra nickel an hour, which provided the fount of George's superior status in the group.

If the professor theme may be regarded as the cream of verbal interaction, the "chatter themes" should be classed as the dregs. The chatter themes were hardly themes at all; perhaps they should be labelled "verbal states," or "oral autisms." Some were of doubtful status as communication; they were like the howl or cry of an animal responding to its own physiological state. They were exclamations, ejaculations, snatches of song or doggerel, talkings-to-oneself, mutterings. Their classification as themes would rest on their repetitive character. They were echolalic utterances, repeated over and over. An already mentioned example would be Sammy's repetition of "George is a good daddy, a very fine man! Ike is a bad man, a very bad man!" Also, Sammy's repetition of "Don't bother me! Can't you see I'm busy? I'm a very busy man!" for ten minutes after Ike had dropped a weight behind him would fit the classification. Ike would shout "Mamariba!" at intervals between repetition of bits of verse, such as:

> Mama on the bed,
> Papa on the floor,
> Baby in the crib
> Says giver some more!

Sometimes the three operators would pick up one of these simple chatterings in a sort of chorus. "Are you man or mouse? I ask you, are you man or mouse?" was a favorite of this type.

So initial discouragement with the meagerness of social interaction I now recognized as due to lack of observation. The interaction was there, in constant flow. It captured attention and held interest to make the long day pass. The twelve hours of "click, ——— move die, ——— click, ——— move die" became as easy to endure as eight hours of varied activity in the oil fields or eight hours of playing the piecework game in a machine shop. The "beast of boredom" was gentled to the harmlessness of a kitten. . . .

Footnotes

[1] Charles R. Walker and Robert H. Guest, *The Man on the Assembly Line,* Harvard University Press, Cambridge, 1952.

[2] *Ibid.,* p. 77.

[3] *Ibid.,* p. 68.

[4] Donald F. Roy, "Work Satisfaction and Social Reward in Quota Achievement: An Analysis of Piecework Incentive," *American Sociological Review,* XVIII (October, 1953), 507–514.

[5] All names used are fictitious.

[6] Henri de Man, *The Psychology of Socialism,* Henry Holt and Company, New York, 1927, pp. 80–81.

[7] *Ibid.,* p. 81.

[8] Roy, *op. cit.*

[9] Lucille Milner, *Education of An American Liberal,* Horizon Press, New York, 1954, p. 97.

[10] This spelling is the closest I can come to the appellation given me in George's broken English and adopted by other members the group.

Petroleum Landmen

Brothers in the "Oil Fraternity"

CLIFTON D. BRYANT

Western Kentucky University

Introduction

Petroleum landmen, along with several other occupational specialists, including geologists, geophysicists, oil scouts, and petroleum engineers, comprise the exploration and production component of the oil industry. They explore for oil, locate it, drill for it, and produce it. In the minds of many (and especially themselves) these individuals *are* the oil industry. They are members, as they themselves put it, of the "oil fraternity."

The "oil fraternity" is an occupational complex whose members demonstrate an unusually strong occupational identity and possess a high degree of social solidarity. By implication, the label suggests an eliteness of membership and an aloofness from non-oil people. To some degree both of these characteristics are present. The "oil fraternity," like other in-groups, fosters loyalty to and identity with members, promotes social distance with outsiders, and encourages and facilitates informal interaction among members as a device for building solidarity.

Petroleum landmen with their exploration and production co-workers constitute a work community of unusual cohesion; they and their families interact informally to a considerable degree with each other. In doing so, the members of the "oil fraternity" like members of other fraternities have established a kind of closed social system that is ethnocentric and has social resources largely sufficient to its needs.

A national survey of petroleum landmen several years ago gives some indication of the degree of informal interaction internal to the "oil fraternity."[1] Of the landmen responding to the survey, more than two-thirds reported that when they participated in hobbies such as hunting, fishing, or card playing, they usually did so with other landmen and various individuals in the petroleum industry. Approximately two-thirds indicated that their closest friends were other landmen or persons in the oil business. Approximately two-thirds indicated that when they and their wives entertained they usually invited couples in the oil business. A significant number said that their wives were socially active with wives of oilmen. When asked to assess the social life in the petroleum industry more than 95 percent reported that they felt it was more enjoyable than that in other industries. Perhaps most interesting was the finding that more than two-thirds of the landmen responding did not feel that their social interaction with other oil families was "forced." That is to say, they did not feel that the petroleum industry, with the travel and moving involved, tended to "throw its members together" socially and to prevent them from having many opportunities for meeting individuals and their families who are not in the petroleum industry. Obviously, to some degree petroleum work, like various other kinds of occupational complexes, does tend to force informal interaction among its members, but it apparently does this so subtly and skillfully that the members do not perceive the situation as such. Members of the oil fraternity, it would seem, define their informal interaction as spontaneous and arising out of a genuine "occupational brotherhood."

This paper will examine certain aspects of informal interaction and occupational community among members of the "oil fraternity" and especially among petroleum landmen in terms of some of the means by which this sense of community is effected and maintained.[2]

The Petroleum Industry and Occupational Identity

PETROLEUM LANDWORK: THE DEVELOPMENT OF AN OCCUPATIONAL SPECIALTY

The unusual degree of identity with the occupational complex shared by members of the "oil fraternity" is attributable in a significant way to the glamour and "color" of the oil industry itself. The history of the petroleum industry is relatively short—scarcely longer than the memory of living man —and thus fresh. Its history is tinged with the flavor of the western frontier saga, and the work culture that surrounds the exploration and production of oil boasts refreshing elements of individualism and resourcefulness in a work world otherwise characterized by conformity and drabness.

Petroleum landwork consists of ascertaining the availability of land open for oil exploration in a given area, determining the legitimacy of the title claim of the alleged owner of the land or minerals, securing a conveyance of said land or minerals for oil exploration, and expediting the removal of any hinderances, legal or otherwise, to such oil exploration. Persons who possess the title of petroleum landman may be either salaried employees of petroleum corporations or self-employed individuals who perform the same work on a fee or commission basis. Petroleum landwork represents a highly specialized occupational pursuit, which has developed in its entirety since the discovery of petroleum in this country.

With the discovery of petroleum in the United States in commercial quantities in 1859 and the advent of large-scale petroleum exploration, a need was created for a number of specialized skills among those individuals who would be involved in this exploration for and eventual production of petroleum. Edwin Drake, who was responsible for the first oil well, had brought in his well by a salt driller, and salt and water drillers managed to become sufficiently adept at the task of petroleum drilling to bring in a number of fields in several states within a very few years after the first well in Titusville, Pennsylvania. The rapidity with which the oil industry grew in its early years necessitated the conversion of skills from other lines of work into skills specifically oriented at petroleum production. While Drake had been able to acquire the right to drill an oil well and to supervise and coordinate all of the activities in connection with his well pretty much by himself, the increasing complexity of petroleum exploration in the years that followed began to require specialists in the various phases of exploration and drilling, as well as in refining. One of the activities that soon required specialization was that of acquiring the right to drill.

In the United States, after the Drake well, the question of land titles was somewhat more involved than in other parts of the world. At least it was sufficiently involved to render the acquisition of the right to drill for petroleum a complex activity. The rectangular system of land survey in this country; the American inheritance system, which avoids primogeniture as a basis for land inheritance; and the fact that subsurface minerals could be privately owned and separated from the land for purposes of conveyance were all factors that helped to make the question of land titles quite complex. Loans, tax areas, and other types of liens all tended to cloud the title of the land. The large number of homesteaders extended this title complexity to practically all parts of the nation. By the time of Drake's well and in the years that followed, highly specialized skills were needed to determine land and/or mineral ownership accurately in order to acquire the right to explore for petroleum.

At first the oil operators acquired their own leases much as Drake himself had done, but within a short while, as the size of their operations grew, operators were relying on others to acquire their leases for them.

Attorneys, real estate dealers, and commodity buyers were used as lease takers. All manner of agents and even adventurers appeared on the scene and became engaged in lease trading.

The emerging oil industry was developing unique problems and unique needs in regard to acquiring the right to explore for oil. These new needs, as well as the new skills required by the actual drilling for oil itself, were being met by individuals who were acquiring the necessary skills by actual trial-and-error experience. The leasing arrangements that emerged after the Drake well were in many ways different from earlier leasing procedures for the exploration of other types of minerals.

At first, landmen tended to buy and sell oil leases to companies and individuals much in the role of traders. They were simply the self-employed middle men who, through their acquired skill in the specialized area of lease acquisition, were able to provide this service in the form of leases for sale to the companies.

After the turn of the century, as many of the originally small petroleum companies grew in size, they began more and more to require permanent representation in the various discovery areas in which they were drilling. To meet this need they began employing full-time company landmen. Smaller oil companies also required representation, and this they were able to obtain via independent petroleum landmen who would act as their agents on a temporary basis. Many larger companies, even those with landmen in their permanent employ, would on occasion require supplemental representation, especially in times of unusually active exploration and discovery. They, too, utilized the services of independent landmen who acted as agents on a commission basis.

The oil industry was fiercely competitive, with various firms often drilling simultaneously in the same area. It became important to an oil company that it stay informed of its competitors' progress. The decision to buy leases in a given area might be based in large part on intelligence gathered concerning the drilling activities of other companies. Under these circumstances the nature of landwork began to change, and the nature of the changing and developing oil industry necessitated further changes in the work of the landmen. A degree of specialization became necessary. As one observer put it:

> The landman of the early 1920's and 30's was a jack of all trades—a lease buyer, a scout, he settled claims, bought pipeline right-of-ways, purchased crude oil, and just a little bit of anything else his boss suggested. Since World War II, the picture has changed to one of specialization in various facets of the landman's original trade—oil leases and titles and that administrative work which enters into their handling. Specialization, like education, became the mode of the day. The petroleum industry had changed from a

million dollar baby into a billion dollar giant. As lease costs increased, attorneys recommended additional lease security in the form of joinders, ratifications, and general perfection of title to protect their investment. In short the diversified ability of yesterday's landman succumbed to the monster that created him.[3]

The landman of today, while more of a specialist than his counterpart of the 1920s and 30s, still plays a multi-dimensional work role. The present-day landman, like other occupational practitioners in the oil industry, is heir to an occupational need for generalist skills, and in this sense he continues to retain something of an identity as a "man for all seasons," so to speak, who takes great pride in his ability to do whatever is needed to accomplish the job. A tongue in cheek example of this identity is illustrated in an advertisement published by a landman:

I AM QUALIFIED AS A LEASE BROKER. I HAVE THE FOLLOWING PROCLIVITIES TO MAKE A SUCCESSFUL BROKER.

You have to have vision and ambition, be an after-dinner speaker, and before and after dinner guzzler, night owl, work all day and half the night, drive 200 miles and appear fresh the next day; entertain bankers, farmers, cattlemen, pet widows without becoming too amorous, inhale dust, drive thru snow and sleet and work hard all summer without perspiring or acquiring BO—

Must be a man's man, a lady's man, model husband, fatherly father, a good provider, Plutocrat, Democrat, Republican, Dixiecrat, New Dealer, gin dealer, politician, engineer, mechanic, babysitter, diaper changer, and notary public—

Must be a buying genius, full of misinformation, land scout, and carpenter, visit clients in hospitals, jails, honky-tonks, flop houses, and boudoirs and always be able to step off a couple of thousand miles on 10 minutes notice; must have endurance, wide range of telephone numbers, acquaintances from Cape Cod to the Pecos, own a good car, belong to everything from the Swedish Business Men's Pool Poker and Marching Society to the Petroleum Club—

Must be a hotshot, liar, Rhumba dancer, pitch player, diplomat, financier, capitalist, lawyer, abstractor, and be an authority on dogs, dice, horses, and have peak information on blondes, brunettes, and red heads; must know geology, doodlebugging, and be able to mix drinks with everything from Vodka to corn squeezings—

Maybe the old worn out goat is right—Maybe I'll take up picketing or turtle trapping—Wonder why someone doesn't burst out with a hot oil play up in the cool mountains for the summer?[4]

The story of oil in this country is in large measure simply an extension of the western frontier saga. Although oil was first discovered in Pennsylvania, many of the early strikes were in western states. The boom times of the cattle towns gave way to the boom times of the oil towns with scarcely an interruption. The early days of the oil business were characterized by excitement, adventure, and, above all, risks, both economic and personal. Oil exploration was dangerous; it was expensive; and it involved a gamble since scientific searching for oil was relatively new and relatively unknown. The search for oil was a rugged challenge and it took a staunch individual to meet the challenge. Fast decisions and the need to rely on oral agreements and contracts tended to foster fair dealings and trust between colleagues, and between employee and employer. The early oil business developed a kind of pioneer business morality among oilmen.

From the very earliest days of oil pioneering in Pennsylvania, the men who faced the difficulties and challenges of exploration and production have felt an occupational kinship toward one another, much in the same way as seafaring men or railroaders or scientists. The oil business was different from other business; there was a different language and a different environment, and a different set of skills was required.[5] The search for oil led to isolation in some cases and high geographical mobility in others. More often than not it was with other members of the industry that landmen came into contact most frequently in their work and in their play. A sense of camaraderie emerged which was in later years to draw men of many occupational specialties, but all within the oil business, into a solidified collectivity known to them as the "oil fraternity." The outsider often did not understand or fully appreciate the difficulties or attractions of oil exploration, and thus could not share the identification with the industry. Common and often shared experiences developed a "consciousness of kind" which has persisted through time. Just as the oil industry created the technical innovations and skills it required, it also created its own kind of individual to work in its occupational ranks.

Thus the present-day landmen, like the other exploration and production specialists, are heirs to the short but exciting history of the oil industry with its color and romance. Many of the older oilmen were a part of this history. As inheritors of this work culture, with its traditions of challenge and adventure and its residue of rugged individualism, landmen like their occupational brothers in the oil fraternity have tended to develop to a degree a sense of eliteness and aloofness.

The fact that the nature of present-day landwork has called for increasing specialization and technical expertise has been a significant factor in the professionalization efforts of petroleum landmen. The training or experience and competence required for the work have tended to promote occupational awareness and a closer identity with the oil industry.

Landmen come largely from oil producing states like Texas and Oklahoma where the line of oil culture is perhaps strongest. More than one-
fourth had fathers in the oil business and more one-half had fathers who
were self-employed. Almost one-half obtained their first job in the oil industry through the help of friends or family. All are white and almost 85
percent are Protestant. As white, middle-class Protestants with similar economic and educational origins, they appear to be remarkably homogeneous
as an occupational group.[6] This, no doubt, also contributes to their occupational identity and solidarity.

THE EXPLORATION AND PRODUCTION TEAM

The integrated nature of many petroleum companies necessitates some
sort of internal subdivision along functional lines. The industry as a whole
is in large measure subject to this functional cleavage. Due to this separation of function, different subunits of oil companies may exist and operate
a considerable distance apart geographically. Thus the exploration for and
production of crude petroleum may be centered in some parts of the United
States while the processing and manufacturing of petroleum products will
be centered in other parts of the country, and the marketing and sales
functions carried out primarily in yet other areas.

The functional cleavage and the frequency of geographical separation
between the various kinds of activities in the petroleum industry tend to
produce sub-industrial complexes revolving around specific functions such as
exploration. These sub-industrial complexes are made up of those parts of
petroleum companies directly charged with the function in question, as well
as all of the ancillary individuals and firms providing goods and services in
support of that function. Occupational interdependence, interrelationships,
and solidarity tend to be within the functional area, rather than within the
entire industry.

Exploration and production represents one such functional complex
within the petroleum industry. The exploration and production departments
usually make up a group, and because of the wide geographical range of
oil deposits this group sometimes is located away from the home office of
the corporations and its operations are in many cases decentralized. This
decentralization takes the form of land and exploration *divisions* and *districts*. The *district*, comprising a part of a state or an entire state, is generally the smallest autonomous unit. Activities carried on in the exploration
and production departments include geological work, scouting, land and
leasing operations, drilling, and producing. The petroleum landman usually
works out of the district office.

In the district office the geologist, aided by geophysical, geological, and
other types of intelligence information obtained from higher level offices and

geological archives, as well as that gathered locally, will make recommendations concerning likely areas for oil exploration. He and his staff will also prepare detailed maps and specifications of selected areas to facilitate well location. The oil scout is charged with the function of intelligence gathering. It is his responsibility to obtain information on all drilling and leasing activities in the area. A scout's duties include daily reports to headquarters of the progress of all drilling wells, all strikes of gas or oil, any geological or leasing activities, and the immediate dispatch by telephone or telegraph of news of any important development in the area assigned to him. It is the landman's task, on the basis of information derived from the geologists and scouts, to acquire the right to explore and drill for oil on the prospective lands. This right generally takes the form of an oil and gas lease on the prospective lands, because this involves a smaller amount of money than outright purchase. The exploration department may assign to a landman the task of acquiring oil leases on either a sporadic or systematic basis. Once a lease is acquired, arrangements for the actual drilling of the well are made by the drilling section personnel with private drilling concerns, and should the well produce, the rental section sees that the appropriate royalty is paid to the landowner. The rentals section is also responsible for yearly rental payments being made to landowners whose land has been leased but not yet drilled.

The exploration and production specialties make up a work team that operates somewhat separately and independently from the remainder of oil industry operations. The exploration and production team works in the "glamour" part of the industry and the people on it tend to think of themselves as the only genuine *oil* people.

The symbiotic relationships of team membership, a legacy of colorful and adverturesome work history, and mutual pride in the accomplishment of wresting the petroleum from the earth all tend to generate great cohesion, awareness, and identification with both industry and occupational complex. The exploration and production occupations are all members in good standing of the "oil fraternity."

The Petroleum "In-Group" and Occupational Social Distance

Members of many occupations experience spatial, temporal, or social separation from members of other occupations. Some occupational complexes are physically isolated from others; the military who live and work behind the fences of government bases and camps are a case in point, as are telephone operators who work at unnormal hours and are thus cut off from many other persons. Still others, by virtue of widely divergent occupational value systems or the distinctive nature of the practitioner-clientele status relationship, may establish or experience a significant degree of social distance between themselves and persons in other occupational pursuits. The classic town-gown split of academic and business communities is an example of divergent value systems operating to effect social distance. Members of the oil fraternity tend to enjoy such social distance from members of other occupational complexes by virtue of certain work arrangements that separate them physically from those in other business endeavors as well as an attitudinal reaction to outsiders who are basically unknowledgeable about the nature of oil exploration.

THE UNKNOWLEDGEABLE OUTSIDER

If the oil business possesses a degree of "glamour" for insiders, so too are outsiders often excited by oil exploration. The outsiders, however, often tend to experience the excitement as a kind of "black gold" fever, developing an image of oil exploration as an easy get-rich-quick device. Many outsiders reason that it should be relatively easy for one involved in the exploration and production of oil to profitably invest in oil holdings and become as rich as King Midas. Pursuing this line of reasoning, they imagine all landmen to be so strategically located in terms of "inside information" that they should be able to become rich without difficulty.

Such reasoning, of course, is analogous to imagining that the bank teller, being close to large sums of money, should be able to carry home samples. Oil people and particularly landmen are often asked by friends, relatives, neighbors, and even strangers to invest money for them in oil holdings in order that they may share in the wealth. Unfortunately, outsiders seldom are aware of the risk factor in oil exploration. They refuse to believe that the odds are ten to one that any well drilled will be dry and that even some producing wells must be abandoned because of technical complications or low production. Accordingly, where an oilman does undertake to invest money for an outsider, the person often becomes embittered if the well is dry or does not produce a handsome profit. He may blame the oilman for making a poor investment or claim he was cheated. As a result of this, many oilmen refuse to invest money for outsiders or to let anyone other than oil people buy into their well deals.

Some oil people prefer to avoid fraternization with outsiders lest their relationship lead to the usual request to "let them in on the good thing."

This is similar to the situation Howard Becker has described with respect to jazz musicians who resented their clientele's interference in their work and thought of them as "squares" because they were unknowledgeable about jazz music.[7] These musicians, in their attempt to effect social distance between themselves and their clientele would erect physical barriers of chains around themselves in the absence of a bandstand. The oilman often reacts to the unknowledgeable person outside the oil industry in much the same manner. Having little in common with the outsiders, having different business interests, always wary lest he be importuned to invest money or disclose "inside" information, and immersed in a unique and satisfying work culture, the oilman frequently erects social barriers between himself and those not in the "oil fraternity." A number of circumstances and conditions attendant to oil work undergird the physical separation and social distance from persons outside the field.

Office Segregation

Much of the work involved in the exploration and production of petroleum involves a cooperative effort on the part of many specialists. A company exploration team may well require the services of many ancillary occupational practitioners, including title attorneys, drilling contractors and their rig crews, as well as the employees of electric log or oil well cementing firms, to name a few. Petroleum work is facilitated when all of the ancillary services and other oil specialists are close at hand. As a result there is often a tendency for oil firms and independent specialists to locate their offices near each other. In many cities in petroleum regions there are buildings and office complexes that either were designed to cater to petroleum services or have become such centers over a period of time. Once the process of centralization has begun, it tends to continue with new oil services gravitating toward the existing concentration of offices. Many such buildings or office plazas bear such names as, for example, the Petroleum Building. Such centralization of oil services constitutes occupational segregation, and this is especially the case with the so-called exploration and production specialties. Oilmen see each other frequently and extensively in their day-to-day interaction, both in terms of formal business contacts and informal interaction at meals, during coffee breaks, and in the process of moving back and forth among offices. The landman study showed that more than 90 percent of the respondents told of lunching and sharing coffee breaks with other landmen and other members of the petroleum industry.[8] If a petroleum club is also located nearby, the oilmen are particularly insulated from contact with other occupational groups.

Travel Demands of Work

The nature of petroleum work frequently requires that the oilman and especially the landman travel as part of their job responsibility. It may be necessary that they be away from town for several days each week. Such travel tends to separate them from contact with other kinds of occupations in town. Further, such travel may well throw them into more frequent contact with other oilmen since petroleum specialists often travel together; oil scouts, for example, may on occasion cover their areas together and independent landmen may go on a buying order as a team. In any event, oilmen frequently travel to the same areas, and thus find themselves working alongside each other in the title records office of the local court house, crossing each other's path out in the field, or staying in the same motel at night. Their travel may well provide them more opportunity to interact informally than if they did not travel.

GEOGRAPHICAL MOBILITY

Just as oil work requires travel on the job, it may also require relatively frequent moves from community to community. Landmen, like other oilmen, may find it necessary to move their families to a new town every few years if not more frequently. Thus many oilmen and their families become relative strangers in the new community when they move. Having few contacts outside the oil industry, they often seek out other oil families and old oil friends from previous towns who may have been transferred earlier. Certainly, the various women's petroleum social organizations serve as effective devices for reintegrating the family into the social life of the oil community in the new town. A family can then take up where it left off, so to speak, in terms of social activities. There is even some evidence that oil families may seek out neighborhoods where other oil people live. Or it may simply be that, being in approximately the same general income level, they tend to gravitate to the same housing neighborhoods. The previously mentioned petroleum landmen study, for example, showed that almost 90 percent of the individuals responding indicated that they knew of other members of the petroleum industry living in their neighborhood. Moving from city to city on a relatively frequent basis, then, would not seem to present the oil family with the social crisis that members of some other occupations might experience in such a situation. The oilman instead simply transfers to another "chapter" of his work fraternity in a new community and he and his family continue to enjoy the benefits of occupational brotherhood.

Formal Mechanisms for Facilitating Informal Interaction among Colleagues and Co-Workers

An important element in the development of colleagueship among members of an occupation is the presence of mechanisms for facilitating informal interaction among colleagues.[9] These mechanisms provide the opportunities for frequent interaction among occupational members and serve to strengthen the identity with the occupation. In the petroleum industry generally, and in landwork specifically, there are several such mechanisms that bear examination. These include the local landmen's associations and especially their social programs, the local Petroleum Clubs, and various organizations for the wives of landmen and other persons in the exploration segment of the petroleum industry.

THE LOCAL LANDMEN'S ASSOCIATION

In recent years there has been considerable activity among petroleum landmen to organize themselves into various local and regional occupational associations. The first such local association was the Tri-State Landmen's Association, organized in Evansville, Indiana, in 1939. This first association announced its goal as follows:

> The purpose of this organization is a closer association and acquaintanceship among the landmen of the area and of discussing problems of mutual interest, etc.[10]

The Tri-State Association ceased operations during the Second World War, but reorganized after the war. Because of this break in its continuity, the honor of being the oldest continuous local association goes to the Mississippi Landmen's Association, organized in Jackson, Mississippi, in July 1944. Since World War II, other local landmen's associations have been organized throughout the country.[11] Local associations have been formed in practically all areas of the country where there is any appreciable oil activity or concentration of petroleum industry personnel. As a result, almost all landmen have the opportunity to associate themselves with local organizations, and most apparently do so. The previously cited study of several years ago showed that almost 95 percent of the landmen surveyed indicated the presence of a local landmen's association in their area.[12] Furthermore, more than two-thirds of those questioned were members of the local association, and of these the majority revealed that they attended most of the meetings and participated in social activities sponsored by the association. These local groups have afforded educational opportunities for their members in the form of guest speakers and landwork seminars. In addition, the local associations have engaged in numerous civic activities and fund-raising drives, as well as setting up scholarship funds for students in the Petroleum Land Management Curriculum in various western universities. Local associations also sponsor a wide variety of social affairs and sports events (golf tournaments for example) for the members and their wives. Frequently Landmen's

Associations arrange for outings, parties, and dances at Christmas time or other festive occasions. Even social affairs for the children of members are sometimes sponsored by the associations. Much of the social life of petroleum landmen and families revolves around the local landmen's association and the informal interaction that it promotes.

In addition to serving as a social organization, the local association also attempts to be a professional organization, and so the programs at many of the meetings focus on topics of professional concern or take up matters that bear directly on the work role of the landmen. The purposes of these local associations would seem, then, to be twofold. One purpose is the furtherment of professionalization objectives and the other is to provide opportunities for informal interaction among colleagues through different kinds of social activities, thereby fostering occupational identification and camaraderie.

THE PETROLEUM CLUB

In a number of areas across the country where there are large concentrations of individuals in the petroleum industry, social clubs known as Petroleum Clubs are found. These clubs are frequently uptown clubs with dining, lounging, conference, and bar facilities for their members. Membership, in most cases, is restricted to persons in the petroleum industry proper, although persons in ancillary industries are sometimes admitted. Persons in the production and exploration segment of the industry perhaps contribute most heavily to the membership of most of the clubs. Petroleum landmen, along with other oilmen, can meet and interact with each other at lunch or afternoon cocktail time. Most clubs have television rooms as well as card rooms, and an individual can usually locate some of his friends and associates at the club day or night. In this sense the petroleum club resembles the traditional men's clubs of the large cities. In addition to providing opportunities for interaction among colleagues and co-workers on the premises itself, the clubs frequently sponsor other activities such as golf tournaments, dances, and trips to football games with block tickets. The previously mentioned survey of landmen showed that almost 90 percent had a Petroleum Club available in their area, and almost one-half were members. Landmen over forty years of age and independently employed landmen appeared to be more likely to be members than were younger landmen and company employed men. This can be accounted for by two factors. First, inasmuch as membership entailed a significant economic outlay, the landmen over forty in all likelihood were better able to afford the expense. Secondly, the higher membership among independents than among company men is probably the result of the fact that club membership is functional in providing business contacts with other oil people. The Petroleum Clubs, then, like the Local Landmen's Associations, appear to be important mechanisms in facilitating informal interaction among colleagues.

WIVES' AUXILIARY ORGANIZATIONS

In towns where there are local or regional landmen's associations, there frequently are also auxiliary clubs or organizations for the wives of the landmen. In addition to these auxiliary clubs, there are also other women's social organizations for the wives of individuals in the petroleum industry —especially those in exploration and production activities. Some of these women's clubs are associated with the Petroleum Clubs, while still others may be completely independent of any other organization. The same study of landmen revealed that more than one-half of their wives belonged to some kind of women's petroleum social organization. The wives of company men seemed to be somewhat more prone to be members than were the wives of independent landmen. This is no doubt a result of the fact that company men are geographically more mobile than independents and the women's clubs offered an opportunity for the wives to meet other women in the community. In addition to bridge games, luncheons, and other social activities for women, these clubs also undertake charitable and community projects, arrange golf tournaments for their members, and give dances and parties for their members and their husbands. These social organizations for wives of landmen (or oilmen generally) serve to promote informal interaction as well as cohesion in and identification with the "occupational community."

THE AMERICAN ASSOCIATION OF PETROLEUM LANDMEN AND ITS ANNUAL CONVENTION

Like some other occupational groups, landmen have a national occupational association. The purpose of this organization is to promote the professionalization of the occupation and to encourage the growth of occupational identity among the members. It holds an annual convention (usually at some attractive resort location) and many of its members attend and bring their wives and children. At the convention a number of activities are planned for the wives and a number of social events for couples are scheduled. The convention allows considerable opportunity for informal interaction among landmen and their wives and the event represents a significant recreational occasion for many of them. The annual convention not only promotes the professional identity, it also fosters a strong sense of occupational community.

Summary

Petroleum landmen and the other members of the exploration and production team make up an occupational complex with a unique work culture and a strong sense of occupational community. This sense of occupational community manifests itself in the tendency of these oilmen to think and speak of themselves as members of the "oil fraternity."

Much of their identification with the "oil fraternity" results from the relatively recent colorful and adverturesome history of petroleum exploration in this country and the still "glamorous" nature of the industry today. The tradition of rugged individualism, excitement, challenge, and work camaraderie has produced occupational images with which one can identify comfortably.

Landmen, like other members of the "oil fraternity," tend to confine their informal interaction and their social activities largely to fraternity members. This includes lunching, coffee klatching, family entertaining, and hobby participation. The "Oil Fraternity" is indeed clannish and a number of work arrangements and conditions contribute to this clannishness, including some degree of suspicion and hostility toward outsiders unknowledgeable about the oil business, and a significant measure of occupational segregation brought about by physical separation, frequent transfers from one community to another, and the fact that the work requires much travel.

In addition, several formal mechanisms exist that tend to facilitate informal interaction among oilmen and their families. These include petroleum clubs, social clubs for wives of oilmen, national conventions of professional organizations, and local professional groups.

The closed nature of this occupational social system in terms of internal cohesion, occupational identity, and patterns of informal social interaction would indeed seem to justify the label "fraternity."

Footnotes

This article is a modification and condensation of portions of Clifton D. Bryant's "The Petroleum Landman: A Sociological Analysis of an Occupation" (unpublished doctoral dissertation, Louisiana State University, Baton Rouge, Louisiana, 1964). This dissertation was subsequently published by the American Association of Petroleum Landmen in serial form in seven issues of their official journal, *The Landman*, from Vol. IX, No. 5 (April 1964) to Vol. IX, No. 11 (October 1964).

[1] Clifton D. Bryant, "The Petroleum Landman: A Sociological Analysis of an Occupation" (unpublished doctoral dissertation, Louisiana State University, Baton Rouge, Louisiana, 1964), especially Chapter VI.

[2] For another examination of "Occupational Community" see Joel E. Gerstl,

"Determinants of Occupational Community in High Status Occupations," *The Sociological Quarterly*, 2, No. 1 (January 1961) 37–48.

[3] Joseph H. Mills, "From Oil Smeller to Landman," *The Landman*, IV (August 1959), 49.

[4] L. A. Hawkins, "I am Qualified as a Lease Broker," *Mississippi Oil Review*, July 29, 1952, p. 3. This ad is apparently a variation of a short essay that was originally used by the late Dana H.Kelsey, once vice-president of Sinclair Oil and Gas Company.

[5] As part of the subculture associated with the exploration segment of the oil industry, a highly distinctive occupational language or argot has developed. For the most part the professional and technical occupations employ the same occupational argot as do the drilling crews. Naturally the lawyers, geologists, geophysicists, etc., employ certain technical vocabularies, but basically "oil" language is "oil" language. For a detailed examination of the unique vocabulary of the oil industry, see Lalia Phipps Boone, "Patterns of Innovation in the Language of the Oil Fields," American Speech (February 1949), pp. 26–35, and Gerald W. Haslam, "The Language of the Oil Fields," *Etc.* (June 1967).

[6] Bryant, *op. cit.*; for a detailed discussion of the socioeconomic characteristics of petroleum landmen, see Chapter IV.

[7] See, for example, Howard S. Becker, "The Professional Dance Musician and His Audience," *American Journal of Sociology*, LVII, No. 2 (September 1951). Not only were oilmen suspicious of outsiders; outsiders (at least in the early days) were suspicious of oilmen. Too many "hokus" deals and failures to strike oil after exaggerated promises existed to engender much confidence among outsiders.

[8] Bryant, *op. cit.*, Chapter VI.

[9] For a detailed discussion of such mechanisms see Edward Gross, *Work and Society* (New York: The Thomas Y. Crowell Company, 1958) pp. 229–30. As specific examples Gross mentions clubs and outings.

[10] "Tri-State 1st Landmen's Group Organized," *The Landman*, III (July 1958), 51.

[11] There are several score of these local associations today, located throughout North America.

[12] Bryant, *op. cit.*, Chapter VI.

Practitioner and Clientele

The Cabdriver and His Fare

Facets of a Fleeting Relationship

FRED DAVIS
University of California Medical Center
San Francisco

Even in an urban and highly secularized society such as ours, most service relationships, be they between a professional and his client or a menial and his patron, are characterized by certain constraints on too crass a rendering and consuming of the service.[1] That is to say, in the transaction, numerous interests besides that of simply effecting an economic exchange are customarily attended to and dealt with. The moral reputation of the parties,[2] their respective social standing, and the skill and art with which the service is performed[3] are but a few of the non-instrumental values which are usually incorporated into the whole act.

Tenuous though such constraints may become at times, particularly in large cities where anonymous roles only, segmentally related, occur in great profusion, it is at once evident that for them to exist at all something approximating a community must be present. Practitioners and clients must be sufficiently in communication for any untoward behavior to stand a reasonable chance of becoming known, remarked upon, remembered, and, in extreme cases, made public. And, whereas the exercise of sanctions does not necessarily depend on a community network[4] that is closely integrated (or one in which there is a total identity of values and interests), it does depend on there being some continuity and stability in the relationships that make up the network, so that, at minimum, participants may in the natural course of events be able to identify actions and actors to one another.[5]

It is mainly, though not wholly, from this vantage point that big-city cabdriving as an occupation is here discussed, particularly the relationship between cabdriver and fare and its consequences for the occupational cul-

Reprinted from *The American Journal of Sociology*, Vol. 45, No. 2 (September 1959), 158–65, by permission of the author and the University of Chicago Press. Copyright © 1959 by The University of Chicago.

ture.[6] Approximating in certain respects a provincial's caricature of the broad arc of social relations in the metropolis, this relationship affords an extreme instance of the weakening and attenuation of many of the constraints customary in other client-and-patron-oriented services in our society. As such, its analysis can perhaps point up by implication certain of the rarely considered preconditions for practitioner-client relations found in other, more firmly structured, services and professions.

In a large city like Chicago the hiring of a cab by a passenger may be conceived of in much the same way as the random collision of particles in an atomic field. True, there are some sectors of the field in which particles come into more frequent collision than others, for example, downtown, at railroad depots, and at the larger neighborhood shopping centers. But this kind of differential activity within the field as a whole provides little basis for predicting the coupling of any two specific particles.

To a much more pronounced degree than is the case in other client-and-patron-oriented services, the occupation of cabdriver provides its practitioners with few, if any, regularities by which to come upon, build up, and maintain a steady clientele. The doctor has his patients, the schoolteacher her pupils, the janitor his tenants, the waitress her regular diners; and in each case server and served remain generally in some continuing or renewable relationship. By contrast, the cabdriver's day consists of a long series of brief contacts with unrelated persons of whom he has no foreknowledge, just as they have none of him, and whom he is not likely to encounter again.

Furthermore, by virtue of the differential spatial, social, and organizational arrangements of the community, it is also likely that the clients of these other practitioners will, in some manner at least, know one another and be related to one another in ways that often transcend the simple circumstance of sharing the same services: they may also be friends, kin, neighbors, or colleagues. For this reason the clientele of most practitioners is something more than an aggregate of discrete individuals; it is, as well, a rudimentary social universe and forum to which the practitioner must address himself in other than purely individual terms.[7]

The cabdriver, by comparison, has no such clientele. He has no fixed business address, and his contacts with passengers are highly random and singular. To a striking degree he is a practitioner without reputation because those who ride in his cab do not comprise, except perhaps in the most abstract sense, anything approximating a social group. They neither know nor come into contact with one another in other walks of life, and, even if by chance some do, they are unaware of their ever having shared the services of the same anonymous cabdriver. Even were the driver deliberately to set out to build up a small nucleus of steady and favored passengers, the time-space logistics of his job would quickly bring such a scheme to nought. Unable to plot his location in advance or to distribute time according to a schedule, he depends on remaining open to all comers wherever he finds himself. Much more so than other classes of service personnel, cabdrivers are both the fortuitous victims and the beneficiaries of random and highly impersonal market contingencies.

This set of circumstances—fleeting, one-time contact with a heterogeneous aggregate of clients, unknown to one another—exerts an interesting influence on the role of cabdriver.

Unable, either directly through choice or indirectly through location, to select clients, the cabdriver is deprived of even minimal controls. His trade therefore exposes him to a variety of hazards and exigencies which few others, excepting policemen, encounter as frequently; for example: stick-ups, belligerent drunks, women in labor, psychopaths, counterfeiters, and fare-jumpers. Unlike the policeman's, however, his control over them is more fragile.

Nor, incidentally, is the cabdriver's social status or level of occupational skill of much help in inducing constraint in fares. Patently, his status is low, in large part precisely because, unlike the professional and other practitioners commanding prestige, he can hardly be distinguished from his clients in task-relevant competence. Not only is the operation of a motor car a widely possessed skill, but a large proportion of fares have, for example, a very good idea of the best routes to their destination, the rules and practices of the road, and the charges for a trip. Though they are rarely as adept or sophisticated in these matters as the cabdriver, the discrepancy is so small that many think they know the driver's job as well as he does. Periodically, a cabdriver will boldly challenge a difficult and critical passenger to take over the wheel himself. Others, wishing to impress on the fare that theirs is a real service requiring special talent and skill, will resort to darting nimbly in and out of traffic, making neatly executed U-turns, and leaping smartly ahead of other cars when the traffic light changes.

Goffman[8] speaks of a category of persons who in some social encounters are treated as if they were not present, whereas in fact they may be indispensable for sustaining the performance. He terms these "non-persons" and gives as an example a servant at a social gathering. Although cabdrivers are not consistently approached in this way by fares, it happens often enough for it to become a significant theme of their work. Examples are legion. Maresca[9] tells of the chorus girl who made a complete change from street clothing into stage costume as he drove her to her theater. More prosaic instances include the man and wife who, managing to suppress their anger while on the street, launch into a bitter quarrel the moment they are inside the cab; or the well-groomed young couple who after a few minutes roll over on the back seat to begin petting; or the businessman who loudly discusses details of a questionable business deal. Here the driver is expected to, and usually does, act as if he were merely an extension of the automobile he operates. In actuality, of course, he is acutely aware of what goes on in his cab, and, although his being treated as a non-person implies a degraded status, it also affords him a splendid vantage point from which to witness a rich variety of human schemes and entanglements.

The fleeting nature of the cabdriver's contact with the passenger at the same time also makes for his being approached as someone to whom intimacies can be revealed and opinions forthrightly expressed with little fear of rebuttal, retaliation, or disparagement. And though this status as an accessible person is the product of little more than the turning inside-out of his non-person status—which situation implies neither equality nor respect for his opinion—it nevertheless does afford him glimpses of the private lives of individuals which few in our society, apart from psychiatrists and clergy, are privileged to note as often or in such great variety. It is probably not a mistaken everyday generalization that big-city cabdrivers, on their part, feel less compunction about discussing their own private lives, asking probing questions, and "sounding off" on a great many topics and issues than do others who regularly meet the public, but less fleetingly.[10]

In cabdriving, therefore, propriety, deference, and "face" are, in the nature of the case, weaker than is the case in most other service relationships. This absence contributes to a heightened preoccupation with and focusing on the purely instrumental aspect of the relationship which for the driver is the payment he receives for his services. This perhaps would be less blatantly the case were it not for the gratuity or tip. For the non-cab-owning company driver, the sum collected in tips amounts roughly to 40 percent of his earnings. Considering, for example, that in Chicago in the late forties a hard-working cabdriver, who worked for ten hours a day, six days a week, would on the average take home approximately seventy-five dollars a week including tips, the importance of tipping can readily be appreciated. For the family man who drives, tips usually represent the difference between a subsistence and a living wage. Also, tips are, apart from taxes, money "in the clear," in that the driver does not have to divide them with the company as he does his metered collections.[11] Sum for sum, therefore, tips represent greater gain for him than do metered charges.

It would probably be incorrect to hold that pecuniary considerations are the sole ones involved in the cabdriver's attitude toward the tip. Yet in such tip-sensitive occupations as cabdriving, waiting, and bellhopping to suggest[12] that the tip's primary significance is its symbolic value as a token of affection or appreciation for a service well performed would be even wider of the mark. Vindictive caricatures abound among cabdrivers, as they do among waiters, waitresses, and bellhops, of the "polite gentleman" or "kind lady" who with profuse thanks and flawless grace departs from the scene having "stiffed" (failed to tip) them. In occupations where the tip constitutes so large a fraction of the person's earnings, the cash nexus, while admittedly not the only basis upon which patrons are judged, is so important as to relegate other considerations to a secondary place. Will the fare tip or will he "stiff"? How much will he tip? The answers remain in nearly every instance problematic to the end. Not only is there no sure way of predicting the outcome, but in a culture where the practice of tipping is neither as widespread nor as standardized as in many Continental countries, for example, the driver cannot in many cases even make a guess.

No regular scheme of work can easily tolerate so high a degree of ambiguity and uncertainty in a key contingency. Invariably, attempts are made to fashion ways and means of greater predictability and control; or, failing that, of devising formulas and imagery to bring order and reason in otherwise inscrutable and capricious events. In the course of a long history a rich body of stereotypes, beliefs, and practices[13] has grown up whose function is that of reducing uncertainty, increasing calculability, and providing coherent explanations.

A basic dichotomy running through the cabdriver's concept of his client world is of regular cab users and of non-cab users, the latter referred to as "jerks," "slobs," "yokels," "public transportation types," and a host of other derogatory terms. The former class, though viewed as quite heterogeneous within itself, includes all who customarily choose cabs in preference to other forms of local transportation, are conversant with the cab-passenger role, and, most of all, accept, if only begrudgingly, the practice of tipping. By comparison, the class of non-cab users includes that vast aggregate of persons who resort to cabs only in emergencies or on special occasions, and are prone too often to view the hiring of a cab as simply a more expensive mode of transportation.

Take, for example, the familiar street scene following a sudden downpour or unexpected breakdown in bus service, when a group of individuals cluster about a bus stop, several of whom dart from the curb now and then in hope of hailing a cab. Such persons are almost by definition non-cab users or they would not be found at a bus stop in the rain; nor would they be keeping an eye out for a possible bus. A potential fare in this predicament is to the cabdriver a foul-weather friend, and drivers are on occasion known to hurdle by in spiteful glee, leaving the supplicant standing.

He who hires a cab only on special occasions, frequently to impress others or, perhaps, himself alone, is another familiar kind of non-cab user. Writing of his experiences as a London cabdriver, Hodge relates a by no means uncommon encounter:

> But tonight is different. Perhaps the Pools have come up for once. Anyhow, he's got money. He signals me with exaggerated casualness from the cinema entrance. . . . She steps in daintily, the perfect lady, particularly where she puts her feet. As soon as she's

safely inside, he whispers the address ... and adds, as one man of the world to another, "No hurry, driver." Then he dives in with such utter *savoir faire, comme il faut*, and what not, that he trips over the mat and lands face first on the back seat.[14]

Perhaps the most obvious kind of non-user is the person who, after hailing a cab, will ask the driver some such question as, "How much will it cost to take me to 500 Elm Street?" By this simple inquiry this person stands revealed as one who takes a narrow view of cab travel and from whom not much, if anything, can be expected by way of tip. On the other hand, regular cab users demonstrate in a variety of ways that for them this is a customary and familiar mode of travel. The manner in which they hail a cab, when and how they announce their destination, the ease with which they enter and exit, how they sit—these, and more, though difficult to describe in precise detail, comprise the Gestalt.

There exists among drivers an extensive typology of cab users, the attributes imputed to each type having a certain predictive value, particularly as regards tipping. Some of the more common and sharply delineated types are:

The Sport.   The cabdriver's image of this type combines in one person those attributes of character which he views as ideal. While the Sport's vocation may be any one of many, his status derives more from his extra-vocational activities, e.g., at the race track, prize fights, ball games, popular restaurants, and bars. He is the perennial "young man on the town." Gentlemanly without being aloof, interested without becoming familiar, he also is, of course, never petty. Most of all, his tips are generous, and even on very short rides he will seldom tip less than a quarter. A favorite success story among cabdrivers describes at length and in fine detail the handsome treatment accorded the driver on an all-night tour with a Sport.[15]

The Blowhard.   The Blowhard is a false Sport. While often wearing the outer mantle of the Sport, he lacks the real Sport's casualness, assured manners, and comfortable style. Given to loquaciousness, he boasts and indiscriminately fabricates tales of track winnings, sexual exploits, and the important people he knows. Often holding out the promise of much by way of tip, he seldom lives up to his words.

The Businessman.   These are the staple of the cab trade, particularly for drivers who work by day. Not only are they the most frequently encountered; their habits and preferences are more uniform than those of any other type: the brisk efficiency with which they engage a cab, their purposefulness and disinclination to partake of small talk. Though not often big tippers, they are thought fair. Thus they serve as something of a standard by which the generosity or stinginess of others is judged.

The Lady Shopper. Although almost as numerous as businessmen, Lady Shoppers are not nearly as well thought of by cabdrivers. The stereotype is a middle-aged woman, fashionably though unattractively dressed, sitting somewhat stiffly at the edge of her seat and wearing a fixed glare which bespeaks her conviction that she is being "taken for a ride." Her major delinquency, however, is undertipping; her preferred coin is a dime, no more or less, regardless of how long or arduous the trip. A forever repeated story is of the annoyed driver, who, after a grueling trip with a Lady Shopper, hands the coin back, telling her, "Lady, keep your lousy dime. You need it more than I do."[16]

Live Ones.[17] Live Ones are a special category of fare usually encountered by the cabdriver who works by night. They are, as a rule, out-of-town conventioneers or other revelers who tour about in small groups in search of licentious forms of entertainment: cabarets, burlesques, strip-tease bars, pick-up joints, etc. As often as not, they have already had a good deal to drink when the cabdriver meets them, and, being out-of-towners they frequently turn to him for recommendations on where to go. In the late forties an arrangement existed in Chicago whereby some of the more popular Near North Side and West Madison Street "clip joints" rewarded cabdrivers for "steering" Live Ones to their establishments. Some places paid fifty cents "a head"; others a dollar "for the load." As do the many others who regularly cater to Live Ones—e.g., waitresses, bartenders, female bar companions (B-girls), night-club hosts and hostesses, entertainers, prostitutes—cabdrivers often view them as fair game. And while their opportunities for pecuniary exploitation are fewer and more limited than those open, for example, to B-girls and night-club proprietors, many drivers feel less inhibited about padding charges and finagling extras from Live Ones than they do from other fares. Often extravagant in their tips because of high spirits and drink, Live Ones are also frequently careless and forget to tip altogether. Knowing that Live Ones are out to "blow their money" anyway, many drivers believe they are justified in seeing to it that they are not deprived of a small portion.

Although the cab culture's typology of fares stems in a large part from the attempt to order experience, reduce uncertainty, and further calculability of the tip, it is questionable of course as to how accurate or efficient it is. For, as has often been remarked, stereotypes and typologies have a way of imparting a symmetry and regularity to behavior which are, at best, only crudely approximated in reality. Too often it happens, for example, that a fare tabbed as a Sport turns out to be a Stiff (non-tipper), that a Blowhard matches his words with a generous tip, or that a Lady Shopper will give fifteen or even twenty cents. The persistence of the typology therefore has perhaps as much to do with the cabdriver's a posteriori reconstructions and rationalizations of fare behavior as it does with the typology's predictive efficiency.

To protect and insure themselves against an unfavorable outcome of tipping, many drivers will, depending upon circumstances, employ diverse tactics and stratagems (some more premeditated than others) to increase the amount of tip or to compensate for its loss should it not be forthcoming. Certain of these are listed below. It should be understood, however, that in the ordinary instance the driver makes no attempt to manipulate the fare, believing resignedly that in the long run such means bear too little fruit for the effort and risk.

Making Change.   Depending on the tariff and the amount handed him, the driver can fumble about in his pockets for change, or make change in such denominations as often to embarrass a fare into giving a larger tip than he had intended. The efficacy of this tactic depends naturally on the determination and staying power of the fare, qualities which many fares are averse to demonstrate, particularly when it comes to small change.

The Hard-luck Story.   This is usually reserved for young persons and others who, for whatever reason, evidence an insecure posture vis-à-vis the driver. Typically, the hard-luck story consists of a catalogue of economic woes, e.g., long and hard hours of work, poor pay, insulting and unappreciative passengers, etc. In "confiding" these to the fare, the driver pretends to esteem him as an exceptionally sympathetic and intelligent person who, unlike "the others," can appreciate his circumstances and act accordingly. Most drivers, however, view the hard-luck story as an unsavory form of extortion, beneath their dignity. Furthermore, while it may work in some cases, its potential for alienating tips is probably as great as its success at extracting them.

Fictitious Charges.   The resort to fictitious and fraudulent charges occurs most commonly in those cases in which the driver feels that he has good reason to believe that the fare will, either through malice or ignorance, not tip and when the fare impresses him as being enough of a non-cab user as not to know when improper charges are being levied. Once, when I complained to a veteran cabdriver about having been "stiffed" by a young couple, newly arrived in Chicago, to whom I had extended such extra services as carrying luggage and opening doors, I was told: "Wise up kid! When you pick up one of these yokels at the Dearborn Station carrying a lot of cheap straw luggage on him, you can bet ninety-nine times out of a hundred that he isn't going to tip you. Not that he's a mean guy or anything, but where he comes from, they never heard of tipping. What I do with a yokel like that is to take him to where he's going, show him what the fare is on the meter, and tell him that it costs fifteen cents extra for each piece of luggage. Now, he doesn't know that there's no charge for hand luggage, but that way I'm sure of getting my tip out of him."

The "Psychological" Approach.   Possibly attributing more art to their trade than is the case, some drivers are of the opinion that a cab ride can be tailored to fit a passenger in much the same way as can a suit of clothes. One cabdriver, boasting of his success at getting tips, explained: "In this business you've got to use psychology. You've got to make the ride fit the person. Now, take a businessman. He's in a hurry to get someplace and he doesn't want a lot of bullshit and crapping around. With him you've got to keep moving. Do some fancy cutting in and out, give the cab a bit of a jerk when you take off from a light. Not reckless, mind you, but plenty of zip. He likes that.[18] With old people, it's just the opposite. They're more afraid than anyone of getting hurt or killed in a cab. Take it easy with them. Creep along, open doors for them, help them in and out, be real folksy. Call them 'Sir' and 'Ma'am' and they'll soon be calling you 'young man.' They're suckers for this stuff, and they'll loosen up their pocketbooks a little bit."

In the last analysis, neither the driver's typology of fares nor his strata-gems further to any marked degree his control of the tip. Paradoxically, were these routinely successful in achieving predictability and control, they would at the same time divest the act of tipping of its most distinguishing characteristics—of its uncertainty, variability, and of the element of revela-tion in its consummation. It is these—essentially the problematic in human intercourse[19]—which distinguish the tip from the fixed service charge. And though another form of remuneration might in the end provide the cab-driver with a better wage and a more secure livelihood, the abrogation of tipping would also lessen the intellectual play which uncertainty stimulates and without which cabdriving would be for many nothing more than un-relieved drudgery.

That the practice of tipping, however, expressively befits only certain kinds of service relationships and may under slightly altered circumstances easily degenerate into corruption or extortion is demonstrated, ironically enough, by the predicament of some cabdrivers themselves. To give an example: In the garage out of which I worked, nearly everyone connected with maintenance and assignment of cabs expected tips from drivers for performing many of the routine tasks associated with their jobs, such as filling a tank with gas, changing a tire, or adjusting a carburetor. Although they resented it, drivers had little recourse but to tip. Otherwise, they would acquire reputations as "stiffs" and "cheapskates," be kept waiting inter-minably for repairs, and find that faulty and careless work had been done on their vehicles. Particularly with the dispatcher did the perversion of the tipping system reach extortionate proportions. His power derived from the assignment of cabs; to protect themselves from being assigned "pots" (cabs that would break down in the middle of the day), drivers tipped him fifty cents at the beginning of every week. Since nearly every driver tipped the dispatcher and since there were more drivers than good cabs, a certain number of drivers would still be assigned "pots." Some, wishing to insure doubly against this would then raise the bribe to a dollar and a half a week, causing the others to follow suit in a vicious spiral. If little else, this shows how the tip—as distinguished from the gift, honorarium, inducement, or bribe—depends for its expressive validity on there not being a too close, long sustained, or consequential relationship between the parties to a service transaction.

Among service relationships in our society, that between the big city cabdriver and his fare is, due to the way in which they come into contact with each other, especially subject to structural weakness. The relationship is random, fleeting, unrenewable, and largely devoid of socially integrative features which in other client and patron oriented services help sustain a wider range of constraints and controls between the parties to the transaction. (Much the same might be said of such service occupations as waitress, bellhop, and hotel doorman, the chief difference being, however, that these operate from a spatially fixed establishment, which in itself permits of greater identifiability, renewability, and hence constraint in one's relationship to them.) As a result, the tendency of the relationship is to gravitate sharply and in relatively overt fashion toward those few issues having to do with the basic instrumental terms of the exchange. The very fact of tipping, its economic centrality, and the cab culture's preoccupation with mastering its many vagaries reflect in large part the regulative imbalance inherent in the relationship.

By inference, this analysis raises anew questions of how to account for the many more formidable and apparently more binding practitioner-client constraints found in other personal service fields, in particular the professions. To such matters as career socialization, colleague groups, socially legitimated skill monopolies, and professional secrecy there might be added a certain safe modicum of continuity, stability, and homogeneity of clientele.[20] For, given too great and random a circulation of clients among practitioners, as might occur for example under certain bureaucratic schemes for providing universal and comprehensive medical service, the danger is that informal social control networks would not come into being in the community, and, as in big-city cabdriving, relations between servers and served would become reputationless, anonymous, and narrowly calculative.

Footnotes

This article is based largely on notes and observations made by me over a six-month period in 1948 when I worked as a cabdriver for one of the larger taxicab firms in Chicago. I am greatly indebted to Erving Goffman, Everett C. Hughes, and Howard S. Becker for their comments and criticisms.

[1] Talcott Parsons, *The Social System* (Glencoe, Ill.: Free Press, 1951), pp. 48–56.

[2] Erving Goffman, *The Presentation of Self in Everyday Life* (Edinburgh: University of Edinburgh Social Science Research Centre, 1956), pp. 160–62.

[3] Everett C. Hughes, *Men and Their Work* (Glencoe, Ill.: Free Press, 1958), pp. 88–101.

[4] Because it better delineates the boundaries and linkages of informal sanctioning groups found in larger cities, the term "network" is used here to qualify the more global concept of "community." See Elizabeth Bott, *Family and Social Network* (London: Tavistock, 1957), pp. 58–61.

[5] Robert K. Merton, "The Role Set: Problems in Sociological Theory," *British Journal of Sociology*, VIII, No. 2 (June, 1957), 114.

[6] Parallel studies of this aspect of occupational culture are: Hughes, *op. cit.*, pp. 42–55; Howard S. Becker, "The Professional Dance Musician and his Audience," *American Journal of Sociology*, LVII (September, 1951), 136–44; Ray Gold, "Janitors versus Tenants: A Status-Income Dilemma," *American Journal of Sociology*, LVII (March, 1952), 486–93.

[7] Merton, *op. cit.*, pp. 110–12.

[8] Goffman, *op. cit.*, p. 95.

[9] James V. Maresca, *My Flag Is Down* (New York: E. P. Dutton & Co., 1945). Essentially the same incident is related by an unidentified cabdriver on the documentary recording of Tony Schwartz, *The New York Taxi Driver* (Columbia Records, ML5309, 1959).

[10] Cf. Schwartz, *op. cit.* In fact, these characteristic qualities, with a work-adapted, bitter-sweet admixture of cynicism and sentimentality, comprise the core of the personality widely imputed to cabdrivers by the riding public. Cf. Hughes, *op. cit.*, pp. 23–41.

[11] In Chicago in 1948 the company driver's share of the metered sum was 42½ percent. Since that time the proportion has been increased slightly.

[12] Cf. William F. Whyte, *Human Relations in the Restaurant Industry* (New York: McGraw-Hill Book Co., 1948), p. 100.

[13] Cf. here and in the section to follow the pertinent remarks of Hughes on "guilty knowledge" developed by those in a service occupation with reference to their clientele. Hughes, *op. cit.*, pp. 81–82.

[14] Herbert Hodge, "I Drive a Taxi," *Fact*, No. 22 (January, 1939), pp. 28–29.

[15] As in the past, the Sport still serves as something of a hero figure in our culture, particularly among the working classes. A type midway between the Playboy and the Bohemian, his unique appeal rests perhaps on the ease and assurance with which he is pictured as moving between and among social strata, untainted by upper-class snobbishness, middle-class conventionality, and lower-class vulgarity. In *The Great Gatsby*, Fitzgerald gives us a penetrative exposition of the myth of the Sport and its undoing at the hands of the class system.

[16] The stereotype of women as poor tippers is widely shared by other tip-sensitive occupations. Cf. Frances Donovan, *The Woman Who Waits* (Boston: Badger, 1920).

[17] The term "Live Ones" is employed in a variety of pursuits as apparently diverse as retail selling, night-club entertainment, traveling fairs, and panhandling. Generally, it designates persons who are "easy touches," eager to succumb to the oftentimes semifraudulent proposals of the operator. Cf. W. Jack Peterson and Milton A. Maxwell, "The Skid Row Wino," *Social Problems*, V (Spring, 1958), 312.

[18] Cf. Hodge, *op. cit.*, p. 17.

[19] Cf. Donovan, *op. cit.*, p. 262.

[20] William J. Goode, "Community within a Community: The Professions," *American Sociological Review*, XXII, No. 2 (April, 1957), 198–200, and Eliot Freidson, "Varieties of Professional Practice," draft version of unpublished paper, 1959.

The Lawyer-Client

A Managed Relationship?

JOHN P. REED
Western Kentucky University

Do lawyers manage their clients or merely serve the legally ailing? In spite of the institutionalized image, the suspicion persists that the lawyer's business is not to be equated with his service or his profits with his ethic. While the twain must sometimes meet, they are as likely to diverge as any ideal from accompanying practice.

The lawyer-client relationship is no exception. Canons of professional ethics to the contrary, it is hypothesized that the relationship is subject to managerial skills and situational variables from inception to termination. How else is one to account for the selective nature of a clientele or the growth of public or collective arrangements to serve the legally indigent? Either the lawyer manages or, *sui generis*, the latter create their own clients.

Not only is the theme new but the mechanics have never been spelled out. Most of the legal and sociological literature, in fact, fails to treat of the problem. There the relationship is viewed from a strictly ethical, substantive, or procedural law vantage point[1] or else from nonclient (the community, the profession) and nonbusiness referents.[2] Other referents[3] suggest additional qualities of the relationship which further research may show has important consequences for the lawyer's ethic, image, and his profession.

Population and Design

To test the management hypothesis, a population was obtained from the 1966–67 "Official and Legal Directories" for Duval County, Florida. Lawyers listed in the Directories were first contacted by phone, then clas-

Reprinted from *Academy of Management Journal*, Vol. 12, No. 1 (March 1969), 67–80, by permission of the author and the publisher.

sified as "civil" or "criminal." From the classified list, 125 civil lawyers were randomly selected and forwarded a mailed questionnaire. Civil lawyers were preferred because they are normally more numerous than criminal lawyers and less subject to juridical limitations.[4]

Format for the questionnaire consisted of a cover sheet, the Eysenck-Nagel "Survey of Opinion,"[5] and sequentially arranged items which dealt with managerially-promising aspects of the relationship. If a lawyer failed to respond, he was periodically sent a follow-up letter or another questionnaire. Six letters and two questionnaires generated 71 returns. The remainder either refused to participate (27) or else outlasted all attempts to solicit a response (27).

Frame of Reference

Analytically the lawyer-client relationship may be broken down into a number of parts. What comes most readily to mind, in this respect, is that the relationship has a beginning, an ending, a life span, and a tone or texture. If the parts are, in turn, linked with attributes of the lawyer's role, they produce variables which can be examined and measured. Functions of the role, for example, include advocacy, counsel, and negotiation. In advocacy the lawyer is pleading his client's case while in negotiation and counsel he is either trying to settle an existing controversy or giving predispute advice.[6] Whether one or another function is involved, however, the lawyer is basically making decisions, taking action, or initiating or terminating relations. Functions thus are but composites of the kind of work the lawyer does for his client. By arriving at the elemental work variables, a relationship with others or with the client resolves itself into a rather definitive form. One can now treat of initiating and terminating the relationship as well as the decisional and actional aspects of the relationship.

To work variables may be added others which are derived from the positional nature of the lawyer's role. The role is positional in that it gives access to services, competencies, and legal redress. Access is founded upon the lawyer's monopoly of knowledge and process which ensures that the client is legally ignorant and ultimately dependent upon the lawyer for resolution of his problem.[7] From its positional nature and base, the role acquires a series of power variables that may be paired with parts and work variables to comprise a framework for dealing with a managed relationship. In initiating the relationship those variables would seem to be refusal, acceptance, maneuver, and influence. In other words, a lawyer may accept or refuse a commitment; influence a prospective client's choice of lawyers or course of action; or endeavor to make himself more visible (maneuver) to the legally ailing.

Particular linkages, however, are not mutually exclusive. Variables like decision, action, and influence undoubtedly are operative over the life of the relationship. Others may have a more limited range or simply be restricted to a specific phase of the relationship. Two positional variables with perhaps solitary linkages are prolongation and withdrawal. In the case of the former, the relationship is continued beyond the client's desire to maintain it or the requirements of an adequate performance; in the latter, it is terminated by removal of the lawyer's presence and services.

A number of additional variables—such as perception of the client's role, conference, and discretion—are perhaps merely reflective of work and positional differences. For example, perception and discretion imply positional differences although they have decisional and actional consequence. It would apparently follow that if the lawyer perceives his client as wholly dependent or conceives of himself with considerable discretion, there is little need for conference with his client. He can set out on the course of action he decides to pursue. To confer about an item, on the other hand, implies functionally recognizable differences in lawyer-client roles. Whether the lawyer confers with his client or not depends on the nature of the item or the need to obligate his client. If the item is viewed as lawyer's work or intermediary in a logico-legal sequence that has already been initiated, one would expect the lawyer to proceed without a conference. Because of their apparently dual character, perhaps it would be best to call these variables mixed.

Having focused the approach in terms of work, positional, and mixed variables we can now examine the data.

Initiating the Relationship

Management implies the husbanding of one's resources and their application to designated ends. The lawyer's resources are chiefly his time, skills, and knowledge. If lawyers manage clients, one would expect them to selectively apply their resources. Selective application may be in terms of ethical, economic, or other ends but to qualify as management should consistently evidence a harmony of ends and means in the conduct of a practice.

REFUSAL-ACCEPTANCE

In the formative phase of the relationship, lawyers were fairly consistent in this respect. All would-be clients were not acceptable to respondents for mainly economic reasons. Refusals to enter a lawyer-client relationship ranged from 5 to 200 per individual per year. For all respondents the median number of refusals was 20, with a decreasing number as the occupational status of the prospective client increased. According to a list of 27 items, the more frequently checked grounds for refusing a relationship were "inability to pay" (28), "small money claim" (25), "nominal damages" (24), and "suit against a person who periodically is your client" (47). Unpopular and unethical items were less often encountered in practice and, therefore, not as likely to be accepted or refused. Of the unpopular items, refusals were highest in the case of a "malpractice suit against a member of the local bar association" (10) and representation of a "civil rights demonstrator" (7).

In accepting a client, the "most" and "least" important considerations were "the problems involved" and "the adverse party." Between these two extremes, general legal fare constituted the bulk of lawyer acceptance—with the more remunerative problems preferred. A negative measure of what was "most" important in lawyer acceptance produced a somewhat similar result. Using "least" important as an indicator of the "most" important factor suggests that the client's "ability to pay" is not likely to be overlooked in the formation of the relationship. Of all factors presented, "ability to pay" was checked the fewest number of times as "least" important.

From the data, one might conclude that, within the limits of specialization, the refusal is essentially a screening device for determining which relationships the lawyer will enter. His ethic exhorts him not to avoid the unpopular but, except for a number of prohibitory relationships, leaves the matter largely to him. With this kind of latitude, he may apply resources where he can maximize his return—to the financially able and to the more rewarding legal problems. The "screen" makes for selectivity and in the long run undoubtedly facilitates the building and maintenance of a practice without too many unprofitable relationships.

MANEUVER

Refusal and acceptance, then, are means of effecting client choice. To select clients, however, presupposes a flow. One cannot accept or refuse clients unless there is a recurring demand for services. While that demand may emanate from present, former, or new clients, it is more likely to materialize if cultivated than left to chance. A cultivated demand is the special consequence of visibility techniques that enable the lawyer to create a "presence" among prospective clients. For operational purposes a "presence" is a form of advertising which permits the lawyer to intrude his reputation, specialty, personality, or name into a variety of groups or publics without unduly violating his ethic. Since ethical strictures forbid advertisement,[8] the nature of this intrusion is more in terms of the lawyer's person than extension of his person through communication media. Instead of a "spot commercial" he has a group membership, a physical existence, a working arrangement, or previous contacts which put him into the consciousness of a potentially serviceable population. While they vary with the lawyer, the techniques are his means of "commercializing" in the antiseptic atmosphere of professionalization.

In Tables 1[9] and 2, intergroup and interpersonal techniques are suggested. Intergroup techniques are aimed at more distant prospects who may

TABLE 1

VISIBILITY TECHNIQUES AS USED AND RANKED BY
RESPONDING CIVIL LAWYERS ACCORDING TO THEIR
IMPORTANCE IN OBTAINING CLIENTS

Techniques	As Used (Frequencies)*	Ranked**
Questions 37–38		Questions 35–36
1. The "grapevine" (including satisfied clients)	56	1
2. Referrals from lawyers	47	2
3. Joining organizations	39	3
4. Making talks and speeches	35	4
5. Centrally locating office	22	5
6. Court appointment	20	7
7. Verbal advertising (interpersonal)	12	10
8. Sideline work or business	10	8
9. Taking money-losing but high-publicity cases	7	8
10. Running for office	4	6
11. Hanging around the courthouse	2	11
Questions 47–48		Questions 45–46
1. Contingent fee	35	2
2. Retainers	33	1
3. Fitting fee to pocketbook	28	3
4. Estate and property management	20	4
5. Contacting former clients	8	5
6. "Fear-seeding" clients	5	8
7. Offering to handle problem	5	6
8. Promising profitable outcome	4	7
9. Buying legal practices	2	9
10. Other	6	Mixed

*Questionnaire and question response are not in balance. A number who returned the questionnaire failed to answer specific questions.
**Disparities in rank and frequencies suggests that many who thought a particular technique was important to others didn't use it themselves in obtaining clients or *vice versa*.

not as yet be differentiated from the general public or even membership groups to which the lawyer belongs. Interpersonal techniques involve specific others whom the lawyer is attempting to obligate for his services. In Table 2, "cut-off points" are proposed for "offering one's services" to specific others which limits "offer" for the bulk of the lawyers in the sample to relatives, business associates, and to those who assume a client stance (8, 9, 10). As with other interpersonal techniques (promise, fear-seeding, etc.) "offer" is more likely to occur in either restricted situations or with intimate parties.[10]

If anything the tables demonstrate that the lawyer advertises and occasionally solicits and promotes litigation. His advertising form is the "presence" which is an offshoot of his ethic and the exigencies of practice. Since he is denied standard business and industrial techniques, he creates "presence" to generate client flow. Through flow he obtains client selectivity

TABLE 2

Cut-off Points* for Offering Service to Others
(Frequencies)

Party or Party and Situation	Would Offer	Would Not
Questions 43–44		
1. To parents in auto collision	53	14
2. To wife in auto collision	52	15
3. To in-laws in auto collision	37	29
4. To business associate in auto collision	28*	39*
5. To next door neighbor in auto collision	12	52
6. To former client in auto collision	8	57
7. To a stranger in auto collision	6	59
Question 66		
8. Where party brings his problem for discussion	51	16
9. Where party is seeking advice	50	15
10. In case of anyone who comes to office with legal problem	44	22
11. In case of close relative with problem in area of competence	28*	38*
12. Where retainer has lapsed but party failed to communicate	22	43
13. Where party is former client with legal problem you hear about	19	47
14. Where you overhear party discussing his problem with another	0	71
15. Where you witness a party acquire a legal problem	0	71

*Suggested by declining frequencies in lawyer response and Chi-Square values (see Table 4).

and approaches such other managerial objectives as growth and the profitable operation of his practice.

INFLUENCE

One other aspect of the initiatory phase of the relationship remains to be examined. While "flow" may produce prospects, they have to be somehow obligated to receive the lawyer's services before they can be called clients. Legally, obligation in this context is a function of contract. In the language of contract one party makes an offer, the other has a power of acceptance, which if exercised binds the parties to their agreement. The power to accept is normally with the lawyer[11] but to dwell on the legal intricacies of contracting bypasses the focus of this paper. "Obligating" is also a social-psychological phenomenon in which the uncertainties of the prospective client about his problem or retaining the lawyer are resolved. To resolve uncertainties is to lead the prospect into the relationship. "Leading" is accomplished through verbal and behavioral processes which link a particular lawyer with a potential solution of the prospect's problem. If we call these processes of obligation management, client flow is understandably translatable into a select clientele which conforms to the lawyer's specialty or to his practice objectives.

In pure form, obligating is best observable in the case of the new client. For others (the former client or those specially situated) the presumption

TABLE 3
LINEAR MEASURES OF OBLIGATION MANAGEMENT IN ESTABLISHING THE LAWYER-CLIENT RELATIONSHIP WITH A NEW CLIENT (FREQUENCIES)

Points on Linear Scales	Persuasion	Suggestion	Sympathy	Power	Praise
1	3	1	2	2	1
2	3	3	6	3	7
3	5	3	5	6	5
4	2	3	1	3	2
5	16	25	13	12	10
6	0	2	1	0	0
7	3	2	1	2	0
8	3	4	1	2	1
9	2	1	0	0	0
10	4	7	3	1	0
Totals	41	51	33	31	26

would be not only some variation in the use of the processes but also other means of obligation management. The new client, at least, is unaffected by the residue of a former relationship and must face the lawyer without a crystalized role.

Use of the processes was indicated in answer to general questions and on linear scales $(0''''5''''10)$ which were intended to measure the extent of their involvement in the establishment of the relationship. In Table 3 widespread and multiple use is evident for persuasion, suggestion, sympathy, power, and praise, each of which may be taken as summary labels for connected activity (verbal and behavioral) designed to influence the client's choice of lawyers.

Associations Between Variables

Influence thus completes the initiatory phase of the relationship. In our concern with mechanics (or how the lawyer manages), however, the relationship between variables has not been fully elaborated. Still to be differentiated is the lawyer population—or more precisely, which lawyers use which aspects of the management sequence discussed so far. Confining itself to the more promising associations between variables, Table 4 segregates a lawyer aggregate for closer study. That aggregate consists of liberals, small firm, and defendant and mixed lawyers (handle either side of controversy) who rather consistently resorted to select aspects of screening, techniques, and processes. For their counterparts the management sequence held less attraction but only a small group completely abstained.

In accounting for volatile categories, two factors seem to be of prime importance—the lawyer's ethic and competition. Less ethical involvement was perhaps characteristic of the liberals' excursion into border areas but the converse could not be said to be true of their "acceptance of unpopular causes." While ethically conforming, acceptance more than likely has its motivational base in overriding liberal attitudes than observance of professional norms. "Plaintiff-Other" categories, by way of contrast, were more representative of ethically-oriented behavior. The support for this view lies in the concentration of chi-square values in the defendant and mixed lawyer category. If we assume a defensive set, the "offer" to defend an intimate is a normal expectation, but to promote (the plaintiff category and an offensive set) their causes too often and too vigorously not only raises the suspicion of solicitation and promoting litigation but risks the loss of economic gain and their good will as well. For whatever is handled the intimate's expectation is that it will cost him "next to nothing at all." The

TABLE 4*

Differentiation of Lawyer Population Through
Meaningful Associations Among Select
Variables (Chi-Squares)

	Pltf-Other** (df_1)	Small-Large** (df_1) Firm	Liberal-Conservative** (df_1)
Would offer to handle problem for:			
Wife	9.31		
Parents	7.24		5.36
Close relative	9.11		4.50
In-laws	4.01		4.37
Bus. associate			3.86
Party seeking advice			6.80
Party seeking to discuss			5.00
Anyone who came to office		5.19	
Use persuasion in obligation mgmt			4.12
Use sympathy in obligation mgmt		7.54	
Use power in obligation mgmt	3.89	6.64	
Use three or more processes in obligation mgmt		4.60	
Join organizations			6.48
Make talks and speeches		4.07	
Would accept unpopular causes	4.12		4.25

*Based on items appearing mainly in Tables 1, 2, and 3.
**Pltf-Other as Plaintiff-Other with Other as defendant and mixed lawyers who handle either side of controversy; Small-Large Firm as based on number of members in firm with five or less as small; and Liberal-Conservertive as determined by Eysenck-Nagel "Survey of Opinion."

same assumption could well be used to account for the remaining values in the category, unpopular causes and power. From a defensive set, one (acceptance of unpopular causes) is ethically recommended behavior; the other (as a power of acceptance) creates the lawyer-client relationship. From an offensive set, both could well entail adverse ethical and career consequences. Small firm values, on the other hand, seem more explainable in terms of competition than anything else. Whether creating "presence" or "obligating clients" one gets the impression that "they have to try harder" for what they get than the large specialized firm whose reputation has already been made.

Other combinations failed to provide meaningful associations. Specialization and years in practice yielded values at the 10 percent level of significance, but the smallness of the sample precluded an adequate test of their effectiveness.

Decisions and Action Within the Relationship

Once established a managed relation implies control. Unless the lawyer makes decisions and is free to pursue the course of action he deems necessary, he cannot be said to manage. Control involves power by the lawyer over the client and the subject matter of the relationship. How power is distributed we may call the *power balance* and, through perception of the client's role, lawyer discretion, and conference—which are reflective of that balance—try to ascertain the nature of the lawyer's managerial role.

PERCEPTIONS OF THE CLIENT'S ROLE AND LAWYER DISCRETION

One indicator of the lawyer's control is how he perceives his client. If he perceives him as wholly dependent, the power of decision and action is likely to be with the lawyer. In response to the question "What part does the client play in the solution of his problem," lawyers generally indicated that the client's role is relatively impotent in generating solutions or, for that matter, anything besides consent and the broadest of directives. According to 52 percent of the lawyers in the sample, "the client is asked to consent to individual moves or action taken in his behalf." The remaining 48 percent were split between "the client sets the limits for what can be done" (18 percent) and the lawyer being in charge of problem solution (30 percent). No lawyer thought his client "decided how to solve the problem" or "told him what action to take."

The response suggests a consenting role for the client and an initiating and resolving role for the lawyer based on his monopoly of knowledge. Consent, however, may not always be necessary. A perceived dependence in the client's role may enhance the lawyer's discretion in problem resolution. In racial and occupational rankings, lawyers indicated Negroes and laborers allowed more discretion than whites, managerials, and professionals. An obvious knowledge gap gives the lawyer wider latitude in working with his client's problem. In fact, it may well be that at the extremes consent itself has little substance: the lawyer proceeds with his own assessment of what must be done.

CONFERENCE

A final indicator of the lawyer's control of the relationship is conference. Like perceived role and discretion, conferring is indicative of work and positional differences in the roles of the lawyer and client. If the client's role is consentaneous, he should be approached from time to time for approval of lawyer activity. Items considered lawyer's work would ordinarily be exempt, but only in cases of an extreme power imbalance or an earned confidence would there be nothing to confer about.

In Table 5, the nature of the roles becomes more evident. By having lawyers check a list of recurring types of activity we can get some idea of when they think a conference is necessary.

According to the majority, a conferrable item is one which involves considerable cost, inconvenience, and consequence (items 1–9). Conference in this context is environed by practicality and weighted by necessity. If he doesn't confer, the lawyer may be getting his client in "over his head" or failing to initiate or complete a logico-legal sequence on which the ultimate solution of the problem depends. The roles then are reciprocals but only to the extent of ensuring a managed outcome. Through consent the lawyer is obligating the client to his resolution of the problem.

Differentiation of the Population

In Table 6, the lawyer population is again differentiated through select

TABLE 5

Where Conference would Precede Action According
To Responding Civil Lawyers
(Frequencies)

Items	Would Confer
1. Out-of-court settlement	66
2. Appeal to higher court	64
3. Refusing an out-of-court settlement	64
4. Filing suit	61
5. Filing criminal charges	58
6. Setting fees for services	54
7. Hiring an investigator	51
8. Seeking a change of venue	45
9. Using expert witnesses	33
10. Contacting the adverse party	30
11. Asking for a jury trial	30
12. Daily transcription of trial testimony	29
13. Taking a deposition	20
14. Asking for a continuance	19
15. Subpoenaing witnesses	11
16. A meeting with opposing counsel	6
17. Applying trial strategy	4
18. Excepting to judge's ruling	4
19. Requesting a pre-trial conference	3
20. Preparing a brief	0

variables. Unlike Table 4 values were not as numerous and somewhat differently distributed. Concentrations appeared in the "plaintiff-other" category but the remainder were not as productive of meaningful associations. Both small firm and conservative values (particularly if coupled with generally higher frequencies on similar conference items) could be interpreted as a practical orientation to "less well-heeled" clients or to legal practice itself, but "plaintiff-other" values perhaps have another meaning. If we again assume an offensive-defensive set, one or both of the following explanations might adequately account for defendant and mixed lawyer values. Either the items have to be viewed as primarily defensive or the client's consenting role would have to be said to have more substance as a defendant. Certainly the latter is an intriguing possibility.

Perceived role, discretion, and conferring set the tone of the relationship. Where perceived role is highly subordinate control would be expected to be at a maximum. If the roles are otherwise aligned, differences should be reflected in the quantity and quality of conference. With a knowledgeable client, conference may well take on the character of a colleagueship in the search for information and alternative solutions to the client's problem.

Terminating the Relationship[12]

In a managed relationship, terminating is a matter of achieving a planned outcome. The outcome may relate to the problem or disposition of the relationship. If it relates to the problem the supposition is that the

TABLE 6

DIFFERENTIATION OF THE LAWYER POPULATION FOR
DECISIONAL AND ACTIONAL PHASE OF THE RELATIONSHIP
(CHI-SQUARES)

	Pltf-Other (df_1)	Small-Large Firm (df_1)	Liberal-Conservative (df_1)
Client is asked to consent		4.34	
Would confer before:			
Contacting adverse party	3.85		
Seeking a change of venue	4.37		5.32
Hiring an investigator	7.26		
Using expert witnesses	4.07		
Making daily transcription of trial testimony	5.29		

problem is resolved whether favorable or unfavorable to the client. Among respondents termination was usually "by performance of acts for which the lawyer was hired" (58) and infrequently by out-of-court settlement (8) or by court decision (2). In disposing of the relationship the lawyer is withdrawing[13] his presence and services. Withdrawal by the lawyer presupposes some basic deficiency in resources, the client, or his problem which screening failed to reveal or which developed unexpectedly. To control outcome he has to terminate or face undesirable consequences.

For lawyers in the sample the median number of times they withdrew was six, with a range from zero (3) to forty (2). What prompted their withdrawals included ethical, economic, and personal considerations, which they ranked in Table 7. From the rank order one is inclined to conclude that "screen" and management are economically effective although not always interpersonally successful.

Whether solving the problem or withdrawing from the relationship, the lawyer is playing a resolving role. What may have been nurtured in technique and process is being brought to a conclusion. The client gets his *quid pro quo* but only as his lawyer designs it.

Conclusions

Whatever else the lawyer-client relationship may be called it is also a business relationship. As a business relationship it antedated its professionalization with its organized bar, code of ethics, and tests of admission. What the sociology of professions' approach seems to overlook is that professionalization does not create a new relationship, it is only modifying an old one which has continued to evolve from its economic base. Persistence

TABLE 7

LAWYER RANKING OF ITEMS INVOLVED IN WITHDRAWALS

Items	Ranking
No cause of action	1
Couldn't get along with client	2
Client couldn't make up his mind	3
Client was of questionable moral character	4
Client settled with other party	5
Other business was more pressing	6
Client hired another lawyer	7
Client ran out of money	8

and new accretions for that aspect of the relationship create ethical problems, "schizoid images," and professional malaise. We may speak of "stresses and strains from formal institutional patterns as manifesting themselves in informal patterns,"[14] but it seems to be putting the cart before the horse. The lawyer-client as a managed relationship, at least, acknowledges its past and suggests that its present form is a product of both business and professional foci.

In a management sequence (though not in the order elaborated) and role performance some rapprochement is sought, points of stress are indicated, and the highly rational quality of business and profession are accentuated.

Footnotes

[1] Elliott E. Cheatham, *Cases and Materials on the Legal Profession* (2d ed.; Brooklyn: The Foundation Press, 1955); Vernon Countryman, *The Lawyer in Modern Society* (Chicago: The National Council on Legal Clinics, American Bar Center, 1961); Henry S. Drinker, *Legal Ethics* (New York: Columbia University Press, 1963); *American Jurisprudence* (2d ed.; New York: The Lawyers Cooperative Publishing Co., 1963), Vol. 7, pp. 105–152.

[2] Albert P. Blaustein and Charles O. Porter, *The American Lawyer, A Summary of the Survey of the Legal Profession* (Chicago: University of Chicago Press, 1954); Jack P. Gibbs, "The Sociology of Law and Normative Phenomena," *American Sociological Review*, XXXI (June, 1966), 315–325; Erwin O. Smigel, "The Impact of Recruitment on Organization of the Large Law Firm," *American Sociological Review*, XXV (Feb., 1960), 56–66; Arthur L. Wood, "Informal Relations in the Practice of Criminal Law," *American Journal of Sociology*, LXII (July, 1956), 48–55; Arthur L. Wood and Walter I. Wardwell, "The Lawyer and Community Leadership," *Journal of Legal Education*, IX (1956), 162–176.

[3] Other referents are used in the following: Jerome E. Carlin, *Lawyers on Their Own* (New Brunswick: Rutgers University Press, 1962), pp. 123–149; Martin Mayer, *The Lawyers* (New York: Harper and Row, 1966), pp. 305–414.

[4] For example, constitutional guarantees and legal presumptions favoring the accused which might affect the relationship.

[5] Stuart S. Nagel, "Off-the-Bench Judicial Attitudes," *Judicial Decision-Making*, ed. Glendon Schubert (Glencoe: The Free Press, 1963), pp. 50–53.

[6] Countryman, pp. 1–52.

[7] Arthur L. Wood, "Professional Ethics Among Criminal Lawyers," *Social Problems*, VII (Summer, 1959), 71.

[8] *Your Privileges and Responsibilities as a Lawyer in Florida* (Tallahassee: The Florida Bar, 1956). See particularly Canon 27 of the *Canons of Professional Ethics* adopted by the American Bar Association.

[9] Table 1 does not pretend to exhaust the lawyer's "visibility techniques." Others could be determined through the use of a larger sample. For a discussion of some of these items see Carlin, pp. 123–149.

[10] Where it is assumed there would be low public and professional visibility

considering canonical imperatives, such as ABA Canons 27 and 28. See also *American Jurisprudence*, pp. 66–72.

[11] *Ibid.*, p. 105. In restricted instances the lawyer may make the offer.

[12] No treatment of prolongation as a variable appears in the text of the paper. Apart from questionnaire discrepancies between attempts and actual withdrawals by clients, it is postulated some aspects of estate practice might qualify.

[13] On termination consult *American Jurisprudence*, pp. 132–141.

[14] Wood, *American Journal of Sociology*, p. 48.

Work and the Family

A Doctor in the House

Janet Kern
Highland Park, Illinois

Father was a doctor, but Mother was his wife—which made for a nice balance of parental attitudes, training, temperaments and viewpoints. And, let the record show, throughout nearly thirty-six years of marriage and near-inseparability, neither ever changed in the least. Mother remained gay; Father remained solemn. Mother remained confidently optimistic; Father remained suspicious and pessimistic. Mother remained thoughtful and cautious; Father remained impulsive, to put it mildly. . . .

Handwashing was a vital and perpetual ritual at our house, where cleanliness was a frequent topic of conversation and a constant matter of examination. In our family, dirt was synonymous with germs, and germs were the worst bogeymen extant. In most houses, when the host inquires whether you want to wash your hands, he is employing a delicate euphemism designed to find out if you're getting curious about the location of the plumbing. But when Father asks if a guest wants to wash his hands, he means precisely what he is asking; and it's really not an inquiry at all —it's an order. Hygiene was our religion and it permeated our home environment like true religious fanaticism.

It took years for me to realize that most people do not consider every kiss a cue to rush to the washbasin. During all those years, the embraces which I saw in the movies confused and disturbed me. Father had pounded

into me from infancy the fact that kissing involves germs and, when absolutely unavoidable, must be limited to the cheek—a kiss on the lips being
the ultimate in unsanitariness.

There was a period, after I'd grown up some and learned a little—very
little—about life and love, when I would speculate anxiously to myself
about how Father had succeeded in wooing and winning Mother, and even
had managed to produce me, without ever indulging in any love life less
sanitary than a peck on a quickly scrubbed cheek.

Of course, cleanliness and hygiene were not limited to matters of affection and its expression. Sanitation was of prime import in every area of our
life and household. Doctors see too much illness, injury, and suffering, from
too many causes, to be able to glide gaily through this dirty world and this
dangerous life. Slowly but surely they become ridden by the fear of dirt and
danger striking in their homes or at their families.

My father once treated a man for a spinal fracture, the result of tipping
too far backwards in a chair. As a result, the rule in our house always was:
"All four legs of the chair flat on the floor!" That rule was so severely
stressed, and buttressed by such graphic descriptions of the condition of the
poor man with the spinal fracture that, to this day, I break out in a sweat
of sheer panic when anyone within my view tilts a chair back on two legs.
I've never yet managed to wait for more than ninety seconds before im-
politely crying out: "Don't *do* that!"

One of Father's close friends and colleagues developed an awful fear
of bicycle accidents and refused to permit his children to possess such
dangerous vehicles. When his son was carried home with a broken leg, the
result of a fall from another youngster's bike, that medical father was forced
to change his mind slightly. He decided it might be wiser to supply one's
children with their own lethal toys, thereby retaining the right to enforce
rules of operation.

One of the rules which that doctor instituted, and which all his medical
friends copied, required that bikes be ridden only on the sidewalk; *never*
in the street. This posed something of a problem, since the city ordinances
forbade bicycle riding on the sidewalks. . . .

Another doctor in my parents' social set came to the conclusion that
ice-cream bars couldn't possibly be sanitary. As a result, all the children
in our medical set promptly were forbidden such delicacies. This prohibition struck me as pretty silly. Like all children my age, I spent a large
portion of my free time chasing the horse-drawn ice wagon for chips of
ice which the iceman gave us to suck after he'd chopped off the proper
sized block of ice for each customer. Those chips, I'd observed, came from
the very unsanitary floor of the ice truck. Having already survived several
years of sucking dirty ice, I felt sure that my stomach could cope with whatever germs an ice-cream bar might conceivably possess.

I mentioned this logical comparison to Mother, who lost no time in forbidding me to mention the subject to Father. All poor Mother needed was for Father to decide that our *ice* was unsanitary. But apparently Mother had a little talk with Father, for he suddenly informed me that I could buy and eat Good Humors and Popsicles. This was a fortunate change of the paternal mind, for shortly thereafter we got a refrigerator and the iceman rarely stopped at our house any more.

The advent of the refrigerator brought a new source of paternal worry into our house—Father's fear of escaping ammonia gas! So far as I know, we never had any gas escape from our refrigerator, but for years we conducted nightly promenades around the kitchen in olfactory search of the leak Father suspected.

All such fondly intentioned excesses of fatherly caution made life considerably more complex and difficult for the doctor's child than it was for children from nonmedical households. But by the time we were old enough to notice that our homes and lives were different from the norm, we already were used to it. Life starts being different for the doctor's child the moment the poor little thing is born—and sometimes even earlier. . . .

My father expected me to make my appearance in this world on schedule, the fourteenth day of November, and he preferred that I select a "decent moment"; that is, a daylight moment which would not interfere with office hours. Accordingly, on the Thursday night of November 13, several years ago, he and my mother went out for a drive. After several hours of aimless riding, Father decreed a stop at the delicatessen, where he prescribed corned beef sandwiches for Mother. Then they rode awhile longer, until Father inexplicably announced: "*Now*—we go to the hospital!"

Father knew whereof he announced. At 6 A.M. on November 14, I made my appearance, precisely as Father had planned and intended. Mother considered corned beef sandwiches pretty potent stuff from then on.

It took a while for me to wake up to the difference between my life and that of other children. It never occurred to me that most of my playmates never had heard of a sphygmomanometer, let alone know how to spell it. It never dawned on me that they never were awakened to go on a midnight call, and had not been schooled in the daily achievement of that engineering miracle known as "making a hospital bed." I thought that all the neighborhood children were slow eaters. No one had told me that most people don't bolt their meals in a grim race to finish before the phone rings.

The first awakening came one long day, when Mother and I were waiting in the lobby of a hotel while Father delivered a speech. Suddenly I saw a bellboy hurry into the room where Father was speaking. In a moment he hurried out, with Father dashing right behind him—straight into the ladies' room!

Grabbing Mother, I shouted, "Do something—Daddy's going into the *ladies'* room!" Mother glanced up, murmured "Oh?" or something equally unperturbed, and returned to her reading.

I grabbed her again, harder, and shouted louder: "Mo-th-*er!* He's in the *ladies'* room! Men *can't* go in there!"

Mother glanced up again and smiled calmly. "It's all right, dear," she explained, "your father isn't a man. He's a doctor." . . .

The Depression was horrible for the very poor and hell for the very rich, whom it catapulted without warning into the ranks of the poor. The only group for whom the Depression did not spell absolute disaster was the so-called "comfortable" class of folk who had enough money to live comfortably but never had been rich enough to invest heavily.

Fortunately for us, this was the economic group into which most doctors fell. In a sense, national economic trends affect doctors in exactly the opposite way they do other people. In prosperity, everything costs a doctor more of his inflated dollars, but his fees cannot be increased accordingly. Conversely, during a depression, the doctor's trade is one of the few which still is in demand.

People get sick no matter how healthy or unhealthy the stock market may be. If they cannot afford to pay money for medical services, they resort to something closely akin to the barter system, and the doctor, being an individual human being rather than a corporation or a store, is in both a mood and a position to accept payment in merchandise, services, and so on.

When I was a child, doctor's phones were usurped by their children on Christmas morning, as the youngsters in medical homes phoned one another to report—and gloat—over what they and their parents got from "the G.P.'s." In medical family code, "G.P." meant "Grateful Patient," and their Christmas gifts were wonderful indeed. For months, one M.D.'s child would spot another in a fancy new dress, or carrying a beautiful purse, or riding a wonderful bike, and would inquire jealously, "From a G.P.?" The answer, during the Depression at least, invariably was "Yes."

Christmas and birthdays, especially the former, still bring gifts from Grateful Patients, but there aren't as many and they aren't as all-important as they were in my childhood. Today most people can pay their doctor bills. But during the Depression, most people were genuine Charity Patients and they paid the doctor to the best of their ability with a gift, frequently the very best they had in stock in whatever business they happened to be in. Even when the head of the doctor's house didn't know how he was going to pay the milk bill, his children were the best and most expensively dressed kids on the block; the Grateful Patients—one in the dress business, one a shoe clerk, one in pocketbooks—saw to that. Thanks to the Grateful

Patients, I grew up looking, thinking, and feeling "rich," while Father wrestled the wolf at the door.

Only once did the Depression, as a personal deprivation, come home to me with full impact. There came a winter when it seemed to my parents that the bills were so far beyond the foreseeable income that an impassable cul-de-sac had been created. Of this fear and worry I knew nothing. I only knew that Father was even more irritable than usual, and that Mother was employing more euphemisms, and beating around the conversational bush, even more than usual—especially when the conversation got around to the fast approaching celebrations of my birthday and Christmas.

Finally, Mother announced that she wanted to talk to me.

"I don't want you to mention this conversation to your father," she began. "He would be very angry at me for telling you this. But you're a big girl now and you're a member of this family and I think it's only fair to give you a chance to do your part."

This sounded intriguing and grown-up, and I was fascinated.

"Your father has a lot of bills to pay just now," Mother continued, "and he doesn't have enough money to pay them, because people aren't able to pay his bills at the moment. So, much as we hate to do this to you, we simply cannot afford to give you much of a birthday or Christmas this year.

"I hope you will understand and not make this whole thing even more painful for us by making a fuss about it."

Under the circumstances, what could any nine-year-old say, except that she didn't mind (which, of course, she did, terribly). Under the impetus of Mother's solemnity and persuasive power, I volunteered to forego my birthday and Christmas altogether.

"Oh, heavens, that won't be necessary!" Mother groaned. "It would just make your father feel even worse. What you have to do is see to it that you don't *want* very much this year.

"When your father asks you what you want for your birthday and Christmas, forget about the bicycle and all those expensive things and ask for just one or two cheap little gifts.

"If he urges you to think of more, tell him you've tried, but you just don't want anything else. And when he asks you who you want to have celebrate your birthday with us, tell him you're tired of those big parties and couldn't we just have one or two people this year.

"And Janet," Mother urged, "make it *convincing!* Don't pout about it or go through it like something you *have* to do. Make your father believe you *really* don't want the things he can't afford to give you—and *don't* let on that you know he can't afford it. It won't make any difference in the long run, you know. You'll only get what we can afford to buy you anyway.

The only difference is that if you do it my way, your father won't feel so bad about it."

Mother turned and started out of the door. Then, as though struck by an afterthought, she turned around and added wistfully:

"I'm sorry about this, dear, but we'll make it up to you someday."

Whether my "act" really convinced Father I don't know. But I went through it dutifully and he certainly seemed convinced.

My birthday "loot" that year was rather skimpy, but a few weeks later, when Christmas rolled around, skimpy was the last word that would have been applicable. A couple of patients had come through with unexpected payments on their bills and my parents had gone berserk in toy stores. It was quite a Christmas, and it seemed even more extravagant than it was, because I'd been expecting very little. But I had become aware that the Depression applied to us, too. . . .

Probably the most obvious and deep-set difference between life in a medical household and that in any other kind of home is the difference in attitude towards the telephone.

Ordinary homes may have problems with the youngsters monopolizing the phone, but long before adolescence sets in, the doctor's child is fully aware that the phone belongs to Daddy.

Only recently, a business acquaintance, watching me use the phone in my office, inquired in surprise, "I thought you were a doctor's daughter, so how come you're using the phone? My wife is a doctor's daughter; she was brought up on '*Don't tie up the phone!*' and she still acts as though the telephone might bite her."

"*Don't tie up the phone!*" is the national anthem of medical households. Even the dullest toddler is soon aware that the telephone must never be used unnecessarily and, when it is used, the conversation must be brief. In later life, doctors' children have to struggle against a compulsion to cut short every phone call with the habit-ingrained declaration: "I'm sorry, but I have to hang up now. My father is expecting a call." In a doctor's house, your father *always* is expecting a call!

A doctor's child learns early in life that the telephone is not for her convenience; that it is, rather, a chore at which she cannot fail. Doctors' children are taught how to "take a message" before they learn to tie their shoelaces, and the necessity of promptly answering the phone is a responsibility which such children shoulder the moment they can talk.

Moreover, long before most children become aware of the existence of evil, the doctor's child has been made acutely conscious of it. In my childhood, narcotics and dope addiction seldom were in the headlines or in the thoughts of the majority of Americans. But even the youngest in a doctor's family knew all too well how often a physician, summoned on a supposed emergency call, drove into a fatal ambush set by addicts trying to steal narcotics (which, ironically, doctors almost never carry or keep on hand). We were taught from toddlerhood to recognize the voices of patients, other doctors, and so forth. For the unfamiliar voice might belong to a stranger planning to break into the house, or to waylay Father, in search of narcotics or, during my childhood, liquor prescriptions.

The telephone was a responsibility and a hazard in homes like mine. It also was, and is, a headache. In medical households, we can't eat a meal or sleep a night through; we can't play a card game, plan an evening out, or even talk to one another without being interrupted by phone calls.

Every doctor, and every doctor's family, knows that when a patient is taken suddenly ill, he—quite properly—will call his doctor. But how many patients can any one doctor have? And how many of those patients can be taken suddenly ill between the hours 6 P.M. and 6 A.M.?

If doctors' disturbances at home were limited to legitimate calls from suddenly stricken patients, each doctor might be bothered six or eight times in the course of a year. On the contrary, four and five nights per week, the medical family's sleep is fractured. Night after night, their dinners are ruined with the regularity of clockwork. In the kitchen, we bet grimly: "Watch! Just as I put the food on the table, the phone will ring." There can't be that many suddenly stricken people in the world. And there aren't.

Most late-night calls are from people complaining that they feel just awful, and, "Doctor, it's been like this ever since I woke up this morning!"

Ask such callers why they suffered in silence for eighteen hours or so. Invariably the answer will be "I didn't want to bother you!"

The rash of calls which come just as the sizzling, rare steak is put on the table usually are from patients seeking academic information about their condition, medication, or what have you. These people frequently announce proudly: "I called now because I knew this is when you have dinner so you'd be sure to be home."

Doctors, of course, are human beings. They become fathers in the usual fashion and the children they father are no different from any other young human beings. But schoolteachers, somehow, always have seemed to have an unshakable belief that doctors' children just naturally are brighter, harder-working, and more efficiently scholarly than other youngsters.

Let me make a mistake in recitation, and the teacher would tsk-tsk: "And you a *doctor's* daughter!"—as though I had besmirched the entire medical profession.

Other peoples' children have the privilege of being sick on occasion. They can miss school and return with a note from home and that's that. But when I missed school, the teacher would eye my mother's note suspiciously and say, "*You* were sick? A *doctor's* daughter?"

Actually, and perfectly logically, nobody gets sick as often as doctors' families. No matter what epidemic is raging, doctors must enter infected homes, stick their faces into germ-ridden throats, get breathed on by feverish patients. Then they come home, bearing the day's invisible harvest of germs and infection on their persons, their breath, and their clothes. If there's any disease going around, it's sure to be going around a doctor's house.

Back in the epidemic-ridden days of my childhood, before sulfa and penicillin and Salk vaccine were discovered, doctor fathers frequently came through the door in the evening shouting the warning: *"Don't* kiss me!"

This was the signal that an epidemic was on the loose. Immediately, Mother began putting small bottles of alcohol and small stacks of sterile gauze beside every telephone. Every time Father finished talking on the phone, he would saturate a wad of gauze with alcohol and wipe out the mouthpiece. Whenever one of the rest of us used the telephone, we rinsed it with alcohol before beginning to talk and exercised even greater care than usual to obey the house rule against ever touching our mouths to the mouthpiece.

While the epidemic remained in force (and, in those days, they remained in force for quite a while) hand-washing was stepped up to a several times hourly procedure, and only the smelly, doctor's-office green soap was used. Everyone in the household was charged with taking his or her temperature three times a day, no matter how healthy we might feel. The doctor's children invariably were sent to school with notes excusing them from gym class and they were forbidden to go to movies, parties, or other crowded places.

Melodramatic though it may sound, it is nonetheless true that no soldier ever answered the bugle call to a losing battle with more panic, or more sheer heroism, than the family doctors of the 1920's, '30's, and '40's who answered calls from parents reporting a child with a sore throat and stiff neck . . . "And, Doctor, he says he can't move his arms."

Every doctor knew full well that he could do nothing for that child except to summon an ambulance to transport the youngster to the prison-like Hospital for Contagious Diseases, and then notify the Board of Health that another human statistic must be added to the long roster of the polio-stricken. But knowing this, the doctor still went to the child's bedside. He went, feeling not unlike Abraham on his way to sacrifice Isaac; painfully aware that only a miracle from heaven could prevent the aftermath of this call being the infection of the doctor's own home and his wife and children. Despite all the most stringent precautions and astringent scrubbings and boilings, it was almost inevitable that the doctor's family eventually fell victim to the disease of the moment.

That, as they say, is when the fun began. Just as the cards are stacked against the doctor's family escaping illness, so is the deck stacked against the doctor's family getting useful treatment.

Many a doctor's child has good reason to bless the custom of illustrating medical textbooks with detailed color photographs of the diseases described, for those photographs were the doctors' wives' most useful tool in diagnosing their children's measles, chicken pox, and so on.

Most of the medical treatment I got in my childhood, I got from Mother. All she had to do was match my rash or other symptom to the proper picture in one of Father's medical books and then phone the office to tell Father that "Janet has the measles [or whooping cough, or whatever Mother had decided that Janet had]. . . . Please bring home some medicine."

There was only one essential medical service which Mother couldn't provide on her own. In those days, practically everything which a child might get required official quarantine of the house, complete with a big, black-lettered announcement sealed onto the front door. But the Health Department shortsightedly failed to recognize Mother's marriage license as a license to practice medicine. As a result of this governmental oversight, whenever Mother diagnosed a quarantinable disease, she was forced to phone a pediatrician of our acquaintance to have me included in his report to the Health Department. Sometimes the pediatrician was so busy with real patients that I slipped his mind—and his report—for several days. On one occasion, the Health Department man didn't come around to slap the big "*Quarantined!*" sign on our door until three days after I'd returned to school, fully recovered.

This do-it-yourself medical treatment is not simply an extension of the "shoemaker's children go barefoot" concept. I did not lack professional medical care because my father was too busy, or uninterested, to take care of his family as he did his patients. Quite the contrary. It is an unwritten rule of the medical profession that a doctor does not treat his own family. This is a rule by which most M.D.'s abide so stringently that they all deserve gold stars for obedience.

To the lay mind, this often seems a foolish and mystifying rule. If a doctor doesn't trust himself to treat his own family, they often figure, why on earth should I trust him to treat my family? Actually, however, physicians, being human beings, simply are too emotionally involved with their own loved ones to be able to treat them with proper scientific objectivity. They are not unconcerned with the health of their families—they are too doggone concerned.

Occasionally, of course, if I looked sick enough, or if my hourly temperature chart hit a high enough peak, Father would ask Mother anxiously, "Do you think we ought to call a doctor?" But they hardly ever did call one. When you live in a doctor's house, you don't go around bothering other doctors without grave reason.

For along with the rule against treating one's own family, there is a well-intentioned little medical ethic which prohibits one doctor from charging another for medical services rendered. This makes doctors' families fanatically unwilling to summon a physician. We know how *we* hate the sound of the ringing telephone and the dire, plan-destroying aftermath when Father announces wearily, "I have to make a call." To do this to another doctor's family without even being permitted to pay for the imposition is more than we can bring ourselves to do, unless forced by the most acute of crises.

Moreover, given a really acute crisis, there's the equally acute problem of which doctor to call. Much as a physician dislikes being summoned to another doctor's home, even more—because of the implied endorsement of skill involved—does he hate to see someone else called in his stead. Thus, if Dr. Jones calls Dr. Brown rather than Dr. Smith, immediately Dr. Smith feels like a wallflower at an A.M.A. smoker.

When there's acute illness in a medical household, years of professional relationships hang by a suture while the doctor and his wife debate which colleagues should be offended and which one inconvenienced. They usually end by deciding not to call a doctor at all. Instead, they fall back on the old medical family stand-by treatment: Let Nature Take Its Course and See What Happens! Which brings all too vividly to mind the night of my appendicitis attack.

As a well-indoctrinated doctor's daughter, I tried to struggle through the night on my own, letting nature take its painful course. After a few rule-of-thumb tests seemed to confirm my self-diagnosis, I cast aside my hot water bottle (heat is *not* prescribed for an ailing appendix) and staggered to the kitchen to make an ice pack. By 3 A.M., however, the situation had gotten out of control—my control, at least. There was no avoiding the emergency move of bothering Father.

Both parents came quickly and held the inevitable bedside conference. "I think she's right . . . it may *be* her appendix!" Father muttered.

"Should we take her to the hospital?" Mother inquired.

Father scowled. "That won't accomplish anything unless we operate right away. And three A.M. is awfully early to wake a surgeon."

Mother leaned over the bed and inquired solicitously, "Do you think you can stand it till six or seven o'clock? It's only a few hours."

From the depth of my agony, lifelong medical daughterhood came to the fore. We *couldn't* call a doctor in the middle of the night! "If I could just get to sleep. . . ."

Father turned to Mother and sighed, "Go sterilize a needle. I'll give her a shot that'll hold her till morning."

By all odds, I should have suffered a ruptured appendix, peritonitis, and my own funeral. Any ordinary daughter would have. But I was a doctor's offspring, over whom heaven must keep special watch. Or perhaps it wasn't appendicitis at all (we don't disturb laboratories at 3 A.M. either). In any event, by morning the pain had subsided, the stomach had settled, no doctor had been disturbed in the middle of the night—and I still have my appendix.

There are occasions, of course, when even the doctor's family figures that a doctor really must be called. When thus forced to solve that thorny problem of whom to call and whom to leave undisturbed and insulted, the medical paterfamilias has several alternatives. He can give everyone he knows a whack at the case, or his wife can throw together a quick party, in the course of which a doctor-guest will be lured into the sickroom to take a quick, casual look at the patient. No matter which alternative is chosen, the resultant treatment resembles nothing ever experienced by a nonmedical family.

The year I had whooping cough was a bad year for us, medically speaking. Whopping cough was the third childhood disease I had in a matter of months and it caught me in so run-down a condition that my case seemed severe enough to require something more professional than Mother's medical reference-book treatment. This was one of the times when my parents chose the "Why don't you and Clarissa come over this evening?" gambit. The doctor and Clarissa arrived at eight-thirty, carrying all the makings of plaster masks, the big game sensation among adults that year.

Out of regard for my serious state of health, the mask-making para-phernalia was set up on the sun porch adjoining by bedroom and the door was left open so that I'd be sure to hear the doctor's shouts, through wet plaster, "Janet—take your temperature!" and "What's your pulse now?"

I wanted to make a mask, too, but they said I was much too sick to get out of bed; I must stay there and take my temperature and, "Why don't you go to sleep? It's way past your bedtime!" Shortly after midnight they left, enabling me at last to go to sleep without the porch light shining in my face and the grownups' laughter tantalizing my ears. As they left, the doctor said that Mother's treatment was just fine, and, "Don't hesitate to call, if you want me to come and look at her again." In due course, I recovered and got out of bed, but by then the mask-making fad was over so I learned mahjong instead.

The "Why don't you and Clarissa come over this evening?" method of medical treatment may seem somewhat unsatisfactory but it's 100 percent better than the "give everyone a whack at it" method. When the latter is chosen, doctors descend upon the bedside the way locusts descended upon Egypt when Moses raised the rod.

Needless to mention, no doctor bothers wasting his "beside manner" on a bedside in a physician's house!

Anyone who ever has faced a serious illness, hazardous surgery, or sudden disability can testify to the efficacy of the firm, spirit-buoying guid-ance of an experienced doctor with a good bedside manner. But what a shock it would be for such patients to get a keyhole peek at their medical

Rock of Gibraltar—that pillar of stability, resignation, and adaptable good cheer—when he is reacting to even the most minor ills and injuries within his own family. . . .

To put it briefly and bluntly, all doctors are hypochondriacs, dedicated to converting their families to hypochondriasis, too. In restaurants they examine the silverware for symptoms of nonsterility; they insist on moving from table to table for fear of a cold developing from a suspected draft; they go into a close approximation of hysterics should anyone cough or sneeze behind them in a theater or on a train or bus. The common cold is forever on a doctor's mind, but never will he believe that any relative of his is suffering from anything so minor or common as a cold. Such sneezing and coughing must be incipient pneumonia, at the very least. More likely, he figures, it's the beginning of a rare and lethal disease which hasn't occurred since the Middle Ages but still gets a paragraph in medical reference books. A doctor in the state of Maine has no trouble convincing himself that his Maine-bound offspring somehow have managed to contract a case of Rocky Mountain spotted fever.

For weeks and months after the simple, common cold has passed, the doctor's relative is subjected to complex blood tests, barium X-rays, electrocardiograms, and the like. During all those perfectly healthy weeks and months, the doctor flits worriedly around his recovered relative, watching anxiously for signs of a relapse.

But, oversolicitous as the doctor is when short-term, acute illness occurs in his family, his reaction is exactly the opposite when anything serious, chronic, or incurable strikes. Chronic ills and permanent disabilities are forbidden to the doctor's wife and children. His parents, brothers, sisters, and others would be wise not to sully *themselves* with such ailments either. The more serious or obvious the condition, the more casually the doctor shrugs it off. He simply refuses to admit its existence. Or, if forced to admit that such a condition does exist within the sacred precincts of his household, he angrily holds the afflicted relative personally to blame. Anything short of 100 percent physical perfection is a gross violation of the medical house rules.

This peculiar attitude, so widespread among doctors, is rooted in the soil of solvency. Nonmedical folk, especially a doctor's patients, are deeply and adversely impressed by illness or disability in a doctor's intimate circle. Frequently, they will demand in accusing tones, "How come you can't do anything for your wife [or for your daughter, mother, or whomever]?" The clear implication is that you must be a pretty poor doctor, and this is an implication which most physicians resent.

Legitimate physicians, of course, are not permitted to advertise their services. But the doctor's bride and, later, his children are very quickly made aware that they constitute the doctor's living, breathing, walking advertisements—and that there are few sins more dire or less forgivable than the sin of "being a bad ad." My own father had the misfortune to acquire, by way of a family, the worst ads with which a doctor could be afflicted.

Mother was an asthmatic—and just try to hide coughs, wheezes, and almost total lack of breath during an asthmatic attack. Father frequently expressed the fear that I, too, would develop asthma and that I "wouldn't be as good at it" as Mother was.

Mother, I must admit, was extremely good at it. Despite the fact that, for most of my early childhood, she was so incapacitated by asthma that she had to be carried up and down stairs (and most of the people we visited lived in upstairs apartments), Mother somehow made it seem normal to be short of breath, heavily wheezing, constantly convulsed with wracking coughs and, of course, carried up and down stairs. In Mother's presence you got the idea that this was all a gay, new fad and that people who breathed and walked normally were just a bunch of old fuddy-duddies, doing things the old-fashioned way.

As it turned out, I developed hay fever instead of asthma, so all that was required of me was not to sneeze. "Do you want people to think you've got a cold and I'm letting you run around spraying germs all over the place?"

Hay fever I managed to carry off pretty much to Father's satisfaction, except on a few days out of each summer when I was advised, "Don't let anyone see you—you look *pathetic*."

It had not required any prophetic talent for Father to anticipate that I would one day fall victim to hay fever or asthma or both. The inoculations which are a regular part of American infancy had made it quickly apparent that I was one of the earth's fortunates given to allergies. In fact, one of my very first babyhood shots had resulted in an extreme and long-lingering case of eczema which necessitated the removal of most of the hair from the left side of my head.

Father did the barbering himself, leaving the hair on the right side of my head long and wavy. Then he told everyone—including me, when I became old enough to ask—that this was a special, highly fashionable French hair style called a "boyish bob." I was in high school before Mother let it slip to me that I had worn my hair in that "boyish bob" for the first several years of my life only because I *had* to wear it that way.

I don't know how nonmedical parents react to the innumerable tumbles, sprains, and fractures which beset young human beings. In our house, every such accident ushered in a long period of paternal commands: *"Don't limp!"* Any doctor's child worth his salt is an expert limp-camouflager by the age of ten.

One doctor's wife of my acquaintance suffers from a fairly common and clearly apparent disability. If anyone makes the *faux pas* of commiserating with that doctor about his wife's painful condition, he invariably becomes annoyed and replies angrily: "She's all right!"

This medical ire at anyone in the family who dares to be sick for a prolonged period is difficult for doctors' children to understand when they are young. When a child is hurt, he doesn't want to be punished for it. When a child is sick, he does not want to have Father get angry about it. But invariably, the doctor's child is punished for accidents and scolded for illnesses.

Eventually, you learn the fundamental fact of life in a medical household. You realize that, if there's a doctor in your family, whatever is wrong with you is *your* fault, and you'd better learn to keep your "abnormality" well hidden from public view. There'd better not be any joking about such serious, career-impeding matters, either. Secretly or openly, most doctors are in perfect accord with my father, who frequently points out sternly: "When it comes to medicine, I have *no* sense of humor!" Even without this frequent declaration, Father had plenty of occasion to remind us of this phase of his character.

Mother had migraine headaches as long as I knew her. I started having them when I was sixteen. A really major migraine attack is preceded, as all real migraine victims know, by a perfectly gorgeous "aura"—a kaleidoscopic panorama of whirling disks, shooting stars, blazing skyrockets, and intriguing geometric designs, all in the most vivid and exquisite colors imaginable. There's not a great deal to be said for having migraine, but that preliminary aura *is* a beautiful sight to behold. Father, however, did not appreciate our note-swapping enjoyment of our auras.

"If we've got to have them, we might as well enjoy them," Mother argued, without much success.

Since migraine attacks can come so frequently and can be so acute— and so obvious—it is fortunate that this is one of the few chronic ills approved for doctors' families. It is approved because, it happens, an astonishing number of doctors themselves suffer from migraine. These migrainous physicians—and those, like my father, who have migrainous wives and children—find comfort in the carefully scientific theory developed by one noted medical authority (himself a migraine victim) that this is a "disease of genius" suffered only by people of extraordinary intellect. . . .

Father had a number of close friends who were migraine-afflicted doctors and all of them, like Mother and myself, were experts at prescribing the sole migraine treatment then accepted (still the most effective, for my money), namely: black coffee, a hot bath, and a dark room. Since migraine sufferers frequently get attacks at about the same time, we had some interesting social get-togethers when the wind was right for migraine.

At one record-breaking dinner party, three doctors, two doctors' wives, and one doctor's daughter all got hit hard and simultaneously with acute migraine. Fortunately, we were guests in a big, old-fashioned house which at one time had contained a very large family. As a result, three bathtubs and four bedrooms (containing six beds) were available. We took our hot baths in two shifts; paired off in the dark bedrooms; and the hostess made black coffee by the gallon.

Had any laymen been present, we six bad ads probably would have set the medical profession back thirty years.

What makes the medical father's attitude towards familial health particularly difficult is the fact that medical fathers consider the term "health" so all-embracing. A multitude of matters not at all related to illness fall into this touchy category; posture, for instance. Doctors are painfully posture-conscious and their children are the most posture-sensitive and posture-hounded children in the world.

All my life, Father has kept up a steady stream of commands to "*Walk proud!*" For his own part, Father walks "proud" and with the ingrained stiffness which a childhood in an Imperial Austrian military school and a young manhood in the United States Army embossed upon his ramrodian personality. Father says that he hated being in the service and didn't much enjoy military school either, which is a pity, because he's a born drill sergeant.

Along with Father's super-stiff, doctorly posture, he has a typically medical gait—those long, hurried, flatfooted, strictly purposeful strides which practically scream at onlookers: "Don't bother me! I'm in a terrible rush!"

Doctors always walk as though they've got an emergency just around the corner. Rushing is such a habit with them that they do it even when they're not going anywhere. They can't bear the thought of wasted time, and to be late for anything—or for nothing—is sheer agony. Woe betide the doctor's wife, daughter, or date, whose last-minute nose-powdering entails the most remote risk of entering a theater thirty seconds after the curtain's rise.

"If we're going, let's go!" is Father's oft-stated philosophy, even if where we're going is only for a leisurely, aimless drive. Father never makes even the most casual appointment without commanding: "All right, let's synchronize watches!"

Most doctors are inclined to be somewhat rigid and inflexible of habit. In Father, this inclination has been elevated to an all-embracing way of life. Once in my lifetime, Father decided that a change in office location was called for, so he moved from one office building to another—right next door. That was in January, 1928. He's been there ever since. Every two years, like Old Faithful on a toot, Father redecorates the office. Sometimes the beige comes out a little lighter and sometimes the green comes out a little darker, but most of the time both come out exactly the same as they were before the decorators arrived.

Every day, Father leaves his beige-and-green office on the stroke of twelve noon, and not one minute later, and goes to lunch at the same table, in the same restaurant, where the same waiter serves him.

It is a long-standing joke in our family that when Father sits with woman (any woman) in a theater, he automatically reaches to hold her hand and, equally automatically, his fingers creep upward until he is taking her pulse. That his medical preoccupation extends quite this far, Father vehemently denies, but the time came when he unwittingly proved the point of that family joke.

We were sitting together, watching "I've Got a Secret" on TV.

The *pièce de résistance* of that night's show was the appearance of a bevy of scantily clad young ladies from the circus. Their "secret" was that one of them was to marry a celebrated clown the next morning.

"I'll bet it's the second from the right," Mother challenged.

"Nope, I think it's the one on this end," I countered.

"It's the third from the left," Father declared authoritatively.

Mother and I kept switching our choices. Father shrugged off all our guesses and dogmatically maintained that it was the third from the left.

As it turned out, Father was absolutely right.

"*How* in the world did you guess that?" I asked and the word "guess" brought a scowl to Father's face.

"I *didn't* guess!" he roared. "I said it *was* that one . . . I don't usually make positive statements unless I know what I'm talking about!"

"Just how did you 'know'?" I challenged.

"It was easy," he replied, "I counted their respiration—she was breathing faster than the others."

Come to think of it, I really should have figured that out. What else could you expect from a father who yawns, stretches, and picks up a magazine when a well-curved glamour girl glides onto the TV screen, clad in the manner most efficiently designed to display the most curves where they'll do the most good. If you force the issue by suggesting that Father really should look—"That's Marilyn Gabor, you know"—he takes a quick, bored glance and mutters: "I charge women to look at them like that." . . .

Nine times out of ten, the prescription for the patient who lives in a doctor's house is aspirin and bed rest. For more potent medication there's a wonderful institution known as the Sample Drawer. Pharmaceutical houses send a multitude of samples to doctors, and most of them go into the Sample Drawer against the day of need. It is from this drawer that the family ills are treated.

This, of course, imposes something of a problem, for it is incumbent upon doctors' families to bend every effort toward matching their ailments to the medicines available here. Sometimes the doctor's family rebels. One physician of my acquaintance, an eminent authority on disturbances of the skin, was quite put out when his teen-age daughter announced that she wanted to take her acne to a "real doctor."

"Just what," her injured father demanded, "do you consider a real doctor?"

The youngster's answer was straightforward: "A doctor who will treat me with a prescription instead of samples."

Once while cleaning out the Sample Drawer I picked up an unfamiliar bottle of huge, green pills. "What's this?" I asked.

Father took the bottle, read the label, and handed it back. "Take it," he said. "It might be good for you."

There's no sport in the world that can hold a candle to being a doctor's daughter if you like to live dangerously. Statisticians may not have figured the mortality rate among physicians' offspring, but I'll wager this is one segment of the population in which the jungle law of survival of the fittest holds good. A doctor's child has to be fit to survive. . . .

The Role of the Ambassador's Wife

An Exploratory Study

ARLIE HOCHSCHILD
University of California, Santa Cruz

The wife of the Mauritanian ambassador gave a tea last Thursday for the diplomatic corps wives. The Red Chinese came—as usual there were three of them—and shook hands with me and found the Yugoslav. The Pakistani kissed the Red Chinese on the cheek, while the Indonesian, formerly the Chinese' best friend, turned her back and sat down with the Swede and the South Vietnamese.[1]

As an unofficial representative of American foreign policy and American people, the ambassador's wife has a full-time position made up of responsibilities, restrictions, and privileges which carry over from her husband's official position. In this "vicarious role" (a role by virtue of one's association with another person's role) she must not only meet, know, and entertain a large variety of politically relevant people, she must communicate political and social messages to them.

Thus, here is a particular kind of vicarious role.[2] It involves being a symbol to others and dealing with the symbolic side of other people, for in diplomatic life, public behavior even in apparently private places is "diplomatically significant" and carries with it messages which have less to do with personal feelings than with the decisions of higher state department officials in Washington. Furthermore, the ambassador's wife, because she has no *official* rights and responsibilities, tends to specialize in the more purely symbolic aspects[3] of diplomatic life and in the communication of political messages through nonofficial channels.

The nonofficial channels of diplomatic communication through which

From *Journal of Marriage and the Family*, Vol. 31, No. 1 (February 1969), 73–87. Reprinted by permission of the author and the National Council on Family Relations.

she works involve a set of rules, some informal and others formally codified
into protocol. Deviations from these rules—for example, the intentional
breaking of protocol in assigning seats at a diplomatic party—can thus be
a means of communicating indirect or covert diplomatic messages. There
are other means aside from the manipulation of protocol by which to communicate covert messages—omissions from and additions to guest lists; accepting, rejecting, or giving gifts; or "formalizing" and "informalizing"
diplomatic occasions. In addition to these *methods* of communication, we
examine two *types* of "message system," as Edward Hall[4] calls them, defined
by the nature of the message. The first is the political message system used
mainly to communicate messages about governmental positions on various
issues. It is used primarily between members of different diplomatic missions
or between one diplomatic mission and foreign government officials. The
second is the social message system which communicates messages about
status differences and is used primarily between people of different social
rank within "the American diplomatic team."[5]

Thus, this paper focuses on some mechanisms through which political
and social messages are conveyed in social settings, as used by people in a
vicarious role, without official responsibility for such communications. It
focuses particularly on the functions of the ambassador's wife as chief of
American embassy wives and as diplomatic hostess. Some of the examples
of these mechanisms of diplomatic communication at work also illustrate
unintended consequences. For example, the very art of interpreting messages
—in that it enables one to discriminate between impersonal messages to the
role as representative, and personal messages to the self—can be a means
of preserving role distance (distance between self and role). Also, protocol
by its very impersonality can have the unintended consequence of providing
some measure of social distance (distance between self and a variety of
socially required acquaintances). Hopefully, the focus of this paper on the
details of one unusual role can shed some light on the broader issue of the
ways in which public symbols attached to roles, acts, and words pervade
private lives.

Methodology

This study relies mainly on participant observation and secondarily on
survey data. I began taking systematic notes of my observations in the summer of 1964 when I lived with an ambassador and his wife for a period of
six months. I went to many diplomatic luncheons, dinners, teas, and cocktail parties given by other diplomats and by foreign officials and observed
preparations for similar functions in the home of my host. (Although I have

lived for ten years as the child of a diplomat, in larger and smaller embassies than this one, I did not make systematic records of my observations in those posts.) Much of this analysis, then, is based on an intensive case study of one moderately sized embassy, but the findings of the questionnaire study suggest that these findings can be generalized to all American embassies and, with some qualifications, to diplomatic life in general.

The survey was designed to elicit attitudes toward the role of ambassador's wife. An open-ended questionnaire was sent out in 1965 to wives at 116[6] Chief of Mission posts, on active duty in foreign capitals around the world. Of the 30 questionnaires returned, most were from wives at small posts in Europe and Latin America; the rest were evenly distributed between wives at posts in the Far East, the Near East, and Africa. Fourteen percent did not specify the country to which the husband was assigned, apparently in order to assure anonymity.[7]

Thus, the survey part of this report does not reflect the attitudes of all American ambassadors' wives, but rather an unrepresentative third of them. Although the responses of wives at large and at small posts bear a remarkable similarity,[8] further research is necessary to know how far we can safely generalize about the results reported here.

The Role of the Ambassador's Wife

Officially the role of the ambassador's wife is not a job.[9] It is not mentioned in the *Dictionary of Occupational Titles* and there is no direct pay. Were she not married to an ambassador, she would not normally go to or give innumerable diplomatic functions, ride in the diplomatic car, live in an embassy residence, carry a diplomatic passport, and enjoy diplomatic privileges, nor would she have to answer to a large number of diplomatic obligations and restrictions on behavior. Yet these privileges, obligations, and restrictions, while they lack official recognition and title, nontheless constitute a full-time "vicarious role," similar to that of the wives of high military officials, politicians, government officials, college presidents, and ministers. Before discussing the role itself, we shall take a brief glimpse at *how* her husband's position influences hers.

The occupational role of one individual often affects the expectations held of his (or her) spouse or other associates, but the influence is more profound,[10] the more symbolic or representative the role of that individual is. (By "representative" role I will mean a role which is concerned with the relations of one collectivity to another.)[11] The role of the diplomat, a representative role par excellence, has a special concern with the relations between the United States government and people, and foreign governments and the people they represent. Thus the role of ambassador involves more "carry-over" to his wife's role in the form of restrictions, obligations, and privileges than does the role of dentist, or lawyer, or shopkeeper. This is in part because the role of the diplomat, like that of the college president, is functionally diffuse. What contributes to good relations between countries and what does not are not as finely defined as what contributes, for example, to dental hygiene and what does not. Thus, for people in representative roles, there is a blur between official and nonofficial life and between representative and nonrepresentative acts.

As de Callieres, an eighteenth century expert in diplomacy, pointed out:

> The diplomatist must . . . bear constantly in mind both at work and at play the aims which he is supposed to be serving in the foreign country, and should subordinate his personal pleasure and all his occupations to their pursuit.[12]

Just as the diplomat considers most acts relevant to his diplomatic purpose, so most of his behavior is interpreted in this light and, more importantly, so also is the behavior of his wife. Other associates such as secretaries, chauffeur, and servants, through their association with him, also reflect on him and on the country he represents in their leisure as well as their work. In general the closer the association, and usually also the more equal to him in status, the more the associate shares his representative function. For example, if his personal secretary has an illicit affair this indirectly affects his reputation, but if his wife has the affair it affects his reputation more. Similarly, if his chauffeur is unfriendly to the chauffeur of other ambassadors, the ambassador's reputation is affected, and if his wife refuses invitations from the wives of other ambassadors, it is affected more.

Since the behavior of the ambassador's wife affects her husband's position, his job indirectly defines the limits of appropriate and permissible behavior for her, in order to avoid the misreading of diplomatic messages which might be inadvertently communicated through associates such as his wife. And, in fact, there is a quasi-informal system of socialization for the ambassador's wife in order to assure against such hazards. Most of her knowledge about how to entertain, to befriend foreign officials and their wives (in their own vicarious roles) has traditionally come from experience on the job and from informal "hints" from more experienced officers' wives. The Association of American Foreign Service Women, headquartered in Washington and with branches abroad, provides channels for passing on such advice, as does the *Department of State Newsletter* in which a senior officer's wife suggested to her younger colleagues:

> In the junior ranks . . . keep your entertaining simple . . . however you will have to attend formal affairs and then you can see how they are done and learn from experience for future use.[13]

Yet, her training has become more formal as the representative character of her role has grown more important with the decline of nineteenth century "secret diplomacy"[14] and the growth of "grass-roots" (people to people) diplomacy. Accordingly, the Foreign Service Institute now offers briefing sessions for wives, including lectures on American culture and history and foreign policy, guided tours to art museums, and language courses in almost everything from Russian to the Ghanaian dialect, Twi. In addition, a general bibliography is given to all ambassadors' wives which suggests both the political nature of her vicarious role and the consequent importance of knowing the rules that define politeness in international gatherings. The bibliography includes a book on American etiquette by Emily Post and two books on diplomatic etiquette—Satow's *Guide to Diplomatic Practice* and *Social Usage, A Guide for American Officials and Their Families*—which are mainly based on official instructions on protocol given by the State Department. (It also includes three books on communism, including J. Edgar Hoover's *The Study of Communism*, two books on American history, and two on the nature of the non-Western world.) Some ability to speak the local language and to appear knowledgeable about American history and culture as well as American and international etiquette are considered minimal requirements demanded even of those who treat the role most passively. The ambassador's wife is encouraged to do more, and in some instances she may, in her vicarious role, go beyond her husband in "representing America." For example, in a speech by the wife of the head of the Foreign Service Institute, one exemplary American diplomatic wife was described as holding classes for the wives of local officials on "the American way of life[15] in different rooms in her home, focusing conversation on things pertaining to the particular room. . . . She then served her class American style food, while teaching them about U.S. eating habits and customs."[16]

Training for this vicarious role prepares the ambassador's wife not only for certain obligations but certain restrictions on her life, some of which are suggested in an article in the *Department of State Newsletter:*

> We begin by remembering what all Foreign Service wives learn early in their careers: that the behavior of any American living abroad will invariably be considered typical of most Americans—our attitudes, our cultural values, our personalities and sensitivities.[17]

Most Americans abroad, are indeed, compared in the foreigner's mind to a stereotype of Americans. To non-diplomatic Americans, this fact usually involves fewer restrictions on behavior. For diplomats and their wives,

> Scrupulous observance of local laws, . . . and careful attention not to offend local customs are urged. [But] "going native" is as unwelcome in most countries as aggressive Americanism.[18]

The requirements for being considered typically American should, according to the *State Department Newsletter*, touch not only one's behavior, but one's attitudes, values, and personality. Either attitudes must accord with behavior, or real attitudes must be acceptable.

> To announce an attitude and then not seem to live up to it is to many people in the host country a form of dishonesty that reflects against the United States. For example, to say that you like the local food and then refuse to touch it does not win friends.[19]

Moreover, while she is not an official representative, she is seldom in the realm of the "unofficial," and this largely cuts out the practice of other non-diplomatic professions, even if time were no obstacle. The wife of the envoy to Iceland explained in response to the questionnaire:

> A specific profession such as a lawyer, doctor or work in any commercial field would be well nigh impossible, for your official position would prejudice any action and would cause resentment and criticism.[20]

Only those professions, typically cultural, which are remote from public social life and which do not require acts which could possibly be interpreted as political are exempt.

The same holds for her memberships in organizations. As one speech warned,

> Caution is urged when joining new organizations; sometimes groups seek both the prestige and the cover afforded by participation of wives of American officials, so it is suggested that Embassy officials be consulted before joining unknown groups, signing petitions, or taking part in programs which involve innocent Americans in international political activities.[21]

In fact, most formal and informal social relations are affected by the representational character of the role. The ambassador's wife is advised to "confine the guest list to those whom your husband should know and with whom he works." In her choice of informal friends, she may choose according to her predispositions and interests—but only to a limited extent.[22] Political relevance is often a stronger criterion than interest or affinity in the allocation of social time. As the wife of the ambassador to a small European country noted,

> Naturally it is difficult to be closer to the wife of the French ambassador than to the wife of the British ambassador—or to spend

more time with the Russian wife than the Italian wife; we must be "diplomatic."

The diplomat's wife is urged to observe caution especially with foreigners, whether they are socially required guests or friends. In one speech embassy wives were told:

> Remember . . . when you are invited to a party given by other than Americans, it is usually because of your husband's position in the embassy and his work. Therefore look upon yourselves as representatives of the United States even when your hosts are good friends.[23]

There are certain categories of American audiences, for example, visiting congressmen or State Department inspectors, for whom she must represent America. In general, however, this demand on her behavior and demeanor applies to occasions shared with non-Americans.[24] In addition to the obligations and restrictions inherent in the role of ambassador's wife, there are certain vicarious honors and privileges, such as being given a seat of honor at dinner parties, having American wives of lower ranking officials stand when she enters a room, and having all invitations made to subordinates almost always accepted. In addition she enjoys diplomatic privileges such as immunity from legal prosecution, parking tickets, and customs inspection when she travels. Finally, her house and servants and chauffeured car reflect a materially high standard of living, which suggest a new variation on what Thorstein Veblen in his *Theory of the Leissure Class* called "vicarious conspicuous consumption." But it is not so much that his wife's furs reflect the ambassadors wealth, as that their limousine[25] reflects America's wealth.

Communicating Messages

We have said that while the ambassador communicates diplomatic messages through both direct and indirect channels, his wife must consciously avoid the direct and specialize in indirect ways of communicating political and social messages. In examining these messages, it is important, as Hayakawa has pointed out, to look "not at the words or the gestures themselves, but at the semantic reactions, that is human responses to symbols, signs and symbol systems including language."[26] Hayakawa has distinguished on the verbal level between occupational language and public language.

When two physicists talk about "positrons" . . . they can be presumed to have enough of a common background of controlled experience in their fields to have few difficulties about understanding each other. But most of the words of artistic and other general discussion are not restricted to such specialized frames of reference. They are part of the language of everyday life—by which I mean that they are part of the language in which we do not hesitate to speak across occupational lines.[27]

Within diplomatic circles, there is also an agreement about meaning of words and also of gestures. Just as scientists among themselves know what they mean by the word "positron," so diplomats know what they mean by "We are unable to accept the kind invitation of ———— to the National Day Celebration." The difference is that while much of scientific language deals with the nature of physical matter, much of diplomatic language deals with the nature of relations between roles and the symbols attached to them.[28]

Diplomatic language can be either overt or covert. The covert diplomatic language shares some characteristics with its overt counterpart. According to Harold Nicolson, "the expression 'diplomatic language' is often used to describe that guarded understatement which enables diplomatists and ministers to say sharp things to each other without becoming provocative or impolite."[29] In actions as well, messages are communicated in the form of a guarded understatement. And for this reason the ambassador's wife must develop a keen ability to communicate and interpret, through all her interactions, covert political and social messages, as well as personal messages. To give messages in this communications system requires a facility in what Goffman has called impression management. To interpret these messages given by others, she must be able to discern not only messages which are given but those which are "given off." As de Callieres pointed out:

> The negotiator must possess that penetration which enables him to discover the thoughts of men and to know by the least movement of their countenances what passions are stirring within, for such movements are often betrayed even by the most practiced negotiator.[30]

Facility in this occupational language goes with her role as much as speaking French does for a representative to France, and it may go not much deeper psychologically. She may come to be as unaware of her peculiar specialization as she is of speaking a second language. Just as she begins to dream in French when in a French-speaking country, she may automatically think in the occupational language. If her husband has been promoted to the top, the chances are that she, as his chief aide, has made this facility into an art.

There are two primary covert message systems: (a) the political message system associated with her capacity as unofficial government representative and (b) the social message system attached to the role as chief of embassy wives. Usually these message systems are in use simultaneously.

For each message system there is a reference group, composed of those to whom the ambassador's wife is speaking and those on whose behalf she speaks. As an unofficial diplomat she is, as we have noted, only indirectly implicated in a communications system between the United States government on whose behalf the ambassador speaks and the foreign government to whom he addresses himself. She has no direct say in this communications system, and there is a negative proviso *not* to discuss official diplomatic business since she is not supposed to be told diplomatic secrets and her word may mistakenly be taken as official. However, at the same time, she deals constantly with politics indirectly.

She learns to interpret indirect political gestures, and she can also convey messages indirectly, for example, by the invitations and gifts she does or does not accept, the guests she invites, where she seats them, and her manner toward them. Thus, what are normally social gestures are interpreted in a political light. Did the Yugoslav ambassador come to our Fourth of July party or not? Did he leave early without having another function to attend?[31] Did he send a junior officer instead of showing up himself? Or was he unusually friendly to us tonight, and did he snub the Russian official? A typical question interpreting these kinds of actions is: Are we stepping up the aid program to Yugoslavia, or did the Yugoslav get a recent communiqué from his government to take a harder line against the war in Vietnam? Diplomats and their wives thus learn to "read" behavior. Two questions pose themselves at this point. First, why should an indirect form of communication be necessary at all? Why is it that the diplomat or his wife does not simply and openly say, "I do not like your policy in Vietnam and I am expressing this by not coming to your party tomorrow night"? Or why not simply say, "I oppose your policy in Vietnam but I like you as a friend and will come to your party tomorrow night"?

One plausible explanation for why a seasoned diplomat usually avoids the first alternative is, in fact, its very directness. There is some use in being indirect. One of the possible functions of the covert political language is its very ambiguity. It leaves room for doubt, for multiple interpretations by both parties thus leaving a way out, should the political winds change. The diplomat who chooses the second alternative, given the homogenized nature of his or her public and private life, risks having a private gesture interpreted as an official one.

Second, how can behavior perform some of the functions of a verbal language in diplomatic circles? In part, it does so through the various meanings universally attached to certain actions, through the dictionary of protocol,[32] much as meanings are attached to nouns and verbs in speech. Just as there is a commonly accepted standard of grammatical correctness in language, so there is in diplomatic behavior. As one ambassador's wife explained in a speech,

> "Protocol" is a set of rules of the game—the game of diplomatic life where you meet people of different cultures, backgrounds and so on. If we all acted the way we did in our home towns, it might not be completely understood in Bangkok or Leopoldville or Lima or Paris. So there is "protocol" which tells us the right international way for an ambassador to present his credentials, to meet a visiting Royalty or a President, to arrange conferences and in what order to rank officials of countries, big or little.[33]

Protocol, then, is a set of rules which define what is polite and impolite conduct in a given context. It provides guidelines not only for ambassadors but for their wives, and it regulates not only the most formal of ceremonies but, as we shall see shortly, most of the more minor diplomatic encounters in fairly detailed fashion. Its manifest function is to provide a universally understood and agreed upon set of formal norms, a behavioral Esperanto. There are other formal norms, which are not codified in the form of protocol but which function in the same way.

Since protocol defines what is impolite behavior in certain contexts, and since impolite behavior often carries with it a political message, conformity with or deviation from protocol can be a means of conveying political messages. Thus, since those in diplomatic circles are assumed to understand and speak this behavioral Esperanto, the breaking of protocol is often interpreted as an intentional gesture—usually an intentional political gesture. The norms of protocol offer a choice: one can either follow protocol to the letter (although this in itself, as we shall see, is insufficient to meet the criteria of ideal diplomatic behavior) or one may deviate from it. If the individual chooses to "break protocol," he or she may do it with the effect of increasing social distance or decreasing it. In either case the individual does not escape the risk of having a personal gesture interpreted as a diplomatic one or an expressive gesture interpreted as an instrumental one. The same goes for the breaking or non-breaking of less formal norms of conduct.[34] I should add parenthetically that protocol offers some of the advantages of other formal cultures. For example, when paying a personal call to the ambassador's wife (an example we return to later), the caller is told in *Social Usage*, the official document of protocol, that when her hostess says, "Must you go now?" she is not actually urging the guest to stay but rather being polite. When meanings are spelled out so finely, many of the ambiguities of social intercourse are clarified and a whole set of small decisions prescribed. As Edward Hall has pointed out, because the boundaries of behavior are so clearly marked even to the permissible deviation, "there is never any doubt in anybody's mind that, as long as he does what is expected, he knows what to expect from others."[35] Hall suggests that those in a formal culture tend to have a relaxed view of life, and while this is probably true, the situation is also probably different for those such as diplomats who live part of their lives in a formal culture of diplomacy and part of it outside that formal culture. Yet, the rules of protocol probably do reduce a number of anxieties which would otherwise be inherent in a situation in which expectations are unpredictable, the individuals are not well known, and there is a premium on avoiding offense.

Entertaining appropriate people is the chief business of the ambassador's wife, and dinner parties, cocktail parties, luncheons, and teas provide a continual forum in which those in vicarious roles do not "talk politics" though their presence or absence at such functions is diplomatically "significant." Several characteristics of the guests and the hosts (hostesses) in diplomatic life reduce the probability that deep personal friendship will obscure the "diplomatic significance" of encounters.

The first such characteristic is the sheer number of people with whom an ambassador's wife deals. One wife reported, "At this small post I average 14 'must' social functions a week, not counting entertaining an average of 40 people a week, large receptions excluded. [In the summer time it's usually much less.]" Eighty percent of the ambassadors' wives reported either giving or going to ten or more dinners, luncheons, or receptions a week, and the average wife attended at least one function a day in someone else's home. The time it takes to entertain a large number of people is, ironically, a barrier to or protection against intimacy. As one ambassador's wife notes, "You have so many friends and acquaintances that you find yourself spread too thin—even if you enjoy people." Or, as another put it, "Your husband's position, and responsibilities connected with your husband's position don't leave you much time to cultivate close friends."

Of the ambassadors' wives sampled, 36 percent spent most of their time with other Americans (of that, 23 percent with other American embassy wives), 12 percent with foreigners not from the assigned country— mostly diplomats from other embassies, and 52 percent with locals.[36] The Americans and the foreigners with whom half of the wives spent most of their time are usually on two- to four-year tours of duty. She may arrive at a post just as someone she knows and likes is leaving. According to one wife, "it depends on the post. In one post I made extremely close friends. In Paris it was harder for the social life was so extremely active and Americans were passing through all the time." The transiency goes for local officials too; for if they lose office or are demoted, they also lose their priority on her guest list.

In addition, many of the people with whom she deals are younger than herself. She and her husband are at the pinnacle of a small hierarchy and as one ambassador's wife explained, "Ambassadors' wives, having gone up the ladder, are usually older and find few contemporaries at the same stage of life." Her contemporaries are generally other ambassadors' wives at the post and high local government officials. Yet in a young developing nation, where the educated political elite is young, many of the top officials and their wives are twenty or thirty years younger than the ambassador to the country and his wife.[37]

Thus, the characteristics of people she deals with, their transience, their age, social position (which we shall go into shortly), as well as the sheer numbers of them reduce the probability of intimate friendships which might obscure the more purely diplomatic function of entertaining. This is true not only in her public life, but in her private life as well. The weekend is not experientially set off from the rest of the week; activities such as going to church or to the races in countries such as England, Australia, or New Zealand are partly work. In most posts, golf and tennis are also partly work since the people one meets on the course or the court are usually the same people it is one's job to cultivate. Thus, public and private life, leisure and work are finely woven into each other and bound to the pervasive diplomatic task.

In the face of the demands of diplomatic life, there appears some need, in order to maintain the integrity of the self, to limit the level of involvement. An ambassador's wife could not and usually does not want to become closer or more intimate with *all* the people she meets in the course of a month. There are social barriers which both limit her and protect her from unwanted intimacy with a variety of diplomatically necessary acquaintances. One means of maintaining social distance, as we shall see, is adherence to protocol. It is in light of the nature and purpose of her sociability and the quality of her relations that we now look at the means by which she communicates political and social messages, and it is in light of her need for social distance that we look at some of the functions of diplomatic communication.

CHIEF OF AMERICAN EMBASSY WIVES

We can now look at the ambassador's wife as chief of the hierarchy of embassy wives and as diplomatic hostess, to illustrate and amplify the basic arguments made above.

When the ambassador's wife is alone with other American officers' wives, the political symbolism of her role and the message system associated with it tend to disappear. On the other hand, the social message system comes into use and protocol is more often used to communicate social than political messages. It helps preserve social distance between those of unequal status within the embassy hierarchy.

By the same token, in the company of foreign guests the social distance between wives of different ranks within the embassy hierarchy tends to fade out, and the social message system associated with those status differences tends to fall into disuse. For example, at a dinner party protocol governs the seating of Americans vis-à-vis each other, taking into account their relative rankings, and *Social Usage* suggests that Americans "should forget precedence among themselves and be prepared to be seated in any way which will make conversation easier and which will take into account language qualifications."[38]

Thus, relations between Americans vary according to whether or not foreigners are present, and this affects the kind of message system used. It is not that the social distance between people declines depending on the presence of foreigners, but rather that the basis on which it rests changes. Correspondingly, while one message system is used to express political messages to foreigners, and another message system is used to express status differences among Americans, one message system or another is usually in use.

In order to understand the use of the social message system as a means of keeping social distance, we will have to back up and discuss why her vicarious role as chief of American officers' wives means keeping a proper distance from those wives. Then we look at *how* the distance is kept.

Her relationship to the wives of subordinates in the embassy and theirs to her is defined by the rank of their respective spouses in the embassy hierarchy. The social hierarchy within the embassy is symbolized by the order in which American officials and their wives line up in a receiving line at a diplomatic function; the ambassador and his wife first; the political counselor and his wife; then the economic counselor, the administrative counselor, on down to the junior officers and their wives.[39] The ambassador's wife, like the corporation executive's wife, is not formally in the organizational structure but is nevertheless covered by its bureaucratic ranks. This shadow hierarchy of wives is formally recognized and institutionalized in the American women's clubs,[40] and in some cases in binational women's groups or international women's organizations which includes resident foreign nationals. In large embassies there is usually a formal wives' group to which all embassy wives automatically belong, and these provide formal channels through which to observe and supervise subordinates and exercise social control. The ambassador's wife is automatically either the chairman or the honorary chairman.[41]

The nature of the relation between the ambassador's wife and her subordinates depends among other things on the size of the embassy, the pace of the social life, and the various personalities involved. European embassies typically have larger staffs, embassies in the newly developing countries typically smaller ones.[42] One ambassador's wife distinguished between the way relations with wives should be handled in a small and in a large embassy:

I have always assumed that the morale and efficiency of the distaff side of the Embassy is largely the responsibility of the ambassador's wife. . . . In small embassies one can bring the senior wives in for a monthly coffee or lunch and discuss the general problems of the local scene. Informal talks about how the different wives are getting on, whether there are any problem children and what can be done about them, enable the ambassador's wife to keep her finger on the pulse of things without becoming unnecessarily involved in individual problems. In a large Embassy, of course, this is more difficult, but it is usually possible for even the busiest ambassador's wife to set aside one morning every four or six weeks to talk with the senior wives, who should be prepared to talk briefly and knowledgeably about the junior wives in their sections of the Embassy and whether the general morale is good or bad.

In most embassies the wives like to refer to themselves as a "team" or as "one big family." According to one wife, "To be in a foreign post is to be a member of a larger family and the differences of interests between me and my old friends [presumably in the United States] who do not belong to it, makes a large gap in our relationship." In many embassies, especially the small ones, the collective morale associated with a team is strong.

However, given the occupational relations between the ambassador—whose evaluation is important in getting a promotion—and subordinates in the embassy, some impersonality and social distance are required not only between the two men but between their two wives. For example, it would be very difficult for an ambassador to fire or recommend against promotion for an officer who has been a close friend but an incompetent officer. A friendship between the two wives would present the same obstacle against applying a universalistic standard in recommending promotions.

In practice it is not only the ambassador's wife who guards against too close a relationship, but also the wives of embassy subordinates. One ambassador's wife put the situation this way:

It has been my experience as a Consul-General's wife in the past too, that the moment one's husband is in charge, both American and local residents do not feel so free to drop in or to invite one for informal activities on the spur of the moment. Americans are particularly loath to do so.

One possible explanation for this is that since it might benefit their husband's careers, there is a strong temptation for embassy wives to befriend the ambassador's wife on grounds which are not strictly personal. For this reason, any subordinate's wife who does try to become a favorite is bitterly resented for "currying favor" and strongly censured by other wives.[43]

The norms which dampen intimacy between the ambassador's wife and wives of his subordinates also call for an ability to discriminate between socially required and personal gestures, or between the instrumental and the expressive character of a particular gesture. As the same woman continued:

> The principal officer's wife must make the first move, most of the time, and then she can never be sure that an invitation of hers is accepted because it *must* be accepted. There seems to be an unwritten regulation that the lower ranking officers cannot refuse invitations from their superiors—a custom of which I do not approve incidentally.

Of the wives who replied to the question concerning their relations with other embassy wives, three-fourths mentioned the barriers which the social requirements of the embassy hierarchy set up. It is no surprise, then, that of the 52 percent who said that most of their best friends were in the American diplomatic service, only 5 percent said their best American friend was an American at the same post.

Ironically, the incentives are structured so that wives seek friendships either among foreign nationals or among social equals. As one ambassador's wife put it,

> One's position of authority with other Americans precludes closeness. One shouldn't have "favorites" although inevitably they exist. *The incentive to having friends . . . among the locals is higher.* It is your profession to develop friends. If you fail, you're sent home.[44]

Another put it simply, "One's chances are better with the local officials and their wives." But she added, "In general, one makes friends but not close ones." One ambassador's wife concluded, "It is, much of the time, a lonely job."

However, usually the ambassador's wife does tend to have favorites or confidantes within the diplomatic "team," and one central problem is to avoid the jealousy that results. If she chooses a close friend from within the team, she must usually cross not only age but also status boundaries. The more status boundaries she crosses, the more social tension she is likely to create.

As one wife observed, "The higher one's rank, the harder it is [to make friends]. Any chief officer's wife—be she that of a Consul, Consul-General, Minister, or Ambassador—probably has this experience."[45]

According to another,

> Among your own wives you have to take care to treat all care-
> fully to avoid jealousies and rivalries.

Or,

> Within the Embassy family it's a delicate matter. I feel my rela-
> tionships with all the other Embassy wives should be on an equally
> friendly but not intimate footing. My best friend is the wife of
> another ambassador at the Post.

The structural barriers which guard or protect against close friendship
apply also to American wives whose husbands work for parallel hierarchies
of wives in USIS and AID, which are under the general supervision of the
ambassador.

> Jealousy and rivalry among the services and missions is a prob-
> lem if one devotes too much time and attention to any [agency].

Thus her talking, telephoning, and visiting time should be distributed
equitably among all the wives of subordinate officers in a number of local
American organizations.

Again, the message system of protocol serves as a set of impersonal rules
that remind those to whom they apply of the status differences between
wives. Its very impersonality helps guard against intimacy and thus against
jealousies and rivalries. For example, according to protocol, a newly arrived
embassy wife should pay what is called "a personal call" on the ambassador's wife.

> One of the first things you must do at a new post, is to call . . .
> "calling" is an easy way of getting to know people. Here in the
> U.S.A., neighbors drop in for coffee on a new-comer in the area.
> It is the same thing in a slightly different form in a foreign post,
> only more important abroad as your length of stay is limited and
> you must not waste time in establishing friendships.[46]

The requirements of the personal call are given in *Social Usage*, spelling
out what is proper even to the point of defining a socially polite gesture as
opposed to a personal one by the hostess.

> One stays for approximately 20 minutes, unless strongly urged
> by the hostess to stay longer, ("Must you go now?" does not con-

stitute urging) . . . or if refreshments are served, and on leaving one shakes hands with and thanks the hostess. If no appointment has been made, one asks at the door if Mrs. X is "at home" or "receiving." . . . If not, upon departure, leave the proper number of cards to the individual who answers the door. . . . Cards must not be handed to the person on whom one is calling. Turning down either upper corner of cards indicates a personal call.[47]

The boundaries of minimal courtesy are explicit, and the ambiguity attached to what sorts of gestures are those of friendship and what sorts are socially required is largely cleared up. Thus, the necessary social distance is maintained through the behavioral language of protocol, the level of personal involvement is minimized, and the system of formality ironically appears to help the individual from "being spread too thin."

Hostess

In her capacity as hostess, the political message system between American and foreign officials and their wives comes into play, while the social message system used between people of different status within the American embassy hierarchy tends to recede. Her guest list in itself is a means of communicating political messages, and consequently whom she invites is not a matter of whim or chance. One ambassador's wife recommended keeping a file:

> A card file, with a thumbnail sketch of the person being documented, his language abilities and general interests on one side, and on the other side, the dates and functions at the Embassy to which he has been invited, as well as the invitations accepted from him, has been of the greatest use to me.[48]

A speech given by the wife of a high government official in Washington also suggested listing those guests who have been invited with the person and listing what was served "in order to avoid duplication."[49]

Conversely, in her role as guest, she herself is on a comparable list of potential guests. One wife reported the difficulty American diplomats in her assigned country had in getting onto the guest lists of foreign nationals. "There is a problem in this country, since they are neutralist, and do not want to be tagged as Pro-American." Thus, local officials with whom she deals must apportion their sociability according to similar impersonal mandates.

Since the ambassador's wife is much of the time either a hostess or a guest, and since much of her important work is performed in those roles, she finds that often she is stationary, either on her "turf" or on someone else's.[50] There is not much time for walking around in public. Rather, in private places she is in public. She entertains at "the residence," a large house which looks and feels like a public building and literally owned, as it were, by the role rather than the occupant. Furnishings such as chairs, rugs, and curtains are provided by the State Department, and the United States seal appears on all the glasses and plates. The house and the objects in it usually remind guests that they are visiting "the residence" as well as its occupants.[51] Often one or two rooms in the mansion are "home rooms," furnished with familiar personal objects and pictures, and are kept largely exempt from public use or observation. The rest of the house is explicitly designed for formal entertaining, with large hallways for overflow crowds, closet space ample enough to hold dozens of coats, large doorways and servant quarters to house servants who sometimes "come with the house."

Entertaining, like the house in which it is done, is largely formal. The farther up one's husband goes in the diplomatic hierarchy, the more formal it becomes.[52] It takes place at designated times and is tightly scheduled. One woman commented, "local residents . . . feel that a diplomat's wife is always busy and [they] are embarrassed if they drop in and find guests at the residence." Servants, as suggested earlier, add to the air of formality since, unless they are known to speak no English at all, they tend to cramp intimate conversation.[53]

The dinner party is prototypic of much of the style of diplomatic life, for it illustrates the indirect ways in which political and social messages are communicated through the use of protocol. The general purpose of the diplomatic function itself is usually well understood on all sides: to create a good will between countries and, as de Callieres has put it, to help "to conduct the affairs of his [the diplomat's] master to a prosperous issue, and to spare no pains to discover the designs of others."[54] Furthermore,

> If people of this kind [the deputies in a democratic state] have a freedom of entree to the ambassador, a good table will greatly assist in the discovery of all that is going on.[55]

Certain norms of protocol are always observed in such matters as who precedes whom in entering the dining room and in the table seating. Each embassy has a protocol officer whose job it is to assure that, as the saying goes, "everything goes according to protocol." The place of honor for male guests is to the right of the hostess, while that of the highest ranking lady at the dinner is to the right of the host, and protocol spells out the seating on down to the middle of the table.[56] To avoid offense, it is suggested in *Social Usage* that

> it is sometimes more convenient to entertain at 2 or more tables of 6 or more persons. The host and hostess would not then be seated at the same table. The advantage of this arrangement is that it affords more places of honor.[57]

If for some reason protocol cannot be followed, the host or hostess should inform the guests involved, according to *Social Usage*, "to avoid any misunderstanding."[58] Since the norms are so explicitly spelled out and universally understood, the "misunderstanding" often concerns whether or not the breaking of protocol is intentional or not.

A set of less formal norms governs the content of conversation for the hostess. Usually her conversation should steer a middle course between politically relevant subjects on the one hand and trivial matters on the other. It should not be too serious nor too light.[59]

The para-political nature of her role vis-à-vis foreign officials' wives is illustrated by the remarks of one ambassador's wife:

> Most of my friends are among the local wives, but there too I must be extremely careful of carefree conversation which can always be misinterpreted. An innocent remark can be carried (equally innocently) by my friend to her husband—and there hangs many a diplomatic blunder.

Thus, not only whom she talks to but what she says is filtered for political relevance. She talks to politically relevant people, but often on politically nonsignificant subjects. For even if the wife of a local official, for example, is not consciously scouring the conversation for information useful to her husband, the result may be the same as if she were. The content of conversation may also affect her relations to her husband. One ambassador's wife reported,

> You must avoid politically sensitive areas as your words will be taken as government policy in spite of the fact you never see the telegrams or are privy to secret information. If you slip once, or god forbid, twice on secret information your husband has confided in you, his job is at stake, and worse—he watches every word he says to you thereafter.

Ironically, formal entertaining often calls for the hostess to "take off" some of the formality. The hostess may "informalize" a formal setting indirectly through her servants. For example, if a guest arrives at the door, she may open the door and greet the guest herself, while letting the servant take the guest's coat. She can in this way silently communicate the message, "My servant usually answers the door for other kinds of guests, but you are special, so I answered if myself." She may also mention some eccentricity which relaxes the expectations of her guests. She may thus jar the strictures of formality by making light of protocol but usually without deviating from it. For example, one ambassador's wife complained playfully, "I don't know where people sit here," having provided neatly printed names in front of each guest's plate, thus assuring that the guests found their proper places but somehow in spite of her ineptitude. She is thus seen as informal and "genuine" within a formal and not very genuine setting— the ideal diplomatic combination.

Yet, while she must be gracious and informal within a formal setting, the formal setting itself offers her the choice of being as formal as her surroundings (maintaining the ice) or being informal (breaking the ice). Indeed, this is what de Callieres recommended to eighteenth century diplomats:

> The diplomatist will readily understand that at certain times he can win the good grace of those around him by living in an easy, affable and familiar manner among his friends. To wrap one-self in official dignity, at all times is mere preposterous arrogance, and the diplomatists who behave thus will repel rather than attract.[60]

Beyond this covert communication with guests, the hostess maintains subterranean communication with her servants.[61] Since most entertaining involves feeding large numbers of people, the hostess often shares many techniques with the professional restaurant manager who has a personal interest in the contentment of the clients and a professional stake in their enjoyment of the occasion. In this respect she shares many of the characteristic requirements of non-diplomatic hostesses. Good communication between hostess and servant usually presupposes agreement on whose national customs will be respected on what occasions. According to one diplomat's wife, stationed in India, the tasks which were thought proper for various categories of servants differed depending on whether guests were present or absent:

> It was a different matter if guests were present. A plate of food might be spilled on the floor. The bearer would see it, might put a stool in front of it so that guests wouldn't stumble onto it but he would walk with dignity out of the room to get the sweeper to come and clear it away. He wouldn't embarrass me in front of my guests

by behaving as if he didn't know the proper way for a respectful Hindu man to act. If there guests, I wouldn't embarrass the butler by doing the job myself as any American housewife would be inclined to do.[62]

Implications and Conclusion

The role of the ambassador's wife, as it involves heading a group of American embassy wives and playing hostess to foreign nationals, illustrates several dimensions of many other roles. It exemplifies a type of vicarious role, the social requirements of being a representative, and the use of political and social message systems. It shows also the function of formality, not only as a means of communicating covert political and social messages, but also as a way of maintaining social distance.

Many wives as well as their husbands complain and joke among themselves about what they recognize as a system of mutual expectations which appears to exist above and beyond their own personal predispositions. They may abide by protocol or not, but they ignore it only at grave risk to their relations with others in their diplomatic circle. Yet, protocol and other unspoken rules of diplomatic conduct which in part make up this system can provide protection and help maintain the sanctity of one's inner self from the more impersonal encroachments by the symbolic aspects of the role. Formality assures that relations which are in large part instrumental are guided by norms which are distinctly different from those guiding the essentially expressive relationships which characterize intimacy and close friendship.

It is not that by virtue of her representative role the ambassador's wife is closed off from expressive relationships, but rather that the sphere of potential intimates is narrowed. Indeed, her relations to close friends may be even closer. It is likely that the intimate working relationship she has with her husband goes with an even closer personal relationship with him. One wife put it, "One makes hundreds of 'friends' and few close friends but my close friends mean a lot to me."[63] Although I do not have data on divorce, further research may verify my impression that it is extremely rare compared to that of other American women of the same social background.[64]

Given the characteristics of diplomatic life and the ways in which they influence the role of the ambassador's wife, what do most wives think of their role? Most enjoy it. Only 7 percent of those questioned said that if they could choose their husband's profession they would not have him be-

come an ambassador. All things considered—the travel, the variety of interesting people, the style of life—they would not leave it for any other
life.[65]

Because the intricate set of shared symbols into which the ambassador's
wife is socialized and into which she socializes others, calls for a working
relation between her own personal feelings and the front she must present,
between a personal sublanguage and covert political and social ones, the
distinction between these two aspects of her role and mode of communicating often becomes hard to maintain.

Since the ambassador, like Merton's bureaucrat, picks a profession for
which he is likely to be personally suited and is molded in a direction which
does not painfully cramp his personal style, he may not consciously or unconsciously feel any "pinch" between personality and role. However, the ambassador's wife in most cases selected, not the role, but rather the husband
whose professional role so profoundly influences her own. Thus, it is probable that among diplomatic couples the wife, although she may in many
ways enjoy her role, is more likely to feel the "pinch."

For purposes of exposition I have erased some of the ambiguity which
in reality shrouds her role. Questions around which confusion concerning
communication may arise are: Who shares the diplomatic system of symbols
and who does not, e.g., who would take a political gesture personally? When
does a veteran linguist stop communicating in the political message system?
When does the vocabulary of the diplomatic message system differ from
that of a particular culture,[66] and when is one language to be observed
rather than another? Other ambiguities involve the point at which an
autonomous social or professional life is felt to encroach on the demands
of the diplomatic role. More generally, to what extent can an ambassador's
wife carve out her own role and to what extent is it "made" for her?

I have stressed the formal at the expense of the informal aspects of her
diplomatic role and the social requirements of it over the freedom it offers.
But in doing so, I mean to show how mechanisms such as covert message
systems arise which can help to preserve some measure of freedom and some
differentiation between occupational and personal roles, occupational and
personal communication. In a life as transient, socially fractionalized, and
spread thin as hers, there is a greater need for such differentiation than in
the case of many other roles. Yet, most people to some extent fill roles
which are in part representative and which require some protection from
the "pinch." The more greatly the role demands differentiation between
personal and impersonal messages, the more need there is for the political
and social and occupational equivalent of the psychiatric eye for the larger
meanings of small signs. The role of the ambassador's wife, because she
specializes in this language and in the art of interpreting it, simply accentuates the diplomacy of everyday life.

Footnotes

Research for this paper was done from June through November, 1964. The author is grateful to Neil Smelser, Robert Blauner, and Harold Wilensky for valuable comments on an earlier version of the paper.

[1] Correspondence from an ambassador's wife.

[2] See Ralph Turner, "Role-Taking: Process versus Conformity," in *Human Behavior and Social Processes, an Interactionist Approach*, ed. by Arnold Rose (Boston: Houghton Mifflin Co., 1962). The norms which govern role behavior and expectations, in this case, define a limited range of behavior from which deviation is not tolerated. The role of the ambassador is much more clear-cut, and it involves a range of sanctions attached to certain kinds of behavior, which are absent in the case of the role of the ambassador's wife. The sanctions attached to her role are indirect, i.e., if she insults a leading official, it is her husband who is punished, and through him, she is.

[3] See Talcott Parsons, *The Social System* (London: The Free Press of Glencoe, 1951), p. 100. Parsons distinguishes between the instrumental aspect of the executive role and the expressive element of leadership. "The position and the actions in his role of an expressive leader serve to symbolize to outsiders the nature and the solitary sentiments of the collectivity he represents, and to organize its relations to other collectivities. All of this is of course clearly evident in various aspects of international relations." *Ibid.*, p. 401.

[4] See Edward T. Hall, *The Silent Language* (Greenwich, Conn.: Fawcett Premier Books, 1959). Hall distinguishes between ten kinds of "message system." I am adopting here only his term, not his classification scheme.

[5] There is also a technical message system between hostess and servants. At a diplomatic function, her communication with waiters is often by use of the hand and eye. As a technician of elegance, she has a watchful eye on the water glasses and soup spoons under the soup bowls, in order to be able to signal the next move. She may do this by stepping on an inconspicuous buzzer lodged under the table which rings out in the kitchen and signals the cook to heat the dinner plates. She thereby avoids the necessity of eye signals which can disrupt the flow of conversation with the guests seated next to her, usually the most important guests there. (Often it is only to her that servants are not what Goffman has called "nonpeople," although the less educated wives of local officials may occasionally feel closer to servants who are the same race, speak the same language, and share the same customs.)

[6] When the questionnaires were mailed in 1965, there were 116 embassies, two of which were headed by women, some by bachelors, and six were vacant. Two-thirds were held by career diplomats and a third by political appointees. Interestingly, the responses from wives of political appointees did not differ significantly on any question from those of the wives of career men. This suggests the underlying similarity of the role of wives of business executives and career diplomats.

[7] While the sample is thus unrepresentative, most of what follows goes for the wives at larger posts who probably lacked time to fill out the questionnaire. Of those who replied, 24 percent were from Europe, 14 percent from the Far East, 20 percent from Latin America, and 14 percent from Africa. In 1958, 42 percent of all State Department personnel abroad were stationed in Europe, 34 percent in the Far East and Southeast Asia, 9 percent in the Near East, 8 percent in Latin America, and 6 percent in Africa. See Harlan Cleveland *et al.*, *The Overseas Americans* (New York: McGraw-Hill Book Company, 1964), p. 71. Thus Europe and the Far East were under-represented in the sample; and the Near East, Latin America, and Africa were over-represented. There were five returned empty questionnaires from single or divorced ambassadors and from women new to the job who did not feel they could comment yet.

[8] The large posts and especially the European large posts which are under-represented in this sample are more likely to be filled by political appointees who can dip from their own pockets to supplement entertainment allowances. Their wives are more likely to be new to embassy life, but their experience as corporation wives is not strikingly different. See William F. White, Jr., *Is Anybody Listening* (New York: Simon and Schuster, 1952), chap. 8, "The Wives of Management."

[9] It is a role but not an occupational role.

[10] There are many ways in which the occupational role of one individual affects his or her spouse or other associates. The wife or son of a famous scientist, for example, may be known to many others by virtue of their association with him. But the occupational role may have other effects too in the form of new obligations, restrictions, and privileges on those in vicarious roles.

[11] See Footnote 3.

[12] Monsieur de Callieres, *On the Manner of Negotiating with Princes: On the Uses of Diplomacy, the Choice of Ministers and Envoys; and the Personal Qualities Necessary for Success in Missions Abroad,* trans. by W. F. Whyte, (Boston and New York: Houghton Mifflin Co., 1919; originally published 1716), p. 127. De Callieres noted another rule of thumb: "The more powerful the prince, the more suave should his diplomatist be, for since power of that kind is likely to awaken jealousy in his neighbors, the diplomat should let it speak for itself and rather use his own powers of persuasion by means of moderation to support the just rights of his prince than to vaunt his power or the extent of his dominions." *Ibid.,* p. 125.

[13] A speech given by Mrs. Charles Bohlen, "Young Foreign Service Officers' Wives," March 20, 1962. Also see, "Esther Peterson Discusses the Foreign Service Wife," *Department of State Newsletter,* No. 48 (April, 1965), p. 20.

[14] In this respect the wife's role, compared to that of her eighteenth or nineteenth century counterpart, has become more important. James Westfall Thompson and Saul K. Padover, *Secret Diplomacy, Espionage, and Cryptography, 1500–1815* (New York: Frederick Ungar Publishing Co., 1963); John W. Foster, *The Practice of Diplomacy as Illustrated in the Foreign Relations of the United States* (Boston and New York: Houghton Mifflin, 1906); Charles Roetter, *The Diplomatic Art: an Informal History of World Diplomacy* (Philadelphia: Macrae Smith, 1963). Judging from de Callieres, eighteenth century diplomatist, the role of women in eighteenth century diplomacy is more as a source of influence upon powerful men than as a source of information or as a skilled information gatherer: "If the custom of the country in which he serves permits freedom of conversation with the ladies of the court, he must on no account neglect any opportunity of placing himself and his master in a favorable light in the eyes of these ladies, for it is well known that the power of feminine charm extends to cover the weightiest resolutions of state." De Callieres, *On the Manner of Negotiating with Princes,* p. 23.

[15] While her main task is to represent the "American people" (as distinct from the American government) to the local country, she actually represents a small segment of American people to local officials. By and large she is untypical of the living standard or values of lower-class Negroes, Chinese, Italian Americans, not to mention the American insane, blind, or handicapped. There are no hominy grits every tenth night or spaghetti every twelfth, for example. For the most part she represents the life style of the upper-class Protestant East Coast. The servants, the mansion, the chauffeured car, the six-course meals represent in fact a small elite. This is, of course, equally true for the diplomats from most other countries.

[16] Mrs. George A. Morgan, "Language and the Foreign Service Wife," *Department of State Newsletter,* No. 45 (January, 1965); No. 47 (March, 1965).

[17] "Esther Peterson Discusses the Foreign Service Wife," p. 20.

[18] Morgan, "Language and the Foreign Service Wife," parentheses mine.

[19] Mrs. George A. Morgan, "The Foreign Service Wife Serves Her Country Well," *Department of State Newsletter*, No. 37 (May, 1964), p. 30.

[20] However, she went on to explain that she felt that being an ambassador's wife is a profession. "I'm still practicing my profession [she was a cultural officer in the Foreign Service before marriage] but in an unpaid and unacknowledged capacity." Of the wives sampled, slightly over half had been trained for and had practiced an occupation—typically a "cultural" one. This group included journalists, teachers, executive secretaries, a cultural officer, hospital dietitian, a public relations officer for an investment firm, musicologist, artist, and an editor. Others, while not professionally trained, took a strong interest in their hobbies of music and teaching dance. Of the occupationally trained, half said that, in a way, they were still practicing their professions. For example, one former hospital dietitian said that she practices her profession "every day in the home" and "outside the house in under-developed countries by talking over nutritional problems. . . . My college and internship training and my two years of work before marriage are very valuable for my life in the foreign service and as the mother of six children." Another, formerly an investments public relations officer reported, "I have a chance to practice my profession, as an ambassador's wife and must try to be all things to many types of people."

On the other hand, a former journalist said about keeping up her profession, "It's okay back in the United States but never while abroad." A trained nurse who said she was not continuing her profession said, "I think being an ambassador's wife is a full time job and should not be delegated to junior wives. I retain my interest by encouraging wives to participate in volunteer work at hospitals and arranging benefits for hospitals." Most agreed with one wife who warned, "If an ambassador's wife wishes to practice her profession, she can't be too careful."

[21] Bohlen, "Young Foreign Service Officers' Wives."

[22] Some wives do not feel hampered by this in their choice of friends. When asked, "What do you feel about the chances to make close friends in your present position?" one wife stationed in east Africa replied, "Excellent among those in the community who have my interests in museology and art."

[23] Bohlen, "Young Foreign Service Officers' Wives."

[24] When she travels around the country with her husband, dedicates museums, hands out school prizes, or goes to concerts where the people present are not directly involved in political decision making, she observes certain norms of dress and demeanor. Even going to the movies with her husband, she watches her appearance and behavior. One ambassador's wife commented (referring to dress), "You never know whom you'll meet when you go out, it's best to always be presentable."

[25] The official car is actually the property of the American government, not the ambassador.

[26] S. I. Hayakawa, *Symbol, Status and Personality* (New York: Harcourt, Brace and World, Inc., 1953), p. 30.

[27] *Ibid.*

[28] Scientific language is, according to Hayakawa, a "time-binding activity" in that it links the past to the future. A scientist may seek to add to the research of the past for the benefit of future scholars. Similarly diplomatic language is "time-binding" and it is also "space-binding." Two countries talk to each other through their diplomatic middlemen. Actually it is not diplomats but countries which are communicating. So to facilitate this "space-binding" function of diplomatic encounters, semantic conventions are observed.

[29] Harold Nicolson, *Diplomacy* (London and New York: Oxford University Press, 1952), chap. 10, p. 219.

[30] "It is not enough to think aright, the diplomatist must be able to translate his thoughts into the right language, and conversely he must be able to pierce behind

the language of others to their true thoughts." De Callieres, *On the Manner of Negotiating with Princes*, p. 62.

[31] To avoid an interpretation which is not intended in the covertly political language but which might be interpreted in that language, the ambassador's wife and her husband may devise certain formulas. For example, one couple who were invited to only one diplomatic function on a particular night went to that cocktail party in full dress and tuxedo and excused themselves early without need for explanation. The host, assuming the ambassador and his wife were leaving early to go to another function (which is often necessary), did not interpret the early departure in a quasi-political or personal language. The couple thus avoided offense and got home early.

[32] See Luis Moreno Salcedo, *A Guide to Protocol* (rev. ed.; Manila, Philippines: University Book Supply, 1959); and *Guide to Social Usage*; *A Guide for American Officials and Their Families* (Washington, D.C.: Department of State, Office of the Deputy Under Secretary for Administration, no date). This is required reading for foreign service wives. The major sources for this pamphlet are the official instructions of the Department of State on "Protocol, Precedence and Formalities," in *Foreign Affairs Manual*, Vol. 2, *General*, chap. 300. Much of the protocol cited was set down in the Congress of Vienna in 1815, though these rules were revised in 1961 by a meeting of plenipotentiaries of 80 countries who convened under the auspices of the United Nations.

[33] Bohlen, "Young Foreign Service Officers' Wives."

[34] Norms of dress, for example, can communicate political messages. The modest way in which early American and post-1917 Russian diplomats' wives dressed was "an expression of scorn for the pomp and flummery of bourgeois manners and dress of diplomates from other countries." See Roetter, *The Diplomatic Art*, p. 167.

[35] Hall, *The Silent Language*.

[36] Thirty-eight percent spend most of their time with local officials and/or their wives, 23 percent with American embassy wives, 8 percent with other Americans (mostly businessmen), 3 percent with their families, 10 percent with foreign envoys, 3 percent with servants (who are usually local), 3 percent with Peace Corps volunteers, 2 percent with local artists and intellectuals, 2 percent with foreign visitors, 5 percent with other local women, 2 percent with local students and 2 percent with local wives married to American officers. Three said it was "hard to tell." Altogether, 36 percent spent most of their time with other Americans of some sort or another, 12 percent with foreigners not from the assigned country, and 52 percent with locals.

[37] The average age of the career chief of mission is 53. For the political appointee it is slightly younger, 51.9. In 1963 the youngest ambassador was 38 years old. *Department of State Newsletter*, No. 33 (January, 1964), p. 18, "Anatomy of the Ambassador." The average age of the Foreign Service Officer is 41.

[38] *Social Usage Abroad, A Guide for American Officials and Their Families* (Washington, D.C.: Department of State, Office of the Deputy Under Secretary for Administration, August, 1963), p. 8.

[39] See, *The Country Team*, Department of State Publication 8193, Dept. and Foreign Service Series 136 (Washington, D.C.: U.S. Government Printing Office, 1967), p. 9. Also see Glen H. Fisher, "The Foreign Service Officer," *Annals of The American Academy of Political and Social Science* (November, 1966).

[40] It excludes female officers and lower-scale female embassy employees.

[41] If she does not actively participate, she keeps herself informed about their activities which include preparing booklets and directories, shopping guides, setting up thrift shops, holding bazaars to raise charity money, holding flower shows, teaching (usually English) or doing social work.

[42] In Paris alone there were 21 people in the agricultural attaché's office in

1967, while in Nairobi there was one man and a secretary reporting on agriculture in seven African countries. The size of the community of wives varies accordingly.

43 Robert K. Merton, "Bureaucratic Structure and Personality," *Social Theory and Social Structure* (New York: The Free Press, 1965). As Merton points out, the formal secondary group does not allow for primary relations which are disdainfully labeled as "apple polishing" or nepotism, or favoritism.

44 The emphasis is mine.

45 Parentheses mine. According to another wife, "It is easier when you're in more junior positions. The main obstacle is the necessity to maintain as even a balance as possible in one's relationship to many groups and there is also lack of time to spend intimately with individuals." W. F. Whyte has noted the same structural barriers to friendship among corporation wives. "The wife must now learn to make 'constructive' friendships, to become consciously aware of the vagaries and gradations of the social structure of business." Whyte, *Is Anybody Listening*, p. 160.

46 Bohlen, "Young Foreign Service Officers' Wives."

47 *Social Usage*, "The Personal Call," p. 4 According to protocol, everyone rises whenever the Ambassador or his wife enters a room, even when many people are present. Chiefs of mission and their wives precede others in entering or leaving rooms. And no one should leave a function before the Ambassador and his wife leave. This means that, out of courtesy to restless subordinates, the Chief of mission and his wife usually leave fairly early, in order to allow their subordinates to go home.

48 Anne Penfield, "The Ambassador's Wife," *Foreign Service Journal* (August, 1963). She continued, "Naturally this file is given to one's successor . . . ," suggesting the passing on of the social requirements to the next occupant of the role.

49 Bohlen, "Young Foreign Service Officers' Wives." She suggests to young wives, "In the junior ranks you will not have to invite senior officials; keep your entertaining simple and confine the guest list to those whom your husband should know and with whom he works."

50 Even the embassy-furnished car and chauffeur are associated with a sense of territoriality. In 1661, "The attendant of the Spanish Ambassador in London fell upon the French Ambassador's coach, killed the postillion, beat up the coachman and hamstrung two horses in order to make certain that the Spanish Ambassador's coach went first." Roetter, *The Diplomatic Art*, p. 162. While this is no longer such a symbolic object, there are still some rules of protocol attached to car seating. The official guide, *Social Usage*, suggests, "In order to have the ranking person sit there [at the place of honor on the right] it may be necessary for the junior person to enter the car first, or to go behind the car and enter from the other side," p. 23. *Social Usage* also suggests that in many countries, the right side of the sofa is "considered the seat of honor" and "should not be occupied by the junior wife or husband unless specifically invited to do so," p. 23.

51 While most of the furnishings are supplied by the State Department and are not of her choosing, the house often reflects American standard of living and customs. It has airconditioning or heating, the windows usually have screening so that rooms are free of flies and other insects; and there are carpets on the floor. Even the smells (from the furniture and the cooking) are American and make Americans feel at home and foreigners feel to some extent not at home.

52 Bohlen, "Young Foreign Service Officers' Wives."

53 Parentheses mine. Servants provide a middleman between hostess and guest, and as such the servant can protect the hostess from unwanted callers, or at least permit her some stalling.

54 De Callieres, *On the Manner of Negotiating with Princes*, p. 127, parentheses mine.

55 *Ibid.*, p. 118, parentheses mine. He elaborates, "Indeed it is the nature of

things that good cheer is a great conciliator, that is, fosters familiarity, and promotes a freedom of exchange between the guests, while the warmth of wine will often lead to the discovery of important secrets," p. 119.

56 Often the problems of seating determine who is omitted from the guest list, since protocol might seat people next to each other who are known to dislike each other or whose countries are in major disagreement on an important issue at the time.

57 The host and hostess can each have a co-hostess and co-host at their respective tables. *Social Usage*, p. 7.

58 *Ibid.*, p. 8.

59 See Kurt Wolff, *The Sociology of Georg Simmel* (New York: Free Press, 1951), p. 51. There are also certain rules of thumb concerning whom one talks with. "Talk to foreign guests and not with Embassy friends, introduce yourself to people you have not met. At dinner parties be sure to talk to your neighbor—even when language barriers exist you can usually manage something with your hands . . . or just be friendly, but above all try—a hostess cannot bear pools of silence halfway down her table." Bohlen, "Young Foreign Service Officers' Wives."

60 De Callieres, *On the Manner of Negotiating with Princes*, p. 132.

61 If it is a fairly large embassy, there may be a staff of up to five or six, one being the head steward. She may take them with her from post to post or train each staff as she meets them at a new post. In some cases, they may provide her only deep insight into the indigenous culture. One of the biggest problems with her staff is petty stealing or "borrowing." As one ambassador's wife reported, "Your staff are your biggest problem. Without their loyalty and respect you cannot entertain. In spite of this you must constantly safeguard against stealing—thus insulting them. Thievery is common. We've just caught our cook at it. The guardienne and the other steward reported it. If I fire him, two years of training in a hot kitchen goes down the drain as well as a good cook. If I keep him, the morale of the others goes down and they think it's acceptable to steal. I've learned to accept cheating up to a certain point. Cooks are hard to find in————.''

62 Louise Winfield *Living Overseas* (Washington, D.C.: Public Affairs Press, 1962). Her communication with embassy wives is similar to the advice given to junior wives: "Keep your eye on the hostess, she may need an errand done or want some information."

63 According to one ambassador's wife, "Old friends may become more precious also." Said one wife, "Maintaining friendships with old friends in the Service in previous posts, by correspondence, is one of my pleasures. Old friends have almost become my roots in this nomadic life of ours, and becoming a principal officer's wife does not change one's contact with them."

64 Louise Winfield, *ibid.*, notes, "Another thing which frequently is revealed is that in a new and strange situation family members are pulled closer together and there is a closing of the ranks," p. 96.

65 Some indication of their attitude toward one aspect of the role—the head of the hierarchy—is given in response to the question, "Which do you prefer, the role as the wife of a junior officer or that as the wife of an ambassador?" For those to whom the question applied, a fifth said they preferred the life of a junior officer; 40 percent thus preferred the Ambassador's wife from their own point of view, and 40 percent said they could not say. Thus for their husbands they were satisfied; for themselves a bit less so.

66 For example, according to protocol, one should arrive promptly at a designated time for a dinner party. Is a Ghanaian guest who arrives three hours late necessarily gesturing in the covert political language, or is he being purposely rude? Is he conforming to his own national customs, or is he covertly saying, "Conform to our customs of informal dinners and indefinite meal times now that you are in Ghana"?

6

THE DYSFUNCTIONS

AND

DISAFFECTIONS OF WORK

INTRODUCTION

If man lives by his work, so too may he sicken and die by his work, as well as suffer injuries and develop mental illnesses as a result of it. Too often we overlook the fact that man's physical and mental condition and frequently his appearance are significantly related to his occupational specialization. Many individuals wear the physical imprint of their work. The relationship between physical condition and work is often obvious and direct, but in some instances it is more subtle and less recognizable. In the case of an obvious relationship between work and physical effect, we even incorporate some recognition of it into our very language and accept it as a matter of course, although we may also tend at times to overlook or forget it by simply taking it for granted. As a case in point, consider the "flatfoot" or policeman who, according to popular belief, develops fallen arches as a result of walking his beat. Just as we have traditionally spoken of the erect posture and carriage demanded by military training as the "military bearing" when referring to a soldier, so too have we characterized the sloppier posture of the preoccupied professor as the "scholar's stoop." Of course we know that all blacksmiths had strong muscular right arms, and that agricultural workers whose necks (as well as other uncovered epidermis) become weathered and sunburned are "rednecks," and for that matter that white-collar workers often have an "office pallor" as a result of working indoors away from the direct sunlight. Boxers will eventually have "cauliflower ears" as a result of repeated blows to the head and will also unfortunately in many instances become "punch-drunk" for the same reason. Nor must we forget the "dishpan hands" of the housewife. (This was of course prior to the new miracle soaps.)

Thus we come to expect the inevitability of the physical effect of work. By our very language we recognize that work does in fact leave its physical mark on us. Manual labor will produce calloused hands just as a ballet dancer will develop muscular calves. Persons who work around loud noises sometimes become partially deaf in certain hearing ranges. And if certain types of work produce certain physical effects, conversely entry to an occupation may hinge on some physical attribute. Jockeys must, of course, be small; basketball players should ideally be tall; airlines stewardesses should neither be too short nor too tall. In the field of modeling, the "California type" model should look well fed, tanned, and natural while the "high fashion" or "Harper's Bazaar" type model must appear slender and emaciated in order to get a job. The Naval Academy at Annapolis will not admit a person to its program who is "grossly ugly." Prize fighters must meet a precise weight classification or find themselves matched with opponents far larger than themselves. For the fighters as well as the jockeys and the fashion models, to name only a few occupations, there is a constant struggle to maintain a particular weight and shape—a sort of perpetual "battle of the bulge," so to speak. The English author Sir Arthur Conan Doyle had his fictional detective hero Sherlock Holmes once correctly identify a man walking across the street from where he was standing as a retired sergeant of the Royal Marines on the basis of the individual's military carriage, regulation side-whiskers, and a "certain air of command." He also deduced from the fact that a man he met had a right hand larger than his left that he had done manual labor (a ship's carpenter as it turned out) in the past. In a similar vein, Holmes was able to identify a ship's sail maker from the location of a certain kind of callus on the palm of the individual's hand. Conan Doyle even had his fictional hero Holmes author a monograph on "the influence of a trade upon the form of the hand," including "lithotypes of the hands of slaters, sailors, corkcutters, compositors, weavers, and diamond-polishers."[1]

With regard to disease and disability, work often takes its toll in singular and unique fashions. Sales clerks and others who must remain on their feet in their work (including crap table operators), often have leg and foot complaints, including varicose veins, which are sometimes even partially disabling. Many salesmen who, of necessity, are seated behind the wheel of their car often complain of lower back pains. At a more serious level, tunnel building workers or "sandhogs" traditionally developed "caisson disease" and coal miners and rock-quarry workers have tended to be the victims of silicosis, pulmonary tuberculosis, fibrosis, and bulbous emphysema. Recently national attention has been drawn to the so-called "black lung syndrome" or "coal worker's pneumoconiosis." Recent studies have established a significantly higher rate of lung cancer among asbestos workers than among most other occupational groups. It also seems that card players and gamblers are likely to be afflicted with "blackjack dermatitis," a skin irritation caused by a substance in green felt table coverings.

Seafaring men "go down to the sea in ships" and sometimes drown, or freeze in a lifeboat if their ship sinks. Coal miners go down to the pits and tunnels and are sometimes injured, maimed, or killed there. The first reading in this chapter, Ben. A. Franklin's "The Scandal of Death and Injury in the Mines," looks at the hazards of coal mining as an occupation. Miners run the risk of entrapment in a mine and slow asphyxiation from lack of oxygen or from poisonous gas. Methane and coal dust explosions, fire and falling timbers and coal chunks all compound the dangers of working underground. Over and above the accident hazard conditions there is the ever-present danger of pneumoconiosis (black lung disease) or other respiratory ailments that result from inhaling coal dust. Many of the hazards of coal mining could be removed or reduced but, according to the author, safety improvements and other attempts to make mining a safer and less disease-prone vocation have been both few and slow in reaching the mines. This, he concludes, is the result of public apathy, governmental indifference, coal industry profit motives, and fatalism on the part of the miners themselves.

Just as physical illness or death may be a function of occupation, so too may mental illness. In referring to the military psychiatric victim of war, we speak of "shell shock" and "combat psychosis." Pathological idiosyncratic patterns, neurotic tendencies, and mental breakdowns among entertainers and persons in show business are legendary and the pressures of bureaucratic existence may produce "executive stomach" and accompanying nervous disorders. Similarly, the relationship between the monotony and the meaninglessness of work in a factory and mental malaise has long been recognized. In the next selection, "Toward an Assessment of the Mental Health of Factory Workers: A Detroit Study," Arthur Kornhauser compares the mental health of several occupational groups in the Detroit automobile industry. Classifying workers by skill level and variety in the work task within skill level, and using the mental health scores of these workers, he compared the scores of these several groups while controlling for education and age. He found in his analysis than there appears to be a "genuine" relationship between mental health and occupation. Among the groups of factory workers that he studied, it appeared that mental health was progressively poorer moving "from more skilled, responsible, varied types of work to jobs lower in these respects." Kornhauser concludes that "mental health is dependent on factors associated with the job," but also warns of attempting to single out one job-related characteristic as the principal causal factor in poor mental health. Instead he suggests that to adequately understand the relationships of a job to the worker's mental health it is necessary to "look at the entire pattern of work and life conditions" of the worker.

Many occupational endeavors endanger the practitioner with a variety of distinctive hazards both real and potential as well as expose him to conditions that may promote illness or extreme stress, tension, and anxiety. The insurance companies, in recognizing these hazards, have been able to develop some elaborate mortality tables which suggest a considerable degree of differential mortality among various occupations. Whereas the bullfighter, it seems, may be *gored* to death, the office worker may be *bored* to death. The more obvious occupational dangers may not be as significant as the latent hazards; according to statistical mortality tables, for example, it appears that the life of a musician is far more hazardous than is that of a person who washes windows on skyscrapers. The individual who travels a great deal in his work may be more prone than average to falling victim of a fatal traffic accident. In a similar fashion, the sedentary life demanded by certain occupations may be more likely to produce overweight and perhaps a coronary attack. Occupational specialization and the grim reaper would seem, then, to have a compact.

One might even say that occupation follows a person to the grave, as witness, for example, the "military funeral," complete with firing squad, flag-draped coffin, and the playing of "taps" for the soldier, while the seafaring man will, in all probability, by common custom be "committed to the deep six," sewn up in his weighted hammock.

It can be said then that health, both physical and mental, bodily condition and appearance, and perhaps even the mode and manner in which men meet their demise are all significantly affected by their occupational specialty.

Looking at another aspect of this phenomenon, we note that within the social organization of work certain persistent patterns of deviant behavior are often to be found. This relationship between work and deviant behavior is not always recognized, for the deviant behavior configurations are frequently buried, like an iceberg, beneath the surface of occupational structure.

At a surface level, we are quick to recognize the deviant occupations and the practitioners of deviant activities who pursue their work in defiance of legal code and social norm. Included here are the so-called "professional" criminals who have made a career and earn their livelihood from their criminal specialty. Although as a general rule, such occupational practitioners operate completely outside the pale of popular support, the Robin Hoods and Jessie Jameses (not to mention the more recent "Bonnie-and-Clyde" types), by only "robbing the rich" in order to be able to "help the poor," have received aid and comfort from the public on occasion and have been elevated to the pedestal of folk heroes. Other criminal occupation practitioners such as prostitutes, dope peddlers, and bootleggers have to depend on the cooperation and patronage of their customers in order to practice their trade. Moreover, the local community may view the presence of such deviant occupations as both desirable as well as necessary, and the rendering of their services as an essential component in the division of labor. Once in a dry county in the deep south, when it became evident that the leading wholesale bootlegger was contemplating retirement just prior to the Christmas season, the local newspaper ran a front page editorial openly asking the bottlegger to postpone his retirement until after the holiday season so as to not disaccommodate the public who would otherwise be shut off from their supply of "Christmas Cheer."

Many other occupations, while marginally legal, may have criminal intent as an integral part of their occupational goal, and these, perhaps even more than prostitution and bootlegging, depend on their clientele and certain segments of the population to support and tolerate their activities. Included here might be "pool hustlers," "card sharks," "B girls," medical "quacks," fortune-tellers, and spiritualists. Such persons may walk a razor thin line of legality, but they have a considerable following, especially among the poorer and less sophisticated elements of society. (The recent astrology fad, in contrast, is essentially a middle-class preoccupation.) But despite this toleration, they are frequently stigmatized as occupational deviants of an objectionable variety by much of society and especially by the so-called "respectable" elements of the population.

In addition to deviant occupations, deviant behavior in work also occurs in the form of work norm violations (which are not necessarily illegal acts) within a work system. Examples might include "rate busting," quota restriction, the use of forbidden procedures as a shortcut technique or to cover up mistakes or shoddy workmanship, and unethical professional behavior.[2] Some occupational structures or cultures appear to attract, harbor, induce, or facilitate certain kinds of deviant behavior; alcoholism among executives and carnies, narcotic addiction among physicians and nurses, marijuana smoking among musicians, and lesbianism among strippers are all illustrations of such a situation. One of the more frequently encountered forms of deviant behavior in work is that of illegal activities committed within the framework of a conventional legal occupational structure. Example of such activities include illegal rebates, pilfering, expense account padding, embezzling, misappropriation of property, and criminal misrepresentation of product—to name a few.

The first selection taking up the question of occupational deviancy is Richard Quinney's "Occupational Structure and Criminal Behavior: Prescription Violation by Retail Pharmacists." Although there are many professional aspects of pharmacy operation, most of its occupational activities occur in a business establishment—the drugstore. Accordingly, the pharmacist often must attempt to play two occupational roles—a professional role and a business role. Quinney hypothesized that such a role dilemma and its attendant strain are structural components of retail pharmacy and "that prescription violation may result, depending upon the individual mode of adaptation." Using interview data from two groups of pharmacists, one consisting of known prescription violators and the other of non-violators, Quinney concluded that prescription violators tended more to have a business orientation while non-violators tended to have more of a professional or professional-business orientation. The business-oriented pharmacists stressed "the merchandising aspects of pharmacy" and were "primarily interested in monetary gains." They also felt less bound by professional norms. Quinney concluded that prescription violation appeared to be related to the structure of the pharmacy occupation and was an "expression of that structure." It was his feeling that "the structure of the occupation and criminal behavior within the occupation can be better understood if they are considered together."

In the next reading on deviant behavior and work, "The Informal 'Code' of Police Deviancy," Ellwyn R. Stoddard provides some insights concerning deviant activities among policemen, or "Blue-Coat Crime" as he calls it. According to Stoddard, some policemen engage in a variety of illegal activities, including "shopping" (larceny), extortion, bribery, and shakedowns, as well as unethical practices such as mooching, chiseling, and practicing favoritism. The police recruits are socialized into these illegal or unethical practices of the "informal code," for the policemen who practice the "code" would feel threatened if they failed to effectively socialize the new recruits. Either exceeding the limits of the "code" or failing to conform elicits sanctions from the group. These deviant patterns were encouraged and maintained by various group processes. According to Stoddard, deviancy of this variety found in a police department "is a reflection of values which are habitually practiced and accepted within that community."

As we have seen from earlier chapters, for many individuals—especially those who occupy professional or other high prestige occupations—work may be a central life interest, a source of significant social and psychological gratification, and a stimulating and pleasurable pastime. For many other persons, however, work may fail to provide either intrinsic stimulation, social adulation, or personal satisfaction. For such persons work may, on the contrary, provide tedium or stress and tension, be a source of embarassment or debasement, or be disruptive of their personal, familial, and social lives. The instance of the monotonous and stultifying nature of assembly line work and other menial forms of work is well documented. Some experiments with pigeons several years ago revealed that the birds could be trained to detect cracks in metal castings as they passed by on a moving conveyor belt. A task that can be adequately performed by a pigeon can hardly hold much excitement or challenge for a man. Several years ago in a tour of a battery plant, the editor came across an instance where an assembly line worker who had formerly had the job of moving carbon blocks from one conveyor belt to another had discovered by accident that by holding her finger in a particular position just above one of the belts, she could cause the carbon blocks to ricochet to the other conveyor belt. Armed with this discovery, the following day she devised two sticks that accomplished the same ricochet movement of carbon blocks that she had been able to effect with her finger. A simple device made of two sticks was doing her job better than she could do it. When the plant superintendent discovered what the worker had done, he removed her from the line, thereby saving cost on the battery assembly. (She was, however, given another task on another line.) Obviously a job like this that calls for machine-like behavior provides little in the way of intrinsic gratification. As Harvey Swados has put it:

> The plain truth is that factory work is degrading. It is degrading to any man who ever dreams of doing something worthwhile with his life; and it is about time we face the fact. . . .
> Almost without exception, the men with whom I worked on the assembly line last year felt like trapped animals. Depending on their age and personal circumstances, they were either resigned to their fate, furiously angry at *themselves* for what they were doing, or desperately hunting other work that would pay as well and in addition offer some variety, some prospect of change and betterment. They were sick of being pushed around by harried foremen (themselves more pitied than hated), sick of working like blinkered donkeys, sick of being dependent for their livelihood on a maniacal production-merchandising setup, sick of working in a place where there was no spot to relax during the twelve minute rest period.[3]

It has been said that at one time the craftsman might psychologically "own" his product. It is difficult to imagine "owning" a tightened wheel nut on the left rear wheel of green Oldsmobile two-door automobiles if that happens to be one's highly specialized and routinized task (or for that mat-

ter "owning" tightened jar tops on fruit jars, at the rate of 48,000 per shift
—a job this editor once had).

Some work may be demeaning and thus unsatisfying because it involves
dirty or disagreeable tasks or because it requires a subservient posture
toward the clientele being served. In other instances, work may be unsatisfying or stressful because of status dilemmas or role conflicts. In
T. E. Levitin's article, "Role Performance and Role Distance in a Low-
Status Occupation: The Puller," attention is focused on the plight of the
puller, the store salesman who works outside on the street in front of a
store and attempts to attract customers into the establishment. The puller
often works in rundown commercial areas, is paid a relatively modest salary,
and views his occupational role as one of low status. The puller must attempt to interact with pedestrians who are walking past the store, in the
hope of luring them into the store with offers of exceptional values in
merchandise. He uses a variety of approaches in his encounters with these
people, including humor directed at himself, self-abasement, affecting an
accent similar to that of the passers-by, and ludicrous flamboyant gestures.
He must deal with any kind of person regardless of sex, race, or ethnic
background and is frequently rebuffed, ignored, or insulted. To be effective
the puller may have to feign deference or demean himself to people he
considers to be his inferiors. As one puller said: "I havta act like niggers
are as good as me to make a sale." Faced with the difficulty of maintaining
self-esteem and an acceptable self-image in the face of having to relate on
an equal basis to persons perceived as inferior, and to play a subordinate
and deferential role to persons who perceive themselves as superior to him,
the puller relies on the mechanisms of *role distance*. Role distance was
evidenced by such manifestations as self-communication, frequent retreats
from the role, and communication with the interviewer on a detached-
from-the-role basis. The puller, in effect, separates himself from his role.
It is he as the *puller* and not he as *himself* who is interacting with the
passers-by. By developing appropriate adaptive defense mechanisms, the
puller is able to handle the work discomforts resulting from his perceived
low status and threatened self-esteem.

Looking at another situation of occupational discomfort, Harold L. Nix
and Frederick L. Bates, in their "Occupational Role Stresses: A Structural
Approach," examine the situation of the vocational agriculture teachers.
Using the stresses experienced by "Vo-Ag" teachers as examples, they develop a conceptual typology of five analytically distinct types of structural
stress, including role conflict, role inadequacy, role frustration, role superfluity, and role incongruity. The Vo-Ag teacher is under the supervision
of both the public high school and the state-federal Vo-Ag organization.
Accordingly he is "subject to both bureaucratic pressures and pressures
from his clientele," and is also "expected to perform multiple functions" in

his job. To further compound his work situation, the Vo-Ag teacher is legally charged with the responsibility of training "present and prospective farmers for proficiency in farming," in the face of rapidly changing economic conditions that may limit farming opportunities in the future. Despite these stresses, the Vo-Ag teacher still expresses role satisfaction. This appears to be partly the result of several mechanisms for alleviating the structural strains, as well as other compensating rewards available to the Vo-Ag teacher, such as a "sense of public service" and "recognition."

The military intelligence agent is also subject to certain role structured discomforts in connection with his work, as Ellwyn R. Stoddard points out in the final article in this chapter. Some of the strains associated with the agent's role revolve around the particular dress required in the performance of his job. Unlike other military personnel, the intelligence agent wears civilian attire, which frees him in large measure from "restrictive military courtesy customs," and lets him better assume, on occasion, a "cover" identity. Some officers experience deprivation "of their privileged position by the standardization of civilian clothing." The civilian clothing forces a kind of equalitarianism on the officers vis-à-vis the enlisted personnel because military courtesy is usually directed at the badges of rank rather than the bearer. Enlisted agents, on the other hand, enjoy this anonymity of rank when interacting with regular military officers as part of their assignment and enjoy the "increased status achieved while operating as an agent in the field." When the agent assumes his enlisted identity at headquarters, he may be required to perform menial maintenance tasks appropriate to his rank and he may experience role ambivalence strain. This problem of rank identity may in turn lead to interactional difficulties with both enlisted and officer personnel. Persons who deal with agents are uncomfortable when they do not know the agents' ranks because they do not know how to appropriately relate to them.

The assumed "cover" may cause special problems in that the agent may have to give up certain military privileges in the process of taking on a new civilian identity. If the agent's cover is "blown" it may prove awkward for him thereafter to interact with people with whom he had been dealing under the guise of that cover.

The military intelligence agent lives in two or more social worlds and is marginal to all. Trying to cope with multiple and contradictory or conflicting role demands often results in occupational role strains and work discomfort.

The dysfunctions and disaffections of work are simply the other side of the coin, and any serious inquiry into the social nature of work must, of necessity, include an examination of the unpleasant and undesirable dimensions therein. The selections in this last chapter were included for the purpose of acquainting the neophyte student of work with the fact that in some situations and under certain circumstances, man may fall casualty to his work, use his work as a device to victimize others, or find that work is psychologically stressful or ego damaging to himself, as well as erosive and disruptive to the social enterprise.

Footnotes

[1] Sir Arthur Conan Doyle, *Famous Tales of Sherlock Holmes* (New York: Dodd, Mead, & Company, 1958), pp. 174–75.

[2] See, for example, Joseph Bensman and Israel Gerver, "Crime and Punishment in the Factory: The Function of Deviancy in Maintaining the Social System," *American Sociological Review*, XXVIII, No. 4 (August 1963), 588–98.

[3] Harvey Swados, "The Myth of the Happy Worker," in *A Radical's America* (Boston: Little, Brown and Company, 1962), p. 117.

Work and Physical and Mental Illness and Injury

The Scandal of Death and Injury in the Mines

More Than 120,000 Miners Have Died Violently

BEN A. FRANKLIN
The New York Times
(Washington Correspondent)

Of the 54 men in the mine, only two who happened to be in some crevices near the mouth of the shaft escaped with life. Nearly all the internal works of the mine were blown to atoms. Such was the force of the explosion that a basket then descending, containing three men, was blown nearly 100 feet into the air. Two fell out and were crushed to death, and a third remained in, and, with the basket, was thrown some 70 to 80 feet from the shaft, breaking both his legs and arms.

These sentences matter-of-factly describing the pulverization of a shift of coal miners, including the three men grotesquely orbited out of the mine shaft as if launched from a missile silo, are from the first detailed record of an American mine disaster. Antiquity probably explains the nursery rhyme quality—*"two fell down and broke their crowns . . ."* For this earliest remembered mine catastrophe, in the Black Heath pit near Richmond, Va., occurred March 18, 1839.

A primitive time, no doubt. The nation was then so new that Martin Van Buren, warming his feet at the coal-burning grates in the White House, was the first President to have been born a United States citizen. The daguerreotype was introduced here that year by Samuel F. B. Morse, while awaiting the issuance of a patent on his telegraph. Half the coal-producing states were not yet in the Union.

The coal mines, on the threshold of fueling a manufacturing explosion that was to make this country an unmatched industrial power, produced barely one million tons in 1839, less than 1/500th of the output today. In the absence of all but the crudest technology, men relying on the death flutterings of caged canaries to warn them of imminent suffocation obviously would die in the mines. Some mines employed suicidal specialists known as "cannoneers," whose mission was to crawl along the tunnel floors under a wet canvas before a shift, igniting "puffs" of mine gas near the roof with an upraised candle. Dead miners were not even counted. Their enormous casualty rate was not archived until less than 100 years ago.

A glimpse into this dim crevice of American industrial history is necessary to put into perspective the myths and realities of the men who work in the mines today. For the real story of coal is not its multiplying inanimate statistics—tons and carloadings and days lost in strikes. It is the agony of those men—a tale as old as Black Heath and one that is so full of extravagantly evil personalities and atrocious acts that Charles Dickens would have loved to tell it. For behind and beneath the mountains of the Appalachian coalfield, miners have remained since Black Heath the most systematically exploited and expendable class of citizens (with the possible exception of the American Indian and the Negro) in this country.

The story at last may have an unDickensian ending. For now, coal miners can see light at the end of the tunnel. In this 1969 spring, 130 years after the Black Heath disaster, the mining industry may finally agree to pay the modest cost of keeping its work force alive, of abandoning the embedded idea that men are cheaper than coal. And—small pittance—we may all be involved in helping pay what it costs to write this long delayed postscript to the industrial revolution; the price of bringing miners into the 20th century probably will appear, as we shall see, as pennies on our electric bills.

In the context of technological advancement in nearly every other area of human enterprise, very little has changed for men who go down to the mines in shafts. Only four months ago, 78 coal miners were trapped and killed below ground in West Virginia in one of the most volcanic eruptions of explosion and fire in the memory of Federal mine inspectors. As at Black Heath, the explosion at the Consolidation Coal Company's 27-square-mile No. 9 mine at Farmington, W. Va., almost certainly was caused by an ignition of methane gas, a volatile, highly flammable, usually odorless and invisible hydrocarbon gas liberated from virgin coal.

At Consol No. 9, a modern, "safe" mine operated by one of the wealthy giants of the industry, the daily methane emission was 8 million cubic feet, enough to supply the heating and cooking needs of a small city if it were captured and sold. The explosion hazard was dealt with there as it is generally in mining today, by only modestly more sophisticated methods than those at Black Heath.

Fresh air is drawn into the mines by giant fans and circulated and directed constantly through the honeycomb of tunnels by means of doors, ducts or sometimes by curtains called brattices (miners call them "braddishes"). The intake air is supposed to dilute and, by law, "render harmless or carry away" the methane and hold the mine atmosphere to less than the legal limit of 1 percent gas. Unless coal dust is mixed with it—in which case the explosion threshold drops significantly—methane will not ignite or explode in concentrations of less than 5 percent. Miners live and die today on a margin of 4 percentage points—or less if coal dust is suspended in the air.[1]

It is known that the giant electric mining machines in use for the last 20 years—machines that chew up and claw coal from the face with rotary bits the size of railroad wheels—churn up an immense amount of dust. The machines have water sprays to settle the dust. But the machines' rapid rate of advance through the seam also liberates much methane.

The first explosion at Consol No. 9 came at 5:25 A.M., Nov. 20, during the cateye shift. It was a day after the passage over northern West Virginia of a cold front accompanied by an abrupt drop in barometric pressure. In the primitive mythology of mine safety, these natural events—the arrival of cold, dry air and a barometric low, which increases the methane liberation in a mine—have been associated for years with disasters. The legendary great mine explosions, from Monongah and Darr in 1907, Rachel & Agnes in 1908 and on up to Orient No. 2 in 1951, have occurred in November and December and in cold, dry weather. The dry air dehumidifies a mine and sets coal dust in motion.

Every fall through 1967, the United Mine Workers Journal had published a fraternal warning to union brothers to observe special precautions in "the explosion season." But, no research having been done in a century of such meteorological coincidences, the industry can and does take no account of what it, therefore, regards as a folklore factor—which might interfere with production. The U.M.W. Journal had not got around to running the 1968 warning when Consol No. 9 blew up. "We figured afterward it would be no use," a Journal editor said later.

No one yet knows what death befell the 78 men in No. 9. Miners who survive the shock wave, heat and afterdamp (carbon monoxide) of an underground explosion are instructed to barricade themselves in good air, if any, and await rescue. But during the nine days and nights that rescue teams stood by helplessly on the surface at Farmington, there were at least 16 further explosions in the mine. The first blast had burst up 600 feet through the portals and ventilation shafts, blowing the internal works of the mine to atoms and knocking out ventilation circuits. At the top, the main shaft became the muzzle of a mammoth subterranean cannon. The massive headframe, a trestled structure of bridge-size steel I-beams that supported the main hoist, was blown apart. For days, a boiling plume of poisonous black smoke alternately belched from the shaft and then unaccountably reversed its flow and inhaled, bursting forth again with renewed detonations below.

Finally, on Nov. 29, all five shafts and portals at the mine were sealed —capped and made airtight with tons of rock, steel and concrete. Not for months, until engineers are certain that restoring ventilation will not reignite coked embers and trigger the millions of cubic feet of methane collecting in the primordial atmosphere below, will Farmington's dead be disinterred from their gassy grave. The same mine was sealed for more than a year following a less violent explosion in 1954 that killed 16 men (including one, Black Heath-style, topside near the mine mouth), and fires continued to burn in sealed sections of the mine even after production was resumed.

If entombing a mine fire to control it seems primitive in this day of chemical fire fighting agents and automatic deluge sprinkler systems, it is futuristic, compared with the industry's performance in disaster *prevention*. There have been profitable technological advances in the extraction of coal from the seam, and today the industry is on the brink of such a long, secure production boom that big oil companies, with some of the sharpest eyes for markets and profits in the business world, are buying up and merging with coal companies at a rapid rate. But production economies in the past have more often than not been at the expense of human economies, and Big Oil may be surprised to find itself saddled with coal's amazing insensitivity to mayhem and death. It was the fatalistic acceptance of Farmington more than the disaster itself (President Nixon has since criticized this acceptance of death as "as much a part of the job as the tools and the tunnels") that finally started the mine-safety revolution.

At first, at the daily post-explosion news conferences in Consol's cinderblock company store near Farmington (many miners are *still today* in debt to their employers' merchandising subsidiaries for nearly a full paycheck before they are paid), William Poundstone, Consol's executive vice president for mining operations, insisted that the mine was "only technically gassy." W. R. Park, a senior Federal mine inspector familiar for years with the mine, insisted it was "extremely gassy," and John Roberts, a Consol public relations man, called it "excessively gassy." Roberts, a master of malapropism who greeted the news corps before one vigil news conference by asking cheerily, "Are all the bodies here?", also described the No. 9 explosion hazard as "something that we have to live with."

Then came the parade of V.I.P.'s. U.M.W. president W. A. (Tony) Boyle came to the mine head not only to congratulate consol on being "one of the better companies as far as cooperation and safety are concerned," but to add that if this "safe" mine blew up, "you can imagine what the rest are like." "As long as we mine coal," said Boyle, the philosophical miners' ombudsman, "there is always this inherent danger of explosion." The then assistant Secretary of the Interior, J. Cordell Moore, the department's top minerals man, flew up from Washington to add that "unfortunately—we don't understand why these things happen—but they do happen," and to venture that "the company here has done all in its power to make this a safe mine." (In fact, Moore's own Bureau of Mines had reported substandard rock dusting at Consol No. 9—the most basic of explosion-prevention measures involves rendering coal dust inert with 65 percent crushed limestone—in all 24 of its inspections there since 1963. The bureau had cited No. 9 for 25 other safety violations since December, 1966. Moore probably saw nothing unusual in that because violations are the norm in most mines.)

Hulett C. Smith, then the Governor of West Virginia, also stood before the television cameras and observed more in sadness than in anger that "we must recognize that this is a hazardous business and what has occurred here is one of the hazards of being a miner."

With that, the fuse, delayed so long, finally blew in Washington. The then Secretary of the Interior, Stewart L. Udall, after eight years of more concern for California redwoods than for miners, denounced the whole system of coal mining—the technological *and* moral systems—as "unacceptable." As an astonished layman, Udall noted that Consol was mining "in an area that really is a low-grade gas field" and that "obviously it is not a solution that is completely adequate to dilute the gas by pumping in air." Within three weeks, Udall summoned a national coal-safety conference which turned out to be one of the most amazing gatherings in bureaucratic history. In a Soviet-style mood of confession, Udall publicly admitted that "we have accepted, even condoned, an attitude of fatalism that belongs to an age darker than the deepest recess of any coal mine. At every level of responsibility, from the individual miner to the highest councils of Government, we have looked with horror on the specters of death and disease that haunt our mines. Then we have shrugged our shoulders and said to ourselves, 'Well, coal mining is an inherently hazardous business' or 'It's too bad, of course, but as long as coal is mined men inevitably will die underground.' These easy rationalizations are no longer acceptable in this time in history."

The stubborn Black Heath syndrome—so costly in human life and so profitable to the industry—finally was broken. Within a week, Bureau of Mines Director John F. O'Leary, on the job one month, issued orders to his inspectors. They were to cease immediately giving prior notification of impending inspections to the operators, a practice known for years to encourage a sudden, temporary kind of mine housecleaning for the benefit of the inspector—"baking a cake," one inspector called it. They were to cease reviewing mine violation reports with owners. Where violations occurred involving imminent danger of explosion, they were no longer merely to write them down as before, they were to close the mine. The list was startling for what it said about past practices.

It is hard to tell which is more gripping—the penny-pinching, corner-cutting and profiteering waste of human life in mines still operated today —Black Heath-style—with bland abandon of what the U.S. Bureau of Mines calls "ordinary regard for safety," or the callous result, the history of human carnage in the mines. The record to date, even the most contemporary chapters of it, is appalling. In the 100 years that partial records of fatal mine accidents have been kept (the early figures are incomplete) more than 120,000 men have died violently in coal mines, an average of 100 every month for a century. The total does not include those who died of what passes for "natural causes" in work that is as notoriously hazardous to health as it is to life and limb. Today, among men aged 60 to 64, the "natural" death rate of miners is eight times that of workers in any other industrial occupation.

Chronic lung disease may, in fact, turn out to be a far worse killer of miners than accidents. The U.S. Public Health Service, in unfinished research that is 25 years behind completed medical findings in British mines, has recently documented that coal dust—not the rock dust associated for decades with miners' silicosis—has become perhaps the pre-eminent threat to survival in the mines.

A prevalence study completed in 1965 found that, conservatively, 100,000 active and retired American coal miners suffered from the progressive, gasping breathlessness associated with prolonged inhalation of fine coal dust, a condition known (from autopsy observation) as "black lung" or pneumoconiosis. The U.M.W. estimates that in the 20 years that electric mining machines have been churning up greater and greater clouds of dust at least one million men have been exposed to an occupational disease whose ravages do not stop with removal to a dust-free environment.

The black-lung hazard—as the coal industry and physicians in its employ constantly point out—is as yet a qualitatively and quantitatively uncertain threat to life. It is real enough, however, to have caused more than 30,000 West Virginia miners, normally among the last in the industry to engage in wildcat strikes, to walk off their jobs for three weeks in February of this year [1969] to demand that the State Legislature include black lung in the list of injuries and diseases for which disabled miners are eligible to collect workmen's compensation benefits. Until then, only three coal-producing states—Alabama, Virginia and Pennsylvania—authorized work-men's compensation payments (generally financed by the industry) to black-lung victims, and only Pennsylvania has paid any claims. (In Penn-sylvania, the benefits are paid for by the taxpayers, *not* the industry, which may explain how the legislation survived there. Coal has a history of very aggressive lobbying to protect its economic interest.)

In West Virginia's Statehouse last month, a doctor testifying in support of the industry's proposal of further medical studies of black lung before changing the compensation law "in haste," charged that Drs. I. E. Buff, Donald L. Rasmussen and Hawey Wells, the three crusading physicians in that state who had galvanized the miners to strike for health reform, had done more damage as "alarmists" than the disease itself. There was nothing more pathetic, the lachrymose industry witness testified, than a coal miner told to quit the only work he knows just because he is a little breathless. It was a Dickensian performance.

The coal operators, or some of them, have taken the position that pneumoconiosis does not exist. But sudden violence in the mines has been documented monotonously since Black Heath. Last year, alone, 309 miners died in accidents—"needlessly," according to O'Leary, the new and aggres-sively safety-conscious director of the Bureau of Mines—and the miners' death and injury rates, already the highest of any industry, are on the rise this year.

The injury *severity* rate in mines, also the highest, is two and a half times that of lumbering, nearly four times that of trucking. Since records of nonfatal accidents began to be archived in 1930, the number of men temporarily or permanently disabled digging coal has risen to 1.5 million. Today, a miner surviving a lifetime in coal (and there is one chance in 12 that he will not) can expect three or four lost-time injuries, not counting one chance in 5 or 10 of serious and eventually fatal lung disease.

Mining, like prostitution, is one of the oldest occupations in the world and is probably as impossible to stop. From the beginning, coal has been a curse on the land from whence it came, blighting the landscape with strip mines and culm banks and polluted streams, extracting for absentee owners vast fortunes from Appalachian states that are today synonymous with poverty, and plunging generations into despair.

But the scandal of gratuitous death and injury in the mines—almost all of it recognized, as the Interior Department report put it recently, as the result of the operators' "tendency to cut safety corners when profits are low and ignore good safety practices when profits are high"—has finally reached the point at which a Republican Administration in Washington is talking about limiting coal production to save lives.

In testimony this month supporting the sudden rush of mine-safety bills in Congress following the explosion at Farmington, this radical notion was put forth by none other than Secretary of the Interior Walter J. Hickel. "It is clear that our society can no longer tolerate the cost in human life and human misery that is exacted in the mining of this essential fuel," Hickel said. "Unless we find ways to eliminate that intolerable cost, we must inevitably limit our mining of coal, which has an almost inexhaustible potential for industrial, economic and social good."

Republican coal barons must have rolled in their graves. Even from Democratic Administrations, this most destructive of industries had never received such a radical warning. In fact, Democrats in Congress have been the protectors of the industry's economic interests over the survival interests of its workers.

In 1941, at the end of three decades during which miners died at an average rate of better than 2,000 a year, a series of terrible disasters which had killed 276 men during the closing months of 1940 finally forced passage of the so-called Coal Mine Inspection and Investigation Act. It was conceded, as the Bureau of Mines timidly put it then, that "speed of operation and demand for maximum tonnage at a minimum cost resulted in a neglect of ordinary safety measures."

In 1941, when technology in the United States had advanced to the threshold of the atomic era, the gross and calculated neglect of ordinary prudence in the powder-house atmosphere of coal mines was evidenced by the fact that barely half the underground coal miners had been equipped with battery-powered electric cap lamps, approved by the Bureau of Mines for the absence of spark hazards. Incredibly, the rest still wore carbide lamps, which gave their light by generating acetylene gas and emitting an open, two-inch jet of flame.

In 1941, half the mines still used unstable black powder for blasting rather than the safer "permissible" explosives recommended for 30 years by the bureau. The carbide lamps were handy for lighting fuses. Some mines had advanced to the employment of "shot firers," solitary men whose job was to shoot down the drilled coal after everyone else had left the mine. It was a concession to modernity. If the mine blew up, only one man was lost.

Everyone knew that disasters could be stopped. "In view of the present knowledge of preventing explosions, disasters are inexcusable and discredit the mining industry," the Bureau of Mines said in 1940. Everyone knew that more improvements in the feeble state mining laws were being blocked than passed. But Congress heeded the industry's states' rights argument. The 1941 act gave the Bureau of Mines for the first time authority to enter and inspect mines and write reports containing noncompulsory safety recommendations, but no powers of enforcement. The states would take care of that.

Since 1910, when the Bureau of Mines was established, its engineers have been testing and recommending to the industry as approved or disapproved—as "permissible" or "nonpermissible" (words that convey more authority than the bureau had then or has today to require their use)—a whole range of mining equipment, including explosives and electric wiring, lights, drills, cutting machines and haulage devices. Such safety-designed machinery is obviously the key to disaster prevention in mines full of a mixture of inflammable methane gas and explosive coal dust.

Yet, nearly half the explosions—835 miners dead—between May, 1941, when the bureau got its authority to inspect and recommend, and July, 1952, when Congress next amended the mine-safety law, were caused by electric arcs from nonpermissible mine machinery. Most of the rest involved nonpermissible—but still not illegal—use of explosives.

Unbelievably, when the misnamed Federal Coal Mine Safety Act of 1952 finally emerged from the coal lobby's permissible cutting machine, it contained a "grandfather clause" which allowed the indefinitely continued use of knowingly dangerous nonpermissible electrical machinery "if, before the effective date of this section . . . the operator of such mine owned such equipment . . . or had ordered such equipment." The law also set up two classes of mines—gassy and nongassy—and it stretched the loophole for nonpermissible equipment even further for the 85 percent of mine owners lucky enough to meet the nongassy standard.

In effect, Congress told the mine operators that "if you were creating an avoidable explosion hazard before we passed this law, it's all right to go on doing so until the dangerous machinery wears out." Today, this means that spark-hazard machines—some of them rebuilt twice and three times over under the same serial numbers—are still in use in some mines 17 years after the law was passed. A count by the Bureau of Mines in 1967, when the law had been on the books 15 years, showed 1,117 pieces of nonpermissible electrical equipment in use in 159 mines.

The 1952 mine-safety act may have been one of the great legislative mirages of all time. It specifically exempted small mines, those with fewer than 15 employes. Although the small mines were depicted in the industry's testimony as too inefficient and limited in capital resources to bear the cost of retooling for the most basic disaster prevention, their number immediately doubled after the law was passed. Large mines were simply separated into smaller units to evade the law. (In 1966, the small mines were finally brought in—with all "grandfather clauses" still intact.)

Moreover, the law was deliberately written to apply to, and to give Federal mine inspectors jurisdiction over, only certain kinds of "major disasters"—defined by Congress as those killing five or more miners in one stroke. More than 90 percent of mine deaths then occurred in lonely ones, twos and threes. Far more than half were caused by rock falls from the mine roof, largely at the working face. The 1952 law established roof-control standards, but only for established tunnels used as haulageways where such accidents were least common.

Having extended Federal safety jurisdiction to the kinds of "major disasters" that made the news wires and brought discrediting publicity, Congress emphasized that the new law was *not* to protect the miners from "the lack of, or inadequacy of, guards or protective devices." It was totally silent on hazards to health.

In signing the act into law, former President Truman obviously did not overstate the facts in observing that "I consider it my duty to point out its defects so that the public will not be misled into believing that this is a broad-gauge accident-prevention measure . . . I am advised that loopholes in the law were provided to avoid any economic impact on the coal-mining industry."

Congress has considered mine-safety legislation only three times in the last three decades. But in the years between enactments, there was activity. In 1962, after explosions in the Robena and Compass mines had killed 59 men, President Kennedy commissioned a task force to review the situation. Its report concluded that the industry's continuing disregard of the most basic hazards to life and limb deserved Congressional attention. For one thing, the task force proposed to put a deadline—one year after enactment of an implementing amendment by Congress—on the nonpermissible machinery "grandfather clause." It also noted that Britain, producing only a fraction of the coal output of the United States, was spending more than twice as much on mine health research.

But then in a series of private conferences with Bureau of Mines and Interior Department officials, the Bituminous Coal Operators Association, the union-negotiating arm of the coal industry, persuaded them to recommend to Congress a "grandfather clause" deadline of *five* years. Since Congress took no action on it, the B.C.O.A. had another opportunity last year to persuade the Bureau of Mines to propose an even further extension to *ten* years. The capitulation was so flagrant that the White House, overseeing the draftsmanship of the 1968 mine-safety bill, demanded its exclusion from the bill, which went up to Congress in September. It died without hearings.

Other capitulations to the industry have perpetuated the Bureau of Mines's reputation as the submissive captive of the industry it is supposed to police. As recently as a year ago, a long-proposed revision of the 1952 law specifically requiring diversion of a minimum flow of dust- and gas-diluting forced air ventilation to the working face of coal mines—a point beyond the last moving air current in the established workings—was dropped by the bureau upon the B.C.O.A.'s complaint that it would be too costly.

It has been known for years that progressive contamination of mine ventilation air—a pickup of dangerous amounts of methane or coal dust, or both—results from coursing air from one working section of a mine to another before routing it to the surface. The practice is known to have caused explosions and deaths. Yet a year ago the B.C.O.A. was still dickering privately with the bureau, demanding language in the bureau's proposals for tougher mine ventilation standards which would say that if it cost too much to provide a separate "split" of air to each active working place it would not be required until after "a reasonable time"—not, of course, defined.

It is not that any of these proposals were new. The industry could claim no element of surprise—except at the idea of being compelled to adopt them after so long a history of lethal *laissez-faire*. Mine technology has been equal to all of these proposed measures for at least all of this century—for 101,000 mine deaths.

The inclusive almanac of mine disasters published by the Bureau of Mines in 1960 (it is now out of print) says that the violently explosive and unpredictable characteristics of suspended coal dust in mines were known as long ago as 1886. A team of mining engineers which visited all the major coalfields in 1908, a year after the worst mine explosion in American history had killed 362 men at Monongah, W. Va., published a detailed report identifying every source of all the subsequent mine disasters (72,501 deaths—1909 through 1968) and recommending disaster-prevention standards which are *still* not observed.

While lobbying privily against safety, the industry has publicly promoted the idea that the death and multilation of its workers was a cost of doing business. It got a depletion allowance on its taxes. Its workers got none for their depletion. The industry reaction to disaster was in the brave tradition of "what can you expect in an inherently risky business"—*and* with some of the most effective lobbying in legislative history to perpetuate the trade-off of cheap life for cheap coal. And it has not been alone.

Even on the left in this medieval atmosphere, the miners' union, the United Mine Workers of America, has been so concerned with helping the industry survive its postwar slump and with preserving coal's low-cost competitive advantage over other basic fuels—oil, natural gas and nuclear energy—that it long ago sacrificed what could have been the leadership of a mine-safety crusade for high wages, mechanized high production, and the highest accident rate of any industry.

Some of the accidents were no accident. In 1947, the U.M.W. in Illinois was found to have voluntarily signed a labor contract with coal operators in that state whose terms forbade the union from seeking improvements in Illinois' mine-safety law, upon which the industry placed such store in opposing greater Federal control. The Federal law of 1941, then in effect, was no threat to the cheapest production economies; the 1941 act had been so considerate of the industry's faith in state regulation that Federal mine inspectors were denied enforcement powers.

Since 1946, moreover, the U.M.W. had become locked in an embrace with the operators nationally. Through the 1946 coal labor contract, which set up the U.M.W. Welfare and Retirement Fund and financed it by an industry royalty—now 40 cents a ton for all coal taken out of union mines —the U.M.W. also acquired an immense interest in production. The Welfare and Retirement Fund collects income from *operating* mines, not from those harried by mine inspectors or closed down for safety violations.

The U.M.W.'s obvious conflicts of interest are a legacy of John L. Lewis, the 89-year-old former president. Lewis's postwar decision to help the coal industry survive by sacrificing 400,000 miners' jobs to mechanization in return for the company royalties was regarded then as a modernizing act of industrial statesmanship. But it established alliances that obviously are not in the best interests—on mine safety, if nothing else—of the rank-and-file membership. For example, under Lewis the U.M.W. bought control of the National Bank of Washington, a profitable sideline that has furthered the appearance, if not the fact, of shared interests by making loans to coal companies.

Since Congress was no help, in 1946 the Interior Department, which was then operating the mines under President Truman's strike-induced Federal seizure order, negotiated with the unions (as a condition in the contract) safety standards unobtainable by other means. Compliance with the contract's so-called Mine Safety Code, which incorporates many of the reforms talked about since the early nineteen-hundreds, is monitored by Federal mine inspectors. But its enforcement depends on the union, through its contractual right to withdraw men from mines in violation of the code.

Compliance, according to Bureau of Mines Director O'Leary, "leaves much to be desired." The compliance average in 20 of the largest mines is 65 percent, O'Leary has told Congressional committees, but in some states (depending on coal operator attitudes and union militance) it is as low as 30 percent and in one state as low as 7 percent. The U.M.W.'s "safety division" at its headquarters in Washington consists of one man.

The Welfare and Retirement Fund is not the only loser when the men walk out of an unsafe mine. The miners lose wages. When I asked him several months ago whether the U.M.W. had considered negotiating with the companies a requirement that they pay regular wages to men who left a shift while demonstrable code violations were corrected, the U.M.W.'s

Boyle, a slight, normally combative Irishman from Montana, told me that that would be impossible because even among miners there were "lazy men"; there would be abuses to get pay for no work. Later, in a safety proposal prepared by the U.M.W., the union finally supported the idea that miners should be paid for time off the job if *a Federal inspector* closed a mine.

But more than any other witnesses on this year's crop of catch-up mine-safety bills, Boyle has agreed with the industry's position. On the proposed revision that Secretary Hickel and O'Leary have called the reform of "paramount importance," Boyle's stand is significantly less reformist than the industry's. In view of the miserable record of Congressional inaction and protection of the industry, the Administration this year is asking Congress to give the Secretary of the Interior the flexibility of administrative rule-making authority. After hearings, *he* would establish the safety standards. There would be the right of appeal. It is the system in use since 1938 in nearly every other area of Federal regulatory activity, and the coal industry now says it will go along with it if the Secretary's authority is suitably circumscribed to prevent "arbitrary" decisions. Boyle, however, has said he "would rather take our chances with Congress."

Those chances this year are very good indeed, partly because Boyle himself has underlined the unequal forces working for mine safety in the private sector. The U.M.W. is clearly embarrassed by the reformist zeal of what it calls "Johnny-come-lately experts" since Farmington, like Udall, Ralph Nader and Representative Ken Hechler of West Virginia. For suggesting that the union bears some responsibility and that it has compromised and "snuggled up to" management on safety issues, the U.M.W. Journal recently labeled Nader and Hechler as "finks" in a front-page editorial. And the union magazine has engaged in such a Mao Tse-tung glorification of Boyle and his record as a safety crusader—it refers to him as a "union chieftain"—that the U.M.W. has become an embarrassment to its friends in Congress. While fulminating at the charges of collaboration with the industry, The Journal has *not* reported that weeks before the Consol disaster, the U.M.W. was convicted along with the Consolidation Coal Company in a Federal court in Lexington, Ky., of conspiring to create a monopoly in the soft coal industry. With the conviction, which is being appealed, went a $7,300,000 damage award, to be paid half by the union and half by the company that Boyle has praised for "cooperation." The case involved Consol's alleged withdrawal of coal marketing services from South-East Coal Company after the company went nonunion.

Moreover the coal industry can hardly cry poor this year. Because of its secure grip on a growing share—now more than half—of the fuel market in the surging electric utility business, even the National Coal Association is calling the future "glittering." It turns out that local boosters who, through depression upon depression, have been calling the state of West Virginia "The Billion Dollar Coal Field" were not far from wrong.

As Senator Harrison A. Williams Jr. of New Jersey noted in starting mine-safety hearings, coal has become so profitable that since 1966 the three largest coal producers have been taken over by other giant mineral corporations—Peabody Coal Company by Kennecott Copper, Consolidation by Continental Oil Company, and Island Creek Coal Company by Occidental Oil. According to the National Coal Association, the list of oil corporations that have acquired coal-mining companies now includes at least 20 of the major petroleum producers—Gulf, Shell, Humble, Standard of Ohio, Atlantic-Richfield, Sun, Ashland and Kerr-McGee among them. It was a relief to know, Senator Williams noted, that the safety hearings would not be "complicated" by the usual coal claims of imminent bankruptcy. To the oil owners of coal, Williams pointedly observed that the spectacle of oil-well pollution of the Pacific Ocean off Santa Barbara, Calif., and new evidence of "lung pollution" in the mines "may be trying to tell us something." "In both cases," he said, "we find at the top of the ownership structure big oil companies."

Whether or not by corporate edict from these powerful new coal owners, the fact is that the National Coal Association, the largest industry group, is taking a remarkably calm and even welcoming view of the strenuous safety legislation before Congress this year. By enacting the Nixon Administration bill, which is among the strongest of the lot, Congress could close all the old loopholes at once and take—for coal—a daring new step into industrial human ecology. The Nixon bill would require mine operators to attack the black-lung epidemic among miners by reducing coal dust contamination in mine air to 4.5 milligrams of respirable dust per cubic meter of air, as a starter. The standard is a compromise of the U.S. Public Health Service's 1968 recommendation—3 milligrams. It would become effective six months after passage of the law and could be lowered later by decision of the Secretary of the Interior. The dust-control problem is publicly pictured as a cost nightmare by the industry. The Bureau of Mines estimates that the cost will be only pennies per ton.

The economics of mine safety are the one great unknown in this year's reform spree. No one knows what the cost of a century of neglect has been. Lee White, the chairman of the Federal Power Commission, which regulates wholesale electric power rates, opened the door a crack during Secretary Udall's post-Farmington *mea culpa* last December by observing that, as a nation, we have lost money as well as life in the mines, "and we must pay." The F.P.C. is anxious to pass on to consumers "all savings in costs that are properly made," White said. But if it takes an increase in the cost of electricity to indemnify the miners who dig the coal for steam-electric power, "I believe the American people are willing and should be willing to pay that extra cost . . . For all I know, we are not talking about increased rates but only a smaller decrease in rates."

Some but not all of coal's new 20-year and 30-year contracts to supply the huge fuel demands of electric power contain escalator clauses, which would permit certain price increases to pay for safety. But a share-the-cost program may not be as easy to work out as White made it seem; one reason that the coal industry is so mercilessly cost-conscious has been the strong downward pressure on prices exerted by the electric utilities, including the Government's own Tennessee Valley Authority, the biggest of all coal consumers. The average value per ton of coal at the mine has dropped from $4.99 in 1948 to $4.62 last year.

It may be significant that John Corcoran, the president of Consol—a moderate man to start with, by coal industry standards, and one who has been deeply affected by the Farmington disaster—also is chairman of the National Coal Association and a director of the American Mining Association and the Bituminous Coal Association. The industry does seem to be speaking with a new voice. But the coal industry is still a very loose coalition of new humanists and old buccaneers. And as one of its publicists put it recently, "We are like any association—we reflect the lowest common denominator. We have a few members who think the world is flat, so we have not publicly endorsed the use of globes."

Footnotes

[1] One example of the retarded technology of mine safety is that miners testing for gas still rely today on the Glame safety lamp of Sir Humphrey Davy, perfected more than 150 years ago. The safety lamp is rugged and safe if used properly, but it requires highly skilled operators to read it accurately, and then its accuracy is no more than half a percentage point—or 10 percent of the margin between survival and explosion.

Toward an Assessment of the Mental Health of Factory Workers

A Detroit Study

ARTHUR KORNHAUSER

Industrial psychology in America has been most concerned with productivity and organizational effectiveness. Working people are studied primarily as means to the ends of efficiency, whether of the single enterprise or of the larger society. Even when attention is directed to attitudes, feelings, and morale, interest usually centers on how these subjective states affect performance.

An alternative orientation focuses upon working people as themselves the significant ends. Interest attaches to the personal development and wellbeing of the men and women in industry, the improvement of their individual and social health—especially their "mental health." The present study belongs to this second category. It inquires about the impact of modern economic organization, particularly the demands of mass production manufacturing, on the people involved. What does the industrial way of life do to, and for, the men who man the machines? What does their work mean to them and what are the effects of their factory occupations on their spirit and their life adjustments?

Are factory workers—specifically Detroit auto-workers—happy and well-adjusted in the main? Or are they predominantly bitter or depressed or anxious or apathetic? Are they enthusiastic, idealistic, self-reliant, zestful? Or cynical, alienated, dispirited? One can find assertions that they are all these contradictory things and many more. Evidence to support the assertions is scarce indeed. Even less is known about subgroups, for example by job levels, age, income, and education. Are assembly line jobs peculiarly monotonous, frustrating, deadening—and hated? Does work on the

Reprinted from *Human Organization*, Vol. 21, No. 1 (Spring 1962), 43–46, by permission of the author and The Society for Applied Anthropology.

line produce poor mental health? On this question, too, violent disagreement continues despite the debates which go on decade after decade.

In this article I shall sketch a few partial results from a study which attempted to secure evidence bearing on these issues. Along with the findings I shall briefly mention some possible implications and interpretations —and unanswered questions.

The research focuses on comparisons of the mental health of occupational groups in the Detroit automobile industry. The factory workers studied were selected by a systematic sampling procedure from the personnel files of 13 large and medium-sized automotive manufacturing plants. The sample includes only white, American-born men who had been with their present employer three years or more.

In reaching for methods to assess the mental health of these people we adopted two guiding principles: (1) We would begin with a variety of simple, commonly accepted ideas as to what constitutes good versus poor mental health and would proceed in subsequent steps to interrelate, test, and in some sense "validate" these ideas; and (2) we would rely primarily on data obtainable by means of interviews with the working people themselves, supplementing these findings by reports from interviewers, wives of respondents, and company records of absenteeism and medical department visits. Accordingly, several hundred detailed interviews were completed with workers and their wives, all at the homes of the interviewees.

The rationale of our mental health measures is this: We conceptualize mental health not as representing any psychodynamic unity but as a loose descriptive designation for an overall level of success, effectiveness, or excellence of the individual's functioning as a person. The emphasis is on mental health in a "normal" and positive sense; the inquiry does not deal with mental disease or illness. We proceed on the assumption that mental health is multi-dimensional—although this is not at all to imply that there are not certain dimensions of especially great importance relative to others. On the side of practical procedures, our search is not for any peculiarly crucial key measures of mental health but for useful indicators chosen from innumerable possible ones.

More specifically, the study relies upon reports by working men and their wives in regard to the workers' feelings of satisfaction and happiness; their attitudes and sentiments toward themselves, other persons, their world, and their future; their personal and social activities (at work, at home, and in the community); and their psychological and bodily manifestations of disturbing stress or tensions. The interviews also included responses to lists of selected personality inventory items.

A number of indexes were derived from the interview responses. Those which enter into our general measure of mental health are indexes of:

Anxiety and emotional tension

Hostility versus trust in, and acceptance of, people

Sociability and friendship versus withdrawal

Self-esteem versus negative self-feelings

Personal morale versus anomie or social alienation

Overall satisfaction with life

"Validity" of the Mental Health Index

These component indexes were combined to form a total index of mental health. We then classified workers according to their scores on this general index. Although I shall freely refer to the "better" or "poorer" mental health of the men so classified, the statements are necessarily limited by the particular way in which the assessments are made. The meaning and justification of the appraisals must rest largely upon the "face validity" of the indexes—that is, upon the apparent reasonableness of the response material as indicative of what is ordinarily believed to characterize mental health in our culture (positive self-feelings, relative freedom from anxiety symptoms and hostile attitudes, and other qualities suggested by the above list of indexes).

An important additional type of evidence was obtained, however, as a check on whether our measure of mental health does in fact correspond with evaluations used and accepted by professional persons directly concerned with mental health in our society. Does the proposed index of mental health actually measure what the "experts" mean by mental health? Before proceeding to use the index we set up a small-scale "validation" study to answer this question. We arranged to have six experienced, highly qualified clinical psychologists and psychiatrists read the complete interview records of 40 cases and give their overall evaluation of each individual's mental health. Comparison of our quantitative indexes with these independent global ratings reveals that the indexes do, in fact, agree decidedly well with the clinicians' judgments. The tetrachoric correlation is .84; the Pearson coefficient is .76. It is thus apparent that the meaning of mental health represented by our index corresponds closely to what the clinicians also conceive to be better or poorer mental health.

A different type of validity check compared workers' responses with reports by their wives. These comparisons justify the further conclusion that the interview content represents behavior and attitudes possessing some reality in the eyes of another observer. When wives' estimates of whether their spouses are nervous, well satisfied with life, etc. are compared with adjustment-indexes based on the man's own replies, the median correlations are above .50. When these several findings are taken together, they appear to offer considerable justification for employing our indexes for present purposes as presumptive measures, albeit crude ones, of mental health.

Mental Health Differences
by Factory Occupational Categories

Our first question here is whether there are, in fact, differences of mental health associated with different types of factory jobs. If it is established that such differences exist, the next task is to search for explanations. As to the occurrence of significant differences our results are clear and unambiguous. When workers are classified by skill level and variety of work operations, mental health scores do show consistent correlation with the occupational hierarchy. The higher the occupational level the better the mental health.

TABLE 1

COMPARISON OF OCCUPATIONS BY THE PERCENTAGE OF
WORKERS ENJOYING "GOOD" MENTAL HEALTH

	Percentages with scores indicating "good" mental health	No. of workers
298 men in their 40's		
Skilled workers	56	45
High semi-skilled	41	98
Ordinary semi-skilled	38	82
Repetitive semi-skilled	26	73
Repetitive, machine-paced only (subdivision of preceding category)	16	32
109 men in their 20's		
Skilled and high semi-skilled*	58	33
Ordinary semi-skilled	35	46
Repetitive semi-skilled	10	30
Repetitive, machine-paced only (subdivision of preceding category)	7	15

*The two categories are combined here because of small numbers.

One simple set of figures will suffice to make this more concrete. Let us compare occupations by the percentage of workers enjoying "good" mental health—i.e., having "high" mental health scores (the cutting point for "high" is, of course, arbitrary). We have two age groups—men in their 20's and those in their 40's. (See Table 1.)

A vital next question is whether these occupational differences are due to *effects of the jobs* and their associated conditions, or alternatively, do the differences result from *selection of certain kinds of persons* who go into and remain in the several types of work. Before I consider a little of our evidence on this second question, I wish to emphasize the importance of the first results themselves. If more thorough studies confirm the findings I have reported, the social knowledge thus established may have large consequences. The poorer mental health of workers in lower level occupations cannot fail to affect not only their industrial behavior, as employees and labor unionists, but likewise their roles as citizens and as family and community members. As the knowledge of such differences becomes known (and again I repeat, if confirmed by additional studies), one may anticipate intensified efforts by the lower-placed groups, their leaders, and agencies concerned with their welfare to bring about social and industrial changes intended to eradicate the condition. Such social action programs will sorely need expanded research knowledge regarding crucial determining conditions and promising correctives. But demonstration of the existence of the problem is the first requirement.

These last comments are in no way intended to minimize the importance of the second question—the issue of whether and to what extent the observed occupational differences are attributable to the influence of the work and its correlates. We now turn to a brief analysis of this question. If the mental health differences are due to the type of persons in the occupations, differences among these people ought to be detectable in the pre-job period of their lives. A first suspicion that crosses one's mind, for example, is that the mental health results may all be "explained away" as due to educational differences. This could occur by reason of the direct association of schooling with both occupational level and good mental health scores (the latter possibly meaning merely greater sophistication and self-protection in answering questions, thus giving the *appearance* of mental health).

Amount of schooling, then, affords one good test of the *selection* explanation of occupational mental health differences. Since substantial educational differences do occur between occupations and since education is also associated with better mental health, the possibility has to be examined whether this association is sufficient to produce the obtained results. Conversely, do occupational mental health differences persist apart from the influence of education—i.e., when only persons of like amounts of education are compared? Our findings strongly suggest that the latter is true. Proportions of workers having good mental health consistently decrease from higher to lower level occupations *for each of three educational categories separately*. Moreover, the magnitude of the differences is very nearly the same as when education is not controlled but is permitted to add its influence (see Table 2).

For the middle-age group (in which there are enough cases to permit more adequate analysis) occupation and education show a small additive effect on mental health as may be noted in Table 2A. Mental health is best among those high in education *and* occupation, poorest for those low in

TABLE 2

PERCENTAGE OF HIGH MENTAL HEALTH SCORES BY GROUPS
HAVING SPECIFIED OCCUPATION AND EDUCATION
A. MIDDLE-AGE FACTORY WORKERS

	Education			
Occupation	Grade School	Some H.S.	H.S. Grad.	Total
Skilled	43%(7)	45%(20)	72%(18)	56%(45)
High semi-skilled	33 (46)	45 (33)	53 (19)	41 (98)
Ordinary semi-skilled	31 (35)	39 (36)	55 (11)	38 (82)
Repetitive semi-skilled	24 (46)	29 (21)	33 (6)	26 (73)
Total	30%(134)	40%(110)	57%(54)	39%(298)

Figures in parentheses show the number of cases in each cell on which the accompanying percentage is based.

B. YOUNG FACTORY WORKERS

	Education		
Occupation	Some H.S. or less	H.S. Grad.	Total
Skilled and high semi-skilled	57%(14)	58%(19)	58%(33)
Ordinary semi-skilled	33 (36)	40 (10)	35 (46)
Repetitive semi-skilled	10 (21)	11 (9)	10 (30)
Total	31%(71)	42%(38)	35%(109)

Because of small numbers, we here combine the two lower educational groups and the two upper occupational groups.

both education and occupation. This is contrary, of course, to the psychologically plausible hypothesis that mental health is adversely affected by lack of congruency between educational status and occupational status— the view that poorest mental health occurs among persons of better education in low-level jobs (and perhaps also among those of low education in high-level jobs). This hypothesis receives no support at all from our data, either for the middle-age group or the younger workers. In fact, the percentage of "good" mental health in lower-level jobs is *greater* for persons having more schooling.

Conclusions

The analysis of our data as a whole leads to the conclusion that educational differences, either by themselves or in interaction with job level, do not account for the observed mental health variation by occupation. To the extent that this conclusion is confirmed and to the extent that other pre-job personal characteristics (possible job *selection* factors) yield similar negative findings, it would indicate that the influences determining occupational mental health differences among factory workers are to be found in the jobs themselves and their associated life conditions.

We have analyzed a few other pre-job characteristics of workers in a manner parallel to that employed in respect to education. The material consists of responses to an extensive series of questions about the workers' boyhood conditions, behavior, attitudes, and aspirations. In a word, the findings are similar to those for schooling though less clear-cut. That is to say, the occupational groups do differ by childhood characteristics (such as reported anxiety symptoms, success in school, self-confidence, economic deprivations, degree of happiness) but when occupations are compared for individuals having the same degree of these pre-job characteristics, occupational mental health differences persist even if somewhat reduced. In respect to childhood goals and values, the occupational groups show only minor differences and there is no evidence that these differences are responsible for any large part of the observed mental health variations.

In sum, then, the indications from our present data are: (a) that mental health (as here assessed) is poorer among factory workers as we move from more skilled, responsible, varied types of work to jobs lower in these respects, and (b) that the relationship is not due in any large degree to differences of pre-job background or personality of the men who enter and remain in the several types of work. The relationship of mental health to occupation, in other words, appears to be "genuine"; mental health is dependent on factors associated with the job.

This conclusion at once presents the further challenging question of what *aspects* of occupations are important. Which of the myriad characteristics of higher- and lower- level jobs and associated conditions of life are the salient determinants of better or poorer mental health? More simply, *why* do we find poorer mental health in low-level occupations? I can do no more than touch upon these questions at this time.

One can readily offer a long list of plausible explanatory factors—from lower pay, economic insecurity, and disagreeable working conditions to the more intangible influences of status, promotion opportunities, type of supervision and work-group relations, simplicity and repetitiveness of job operations and lack of personal control over them, non-use of abilities with consequent feelings of futility, and many more such possible influences on and off the job. Some of these obviously may be more significant than others. We have analyzed data pertaining to many of these variables in an effort to estimate their saliency but I must leave these analyses for reporting at a later date.

Here, I wish merely to suggest that it would be a mistake to think in terms of this *or* that causal factor as important. Mental health is surely a product of complex combinations of influences—varied and shifting, dependent on the values currently emphasized and the expectations aroused as well as on the existing conditions of gratification and deprivation. Mental health is probably not so much a matter of freedom from specific frustrations as it is an overall orientation and balanced relationship to the world which permits a person to maintain realistic, positive belief in himself and his purposeful activities. Insofar as his entire job and life situation facilitate and support such feelings of adequacy, inner security, and meaningfulness, it can be presumed that mental health as we have assessed it will tend to be "good." The question becomes one of whether lower-level factory jobs do offer generally less favorable circumstances for the development and maintenance of this "healthy" personality than do "better" jobs—less favorable in many and varied ways a number of which I have mentioned. It appears to me there can be little doubt that this is true.

Furthermore, both on rational grounds and from our empirical evidence, I see no reason to think that it is useful to single out one or a few of the job-related characteristics as distinctively important—whether it be status, human relations at work, specialization of operations, lack of independence and control, or any other particular variable. What is important is *everything* that deprives the individual of purpose and zest, that leaves him with negative self-feelings, anxieties, tensions, a sense of lostness and futility, which distorts his thinking and obstructs effective behavior. If we are to understand why mental health is poorer in less skilled, more routine factory jobs, we must look at the entire pattern of work and life conditions of the people in these occupations—not at single variables.

Footnote

This is a slightly revised form of a paper read at the American Psychological Association meetings in Chicago in September, 1960. It is a preliminary report of one part of a more extensive study. A detailed publication covering the entire project is in preparation. Principal support for the research was provided by the National Institute of Mental Health (Research grant M-460, 1951–57). Grateful acknowledgment is made to that agency and, for other assistance, to the Wayne State University College of Liberal Arts, the Computing Center, and the Wayne State Fund; also to the Institute of Labor and Industrial Relations of Wayne State University and the University of Michigan. Special thanks go to Dr. Otto M. Reid who shouldered a large share of responsibility for the conduct of the study.

Work and Deviant Behavior

Occupational Structure and
Criminal Behavior
Prescription Violation by Retail Pharmacists

RICHARD QUINNEY
New York University

An increasing number of sociologists have become interested in the study of occupations, noticeably neglecting at the same time the criminal behavior which occurs within occupations.[1] On the other hand, sociologists concerned with the study of white collar crime have not made any systematic attempt to consider the social structure of occupations in their explanations of white collar crime.[2] The purpose of this study is to demonstrate that an analysis of the occupation should be considered in the attempt to explain violations of laws and regulations which control occupational activities and that such an approach makes it possible to learn more about both the structure of the occupation and the criminal behavior which occurs within the occupation. More specifically, the principal problem of the study is to offer an explanation for a type of criminal behavior which occurs in retail pharmacy in terms of an analysis of the occupation.

Research Procedure

For a study of occupational violation among pharmacists employed in retail establishments—retail pharmacists—it was first necessary to limit the violation to a type which might form a homogeneous unit of behavior and be subject to a common explanation.[3] While violations of the many state and federal statutes and administrative regulations pertaining to retail pharmacy are all regarded legally as misdemeanors and are subject to particular punishments, the behaviors involved are by no means homogeneous. In the attempt to delineate a specific type of behavior which could be ex-

Reprinted from *Social Problems*, Vol. 11, No. 2 (Fall 1963), 180–85, by permission of the author and The Society for the Study of Social Problems.

plained by a single theory, the various laws and regulations were subjected to a content analysis in terms of basic occupational activity.[4] The laws and regulations (and their accompanying violations) can be classified into three types: regulation of licensure, regulation of the drugstore, and regulation of prescriptions. Although any one type appeared to represent homogeneous behaviors, the most important type of violation both in terms of public welfare and frequency of occurrence is the violation of laws and regulations that control the compounding and dispensing of prescriptions. Prescription violation was therefore selected as the type of behavior for which an explanation would be sought and thus became the dependent variable of the study.

One of the primary aims of the research design was to provide a comparison of prescription violators and non-violators. These groups of retail pharmacists were drawn from the population of retail pharmacists within the city limits of Albany, New York. Through the cooperation of the New York State Board of Pharmacy, the names and addresses of the pharmacists, as well as their violation records over a five year period, were secured. The twenty prescription violators who had been officially detected by state and federal investigators as violating a prescription law or regulation made up the group of prescription violators. The non-violator group consisted of 60 pharmacists randomly selected from the remaining retail pharmacists who had been investigated but had never been found to violate a prescription law or regulation. The final study group, then, consisted of 80 retail pharmacists, 20 prescription violators and 60 non-violators.

Data were collected through structured interviews with the retail pharmacists. The interview schedule, designed also for a broader range of problems, obtained information about the pharmacist's background, career in pharmacy, experiences in pharmacy, and attitudes about the occupation.[5] The respondents were not informed that their violation record was known to the researcher, and any idea that the study was partly concerned with violation could not have occurred until the last few minutes of the interview, after the major information had been secured. In addition to the formal interviews, throughout the study there were informal discussions with persons related in various ways to retail pharmacy, including members of the state board of pharmacy, instructors in pharmacy, pharmacy students, physicians, and customers.

Occupational Roles in Retail Pharmacy

Most of the sociological studies of occupations have either assumed or demonstrated that occupations are characterized by patterned expectations internalized by the incumbents and reflected in their occupational behavior.

On the three occasions that retail pharmacy has received sociological attention, it has been observed that the occupation incorporates two different
roles, professional and business. Weinlein noted that the professional aspects of retail pharmacy are vitally influenced by the fact that most of the
occupational activities take place in a business establishment, the drugstore.[6]
In addition to filling prescriptions, he observed, the pharmacist is involved
in many activities of a business nature. Likewise, Thorner described retail
pharmacy as an occupation which has the characteristics of both a profession and a business.[7] McCormack defined retail pharmacy as a marginal
occupation because it contains the conflicting goals of a profession and a
business.[8] These observations were given support in the present research
when it was found that 94 percent of the pharmacists replied in the affirmative to the question, "Do you find that the public expects the pharmacist
to be *both* a business man and a professional man?"

From what was known about retail pharmacy, then, it appeared that
various aspects of the social and cultural structure of the occupation would
have implications for the study of prescription violation, particularly the
status of retail pharmacy as both a profession and a business.[9] Thus, the
research was guided by the general hypothesis that social strains in the form
of divergent occupational role expectations are structured in the occupation
of retail pharmacy and that prescription violation may result, depending
upon the individual mode of adaptation. Such a conception that crime (or
deviant behavior in general) is structured finds support in Sutherland's idea
of "differential social organization," which proposes that in a heterogeneous
type of structure alternative and possibly inconsistent standards of conduct
are held by the various segments.[10] A similar idea is found in the sociological tradition of functionalism.[11] Both approaches attempt to account for
variations in rates of crime between or within social structures. The strategy
taken in the present study was to account for variations in rates of criminal
behavior within an occupation.

Structural Strain and Adaptation

To the retail pharmacist, the existence of two different occupational
roles can present a personal dilemma in terms of appropriate occupational
behavior. The retail pharmacist is faced with the task of performing his
occupational activities with definitions which are not always clear, consistent, and compatible. Structural strain is built into retail pharmacy. The
pharmacist must, therefore, make some sort of a personal adjustment to the
situation.[12]

It was hypothesized that retail pharmacists resolve the dilemma of
choosing between different occupational roles—professional and business—

by adapting to an *occupational role organization*. Occupational role organization refers to the relative orientation of the retail pharmacist to both the professional and business roles.[13]

The degree to which pharmacists were oriented to the business and professional roles was then measured. By asking the respondents to indicate how important they regard certain activities and goals in pharmacy, it was possible to determine the relative orientation of pharmacists to the two roles.[14] The results suggest that pharmacists orient themselves in different ways to the available roles. It was thus possible to construct a typology of occupational role organizations based on these differences in orientation. Some pharmacists are oriented more to the professional role than to the business role (Professional Pharmacists—16 percent of the sample), while others are oriented more to the business role (Business Pharmacists—20 percent). Other pharmacists are oriented to both roles (Professional-Business Pharmacists—45 percent), while a few appear not to be oriented to either of the roles (Indifferent Pharmacists—19 percent).[15] Therefore, since there are two possible occupational roles for the retail pharmacist rather than a single, well-defined role, there appears to be a patterned response in orientation to the two different roles. Retail pharmacists resolve the dilemma of choosing between different occupational roles (or, more generally, adjust to role strain) by adapting to an occupational role organization.[16]

Prescription Violation

The foregoing analysis provides a point of departure for an investigation of the possible behavioral consequences of structural strain. Prescription violation may be related to the types of occupational role organizations. More specifically, it was hypothesized that prescription violation occurs with greatest frequency among business pharmacists and least among professional pharmacists, with professional-business pharmacists and indifferent pharmacists being intermediate in the frequency of prescription violation.

The hypothesis was tested by cross-tabulating the prescription violation records and the occupational role organizations of the retail pharmacists. As shown in Table 1, there is a significant association between prescription violation and occupational role organization in the direction predicted. Prescription violation occurred with greatest frequency among the business pharmacists—75 percent of these pharmacists were violators—and occurred least among professional pharmacists. None of the professional pharmacists were violators. The professional-business pharmacists and indifferent pharmacists were intermediate in violation: 14 percent of the professional-business pharmacists and 20 percent of the indifferent pharmacists were

TABLE 1

RELATIONSHIP BETWEEN PRESCRIPTION VIOLATION AND
OCCUPATIONAL ROLE ORGANIZATION

Prescription Violation	Occupational Role Organizations							
	Professional		Professional-Business		Indifferent		Business	
	No.	Pct.	No.	Pct.	No.	Pct.	No.	Pct.
Violators	0	0	5	14	3	20	12	75
Non-Violators	13	100	31	86	12	80	4	25
	13	100	36	100	15	100	16	100

$X^2 = 28.6$, df $= 3$, P $< .001$.

prescription violators. Therefore, in verification of the hypothesis, it was concluded that prescription violation varies according to the types of occupational role organizations in retail pharmacy.

The research findings suggest that pharmacists vary in the degree to which they are affected by the controls of the occupation. Location within the structure of the occupation determines the effectiveness of the controls on the individual pharmacist. Pharmacists with an occupational role organization that includes an orientation to the professional role are bound by a system of occupational control which includes guides for the compounding and dispensing of prescriptions. Pharmacists who lack the professional orientation and are oriented to the business role are less bound by the occupational controls. They stress the merchandising aspects of pharmacy and are primarily interested in monetary gains. The formal controls (particularly legal controls) are made effective by the operation of informal controls (in terms of role expectations) which come mainly from within the occupation.[17]

The results, thus, indicate that prescription violation is related to the structure of the occupation and is an expression of that structure. Furthermore, from the standpoint of the individual pharmacist, prescription violation is related to orientation to the different roles in the occupation. From a social psychological position, then, prescription violation is a matter of *differential orientation*. That is, for each pharmacist, orientation to a particular role more than to another provides a perspective in which violation may seem appropriate.[18] Prescription violation is thus explained in terms of the existence of structural strain in the occupation, because of the existence of divergent occupational roles, and differential orientation of the pharmacists to the roles in the form of adaptations to occupational role organizations.

Conclusion

A theory of prescription violation by retail pharmacists was formulated and verified in this study. There are two divergent occupational role expectations in retail pharmacy—professional and business. Pharmacists adjust to this situation of structural strain by orienting themselves in varying degree to the roles, by adopting an occupational role organization. The types of occupational role organizations in turn differ in the extent to which they generate tendencies toward prescription violation. The occupational role organizations which include the professional role orientation restrain the pharmacist from violating, while the occupational role organizations which do not include the professional role orientation do not exercise this restraint on the pharmacist. Therefore, prescription violation occurs with greatest frequency among business pharmacists and least among professional pharmacists, with professional-business pharmacists and indifferent pharmacists being intermediate in frequency of prescription violation. It was thus concluded that prescription violation is related to the structure of the occupation and the differential orientation of retail pharmacists.

In an attempt to explain a homogeneous unit of behavior, this study was limited to only prescription violation by retail pharmacists. It is possible, however, that the theory as developed has implications both for other types of violation in retail pharmacy and for violations which occur in other occupations.

Occupational role strain is a common phenomenon in modern society, due in part to the frequency and rapidity with which changes in occupational role definitions occur and new occupational roles appear.[19] Particularly, it seems evident that the occupational roles of business and profession are by no means unique to retail pharmacy. Numerous observations show that some businesses are in the process of becoming professions, some professions are taking on some of the characteristics of business, and other occupations (similar to retail pharmacy) have already firmly incorporated the business and professional roles. For example, such occupations as dentistry, optometry, chiropody, osteopathy, and even independent general medicine are similar to retail pharmacy in that they possess the characteristics of both a profession and a business. Such occupational careers as real estate agent, accountant, and electrician, while traditionally business oriented, are now taking on some professional characteristics. Similarly, some of our traditionally professional careers—such as that of the psychologist—are taking on business characteristics as members become private consultants and counselors.

Also, by way of relating occupational role strain to occupational violation, many of these occupations are subject to laws and regulations similar to those of retail pharmacy. The violation of these laws and regulations is similar to prescription violation in that illegal behavior occurs in the course of serving the customer, as in the failure to retain a dental prescription by the dentist, alteration of a prescription for lenses by an optometrist, and the use of a secret method or procedure of treatment in the case of both osteopathy and medicine. It appears likely that the theoretical orientation employed in this study and the research findings of the study are applicable to other occupations and violations.

Finally, the study of prescription violation adds credence to the increasingly popular conception that deviant behavior is a reflection of social structure.[20] A demonstration of this assumption has been accomplished by bringing together a study of the occupation and a study of criminal behavior in the occupation. If white collar crime is illegal behavior in the course of occupational activity, then it is reasonable to assume that the occupation itself must become the object of study as well as the illegal behavior which occurs within the occupation. White collar crime reflects the particular structure of the occupation and is a normal response to one's particular location within the occupation. Criminologists might consider the importance of understanding the occupation in the process of formulating theories of criminal behavior; and, on the other hand, sociologists who study occupations might give some attention to understanding the occupation by an investigation of the criminal behavior in the occupation. Both the structure of the occupation and criminal behavior within the occupation can be better understood if they are considered together.

Footnotes

Presented at the annual meeting of the Southern Sociological Society, Durham, North Carolina, April, 1963.

[1] Approaches to the sociological study of occupations are presented in Sigmund Nosow and William H. Form (eds.), *Man, Work, and Society: A Reader in the Sociology of Occupations*, New York: Basic Books, 1962.

[2] There are several significant studies of white collar crime: Marshall B. Clinard, *The Black Market*, New York: Rinehart, 1952; Donald R. Cressey, *Other People's Money*, Glencoe, Ill.: The Free Press, 1953; Frank E. Hartung, "White Collar Offenses in the Wholesale Meat Industry in Detroit," *American Journal of Sociology*, 56 (July, 1950), pp. 25–34; and Edwin H. Sutherland, *White Collar Crime*, New York: Dryden Press, 1949.

[3] The importance of delineating homogeneous units of criminal behavior for the purpose of explanation is discussed, among other places, in Marshall B. Clinard, *Sociology of Deviant Behavior*, New York: Holt, Rinehart, and Winston, 1963, pp. 204–216; Donald R. Cressey, "Criminological Research and the Definition of Crimes," *American Journal of Sociology*, 56 (May, 1951), pp. 546–551; and A. R. Lindesmith and H. Warren Dunham, "Some Principles of Criminal Typology," *Social Forces*, 19 (March, 1951), pp. 307–314. For application of this approach see Marshall B. Clinard and Andrew L. Wade, "Toward the Delineation of Vandalism

as a Subtype of Juvenile Delinquency," *Journal of Criminal Law, Criminology, and Police Science,* 48 (January-February, 1958), pp. 493–499; and Cressey, *Other People's Money, op. cit.* The suggestion that homogeneous units be delimited within white collar crime has been made in Vilhelm Aubert, "White Collar Crime and Social Structure," *American Journal of Sociology,* 58 (November, 1952), pp. 263–271; and Gilbert Geis, "Toward a Delineation of White-Collar Offenses," *Sociological Inquiry,* 32 (Spring, 1962), pp. 160–171.

[4] The laws and regulations pertaining to pharmacy in New York are compiled in the University of the State of New York, *Pharmacy—Laws, Rules and Information,* Albany, New York, 1959.

[5] For the larger study see the writer's unpublished Ph.D. dissertation, "Retail Pharmacy as a Marginal Occupation: A Study of Prescription Violation," University of Wisconsin, 1962. I am indebted to Marshall B. Clinard, under whose guidance this study was formulated and completed. Michael Hakeem and Thomas J. Scheff also provided valuable assistance.

[6] Anthony Weinlein, "Pharmacy as a Profession with Special Reference to the State of Wisconsin," unpublished M.A. thesis, University of Chicago, 1943.

[7] Isador Thorner, "Pharmacy: The Functional Significance of an Institutional Pattern," *Social Forces,* 20 (March, 1942), pp. 321–328.

[8] Thelma H. McCormack, "The Druggists' Dilemma: Problems of a Marginal Occupation," *American Journal of Sociology,* 61 (January, 1956), pp. 308–315.

[9] Discussions of profession and business as two separate occupational institutions are found in Talcott Parsons, "The Professions and Social Structure" and "The Motivation of Economic Activities," *Essays in Sociological Theory,* Glencoe, Ill.: The Free Press, 1949, pp. 185–217; and Theodore Caplow, *The Sociology of Work,* Minneapolis: University of Minnesota Press, 1954, pp. 100–123. Accounts of the historical development of retail pharmacy which document the existence of both professional and business roles may be found in Richard A. Deno, Thomas D. Rowe, and Donald C. Brodie, *The Profession of Pharmacy,* Philadelphia: J. B. Lippincott, 1959; and Edward Kremers and George Urdang, *History of Pharmacy,* Philadelphia: J. B. Lippincott, 1951.

[10] Sutherland discussed "differential social organization" or "differential group organization" in "Development of the Theory," in Albert K. Cohen, Alfred R. Lindesmith, and Karl F. Schuessler (eds.), *The Sutherland Papers,* Bloomington: Indiana University Press, 1956, pp. 13–29; and Edwin H. Sutherland and Donald R. Cressey, *Principles of Criminology,* Philadelphia: J. B. Lippincott, 1960, pp. 79–80, 82–85. This aspect of Sutherland's theory has been pointed out by Donald R. Cressey in "Epidemiology and Individual Conduct: A Case From Criminology," *Pacific Sociological Review,* 3 (Fall, 1960), pp. 38–58.

[11] Robert K. Merton, "Social Structure and Anomie," *American Sociological Review,* 3 (October, 1938), pp. 672–682; and Talcott Parsons, *The Social System,* Glencoe, Ill.: The Free Press, 1951, pp. 249–325.

[12] The idea of structural strain is found in Parsons, *The Social System, op. cit.* The concept has been recently employed in Neil J. Smelser, *Theory of Collective Behavior,* New York: The Free Press of Glencoe, 1963. Discussions of adjustment to structural role strain (and role conflict) are found in Leonard S. Cottrell, Jr., "The Adjustment of the Individual to His Age and Sex Roles," *American Sociological Review,* 7 (October, 1942), pp. 617–630; J. W. Getzels and E. G. Guba, "Role, Role Conflict, and Effectiveness: An Empirical Study," *American Sociological Review,* 19 (February, 1954), pp. 164–175; William J. Goode, "A Theory of Role Strain," *American Sociological Review,* 25 (August, 1960), pp. 483–496; Neal Gross, Ward S. Mason, and Alexander W. McFachern, *Explorations in Role Analysis,* New York: John Wiley & Sons, 1958, chaps. 16–17; Samuel A. Stouffer, "An Analysis of Conflicting Social Norms," *American Sociological Review,* 14 (December,

1949), pp. 707–717; Jackson Toby, "Some Variables in Role Conflict," *Social Forces*, 30 (March, 1952), pp. 323–327; Walter I. Wardwell, "The Reduction of Strain in a Marginal Social Role," *American Journal of Sociology*, 61 (July, 1955), pp. 16–25; and Donald M. Wolfe and J. Diedrick Snoek, "A Study of Tensions and Adjustment Under Role Conflict," *Journal of Social Issues*, 18 (July, 1962), pp. 102–121.

[13] See Ronald G. Corwin, "The Professional Employee: A Study of Conflict in Nursing Roles," *American Journal of Sociology*, 66 (May, 1961), pp. 605–615.

[14] After pertinent materials in the sociology of occupations and retail pharmacy were studied, several items were selected through their construct validity to measure professional and business role orientation. The interview schedule contained the question: "In terms of your pharmacy career, how important is each of the following?" (with the possible response categories of very important, important, of minor importance, of no importance). There followed ten items, randomly placed (selected after the discriminative power of each item had been determined in the interview pretest), which measured the respective role orientations. The professional role items were: (1) reading the professional literature, (2) being a part of the public health team, (3) using and encouraging the use of official drugs, (4) attending professional meetings, and (5) compounding and dispensing prescriptions. The business role items were: (1) maintaining a business establishment, (2) being a successful business man, (3) arranging window and counter displays, (4) being a good salesman, and (5) handling a variety of sundry goods. Each respondent had two role orientation scores (professional and business), and each respondent was given a low or high rating for each role. The pharmacists were then categorized according to the four types of occupational role organizations as based on relative orientation to the professional and business roles.

[15] It should be noted that this distribution is skewed slightly in the direction of business pharmacists. The reason for this is that the number of prescription violators in the study sample over-represents the proportion of violators in the population of retail pharmacists; and, as it will be shown, the group of prescription violators contains a disproportionate number of business pharmacists. Thus, an entirely random sample of retail pharmacists would contain a few more professionally oriented pharmacists.

[16] An occupational role organization may be regarded as the integration of the individual's total occupational role system. See Goode, *op. cit.*, pp. 485–487. Each type of occupational role organization represents a particular method for "ego's manipulation of his role structure" in an attempt to reduce role strain.

[17] This interpretation finds support in Howard S. Becker and James W. Carper, "The Elements of Identification with an Occupation," *American Sociological Review*, 21 (June, 1956), pp. 341–348; Caplow, *op. cit.*, pp. 113–121; Edward Gross, *Work and Society*, New York: Thomas Y. Crowell, 1958, pp. 134–139; Oswald Hall, "The Informal Organization of the Medical Profession," *Canadian Journal of Economic and Political Science*, 12 (February, 1946), pp. 30–44; Louis Kriesberg, "Occupational Controls Among Steel Distributors," *American Journal of Sociology*, 61 (November, 1955), pp. 203–212; and Tamotsu Shibutani, *Society and Personality: An Interactionist Approach to Social Psychology*, Englewood Cliffs, New Jersey: Prentice-Hall, 1961, especially pp. 60, 91–94, 276–278.

[18] This is essentially the same as Glaser's concept of "differential identification." Daniel Glaser, "Criminality Theories and Behavioral Images," *American Journal of Sociology*, 61 (March, 1956), pp. 433–445.

[19] See Walter I. Wardwell, "A Marginal Professional Role: The Chiropractor," *Social Forces*, 30 (March, 1952), pp. 339–348.

[20] A recent textbook in criminology uses this as a major theme: Herbert A. Bloch and Gilbert Geis, *Man, Crime, and Society*, New York: Random House, 1962.

The Informal "Code" of
Police Deviancy

A Group Approach to "Blue-Coat Crime"

Ellwyn R. Stoddard
University of Texas at El Paso

It has been asserted by various writers of criminology, deviant behavior, and police science that unlawful activity by a policeman is a manifestation of personal moral weakness, a symptom of personality defects, or the recruitment of individuals unqualified for police work. In contrast to the traditional orientation, this paper is a sociological examination of "blue-coat crime"[1] as a functioning informal social system whose norms and practices are at variance with legal statutes. Within the police group itself, this pattern of illicit behavior is referred to as the "code."

Following an examination of these contrasting viewpoints, this case study will provide data to ascertain the existence of the "code," its limitations and range of deviancy, and the processes through which it is maintained and sanctioned within the group. The guiding hypothesis of this study is that illegal practices of police personnel are socially prescribed and patterned through the informal "code" rather than being a function of individual aberration or personal inadequacies of the policeman himself.

The Individualistic Approach

Three decades ago August Vollmer emphasized that the individual being unsuited to police work was the factor responsible for subsequent deviancy among officers. This approach implicitly assumes inherent per-

Reprinted by special permission of the *Journal of Criminal Law, Criminology and Police Science* (Northwestern University School of Law), Copyright © 1968, Volume 59, Number 2.

sonality characteristics to be the determinant which makes a police recruit into a good officer or a bad one.[2] A current text of police personnel management by German reaffirms the individualistic orientation of Vollmer, and suggests that the quality of police service is ultimately dependent upon the individual police officer. There is no evidence of an awareness of group pressures within his analysis.[3]

A modified version of this individualistic approach is the view that perhaps the individual chosen had already become "contaminated" prior to being hired as a member of the force, and when presented with chances for bribery or favoritism, the "hard core guy, the one who is a thief already, steps in."[4]

A third factor, stressed by Tappan,[5] is the poor screening method at the recruitment stage. Such an officer might have had inadequate training, insufficient supervision, and poor pay and is ripe for any opportunity to participate in lucrative illicit enterprises. This author then goes into great detail to show the low intelligence and educational level of police officers. Another author adds that improved selection and personality evaluation have improved the quality of the police considerably over the past 20 years,[6] thereby attacking this problem directly. One recent author wrote that low salaries make more difficult the attraction of applicants with the moral strength to withstand temptations of "handouts" and eventual corruption.[7] Sutherland and Cressey, although aware that graft is a characteristic of the entire police system[8] rather than of isolated patrolman, stress the unqualified appointments of police officials by corrupt politicians as the source of police deviancy. They state:

> Another consequence of the fact that police departments often are organized for the welfare of corrupt politicians, rather than of society, is inefficient and unqualified personnel. This is unquestionably linked with police dishonesty, since only police officers who are "right" can be employed by those in political control. Persons of low intelligence and with criminal records sometimes are employed.[9]

The Group Approach

In contrast to the individualistic approach of these foregoing authors, the emphasis on the social context in which police deviancy flourishes has preoccupied the sociological criminologists. The present case study would clearly reflect this latter orientation.

Barnes and Teeters mention police deviancy in conjunction with organized syndicated crime.[10] Korn and McCorkle,[11] Cloward,[12] and Merton[13] see political and police corruption as a natural consequence of societal demand for illegal services. When these desired services are not provided through legal structures, they are attained through illegal means. However, documentation in support of these theoretical explanations is sketchy and limited in scope. Bell suggests that "crime is an American way of life." In the American temper there exists a feeling that "somewhere, somebody is pulling all the complicated strings to which this jumbled world dances." Stereotypes of big crime syndicates project the feeling that laws are just for "the little guys." Consequently, while "Americans have made such things as gambling illegal, they don't really in their hearts think of it as wicked."[14] Likewise, the routine discovery of an average citizen in overt unlawful activity rarely inflames the public conscience to the degree that it does when this same deviant behavior is exhibited by a police officer. Thus, the societal double standard demands that those in positions of trust must exhibit an artificially high standard of morality which is not required of the average citizen.

A measure of role ambivalence is an inevitable part of the policeman occupation in a democratic society. While he is responsible to protect the members of his society from those who would do them harm, the corresponding powers for carrying out this mandate are not delegated.[15] To perform his designated duties, the conscientious policeman often must violate the very laws he is trying to enforce. This poses a serious dilemma for the police officer since his attempt to effectively discourage violation of the law among the general public is often hinged to extra-legal short-cut techniques[16] which are in common practice by his law enforcement cohorts. For example, the use of "illegal" violence by policemen is justified by them as a necessary means to locate and harass the most vicious criminals and the Organized Syndicates.[17] These procedures are reinforced through coordinated group action.

> The officer needs the support of his fellow officers in dangerous situations and when he resorts to practices of questionable legality. Therefore, the rookie must pass the test of loyalty to the code of secrecy. Sometimes this loyalty of colleagues has the effect of protecting the law-violating, unethical officer.[18]

Such illegal practices which are traditionally used to carry out a policeman's assigned tasks might well be readily converted to the aims of personal gain.

In these tight informal cliques within the larger police force, certain "exploratory gestures"[19] involving the acceptance of small bribes and favors can occur. This is a hazy boundary between grateful citizens paying their respects to a proud profession, and "good" citizens involved in corruption wishing to buy future favors. Once begun, however, these practices can become "norms" or informal standards of cliques of policemen. A new recruit can be socialized into accepting these illegal practices by mild, informal negative sanctions such as the withholding of group acceptance. If these unlawful practices are embraced, the recruits membership group—the police force—and his reference group—the clique involved in illegal behavior—are no longer one and the same. In such circumstances the norms of the reference group (the illegal-oriented clique) would clearly take precedence over either the formal requisites of the membership group (police department regulations) or the formalized norms (legal statutes) of the larger society.[20] When such conflicts are apparent a person can

> (1) conform to one, take the consequences of non-conformity to the other. (2) He can seek a compromise position by which he attempts to conform in part, though not wholly, to one or more sets of role expectations, in the hope that sanctions applied will be minimal.[21]

If these reference group norms involving illegal activity become routinized with use they become an identifiable informal "code" such as that found in the present study. Such codes are not unique to the police profession. A fully documented case study of training at a military academy[22] in which an informal pattern of behavior was assimilated along with the formal standards clearly outlined the function of the informal norms, their dominance when in conflict with formal regulations, and the secretive nature of their existence to facilitate their effectiveness and subsequent preservation. The revelation of their existence to those outside the cadet group would destroy their integrative force and neutralize their utility.

This same secrecy would be demanded of a police "code" to insure its preservation. Although within the clique the code must be well defined, the ignorance of the lay public to even its existence would be a requisite to its continuous and effective use.[23] Through participation in activity regimented by the "code" an increased group identity and cohesion among "code" practitioners would emerge.

> Group identity requires winning of acceptance as a member of the inner group and, thereby, gaining access to the secrets of the occupation which are acquired through informal contacts with colleagues.[24]

Lack of this acceptance not only bars the neophyte from the inner secrets of the profession, but may isolate him socially and professionally from his colleagues and even his superiors. There is the added fear that, in some circumstance in which he would need their support, they would avoid becoming involved, forcing him to face personal danger or public ridicule alone.

The social structure in which law enforcement is maintained has a definite bearing on what is considered normal and what is deviant behavior. The pattern of "Blue-Coat Crime" (i.e., the "code") seems far more deviant when compared to the dominant middle-class norms of our society as when compared to lower-class values. Whyte maintains that in the Italian Slum of Cornerville, the primary function of the police department is not the enforcement of the law, but the regulation of illegal activities...

> ... an outbreak of violence arouses the "good people" to make demands for law enforcement... even when they disturb police racketeer relations. Therefore, it is in the interest of the departments to help maintain a peaceful racket organization... By regulating the racket and keeping peace, the officer can satisfy the demands for law enforcement with a number of token arrests and be free to make his adjustment to the local situation.[25]

Since an adjustment to the local situation might well involve adopting some of the "code" practices, the successful police rookie is he who can delicately temper three sets of uncomplementary standards: (1) the "code" practices adopted for group acceptance, (2) the societal standards regulating the duties and responsibilities of the police profession, and (3) his own system of morality gained from prior socialization in family, religious, educational, and peer-group interaction.

METHODOLOGICAL CONSIDERATIONS

The difficulties connected with any intensive investigation into the "code" are self evident. The binding secrecy which provides the source of its power would be disrupted if the "code" were revealed to an "outsider." Thus, standard sociological research methods were ineffective in this type of investigation. The traditional ethnographic technique of using an informant familiar with the "code" and its related practices made available the empirical data within this study. Obviously, data from a single informant do not begin to meet the stringent scientific criteria of reliability for the purpose of applying the conclusions from this case to police agencies in general. It is assumed that subsequent research will establish whether this is a unique episode or more of a universal phenomenon. However, the decision to enrich the literature with this present study in spite of its methodological deficiencies was felt to be justified inasmuch as an intensive search through the professional literature revealed no empirical accounts dealing directly with deviant policemen.[26]

Because of the explosive nature of such materials on the social, political, and economic life of the persons involved, the use of pseudonyms to maintain complete anonymity is a precaution not without precedent, and was a guarantee given by the director of this study in return for complete co-operation of the informant.[27] The informant was a police officer for 3½ years before he was implicated in charges of Robbery and Grand Larceny. He was subsequently tried and convicted, serving the better part of a year in prison. At the time of these interviews, he had been released from prison about three years.

The initial design of this study attempted to correlate these empirical data with two journalistic accounts[28] but the subjective handling of those stories neutralized any advantage gained from an increased number of informants. The present design is based exclusively on the single informant.

THE CODE AND ITS PRACTICES

Some of these terms used to describe police deviancy are widely used, but because of possible variations in meaning they are defined below.[29] These practices are ordered so that those listed first would generally elicit the least fear of legal prosecution and those listed last would invoke major legal sanctions for their perpetration.

> Mooching—An act of receiving free coffee, cigarettes, meals, liquor, groceries, or other items either as a consequence of being in an underpaid, undercompensated profession *or* for the possible future acts of favoritism which might be received by the donor.
>
> Chiseling—An activity involving police demands for free admission to entertainment whether connected to police duty or not, price discounts, etc.
>
> Favoritism—The practice of using license tabs, window stickers, or courtesy cards to gain immunity from traffic arrest or citation (sometimes extended to wives, families, and friends of recipient).
>
> Prejudice—Situation in which minority groups receive less than impartial, neutral, objective attention, especially those who are less likely to have "influence" in City Hall to cause the arresting officer trouble.
>
> Shopping—The practice of picking up small items such as candy bars, gum, or cigarettes at a store where the door has been accidentally unlocked after business hours.
>
> Extortion—The demands made for advertisements in police magazines or purchase of tickets to police functions, or the "street courts" where minor traffic tickets can be avoided by the payment of cash bail to the arresting officer with no receipt required.

Bribery—The payments of cash or "gifts" for past or future assistance to avoid prosecution; such reciprocity might be made in
terms of being unable to make a positive identification of a criminal, or being in the wrong place at a given time when a crime
is to occur, both of which might be excused as carelessness but
no proof as to deliberate miscarriage of justice. Differs from
mooching in the higher value of a gift and in the mutual *understanding* regarding services to be performed upon the acceptance
of the gift.

Shakedown—The practice of appropriating expensive items for personal use and attributing it to criminal activity when investigating
a break-in, burglary, or an unlocked door. Differs from shopping
in the cost of the items and the ease by which former ownership
of items can be determined if the officer is "caught" in the act of
procurement.

Perjury—The sanction of the "code" which demands that fellow
officers lie to provide an alibi for fellow officers apprehended in
unlawful activity covered by the "code."

Premeditated Theft—Planned burglary, involving the use of tools,
keys, etc. to gain forced entry or a prearranged plan of unlawful
acquisition of property which cannot be explained as a "spur of
the moment" theft. Differs from shakedown only in the previous
arrangements surrounding the theft, not in the value of the items
taken.

Mooching, chiseling, favoritism, and *prejudice* do not have rigid interpretations in the "code." Their presence appears to be accepted by the
general public as a real fact of life. Since the employment of one of these
practices can be done while in the normal routine of one's duties, such
practices are often ignored as being "deviant" in any way. Ex-Officer Smith
sees it in this light:

> ... the policeman having a free cup of coffee? I have never thought
> of this as being corrupt or illegal because this thing is just a courtesy
> thing. A cup of coffee or the old one—the cop on the beat grabbing
> the apple off the cart—these things I don't think shock too many
> people because they know that they're pretty well accepted.

But when asked about the practice of *mooching* by name, it assumed a
different character of increased importance to Smith!

> I think mooching is accepted by the police and the public is
> aware of it. My opinion now, as an ex-policeman, is that mooching
> is one of the underlying factors in the larger problems that come ...
> it is one of the most basic things. It's the easiest thing to accept

and to take in stride because it's so petty. I think that it is the turning point a lot of times.

The "Sunday Comics" stereotype of policemen initiating mooching, bribery, and favoritism is incorrect according to Smith's experience:

> Generally, the policeman doesn't have to ask for things, he just finds out about them. Take for example the theaters. I know the Roxy theaters would let the policeman in on his badge, just about anytime. It's good business because it puts the owner in a closer relationship with the policeman, and the policeman is obligated to him. If they had a break-in, a fire, or a little favor such as double parking out front to unload something, they'd expect special consideration from the policeman.
>
> When I walked the east side beat the normal thing was for bartenders to greet me and offer me a pack of cigarettes or a drink. When I walked the beat I was pretty straight-laced, there were a few bartenders that I felt were just trying to get along with me, and I loosened up a little with those people. One bartender gave me cigars when he found out that I didn't smoke cigarettes. I always accepted them; he always pointed out there wasn't any obligation. Some of the beat men accepted cigarettes, some cigars, some took cash, and these men know when they're dealing with bootleggers, and why they're being paid. Different businessmen in the loop area give policemen Christmas presents every year.

Shopping and *shakedown, extortion* and *bribery* are all clearly unlawful, but in these practices the manner in which they are carried out contains a measure of safety to the policeman should his presence or behavior be questioned. A policeman's investigative powers allows him entry into an open building in which a "suspected robbery" has occurred, and various types of articles such as cigarettes and the like cannot be traced to any given retail outlet. Hence, his presence on such occasions is not *suspected*; rather, it is *expected!* Also, should a clumsy job of *shopping* or *shakedown* result in witnesses reporting these unlawful practices, the "code" requires that participating officers must commit *perjury* to furnish an alibi for those colleagues observed in illegal activities. This is both for the protection of the deviant officer and to preclude public disclosure of the widespread involvement of fellow officers in "code" practices. How extensive are *shopping* and *shakedown* as practiced by a department?

> As far as the Mid-City department is concerned I would say that 10 percent of the department would go along with anything, including deliberate forced entries or felonies. But about 50 percent of them would openly go along with just about anything. If they

found a place open or if there had been a break-in or if they found anything they could use and it was laying there, they'd help themselves to it.

Whenever there's an open door or window, they call for all the cars and they shake the whole building down—loot it!

Would those policemen involved in shopping and shakedown participate in something more serious? According to ex-officer Smith, they would.

Most of the policemen who shop or go along with shopping would go along with major theft, if it just happened. I think where you've got to draw the line is when you get into premeditated, deliberate thefts. I think this is where the big division comes.

In shopping, the theft just happens. Premeditated theft is a cold, deliberate, planned thing.

Here Smith points out the limits of the "code" which, through condoning any level of theft that "just happens," cannot fully support *premeditated theft*.

I think in premeditated theft that the general police attitude is against it, if for no other reason just for the matter of self-preservation, and survival. When you get to a premeditated, deliberate thing, then I think your police backing becomes pretty thin.

At the time when Smith was engaged in the practice of *premeditated theft* in Mid-City, it looked somewhat differently to him than it did later. When he took an objective look, he was aware of just how little this extreme deviancy *actually was practiced*.

When I was involved in it, it seemed like all the people around me were involved in it, and participating in it. It looked more to me like the generally accepted thing then, than it does now, because actually the clique that I was in that did this sort of thing was a small one. I'm not discounting the fact that there may have been a lot of other small cliques just like this.

Looking at his behavior as an outsider, after his expulsion, Smith saw it in this light:

After taking a long, hard look at my case and being real honest about it, I'd have to say that this [premeditated theft like mine] is the exception. The longer I'm away from this thing the more it looks like this.

In Mid-City, *extortion* was not generally practiced and the "code" prescribed "street courts" (i.e., bribery for minor traffic offenses) as outside the acceptable pattern.

> [Extortion is] something that I would classify as completely outside the law [here in Mid-City], something that in certain areas has been accepted well on the side of both the public and the police. There's a long standing practice that in Chicago if you are stopped for a traffic violation if you had a five dollar bill slipped in your plastic holder, or your billfold, the patrolman then asks for your license, and if that's in there you'll very rarely be issued a summons. Now this thing was something that was well known by truck-drivers and people who travel through that area.

Smith maintains that the "code" is widespread, although from the above analysis of extortion it can be clearly seen that specific practices have been traditionally practiced and accepted in certain areas, yet not found acceptable in another community. Would this mean that the bulk of these "code" practices occur in police departments other than the one in which Smith served his "apprenticeship" in "Blue-Coat Crime"? Our informant says "yes" and offers the following to substantiate his answer:

> I think generally the Mid-City police department is like every police department in the world. I think the exceptions are probably in small towns or in a few cities that have never been touched by corrupt politics, if there are any. But I think that generally they are the same everywhere,[30] because I have talked to policemen from other cities. I know policemen in other cities that I've had contact with that were in those things. I've discussed open things, or out and out felonies, with policemen from Kansas City on. And I know that at least in that city that it happens, and it's a matter of record that it happens in Denver and Chicago. And I think that this happens in all cities.

From a scientific point of view, other than the incidence of police scandals from time to time, there is no evidence to confirm or deny this one ex-officer's opinion regarding the universal existence of the "code."

The Recruit's Initiation into the "Code" Clique

Bucher describes a profession as a relatively homogeneous community whose members share identity, values, definitions of role, and interest. Socialization of recruits consists of inducting them into the "common core."[31] This occurs on two levels: the formal, or membership group, and the informal, or the reference group.

In the Mid-City police department the failure to socialize most of the new recruits into the "code" would constitute a threat to those who presently practice it. Thus, all "code" practitioners have the responsibility of screening new recruits at various times to determine whether they are "alright guys," and to teach by example and mutual involvement the limitations of "code" practices. If the recruit accepts such training, he is welcomed into the group and given the rights and privileges commensurate with his new status. If he does not, he is classified as a "goof" and avoided by the rest.

In a journalistic account of police deviancy, it was argued that if corruption exists in the political structures controlling police department appointments, this "socialization" into deviancy begins at the point of paying for the privilege of making an application or of buying an appointment.[32] Although Smith did not "buy" his appointment, he cited the existence of factions having influence in recruit appointments, even within the structure of a Civil Service Commission.

> There are four different requirements to the whole thing. One is your written test, one is your agility, one is your physical examination, and the fourth is the oral examination which is given by the civil service commission. I really crammed before I took the test. When I took the test it was a natural for me, it was a snap. I scored a 94 on my test for the police department. With my soldiers preference, which gives you 5 points, I scored a 99.[33] I passed my agility test and my physical. I could have had a 100 score, I could have been a gymnast, gone through the agility test and made everyone else look silly and still I could have failed in the oral exam. And this is the kicker where politics comes in.
>
> There are three old men that are aligned with different factions, different people on and off the department, different businessmen that have power, different groups, different lodges and organizations and all these things influence these men, these three people that make up the civil service board.

The existence of the "code" had hurt the level of morale generally in the Mid-City department. In fact, the breakdown of each new recruit's morale is an important step in gaining his acceptance of the "code."[34]

> The thing that hurt the morale was the fact that a large percentage of the people on the department were involved in illegal practices to some degree. And actually you take a man that has just joined the department, has good intentions[35] and is basically honest, and in this, to a man that's never been dishonest and hasn't stepped over the line, there aren't degrees. It's all either black or white. And the illegal activity I know shocks a lot of these young men . . . because it was the thing to do. It's a way to be accepted by

the other people. It's a terrible thing the way one policeman will talk about another. Say an old timer will have a new man working with him and he'll tell you, "You've got to watch him, because *he's honest!*"

For a recruit to be accepted in the Mid-City police department he must accept the informal practices occurring in the department. Illegal activity is pursued within the police force as the dominant "norm" or standard.

To illustrate the group pressure on each policeman who dares to enforce the law as prescribed in the legal statutes, the following account is typical.

> We'll take a classic example—Mr. Sam Paisano. Now when I was on the force I knew that whenever I worked in the downtown area, I could go into Sam's restaurant and order my meal and never have to pay a dime. I think that just about every patrolman on the force knew that. If I had run across Sam doing anything short of murder, I think I would have treaded very lightly. Even if I hadn't accepted his free meals. Say I had turned it down; still, if I stopped this man for a minor traffic violation, say I caught him dead to rights, I'd be very reluctant to write this man a ticket because I'd suffer the wrath of the other men on the force. I'd be goofing up their meal ticket. Now he in turn knows this. The rest of the officers wouldn't waste any words about it, they'd tell you right off —"You sure fouled up our meal ticket." The old timers would give you a cold shoulder. If it came to the attention of the gold braid, your immediate superiors, they'd make sure you had a little extra duty or something. In most cases if you did this just to be honest, just to be right, it would go badly for you.
>
> This special treatment of Mr. Paisano wasn't something that you concealed, or that you were ashamed of because it was the normal accepted thing to do. I'd have been more ashamed, and I'd have kept it quiet if I'd stopped such a man as this, because I'd have felt like some kind of an oddball. I would have been bucking the tide, I'd been out of step.

Yes, such general practices must be converted to individual participation at some point, and to be effective this involvement must be on a primary group relationship basis. Smith's account of his introduction to the "code" follows the first steps of the assimilating process.

> The first thing that I can recall seeing done [which was illegal] was on the night shift when I first went on patrol. The old timers were shaking buildings down and helping themselves to whatever was in the building. The first time I saw it happen I remember filing through the check-out counter at a supermarket, seeing all

the officers grabbing their cigarettes or candy bars, or whatever they wanted and I passed through without anything.

I got in the car and this old timer had, of all the petty things, two of these 25 or 30 cent candy bars and he sat them down in the seat and told me to have some. I told him I really didn't want any. And he asked me if "that shook me up" or something. And I told him, "Well, it sort of surprised me." He said that everybody did it and that I should get used to that.

And as it went on it progressed more. Well, in fact, he justified it at the time by telling me he had seen the same market one time, when there had been a legitimate break-in and one particular detective had been so busy loading the back seat of his car full of hams and big pieces of beef that he was stumbling and falling down back and from the cooler to the alley, and he didn't even know who was around him he was so busy carrying things out. And he named this officer and I don't doubt it because I've seen the same officer do things in that same nature.

And this was the first direct contact I had with anything like this.

The old timers would test the new recruits with activities which could be laughed off if they were reported, such as the 30 cent candy bar taken from the supermarket in the above account.

The old timers would nose around 'til they found out whether a young guy was going to work with them and "be right" as far as they were concerned, or whether he was going to resist it and be straight as far as the rest of the world was concerned.

If the recruit cooperated, the practices were extended and the rookie became involved. Once he was involved there was no "squealing" on fellow policemen breaking the law. Then he could have some personal choice as to how far he personally wished to go. However, those who were straight-laced and wanted to stay honest had their problems too. Social isolation appears to be a powerful sanction as can be seen from Smith's information.

There are a few policemen that are straight-laced all the way. I can remember one policeman who might have made an issue of another policeman taking something. He had that attitude for the first six months that he was on the force but by that time, he had been brow beaten so bad, he saw the writing on the wall. He knew better than to tell anything. In addition to brow beating, this man in very short order was put in a position where they had him on the information desk, or kicked around from one department to another, 'cause nobody wanted to work with him. This kind of a man they called "wormy," because anything that would happen he'd run to the braid.

This fellow, I knew, wanted to be one of the boys, but he wanted to be honest, too. As it turned out, this guy was finally dismissed from the force for having an affair with a woman in his squad car. Just a couple of years before that he would have had a fit if he thought that somebody was going to take a drink on duty, or fool around with a woman, or steal anything. For this reason this man spent a lot of time on the information desk, working inside, and by himself in the squad car.

Negative sanctions were applied against "goofs" who advocated following the legitimate police ethic. Group acceptance by senior officers was the reward to a recruit accepting the "code," and the "code" was presented to the recruit as the police way of life having precedence over legal responsibilities.

This small fraction that . . . are honest and would report illegal activity, are ostracized. Nobody will work with them. They look at them like they're a freak, talk about them like they're a freak, and they are a freak.

The goofs that would talk about doing things the way they should be done, they had to be ignored or put down. There were older policemen that as they found out I would go along with certain things, pressed to see how much further I would go. And showed me that they went farther, whether I cared to or not. So naturally I went along quite a ways with some of them. And I don't really remember how we first became aware of how far the other person would go. I think this is just a gradual thing.

The existence of a social system of an informal nature working quietly under the facade of the formal police department regulations has been clearly demonstrated in Mid-City. One further note in explaining the motivations of policemen toward illegal activities involves the condition of low salaries. Smith's department pay scale and working conditions would suggest that economic pressures were a factor in condoning or rationalizing "code" practices.

The pay wasn't good. I went on the department and earned $292 a month. The morale of the force was as low as that of any group that I've ever been around. There was constant complaining from all then about everything.

The training programs were set up so that you would have to come in on your own time and weren't compensated for it. . . . They dictated to you how you lived your whole life, not only what you did during the eight hours you were a policeman but how you'd live your whole life. This as much as anything hurt the morale.

But when Smith was asked directly, "With the policeman's low salary, do illegal activities become necessary to keep up financially?" he discounted it as a major factor.[36]

> I don't think this is the case. I don't think there are very many policemen that I knew, and I knew all of them, that were social climbers or that tried to keep up with the Joneses, by illegal activities anyway.
>
> Actually most of the police officers think that they are even above those people that have money, because they have power. Those people with money are pretty well forced to cater to a policeman. And you'll find that very few people ever tell a policeman what they think of him, whether they like him or not. They know that a policeman will do him harm. The businessmen, especially the bigger businessmen, pamper the policemen. They will treat them with respect when they face them.

Sanctions for Preservation of the "Code"

Normally, practitioners of the "code" would consist of a united group working to protect all fellow patrolmen from prosecution. However, Smith had exceeded the "code" limits[37] by committing *premeditated theft*, and in order to protect the "code" from being exposed during the scandal involving Smith and two accomplices, the "clique" socially and spatially isolated themselves from the three accused policemen.

> Everybody ran for cover, when the thing hit the front page of the newspapers. I've never seen panic like there was at that time. These people were all ready to sell out their mother to save their own butts. They knew there was no holding back, that it was a tidal wave. They were grabbing just anything to hang on. The other policemen were ordered to stay away from us, myself and the other men involved. They were ordered to stay away from the trials. They were told to keep their noses out of this thing, that it would be handled.
>
> There were a few policemen who came around during this time. Strangely the ones who came around were the ones who didn't go in for any of the illegal activity. They didn't have anything to worry about. Everybody else ran and hid.

During a time like this, group consensus is required to preserve the "code." A certain amount of rationalization is necessary to mollify past illicit activity in light of present public exposure. Smith continues:

> I think if they had really gone by the book during the police scandal, that 25 percent of the policemen would have lost their jobs. I've talked to some of them since, and the worst violators all now have themselves convinced that they weren't guilty of a thing.
>
> I've never referred to myself as this before, but I was their goat, their scapegoat. The others stuck together and had support. I got what I deserved, but if I compare myself with the others, I got a real raw deal.

Preservation of the "code" occurs when policemen work with another person who has similar intentions and begin to "trust" one another in illegal activities without fear of the authorities being informed. A suggestion of rotating young officers from shift to shift to weaken the "code" had been given public discussion. To this, Smith reacted thusly:

> I think that the practice of rotating young officers will serve a purpose. It will eliminate a lot of things because you just can't take a chance with somebody that you don't know. If you don't know but what the next person they throw you with might be a CID ... short for Criminal Investigation Department. They're spies! Say there are just 10 percent of the men on the department that wouldn't go along with anything, and they are switching around with the new system, you don't know when you're gong to catch one of them, and if you do you're a cooked goose. The old system you were 90 percent sure of the people you were with.

This same process used to preserve the illegal "code" as a group phenomenon is also the same process used to develop and promote the acceptable professional ethics of the police. A situation in which it is "normal" for a policeman to "squeal on his fellow patrolmen," would undermine professional ethics. Personal insecurity would mount with the constant fear of just being accused with or without supporting evidence. Such an anarchical system lends itself to intrigue, suspicion, and an increased possibility of each officer being "framed." Thus, these same procedures which would effectively reduce the continuation of the "code" would also prove dysfunctional to the maintenance of the ethics which are the core of the police profession itself. These concurrent processes reflect the dual standards extant in society at large.

DIFFICULTIES INVOLVED IN BREAKING THE "CODE"

If a "code" does exist in a law enforcement agency, one of the major factors which protects it from attack is secrecy. This factor is compounded by public acceptance of the traditional view of illegal behavior as only an individualistic, moral problem.

Another shield of the "code" from attack is the apathy resulting from the myriad of complex demands and responsibilities placed upon the average citizen. So many things touch him with which he *must* become involved that he does not pursue problems which do not directly concern him. Inextricably connected with this is the realistic fear of retaliation, either through direct harassment by the police or indirectly through informal censures.[38]

Smith says that only a real big issue will provoke an apathetic public to action.

> Everybody's looking out for number one. And the policeman can do you harm. It's such a complex thing, there are so many ways, so many different people are affected by the police—Most people will back off. Most people are afraid to do anything, if it looks like it's going to affect them adversely.

If the police have carefully practiced *prejudice*, in their day-to-day operations, the chances are slim that the persons against whom these illegal practices were committed possess either the social or political power to break the "code" before the system could retaliate. Knowing this fact keeps most of the persons with any knowledge of the "code's" operation silent indeed.

The rigid procedures of obtaining legal evidence and the dangers of committing a *false arrest* are gigantic deterrents to bringing accusations against any suspicious person, especially a policeman. Ex-Officer Smith discusses the realistic problems involved in attempting to enforce legal statutes against *shopping* or other aspects of the "code":

> I think that any law against *shopping* would be hard to enforce against a police officer. You'd really have to have the evidence against him and really make it public, cause it would be soft pedalled all the way otherwise. Let's say you see a police officer in a restaurant taking a pack of cigarettes or let's say it's something other than a pack of cigarettes, something that you can prove came from the restaurant. And along comes a radio news unit and you stop the unit and say you just saw a policeman steal a pack of cigarettes or something bigger. When other police arrive on the scene the newsman would probably pull the other policemen off to the side and tell them that their buddy just took a pack of cigarettes and that goofball [the informer] wants to make trouble about it. You insist that they shake down the policeman and they find the item. Here you're in pretty good shape. In this case you'd have a policeman in a little bit of trouble. I don't think he'd lose his job or do any time over it, but I'd say there would be some scandal about it. Unless you were real hard headed they'd soft pedal it.
>
> Let's back up a little and say the policeman threw the item

back into the restaurant, and then you made your accusation. Then you're in trouble, 'cause when they shake him down and he doesn't have a thing. Now you're a marked man, because every policeman in town will know that you tried to foul up one of their boys. Even the honest policemen aren't going to like what you did. In other words, they are tightly knit, and they police this city by fear to a certain extent.

In Mid-City only those who are involved in practicing the "code" are equipped with the necessary information to expose its operations. Whether one *can* inform on his fellow officers is directly connected with the degree of his illegal involvement prior to the situation involving the unlawful event.

It all depends upon how deeply you are involved. If you've been a guy who has gone along with a free cup of coffee, the gratuities, the real petty things and you'd happen to drive up on a major theft, drive up on another policeman with his shoulder against the door, then you might take action. However, if you had gone a little farther, say you'd done some shopping, then you're forced to look the other way. It's like a spider spinning a web, you're drawn in toward the center.

It appears obvious that those who are involved in the "code" will be the least useful instruments for alleviating the problem. Only the professionally naive would expect a "code" practitioner to disclose the "code's" existence, much less reveal its method of operation, since his own position is so vulnerable.

Summary of Findings

From data furnished by a participant informant, an informal "code" of illegal activities within one police department was documented. The group processes which encouraged and maintained the "code" were identified. It was found that the new recruits were socialized into "code" participation by "old timers" and group acceptance was withheld from those who attempted to remain completely honest and not be implicated. When formal police regulations were in conflict with "code" demands among its practitioners, the latter took precedence. Since the "code" operates under conditions of secrecy, only those who participate in it have access to evidence enough to reveal its method of operation. By their very participation they are implicated and this binds them to secrecy as well. In this study the public indignation of a police scandal temporarily suspended the "code" but it flourished again when public apathy returned.

Although some individual factors must be considered in explaining police deviancy, in the present study the sanction of group acceptance was paramount. This study clearly demonstrates the social genesis of the "code," the breeding ground for individual unlawful behavior. From evidence contained herein, an individualistic orientation to police deviancy may discover the "spoiled fruit" but only when the "code" is rooted out can the "seedbed" of deviancy be destroyed.

From related research in group deviancy, it can be stated that the social organization of a given community (including its respectable citizens) is the milieu in which a "code" flourishes. Thus, a police department is an integral element of that complex community structure, and deviancy found in an enforcement agency is a reflection of values which are habitually practiced and accepted within that community. This was found to be true in the present study.

The findings of this case study should not be interpreted as applicable to all police departments nor should it be a rationalization for the existence of an illicit "code" anywhere. Rather, it is a very limited effort to probe the very sensitive area of "Blue-Coat Crime" and describe its operation and method of perpetuation in one enforcement agency.

Footnotes

Revision of a paper presented at the Rocky Mountain Social Science Association, Air Force Academy, April, 1967. It was supported in part by a grant from the University Research Institute, University of Texas at El Paso.

[1] This concept is a restricted modification of Sutherland's term "White Collar Crime." Edwin H. Sutherland, "White Collar Criminality," 5 *Amer. Soc. Rev.* 1–12 (1940). However, the stress of Sutherland's thesis is the lowering of social morale *of the larger society* by the violation of trust by those holding these social positions. The present emphasis is upon the group participating in those violations and *their* reactions, morale, and behavior, rather than the consequences accruing the larger society as a result of these illegal actions. The same violation of trust might produce a degree of disorganization and lowering of morale among nonparticipants, while producing a heightened morale and cohesion among all of those in the norm-violating clique.

[2] August Vollmer, *The Police and Modern Society* 3–4 (1936).

[3] A. C. German, *Police Personnel Management* 3–4 (1958).

[4] Mort Stern, "What Makes a Policeman Go Wrong? An Ex-Member of the Force Traces the Steps on Way from Law Enforcement to Violating," by a Former Denver Police Officer as told to Mort Stern, Denver *Post*, October 1, 1961. Reprinted in 53 *J. Crim. L., C. & P. S.* 97–101 (1962).

A similar reaction is given by James F. Johnson, a former state trooper, Secret Service Agent, security officer, and private investigator in *World Telegram and Sun*, March 10, 1953, quoted in Tappan, *Crime, Justice and Correction* 290 (1960).

[5] Tappan, *ibid.* 309ff.

6 Wilson, "Progress in Police Administration," 42 *J. Crim. L., C. & P. S.* 141 (1951).

7 Johnson, *Crime, Correction and Society* 452 (1964).

8 The Lexow Committee in New York (1894–1895), and the Seabury Committee a generation later found the same situation of *departmental* corruption quoted in Sutherland & Cressey, *Principles of Criminology* 338 (6th ed. 1960).

9 Sutherland & Cressey, *ibid.*

10 Barnes & Teeters, *New Horizons in Criminology* 245–247 (2d ed. 1958).

11 Korn & McCorkle, *Criminology and Penology* 85–86, 125–136 (1959).

12 Richard A. Cloward, "Illegitimate Means, Anomie, and Deviant Behavior," 24 *Amer. Soc. Rev.* 167 (1959).

13 Merton, *Social Theory and Social Structure*, Chaps. 1, 4 and 5 (Revised and enlarged ed. 1958).

14 Bell, "Crime as an American Way of Life," 13 *Antioch Rev.* 140–144 (1953).

15 Sutherland & Cressey, *op. cit.* 331.

16 This dilemma is presently being compounded by recent Supreme Court decisions involving police powers and personal civil rights. The fear of an emergent police state (which may or may not be valid) leads the present Justices to feel that freedom of the individual will result when police powers no longer encroach upon individual rights. The paradox is that the police are required to fulfill their traditional protection duties in spite of these new formal procedures designed to limit their investigative activities. To fulfill the social expectations of "catching criminals, dope peddlers, etc.," the policeman must adopt certain extra-legal procedures strictly on an informal basis, while appearing on the surface to be adhering to the formal limitations imposed upon him. See Arthur Niederhoffer's recent monograph *Behind the Shield: The Police in Urban Society* (1967).

17 Westley, "Violence and the Police," 59 *Amer. J. Soc.* 34–41 (1953).

18 Westley, "Secrecy and the Police," 34 *Social Forces* 254–257 (1956).

19 This concept was taken from Cohen, *Delinquent Boys: The Culture of the Gang* 60 (1955).

20 Sherif & Sherif, *An Outline of Social Psychology* 630–631, 638. For a sophisticated treatment of reference group theory see Chapters 4, 16, and 18 (Revised ed. 1956).

21 Stouffer, "An Analysis of Conflicting Social Norms," 14 *Amer. Soc. Rev.* 707 (1949).

22 Dornbush, "The Military Academy as an Assimilating Institution," 33 *Social Forces* 316–321 (1955).

23 Moore & Tumin, "Some Social Functions of Ignorance," 14 *Amer. Soc. Rev.* 791 (1949).

24 Johnson, *op. cit.* 445–446.

25 Whyte, *Street Corner Society* 138–139 (Enlarged ed. 1955). Another author conceptualized this problem by delineating it as two separate police functions. "Law enforcement" has specific formal legal procedures whereas "keeping the peace" is vague and without a clear-cut mandate. This study updates by three decades the classic work of Whyte. See Egon Bittner, "The Police on Skid-Row: A Study of Peace Keeping," 32 *Amer. Soc. Rev.* 699–715 (1967).

26 Many authors have written of police deviancy as tangential to their central theme. However, persistent search failed to reveal recent empirical studies focusing directly on the deviant policeman himself. Most applicable were Westley's, "Violence

and the Police," *op. cit.*, and "Secrecy and the Police," *op. cit.*, although even here the data were gained from policemen still "in favor," who might well have reservations about revealing the full extent to which the "Code" was practiced.

[27] A graduate assistant from the Department of Sociology, Mr. Ivy L. Gilbert approached ex-officer "Smith" as a friend, and under guidance of the present author was able to gain "Smith's" cooperation for a scientific study. Taped interviews over a period of several months were recorded and transcribed by Gilbert. Many of these materials were used in Gilbert's Master's Thesis, "A Case Study of Police Scandal: An Investigation into Illegitimate Norms of a Legitimate Enforcement Agency" (University of Texas at El Paso, June, 1965).

[28] One article is a composite of personal experience as a police reporter, David G. Wittels, "Why Cops Turn Crooked," *Saturday Evening Post*, April 23, 1949, p. 26ff; the other is an account of a former Denver policeman as retold by a news editor, Mort Stern, *op. cit. supra* note 4.

[29] The majority of these terms and definitions are modified from those listed by Gilbert, *op. cit.* 3–4, and discussed by German, *op. cit. supra* note 3 at p. 173.

[30] Smith's evaluations are heavily influenced by his experience. He was a patrolman in a police department totaling about 250 personnel, serving a metropolitan area of a quarter of a million persons.

However, other sources have suggested that when a community gets larger than 80,000 people, political corruption and graft are inevitable. Wittels, *op. cit.* 26.

[31] Rue Bucher and Anselm Strauss, "Professions in Progress," 64 *Amer. J. Soc.* 325–326 (1961).

[32] One Policeman reported having paid $300.00 to take the police examination. He also was required to pledge his family's vote to the "right" party. After some wait, he took a "special exam," then more waiting lists, and a final $300.00 to the party fund was required before he was hired. Then he had to purchase his own uniform on contract at the "right" store. Before this man became a member of the department, by his participation in the recruitment process, he was an involved member practicing the "code." Wittels, *op. cit.* 105–107, 111.

[33] In spite of Smith's remarkable test level, he was left off a list of highest 10 eligible applicants, and some three months later was put on the list through the influence of his father, a respected member of the police department with many years of unblemished service. Otherwise, he may never have been placed on the appointment list.

[34] This is not unlike the planned removal of old civilian standards and values when a new soldier recruit is given basic training. The formal regulations are presented to him, but in company with "old Salts" he learns how the system can be worked and what a person must do to participate in it.

[35] One writer corroborates this by stating that young recruits who show traits of being ambitious, as well as those with family responsibilities, are the most susceptible to graft. The pressures toward success and achievement are clearly indicated by either or both of these factors. Wittels, *op. cit.* 27.

[36] To evaluate Smith's statement on economic pressures, an additional personal datum is relevant. Smith used most of his money from *premeditated theft* for his "habit"—a racing car. He later declared he probably wouldn't have participated in this crime *so much* had it not been for the "habit." His responses did not seem to indicate that he *began* theft for racing money, but that he *continued* it to counter the economic drain created by owning and driving the racing machine.

[37] One officer reports that he wondered why he was not promoted—perhaps they thought he was lazy. He was tagging cars of all violators, and even reported a broken sidewalk belonging to an "organization" man. He couldn't get ahead. He made a couple of outstanding arrests and was made a detective. Later, he ran a

"vice" raid against a "protected" place, and was back as a rookie on a beat in "Siberia." He finally took some payoffs and cooperated and eventually became a Police Captain, but exceeding the "Code" limits, was caught and prosecuted. Either not accepting the "code," or exceeding its limits, had negative effects. Wittels, *op. cit.* 111–122.

[38] The campaigning attack on the "untouchable" image of J. Edgar Hoover and the FBI has made political news. The very act of exposing methods used by Hoover's organization, which though admittedly effective were clearly unlawful, caused the political downfall of an otherwise popular politician in the November 1966 Nevada election.

The Discomforts and
Dilemmas of Work

Role Performance and Role Distance in a Low-Status Occupation

The Puller

T. E. LEVITIN

Many studies, such as those of the waitress and of the janitor, have illuminated some of the social processes and problems of low-status occupations.[1] Examined here is the occupation of the "puller," a salesman who stations himself outside the store for which he works, selects potential customers from passing individuals, and persuades them to enter the store, where other salesmen assist them in selecting merchandise. This study proposes to demonstrate that performance of the role of puller threatens the fulfillment of certain needs of the occupant of that role, particularly the need for self-esteem, and that certain defensive mechanisms, particularly that of *role distance*, have therefore become an integral part of the role performance. Furthermore, it is suggested that both role performance and role distance patterns vary with the specific characteristics ascribed to categories of people with whom the puller interacts. Essentially, with E. C. Hughes, "our aim is to *penetrate more deeply* into the personal and social drama of work, to understand the social and social psychological arrangements and devices by which men make their work tolerable or even glorious to themselves and others."[2]

More than sixty pullers work in an area, two to three blocks long, of small stores in south Chicago. One puller in particular was studied in detail as observations of several of his colleagues indicated his patterns of role performance were similar to theirs and therefore might be considered representative of his occupation. Observation, both with and without the knowledge of the subject, was the chief method by which data were gathered. Information from more than twenty-five hours of observation on five occasions between October, 1963, and February, 1964, was supplemented by

Reprinted from *The Sociological Quarterly*, Vol. 5, No. 3 (Summer 1964), 251–60, by permission of the publisher.

two unstructured interviews, one in October, the other in February. The subject is fifty-one years old, completed the eighth grade of school, and has been pulling for thirty-five years. He is paid $65.00 a week. He is a native American, married, the father of two children, and a member of the Jewish faith.

The significance of noting in detail the behavior of a single member of a low-status occupation is of a dual nature. First, the low-status occupation itself is a legitimate object of study, for "since prestige is so much a matter of symbols, and even of pretensions—however well merited—there goes with prestige a tendency to preserve a front which hides the inside of things; a front of names, of indirection, of secrecy (much of it necessary secrecy). On the other hand, in things of less prestige, the core may be more easy of access."[3] Second, the method of study—assessment through observation—reveals the numerous ways occupational demands can be met, indicates the vast and varied repertoire of responses possible within a narrowly defined occupational role.

That the puller views his occupational role as one of low status is a most basic assumption of this paper, which is supported both by historical fact and by the opinion of the puller himself. The area in which he works, Maxwell Street, is an outdoor market in south Chicago. The narrow, often broken, sidewalks are bounded by small stores on one side and by large wooden panels of store goods on the other. Many tables are set up in the street. Clothing, shoes, jewelry, flashlights, and material are but a few of the items sold. This was once the center of a ghetto of Jewish immigrants who established traditions of commerce little different from those they had left behind in Europe. In 1928 it was noted that Maxwell Street was beginning to pass away.[4] Today this decline is even more evident. The residential area around Maxwell Street contains cold-water flats in what is now one of the worst remaining slums in Chicago. Now only about half of the shops are owned by Jewish merchants. Gypsies, Negroes, and Latin Americans own and operate the rest of Maxwell Street commerce.

Implicit in this paper is the assumption that the need for self-esteem is a vital and potent need. The problem of the puller should, therefore, be patent: his occupational role is such that he sees himself, as viewed by others, in a position dissonant with his self-esteem. His occupational role precludes acting to people in terms of imputed values, status, or potential purchasing power. Proper and legitimate occupational role performance must conform to certain cultural expectations. For example, everyone should be given an equal opportunity to buy, people should be served in order of arrival, sexual or aggressive overtures should be avoided. However, within these general demands, the puller has developed specific ways of acting toward categories of people, ways which are structured into role performance neither by cultural nor by occupational demands.

First, the puller notes: "I havta act like niggers are as good as me to make a sale." "People think I'm a freak, I know they do, but I've gotta be nice to them." Clearly, preservation of self-esteem is threatened by having to relate on an equal status level to those he feels are his inferiors and by having to acquiesce to adverse judgments of those who feel they are superior to him. The psychological mechanisms of response to such constant tension are aggression, regression to an infantile or more primitive mode of behavior, physical or symbolic withdrawal, or some type of accommodative behavior.[5] A mechanism of response allowing both the control and indirect release of some of these tensions without interruption of adequate role performance is also available to the puller. This mechanism is *role distance*, which is defined by Goffman as conduct "that falls between role obligations on one hand and actual role performance on the other"; he notes that these roles which "place an individual in an occupational setting he feels is beneath him are bound to give rise to much role distance," as, indeed, the role of puller indicates.[6] When the puller, more or less deliberately, separates from his role, he is able both to perform his role adequately and to preserve his self-esteem as it is not he *himself* but he *as puller* who is interacting with members of the general category of "customer," and the customer's responses are to him as puller, not to him as a person. Various mechanisms of such role distance were associated with specific patterns of role performance toward different subcategories of customers, which facilitated that performance and increased sales. For "when the customer takes an active part in business activity, the whole organization must be adjusted to his behavior."[7]

The puller interacted with people of greatly different backgrounds. Understanding their expectations of him and acting in accordance with those expectations, even if so doing threatened his self-esteem, elicited positive responses from customers and increased the number of sales. Role performance was more successful when the puller learned the verbal and nonverbal responses favored by particular categories of customers. According to the subject, "the Spanish, they like you to throw your arms around them like a friend; they expect it. But you don't do that to a Jew. Just like you couldn't talk Yiddish to a Spanish." "You gotta do whatever they want to make a sale. Like you have to kid them in their language."

On the other hand, elements of self-abasement were patent in the humorous manner the puller displayed throughout his encounters, particularly with high-status people, for this humor was uniformly directed toward himself. Several times he said in a jocular manner, complete with a smile and laughing tone: "Hey, how come you don't buy a coat? Is it because I'm so ugly?" This comment usually elicited laughter. "Make them laugh at you. Puts them in the mood for a serious pitch and a sale." Introduction of this type of humor into role performance served a dual purpose. First, such comments facilitated the rapport necessary for successful salesmanship. Second, such comments manifested a certain degree of role distance. If the puller made himself, as puller, an object of humor that *both* he and high-status customers found ridiculous, he aligned himself with that customer and separated himself from that ludicrous low-status occupation.

Distance from role also took the form of identifying himself with ideas and activities usually associated with high-status people and of manipulating the symbols thereof: "Hey look! I'm working my way through college by selling coats." "This is a good coat. It's got class like a Cadillac or like fine jewelry like your earrings." Reference to items associated with high status not only established rapport for sales purposes but also indicated that the puller, as a person, was familiar with these items and therefore deserved more respect than his occupational role alone might indicate. "I like to let them know I know about high-class stuff so they won't think I'm a bum like some of the other guys here."

To low socioeconomic status people of either sex, there were also definite types of role performance. Some low-status members were ignored completely. "Hillbillies are the worst type of people. . . . They don't got no money; I never even talk to them." "Gypsies are liars. They're dirty too. We don't want them in our store." In general, with those ascribed to a low status, persuasive speech was directed more toward economy, also toward sexual attractiveness, and less toward quality than with high-status customers. On the other hand, rather than make himself the object of humorous comments, as with high-status people, the puller tended to make those of lower status the objects of that humor. Comments such as, "Hey, you with the ugly husband, why not make him buy you a coat?" were frequent. Several times he initiated interaction by saying, "Your mother-in-law will throw you out of the house if you don't buy your wife a coat"; or "Find yourself a better husband with a new coat, OK?" Such humor allowed him to laugh at, rather than to laugh with, his customers and thereby to distance himself from a role not allowing such disrespect. Yet making lower-status people the objects of this hostile, disrespectful humor did not noticeably alienate people to whom it was directed. Usually, smiles and favorable responses were elicited from members of both sexes. Indeed, this type of humor, though primarily a mechanism of role distance, also served to facilitate role performance. The primacy of humor as a mechanism of role distance was indicated by numerous statements similar to this one: "These people don't know I laugh at them. It makes me feel good that they don't know. That's what's important. Besides, then they buy coats."

However, the puller's most common approach to lower-status people was to indicate by word as well as by gesture that he shares the same socioeconomic status. He said to a white man: "Look, I'm broke too, but I'm willing to let you have this for your wife for only twenty bucks." As he spoke he turned the front pockets of his pants inside out. He told a young Negress: "We can't shop at Marshall Field's where a coat like this there would cost fifty bucks. Here it's only 19.99." Yet the puller by no means felt that he indeed shared this status, only that his occupation made him appear that way and that successful role performance demanded he behave that way. "I'm not like these guys, but they don't wanna think anybody's above them, so I act like we're all big friends to sell more coats."

Those to whom the puller especially acted like "big friends" were people of Latin American origin. With these people, his physical responses were particularly obvious and frequent. He would throw his arms around both men and women as they walked by. "They all hug each other. They just do; so, I hug them too. Everybody's happy then, and they buy a coat."

His encounters with Latin American people had another unique aspect, consciously calculated to introduce familiarity and rapport. The puller addressed all Spanish-looking people, male or female, with the words. "Hey Señor!" He would assume a Spanish accent, saying to one man that his wife would "geeve you a beeg kees" if he bought her a coat, and trilling the r's when he told a woman she "would be so prreety" if she bought "thees coat wheech is a rreel barrgin." He said, "Look, I talk this gibberish to them. *They* don't understand, and *I* don't understand, but it makes them feel good, like I'm gonna give them a real deal or something." Terms of address to Negroes consistently took the form of "Sir" or "Madam," whereas even high-status white people were sometimes addressed with a casual "Hey!" The puller said: "I always call them 'Sir' or 'Madam' even though they're lower than me. But colored people like to be kibbitzed like that; especially when a white man who's better than them talks to them they like it." These specific yet varied approaches were so consistent in role performance that it is not surprising Wirth noted "the 'puller' is a specialist."[8]

Other mechanisms of role distance less conjunctive with successful role performance were also evident. While these mechanisms were not debilitating to ongoing role performance, they did not enhance that performance. But they were necessary to reaffirm self-esteem.

Ceasing to participate in the performance was the most frequent index of role distance. After the initial eye-contact, the puller looked around while talking to the customer. Although his eyes always returned to the customer, these brief periods of looking around were legion. Verbal role performance remained unaffected by his gaze wandering. Even the rather intricate technique of hiking up his pants with one hand and simultaneously holding his elbow with the other while looking at his belt buckle, an arrangement often noted, was performed without interruption of the verbal aspects of role performance. Nothing in his voice indicated the disinterest and distance his gestures evidenced.

Gestures exaggerated to the point of flamboyance were also frequent. These expressive actions occurred more often when the puller encountered lower-status people. There was some overt consideration to improving role performance by means of such exaggeration: "Some people get a kick if you jump around more; some rich customers don't got time for that sort of stuff, so I do it, but not as much." Nevertheless, there seemed to be a more important covert function to these expansive gestures, for, wild though they might be, the very sharpness and repetition of these gestures indicated a large degree of control of, and therefore distance from, such behavior. These gestures were forced rather than spontaneous. Furthermore, there did appear to be a direct relationship between degree of hostility to the customer and manifest wildness of these gestures. For example, after a brief encounter with a buxom Negress, during which the puller had waved and walked jauntily, talked louder and touched far more often than usual, he confided with intense vehemence: "God, she's the *worse* nigger I've met today. You could tell she's dirt. Real dirty dirt!"

Additional evidence of types of role distance came from unexpected customer responses. The puller approached a Latin-American woman. "Señor," he began, placing his hand on her shoulder, "I've got a real bargain for you. . . ." The lady turned and, without losing pace, pushed his shoulder with the palm of a stiffly extended arm and said in a softly menacing voice: "Don't *touch* me, you dirty, ugly man!" The puller stepped back two paces, although her push had not been forceful enough to cause him to do so. A brief blank expression crossed his face, and then he began to sing over and over again in a high voice, "don't touch, don't touch," hopping on alternate feet to the beat of his words as he sang. This regressive behavior, clearly totally out of role performance, lasted for a full minute. Retreat from role to protect self occurred again and again when responses elicited were unexpected and threatening to his self-esteem. A well dressed young man to whom he had said, "I'll be honest with you; this coat cost me $50, but you can have it for $20," interrupted him by saying "Shut up, shithead!" The puller stepped back, and, after the man had walked by, he directed an unmistakable gesture with his middle finger toward the retreating figure and murmured to himself: "The bastard!" This particular incident so upset the puller that he allowed several customers to walk by while he stood there, rocking back and forth, lifting his pants by the belt, one hand on his elbow, and staring at his belt buckle. Temporary divorce from a role through regression seemed the only defense possible as his occupational role did not provide for any type of retaliation to the source of those insults that would not harm role performance.

Interaction with fellow workers is another mechanism of role distance. Several pullers work in the immediate vicinity. All make approximately the same amount of money. None have completed high school. There was no interaction between them outside of their work experience; as lunch hours were irregular, they seldom ate together. Nevertheless, in the long years these men have worked side by side (one has been there 20 years,

another 25, another 28), some definite patterns of noncompetitive interaction have been established. Communication among co-workers took place
both during role performance with customers and during times when no
customers were present. Each type of relationship deserves notice.

Communication with co-workers during role performance was comparatively infrequent. These men were spatially separated, and catching the
eye of a fellow puller was simply a chance encounter. However, there were
definite patterns of communication even in these infrequent chance encounters.

If a customer was particularly rude or insulting, the subject would frequently indicate this by raising his eyes skyward. This gesture was also a
signal to other pullers not to waste time with that particular customer. "If
I see them looking at me, I tell them by the way I look if I've got a real
bum or not." Asked if he raised his eyes to signal them, he responded:
"Yeah, maybe that's what I do because that's what they do to warn me."

When an especially attractive female walked by, no matter what her
imputed status, race, or response to the puller, the gesture of looking from
shoes to hair and down to shoes again with a slight puckering of the lips
was given; an unattractive woman rated a surreptitious thumbs down
gesture.

The appearance of a couple tended to elicit another pattern of distance
from role by co-worker interaction. Here the criteria were youth and sexual
involvement. Especially young couples holding hands or walking arm-in-arm
were subjects of expressive gestures. The puller grinned expansively and
gave what can be described only as a knowing wink to his co-workers, were
they to catch his eye. This action took place after, never during, contact
with the couple, perhaps because an action as obvious as this could be
detected too easily and be destructive to role performance. "Hell, it's no
secret what those kids do when they get home, but they don't want us to
show that we know. But we do (know), boy we do!"

During numerous slack periods of business, the pullers have ample
opportunity to interact outside of their roles as pullers. This interaction was
characterized by a great deal of physical contact, joking, and exchanging
insults. They constantly pushed, poked, made disparaging comments about
each other's personality, wives, legitimacy, and sexual exploits. Such action
was rapidly terminated whenever potential customers appeared and just as
rapidly resumed whenever possible. The facility with which the conversation was picked up at the point at which it had been dropped, whether the
interval between contacts was two minutes or one hour (the shortest and
longest intervals recorded), was demonstrated again and again. It would
seem that the eagerness and ease with which the pullers totally stepped
out of their occupational role at every opportunity might be a function of
dissatisfaction with that role.

Perhaps the hostility displayed toward other pullers through insults and physical aggression was also a result of the requirements of role performance suppressing such activity. Miller and Swanson point out that "given a particular pattern of experiences certain types of moral standards, defense mechanisms, and expressive styles tend to develop. . . . In the working class the reactions are likely to include less extensive standards, defenses like denial and withdrawal and direct expression of aggression."[9] That these departures from role served as a mechanism for the release of occupational tensions seemed clear, for after such activity, subsequent role performances were characterized by noticeably less role distance; there was less looking around, less joking, less attempting interaction with other pullers for the next few minutes.

The puller was also active in much self-communication to create role distance. Self-communication was frequently observed, but no particular patterns following any particular type of encounter were apparent. However, actions such as muttering to self, tugging on slacks, laughing at some private joke, and other indications of awareness of a self apart from role performance were both more frequent and more obvious after negative responses from customers. Role distance thus made failure a part of the structure of the role performance, not a flaw in self.

An additional form of role distance was response to the interviewer. Through explaining his performance, the puller detached himself from his role and appeared to indicate that he and I together could watch him perform a role that was apart from himself: "Like I told you, you gotta treat Spics friendly; that's what I think while I'm talking." "While I was pulling that guy I was wondering what you was writing about me." No significant changes were made by the presence of the interviewer as the same patterns of role performance and role distance were present during times when the pullers were not aware that they were being observed.

Robert E. Park has written that every vocation in a city, even that of beggar, has "the tendency . . . not merely to specialize, but to rationalize one's occupation and to develop a specific and conscious technique for carrying it on."[10] Detailed observation of the puller affirms the statement and indicates to some degree the complexity and specificity of mechanisms, verbal and nonverbal, contrived and spontaneous, possible within a narrowly defined occupational role, mechanisms which both preserve self-esteem and increase the success of the role performance.

Footnotes

First prize in the Manford H. Kuhn Memorial Essay Contest for Students, Midwest Sociological Society, 1964. This article is a greatly condensed version of the original paper. I am grateful to Mayer N. Zald, University of Chicago, who, though not responsible for the ideas and organization of this paper, provided invaluable criticism and encouragement.

[1] See, for example, W. F. Whyte, "When Workers and Customers Meet," in *Industry and Society*, ed. by W. F. Whyte (New York: McGraw-Hill, 1946), Chapter VII, pp. 123–48; R. Gold, "Janitors versus Tenants: A Status-Income Dilemma," *American Journal of Sociology*, 57:487–93 (Mar., 1952).

[2] Everet C. Hughes, *Men and Their Work* (Glencoe, Ill.: Free Press, 1958), p. 48.

[3] *Ibid.*, p. 48–49.

[4] Louis Wirth, *The Ghetto* (Chicago: Univ. of Chicago Press, 1925), p. 240.

[5] Talcott Parsons, *The Social System* (Glencoe, Ill.: Free Press, 1951), p. 70.

[6] Erving Goffman, *Encounters* (Indianapolis: Bobbs-Merrill, 1961), pp. 113–14.

[7] Whyte, *op. cit.*, p. 123.

[8] Wirth, *op. cit.*, p. 233.

[9] Daniel R. Miller and Guy E. Swanson, *Inner Conflict and Defense* (New York: Henry Holt, 1960), p. 66.

[10] Robert E. Park *et al., The City* (Chicago: Univ. of Chicago Press, 1925), p. 14.

Occupational Role Stresses

A Structural Approach

HAROLD L. NIX
University of Georgia
FREDERICK L. BATES
University of Georgia

In our complex and rapidly changing society there are many evidences of social and cultural stresses. To name but a few, there are the increasing rates of crime, divorce, juvenile delinquency, alcoholism, and suicide. It is the sociologist's responsibility to describe the stresses which produce these evidences of social disorganization, to explain their causes, and to determine their consequences.

The primary purpose of this paper is to describe a theoretical approach which will aid in identifying and classifying role stresses within an occupational position. In order to accomplish this purpose, the findings of an occupational study will be used to furnish concrete examples of each category of role stresses. This study is based on data derived from a review of the appropriate literature and from twenty-seven four-hour interviews with "Vo-Ag" teachers in three selected parishes in Louisiana.[1]

Theoretical Approach

Many researchers have dealt in varying ways with what is commonly referred to as "role conflict." Other important types of stresses have been largely overlooked or, at most, given only casual attention. In this discussion we propose to define five analytically distinct types of structural stress and to give concrete examples of these stresses as they apply to the roles of the high school vocational agriculture teacher. We will further attempt to explain why these stresses have occurred, the mechanisms by which they are

Reprinted from *Rural Sociology*, Vol. 27, No. 1 (March 1962), 7–17, by permission of authors and publisher.

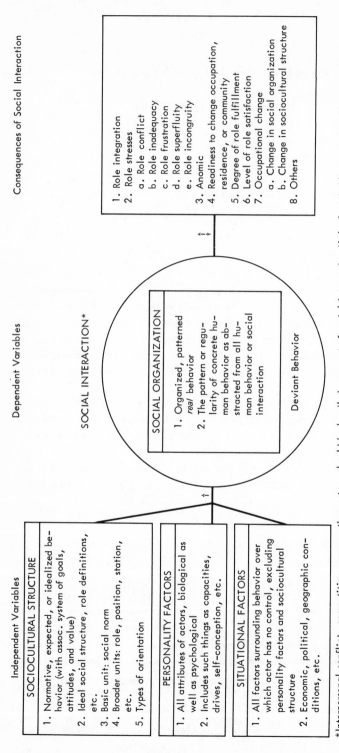

A. STRUCTURE

B. FUNCTION

Independent Variables

Dependent Variables

Consequences of Social Interaction

SOCIOCULTURAL STRUCTURE

1. Normative, expected, or idealized behavior (with assoc. system of goals, attitudes, and value)
2. Ideal social structure, role definitions, etc.
3. Basic unit: social norm
4. Broader units: role, position, station, etc.
5. Types of orientation

PERSONALITY FACTORS

1. All attributes of actors, biological as well as psychological
2. Includes such things as capacities, drives, self-conception, etc.

SITUATIONAL FACTORS

1. All factors surrounding behavior over which actor has no control, excluding personality factors and sociocultural structure
2. Economic, political, geographic conditions, etc.

SOCIAL INTERACTION*

SOCIAL ORGANIZATION

1. Organized, patterned real behavior
2. The pattern or regularity of concrete human behavior as abstracted from all human behavior or social interaction

Deviant Behavior

1. Role integration
2. Role stresses
   a. Role conflict
   b. Role inadequacy
   c. Role frustration
   d. Role superfluity
   e. Role incongruity
3. Anomic
4. Readiness to change occupation, residence, or community
5. Degree of role fulfillment
6. Level of role satisfaction
7. Occupational change
   a. Change in social organization
   b. Change in sociocultural structure
8. Others

*Interpersonal conflict, competition, cooperation, etc., should be handled as a part of social interaction if the form is idiosyncratic. However, if they are institutionalized, they should be treated as a part of social organization.
† Intervening variables are (1) social control or the exchange of sanctions and (2) communication or the exchange of meaning. These are the means by which the relationship between the independent or dependent variables are maintained.
†† Intervening variables are mechanisms by which stresses are alleviated. These mechanisms tend to change or to the prevention of change.

CHART 1
Model of Behavioral Causation

usually ameliorated, and, finally, the consequences of these stresses. In order to accomplish this we first must develop a broad theoretical framework.

The sociologist is primarily concerned with patterns of social behavior. In order to understand these patterns he is concerned also with the components or causative factors that structure behavior, the manner of their coalescence, the patterns and processes that evolve in social action, and finally, the consequences or functions of specific patterns of interaction in specified situations. With these general considerations in mind, we have employed a framework or a "model of behavioral causation" (Chart 1) by which we may analyze not only the similarities in human behavior but also the differences between expected and real behavior as well as the consequences of these differences.

We have attempted to show schematically in Chart 1 that social organization, or "organized real human behavior," as well as social disorganization, emerge from the interplay of three broad groups of factors which operate within a broad cultural context. These groups of factors are: (1) sociocultural structure, that is, ideal behavior, expected behavior, or norms; (2) situational factors or any phenomenon—social, physical, or cultural—which exists outside of the actor, and over which he has no control in the short run; (3) personality factors, that is, the psychological and biological factors.[2]

On the basis of this classification of factors, we can define different types of stresses or structural maladjustments which can aid in answering three basic questions: (1) How does real behavior differ from ideal behavior? (2) How do informal expectations differ from formal expectations? (3) How do structural change and social change take place? Our general view is that all of these questions may be at least partially answered in terms of maladjustments in the social system between and within the three groups of independent variables that structure the system—that is, between and among sociocultural structure, situational factors, and personality factors. We are using Chart 1 to represent an essentially functional model in which we assume an ideal state of equilibrium or adjustment in the system. It is further assumed that various factors lead to a tendency in a social system toward equilibrium—a state in which there are no stresses or strains between or within the various independent variables. Finally, it is postulated that if maladjustments are introduced and stress exists, there will be a tendency to eliminate them.

Classification of Stresses

Various types of stresses are derivable directly from our behavioral model by taking (a) the various types of internal stress within each factor, (*b*) the various forms between two factors, and (*c*) the form incorporating all three factors.

Stresses Within Factors.

1. Maladjustment within the sociocultural structure, that is, between ideal expectations or norms, are of two basic types we call role conflict and role incongruity.

(*a*) *Role conflict* is defined here as a type of stress arising from a condition in which the player of a focal role or roles perceives that he is confronted with incompatible expectations or norms. (These expectations may be felt obligations at the sociocultural level or perceived pressures at the social organization level.)

(*b*) *Role incongruity* of status attributes—refers to the extent to which the various status attributes such as rewards, prestige, authority, and functional importance which are associated with a role are: (1) out of balance with one another or (2) internally inconsistent.[3]

2. Maladjustment between the contents of the personality is called personality disorganization (neurosis, psychosis, etc.). This area is a primary concern of the psychologist.

3. Maladjustment in the contents of the situation may be called a situational crisis—however, since our definition of role stresses is built upon the notion that for role stress to exist it must be felt by the actor—this situational maladjustment must evolve into one of the other types to be classified as role stress. An example of a situational crisis would be an economic depression or a revolution.

Stresses Between Two Factors.

1. Maladjustment between sociocultural structure and personality we call *role inadequacy*. It is defined here as the inability of an actor or class of actors to fulfill their perceived roles due to recurrent personal inadequacies. It may take the form of trained incapacity or biological or psychological incapacity to play required roles. Role inadequacy is of interest to the sociologist only when it applies to a class of actors, as in the case of a failure of socialization to provide large numbers of individuals with training necessary to play roles, or in the case of a stratification system that allocates persons with the wrong abilities to certain roles.

2. Maladjustment between the sociocultural structure and a recurrent situation is called *role frustration*. This stress is defined as the inability of an actor or class of actors to fulfill a perceived role because of situational factors. It is, of course, of interest to our pro-

fession only when it applies to repetitive situations and to a significant number of actors in society.

Stresses Among All Three Groups of Factors Simultaneously.

We have named the type of stress that involves all three groups of factors simultaneously "role superfluity." It occurs when the biological or psychological characteristics of actors combine with situational attributes with the result that difficulty is encountered by actors in fulfilling their roles. Essentially, this type of stress derives from excessive nonconflicting expectations. Expectations are said to be excessive in light of the modal actor's biological and psychological capacities in conjunction with recurrent situational factors. Role superfluity is of interest to the sociologist whenever it applies to a class of actors in a certain type of situation.

How Pattern Variables Were Employed

In order to understand our description of the particular stresses located within the position and roles of the Vo-Ag teacher, it is necessary first to understand the particular scheme for analyzing the contents of roles used in this study. The contents of both the formal and informal structure of the Vo-Ag teacher's roles were analyzed in terms of Parsonian and other lower order pattern variables. Pattern variables are defined by Parsons and his associates as follows:

> A pattern variable is a dichotomy, one side of which must be chosen by an actor before the meaning of a situation is determinate for him, and thus before he can act with respect to that situation. We maintain that there are only five basic pattern variables (i.e.) pattern variables deriving directly from the frame of reference of the theory of action and that, in the sense that they are all of the pattern variables which so derive, they constitute a system.
> They are. . . .
>   1. Affectivity . . . . affective neutrality
>   2. Self-orientation . . . . collectivity-orientation
>   3. Universalism . . . . particularism
>   4. Ascription . . . . achievement
>   5. Specificity . . . . diffuseness[4]

Actors do not orient randomly, according to Parsons, but in some patterned way to these alternatives. It is from this patterning that their general "role definition" or "value orientation" can be determined.[5] It is also from this patterning that we may focus upon social disorganization in the form of role stresses.

Parsonian pattern variables were used in the study of the Vo-Ag teaching occupation as an aid to setting up other pattern variables and subvariables of more concrete nature. Through these concrete variables, roles could be classified into types by asking specific questions relative to selected occupational (1) norms, (2) goals, and (3) attitudes and values.[6] The general role definition as well as role stresses were assessed by noting the patterning of interviewees' specific responses and classifying these responses in terms of the pattern variables and subvariables.[7]

The Parsonian pattern variable scheme was used to provide a convenient way of summarizing the contents of roles in an abstract fashion. It also provided a much needed technique for identifying and classifying certain types of role stresses. This latter use of the pattern variables stems from the fact that each variable represents "paired opposites" in value orientation. Thus, role stress may be said to exist when both of the opposite orientations are present in a role.

General Setting of Vo-Ag Occupation

Before we can proceed to the analysis of role stresses, a very brief description of the general setting of the vocational agricultural occupation is necessary.

The National Vocational Education Act of 1917 established the occupation of "high school vocational agriculture teacher" in the local-state public school systems. The act also provided for the development of a non-public-school bureaucratic structure, a state-federal organization for the administration and supervision of the vocational education program. In this way the Vo-Ag teacher was made a member of dual bureaucracies, that of the public high school, and that of the state-federal Vo-Ag organization. He became subject to the expectations of both. He was also subjected to the expectations of those whom he was supposed to serve—his Vo-Ag students and the rural people of his community.

In addition to being under the supervision of dual bureaucracies and being subject to both bureaucratic pressures and pressures from his clientele, the Vo-Ag teacher was expected to perform multiple functions. That is, he was expected to be not only a regular high school teacher and to perform all the general and special duties pertaining thereto, but he was also expected to be an adult teacher, a community leader, and an agricultural leader. The National Vocation Education Act further provided for an extension of education beyond classroom activities to the farms of the students and, indeed, the total community. Growing out of the traditional view of farming as a "way of life" rather than as just a "means of a livelihood," a philosophy was developed within the occupational group which commits it to the dual responsibility of aiding the student in both his vocational training and his general educational development.

A further difficulty with which Vo-Ag teachers were faced is the legal prescription "to train present and prospective farmers for proficiency in farming." That is, his primary objective is supposed to be to aid present farmers to become more successful in farming and to aid high school students and young farmers to become successfully established in farming. At the same time, the teachers of vocational agriculture, as well as certain other agricultural workers, are faced with rapidly changing economic conditions which permit only a very limited fulfillment of these expectations.

Personal Traits of Vo-Ag Teachers

Certain personal traits of the modal Vo-Ag teachers are significant in viewing occupational stresses. Examination of the sample population revealed that the Vo-Ag occupation is not passed on from father to son, but rather each new generation of Vo-Ag teachers is drawn from the sons of small and part-time farmers. This is no doubt an important factor in the modal respondent's commitment to basic rural values and to farming as a way of life. In order to be a Vo-Ag teacher a person must have a farm background and receive a prescribed four-year college course in technical agriculture and 18 to 20 hours of teaching methods. The dominant themes of the Vo-Ag teaching philosophy which are transmitted during this training involve "leading others, through the scientific thought process, within a democratic setting to learn by doing."

The value orientation thus acquired by the Vo-Ag teacher appears to be unusual for a member of a professional occupation. The conditions of the teacher's employment prescribe a basically achievement, universalistic, and collectivity orientation; but these conditions combined with economic necessity require him to maintain a position of affective neutrality toward methods of farming. On the other hand, the teacher's orientation to the structural elements of *Gemeinschaft* (neighborhood, unity of mind and spirit, and, to a limited extent, kinship)[8] appear to be associated with a positive affectivity toward rural people and toward farming as a way of life. The *Gemeinschaft* orientation appears also to be associated with collective rather than self-interest, and with a strongly diffuse orientation which prescribes a "community of fate" with rural people in which the teacher feels he should share the hardships and sorrows, joys and satisfactions of the people he serves.

Illustration of Stresses

The unique value orientation of the vocational agricultural teaching profession, its dual administration and functions, and the rapidly changing agricultural situation make the occupation a particularly good case with which to illustrate the types of role stresses described earlier. However, due to the limitations of time, we can only illustrate the types of stresses with a few concrete examples taken from the Vo-Ag teaching occupation.

Role Conflict. Role conflict as we have said involves maladjustments within the sociocultural structure or between the patterns of expected behavior. It was defined earlier as a condition in which the occupant of a focal role or roles perceives that he is confronted with incompatible expectations.

At the sociocultural or "ideal structure" level, role conflict appears when felt role obligations appear "logically" or "morally" inconsistent to the actor. To illustrate, the majority of the Vo-Ag teachers interviewed appeared to be "positively affective" in their orientation toward their clients and the traditional rural way of life, on one hand, and affectively neutral (essentially rational) toward methods of farming, on the other. Role conflict exists at the sociocultural level in this case because the teachers felt that out of economic necessity they should promote scientific rational farming; and at the same time, they felt that this type of farming is antithetical to the traditional rural way of life.

At the level of social organization or real behavior, the actor may perceive no contradictions in his felt obligations but may perceive the pressures[9] of different expectations held by different significant reference groups which prevent the fulfillment of his roles without interpersonal conflict. For example, role conflict was evident in relation to a subvariable of the "specificity versus diffuseness" variable, called here "general agriculturalist" versus "agricultural specialist." Although there was general consensus among the responding Vo-Ag teachers that they were and should be generalists, they felt that their "most significant others," that is, their Vo-Ag students and adult farmers, expected them to be both "specialists" and "generalists." Thus pressures existed in opposite and incompatible directions on their behavior.

Role Frustration. Role frustration as defined earlier involves the inability of an actor or class of actors to fulfill perceived role expectations because of recurrent situational factors. In this case strains or inconsistencies exist between the sociocultural structure (norms) and recurrent situational factors. One teacher pointed out the basic role frustration of his occupation in the following statement: "We are supposed to be making farmers and educating them for increased agricultural production. Yet, we are faced with overproduction; many farmers are being forced out of business; and fewer of our students can become farmers." The majority of the respondents expressed in various ways the feeling that the ideal expectations of helping farmers to be more successful in farming and aiding Vo-Ag students to become successfully established in farming are partially frustrated. This frustration derives basically from the rapid scientific and technological advances in agriculture with the resultant overproduction and the economic squeeze placed on the small-scale producer.

Role Inadequacy.   Role inadequacy has been defined above as the inability of an actor or class of actors to fulfill a perceived role because of recurrent personal inadequacies—either biological or psychological.

   In a period of rapid change, especially in a diffusely oriented occupation, it is to be expected that there will be feelings of role inadequacy among members of the occupation. Two thirds of the respondents in this study felt that the four-year training program was inadequate for the proper performance of their jobs. The inadequacy most often expressed was the lack of depth of technical training, especially in the area of farm mechanics. This is understandable in view of the fact that the respondents typically were recruited from the families of small and part-time farmers. These backgrounds often failed to provide a sufficient practical background in the use and maintenance of modern farm machinery.

Role Superfluity.   Role superfluity, the last type of structural stress to be described, is one involving the simultaneous maladjustment among all three groups of factors which pattern human behavior—sociocultural structure, situational factors, and personality factors. More simply this type of stress arises from excessive expectations in view of the personal attributes of the modal actor and recurrent situational factors present in the occupational setting. It is believed that Vo-Ag teachers are one of the most diffusely oriented of the professional groups in the field of science and applied science. When diffuse expectations are added to the affective prescription to love and serve rural people and to the universalistic prescription to share affection and services equally and impartially, the stage is perfectly set for overwhelming expectations or role superfluity.

   An often quoted unknown author has expressed the excessive expectations or role superfluity of the Vo-Ag occupation when he described the characteristics of a good vocational agriculture teacher as follows:

   The strength of an ox, the tenacity of a bulldog, the daring of a lion, the industry of a beaver, the vision of an eagle, the disposition of an angel, the loyalty of an apostle, the heroism of a martyr, the faithfulness of a prophet, the tenderness of a shepherd, the fervency of an evangelist, and the devotion of a mother.[10]

An example of role superfluity within Vo-Ag teaching involves a sub-type of "specificity versus diffuseness." In relation to this subtype, called "general educationalist versus vocationalist," the responding teachers emphasized vocational expectations. Because of their views of farming as a way of life and because of the nature of their particular educational philosophies, Vo-Ag teachers also felt heavy responsibilities toward the general education of their students. At the same time, they did not feel that the general and vocational aims were contradictory. Because of the lack of felt conflict in norms, the resulting broad expectations may be called role superfluity rather than role conflict.

In spite of the structural maladjustments which give rise to these stresses, the modal respondent expressed above average role satisfaction. This may be, in part, explained by the presence of compensating rewards and mechanisms that ameliorate the stresses. The Vo-Ag teacher's greatest rewards appear to be a "sense of public service" and "recognition." The mechanisms for alleviating structural strains seem to be (1) the isolation of role performance, (2) the formation of a semi-official organization, the advisory council, as a buffer between the two bureaucratic structures, (3) the formation of a hierarchy of role importance, and (4) a teaching philosophy which shifts the responsibility for decision making to the client and synthesizes many aspects of vocational and general education.

The stresses in combination with the mechanisms cited are considered as primary factors leading to the following changes within the occupational structure of the Vo-Ag teaching profession: (1) an increasing educational orientation and a rejection of the "service" role, (2) a shift toward a more "localistic" orientation, (3) a tendency for Vo-Ag teachers to broaden the objectives of their profession to fit their accomplishments while holding on to the institutionalized means of accomplishing the former narrower cultural goals (Merton's ritualism),[11] (4) a tendency to assume less responsibility toward vocational goals and to develop a new role in the area of occupational guidance, (5) a growing dominance of the in-school roles at the informal but not at the formal level, and (6) an increasing integration of the position and roles of the Vo-Ag teacher into the public school system.

Footnotes

[1] Harold L. Nix, "A Sociological Analysis of the Roles and Value Orientation of an Occupation: Vocational Agriculture Teaching" (unpublished doctoral dissertation, Louisiana State University, Baton Rouge, 1960).

[2] Note the similarities between this model and the models of Sorokin and Parsons.

[3] For a discussion of this concept, see Roland J. Pellegrin and Frederick L. Bates, "Congruity and Incongruity of Status Attributes within Occupations and Work Positions," *Social Forces*, XXXVIII (1959), 23–28.

[4] Talcott Parsons and Edward Shils (eds.), *Toward a General Theory of Action* (Cambridge: Harvard University Press, 1951), p. 77.

[5] Although Parsons and Shils relate these pattern variables to personality systems, social systems, and cultural systems, they nevertheless, in their analysis of "action" view these pattern variables in terms of alternative "choices" which actors "must" make in combining normative expectations with personal needs in situations before the situations have determinate meaning for them. The study upon which this paper is based did not focus on the idea of "choice" among alternatives, but rather, on one hand, it used pattern variables as a means of classifying the contents of sociocultural structure, and on the other, to a limited extent, social organization.

[6] These "other" pattern variables and subvariables were aspects of the specific role content under study. There are very significant orientations of any group which are less general than orientations classified by the five Parsonian pattern variables. (According to Parsons these may be considered accidents of content rather than genuine alternatives intrinsic to the structure of all action.) In the study of the Vo-Ag teaching profession seven subvariables to the pattern variable "Specificity versus Diffuseness" were used plus an additional pattern variable, "Educational Orientation versus Service Orientation." The seven subvariables which were concrete adaptations of the pattern variables, "Specificity versus Diffuseness," were as follows: (1) community of fate versus limited responsibility, (2) required integration of roles in and out of the system versus irrelevance of roles outside of the system, (3) involvement of actor's family versus no involvement of actor's family, (4) two-way invasion of privacy versus one-way invasion of privacy, (5) farming as a way of life versus farming as a means of making a living only, (6) general educationalist versus vocationalist, and (7) general agriculturist versus agricultural specialist. The first two of these subvariables were utilized by Loomis and Beegle in their *Rural Social Systems*. Number 4 is also an adaptation of a subvariable used by these authors.

[7] No attempt was made to quantify the orientations of either individual respondents or of the group of Vo-Ag teachers. At best it can be said only that the model teacher tended to orient toward one or the other of the paired orientations, toward the middle, or toward both ends.

[8] Ferdinand Tönnies, *Community and Society (Gemeinschaft und Gesellschaft)* trans. by C. P. Loomis (East Lansing: Michigan State University Press, 1957) p. 257.

[9] Neal Gross, Ward S. Mason, and Alexander W. McEachern, *Explorations in Role Analysis* (New York: John Wiley & Sons, 1958), p. 248.

[10] "The Characteristics of a Good Agriculture Teacher," *Agricultural Education Magazine*, VIII (1935), 5.

[11] Robert K. Merton, *Social Theory and Social Structure* (Glencoe, Ill.: Free Press, 1957), pp. 139–152.

The Military Intelligence Agent

Structural Strains in an Occupational Role

ELLWYN R. STODDARD
University of Texas at El Paso

In the world of work, to achieve success, a person must selectively adhere to contradictory expectations within his occupational role. Certain occupations such as that of the military intelligence field agent contain greater "built-in" role strains than other types of work. Therefore, an analysis of this occupation is made with the purpose of revealing the structural-functional elements contributing to structured role strains not accounted for by personality differences or individual variations alone.

To facilitate the analysis of these stresses which occur in the normal performance of one's occupation, various concepts contained in role theory will be employed. Most applicable to this study are those of role strain, role conflict, and role ambivalence.[1] Whereas role strain is an incompatibility of expectations within a single role (Goode, 1960), role conflict occurs between two social roles whose demands are mutually incompatible. Role strain can be only minimized rather than eliminated, and that by selectively performing according to different role expectations under varying circumstances. Role conflict will necessarily result in one role having higher priority being selected to the exclusion of another. Role ambivalence exists when either resource or role priorities are not clearly designated and indecision results. This can be ameliorated by assigning priorities to the allocation of time, energy, and financial resources to roles which also have some heirarchical ranking as more or less important to the specific individual.

Social scientists have previously identified role strain and role conflict in various occupational settings. For example, the industrial foreman is operating within two non-reciprocal expectations based on his position in

Original manuscript printed for the first time in this volume.

the management line of command and his functional contact and daily interaction with the workers under his direction (Whyte and Gardner, 1945:19,23). A study of the physician in the Soviet Union described the strain of meeting Party production quotas by reassigning recently ill workers as fit for duty in direct violation of his medical ethics (Field, 1953). A similar situation would obtain within the American Armed Forces medical teams operating under the battlefield emergency conditions who, in a survival situation, might relegate only those completely incapable of handling a weapon to the dependent sick role status. The occupation of military chaplain likewise exhibits role inconsistencies. His religious emphasis symbolizes peace and brotherhood although his military role is to tacitly support the military goals of killing the enemy. Assigned as an officer, the chaplain must override the officer-enlisted inequality to counsel intimately with the soldier on an equalitarian basis (Burchard, 1954). The disbursing officer in the Navy controls the paychecks of all personnel. He experiences conflicting pressures to adhere strictly to military regulation, to ease the rules for friends or selected superiors, or to realistically use his potential strategic power for extending his own personal influence while rationalizing his deviant behavior (Turner, 1947). Even within the role of the sociology professor contradictions in expectations are extant. Aside from having rank and salary bestowed on the basis of publication while ostensibly being paid for teaching ability, the strain of teaching professionalism as an objective social scientist (Muir, 1968) while being encouraged to become social engineers and reformers in the real world (Horowitz, 1965) induces conflicting demands. The military intelligence field agent experiences some of these strains and in addition encounters some role conflicts peculiar to that specific occupational role. These will now be analyzed in greater detail.

The secretive nature of the mission and functions of military intelligence precludes a direct investigation into its operation and organization. This necessitates a methodology suited to an informal and indirect method of data acquisition. Focused interviews with fourteen Army and Air Force agents or past agents were conducted over a period of four years. In describing their occupational duties with their corresponding pressures, various aspects of role strain were offered by the informants. Thus, no security regulations were breached in this process of data collection.

To understand the unique role of the intelligence agent within the total intelligence organizational structure it is helpful to review briefly the basic organization of three operational levels common to both the Army and Air Force. These are (1) policy, (2) middle administration and command, and (3) field operation. The Assistant Chief of Staff for Intelligence heads up the Army to intelligence policy level. Intelligence command begins at the Army command level consisting of detachments and sections of field agents. The Air Force's Office of Special Investigations (OSI) within the

Inspector General for Security section of its pentagon command directs its area offices, which it calls districts. These in turn have field level detachments containing assigned field agents. In both the Army and Air Force, the top and middle echelons operate basically within traditional military code of R.H.I.P. (rank has its privileges). It is only at the lowest operational level, the field agents and their commanders, that the minimization of military indentification creates the greatest conflicts between military courtesy and operational expediency. While it is true that related civilian occupations, such as the police, experience some of these contradictory pressures between restrictive regulations on the methods of enforcement and "performance demands" (Stoddard, 1968: 202–203), the military service places these occupational duties within a more rigid code of discipline and justice. To clarify the types of role strains experienced in military intelligence, three operational levels will be discussed: (1) The code of military discipline as applicable to tactical and intelligence units; (2) The cohesive and disintegrative processes operating within the intelligence unit itself in its data gathering and security mission; (3) The strains associated with the agent role resulting from standardized military procedures[2] conflicting with expeditious means to accomplish the intelligence mission, including the strains generated in social and familial relationships outside the occupational role.

Tactical vs. Intelligence Unit Organization

The internal organization of military intelligence units differs markedly from tactical ones in spite of the similarities in their formal table of organization. The platoons of a standard combat company are somewhat interchangeable as also are the majority of platoon members. Within the intelligence company, however, the equivalent of the platoon organization does not represent a mere command designation, but rather distinguishes the function or type of missions to which its members are assigned. Usually these consist of three types. Positive intelligence is to gather and penetrate the enemy's information channels. This carries a maximum need for organizational and personnel deception necessitating the use of "cover or fictional backgrounds" to guarantee maximum flexibility for agents assigned to specific cases. Counter-intelligence is a legitimate defensive measure to ensure national security and normally will operate more "in the open" than positive intelligence. The duties involved in the third type, routine investigation and background security checks, involve the need for least security or secrecy beyond the discreet use of confidential personal data.

The tactical and intelligence units differ also in the composition of personnel. Whereas a standard military command might reflect an officer-enlisted ratio of 1 to 20, an intelligence operation may consist of an officer-enlisted ratio of 1 to 5. Since the duties of investigative fieldwork demand men with the qualities of individual initiative, personal responsibility, and being good security risks—qualities which are similar for commissioned personnel or good non-coms—officers are substantially overrecruited for intelligence work and the rank-and-file enlisted man is underrepresented.

The manner and degree of personal involvement between officers and men in the tactical and intelligence units differ substantially, partially as a result of the variation in officer-enlisted ratios indicated above. In the tactical command, officers and men are trained separately. Moreover, their social life is purposely separated and their housing is geographically segregated. To further emphasize the command distinctions, the officer and enlisted uniforms are distinctive as are their rank symbols and the patterns of military courtesy, for instance, saluting. In contrast, the officers and enlisted military intelligence personnel, though in separate classes, are trained together, on occasion housed under the same roof, socialize together, and work together with similar duties and field assignments. Thus, whereas the tactical unit is organized upon the principle of command, the intelligence unit operates more within the concept of leadership (Feld, 1959:15).

Social Organization Within the Intelligence Unit

In the military intelligence operation, technical competency of performance and/or the possession of specific classified information determines the transitory importance or superiority of its personnel. As reported by various agents, it has not been unusual in an intelligence unit for a neophyte officer agent to become subordinate to a trained enlisted agent who might correct him, criticize his mistakes, and make evaluative judgments on his competency as a future agent. It is entirely possible that this officer at a later date might be asked to attest, via the efficiency report, to the military competence of the enlisted man who was his field trainer. This does not resemble the social organization of the tactical unit wherein command responsibilities are maintained even when enlisted personnel are technically more qualified than their commanders.

Within the intelligence unit itself procedural safeguards exist for carrying out its primary mission which directly concerns the obtaining of intelligence and its subsequent security. Such security procedures tend to create functional cleavages between the various sub-units of the intelligence structure based on the type of mission and the type of information collected. As information is consolidated, it still remains the responsibility of that detachment or section to which it pertains until tactical or other intelligence personnel can demonstrate an unequivocable "need to know" the specific data held by that group. It is never released without the requesting source demonstrating fully their "need to know." With the intelligence mission dependent upon secrecy and security, much vital information is never directed to those who could use it best. A vital military campaign could be hampered because a key piece of information is unavailable to the military planners either because they did not know of its existence or did not direct their "need to know" to the appropriate repository of intelligence information.

This cloud of secrecy engulfing the military intelligence operation has not only served to fulfill the primary mission of the intelligence unit but has also resulted in general ignorance of its mode of operations. For many military personnel and the public at large this ignorance perpetuates the stereotypes associated with intelligence functions which are reinforced by the mass media through the "spy plot" and "cloak and dagger" mystery novel or TV series. This continuing ignorance concerning the intelligence operation has a latent consequence. It promotes the privileged and powerful position of intelligence within the overall military establishment, allowing it maximum latitude in exercising its powers while suffering a minimum of resentment from tactical and supportive branches who are unaware of the differential rewards available to military intelligence (Moore and Tumin, 1949).

Strains Within the Agent Role

When an individual receives the training required for an intelligence agent, he immediately becomes aware of some conflicting demands to which he is subjected. Although the military uniform is a symbol of his occupation, he will probably be required to wear civilian clothing while in the performance of the agent role. The civilian attire ostensibly allows him greater freedom from restrictive military courtesy customs by not revealing his rank but this practice has a latent consequence of complicating interpersonal relationships with other military personnel and civilian acquaintances, especially in counter-intelligence operations in overseas war theaters.

Some officer agents may feel relatively deprived of their privileged position by the standardization of civilian clothing. When a potential agent shows a preference for traditional military courtesy over the informally accepted intelligence agent equality, he is dysfunctional to the intelligence operation. The case of a lieutenant recruited for counter-intelligence duties in the Air Force is illustrative. When he insisted on wearing his officer uniform at the unit headquarters to emphasize his superiority over the other non-commissioned intelligence agents, he was quietly returned to the regular ranks prior to his formal intelligence training. Being "too military" interferes with the field requirements of a good intelligence agent.

For the enlisted man who is selected for intelligence duty, his adaptation to the agent role is a classical study of role ambivalence strain. During the course of a single day it would be possible for a competent but low-ranking, highly educated enlisted agent to wash a latrine, shovel snow, correct an officer agent for field incompetency, and confer with a high ranking military officer on a diplomatic case involving the national security. The increased status achieved while operating as an agent in the field may be countered by his resumption of military rank at headquarters with the onerous tasks which are assigned inversely to military rank. It appears that non-career enlisted agents are much less vulnerable to rank-consciousness commanders inasmuch as they can freely disagree with their superiors without worrying about its affecting their future military careers. In some cases, the functional demands for maintaining a "cover" for an agent directly subvert the traditional military codes of courtesy and discipline upon which authority command in the military services depends. A situation in an intelligence unit headquartered in Europe accurately signifies the strain of perpetuating military command authority in light of successfully accomplishing the intelligence mission. A special agent with the military rank of corporal was ordered to join a crew to beautify the grounds around the intelligence headquarters building. Although other non-agent uniformed support troops were assigned to the unit, the uniformed first sergeant gave a direct order for this corporal to join the cleanup crew, which the corporal agent refused to do. His explanation adds some merit for his refusal to obey a direct order of a superior.

> I had been working with a full colonel in the JAG [Judge Advocate General] Corps to return an American defector from a neighboring European country and he was establishing a legal basis for me to extradite the man. I often met this colonel outside of our office as he went to and from his work, and he knew me by name. I refused to clip grass in front of the headquarters building because of the danger of my encountering the JAG colonel while out there working as a *peon*. It would "blow my cover" and endanger the extradition operation.

The first sergeant initiated a court martial proceedings for insubordination which was dismissed by the unit commanding officer because he felt, along with the agent, that the intelligence mission responsibilities clearly took precedence over his military responsibilities corresponding to his corporal rank.

The commander's decision to side with the view of the subordinate agent was a refutation of traditional military command and undermined the support from his superiors expected by the career first sergeant.

The complications surrounding an intelligence unit which attempts to function internally according to traditional military standards while externally in the field demanding expediency can be seen in this situation of another enlisted agent, also stationed in Europe.

> We got in a new Group commander from the Infantry who was very *gung-ho* on acting like a soldier. He decided that all enlisted personnel from our MI unit of corporal grade up would attend the NCO academy at a nearby military base. This complicated the field assignment of one of our enlisted agents. . . . This sergeant from our office subsequently called on a major concerning a liaison case. Upon presenting his credentials he was immediately accorded the respect shown to an officer. Both the cooperation and the rapport was excellent. As the major and the agent strolled through an adjoining office in which privates and corporals were doing routine filing jobs, one young private called out—"Hey, Sarge, how goes it? Hey, fellas, there's a guy that was with me at NCO training in ——. Boy, did we have a blast." From that moment on the mood changed between the major and the agent, and thereafter only routine cooperation befitting a non-com was extended to our agent.

Persons who are being interviewed by intelligence agents, especially other military personnel, are extremely curious about the rank of the agent interviewing them. In many instances this creates an irritation on the part of the officer being confronted inasmuch as he does not know with what measure of respect to approach the agent. If he accords him the dignity due a fellow officer he takes the chance of being over solicitous to an enlisted man. If he treats the agent somewhat indifferently, he might be denying the courtesies due a fellow officer. This ambivalence arising from the absence of superordinate-subordinate cues sometimes results in frustrated interviewees, as an unusual case in Western Europe demonstrates.

> I was making a routine inquiry of a major, being a sergeant at the time, dressed in civilian attire. After making an appointment and identifying myself as an agent to his aide, I stated my purpose for requesting an interview. When the aide informed him of my visit, I entered his office and was surprised to see him salute in the finest military manner after which he awkwardly sat half-way down being uncomfortable until I was also seated and assured him to be at ease.

At an Army base in the U.S., an SFC responsible for the motor pool supplied an agent with a car each morning. After a few weeks, in desperation he blurted out the question whether the agent rated a salute and a "sir" inasmuch as the SFC had been unable to decide whether to treat him as an officer or an enlisted man. This lack of rank symbols which determine normal military courtesy was unnerving for a career military non-com and reflected the strain and ambivalence experienced by the cabdriver toward his "occasional fare" (Davis, 1959).

In gathering information, the civilian dress supposedly allows a non-commissioned agent to move and communicate with the military commanders including those at the field or general grade. At times, however, the military procedures within a given theater of military operations undermine this goal. An enlisted agent in Germany worked in an intelligence headquarters in which it was local regulations to wear the military uniform at all times except when doing courier duty or liaison work. In these cases, agents would change over to civilian clothing only for the period they assumed these duties. An agent declares:

> We put on a coat and tie to go to Heidelberg to talk to top staff officers. Since I had to sign into the higher echelon HQ using my military I.D., they knew that my rank was sergeant. It was very awkward under those circumstances being in civilian clothing.... Although we enlisted men had the best grasp of the intelligence information the top staff wanted in this case, including first-hand knowledge of the current situation, the higher ranking officers—majors, colonels, and even generals—often felt that we should have told our fellow officer agents what we knew and let "their fellow officers" communicate the intelligence directly to them.

An agent whose support functions are provided by the military and who works in close proximity to a military base, but who is required to play a civilian role, finds his agent role in conflict with his military privileges in day-to-day activities with other military functionaries. One Army intelligence agent in Saigon had a civilian "cover" and was issued an I.D. card with civilian status. This excluded him from the U.S.O. which had the most available telephone for stateside calls (and whose policies gave complete priority to military personnel over civilians). In order to draw water rations from an unpolluted source maintained by the military, the intelligence unit commander appealed to the military authorities for special treatment and was given it. The fact that the agents from this "civilian" unit were the only civilians allowed to obtain their water from the military source completely exposed their military connection to even the most superficial observer. Further examples of the awkwardness of wearing civilian clothing and assuming civilian identities in situations not conducive to reducing the conspicuous role of intelligence agent are noted in a large South Vietnamese metropolis in 1968. An intelligence unit commanded by a major, with a warrant officer and two enlisted men with civilian "covers"[3] and civilian I.D.'s, was billeted in a downtown hotel with all of the other uniformed military personnel working with local officials. Their transportation was a repainted, unmarked military "jeep" although no other civilians in that city had a similar "civilianized" military vehicle. During the *Tet* offensive, decrees forbidding civilians from carrying weapons were put into effect. Since these "civilian" intelligence agents were frequently assigned to courier service, they had previously worn weapons on their belts to protect the confidential materials entrusted to their care. Now under the emergency decrees, they were required to fulfill their agent responsibilities within the restrictions placed on civilians. Even with the formal decrees, some safeguard measures were required by the unit commander of the intelligence unit.

> Since our commanding officer said that we could not carry classified information without a weapon with us at all times, we carried our pistol in the briefcase with the classified information. If the briefcase were stolen or taken from us, our pistol would be taken too!

Although the civilian cover for the agents was self-defeating because of their reliance on the military for housing, transportation, and other supportive function, it was maintained as an intelligence regulation and the agents had to conform to civilian rules in public, obey military commands in private, and combine these in public by acting like civilians while marshalling around a security briefcase of classified documents. To maintain these mutually antagonistic role expectations produces ambivalence within the individual, role conflicts within the unit and between the unit and other civilian and military detachments, and role strain in the agent throughout even the most elementary assignments of his daily routine.

The intelligence agent finds it difficult with any degree of freedom to interact socially with military personnel outside his own branch. The secretive nature of his duties restricts his "small talk" to non-occupational activities. Even his rank must not be divulged either by verbal means or by association or demeanor toward other military personnel. Since his presence at an officers' club or NCO club would reveal his military rank, local base directives giving all intelligence agents equal access to club facilities regardless of rank effectively preserve his rank security. In the Air Force, all military intelligence personnel are automatically honorary members of the NCO club. Thus, their presence would not reveal an officer or an enlisted status. In spite of these directives agents sometimes experience role conflict. On one base, an intelligence unit commander denied his non-commissioned agents access to the base officers' clubs (of which there were three) because his military background considered the fraternization of officers and enlisted men on an equalitarian basis to be disruptive to their military performance. Faced with these contradictory regulations but desirous of a social outlet with other military personnel, the agents investigated the club attendance patterns of their own commanding officer and frequented the club which he did not.

Whereas an individual agent dressed in civilian clothing may drive a civilian automobile and appear to have all of the privileges of a civilian, his dual military-civilian status enabling him to operate freely in both worlds in reality may force him to belong fully to neither one. Whereas he may choose to exert his civilian prerogatives or his military privileges, these may not be asserted at the same time. This situation creates a somewhat schizoidal occupational role for an intelligence agent. One agent on assignment at a major military installation in the United States volunteered:

> I live mostly in the civilian community and most of my friends are civilians. I guess I mostly think like a civilian since I haven't been in an Army uniform in more than a decade. . . . Where I live I have a sergeant as my neighbor and a lieutenant colonel down the block. Although I get along with each of them very well without too much strain (neither knows my rank), yet they are miles apart socially and the three of us cannot mix together in a strictly social situation.

This same situation would exist for socializing with a mixture of military and civilian acquaintances simultaneously.

The occupational stresses emerging from assuming the role of an intelligence agent directly affect the agent's private life and that of his family. His residence is usually found in a predominantly military neighborhood near a base or installation and his daily travel parallels that of other military personnel. Yet his civilian clothing and car create a social barrier between him and his neighbors, thus producing suspicion, curiosity, and intrigue. Neighbors constantly inquire of the wife, "What does your husband *really* do? You can trust *me*, I won't tell anyone!" When intimate secrets are not shared with inquiring neighbors, a social cleavage of distrust develops between neighborhood women which is most difficult to surmount. An agent's children are sometimes invited into nearby homes and bribed or "pumped" for details regarding the father's military rank, his intelligence activities, and any "secrets" to which the child might be privy. One agent's son refused to disclose his father's military rank on a routine school registration form and was expelled from school. The principal reinstated him only after a call from the agent's commanding officer clarifying the situation.

Family members and former friends know the father's previous military rank before he was recruited for intelligence duty. The possession of this "classified" information may serve to strengthen family bonds or longtime friendships or it may be a potential "leak" of security. In this circumstance the responsibility and occupational strains from the agent's role are spread to his loved ones and acquaintances. Moreover, family members must be constantly on the alert for accidental releases of privileged information. In such cases, a rapid adulteration of the information or an extention of the information to a level of the ridiculous successfully provides a security protection. Even the isolation of the agent's occupational activities from his familial roles generates latent role strains in an attempt to minimize their contagion of his agent role stresses. At work an agent has daily contact with vast amounts of unclassified information as well as to secret materials. At the end of the day it is difficult or even impossible to remember which piece of information was classified and which was not. To preserve maximum security, an agent will refuse to discuss any of his work activities at home. The resulting consequences are indicated by one agent surveying his dilemma.

> When you begin to make small talk at home you are constantly afraid that you are talking about some of the classified stuff, and it makes uninhibited conversation with those you love very awkward. Since I was recently married and without children, it was a very difficult time in my marriage inasmuch as we ran out of things to talk about.

This security-conscious aspect of the agent role produces an emotional barrier in familial roles. This contrast with the relaxation felt when in the company of other intelligence agents produces a personal identity of "being oneself" at work and being a restricted self when at home. As an Air Force agent remarked:

> The only time I can really be myself and get out from under the constant pressure of being security-conscious is when our detachment or division gets together. We can exchange all types of experience and information within our own ranks, and this helps lower the pressure of being always on guard when talking to others.

But even this agent association outlet is not entirely without risk. Agents with experience in war zones report that during periods of slack duties resulting in a paucity of case assignments, an agent's investigative training becomes randomly directed toward his fellow agents—looking for potential risks or ferreting out possible security leaks within the organization itself. Thus, the freedom from security-consciousness only decreases in company with one's colleagues but in reality never ceases while one is actively engaged as an intelligence agent. One young enlisted agent went so far as to say that after three years of post-agent civilian life, he still felt the effects of maintaining secrecy about his wartime activities as an agent.

In summary, this discussion of occupational role conflicts, role strains, and ambivalence does not infer that these are peculiar to the military alone nor are they the exclusive property of the military intelligence agent role and those persons occupying it. However, it does serve to clearly outline the contradictory expectations occuring within a single role definition. The intelligence agent's functional mission requires the application of expedient means to accomplish his objective, which must be performed and articulated within a somewhat rigid military bureaucratic structure. The secretive nature of the intelligence operation and public ignorance of its activities allow the perpetuation of "cloak and dagger" stereotypes of be disbursed throughout the mass media although such activities are somewhat rare occurrences for the military intelligence agent.

This analysis clearly demonstrates that the pressures associated with performing as a military intelligence agent are those structurally contained within the work role demands. These operate independently of personality friction, personal animosities between individuals, or personal prejudices and incompatibilities which are due to unique personal factors. They arise from the contradictory demands and inconsistencies from mutually antagonistic expectations as reflected in the military intelligence agent role as now constituted—doing a necessary job in the military structure in a nonmilitary manner. Only individuals who are capable of selectively complying with rigorous bureaucratic procedures while pursuing their field functions expeditiously can successfully fulfill these contradictory expectations found within the military intelligence agent role.

Footnotes

[1] Many related role concepts or more precise variations of these used herein are found in the following sources. Seeman (1959); Goffman (1961:85–125); Coser (1966); Paloli (1967) and Taviss (1969).

[2] It is recognized that these formal military regulations are essentially regarded as deviant norms when in conflict with strong informal military traditions (see Dornbusch, 1955). Moreover, in combat situations the military soldier is not as routinized as he is generally believed to be since his survival depends upon constant improvisation on his part (Janowitz, 1959:37). However, even though combat expedience varies from formal regulations, the decisions are made within the milieu of rank symbols and cues of expected behavior which are entirely absent in the case of an intelligence agent dressed in civilian clothing.

[3] "Cover" is an overworked and loosely defined word in intelligence work. Some types of administrative "cover" are not to conceal identity but to facilitate

liaison functions and to operate within the civilian populace. Obviously, the rare few working in the sensitive twilight zone of enemy agent operations are given a stable and complete "cover" which must hold up under all conditions for their mission to succeed.

Selected References

BURCHARD, WALDO W. 1954. "Role Conflicts of Military Chaplains" *American Sociological Review* 19 (October): 528–535

COSER, ROSE LAUB 1966. "Role Distance, Sociological Ambivalence, and Transitional Status Systems" *American Journal of Sociology* 72 (September): 173–187

DAVIS, FRED 1959. "The Cabdriver and His Fare: Facets of a Fleeting Relationship" *American Journal of Sociology* 65 (September): 158–165 [Reprinted in this volume—ED.]

DORNBUSCH, SANFORD M. 1955. "The Military Academy as an Assimilating Institution" *Social Forces* 33 (May): 316–321

FELD, M. D. 1959. "Information and Authority: The Structure of Military Organizations" *American Sociological Review* 24 (February): 15–22

FIELD, MARK G. 1953. "Structured Strain in the Role of the Soviet Physician" *American Journal of Sociology* 58 (March): 493–502

GOFFMAN, IRVING 1961. *Encounters*. Indianapolis: Bobbs-Merrill Co.

GOODE, WILLIAM J. 1960. "A Theory of Role Strain" *American Sociological Review* 25 (August): 483–496

HOROWITZ, IRVING LOUIS (ed.) 1965. *The New Sociology*. New York: Oxford University Press

JANOWITZ, MORRIS 1959. *Sociology and the Military Establishment*. New York: Russell Sage Foundation

MOORE, WILBERT E. and MELVIN M. TUMIN 1949. "Some Social Functions of Ignorance" *American Sociological Review* 14 (December): 788–791

MUIR, DONAL E. 1968. "The Scientific Training of Introductory Sociology Students" *The American Sociologist* 3 (February): 21–25

PALOLI, ERNEST G. 1967. "Organization Types and Role Strains: An Experimental Study of Complex Organizations" *Sociology and Social Research* 51 (January): 171–184

SEEMAN, MELVIN 1959. "On the Meaning of Alienation" *American Sociological Review* 24 (December): 783–791

STODDARD, ELLWYN R. 1968. "The Informal 'Code' of Police Deviancy: A Group Approach to 'Blue-Coat Crime'" *The Journal of Criminal Law, Criminology and Police Science* 59 (June): 201–213 [Reprinted in this volume—ED.]

TAVISS, IRENE 1969. "Changes in the Form of Alienation: The 1900's vs. the 1950's" *American Sociological Review* 34 (February): 46–57

TURNER, RALPH H. 1947. "The Navy Disbursing Officer as a Bureaucrat" *American Sociological Review* 12 (June): 342–348

WHYTE, WILLIAM F. and BURLEIGH B. GARDNER 1945. "The Position and Problems of the Foreman" *Applied Anthropology* 4 (Spring): 17–28